Nature conservation and estuaries in Great Britain

N C Davidson, D d'A Laffoley, J P Doody, L S Way, J Gordon, R Key,
M W Pienkowski, R Mitchell and K L Duff

With additional contributions from H Caldwell, L Farrell, A Foster, S Leach,
C Johnston, D A Procter and D A Stroud

Estuaries Review
Chief Scientist Directorate
Nature Conservancy Council
Northminster House
Peterborough PE1 1UA

1991

This report should be quoted as: Davidson, N.C.
et al. 1991. *Nature conservation and estuaries in
Great Britain*. Peterborough, Nature Conservancy
Council.

Nature conservation and estuaries in Great Britain is
the first major report from the Nature Conservancy
Council's Estuaries Review. Its summary is also
available separately as Davidson, N. C. 1991.
*Estuaries, wildlife and man. A summary of nature
conservation and estuaries in Great Britain*. Further
reports are in preparation.

Contents

Appendices

Foreword

by Sir William Wilkinson, Chairman of the Nature Conservancy Council

For many centuries people the world over have used coasts and estuaries as rich sources of food, other natural resources, and for the sheltered anchorages essential for national and international trade. Such places play a particularly important role in the life of an island such as Britain since there is no place very far from the coast or an estuary.

The seas and rivers meet and mix in estuaries. Their existence being partly land and partly sea leads to their abundance of wildlife but also to many of the difficulties in conserving this wildlife since estuaries cross many administrative and legislative boundaries. Furthermore some estuarine organisms depend for their survival on just a few individual estuaries but others are highly mobile and need a network of different estuaries.

In estuaries much of the load of sediments and nutrients carried down rivers and in from the sea is trapped and deposited. These shallow areas of shoals and creeks rich in food provide the conditions for settlement and growth of an abundance of plants and animals that have become specially adapted to cope with changing conditions of tides, sediments and salinities. Indeed estuaries are some of the world's most productive ecosystems and they play a vital part in the survival of many plants and animals that contribute so importantly to our natural heritage.

In Britain we are fortunate in being particularly well endowed with estuaries of many shapes and sizes around our coasts and these form over a quarter of the whole estuarine resource in western Europe. Each estuary is a complex ecosystem composed of a variety of shallow marine habitats, intertidal flats and saltmarshes and surounding habitats such as sand-dunes and grazing marshes, each with its characteristic wildlife. But we cannot treat each part of an estuary, or indeed each estuary, in isolation. These are places where geomorphological processes are actively moving sediments in complex patterns of erosion and accretion; places where new land is built from sediments eroded from other parts of the coasts, sometimes within the same estuary but often from much further away. So the habitats on an estuary, both above and below the high and low tide lines, are interdependent.

It is difficult to over-emphasize the importance to national and international nature conservation of Britain's estuaries. Their location and size, and their abundance and variety of wildlife, make estuaries one of Britain's most internationally important features. Nationally the Nature Conservancy Council has identified this conservation importance by notifying many estuaries as Sites of Special Scientific Interest, and by managing parts of several estuaries as National Nature Reserves.

Internationally Britain has a particular responsibility for conserving its estuaries for their bird populations. For many people it is the spectacular sight of enormous flocks of thousands of waders and wildfowl wheeling in unison above a flooding tide that is so characteristic of estuaries. Britain lies where the migration routes of these birds from huge areas of arctic Canada, Greenland, and Iceland meet those from northern Europe and the USSR. So birds from a vast area of the northern hemisphere depend on estuaries in Britain and elsewhere in western Europe. Many birds remain to overwinter, whilst for others they are vital places in autumn where they can moult their feathers and feed before flying on to southern Europe and Africa for the winter, returning to British estuaries again on their northwards migration in the spring. Many of these birds do not only depend on international networks of estuaries for their survival. For many individuals a network of sites within Britain is also vital during their year.

These waders and wildfowl occur in such large numbers because of the continued presence and highly productive nature of the whole estuarine ecosystem. It is the conservation of these interlinked estuarine habitats that is crucial to the survival of such mobile species throughout their range. Under the EEC Council Directive on the Conservation of Wild Birds 1979 the United Kingdom is committed to taking the requisite measures to preserve, maintain or re-establish a sufficient diversity and area of habitats for all species of naturally occurring birds in the wild state. In addition the UK is committed to taking special conservation measures for two groups of birds - certain listed vulnerable species and all migratory species - which include many of the waders and wildfowl for which the suite of British estuaries is so important.

Many of the remaining parts of estuaries behave as some of the most natural ecosystems in Britain. Yet during their long history of varied human exploitation much has been irrevocably destroyed or seriously degraded. Like many other types of wetlands in Britain and world-wide, much of the effort directed at coastal wetlands such as estuaries has been the taming, draining and reclaiming of their flats and marshes.

Since Roman times much of the vegetated fringe of estuaries has been claimed for agricultural purposes. More recently urban and industrial society has treated estuaries as convenient 'free land' for the piecemeal development of industry and other urban land-uses. The recent upsurge in water-based recreational pursuits places increasing pressure on the remaining part of many estuaries.

Much of Britain's population lives with estuaries almost on their doorsteps. Yet increasingly these wild and awe-inspiring places with their major contribution to Britain's natural heritage have been ignored or treated as wastelands into which to pour effluents or dump rubbish. The rich and important tidal flats are, regrettably, still too often regarded as an impediment to a high-quality coastal environment - areas of 'stinking mud' to be removed by permanent inundation or infilling. Yet elsewhere these coastal wetlands are treated rightly as beautiful and exciting parts of our natural environment.

In the light of concerns over continuing and widespread attrition on the wildlife of Britain's estuaries and the upsurge of interest in developments such as 'leisure' and tidal power barrages, each of which could make dramatic changes to estuarine ecosystems, the NCC initiated its Estuaries Review in 1988 with the aim of developing an estuarine conservation strategy. This report is intended to provide the basis and direction for such a strategy. Since estuaries are complex places with varied wildlife interest and much happening on them, its preparation has involved the help and co-operation of many people in a wide range of scientific disciplines throughout the NCC around the whole of Britain, and the provision of information and advice by others in a wide variety of organisations. They are thanked elsewhere in this report.

The message from the report is clear. Many parts of Britain's estuaries are continuing to suffer widespread loss and damage to their habitats of national and international conservation importance, a trend inconsistent with commitments to maintain and enhance such habitats so as to ensure the safeguarding of the wildlife that depends on these special places.

Management of healthy estuaries depends on the actions of many people and organisations who use or control land-based and marine activities. For many the maintenance of the estuarine resource is a shared need. To develop ways of ensuring that estuaries are used in a sustainable way in the future demands, however, understanding and imaginative thinking and action from everyone who uses and

benefits from estuaries. This is especially so since estuarine wildlife such as migratory birds knows no boundaries. So each estuary contributes to the great conservation importance of the whole resource. Damaging one part can jeopardise the functioning of much more.

Estuaries and their wildlife are a key part of our natural heritage. Our challenge is to work together to maintain and enhance this common estuarine heritage. We hope that this report helps and encourages this work by providing a comprehensive basis of understanding of the needs of estuarine wildlife and the pressures facing it now and in the future. We have treated estuaries in the past as wastelands. Let us treat them as treasures in the future.

Sir William Wilkinson
Chairman

1 Summary

1.1 Introduction (Chapter 3)

Estuaries are wetlands that form at the margins of the land and the sea. This straddling of boundaries, coupled with the continual movements of the tide and the mixing of fresh water and salt water, makes estuaries complex and varying ecosystems. The continual input, trapping and recycling of sediments and nutrients make estuaries amongst the most fertile and productive ecosystems in the world.

Because of this uniquely varying set of physical, chemical and biological conditions, estuaries support abundant and varied wildlife, much of it highly dependent on estuaries for part or all of their lives, and making them of great conservation importance.

Man has used estuaries for many purposes, such as for renewable sources of food and materials. However estuaries, like many other types of wetland worldwide, are under long-term and continuous threat of damage and destruction.

About one-third of all British intertidal estuarine habitat and about half the saltmarsh area has been claimed since Roman times, as has over two-thirds of coastal grazing marshes in south-east England since the 1930s. In some estuaries man has removed all, or almost all, the intertidal wildlife habitats. Despite these losses the remaining parts of this estuarine resource are amongst Britain's most important nature conservation features.

The Nature Conservancy Council has recognised the conservation importance of estuaries, and has notified many parts of the resource as Sites of Special Scientific Interest (SSSIs). In addition Britain has major international obligations to maintain and safeguard estuarine wetland habitats and their wildlife, notably under the terms of the 'Ramsar' convention on the conservation of wetlands especially as waterfowl habitat, and the EEC Directive on the conservation of wild birds.

1.2 NCC'S Estuaries Review (Chapter 3.4 & 3.5)

The Nature Conservancy Council's Estuaries Review was established in 1988 in response to widespread concern about the threats to British estuarine ecosystems. Its overall aim is to provide guidance for the development of strategies for the conservation of British estuaries in the future.

This report highlights the main features of British estuaries and their conservation, derived from the findings of the Review. *Nature conservation and estuaries in Great Britain* provides a national overview of:

- the British estuarine resource;

- the wildlife of British estuaries;

- the present conservation status of British estuaries; and

- human activities within British estuaries.

The key findings of the review are that:

- British estuaries are of great national and international importance for wildlife conservation;

- each estuary needs to be considered as an entire ecosystem consisting of a mosaic of subtidal, intertidal and surrounding terrestrial habitats;

- both small and large estuaries are vital components of the resource;

- effective conservation of estuaries for their wildlife requires both the maintenance of the range and diversity of the estuarine network, throughout Britain and internationally, and continued safeguard of individual estuaries;

- the various domestic and international conservation safeguards are difficult to apply to estuaries because they occur at the interface between land and sea;

- it appears, from the continuing widespread destruction of British estuarine ecosystems, including internationally important areas, that the existing conservation safeguards are not effective at maintaining the wildlife resource;

- Britain's estuaries and their wildlife will depend for their survival on conservationists, decision-makers and estuary users co-operating with vision over the conservation and management of this important part of Britain's natural heritage.

1.3 What is an estuary? (Chapter 4)

For the Estuaries Review an estuary is a partially enclosed area of water and soft tidal shore and its surroundings, open to saline water from the sea and receiving fresh water from rivers, land run-off or seepage. Deep-water sea-lochs with predominantly rocky shores are excluded.

Each estuary is divided into a *core site* covering the intertidal and subtidal areas, surrounded by areas of *associated terrestrial* maritime and submaritime habitats such as sand-dunes and grazing marshes, linked to the estuary by their physical, chemical or biological processes.

Estuaries are places of constant change on a variety of timescales. Most British estuaries have formed during the rise in sea level since the last ice age. To survive in them, organisms living on estuaries must often tolerate varying salinities and must either move with the tide or tolerate periods of exposure and immersion during its ebb and flow.

Although apparently stable, tidal flats are usually in a dynamic equilibrium of erosion and deposition. Generally the inner, sheltered, parts of estuaries are muddy and the outer parts are sandy. On the upper tidal levels characteristic saltmarsh vegetation develops.

Estuaries usually have relatively few benthic species, but these often occur in large numbers and large biomass compared with marine or freshwater ecosystems. Benthic estuarine animal communities are characterised by worms and molluscs which live in or on the mud and sand.

Estuaries support large numbers of animals, especially invertebrates, fish and birds, because their waters and sediments are rich in nutrients. These are continually brought in from the sea and down rivers.

1.3 Britain's estuarine resource (Chapters 5 & 6)

The Estuaries Review has identified 155 estuaries around the whole British coastline. Half are in England and almost one-third are in Scotland. Four estuaries cross country boundaries, 20 are within two or more counties or regions, and 60 are the responsibility of more than one local authority district.

Estuaries are divided into nine categories on the basis of their geomorphology and topography. Six are types of river discharge estuary. Most widespread are *bar-built estuaries* (47 sites) where sedimentation has kept pace with rising sea levels, and *coastal plain estuaries* (35 sites) with wide sandy mouths. *Fjards* (20 sites) and *fjords* (6 sites) are both glacial features, fjards being shallower inlets, restricted almost entirely to west and north Scotland. There are 15 *rias* (narrow drowned river valleys) in south-west England and south Wales, and 10 estuaries are of *complex* origin.

Of the 22 open coast estuaries, 13 are *embayments*, often with rivers discharging into them, and seven are shallow *linear shores*, mostly in the outer parts of the Greater Thames estuary. There are two *barrier beach* systems (the North Norfolk Coast and Lindisfarne).

Estuaries are a major component of Britain's coastal zone. The 9,320 km of estuarine shoreline is almost half (48%) of the longest estimate of the British shoreline.

Core sites total almost 530,000 ha: 42% subtidal and 58% intertidal flats and saltmarshes. The 308,000 ha of intertidal habitats on estuaries is 83% of the total in Britain.

British estuaries vary greatly in size. The largest are The Wash (66,600 ha) and the Severn Estuary (55,700 ha), with nine others (Maplin Sands, the Humber Estuary, the Firth of Tay, the Moray and Dornoch Firths, the Dee Estuary and North Wirral, the Ribble Estuary, Morecambe Bay and the Solway Firth) each over 10,000 ha. Largest intertidal areas are Morecambe Bay (33,750 ha), The Wash (29,770 ha) and the Solway Firth (27,550 ha). Although much of the estuarine area in Britain is found on these few large sites, many British estuaries are small – for example 80 estuaries have intertidal areas of less than 500 ha. Although totalling less than 5% of the total estuarine intertidal area, these small estuaries support important parts of the wildlife resource.

British estuaries are unrivalled in Europe for their number, size and diversity of form. British estuaries comprise 28% of the entire estuarine area of the Atlantic and North Sea coastal states, more than any other European country, although the international Wadden Sea forms the largest continuous area.

British estuaries are not only extensive; they also freeze less often than estuaries in mainland Europe because of the influence of the Gulf Stream, and their tidal flats are exposed more consistently because of Britain's generally large tidal ranges. These features give British estuaries even greater international significance for some types of wildlife.

1.4 Britain's estuarine wildlife resource (Chapter 8)

Estuaries support a wide range of wildlife, and consist of a complex mosaic of subtidal, intertidal and surrounding terrestrial habitats. Some characteristic estuarine animals are sedentary, depending on just one habitat and estuary throughout their life. Many others depend on more than one estuarine habitat, which are also vital links in the chains of sites used by many migratory species.

1.4.1 Estuarine habitats (Chapter 8.1)

Even small estuaries are typically composed of a mosaic of between four and nine major habitat types of wildlife interest (subtidal, intertidal mudflats, intertidal sandflats, saltmarshes, shingles, rocky shores, lagoons, sand-dunes and grazing marshes/coastal grassland). Tidal flats occur on all, and subtidal areas and saltmarshes on almost all, estuaries.

Tidal flats are a major part of estuarine ecosystems. They vary from soft muds in the sheltered inner parts of estuaries to firm sandflats in outer parts. Mudflats especially support large numbers and biomass of characteristic estuarine invertebrate animals, notably crustacea, molluscs and worms on which fish and many of the nationally and internationally important waterfowl feed. There are over 265,000 ha of tidal flats – over 83% of the intertidal area of estuaries.

Major British tidal flat areas are in Morecambe Bay, The Wash, the Dee Estuary and North Wirral, the Humber Estuary, around the Thames Estuary, and in north-east Scotland.

Tidal flats are vulnerable to progressive land-claim, bait and shellfish collecting, and the impacts of waste discharge and pollution. Maintaining healthy tidal flats is crucial to estuarine conservation since this habitat is the source of much of the richness of the estuarine ecosystem.

Saltmarsh vegetation develops in a series of characteristic zones on fine sediments on the upper shore in sheltered parts of estuaries. Saltmarshes are a major source of nutrients to an estuary.

Extensive saltmarshes with full zonation occur mostly only where there is ample sediment, but land-claim has now removed much of the upper zone vegetation from many saltmarshes.

Saltmarshes larger than 0.5 ha are found on 135 estuaries. They total over 42,250 ha – over 95% of the British saltmarsh resource and almost 14% of the total intertidal area on estuaries. Largest saltmarsh areas are in the Greater Thames estuaries of Essex and Kent, and in Liverpool Bay. Individual estuaries with the largest areas (more than 3,000 ha each) are The Wash, Morecambe Bay and the Solway Firth.

Saltmarsh plant communities are particularly diverse in southern and eastern Britain, where they include plants such as sea-purslane in low-mid marsh, and sea-lavender and shrubby sea-blite in mid-upper marsh.

Cord-grass swards now occur on 82 estuaries and dominate the lowest zones of saltmarsh especially in southern and western England. Overall cord-grass forms over 16% of the British saltmarsh area. It first appeared in Southampton Water in the late 19th century and has spread both naturally and by widespread planting to aid sea defence and land-claim. Cord-grass now appears to be dying back naturally in southern England, but elsewhere its spread is still causing loss of tidal flat feeding grounds for waterfowl.

Saltmarshes are grazed extensively by livestock. Grazed and ungrazed marshes each have conservation value for different types of estuarine wildlife. 39 estuaries have nationally important saltmarshes and 101 estuaries have saltmarshes

within Sites of Special Scientific Interest.

Sand-dunes, an important and widespread coastal feature, are associated with 55 estuaries. They develop in more exposed parts of estuaries than saltmarshes.

Many form spits across estuary mouths and in some places have been a major force in shaping the estuary. Sand-dunes on barrier islands shelter the shore from waves, permitting estuarine intertidal habitats to develop in their lee.

Many sand-dunes are naturally mobile, particularly on their outer edges. On their landward side dune vegetation, especially marram grass, gradually binds the sand together, resulting in grassy swards, wetter slacks and sometimes heath, scrub and woodland. Major areas of once-mobile dunes have been afforested, greatly reducing their wildlife value, which is most often enhanced by grazing and sand mobility. Housing, recreation (including caravan parks), roads, golf courses and intensive agriculture also affect the wildlife interest of estuarine sand-dunes.

There are seven nationally important **shingle** structures in Britain, five of them associated with estuaries. The protection afforded by these shingles, on the Moray Firth, Spey Estuary, North Norfolk Coast, Ore/Alde/Butley Estuary and The Fleet, has been a major influence in the development of these estuaries.

Shingle is an important estuarine feature for its geomorphology, characteristic vegetation and invertebrate animals.

About 83% of the area of British **saline lagoons** is associated with only 37 estuaries in England and Wales.

About half are natural lagoons behind shore barriers, often shingle. They support a highly specialised flora and fauna, often of very local distribution. Natural saline lagoons are very vulnerable to damage from sea defence and other construction work, and from changes in hydrology and water quality.

There are few **sea-cliffs** on estuaries, but soft cliffs including those outside estuaries are often important sediment sources for estuaries such as the Humber Estuary and The Wash. They have an important but neglected invertebrate fauna.

Coastal grazing marsh (much of it originally saltmarsh) and other lowland wet grasslands are associated with at least 53 estuaries, especially in southern England where they are fast vanishing. Coastal grazing marshes have a wide range of salinities, which encourages the growth of a large variety of often rare or scarce plants, especially in the ditches.

Some lowland wet grasslands (especially around The Wash and Severn Estuary) are washlands created to prevent more widespread winter flooding. These are important waterfowl breeding and wintering areas.

Almost all the **nationally rare vascular plant** species of tidal flats, saltmarshes, shingle, sandy shores and sand-dunes are associated with estuaries. One or more rare plant species is found on 36 estuaries, mostly in southern and western England and Wales.

Ten nationally rare plants in Britain are entirely dependent on estuarine habitats. Estuaries and the maritime habitats surrounding them also support populations of four rare or scarce endemic plants.

1.4.2 Terrestrial and non-marine invertebrates (Chapter 8.2)

There are several thousand species of terrestrial and non-marine invertebrates associated with estuarine habitats, with some restricted to estuaries. Species diversity is generally greater on estuaries on south and south-east coasts. Various microhabitats, such as bare substrates, strandlines, reedbeds, brackish and freshwater pools and ditches within saltmarsh, sand-dune, shingle, coastal grazing marsh and mudflats, support assemblages of high conservation interest.

Terrestrial invertebrates of intertidal estuarine habitats cope with the ebb and flow of the tide through a combination of behavioural and physiological mechanisms. Many larvae, for example, burrow into the substrate. The effects of grazing vary with habitat: ungrazed saltmarsh supports a more diverse fauna than grazed areas, whereas grazing that maintains the vegetation of young sand-dunes benefits the specialist dune fauna. In both habitats vegetation structure, as well as plant species composition, determines the invertebrate species present.

Grazing marsh faunas, especially in brackish and freshwater ditches, are dominated by diverse, and often rare, beetles, bugs, snails and fly larvae.

Since many terrestrial invertebrates have complex life-cycles, with different stages depending on different habitats, conservation of estuarine habitat mosaics is vital for their survival.

One of Britain's rarest moths, the Essex emerald, survives on the upper saltmarsh of only one estuary.

1.4.3 Aquatic estuarine communities (Chapter 8.3)

Britain's shallow seas support a rich and varied mosaic of plant and animal communities, the species composition being determined by factors such as substrate type, salinity and degree of wave and tidal exposure. In the intertidal and subtidal parts of estuaries conditions range from exposed marine systems at the mouths of river estuaries and on open coast estuaries, to tidal and predominantly freshwater conditions in the upper reaches. A classification of aquatic tidal estuarine communities, based on the NCC's Marine Nature Conservation Review (MNCR) classification, has been developed for the Estuaries Review and has been used in the description of communities on 102 estuaries.

Seventeen hard shore communities and 16 soft shore communities occur in estuaries. Individual hard shore community types typically occur only intertidally or subtidally, but 63% of soft shore communities occur in both situations. Many hard shore communities are also those characteristic of non-estuarine marine areas. Most are restricted to the outer parts of only a few estuaries: only two hard shore communities occur on more than 20% of Estuaries Review sites.

One is a **sheltered rocky shore community**, typically with dense growth of knotted wrack, found mostly in the outer parts of rias, fjords and fjards in south-west England and northern Scotland.

Rocky shore communities are most diverse on estuaries in south-west England and south Wales, and scattered sites in Scotland. They are largely absent from eastern England, where soft sediments predominate.

Soft shore community types are more widespread, with five communities being found on more than 20% of estuaries. These include an **exposed sand community** dominated by small crustaceans and polychaete worms in outer parts of estuaries; **mussel beds**, widespread around Britain in both intertidal and shallow subtidal parts of estuaries; and **beds of marine grasses** associated with the lower intertidal mud and muddy sand areas within estuaries.

The other two soft shore communities are particularly widespread, occurring on over 80% of assessed estuaries throughout Britain: a **muddy sand community** in areas of variable or normal salinity, and a **mud community** in more sheltered areas of variable or reduced salinity. Muddy sand is dominated by lugworms, although intertidally cockles, Baltic tellins and several polychaete worms are also abundant. Mud in intertidal and shallow subtidal parts of estuaries is dominated by clams and worms, typically ragworms. Small snails and crustaceans are also abundant.

Estuaries of major marine conservation interest are currently those with many different aquatic communities, but some individual scarce communities are also significant.

These include the **maerl beds** (maerl is a delicate coral-like alga) of the Fal Estuary, Helford Estuary and Milford Haven; a **sand or muddy sand community** dominated by razor shells on a few sites in south-west England and Wales and the Outer Hebrides; and the rich fauna of a **muddy gravel community** in outer estuaries and marine inlets of south and south-west Britain.

1.4.4 Fish (Chapter 8.4)

Estuaries play a crucial role for many species of fish, as migration routes, spawning and breeding areas, and habitat for all or part of their lives. Some fisheries, such as for salmon, sea trout and eels, are of considerable economic importance.

Eighteen fish species (out of over 350 species in Britain) are currently considered 'estuarine', since they are dependent on estuaries for part or all of their life-cycle. Five species (sea bass, common goby, thick-lipped and thin-lipped grey mullets, and golden mullet) are truly estuarine and are generally dependent on estuaries in which to complete their life-cycles. Seven species – flounder, sturgeon, allis and twaite shads, houting, smelt and three-spined stickleback – move between estuaries and fresh or sea water. Four species (sea and river lampreys, salmon and humpback salmon) move from the sea through estuaries to rivers to breed. When adult the eel moves from fresh water to the sea to breed.

The sheltered waters of estuaries such as Plymouth Sound, the Humber Estuary and The Wash are also important spawning and nursery areas for flatfish, and at least 32 estuaries in southern and western England and Wales have sea bass nursery areas.

Many other fish species, several of economic importance, occur within estuaries but their national distributions are poorly understood.

1.4.5 Amphibians and reptiles (Chapter 8.5)

There are only 12 species of native amphibians and reptiles in Britain. Over 95% of the British population of one species, the natterjack toad, depend on dune systems associated with nine estuaries, predominantly in north-west England between the Mersey Estuary and the Solway Firth. About 5% of British sand lizards are on estuarine dune systems in north-west England, and others are on heathlands adjoining southern English estuaries.

1.4.6 Birds (Chapter 8.6)

Three groups of birds are particularly striking and abundant: waders and wildfowl (together known as waterfowl), and seabirds. British estuaries are of major national and international importance for migrant and wintering waterfowl. Many species depend wholly or largely on British estuaries for crucial periods of the year.

Many waterfowl that breed across vast areas of arctic, sub-arctic and temperate regions crowd onto British estuaries in winter. Many others use them as vital staging areas before flying south to overwinter in Europe and Africa and then back north to their breeding grounds in spring. Some waders and seabirds breed at high densities on saltmarshes and the habitats surrounding estuaries.

Estuarine birds can be highly mobile, and depend on a network of sites or parts of sites during their annual cycles. Their use of a particular estuary varies from bird to bird, from species to species and from year to year.

Migrant and wintering waterfowl (Section 8.6.2)

Wintering waterfowl depend on the mosaic of habitats within estuaries. Many waders and some wildfowl feed on the intertidal mudflats, sandflats and saltmarshes, and sometimes during high tide on surrounding pools and pastures. Many roost on undisturbed saltmarshes and shingle banks and other surrounding terrestrial habitats. Other wildfowl feed on surrounding marshes and farmland, returning to roost on the estuary.

In January over 1,740,000 waterfowl are present on estuaries – 62% of the British wintering population, and over 10% of the relevant international populations. 581,000 of these are wildfowl (38% of the British and almost 4% of north-west European populations); and almost 1,159,000 are waders – a massive 90% of the British and over 15% of the East Atlantic flyway populations.

Waterfowl are widely distributed around estuaries. Major concentrations are on The Wash (over 180,000 birds), Morecambe Bay (over 140,000 birds) and the estuaries of Essex and north Kent (almost 229,000 birds – over 13% of the British estuarine population). Just 25 estuaries (each with more than 20,000 waterfowl) hold 83% of the estuarine population in midwinter. Estuaries with smaller populations together support over 3% (waders) and 2% (wildfowl) of international populations.

Twenty-six wildfowl species and 18 wader species occur regularly in winter on estuaries. Almost three-quarters of the waders are dunlins, knots and oystercatchers, and over half the wildfowl are wigeon, dark-bellied brent geese and shelduck.

In January estuaries support more than half of 18 British waterfowl populations and more than 10% of 21 international waterfowl populations.

Estuaries are of particular international importance for knots (67% of the international population), redshanks (55%), bar-tailed godwits (50%), *alpina* subspecies dunlins (27%) and oystercatchers (26%). Amongst wildfowl, estuaries support over 75% of the small Svalbard-breeding population of light-bellied brent geese, and major proportions of international populations of dark-bellied brent geese (over 50%) and barnacle geese (100% of the Svalbard population, 70% of the Greenland population).

Five wader species and three wildfowl species (redshank, curlew, oystercatcher, dunlin, ringed plover, mallard, shelduck and wigeon) are particularly widespread on estuaries. In contrast, most goose populations are restricted to less than one-quarter of estuaries.

Estuaries are important for waterfowl not just as wintering sites but also as refuges in cold weather, as moulting sites and as migration staging areas. At these times many other populations and individuals depend on British estuaries. During migration many more waterfowl use British estuaries than are present at any one time – at least 15-20% of the international wader population in autumn and in spring. Maintenance of late spring staging areas is particularly critical as birds are then rapidly storing energy and nutrient reserves for long-distance migration and for survival on their breeding grounds.

The key implications for estuarine conservation of these winter and migratory waterfowl numbers and distributions are that:

● British estuaries overall are of major national and international importance for waterfowl assemblages, and for many individual species;

● although many waterfowl are widely dispersed around estuaries, many are almost entirely dependent on them for their winter and migratory survival, and for some species a few particular sites are crucial;

● wintering waterfowl depend on habitats on both small and large estuaries;

● movements and population turnover, especially during migration, mean that a much greater proportion of the international population of each species depends on estuaries than is present at any one time;

● estuaries are used as a network, and different parts of the network are important for different species and populations, and at different times.

Estuaries support a variety of other wintering birds, notably divers, grebes and sea-ducks (especially in north-east Scotland), gulls, birds of prey (especially hen harrier, peregrine and merlin) and passerines, for example Lapland buntings and twites.

Breeding birds (Section 8.6.4)

Estuaries are of particular conservation importance for their breeding bird assemblages, typically dominated by waders or locally by seabirds.

Saltmarshes around Britain support some very high densities of **breeding waders** – sometimes over 100 pairs per square kilometre. Some grasslands associated with estuaries also support large populations, but generally total densities, and densities of individual species such as redshank, are higher on saltmarshes than on nearby coastal grasslands.

British estuarine populations of redshanks and ringed plovers are particularly important in a national and international context. 7% of the international population of redshanks and 19% of ringed plovers breed around estuaries.

Britain is of major international importance for **breeding seabirds**, supporting over half the European Community population of each of 14 species. Gulls and terns breed on at least 75 estuaries. Most estuarine breeding seabirds are on upper saltmarshes, sand-dunes and shingle, and estuaries support over 1% of the international breeding population of six species. Estuaries support almost three-quarters of the scarce British breeding population of little terns.

The conservation of estuarine birds depends on safeguarding remaining areas of estuarine habitats. The dependence of birds on site networks means that they are particularly vulnerable to piecemeal habitat loss. The loss of one part can destroy the integrity of the network. Maintaining the health of all parts of an estuary is also vital, since breeding and wintering birds depend on the habitat mosaic and are vulnerable to pollution and recreational disturbance.

1.4.7 Mammals (Chapter 8.7)

Three groups of mammals are associated with estuaries: cetaceans (whales and dolphins), seals, and otters. Two species of **dolphins** (harbour porpoise and bottle-nosed dolphin) occur regularly around the outer parts of British estuaries, notably the Moray Firth. Of the two **seal** species, grey seals regularly visit most estuaries in northern and western Britain, and at least one-third of the British common seal population has recently bred on estuaries, although numbers have declined substantially after a viral epidemic in 1988. **Otters** have been recorded recently on or near 59 estuaries, including over 95% of Scottish estuaries. Coasts and estuaries are particularly important for otters as cold weather refuges. The British otter population is of major international importance.

1.5 The conservation status of British estuaries (Chapter 9)

In recognition of the diverse and abundant wildlife importance of Britain's estuaries many parts of the estuarine resource have been designated or otherwise identified under a variety of domestic and international measures, both statutory and non-statutory. Some are designed specifically for nature conservation; others are primarily for landscape and amenity purposes. It is common for several different designations to be applied to parts of a single estuary, and to overlap.

Much of the current approach to nature conservation in Britain is site-based, but wildlife that is largely estuarine needs a wider land-use approach for its future safeguard. Land-use on estuaries is controlled by a great variety of domestic and, more recently, European legislation. This legal framework is particularly complicated, since it includes the local control of land-based activities, especially through the Town & Country Planning Acts, and the control of activities in the marine environment by 18 government departments and agencies. A great variety of consent mechanisms therefore operate on estuaries. Furthermore much of the intertidal and subtidal shore of estuaries is managed by the Crown Estate Commissioners, who control a variety of activities within these areas.

The protection of wildlife within British estuaries currently depends on a mixture of statutory designations, voluntary management agreements and consultation before development.

British conservation measures derive chiefly from the Wildlife & Countryside Act 1981 and its amendments. In addition the UK Government is party to a number of international agreements which oblige Britain to identify internationally important areas for birds and their habitats, especially the wetland habitats and the migrant waterfowl for which British estuaries are so important.

1.5.1 International conventions and directives (Chapter 9.2)

International conservation measures are essential for safeguarding wide-ranging species, for two key reasons. First, the long-term viability of such species depends on the maintenance of their geographic range and genetic diversity. Second, migratory species depend, individually and as groups, on networks of often widely scattered sites. All parts of the network need to be safeguarded, and British estuaries are critically important for many species.

The conservation of these species depends on countries in all parts of their range acting to safeguard habitats used during different parts of the annual cycle.

Estuaries are a recurrent theme of international conservation measures, both as wetlands and as habitat for very large populations of migratory animals, chiefly birds. The continuing worldwide losses of wetlands makes it vital to conserve those internationally important wetlands that remain. So far international wetland waterfowl conservation measures have been applied mostly for migratory bird populations, but their main aim is habitat safeguard since healthy habitats are as essential for birds as for other wildlife.

Some agreements are international conventions; others are European Community Directives, legally binding on member states. So far the most significant for estuarine conservation have been the 'Ramsar Convention' and the EEC 'Birds Directive'. Other international agreements and designations relevant to estuaries include the Council of Europe Convention on the Conservation of European Wildlife and Natural Habitats (the '**Berne Convention**'), the **'Bonn Convention'** on the Conservation of Migratory Species of Wild Animals, the **World Heritage Convention**, and **Biosphere Reserves**. A further EC directive on the protection of plant and animal species is in preparation.

The **Convention on Wetlands of International Importance especially as Waterfowl Habitat** (the 'Ramsar Convention') was adopted in 1971 and ratified by the UK Parliament in 1976. It aims to stem the progressive loss of wetlands, including all parts of estuaries down to six metres below low water.

Contracting Parties are required to designate wetlands of international importance, and to promote their conservation and 'wise use'. Criteria for identifying wetlands of international importance have been agreed by Contracting Parties. So far the most widely applied criteria relate to waterfowl populations and are especially relevant to estuaries. A wetland is regarded as internationally important if it regularly supports 20,000 waterfowl, or 1% of the individuals of a biogeographic population of one subspecies or species of waterfowl. By April 1989 there were 45 Contracting Parties worldwide and 468 Ramsar-listed wetlands (60% being in western Europe). In Britain the NCC is responsible for identifying suitable sites for designation by the UK Government.

Eighteen of the 39 designated British Ramsar sites cover parts of estuaries, and together they comprise almost 90% of the land designated. A further 43 estuarine Ramsar sites are currently amongst the 115 awaiting designation. Some Ramsar sites cover parts of more than one adjacent estuary, so that there are 66 estuaries in the Ramsar site network, 19 of them having designated Ramsar sites.

The European Council of Ministers adopted the **Directive on the Conservation of Wild Birds** (Directive 79/409/EEC) in 1979. It concerns the urgent need for European co-operation in bird conservation policies, and places emphasis on the need to conserve habitats as a means of protecting bird populations. In part this is achieved through the designation of Special Protection Areas (SPAs). 'Wider-countryside' measures are also stressed as complementary to site-based conservation.

The Directive requires Member States to take additional conservation measures for certain rare or vulnerable species, and regularly occurring migratory species. This is related especially to wetlands and migratory waterfowl. The Birds Directive therefore provides a statutory framework for international co-operation on safeguarding wetlands of international importance. It is explicit in the Directive that the network of SPAs must fulfil the overall objectives of the Directive, that population levels of many bird species should be increased, and that sites with particular importance as, for example, cold weather refuges, or where there is rapid turnover of individuals, can be included in the SPA network even where they do not fulfil quantitative criteria (e.g. 1% of the population). In order to safeguard migratory birds in their area of distribution, it is implicit that SPAs on estuaries need to cover subtidal areas, as well as the intertidal and terrestrial habitats.

The implementation of the Birds Directive in Britain is effected through the Wildlife & Countryside Act 1981, but this procedure has proved time-consuming and complex to apply. In particular the requirement that all sites must first have been notified as Sites of Special Scientific Interest has delayed the process, and has meant that SPAs usually cover only terrestrial and intertidal parts of an estuary, and then often only patchily.

In Britain there are 33 designated SPAs, out of a total of 761 designated by Member States by March 1989. British sites cover just over 127,000 ha (less than 1% of the land area), much less than some other states, for example Denmark (111 SPAs covering 22% of its territory) and Belgium (34 sites covering 12% of its area). Fourteen British SPAs are estuarine and comprise 84% of the designated SPA area in Britain. There are currently 47 estuarine proposed SPAs in Britain.

Overall, 68 estuaries (44%) are internationally important on quantitative criteria alone and are wholly or partly within the Ramsar and/or SPA site network.

Ramsar/SPA sites are mostly on large estuaries and so are not fully representative of the diversity of Britain's estuarine resource. Birds which concentrate on large estuaries are well represented, but those that are widely distributed around small estuaries also need effective site designations.

The Ramsar Convention and the EEC Birds Directive have greatly increased awareness of the international importance of Britain's estuaries. However, even where these designations apply, safeguards are not always maintained. Although the identification of internationally important sites has helped to safeguard some areas against damaging development proposals, habitat losses from internationally important sites still occur.

Consent for several recent major development proposals affecting internationally important estuaries, notably docks at Felixstowe on the Orwell Estuary and an 'amenity' barrage on the Taff/Ely Estuary (Severn Estuary), has been sought through Parliamentary Private Bills. Other major developments obtained consent through the local development planning process. Overall, internationally important British estuaries are still being damaged and destroyed rather than maintained and enhanced.

1.5.2 British wildlife conservation designations (Chapter 9.3)

A national policy framework for nature conservation in Britain was first set out in Government White Papers in 1947. In 1984 the NCC published *Nature conservation in Great Britain* which established a strategy in the context of a review of conservation progress. Nature conservation strategy in Britain currently has three main elements: managing key sites as National Nature Reserves (NNRs); notifying statutory Sites of Special Scientific Interest (SSSIs); and maintaining wildlife in the wider countryside. All are relevant to estuaries. In addition there is a variety of other designations, both statutory and voluntary, that apply to estuaries, often in overlapping patterns.

The detailed assessment and description of **Nature Conservation Review (NCR)** sites, which are biological sites of key importance and of NNR quality, was published by the NCC in 1977. By 1989 there were 943 NCR sites in Britain covering a total area of almost 1,057,900 ha. 150 (16%) are classified as coastal, over half of them estuarine.

The **Geological Conservation Review (GCR)**, begun by the NCC in 1977, is assessing and identifying key earth science conservation sites throughout Britain. There are some 3,000 GCR sites in Britain of which 7% are associated with estuaries. 144 GCR sites are cliff and foreshore exposures of rock and Quaternary deposits, on 60 estuaries. Only 58 estuarine GCR sites are geomorphological, on 48 estuaries. Sites include shingle features, sand-dunes, cliffs and shore platforms and saltmarshes, but tidal flats are not represented, nor are whole estuaries treated as single features.

Sites of Special Scientific Interest (SSSIs) are the major statutory site designations by which site-based wildlife conservation is delivered in Britain. SSSIs were first notified to local authorities under the National Parks and Access to the Countryside Act 1949. Subsequently the Wildlife and Countryside Act 1981 and its amendments strengthened the statutory process by which SSSIs are now notified to owners, occupiers, local planning authorities, the Secretaries of State, water authorities and drainage boards. Sites originally notified under the 1949 Act have had to be renotified under the 1981 Act, a process now largely complete.

There are currently 5,495 SSSIs covering almost 1,723,000 ha (about 7% of Britain). By early 1989 there were 334 SSSIs (6% of the total) associated with estuaries. Many estuarine SSSIs are large (averaging 1,166 ha, compared with the national average of 314 ha), so their total area of 389,300 ha is almost a quarter of notified SSSI land in Britain.

SSSIs are associated with 136 estuaries (88% of the total) throughout Britain. 70% of these SSSIs are at least partly intertidal, and the remainder are on associated terrestrial habitats such as sand-dunes, grazing marshes and maritime heaths. Some estuaries have only one large SSSI covering most of the core area; others have several SSSIs each covering part of the intertidal zone. Many estuarine SSSI boundaries have been drawn along the low water mark on intertidal flats, so dissecting the functional unit of an estuarine ecosystem. There are only 19 (mostly small) estuaries on which there are currently no SSSIs. SSSI designation makes consultation mandatory for developments likely to be damaging to the wildlife interest.

Even so, lasting damage to SSSIs continues to occur. In the three years from April 1986 to March 1989 146 SSSIs (about 3% of the total) were reported as permanently or lastingly damaged, and overall 564 (10%) were reported as suffering some damage. Estuarine SSSIs are even more threatened; during this period 56 estuarine SSSIs were damaged (17% of estuarine sites) and 27 of these (8% of the estuarine sites) suffered at least long-term damage. Planning and conservation legislation thus does not appear to be preventing continuing piecemeal habitat loss on estuaries.

National Nature Reserves (NNRs) are nationally important wildlife sites managed, by the NCC or on their behalf, specifically for nature conservation. 47 of the 234 declared NNRs are coastal and almost 90% of these are estuarine, on 35 estuaries.

Areas of Special Protection (AoSPs) (formerly designated as Bird Sanctuaries under the Protection of Birds Act 1954) are intended to safeguard particular bird species, but also protect all bird species for at least part of the year. Ten of the 38 Bird Sanctuaries/AoSPs in England and Wales are on estuaries. They provide strong statutory protection which can extend to open-water areas below the low water mark.

SSSIs and NNRs are terrestrial designations. The introduction of legislation for **Marine Nature Reserves (MNRs)** in the Wildlife & Countryside Act was intended to provide similar protection for marine areas. Designating an MNR is, however, more complex than designating a National Nature Reserve. The two MNRs so far designated are non-estuarine, but one of six proposed MNRs (Menai Strait) includes parts of five estuaries. Since MNRs can cover all parts of estuaries below the high water mark they can potentially help safeguard whole estuarine ecosystems.

In addition to the statutory MNRs two voluntary marine conservation designations have been applied to estuaries. Parts of four **Voluntary Marine Conservation Areas** cover five estuaries in southern England. One of 29 **Marine Consultation Areas (MCAs)** identified by the NCC in Scotland is an estuary (Traigh Cill-a-Rubha).

Local Nature Reserves (LNRs) increase public awareness of the value of estuarine wildlife. LNRs are declared by local planning authorities, can cover both intertidal and some subtidal areas, and can have bylaws controlling damaging activities, making them an effective way of managing estuarine habitats, especially close to urban centres. 33 LNRs (20% of the national total) are on 29 estuaries, mostly in southern England.

Several other conservation designations directed towards wildlife cover estuaries. Five **Environmentally Sensitive Areas (ESAs)** overlap parts of the upper reaches of 15 estuaries. 122 of the 1,800 **Wildlife Trust reserves** are associated with 52 estuaries, chiefly in eastern and southern England. The **Royal Society for the Protection of Birds** acquires and manages land supporting important bird populations. Thirty-four of its reserves are on 25 estuaries, and the RSPB is currently running a major campaign for more effective estuarine wildlife safeguards. Five **Wildfowl and Wetlands Trust reserves** are on estuaries, three of them covering areas for major wintering and breeding waterfowl populations, and a variety of other organisations own or manage estuarine land for wildlife, often as privately run nature reserves, on 19 estuaries.

1.5.3 Landscape and amenity designations (Chapter 9.4)

Coasts and estuaries are important features of Britain's landscape. A variety of landscape designations afford protection to estuaries, including parts of four **National Parks** on 11 estuaries. In Scotland 15 estuaries lie within **National Scenic Areas**, with almost half the Scottish west coast estuaries covered by this Countryside Commission for Scotland designation. Twenty of the 38 **Areas of Outstanding Natural Beauty (AONBs)** designated in England and Wales by the Countryside Commission have coastal frontage, with 15 of them including parts of 38 estuaries, chiefly in southern England and East Anglia. Twenty-two **Country Parks** have been designated by local authorities on 20 estuaries. The only specifically coastal countryside designation, **Heritage Coast**, was first proposed by the Countryside Commission in 1970. Most of the 1,460 km of Heritage Coast coastline is, however, on rocky and sandy shores. None of the largest estuaries is substantially within a Heritage Coast, most of which end at or just within estuary mouths. The North Norfolk Coast is the only major estuary covered. The **National Trust** and **National Trust for Scotland** provide strong protection covering 825 km of coastline, and with 64 properties on 34 estuaries, mostly on the English south coast and the North Norfolk Coast.

1.5.4 Estuarine planning and management (Chapter 9.6)

Although some designations make strong requirements for wildlife safeguard, none yet entirely precludes land-use conflicts. Such conflicts are particularly difficult to resolve in estuaries, where much of the area not already claimed by man is under threat from further development and disturbance.

Recognition of the great wildlife importance of estuaries, and its acknowledgement in the local authority planning and control system, are key components of the future safeguarding of Britain's estuaries. Zoning policies with presumptions against damaging development on estuaries are essential to minimise the potential impacts of proposed developments. Environmental impact assessment, supported by the terms of the 1985 EC Directive on Environmental Assessment, can provide valuable guidance on the effects of estuarine development proposals, although the variety and complexity of estuarine ecosystems can make reliable impact prediction both difficult and costly.

Parliamentary Private Bills have been used instead of the local planning process to seek consent for some recent major damaging estuarine developments, where parts of the development affect statutory rights of access or navigation. The use of this procedure for developments on estuaries (and other habitats) of high wildlife importance causes concern, not least because such domestic legislation is exempt from the terms of the EC Environment Assessment Directive, although there are now proposals to change this.

The multiple pressures on coasts and estuaries have increasingly led to the demands for integrated coastal zone management plans and strategies. On some British estuaries the initiative has come from the NCC, on others from local authorities or voluntary conservation groups. Integrated coastal zone management can help safeguard the remaining estuaries and their wildlife by treating estuaries as functional units.

1.6 Human estuarine activities (Chapter 10)

Man has used estuaries for many centuries, at first mostly for supplies of food, for grazing animals, and as harbours. More recently the development of towns and cities on the shores of many estuaries, and the continuing expansion of industry and shipping, have led to extensive damage and destruction of habitat.

The widespread discharge of effluents produced by this urban and industrial society has caused heavy pollution of estuaries, and has contributed to the perception of estuaries as wastelands – areas of 'free land' suitable for waste disposal, tipping and land-claim for a variety of purposes. Most recently, leisure and recreational use has placed increasing infrastructure and disturbance pressure on the wildlife using the remaining parts of estuaries.

The Estuaries Review has collected information on the presence of over 250 different types of human activity (grouped into 100 major categories) taking place on estuaries in 1989. It has also identified estuaries on which these activities once occurred but have now ceased, and those for which there were proposals current at the time of the survey.

There are five key features of human use of estuaries:

● many different human activities occur on a single estuary at the same time;

● similar activities occur on many different estuaries simultaneously;

● there are many and widespread proposals for further developments on estuaries;

● current activities and new proposals are focussed on the remaining parts of a dwindling resource, large areas of which have already been claimed for human use; and

● many activities can and do have adverse impacts, both individually and cumulatively, on estuarine wildlife.

1.6.1 Overall activity patterns (Chapter 10.2 to 10.4)

Most estuaries have many different human activities: even on estuaries of less than 500 ha about one-quarter of all major activity categories occur. Although no one estuary had all possible activities recorded on it, some of the largest estuaries (Severn Estuary, Humber Estuary and Morecambe Bay) had over 90% of major activities current. Small estuaries had relatively more diverse activities for their size. Activities were particularly diverse in the Greater Thames Estuary, parts of Wales and north-west England, large Scottish firths, and the Humber Estuary, The Wash and the North Norfolk Coast.

Activity proposals were recorded on 108 estuaries, with a similar distribution pattern as for current activities. Proposals were relatively diverse on small estuaries, notably on the Hayle Estuary (where many were part of a single complex development proposal), parts of the Solent, the Greater Thames Estuary, and on the larger estuaries of the Humber and Firth of Forth.

The most widespread uses (on at least 60% of estuaries) were in these categories: linear sea defences and coast protection; dock, port and harbour facilities; bridges and tunnels; recreational activities including angling, dinghy sailing, boat moorings; exploitation of natural resources such as wildfowling and bait-digging; and scientific research and educational work. Docks and jetties are very widespread, on 147 estuaries, as are informal walking and bird-watching (at least 140 sites). Almost 40% of activities were, however, very localised, occurring on less than 20 estuaries each.

Patterns of activity type differ, ranging from typically 'urban' estuaries with over half the categories being urban, industrial and recreational, to 'rural' estuaries with mainly resource exploitation and recreation.

New proposals were diverse, although mostly less widespread than those activity categories are at present, except for tidal energy and 'amenity' barrages. The most widespread proposals (on 20 or more estuaries) were for 'amenity' barrages, dock, port and harbour facilities, capital dredging, road schemes, housing and car-parks, marinas, shellfish farming, and nature trails and information facilities.

The construction of linear sea defences has had a major impact on estuaries. 85% of estuaries have some artificial embankments restricting the tide. Sea defences are particularly extensive in eastern and south-eastern England. Land-claim was also widely promoted in the last century by the planting (on at least 39 estuaries) and subsequent spread of cord-grass.

Over one-third of the British population (18 million people) lives in towns and cities around estuaries. This places great recreational and urban development pressure on the remaining estuarine shores nearby. Seventeen estuaries have current housing and car-park developments, and 36 have proposals. Improved communications also lead to increased recreational pressure on more rural estuaries.

Many widespread human activities have the effect of degrading remaining parts of estuarine ecosystems through, for example, over-exploitation of their natural resources and excessive discharge and spillage of wastes and pollutants. Widespread water-based and land-based recreational use of estuaries is also of increasing concern both for habitat damage (e.g. sand-dune erosion) and its ability to cause severe disturbance to wildlife, particularly nesting birds in summer and feeding and roosting waterfowl during the non-breeding seasons.

Such uses depend, however, on there being estuarine habitats left. The underlying key conservation issue, which also exacerbates the impacts of pollution, over-exploitation and recreation on the remaining parts of estuaries, is progressive habitat loss through land-claim.

1.6.2 Land-claim and habitat loss (Chapter 10.5)

Land-claim is part of a more general estuarine squeeze that is pushing the high water mark seawards (through land-claim, sea defences, barrages and rising sea levels) and low water mark landwards (through effects of dredging, barrages and rising sea-level).

Land-claim has been widespread, cumulative and piecemeal. It has affected at least 85% of British estuaries, and has removed over 25% of intertidal land from many estuaries, over 80% in estuaries such as the Blyth (Suffolk), the Tees and the Tyne.

The largest area (47,000 ha) has been progressively claimed from The Wash since Roman times. On just 18 estuaries at least 89,000 have been claimed – 37% of their former area and overall an almost 25% loss from the British resource. In the last 200 years estuarine land has been claimed at 0.2-0.7% per year.

Widespread land-claim is continuing. 123 land-claims in progress in 1989 affected 45 estuaries. 72 of these cases were affecting the intertidal and subtidal parts of 32 estuaries.

Land-claim was for many purposes, but two-thirds was for rubbish and spoil disposal, transport (chiefly road) schemes, housing and car-parks, and marinas. Many individual claims were of less than 5 ha, but overall at least 1,100 ha are under active claim below high water mark, 61.5% of which is for rubbish and spoil tipping. Over 1,300 ha of associated terrestrial habitats were under claim, almost all for rubbish and spoil disposal.

Much agricultural land-claim in the past created coastal grazing marshes which have since developed substantial conservation interest. Much of this grazing marsh has now been secondarily claimed for intensive agriculture and for urban and industrial developments. Between 30 and 70% of the marshes that remained in the 1930s in different parts of south-east England have now been claimed. There are further major land-claim proposals for the remaining fragments such as Rainham Marshes on the Thames Estuary.

Many other estuarine development proposals would cause further land-claim: in 1989 there were 135 such proposals affecting 55 estuaries. Most are in the Greater Thames estuary, around the Solent, Milford Haven and the Severn Estuary. Housing schemes, marinas and barrage schemes together account for over half the proposals. There are fewer rubbish and spoil disposal proposals.

Overall future habitat losses will be considerable if all proposals are implemented. Barrage schemes alone may remove at least 8% of the remaining British intertidal resource. Continuing habitat loss will further reduce an already much diminished resource, and will force development and recreational land-uses into increasing conflict with wildlife on the remaining areas of estuarine habitat. Rising sea levels, especially in parts of southern Britain, will exacerbate the pressure because estuaries are not able to retreat landward beyond existing sea defences.

The recognised international wildlife importance of an estuary does not appear substantially to deflect land-claim: 26 estuaries in the Ramsar/SPA network have current habitat losses, 21 of these losing intertidal/subtidal areas.

Furthermore, land-claim proposals affect 36 Ramsar/SPA estuaries. In all, over 50% of internationally important estuaries face further habitat losses by direct land-claim. Proposals involve both small piecemeal incursions and major schemes such as barrages and airports.

Continuing land-claim has many impacts on estuarine wildlife, notably the disproportionate loss of saltmarshes and upper tidal flats, the overall reduction of estuarine biomass and production, and the diminution in the size of some internationally important bird populations, on at least individual estuaries.

1.7 Global warming and sea-level change on British estuaries (Chapter 11)

It is now generally thought that levels of 'greenhouse gases' have been rising over about the last 100 years, coincident with a 0.3-0.6°C rise in global temperatures.

Should this global warming continue, one likely consequence is a rising sea level. This would particularly affect the shallow and intertidal parts of estuaries and the low-lying land surrounding them. Average sea-level rise worldwide is currently estimated to have been 10-20 cm over the last 100 years. Current models predict a likely further 20 cm rise by 2030 and a 65 cm rise by the end of the 21st century.

Present and future effects of rising sea levels are complicated in Britain by the effects of movements of the land after the last ice age. In Britain this results broadly in the relative sea level falling in the north and west, and rising in the south and south-east. The low coastlines in south-east England are most at risk from the combined effects of land sinking and any sea-level rise induced by global warming.

A rise in sea level acts as part of the estuarine squeeze, attempting to move the intertidal zone upwards and inland. Under natural conditions estuarine ecosystems are capable of responding to such changes. This inland movement is, however, now generally prevented by sea-defences which 'fix' the coastline. Amongst options under consideration for future coastal defence are 'soft' approaches such as strategic withdrawal of existing defence lines on parts of the coast so as to permit natural buffers of estuarine and coastal habitats to re-establish.

1.8 The future for estuarine conservation (Chapter 12)

Despite the present extensive and diverse site safeguard designations on estuaries, and increasing awareness of the importance of estuaries in the environment, widespread loss and damage continues. The future existence and health of Britain's estuaries and their wildlife now depends on imaginative resource management and on the improved implementation of conservation measures in partnership with decision-makers and estuarine users. The NCC and its successor bodies have a vital role in such partnerships.

1.8.1 The special needs of estuaries

Estuarine conservation is difficult to deliver effectively within the present statutory framework. Estuaries are diverse, often large, areas and straddle the boundary between land and sea. In addition, they are affected by a range of upstream, onshore and marine activities as well as those directly within their core areas.

Many estuaries cross country and county boundaries, and different parts fall within the jurisdiction of different authorities. Hence no one body can act independently to ensure their safeguard. The future health of estuaries depends on the co-operation of local authorities, developers and estuary users as well as conservationists.

Many issues and developments, such as power generation, port and harbour construction and recreational development, are subject to Government or Parliamentary control, consent or guidance. Government itself will have a key role in supporting the appropriate and sustainable use of estuaries without prejudicing their wildlife.

A 'sustainable development' approach is particularly relevant to estuaries since it presupposes that risks of damage to the environment will be anticipated and avoided. It depends on the maintenance of ecological processes and biodiversity in their own right, the establishment of 'minimum standards' for environmental assets, and environmental accounting of the state of those assets.

Since so much of the estuarine resource has already been lost or damaged, and the remainder functions as a nationally and internationally important network, the 'minimum standard' for estuaries is very high, especially in the light of international obligations to maintain and enhance the resource of estuarine habitats and their wildlife.

1.8.2 Directions for the future

To improve the future safeguard of estuaries requires an understanding of the major national and international importance of estuaries in our natural environment, and the involvement and co-operation of many individuals and organisations.

Key issues for the future are:

- the need for a national policy to sustain the estuarine resource;

- the adoption of statutory site safeguard mechanisms on estuaries to ensure that effective conservation of estuarine ecosystems, including both terrestrial and marine features, is in line with international requirements;

- the need to work with individuals and organisations whose activities affect the health of estuaries and their wildlife, so as to ensure a greater awareness and acceptance of the value of estuarine and conservation needs; and

- the need to work with local interests at the level of individual estuaries to develop integrated management and development strategies, in line with the national and international estuarine network and its conservation needs.

Without sympathetic and imaginative future
treatment of these ecosystems, it seems inevitable
that the piecemeal and cumulative damage and
destruction of estuaries and their wildlife by a wide
variety of activities and developments will continue.
The estuarine resource is one of Britain's most
valuable natural assets. We can no longer afford to
treat it as wasteland.

2 Authors, contributors and acknowledgements

Contents

2.1 The Estuaries Review team

The Estuaries Review was established in September 1988, as part of the NCC's Chief Scientist Directorate, as a team of three – Dr N C Davidson (head), Dr D d'A Laffoley and L S Way – under the overall direction of Assistant Chief Scientist Dr K L Duff. The data collection, collation and analysis for *Nature conservation and estuaries in Great Britain* was undertaken by this three-strong review team. The rapid handling and analysis of the large amounts of information collected during by the review was made possible by L S Way's development of a major computer database. Our thanks also to C Manners and particularly E Leck for invaluable clerical assistance of many kinds during the work of the review, and also to the other current members of the Estuaries Review team, A L Buck and Dr S N Freeman.

The work of the Estuaries Review has been guided throughout by a steering group composed of regional, national and Great Britain headquarters policy and scientific NCC staff. We thank all those who, in addition to the authors of this report, have participated: Dr J Baxter, Dr D A Cadwalladr, I Dair, R Goodier, J Heap, Dr R Jones, Dr R Keymer, Dr R Rafe, P Simmonds and Dr S Ward.

2.2 Authors and contributors

To prepare a report covering the very wide range of topics in *Nature conservation and estuaries in Great Britain* has involved drawing on the knowledge and expertise of many people. This report is multi-authored, with chapters written by different authors. In addition, others have contributed further information to parts of particular chapters. The major authors, and the additional contributors, for each chapter are listed below.

Chapter 3 Introduction: N C Davidson

Chapter 4 The nature of British estuaries: N C Davidson, D d'A Laffoley and L S Way

Chapter 5 The locations and classification of British estuaries: J E Gordon, N C Davidson, D d'A Laffoley and L S Way, with contributions from H Caldwell

Chapter 6 The size of the British estuarine resource: N C Davidson

Chapter 7 Review methodology: N C Davidson, D d'A Laffoley and L S Way

Chapter 8 Britain's estuarine wildlife resource

Chapter 8.1 Estuarine habitats: J P Doody, N C Davidson and D d'A Laffoley, with contributions from L Farrell, S Leach, C Johnston and L S Way

Chapter 8.2 Terrestrial and non-marine invertebrates: R Key and M Drake, with contributions from A Foster and D A Procter

Chapter 8.3 Aquatic estuarine communities: D d'A Laffoley

Chapter 8.4 Fish: D d'A Laffoley

Chapter 8.5 Amphibians and reptiles: N C Davidson

Chapter 8.6 Birds: N C Davidson, with contributions from D A Stroud and M W Pienkowski

Chapter 8.7 Mammals: N C Davidson and D d'A Laffoley

Chapter 9 The conservation status of British estuaries: N C Davidson, with contributions from D A Stroud, J E Gordon and H Caldwell

Chapter 10 Human estuarine activities: N C Davidson, D d'A Laffoley, J P Doody and L S Way

Chapter 11 Global warming and sea-level change on British estuaries: J P Doody

Chapter 12 Conclusions: N C Davidson

2.3 Acknowledgements

A great many people and organisations provided assistance, information and helpful comments at various stages of the review process. These contributions are acknowledged below.

We are especially grateful to those who have read and made helpful suggestions on draft versions of part or all of the texts: Dr J Baxter, T Bennett, Prof D Q Bowen, F Burd, Dr L Campbell, D Connor, Dr A S Cooke, R Covey, Lord Cranbrook,

P Crimmen, Dr M Elliot, Dr C Eno, Prof P R Evans, J Heap, Dr K Hiscock, Prof F G T Holliday, T Hornsby, Dr W R Howells, Dr R Jones, Prof J L Knill, Dr D Langslow, Prof J B L Matthews, J Moore, Dr G Mudge, M Nugent, Dr G Owen, Dr G Potts, Dr R Prys-Jones, Dr G Radley, Dr R Rafe, Dr P Reay, Dr E I S Rees, Dr P Rothwell, Dr D F Shaw, D J Stroud, M Tasker, Prof D Taylor Smith, J Teacher, Dr M Usher and Dr M A Vincent.

We gratefully acknowledge the help of the British Trust for Ornithology, the Wader Study Group, the Wildfowl and Wetlands Trust, the Suffolk Wildlife Trust, Dr C Beardall, A J Prater and H Prendergast in making available additional information on wintering and breeding birds; A Crawford, J & R Green, G Liles, Dr J Harwood, H Marshall, S Northridge, H Smith, Dr P Thompson and H Watson for additional information on mammals; and Dr A S Cooke for additional information on amphibians and reptiles.

We are especially grateful to the many NCC regional staff for their considerable time and effort in helping us collect information on the conservation status and human use of estuaries: I S Angus, A K Bachell, Dr D W Bale, C O Badenoch, J Barrett, Dr A Brenchley, R Briggs, J Burlison, A G Carstairs, C R Charles, R G Corns, J R Cox, C Corrigan, C N Crawford, N Crockford, G J Dalglish, P Day, C F Durell, M J D'Oyly, C R J Eccles, R D M Edgar, M H Elliot, F Evans, S B Evans, Dr C C Gibson, Dr P R Glading, N L Gubbins, R M Hamilton, C J Hayes, G Hayes, J W Hickling, M Hughes, K A Irvine, C M T Johnson, Dr R Jefferson, D G Jones, D J Kite, R Lord, J Lunn, R McGibbon, J K McNaught, I K Morgan, R B Ninnes, S G North, J Ostler, A G Payne, B R Pawson, Dr R Rafe, J Robertson, P Sargeant, K J Scott, C J T Shackles, C Shaw, H E Stace, Dr I M Strachan, F L Symonds, N W Taylor, Dr D J Townshend, C R Tubbs, S R Warman, Dr A J Watson, J R White, Dr R J Wolton, and P A Wright. We thank also all those other people and organisations who provided additional information, including: A Henderson, H Watson, Dr C Beardall, the National Rivers Authority, regional water companies, river purification boards, harbour-masters, dock, port and harbour authorities, the British Ports Federation, the National Trust, the Crown Estates Commissioners, the Sports Council, the Scottish Sports Council, the British Canoe Union, the British Sub-aqua Club, the National Diving Council for Scotland, the British Water Ski Federation, the Royal Yachting Association headquarters and regional associations, the Welsh Yachting Association, the Ministry of Agriculture, Fisheries and Food, the Department of Agriculture and Fisheries for Scotland, the Association of Sea Fisheries Committees, Sea Fisheries Officers, the National Trust, the Cornish Biological Records Unit, the Suffolk Wildlife Trust, the Cornwall Wildlife Trust and the Northumberland Wildlife Trust.

We thank Blackie & Son Ltd., Earthscan Publishers Ltd., the Freshwater Biological Association, T & A D Poyser, Suffolk Wildlife Trust, Wiley & Sons Inc., and John Wiley & Son Ltd., and the authors indicated in the figure captions for permission to reproduce illustrations. Some of the maps in this report are based upon Ordnance Survey maps with the permission of the Controller of Her Majesty's Stationery Office. © Crown Copyright.

The NCC Library staff were most helpful throughout the preparation of this report in helping to locate numerous literature sources and other information. J Riggall and S Thomas were also of great help in providing computer support at critical times in the reviewing process, and we thank S Wallace for making the measurements of estuary areas and lengths.

Earlier drafts of the whole text were edited by S Kaznowska. We are particularly grateful to her for help and tolerance throughout.

<table>
<tr><td>

3 **Introduction**

</td></tr>
</table>

Contents

"[Britain] was alive, throbbing through all her estuaries, crying for joy through the mouths of all her gulls and the north wind, with contrary motion, blew stronger against her rising seas. What did it mean? For what end are her fair complexities, her changes of soil, her sinuous coast? Does she belong to those who have moulded her and made her feared by other lands, or to those who have added nothing to her power, but have somehow seen her, seen the whole island at once, lying as a jewel in a silver sea, sailing as a ship of souls, with all the brave world's fleet accompanying her towards eternity?"

E.M.Forster   *Howards End*

3.1 Characteristics of estuaries

Estuaries are wetlands that form at the margins of the land and the sea. This straddling of environmental boundaries, coupled with the continual movements of the tide and the mixing of fresh water and salt water, make estuaries complex and varying ecosystems. The continual input, trapping and recycling of sediments and nutrients leads to estuaries being amongst the most fertile and productive ecosystems in the world.

Estuaries are distinct from other kinds of wetlands in that they link marine, freshwater and dry land ecosystems (Figure 3.1). As a result estuaries are formed of a mosaic of interlinked subtidal and intertidal habitats surrounded by terrestrial habitats such as sand-dunes, shingle ridges and coastal grazing marshes influenced by their proximity to the coast.

The shallow sheltered areas of tidal water in an estuary cause tidal and river currents to slow, so that fine sediments settle out of suspension. Large

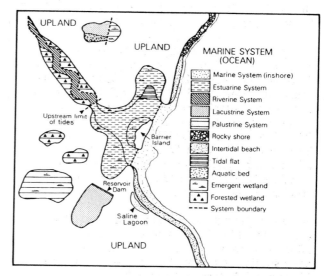

Figure 3.1 The relationship between an estuary and other major wetland types (derived from Maltby 1986).

quantities of these sediments are carried in suspension down rivers from often very large catchment areas and in from the sea. Sedimentation of fine particles carried down rivers is enhanced in estuaries by salt flocculation: salt water causes fine clay particles to stick together, so increasing their effective particle size and accelerating their settlement. This continual trapping and settlement of sediments means that estuaries are generally depositional shores, composed chiefly of fine unconsolidated muds and sands.

With sediments, nutrients are also carried in from the sea and down rivers into estuaries, where they are trapped in sheltered parts and taken up by plants and animals. Here they are continually replenished and discharged by rivers and freshwater run-off from the land and by the repeated ebb and flow of the tide.

Tides ebb and flow over these shallow estuarine shores in a regular and predictable way, covering the shore to different extents on daily, monthly and yearly cycles. In addition, floods occasionally discharge down rivers and storm surge tides funnel into estuaries from the sea. These produce extreme high tidal levels. Such events cause saline or brackish water to extend well beyond its normal zone of influence up river estuaries. With the progressively rising sea-levels on some parts of the coast, there is increasing likelihood of periodic flooding of land behind sea-defences during storm surges. Organisms living on even these parts of the estuarine system, which are very infrequently influenced by the tide or salt water, require adaptations to tolerate estuarine conditions.

This uniquely varying set of physical, chemical and biological conditions enables estuaries to support abundant wildlife capable of exploiting these nutrient-rich but variable conditions. Many of these plants and animals are highly dependent on estuaries for part or all of their lives, and many are of great nature conservation importance.

3.2 Estuaries and nature conservation

Britain has more estuarine habitat than anywhere else in Europe, but even so estuaries form only just over 2% of the British land area. British estuaries, fed by abundant sediments and surrounded by shallow productive seas, also have relatively mild winters under the influence of the Gulf Stream, and so provide particularly favourable conditions for some estuarine organisms when compared with estuaries elsewhere in western Europe. Despite their relatively small share of Britain's area, estuarine habitats and the plants, birds and other animals that they support, were identified by Ratcliffe (1977) in his major review of Britain's wildlife resource as amongst Britain's most nationally and internationally important wildlife features. Britain has a particularly significant international commitment to safeguarding scarce and migrant birds and the network of estuarine habitats upon which they depend for their survival, and Ratcliffe (1977) points out that the destruction of any major estuary would represent a serious loss to nature conservation, not only for Britain, but also on an international scale.

The Nature Conservancy Council has recognised the conservation importance of estuaries, and has notified many parts of the Britain's estuarine resource as Sites of Special Scientific Interest (SSSIs). Britain's major international obligations to maintain and safeguard estuarine wetland habitats and their wildlife, notably under the terms of the 'Ramsar' convention on the conservation of wetlands especially as waterfowl habitat and the EEC Directive on the conservation of wild birds, are recognised by the inclusion of many parts of Britain's estuaries in the network of designated and proposed internationally important sites.

Since Ratcliffe's (1977) review of terrestrial wildlife habitats in Britain, there have been numerous wildlife surveys and reviews that include estuaries. For example, the Nature Conservancy Council's current Marine Nature Conservation Review (MNCR) and Geological Conservation Review (GCR), projects such as the NCC's Coastwatch, and the Coastal Directory for Marine Nature Conservation (Gubbay 1988), include features of estuaries. Other surveys have assessed the distribution of a part of the wildlife resource, for example migrant and wintering birds (Prater 1981), internationally important bird populations (Stroud et al. 1990) and saltmarshes (Burd 1989). Until now, however, there has been no comprehensive assessment of the extent and distribution of all facets of the estuarine resource throughout Britain.

3.3 Estuaries and man

Man has been closely associated with estuaries for many centuries. The contact has been particularly close in Britain which, as an island, has few parts very far from the very long coastline. The sheltered conditions found in many estuaries have provided safe anchorage for boats during storms and seaports for trade with the rest of the world. The highly productive estuarine ecosystems, dependent on the continual input of nutrients down rivers and from the sea, have yielded sustainable harvests of fish, shellfish and waterfowl, supplies of salt, grazing for farm stock and materials for building. The river flows and continual movements of the tide have been harnessed to power mills and, increasingly, to aid the disposal of effluents. More recently the shelter offered by estuaries has also fostered the growth of a wide variety of leisure and recreational activities.

Despite, and sometimes because of, their economic importance, British estuaries are, however, under long-term and continuous threat of damage and destruction. Overall the losses of estuarine habitat, almost entirely attributable to human activity, have been extensive. About one-third of all British intertidal estuarine habitat and about half the saltmarsh area has been claimed since Roman times, as have over two-thirds of coastal grazing marshes in south-east England since the 1930s (Thornton & Kite 1990; Davidson et al. in press). In just the The Wash in eastern England, about 32,000 ha of saltmarshes in the original fenland basin have been claimed for agriculture since Roman times (Doody & Barnett 1987). In some British estuaries man has now removed all, or almost all, the intertidal wildlife habitats.

Estuarine habitat losses are also widespread elsewhere in the world. For example, in France 40% of the coastal wetlands of Brittany have gone in the last 20 years (Maltby 1988). In the USA 54% of all wetlands have been destroyed since colonial times, and the remaining saltmarshes continue to disappear at a rate of almost 1% per year (Maltby 1986, 1988). In south-east Asia the South Korean government has recently identified over 450,000 ha of coastal intertidal land as appropriate for land-claim (Poole 1990).

Such estuarine habitat losses are part of wider damage to wildlife habitats, including other wetlands, that is summarised for Britain in *Nature conservation in Great Britain* (NCC 1984). For example over 84% of the area of lowland raised bog in Britain was lost to agriculture, afforestation and commercial peat cutting between the mid 19th century and 1978 (NCC 1986). In England and Wales between the early 1800s and 1939 about 4.7 million hectares of agricultural land were drained, notably in the fens of East Anglia (Green 1980).

Although uses of estuaries have for centuries been varied and extensive, estuaries are nevertheless difficult and sometimes dangerous places to exploit. Estuaries have acted as an impediment to travel, forcing long detours inland or hazardous crossings of the tidal flats by causeways and fords during short periods of low tide. Such dangers are no respecters even of royalty: many of King John's army died in a disastrous crossing of The Wash in the mid 12th century (Miller & Skertchly 1878), an event that led soon after to the King's death and in which he is reputed to have lost the Crown Jewels. The often shifting sands and mudbanks and the strong currents in estuaries make their navigation or crossing a skilled task. The extreme fluctuations of the physical environment have meant that man's attempts to harness, manipulate and control estuaries have often had limited success, at least until the 20th century, and changes to the gross form of estuaries have been much less obvious than those to many terrestrial systems (see e.g. Rackham 1986). Even so, very substantial modifications to the fringes of estuaries have been under way since at least Roman times, particularly through the alteration and enclosure of saltmarshes for farming, but even now many estuaries remain largely wild and unspoilt areas, even though their shores are often accessible to large numbers of people living close by.

Their unfathomable and untamable nature has led estuaries to be often described in literature as wild and thrilling, but awesome, places (e.g. Dickens 1861; Hill 1983). Estuaries have provided the setting for adventure and excitement for both adults (e.g. Childers 1903) and children (e.g. Ransome 1939). In their more gentle guise they also feature as places of haven and romance (e.g. Du Maurier 1941).

To many people who live and work around estuaries it is the unceasing ebb and flow of the tides and the constantly changing light and seasons that contribute strongly to their attraction. Yet to others, however, these same estuaries and their highly productive tidal flats are regarded as valuable parts of the environment only once the tidal flats have been permanently covered by water, such as by barrage construction, or by infilling as waste disposal sites and for industrial and urban land.

Since the Industrial Revolution man has increased the exploitation of estuaries, and although many human activities have continued to be sustainable, others have increasingly involved irreversible damage to or loss of estuarine habitat. This seems to reflect a shift from the relative harmony of much of man's historical use of estuaries to their now frequent treatment as wastelands. Man's activities include land-claim for a wide variety of purposes and the discharge of slow or non-degradable pollutants. More recently, estuaries have been used to an increasing extent for recreation, particularly the many forms of watersports. In the 1960s and 1970s a number of very large schemes, notably for the construction of water storage barrages, were proposed for several major estuaries in Britain. These would, if built, have substantially damaged the existing wildlife interest of many of these estuaries.

Although these schemes of 15-30 years ago were mostly dropped, in the last 10 years there has been a resurgence of pressure on the wildlife of estuaries from many directions. This has included proposals for barrages for the generation of tidal power, for storm surge control, and to provide for the demands of leisure and recreation. At the same time there have been many other developments, and proposals for developments, which in themselves each affect only a part of an estuary, but which overall can have substantial impact. Furthermore it has become clear that similar proposals can be made simultaneously for many different estuaries.

Although much is know about uses, developments and proposals on individual estuaries, there has been no readily available overall assessment, covering the whole of Britain, of the extent and pattern of human use of estuaries. In seeking to continue to conserve the major wildlife importance of estuaries it is vital to understand both the ways in which wildlife use the estuaries and how man uses the same places, since although man's uses may often be consistent with wildlife conservation, they can also often be highly damaging to wildlife.

3.4 The Nature Conservancy Council's Estuaries Review

In the climate of evident increasing pressure on the remaining estuarine areas and their wildlife the NCC began its Estuaries Review in September 1988. Its purpose is to examine wildlife and human use of estuaries so as to permit the development of a strategy for the promotion of nature conservation in estuaries through the maintenance and enhancement of good wildlife habitat, species populations and earth science features. Such a strategy can only be developed from a sound understanding of the wildlife resource of estuaries, its requirements and what is affecting it.

8.5 Aims and scope of *Nature conservation and estuaries in Great Britain*

This report, *Nature conservation and estuaries in Great Britain*, is the first major product of the Estuaries Review. Its information is presented so as to provide the basis for discussion and the development of strategies to safeguard estuarine wildlife in the future.

Nature conservation and estuaries in Great Britain provides, for the first time in one place, a wide-ranging description of the major wildlife importance of British estuaries, the ways in which the wildlife is protected and the patterns of human activities that affect the wildlife and its conservation.

The timescale of the review and the very extensive range of estuarine features included in it have precluded the detailed examination within this report of the interrelationship between wildlife and man within each estuary. *Nature conservation and estuaries in Great Britain* provides, however, the framework of the distributional information within which more detailed future analyses can be set.

Our approach has not therefore been to provide a detailed site-by-site inventory of each part of the estuarine resource; rather we have chosen to describe features of estuarine wildlife conservation on an overall geographical and numerical basis, identifying the presence or absence of each feature and, where possible, its size distribution around the resource. The report is not intended to be a comprehensive account of the processes and functioning of estuarine ecosystems, although the next chapter provides a brief outline of some of the key physical, chemical and biological features of British estuaries, useful in understanding the conservation needs of estuarine wildlife. There are many general texts that provide such estuarine ecosystem reviews, for example Dyer (1979), McLusky (1981), Barnes & Hughes (1982), Head (1985) and Day *et al.* (1989).

Information has been drawn largely from existing sources, both published and unpublished, and has not involved the undertaking of original wildlife survey work. In some cases our analyses have seemingly, however, provided the first, although sometimes preliminary, distributional assessment of an estuarine feature. The report therefore serves to highlight both the extensive knowledge that already exists about the estuarine wildlife resource and where further information is needed for estuarine conservation. Information on the very wide range of human activities has been drawn largely from the records and experience of the NCC regional staff responsible for the conservation of the estuaries in their part of Britain. Where time has permitted, this has been supplemented with information from a range of other published sources and organisations.

The chapters of this report describe wildlife features and human activities on estuaries in a standardised way, with an assessment of conservation needs and impacts or implications and, where possible, a map showing the distribution. Throughout, our approach has been to treat what man does on and to estuaries as activities rather than as threats, since human modification of estuaries can at different times be beneficial, neutral or threatening to estuarine wildlife. What may be a threat in a sensitive location or at a sensitive time could be neutral or beneficial in other circumstances. The report is intended to provide pointers for the more detailed assessments needed of particular features of estuarine use and conservation, and to provide a reference source to aid understanding of the many facets of estuaries and the conservation of their wildlife.

Nature conservation and estuaries in Great Britain is intended to be of use as a source of information for all those who use estuaries or who are interested in them, including Government Departments, Local Authorities, industry, developers and potential developers, estuarine interest groups, officers of the NCC and its successor bodies and all those who seek the quiet enjoyment of estuaries and their wildlife.

3.6 References

BARNES, R.S.K, & HUGHES, R.N. 1982. *An introduction to marine ecology*. Oxford, Blackwell Scientific.

BURD, F. 1989. *The saltmarsh survey of Great Britain*. Peterborough, Nature Conservancy Council. (Research & survey in nature conservation No. 17.)

CHILDERS, R.E. 1903. *The riddle of the sands*. London, Smith, Elder & Co.

DAY, J.W., HALL, C.A.S., KEMP, M.W., & YANEZ-ARANCIBIA, A. 1989. *Estuarine ecology*. New York, John Wiley & Sons.

DICKENS, C. 1861. *Great expectations*. London, Chapman & Hall.

DAVIDSON, N.C., LAFFOLEY, D.d'A., & DOODY, J.P. In press. Land-claim on British estuaries: changing patterns and conservation implications. *In: The changing coastline*, ed. by J. Pethick. Estuarine and Coastal Sciences Association, Symposium Series.

DOODY, P, & BARNETT, B., eds. 1987. *The Wash and its environment*. Peterborough, Nature Conservancy Council. (Research & survey in nature conservation No. 7.)

DU MAURIER, D. 1941. *Frenchman's Creek*. London, Gollancz.

DYER, K.R., ed. 1979. *Estuarine hydrography and sedimentation*. Estuarine and Brackish-water Sciences Association handbook. Cambridge, Cambridge University Press.

GREEN, F.H.W. 1980. Field under-drainage before and after 1940. *The Agricultural History Review*, *28*, 120-123.

GUBBAY, S. 1988. *A coastal directory for marine nature conservation*. Ross-on-Wye, Marine Conservation Society.

HEAD, P.C., ed. 1985. *Practical estuarine chemistry*. Estuarine and Brackish-water Sciences Association handbook. Cambridge, Cambridge University Press.

HILL, S. 1983. *The woman in black*. London, Hamish Hamilton.

MALTBY, E. 1986. *Waterlogged wealth*. Earthscan, London.

MALTBY, E. 1988. Wetland resources and future prospects – an international perspective. *In: Increasing our wetland resources*, ed. by J.Zelzany and J.Scott Feierabend, 3-14. Washington D.C., National Wildlife Federation.

McLUSKY, D.S. 1981. *The estuarine ecosystem.* Glasgow, Blackie.

MILLER, S.H., & SKERTCHLY, S.B.J. 1878. *The Fenland past and present.* Wisbech, Leach & Son.

NATURE CONSERVANCY COUNCIL. 1984. *Nature conservation in Great Britain.* Peterborough, Nature Conservancy Council.

NATURE CONSERVANCY COUNCIL. 1986. *Nature conservation and afforestation in Britain.* Peterborough, Nature Conservancy Council.

POOLE, C.M. 1990. *A review of coastal development projects in the Republic of Korea.* Kuala Lumpur, Asian Wetland Bureau.

PRATER, A.J. 1981. *Estuary birds.* Berkhamsted, T. & A.D. Poyser.

RACKHAM, A. 1986. *The history of the countryside.* London, Dent.

RANSOME, A.M. 1939. *Secret water.* London, Jonathon Cape.

RATCLIFFE, D.A. 1977. *A nature conservation review.* Cambridge, Cambridge University Press.

STROUD, D.A., MUDGE, G.P., & PIENKOWSKI, M.W. 1990 *Protecting internationally important bird sites: a review of the EEC Special Protection Area network in Great Britain.* Peterborough, Nature Conservancy Council.

THORNTON, D., & KITE, D.J. 1990. *Changes in the extent of the Thames Estuary grazing marshes.* London, Nature Conservancy Council.

4   The nature of British estuaries

Contents

4.1   Introduction

This chapter provides the definition of an estuary used for the NCC Estuaries Review, and then gives a brief introduction to general features of British estuarine ecosystems and their processes. Our intention in this report is not to provide a detailed review of the complex physical, chemical and biological processes of estuaries, but rather to set the scene for the more detailed distributional analyses that follow. Further information on estuarine hydrology, geomorphology and ecosystem processes can be found in many texts such as Steers (1964, 1973), Dyer (1979), McLusky (1971, 1981), Barnes & Hughes (1982), Barnes (1984), Pethick (1984), Head (1985), Kennish (1986), and Day et al. (1989).

4.2 What is an estuary?

There are many ways in which estuaries have been defined, but by their very nature as places of transition between land, sea and fresh water no simple definition readily fits all types of estuarine system. For the Estuaries Review a definition must cover all features that together form the wildlife conservation interest of estuarine systems characterised by a 'functional estuarine unit' of interlinked terrestrial and aquatic tidal habitats.

NERC (1975) regarded an estuary as "a partially enclosed body of water, open to saline water from the sea and receiving fresh water from rivers, land run-off or seepage". This means that some estuaries, where there is a major river inflow, are strongly influenced by fresh water but others are predominantly marine systems. NERC (1975) identify further general characteristics of estuaries: that they are subject to a usually twice daily tidal rise and fall, and that they have mud and sand shoals forming in their shallow basins.

Other characteristic features of estuaries include the presence of saltmarshes, wave shelter, water layering and mixing, temperature and salinity gradients, sediment suspension and transport, high productivity, high levels and rapid exchange of nutrients, the presence of plants and animals particularly adapted to these conditions, and the presence of migrant and seasonally fluctuating populations of animals (NERC 1875). Some of these are features are described further below.

For the Estuaries Review we have followed NERC (1975) in taking a typical estuary as being a partially enclosed area at least partly composed of soft tidal shores, open to saline water from the sea, and receiving fresh water from rivers, land run-off or seepage. This approach is similar also to that of Day et al. (1989) who describe estuaries as a continuum of types ranging from entirely marine-influenced systems such as tidal lagoons formed behind wave-generated sand or shingle bars to deltas created by river processes (see also Davies 1973).

The conditions of large sediment supply and shallow seas surrounding parts of Britain have led to some extensive areas of soft tidal flats, with characteristics typical of the marine end of the estuarine continuum, developing outside river mouths on open coasts. These areas have been included in the Estuaries Review since they have the key features of tidally-influenced extensive soft shores. On a larger scale, most can be regarded as the outer parts of very large estuaries such the Thames. Tidal inlets that have predominantly steeply shelving rocky shores, such as many sea-lochs in Scotland, are not, however, included in the Estuaries Review.

It should be noted that the NERC and Estuaries Review treatment of estuaries is broader than some other widely used estuarine definitions. Fairbridge's (1980) definition ("an inlet of the sea reaching into a river valley as far as the upper limit of tidal rise") includes the tidal, freshwater, upper reaches of a river mouth and also its outer parts under strong marine influence, but still excludes some areas, notably those without major river influence, where marine-dominated estuarine ecosystems have developed. Pritchard's (1967) definition ("an estuary is a semi-enclosed coastal body of water which has a free connection with the open sea and within which sea water is measurably diluted with fresh water derived from land drainage") makes no direct mention of the rise and fall of the tide, and excludes the freshwater tidal reaches of estuaries; zones which can be extensive in the flat lowlands of eastern Britain.

4.3 Estuarine geomorphology

Coastlines are transient in geological time, and the precise physical location of estuaries and other coastal landforms is substantially dependent on sea level and is constantly changing. Present estuaries were formed when sea level rose after the last glaciation, and most estuaries known now did not exist 10,000 – 15,000 years ago. When sea level was low during the last ice age the water's edge was on the steep continental slope so that estuaries were small. However, the rising sea level shallowly flooded the continental shelf so that estuaries are now relatively large and widespread. Even so they still form only a very small part of the land surface even in a country such as Britain which, because of the length of its coastline, is particularly well endowed with estuaries (Chapter 6). The abundance of sediments in the shallow seas surrounding estuaries is both a vital source upon which the abundance and diversity of estuarine ecosystems depends and the cause of change, since many estuaries are gradually becoming filled with deposited sediments. For example, the Teign Estuary in Devon is a ria, formed by the drowning of a river valley by the rise in sea level during the last marine transgression. It has subsequently, however, become filled with soft sediments so that it resembles a coastal plain estuary (Chapter 5).

Although the location of each estuary changes naturally with time, Day et al. (1989) point out that estuarine ecosystems, with their characteristic species composition and adaptations, have also moved back and forth with the edge of the sea. Thus even though estuaries in their particular locations are generally short-lived and, with time, estuaries may coalesce or separate, estuarine organisms and ecosystems themselves are very old. The continued existence of estuaries and their organisms depends, however, on their being able to move with changing sea level. Recolonisation by estuarine organisms can be very slow, and there is evidence that the recolonisation by macrobenthic species of estuaries in the northern North Sea may not yet be complete after the last glaciation (Wolff 1973).

More local movements of estuarine habitats have been increasingly constrained by the construction of retaining walls at high tidal levels and the subtidal dredging of shipping channels. Furthermore the construction of training walls along estuary channels has fixed the natural meandering of the channels, so restricting the natural movement of sediments and nutrients within the estuary. The implications of all these constraints for the survival of British estuaries, particularly in the light of continuing sea-level rise, perhaps accelerated by global warming, are considered further in Chapter 11.

Within estuaries sediments can be cycled on a variety of timescales. For example, changes in the configuration of channels and bedforms can occur over periods as short as days, in addition to the longer-term effects such as changing sea levels.

Abundant suspended sediments reach estuaries on currents from the open sea and down rivers. The relatively sheltered conditions on estuaries, especially where tidal currents are weak, permit sediments to fall out of suspension. These form the characteristic estuarine landforms of mudflats, where the most sheltered conditions allow fine silts to accumulate, and, in the higher energy parts of estuaries, more mobile sandflats. Many estuaries characteristically become sandier towards the outer parts of the system, but there is great variation between estuaries in the pattern and distribution of their soft sediments, depending on the effects of differences in topography, sediment loads and currents. These result in the great variety of types of estuary described in Chapter 5. Very coarse sediments can accumulate around the mouths of estuaries in the form of shingle ridges and spits, characteristic of bar-built estuaries and barrier islands. These shingle features in turn provide the more sheltered conditions that promote deposition of mudflats in their lee. In many places around the mouths of estuaries finer sediments are brought onshore by tidal currents and subsequently blown onto land by the wind to form extensive sand-dune systems.

Although many intertidal mudflats and sandflats appear relatively stable, at least in the medium term, this is generally illusory. Such areas are in a dynamic equilibrium in which rates of deposition and erosion from tidal currents and wave action are

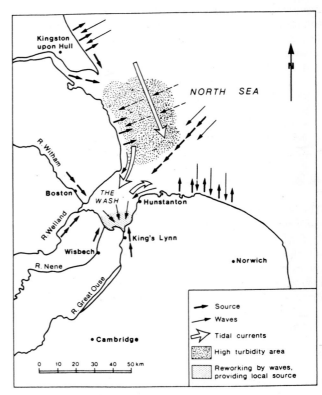

Figure 4.1 A summary of the sources and transport paths of sediment in The Wash and its surroundings, from Evans & Collins (1987). Much of the sediment reaching The Wash comes from outside the estuary mouth, and some reaches the estuary from its extensive river catchment area. Note also that some sediments are eroding and depositing within The Wash.

similar. On accreting shores erosion is slower than deposition, whilst the opposite is true on eroding shores. Many estuaries apparently depend mostly on the open coast as a source of sediment: an example is The Wash (Figure 4.1). In others much sediment is brought down rivers when they are in spate, and in from the sea during periodic storms. Most of the annual sediment supply for some estuaries such as the Tees is trapped in the estuary mouth during just a few storms. Figure 4.1 illustrates another feature of estuarine sediment sources: that much can come from reworking within an estuary. In some places such as the estuaries and coasts of Suffolk and Essex there can be a complex of erosional and depositional shores in close proximity. Here the maintenance of soft shores in estuaries appears to depend on continued erosion of other parts of the adjacent coastline to provide sediment sources for a coastline that is sinking relative to sea level through isostatic change in the aftermath of the last ice age. Eroding soft-rock cliffs are also a frequent feature within estuaries. The conservation significance of all these geomorphological landforms is further described in Chapter 9.

On the upper parts of mudflats a characteristic dense sward of saltmarsh vegetation develops. Estuarine saltmarsh vegetation tends to trap fine sediments among its roots and so increase accretion on these parts of the estuary. The highly invasive fertile hybrid cord-grass *Spartina anglica* has proved particularly effective in encouraging sediment accretion (see Chapter 8.1). Indeed it has in the past been planted for this purpose. It can, however, affect other parts of the estuarine ecosystem since it can colonise open mudflats lower down the shore than other saltmarsh plants can tolerate.

Estuarine saltmarshes can be very extensive and play a vital role in the provision of nutrients into the estuary from the decomposition of their plants. Historically much saltmarsh has been enclosed by sea-walls and converted to coastal wet grasslands (see for example Doody 1987). These coastal grazing marshes have in turn developed into areas of substantial importance to wildlife closely associated with the tidal parts of estuaries (Chapter 8.1). Many have, however, subsequently been converted to more intensive arable farming or to industrial and urban uses. Such areas of former estuary are now generally of little significance for estuarine wildlife.

4.4 Tides

Movements of the tide have a profound effect on the distribution, character and adaptations of estuarine organisms. Tidal movements are largely governed by the gravitational influence of the moon and follow a rather complex cyclical pattern over a number of timescales. The basic tidal cycle in Britain is illustrated in Figure 4.2a. Throughout Britain the tide rises (flood tide) to a high water peak and then falls (ebb tide) to a low water trough

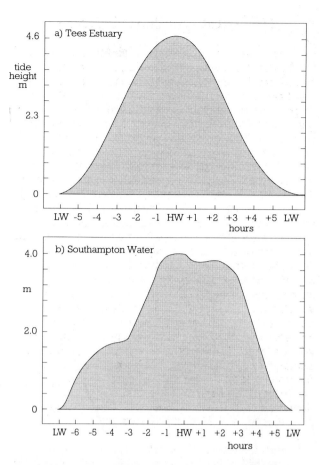

Figure 4.2 Mean spring tide curves for a) the Tees Estuary, and b) Southampton Water. LW = low water, HW = high water

twice in each day. Typically a single flood-ebb cycle takes approximately 12.5 hours. This means that the time at which high water occurs advances by about 1 hour each day. The time at which high water occurs in different parts of Britain differs, with a tidal bulge moving, for example, southwards down the North Sea.

On most British estuaries the tide rises and falls on a fairly steady curve (Figure 4.2a), although in some places the flood period is shorter than the ebb, which encourages a net transport of sediment into the estuary. The tidal pattern is more complex in the Solent estuaries of southern England. An example for Southampton Water is shown in Figure 4.2b. The complex pattern is due to the interaction of the main tidal wave with its higher harmonics, which in the area of the Solent are relatively more important than on other parts of the British coast. This results in there being a pause in the rising tide at about mid-tidal level, followed by a rapid rise to a prolonged high water stand.

The daily tidal cycle means that organisms living on the upper parts of the intertidal generally must be able to withstand prolonged exposure to the air and short periods of inundation with brackish or saline water. Conversely those living at low tidal levels must tolerate prolonged inundation but also short periods of exposure to air. Many organisms living at these lower levels also occur extensively subtidally where they remain covered. Different organisms are capable of tolerating inundation or exposure to varying extents and this results in an often strong vertical zonation on the shore. A good example is in saltmarsh vegetation where upper, middle and lower levels of saltmarsh support quite different saltmarsh plant communities, described further in Chapter 8.1 and illustrated in Figure 8.1.9.

In addition to the diurnal cycle of the tide, there is a monthly pattern of spring and neap tides (Figure 4.3). Spring tides occur when the gravitational pull of the moon and the sun coincide, so exerting a strong force on the water causing it to rise very high and fall very low. Neap tides, when the gravitational forces of the sun and moon are in opposition, reach a lesser height at high water and also drop less at low water. There is thus a tidal

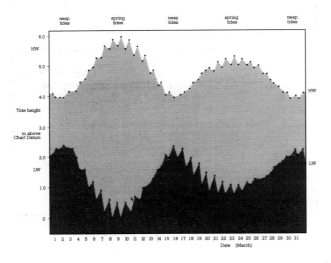

Figure 4.3 Predicted heights of high water (HW) and low water (LW) during a one month period (March 1989) on the Tees Estuary. Heavy shading shows shore heights covered throughout the daily tidal cycle and light shading shows heights covered for only part of the cycle.

height oscillation of varying magnitude around a mid-tide level on the shore that receives a similar period of tidal exposure and coverage regardless of the tidal range.

There are two spring tide and two neap tide series during each month. Typically one spring tide series has larger tidal ranges than the other (Figure 4.3). This means that some of the highest intertidal parts of the shore are covered by tidal water for only short periods on a few days in each month, and conversely those at lowest intertidal levels are exposed for only brief periods on a few days in the month. In contrast, mid-shore levels are inundated and exposed regularly twice daily throughout the month.

In addition to these lunar cycles of approximately a month there is also an annual cycle in tidal range. The very largest spring tides of the year (the highest astronomical tides) occur on a regular

cycle, one in autumn and another in spring. Storm surge tides can, however, force water into estuaries during periods of low atmospheric pressure such that the height of high water exceeds that of highest astronomical tides, even when the predicted high water level is lower. These storm surge events can cause particularly rapid major changes within estuaries.

There is a great variety of physical conditions within a single estuary created by these tidal exposure patterns which, together with the variety of landforms, provides a rich complex of habitats occupied by different specialist organisms. In addition there is considerable variation in the average tidal range on different estuaries in Britain, depending on geographical location and topography of the site (see Chapter 5).

4.5 Salinity

Salinity is the amount of inorganic material dissolved in the water expressed as a weight in grams per kilogram of water, i.e. parts per thousand (‰). The salinity of the sea is approximately 35‰, but that of fresh water is less than 0.5‰. So in estuaries with freshwater inflow, from rivers for example, there is a dilution of sea water down the estuary that produces brackish water conditions. Other review sites such as open shores and large embayments have relatively little freshwater discharge and so have salinities consistently close to that of sea water. In some places, notably coastal saline lagoons, the water can become hypersaline (i.e. saltier than sea water) as a consequence of the evaporative concentration of the inflowing brackish or saline water (see Section 8.1.11).

Where brackish conditions prevail – as in the majority of review sites – salinities, like tides, vary in a complex way. First, there is the geographical variation in dilution down the estuary from fully saline water in the outer estuary to fresh water in the upper parts. In many rivers the saline water fails to penetrate upstream to the tidal limits. This results in there being substantial stretches of tidal freshwater estuary, especially where the gradients of the inflowing rivers are low, as in south-eastern England. This is illustrated in Figure 4.4, which shows that saline water penetrates only a short distance from the main embayment of The Wash into the tidal rivers, so that there are tens of kilometres of freshwater tidal river systems.

Saline water is heavier than fresh water, so it tends to sink below the fresh water flowing down an estuary, forming a salt wedge (Figure 4.5a). This denser saline water then gradually mixes vertically with the outflowing fresh water. As the tide ebbs and floods, this saltwater wedge moves up and down the estuary, so that the salinity at any given point varies throughout the tidal cycle. In some places this can be a variation from almost fresh water to sea water. Salinity gradients such as these are maintained most strongly in estuaries with

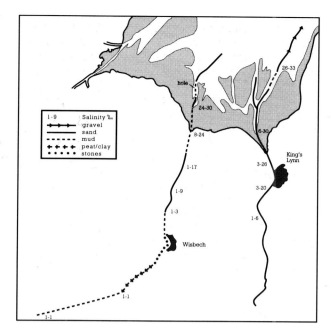

Figure 4.4 Typical salinity ranges in the tidal rivers of The Wash vary from fresh water in the upper reaches to almost fully saline in the main embayment. This figure, from Dyer & Grist (1987), also shows the main substrate types in these rivers.

smooth channel floors. Unlike in these stratified estuaries, there is much more rapid mixing in estuaries with uneven channel floors and here the stratification is destroyed.

In addition to this substantial tidal variation in salinity, there are longer-term, seasonal differences in salinity gradients. In general there are greater volumes of fresh water flowing down rivers in winter than in summer. This results in salt water penetrating considerably further upstream in summer than in winter, a phenomenon illustrated for the stratified Deben Estuary in Figure 4.5b. At any point in the estuary salinities are highest at high water in summer and lowest during winter low water.

4.6 Diversity and distribution of estuarine organisms

In estuaries the variable salinity, coupled with varying periods of tidal inundation and exposure and sometimes highly mobile sediments, provides a harsh physical and chemical environment for plants and animals. Many that occur in estuaries have particular adaptations to, for example, the stresses of varying salinity on the osmotic balance of their body fluids. In general this results in there being fewer species living in estuaries than in either the freshwater rivers above the tidal limit or the truly marine habitats outside estuary mouths. Some freshwater organisms can, however, live in salinities up to about 5‰. Similarly some marine species can tolerate substantially reduced salinities. Indeed it is these euryhaline marine organisms that dominate the estuarine species assemblage, since there are relatively few species

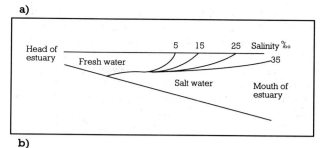

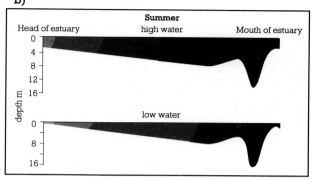

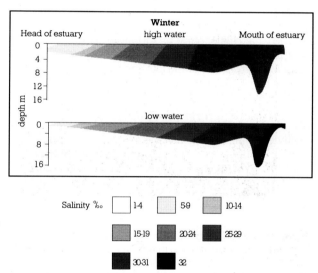

Salinity ‰ 1-4 5-9 10-14 15-19 20-24 25-29 30-31 32

Figure 4.5 Estuarine salinity gradients. a) A generalised gradient in a salt-wedge estuary (after Prater 1981); and b) Tidal and seasonal variations in gradient in the Deben Estuary (after Beardall *et al.* 1988).

restricted only to such brackish waters (Figure 4.6). The lowest species diversity in estuaries occurs where salinities are in the region of 5‰. This results in the diversity of benthic organisms generally decreasing upstream from the mouth of an estuary. Similarly, because at any one place on the estuary higher salinities occur at high water than low water, many of these estuarine animals become increasingly restricted upstream to higher level tidal flats (McClusky 1981).

In addition to salinity the distribution of estuarine organisms is strongly influenced by the type of substrate of the tidal flats. Upstream parts of estuaries are generally both muddier and less saline. Many of the 'typical' estuarine organisms that live in the upper reaches of estuaries, such as the ragworm *Hediste diversicolor* and the

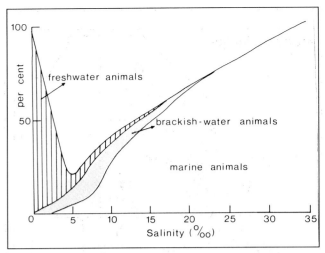

Figure 4.6 The diversity of marine, brackish-water and freshwater animals in relation to salinity (from McLusky 1971)

amphipod crustacean *Corophium volutator*, are adapted to both low salinity and life in soft sediments. Conversely others characteristic of muddy sandflats, such as the lugworm *Arenicola marina* and the bivalve molluscs *Scrobicularia plana* and *Mya arenaria*, cannot tolerate the reduced salinities of upper estuaries (Figure 4.7).

Although estuaries generally contain relatively few benthic species, the abundance and density of individual animals is usually very high. Estuarine species densities are usually greater than densities in marine or freshwater habitats. This is illustrated in Figure 4.8, which also demonstrates that the biomass (the weight of the living matter) is about twice as great in intertidal flats as in marine or freshwater systems.

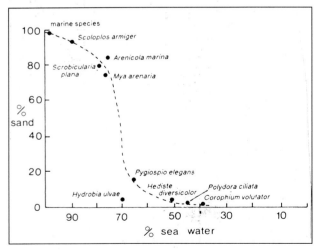

Figure 4.7 The minimum salinity and maximum silt content of the sediment at which different benthic animals were found in the Ribble Estuary (after Popham 1966 and McLusky 1981)

This emphasises one of the key features of estuarine ecosystems – the large mass of plants and animals that live in them and the high rate of energy cycling by these organisms. This is driven by the large quantities of nutrients that enter and

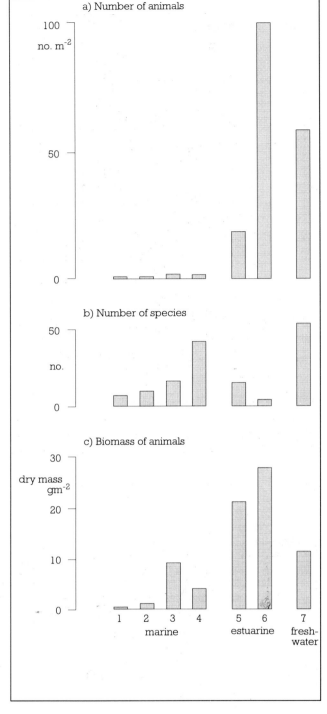

Figure 4.8 The number of individuals, species and their biomass in some marine, estuarine and freshwater habitats in Britain, derived from McLusky (1981). The habitats are: **marine** – 1 exposed intertidal, 2 moderately exposed intertidal, 3 sheltered intertidal, 4 subtidal; **estuarine intertidal** – 5 lower estuary, 6 upper estuary; **freshwater** – 7 loch.

pass through estuarine ecosystems. This is one of three major factors that are believed to limit the numbers of animals living in estuaries – the food supply, the supply of colonisers, and interspecific competition (Wildish 1977; McLusky 1981).

Many typical estuarine benthic species are very widespread and occur throughout the British estuarine resource, and more widely, wherever

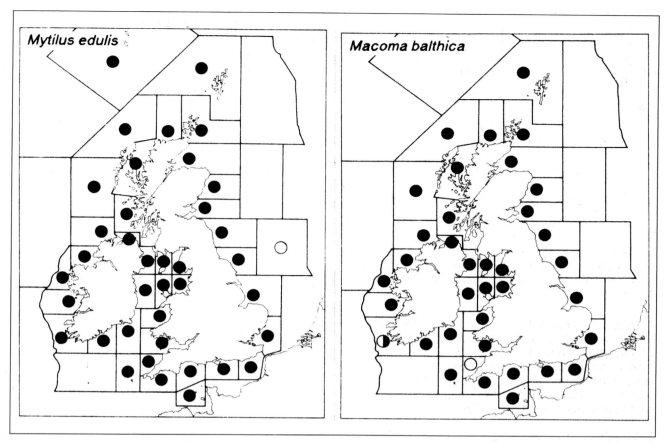

Figure 4.9 The distribution in British coastal waters of two widespread typical estuarine bivalve molluscs, the common mussel *Mytilus edulis* and the Baltic tellin *Macoma balthica*, from Seaward (1982)

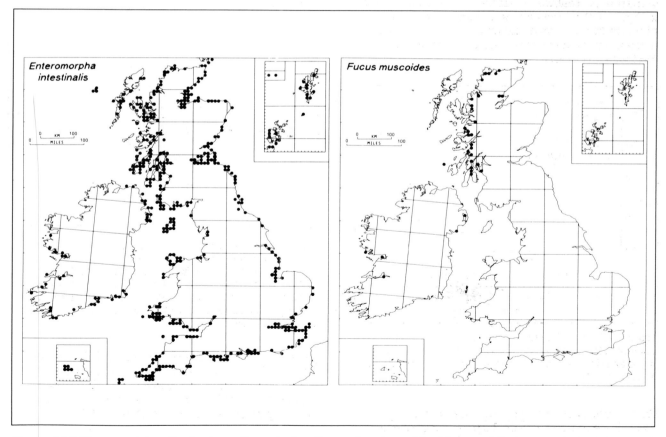

Figure 4.10 The contrasting distributions of two species of estuarine algae, the widespread *Enteromorpha intestinalis*, and *Fucus muscoides*, which is restricted to north and west Scotland, from Norton (1985)

suitable substrates and salinities occur. Two examples are shown in Figure 4.9 – the bivalve molluscs Baltic tellin *Macoma balthica* and common mussel *Mytilus edulis.* Such species also occur much more widely in Europe than just in British estuaries.

Similarly some plants, such as the ubiquitous green alga *Enteromorpha intestinalis,* are characteristic and widespread throughout British estuaries. Other species, such as *Fucus muscoides*, a sterile plant forming moss-like cushions on saltmarshes, are much more restricted in their distribution – in Britain to northern and western Scotland (Figure 4.10).

The benthic animal communities of estuarine tidal flats are characterised particularly by two groups of animals: annelid polychaete worms such as the ragworm *Hediste diversicolor*, *Nereis virens, Lanice cochilega* and *Capitella capitata*; and molluscs. Some of these molluscs, such as *Macoma balthica,* the cockle *Cerastoderma edule* and the clams *Mya arenaria* and *Scrobicularia plana,* are bivalves that live within the mud and feed in a variety of ways, such as by filtering estuarine water or sucking up surface detritus. Other bivalve molluscs form a major part of the epifauna, living on the sediment surface. Predominant amongst epifaunal molluscs in British estuaries is the mussel *Mytilus edulis,* which develops into dense beds on the mud surface. It is in these mussel beds that the greatest biomass in estuaries usually occurs. For example the production on mussel beds in the Ythan Estuary in north-east Scotland was 268 g of dry flesh weight m^{-2} yr^{-1} (Milne & Dunnet 1972).

Another widespread and abundant mollusc is the small gastropod snail *Hydrobia ulvae,* which remains in the upper mud layers when the tide is low, emerging to feed on detritus and algae on the mud surface when the tide is in. *Hydrobia* can occur in huge densities in muddy parts of estuaries, with over 10,000 animals m^{-2} in many places.

One amphipod crustacean, *Corophium volutator,* is particularly characteristic of British estuarine mudflats. Like *Hydrobia*, with which it often occurs, it lives below the mud surface but in a shallow burrow, from which it emerges to feed on surface deposits. Other amphipod and isopod crustaceans are important constituents of the benthic communities of the coarser, more mobile, sediments close to the mouths of estuaries. Such places also support polychaete worms although the biomass of such sandy sediment communities is generally much lower than in the more sheltered muddy parts of estuaries.

Small oligochaete worms can occur in such mudflats in very large numbers, and they thrive especially in areas where oxygen is at low concentration. They are a particularly abundant part of the mudflat community where there is nutrient enrichment of the estuarine ecosystem. In heavily polluted estuaries oligochaete worms may form most of the very low diversity of the mudflat

communities. Although individually small they can make a substantial contribution to the biomass and production of these mudflats. For example on the Firth of Forth McLusky *et al.* (1980) found that in some places the annual productivity of oligochaetes exceeded that of all the mollusc and polychaete populations combined.

In addition to these macrobenthic animals estuaries also provide important spawning areas, nursery grounds and migration routes for fish, described further in Chapter 8.5.

4.7 Food webs and trophic levels

The abundance of animals and plants in estuaries depends on the continual input of energy and nutrients in the form of sunlight and organic materials transported into the estuary from rivers and from the sea. In addition substantial amounts of these organic inputs can be recycled within the estuary, as plants and animals die and are broken down by microbial decomposers. These energy inputs follow complex pathways through the estuarine ecosystem, termed food webs, as illustrated in simplified form in Figure 4.11.

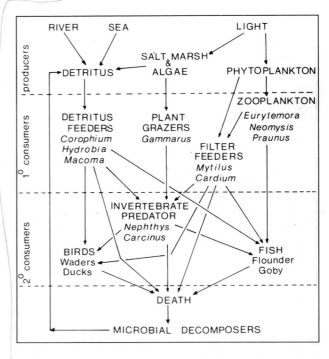

Figure 4.11 A simplified estuarine food web for a typical British estuary, from McLusky (1981). The dotted lines divide the main trophic levels through which energy passes.

As estuarine organisms are eaten by their predators energy is moved through the food web. At each stage some of the energy is assimilated by animals in the next trophic level and some passes back to the producer level of the web, both through excretion by consumers and by death. Such material is decomposed by bacteria and returns to the detritus part of the web. It is the large amounts of nutrients entering the system and being converted into biomass and energy by producers and primary consumers that make estuaries such important places for large populations of secondary consumers. As Barnes (1984) points out, estuaries are amongst the most highly productive ecosystems in the world, in terms of their benthic primary productivities. Other highly productive systems, such as coral reefs and tropical rain forests, differ greatly in how their productivity is achieved. Reefs and rain forests efficiently recycle a limited resource of materials through a very diverse ecosystem. In contrast the low diversity estuarine ecosystems are less efficient at utilising the nutrient inputs but achieve their very high productivities through the continued arrival of new supplies of nutrients.

Plants, in the form of phytoplankton, algae and higher plants on saltmarshes, convert these nutrients through photosynthesis into living material. These producers are then eaten by primary consumers in various ways. Some graze plants, other filter plankton from the water, whilst zooplankton eat the phytoplankton. Other primary consumers such as *Macoma balthica*, *Corophium volutator* and *Hydrobia ulvae* feed directly on the organic detritus.

Primary consumers are themselves in turn eaten by secondary consumers. On estuaries there are three main categories of secondary consumer: invertebrates, fish and birds. Invertebrate predators include mobile polychaetes, such as various species of *Nephthys*, and crabs such as the shore crab *Carcinus maenas*. Fish, notably gobies *Gobius minutus* and flounders *Platichthys flesus*, feed on intertidal macrobenthos when the tide covers the mudflats and may eat very substantial amounts of the invertebrate biomass (see also Chapter 8.4). In one study, on the Ythan Estuary, Summers (1974) found that flounders and gobies ate almost three times the amount of food taken from the same mudflats by birds. In some places much of the food of flatfish such as flounders and young plaice *Pleuronectes platessa* is obtained by grazing the siphons (the filter-feeding apparatus) of bivalve molluscs such as *Macoma balthica* and *Angulus tenuis* (McLusky 1981).

Birds are the third major category of secondary consumer and have been the subject of much study. Most significant in the estuarine food web are the large numbers and variety of species of migrant and wintering waterfowl (waders and wildfowl) that breed throughout a vast area of the northern hemisphere, and depend on the abundant biomass of estuarine producers and consumers as a food supply for winter survival and for further migration to more southerly wintering grounds (see Chapter 8.6).

On British estuaries many of these birds feed on estuarine macrobenthos during the period when mud and sandflats are exposed by the tide. Since many invertebrate species become inactive or withdraw deeper into the sediment once exposed by the receding tide these birds are dependent on

both the density and the activity of their prey to find sufficient food for their energy needs. Most wader species, and some wildfowl such as eider *Somateria mollissima* and shelduck *Tadorna tadorna*, feed chiefly on a wide range of estuarine macrobenthos. Although some species appear to specialise in particular prey species, as do for example eiders and some oystercatchers *Haematopus ostralegus* on mussels, most species are opportunistic. They take a wide variety of different prey species in different estuaries, at different times of year and in different years. Prey selection thus depends greatly on the relative availability of the variety of prey species that may fulfil the energy and nutrient demands of the birds. For further details of the variety of feeding techniques see for example Prater (1981) and Evans *et al.* (1984).

Other waterfowl bypass the primary consumer level of the food web and eat plant material. Some, such as many geese and some ducks (e.g. wigeon *Anas penelope*), graze eel-grass beds and saltmarsh vegetation. Others such as teal *Anas crecca* feed chiefly on the seeds of saltmarsh plants.

These secondary consumers are in turn eaten by top predators (tertiary consumers). On estuaries these are chiefly birds such as birds of prey, that feed chiefly on waders and ducks, and piscivorous birds, such as herons, cormorants and some diving ducks. In addition mammalian top predators such as seals and otters also feed in estuaries.

The distribution of these various groups of estuarine organisms on British estuaries and the importance of this wildlife to conservation are described below in Chapter 8.

4.8 References

BARNES, R.S.K. 1984. *Estuarine ecology*. Second ed. London, Edward Arnold.

BARNES, R.S.K, & HUGHES, R.N. 1982. *An introduction to marine ecology*. Oxford, Blackwell Scientific Publications.

BEARDALL, C.H., DRYDEN, R.C., & HOLZER, T.J. 1988. *The Suffolk estuaries*. Saxmundham, Suffolk Wildlife Trust.

BOLT, S., & MITCHELL, R. In press. Ecological effects of barrages. *In: The changing coastline*, ed. by J. Pethick. Estuarine and Coastal Sciences Association, Symposium 20.

DAY, J.W., HALL, C.A.S., KEMP, W.M., & YANEZ-ARANCIBIA, A. 1989. *Estuarine ecology*. New York, John Wiley & Sons.

DOODY, P. 1987. The impact of 'reclamation' on the natural environment of the Wash. *In: The Wash and its environment*, ed. by P. Doody and B. Barnett, 165-172. Peterborough, Nature Conservancy Council. (Research & survey in nature conservation No. 7.)

DYER, K.R., ed. 1979. *Estuarine hydrography and sedimentation.* Estuarine and Brackish-water Sciences Association handbook. Cambridge, Cambridge University Press.

DYER, M., & GRIST, N. 1987. The ecology of the Great Ouse and Nene estuaries. *In: The Wash and its environment,* ed. by P. Doody and B. Barnett, 138-147. Peterborough, Nature Conservancy Council. (Research & survey in nature conservation No. 7.)

EVANS, G.E., & COLLINS, M. 1987. Sediment supply and deposition in The Wash. *In: The Wash and its environment,* ed. by P. Doody and B. Barnett, 48-63. Peterborough, Nature Conservancy Council. (Research & survey in nature conservation No. 7.)

EVANS, P.R., GOSS-CUSTARD, J.D., & HALE, W.G., eds. 1984. *Coastal waders and wildfowl in winter.* Cambridge, Cambridge University Press.

FAIRBRIDGE, R. 1980. The estuary: its definition and geodynamic cycle. *In: Chemistry and biochemistry of estuaries,* ed. by E. Olausson and I. Cato, 1-35. New York, John Wiley & Sons.

HEAD, P.C., ed. 1985. *Practical estuarine chemistry.* Estuarine and Brackish-water Sciences Association handbook. Cambridge, Cambridge University Press.

KENNISH, M.J. 1986. *Ecology of estuaries.* Volume 1. Physical and chemical aspects. Volume 2. Biological aspects. Boca Raton, CRC Press.

MCLUSKY, D.S. 1971. *Ecology of estuaries.* London, Heinemann Educational.

MCLUSKY, D.S. 1981. *The estuarine ecosystem.* Glasgow, Blackie.

MILNE, H., & DUNNET, G. 1972. Standing crop, productivity and trophic relations of the fauna of the Ythan estuary. *In: The estuarine environment,* ed. by R.Barnes and J.Green, 86-106. London, Applied Science Publishers.

NATURAL ENVIRONMENT RESEARCH COUNCIL. 1975. *Estuaries research.* Natural Environment Research Council Publications series 'B', No. 9.

NORTON,T.A. 1985. *Provisional atlas of the marine algae of Britain and Ireland.* Monks Wood, Institute of Terrestrial Ecology.

POPHAM,E.J. 1966. The littoral fauna of the Ribble estuary, Lancashire, England. *Oikos, 17,* 19-32.

PRATER,A.J. 1981. *Estuary birds.* Calton, T.& A.D.Poyser.

PRITCHARD, D. 1963. Observations of circulation in coastal plain estuaries. *In: Estuaries,* 37-44. Washington, D.C., American Association for the Advancement of Science. (AAAS Publication No. 83).

SEAWARD,D.R. 1982. *Sea area atlas of the marine molluscs of Britain and Ireland.* Shrewsbury, Nature Conservancy Council.

SUMMERS,R.W. 1974. Studies on the flounders of the Ythan estuary. Ph.D. Thesis, University of Aberdeen.

WOLFF, W.J. 1973. The estuary as a habitat. An analysis of data on the soft-bottom macrofauna of the estuarine area of the Rivers Rhine, Meuse and Scheldt. *Zoologische Verhandelingen, 126,* 1-242.

5 The locations and classification of British Estuaries

Contents

5.1 Introduction

The definition of an estuary given in Chapter 4 permits the general location of estuaries around the coast to be established. To review the wildlife usage, the conservation and the human use of estuaries requires, however, more precise delimitation of characteristics and boundaries of estuaries. This chapter describes the criteria under which sites were selected for inclusion in the Estuaries Review, the criteria for the definition of their boundaries, and the distribution of the estuaries covered by the review.

Britain's estuaries are diverse in form and origin. The origins, characteristics and distribution of the nine major estuary types covered by the review are described in Chapter 5.6 and 5.7 below. An understanding of the geomorphological types of estuary is valuable in interpreting the wildlife and human use of estuaries, and in seeking to conserve the diversity of the British estuarine resource.

5.2 Selection of review sites

Site selection was based on the broad definition of estuaries given above, and was a two-stage process: first, the identification of estuarine areas appropriate for inclusion in the review, and second the delimitation of the sites.

Coastlines were selected for inclusion if they had predominantly soft shores and either a) a tidal channel of 2 km or longer, or b) intertidal soft sediment shores of 0.5 km or wider at low water, along a 2 km or longer shoreline.

Application of these criteria selected all the major areas of intertidal soft shores on the British coastline for inclusion in the review, but excluded several types of soft coastline, notably narrow exposed sandy and shingle beaches, small stream and river outflows and most Scottish sea-lochs. These sea-lochs have predominantly narrow shingle or rocky shorelines with steeply shelving beaches, although some do have small areas of saltmarsh and tidal flats where rivers inflow at the head of the loch.

Our size selection criteria exclude, however, the places on the coast where small streams and rivers discharge over rocky or boulder shores, or through short, steeply shelving estuaries. Such freshwater discharges over exposed marine shores often exhibit features of typical estuarine habitats and are of physiographical and marine biological interest, but are outside the scope of this report. The exclusion of these small estuarine systems has little effect on the overall size distributions of estuaries and their wildlife conservation features. Their inclusion would, however, have further emphasised the size distribution pattern, described in Chapter 6, of Britain's estuarine resource being composed of a few very large and many small estuaries.

A few estuaries have been so heavily modified by human activities such as land-claim that they no longer strictly fulfil the selection criteria or have had their natural estuarine form entirely changed. We have, however, included these sites since they are germane to considerations of estuarine habitat loss and other human activities.

The sites selected according to the above criteria

are termed 'review sites' in this report. Review sites are, by our definition, synonymous with 'estuaries', the terms being used interchangeably. In the classification and descriptions that follow, we have divided review sites into two main categories: 'open coast sites', which are the marine-influenced barrier beaches, embayments and linear shores, and 'enclosed coast sites', which are usually under some degree of river influence. These distinctions are consistent with the categories used by the NCC's Marine Nature Conservation Review (MNCR) to describe marine sites.

5.3 Core sites and associated habitats

In its narrowest sense an estuary comprises solely the intertidal and subtidal zones. 'Intertidal' (or 'shore' or 'littoral') features occur between terrestrial vegetation and low water spring tides. 'Subtidal', or sublittoral, features occur below the level of tidal exposure. Although these parts form the focus of attention for many types of estuarine wildlife and for human activities, the estuarine environment is more complex and consists also of a mosaic of maritime and submaritime habitats, which, whilst not directly influenced by the tidal waters of the estuary, are nevertheless inextricably linked to the estuary in a variety of ways (Ratcliffe 1977). For example, terrestrial coastal habitats such as sand-dunes, receive sediments from estuaries and adjacent coastlines, and the hydrology of coastal grazing marshes can be affected by tidal movements of water in the adjacent estuary. Furthermore the natural transitions between intertidal habitats and fringing terrestrial habitats are of particular wildlife interest (e.g. Burd 1989). Estuarine habitats are described further in Chapter 8.1. Many estuarine birds depend on both intertidal parts of an estuary and adjacent terrestrial habitats. For example, many waders feed on intertidal mud and sandflats during low water. Once these feeding grounds are covered by the rising tide, the birds fly to roost on a variety of adjacent habitats such as shingle ridges and coastal grasslands. Conversely many wildfowl feed on such grasslands but fly to roost on the tidal estuary at night (see Chapter 8.6). Human activities affecting tidal parts of estuaries often take place wholly or partly on the adjacent land. Hence this review has considered both the tidal parts of each selected site and the terrestrial habitats surrounding them.

We have therefore treated each estuary as a functional unit and have collected data on estuaries for a 'core site', covering the intertidal and subtidal parts of the estuary, and on the 'associated terrestrial (AT)' habitats surrounding this core site.

Similarly some shorelines outside the mouth of a core site lack the characteristics for direct inclusion within a core site, but are nevertheless strongly linked to the estuary by, for example, the tidal feeding movements of their bird populations (see e.g. Davidson & Evans 1986). These have been included in the review as parts of a review site distinguished as 'associated intertidal' (AI).

5.4 Setting core site boundaries

The upstream limits (for estuaries with river inflows) and shoreline boundaries were defined consistently for all review sites. The great variability of estuarine form has, however, meant that the placing of outer limits of review sites necessarily varies considerably between sites. The types of boundary are illustrated in Figure 5.1.

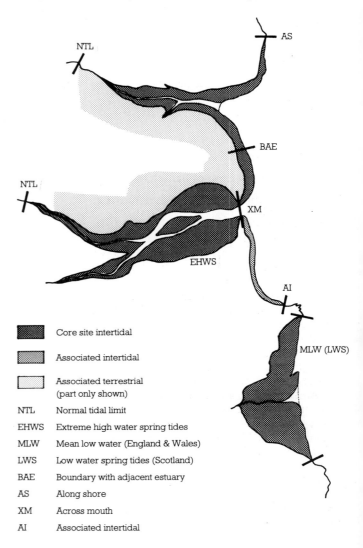

NTL	Normal tidal limit
EHWS	Extreme high water spring tides
MLW	Mean low water (England & Wales)
LWS	Low water spring tides (Scotland)
BAE	Boundary with adjacent estuary
AS	Along shore
XM	Across mouth
AI	Associated intertidal

Figure 5.1 Types of boundary used to define sites in the Estuaries Review

5.4.1 Upstream limits

The upstream limit is the Normal Tidal Limit (NTL) as shown on the 1:50,000 Ordnance Survey (OS) map, except where local information established a substantially different limit to the tidal influence. This means that the core site includes the upper parts of rivers flowing into estuaries that are above the influence of saline water but are subject to tidal movements. On some review sites such as The Wash the upstream limit is over 20 km above the influence of saline water.

5.4.2 Shoreline boundaries

The shoreline upper limit of each core site has been taken as the high water mark of extreme spring tides (EHWS). This is not a mapped feature on OS maps, which mark mean high water (MHW). MHW is not very useful in defining estuaries biologically since it is lower than the landward limits of the upper zones of estuarine habitats such as saltmarshes. EHWS was interpreted on 1:25,000 OS maps and then marked on 1:50,000 maps. Where the high water mark is set by vertical features such as sea defences or cliffs, EHWS is effectively the same as MHW. For shorelines with more gently sloping transitions to terrestrial areas EHWs was interpreted as the upper boundary of mapped saltmarsh, sand, mud, rock or shingle symbols or shading. Where the transition is to sand-dunes, EHWS was taken as the outer limit of sand-dune symbols. In most places EHWS is likely to be located at a broadly similar, or the same, level as highest astronomical tides.

5.4.3 Seaward limits

The variability of estuarine form, and the seasonal variability in the influence of some estuarine features such as salinity, means that the location and type of boundary at the outer limits of core sites depend greatly on the particular geography of each site. In river estuaries the freshwater discharge plume of the estuary can extend a considerable distance out to sea, and the extent of its influence varies with the seasonal variations in the size of the river discharge. This outer zone of estuarine influence in the otherwise marine system corresponds to the 'nearshore mixing zone' of Day et al. (1989). This zone has no precise geographical boundaries and its extent is poorly recorded for many review sites. Since this report looks at the areas and distribution of estuarine features within defined estuary areas we have largely excluded this nearshore mixing zone from the core site. Where appropriate we do, however, note features of conservation significance (e.g. marine wildlife communities) in this outer zone associated with review sites, when the zone is treated in effect as an 'associated subtidal' area, analogous with the associated terrestrial and intertidal areas.

Wherever possible we have defined the seaward limit of the core site as a 'bay closing line' across the mouth of the site. We have used this 'across-mouth' (XM) outer limit for the many sites in which there is a marked narrowing of the estuary at its mouth. An across-mouth limit has also been used for large embayments such as The Wash and Morecambe Bay.

Other estuaries, particularly coastal plain estuaries (see Chapter 5), are funnel-shaped and so have no narrow neck. For these sites an 'alongshore' (AS) boundary has been set along the low water mark as shown on 1:50,000 OS maps: at Mean Low Water (MLW) in England and Wales and Low Water Spring Tides (LWS) in Scotland. The outer limits of

subtidal channels on such sites were set by drawing a line across the channel between the outer points of the adjacent intertidal flats. A similar alongshore treatment has been used for linear shore sites and some sediment-filled embayments. Using this setting of low water mark has the advantages that intertidal areas can be readily measured from Ordnance Survey maps, and that the seaward limits to the intertidal parts of many sites coincide with those of statutory conservation sites.

The Estuaries Review has not covered the outer parts of the large firths in Scotland, since they are effectively non-estuarine in character. On these sites a composite outer boundary has been set in which there is an across-mouth closure of the inner part of the site, outside which is an alongshore boundary. Hence the core site covers both the intertidal and subtidal zones in the inner parts of these estuaries, but in the outer parts only the intertidal zone.

In most cases the alongshore boundary is continued along the coastline of the outer part of the review site to a natural boundary of the soft shore, for example a rocky promontory. Some sites have no such natural limit. For these the alongshore boundary has been set where the intertidal narrows to a width of less than 500 m.

5.4.4 Site boundaries on estuarine complexes

Most estuaries on the British coastline are discrete sites separated from their neighbours by stretches of rocky shore or narrow sandy beaches. Some coastlines, however, are not so simple and have river discharge estuaries or bays joined by broad expanses of intertidal sediments all of which qualify for inclusion in the Estuaries Review. We have set an arbitrary boundary ('between adjacent estuaries' (BAE) between such contiguous sites, usually at either the mid-point of the shore between the sites, or where the intertidal is at its narrowest.

Large estuaries and embayments, for example the Severn Estuary and Morecambe Bay, are often complex and composed of features which can be treated as estuaries at several levels of scale. The rivers flowing into such large estuaries (e.g. the Avon, the Wye and the Taff/Ely on the Severn Estuary; the Wyre, the Kent, the Lune and the Leven in Morecambe Bay) each have an estuarine structure. These 'sub-estuaries' in turn have smaller streams joining their tidal reaches which also show features definable as estuaries in their own right. For the scope and objectives of Estuaries Review we have in general treated these large complexes as single review sites. Similarly Camarthen Bay, with its three confluent river estuaries, is treated as a single site for the purposes of this report. The topography of no two estuaries is, however, identical and for some it has proved more feasible to treat such places as separate review sites, the most complex being the region of the Thames Estuary, described below. Boundaries of such sites have been set so that between them the sites include all relevant core site areas, so that information from them can be combined as a larger-scale site.

On the Thames Estuary there is an almost continuous extensive intertidal area on the southern shore as far east as Whitstable on the north Kent coast and on the northern shore as far north as Colne Point in mid-Essex. This 'Greater Thames Estuary' region encompasses the discharges of five large rivers (Medway, Thames, Crouch, Blackwater and Colne), with areas of broad soft intertidal shores between them. We have chosen here to treat the various components of this area as separate review sites, so as to give proper consideration to the distribution of wildlife interest and human activities in the area. Boundaries between sites have been set with regard to administrative and statutory conservation boundaries, as well as the geography of the areas. We have used a similar approach for some other complex estuarine areas, for example in Swansea Bay in South Wales.

5.4.5 Review sites and statutory site boundaries

Wherever possible review site boundaries have been set to encompass the estuarine parts of statutory wildlife sites, notably Sites of Special Scientific Interest (SSSIs) notified by the NCC under the Wildlife & Countryside Act 1981. As described above, site boundaries between contiguous review sites have, wherever possible, been set to coincide with statutory site boundaries. Many SSSIs that include intertidal areas also include a variety of other terrestrial habitats, so the relationship between Estuaries Review sites and statutory wildlife sites is complex, and it has not been possible for this report to calculate the precise overlaps between review core sites and SSSIs.

5.5 The distribution of British estuaries

The selection procedures of the Estuaries Review have identified 155 review sites that qualify for inclusion. These estuaries are distributed around the whole coastline of Britain (Figure 5.2). There are 27 review sites (17% of the total) in Wales plus two major estuaries – the Severn, and the Dee Estuary and North Wirral – shared with England. 48 review sites (31%) are wholly in Scotland, and again there is also a major estuary, the Solway Firth, astride the border between England and Scotland. A small part of the tidal reaches of the Tweed Estuary is also in Scotland. 76 review sites (49%) are wholly within England. Details of the names and locations of review sites are listed in Appendix 1, and their areas and shoreline lengths are listed in Appendix 2. The characteristics and geomorphological classification of these estuaries are described below, and the classification of each estuary is listed in Appendix 3.

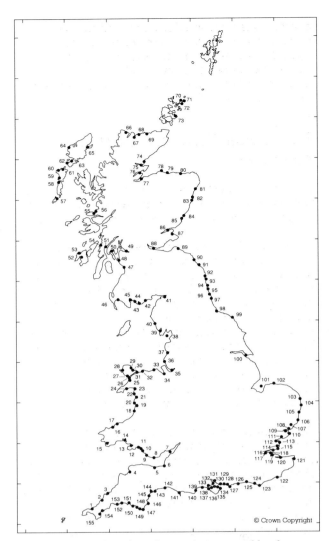

Figure 5.2 The location of estuaries covered by the Estuaries Review. Locations are shown as the central Ordnance Survey grid reference of each site, and numbers are those in Appendix 1, which lists the names used throughout the Review.

Estuaries have long formed natural geographical boundaries, as well as *foci* for human activities. In addition to the four major estuaries forming the country boundaries between England, Scotland and Wales, many others form county or regional boundaries and local authority district boundaries. Each of 15 review sites (10% of the total) is under the jurisdiction of two counties (or regions in Scotland) and six large review sites (Severn Estuary, Dee Estuary & North Wirral, Firth of Forth, Humber Estuary, The Wash and Thames Estuary) are each covered by three different counties/regions. Overall, 60 review sites (39%) are each the responsibility of more than one local authority district. On large estuaries there can be a considerable number of local authorities involved; for example, the different parts of the Thames Estuary are covered by 20 local authorities, the Humber Estuary 14, the Severn Estuary 12, and The Wash and the Firth of Forth eight local authorities each. The fact that an estuary, although a single functional unit, can be covered by a multiplicity of planning authorities has important implications for the relationship between individual coastal zone planning decisions, and for the overall impact of human activities on an estuary and on the overall estuarine resource. Other administrative boundaries subdivide single estuaries; for example, eight review sites are each covered by more than one NCC region.

5.6 A classification of British estuaries

For the Estuaries Review we have adopted a simple two-part classification of estuaries based on their geomorphology and tidal range characteristics.

Since estuaries are active geomorphological systems undergoing continuous change, applying a simple classification to the different parts of the resource is difficult. Some estuaries inevitably do not fit readily into a single category since, for example, their geological history can have involved several phases involving glaciation, sea-level rise and reworking of sediments. Estuaries may also exhibit features of different estuary types at different levels of scale, as for example river discharge estuaries of coastal plain type discharging into a large embayment.

Thus a classification cannot embrace all the attributes of every estuary. Nevertheless it can provide a useful framework for understanding the characteristics of estuaries in general, why they occur where they do, what features they share and, most importantly, how they function. More specifically, as part of the Estuaries Review, a classification allows an assessment to be made of the distribution of the main types of British estuaries and how this distribution is related to the many features on estuaries.

Numerous attempts have been made to define and classify estuaries. These have variously taken account of tides and tidal range; sediment availability, transport and distribution; salinity; and sea-level change. One of the simplest and most effective ways to classify estuaries is through their morphology and origin. The broad definition of an estuary used for the Estuaries Review has been outlined in Chapter 4. Here we develop a classification of review sites included by this definition and describe the Estuaries Review classification in relation to other estuarine descriptions.

Fairbridge (1980) described an estuary in geomorphological terms as "an inlet of the sea reaching into a river valley as far as the upper limit of tidal rise". Fairbridge proposed a morphological classification of estuaries which included elements of the regional history of sea level, tectonic factors, climatic factors and freshwater and sediment supply. The Estuaries Review classification is based on Fairbridge's classification since it provides a relatively simple means of subdividing the estuarine resource.

The basic estuarine types separated by the

classification are illustrated in Figure 5.3. Enclosed coast sites (types 1 to 5) are derived directly from the Fairbridge scheme and are river estuaries, as are type 6 (complex estuaries). Three further categories of review site (types 7 to 9) are open coast sites with extensive expanses of soft sediments (see Chapter 4 for the rationale for the inclusion of these sites). In addition to Fairbridge's morphological classification, we have further classified review sites according to their tidal range as microtidal, mesotidal and macrotidal (see Chapter 5.8). This two-part classification of each of the 155 review sites is listed in Appendix 3.

As is inevitable with evolving structures subject to change through the influence of outside forces, some estuaries in Britain currently have morphological characteristics of more than one estuary type. Such sites are classified here according to their dominant features at the scale of the review. The Estuaries Review's classification outlined here appears to be the first attempt to classify all Britain's estuaries. Other classification schemes have been suggested. For example, Pethick (1984) advocated a classification using present-day processes, which allows the dynamic and changing nature of estuaries to be understood. Detailed information on these parameters is, however, incomplete, and such classifications thus often serve chiefly to illustrate the true complexity of estuarine systems.

Some differences between morphological and process-based classifications should be noted. Pritchard (1967) recognised four types of estuary on the basis of parameters that included dominant mixing force (river flow, tides, wind), mixing energy, width-depth ratio, salinity gradient, turbidity and stability of bottom sediments. The distinction between the Pritchard and Fairbridge classifications is two-fold. First, Pritchard's classification is a short-term, dynamic scheme, and in it an estuary may change frequently in type, for example with seasonal change in river discharge. Fairbridge recognises such short-term effects, but his classification has the advantage that it also accommodates long-term processes such as climatic change and changes in sea level. This provides a key to understanding estuary and coastline evolution.

A second difference lies in the definition of the landward boundary of an estuary. Pritchard's landward boundary is the chemical one: where the chlorinity falls below 0.001% and the ratios of the major dissolved ions change significantly from their values in sea water. Fairbridge's landward boundary is physical: the upstream limit of a measurable tide (NTL). For some estuaries the difference is trivial, but for others the upper limit of the Fairbridge estuary may can be tens of kilometres landward of the Pritchard estuary upper limit. Neither Fairbridge nor Pritchard deals definitively, however, with the geomorphologically important seaward boundary, although both definitions assume that the basic estuary forms a semi-enclosed basin or inlet. Our assessments of

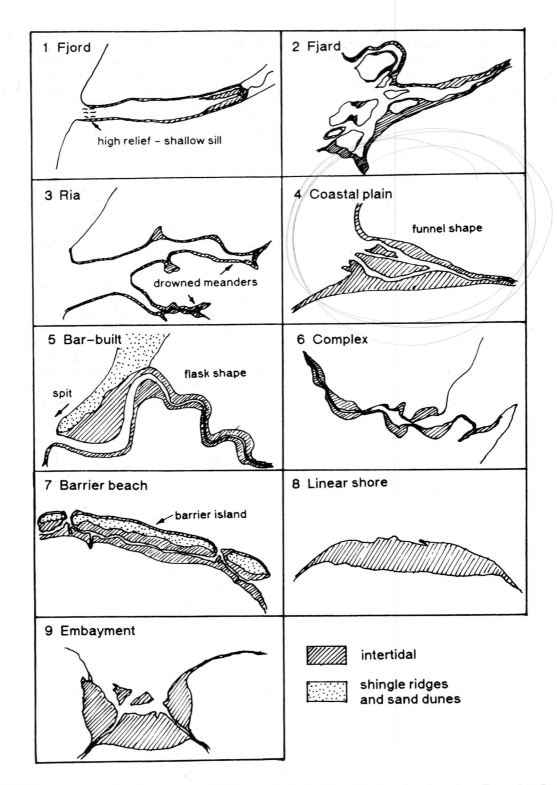

Figure 5.3 The nine categories of estuary used in the morphological classification of review sites. Types 1 to 5 are based on Fairbridge (1980). The classification of review sites by category is given in Appendix 3.

British estuaries indicate that this is not always the case.

5.7 Distribution of estuary types

5.7.1 Fjords

Fjords are essentially drowned glacial troughs, often associated with major lines of geological weakness. They are characteristic of areas once covered by Pleistocene ice sheets where glacial erosion has been intense or selective in its operation (Sugden & John 1976). Erosion by the ice further deepened existing river valleys, but the movement and scouring action of the ice left characteristic shallow rock bars, particularly at the fjord mouths. As a result of glacial overdeepening, fjords have a close width-depth ratio, steep sides and an almost rectangular cross section. Their outline in plan is also typically rectangular, any sharp bends usually reflecting the underlying geological structures. Fjords generally have rocky floors, or a very thin veneer of sediment, and deposition is restricted to the head of the fjord in association with major rivers. River discharge is small compared with the total fjord volume, but as many fjords have restricted tidal ranges, the river flow is often large in relation to the tidal prism (the volume of water between high and low water levels).

The distribution of the six fjords in the Estuaries Review shows estuarine fjords to be confined to north and west Scotland (Figure 5.4). Note, however, that most fjords in Britain are sea-lochs on the west coast of Scotland. These deep-water rocky shore sites fall outside the scope and definitions of the Estuaries Review (see Chapter 4).

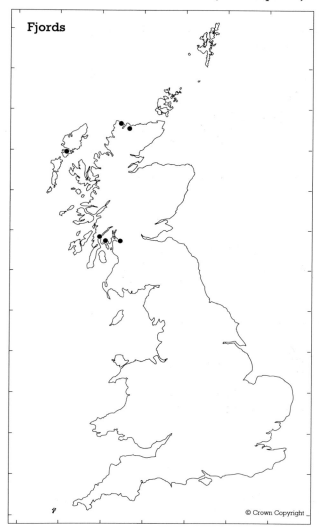

Figure 5.4 Distribution of fjord review sites in Britain. Note that most Scottish sea lochs are excluded from the Estuaries Review by the virtual absence of soft shores.

5.7.2 Fjards

Fjards are typical of glaciated lowland coasts (Embleton & King 1975). They are more structurally complex than fjords, with a more open and irregular coastline and often no main channel.

Their form also frequently reflects the underlying geological structure, and although ice-scoured rock basins and bars are characteristic features, fjards are nevertheless relatively shallow. Numerous low islands may provide localised shelter isolated by current-swept narrows. Although fjards are more exposed to wave action than fjords, they are sheltered in their upper reaches.

The 20 fjards identified in Britain have a wider distribution than estuarine fjords, although they are still confined to western and northern British coasts between Anglesey and Orkney (Figure 5.5). The topography of the offshore area in which most fjards occur is lower and subject to submergence, producing a drowned skerry landscape of small, rocky islands (e.g. Bagh Nam Faoilean). Glaciation produced offshore rock sills particularly around the Western Isles, and an abundant supply of sediment has been available there for the formation of large expanses of dune, machair and strandplain. Many coastal inlets around Scotland have an origin which has been influenced by glacial activity, although the action of subsequent processes and the infills of abundant sediments often mask their true origins. For example, three fjard sites at Oitir Mhor,

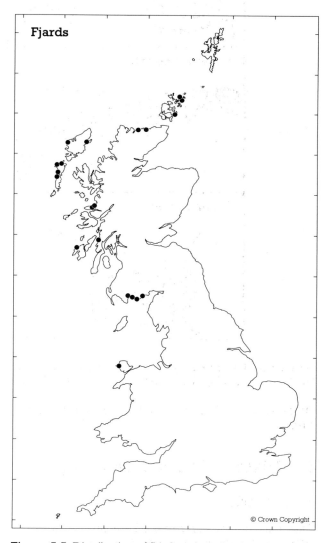

Figure 5.5 Distribution of fjard review sites

Rias

Humber

Figure 5.6 Distribution of ria review sites

15 review sites (9.7%) are identified as rias in Britain (Figure 5.6). They occur predominantly in the Carboniferous and Devonian rocks of Devon and Cornwall, although there are also two rias in south Wales, at Milford Haven and the Neath Estuary. Within the group of rias, the Teign Estuary in Devon is exceptional for the abundance of sediments that have now filled the estuary and the presence of a bar built out from Teignmouth. However, the main features are those of a ria.

5.7.4 Coastal plain estuaries

The Humber is

Coastal plain estuaries were formed during the Holocene transgression through the flooding of pre-existing valleys in both glaciated and unglaciated areas. Maximum depths in these inlets are generally less than 30 m and the central channel is often sinuous. They have the cross-section of normal valleys and deepen and widen towards their mouths, which may be modified by spits. Their outline and cross-section are both often triangular. The width-depth ratio is usually large, although this depends on the type of rock in which the valley was cut. Unlike rias, extensive mudflats and saltings often occur and the estuary is usually floored by varying thicknesses of recent sediment, often mud in the upper reaches, but becoming increasingly sandy towards the mouth. Coastal plain estuaries are generally restricted to temperate latitudes, where the amount of sediment discharged by the rivers is relatively small. River flow in large coastal plain estuaries is also small compared with the volume of the tidal prism, so that salinities in many parts of such estuaries are little reduced from sea water.

Coastal plain estuaries, along with bar-built estuaries, are one of the commonest estuary types in Britain. A total of 35 review sites, forming 22.6% of the total, are identified as coastal plain estuaries by the classification. These estuaries have a wide distribution in England and Wales, particularly in Suffolk, West Sussex, Hampshire, south Wales, and along the north Wales-Lancashire stretch of the west coast (Figure 5.7). Some of Britain's largest estuaries, such as the Severn Estuary, The Dee Estuary & North Wirral, the Humber Estuary and the Thames estuary complex are coastal plain type. Only two examples, the Dee and the Don (both in Aberdeen), occur in Scotland. At least six coastal plain estuaries (Conwy, Clwyd, Don, Dee, Wansbeck and Adur) also contain significant features associated with bar-built estuaries. However, since these features are essentially secondary within the overall estuary morphology, the sites are included in the coastal plain group.

5.7.5 Bar-built estuaries

These estuaries are also in part drowned river valleys which have been incised during the ice ages and subsequently inundated. However, they are distinguished by recent sedimentation which has kept pace with the inundation, and they have a characteristic bar across their mouths. The bar is normally formed where the waves break on the

Torrisdale Bay and Melvich Bay have characteristics of bar-built estuaries, reflecting in part the availability of abundant sediments. However, their overall characteristics are essentially those of fjards and they are classified accordingly.

5.7.3 Rias

Although, superficially, rias have some features in common with fjords and fjards, they have not been formed or modified by glacial processes. They are distinguished as drowned river valleys formed by tectonic subsidence of the land, a rise in sea level, or a combination of both. Sedimentation has not kept pace with inundation and the estuarine topography is still much like that of a river valley. Rias are relatively deep, narrow, well-defined channels which are almost completely marine-infuenced. They have no entrance sill or ice-scoured rock bars and rock basins, and are also shallower than fjords. The predominant substrate of the channel floors of most rias is bedrock, but the sheltered parts of bays and inlets adjacent to the main channels contain soft sediments, and secondary sedimentation elsewhere masks the bedrock.

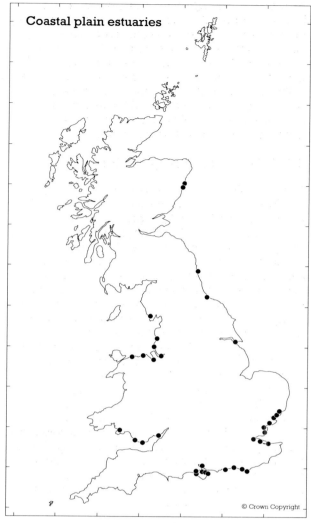

Figure 5.7 Distribution of coastal plain estuaries review sites

mouths by material carried and deposited during long-shore drift (E I S Rees, in lit.)

Because of their restricted cross-sectional area, current velocities can be high at the mouth, but in the wider parts further inland they rapidly diminish. The river flow is large and seasonally variable, and large volumes of sediments are transported during floods. The estuary form is governed by the river regime at the flood stage and may show a basin/bar structure caused by meander scouring. During floods the bar may be swept completely away, but will quickly re-establish itself when the river flow diminishes. The mouth may undergo considerable variations in position from year to year. Many of the naturally formed coastal saline lagoons (see Section 8.1.11) are essentially an extreme form of a bar-built estuary, in which the bar has entirely closed off the mouth of the inlet or embayment, although such entirely enclosed lagoons are outside the definition of estuaries covered in this review.

A total of 47 bar-built estuaries (30.3% of review sites) have been identified. The main areas of their distribution are in west Wales, the south coast of England, East Anglia and eastern Scotland (Figure 5.8).

beach, and for it to develop the tidal range must be restricted and large volumes of sediment must be available. Consequently, bar-built estuaries are generally associated with depositional coasts. These estuaries are only a few metres deep and often have extensive lagoons and shallow waterways just inside the mouth.

A dominant feature of bar-built estuaries is the availability of abundant sediments in the coastal system, allowing tidal dynamics to rework and deposit this material along the coast and across river valley mouths. These sand and shingle bars at estuary mouths can develop from a variety of sediment sources. On estuaries such as the Alde/Ore/Butley in Suffolk and the Ythan in north-east Scotland the bar develops from material carried down the coast by longshore drift. On the Welsh coast the bars on the many bar-built estuaries develop as shingle storm beaches that are largely made up from reworked glacial deposits from subtidal offshore areas. These bars are often formed along the line of old glacial boulder moraines that influence the line of the tidal channels, and so can be considered as 'fossil' compared to the active displacement of estuary

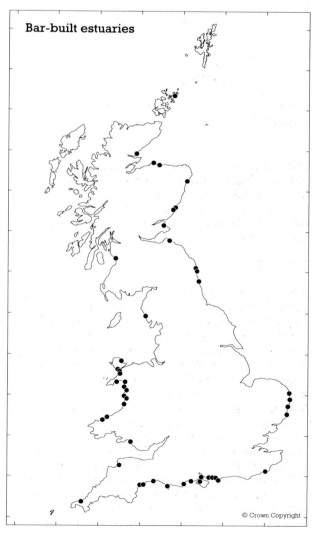

Figure 5.8 Distribution of bar-built estuaries review sites

49

Some general geographical trends are apparent in the characteristics of bar-built estuaries. Along the Welsh coastline, although a variety of deposits are found, sand plays an important part in the formation of bars and the sand-dune systems associated with them. In Scotland, more northerly sites have an abundance of sand, whereas in the Moray Firth area, a combination of sediment supply and powerful current and tidal dynamics has produced extensive shingle bars, for example at the Spey. In East Anglia, banks of deposits from offshore and from the erosion of coastal cliffs have provided sedimentary material of some variety for reworking and deposition in estuary mouths. Along the English Channel coast, shingle is a significant component in the formation of bar-built estuaries, most notably the major shingle system of Chesil Beach that forms The Fleet. Lagoonal systems with seaward openings such as The Fleet are included in the estuary classification as bar-built estuaries, and their wildlife characteristics are described further in Section 8.1.11.

5.7.6 Complex estuaries

Estuaries in this group (Figure 5.9) are river estuaries but are of complex origin and so do not

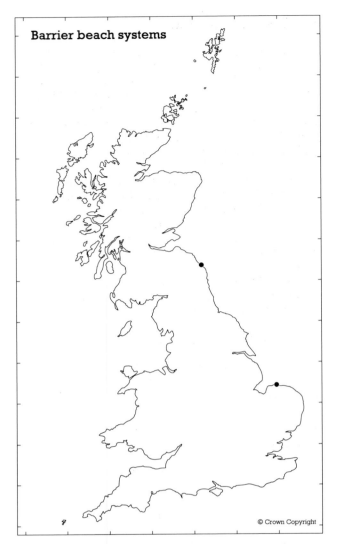

Figure 5.10 Distribution of barrier beach review sites

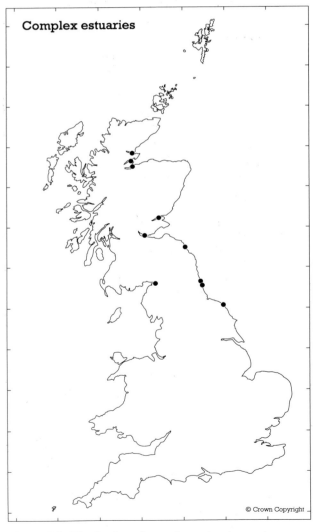

Figure 5.9 Distribution of complex estuaries review sites

easily fit into the other types in the classification. Such estuaries usually result from the influence of a mixture of geological constraints such as hard rock outcrops, glaciation, river erosion and sea-level change. Complex estuaries do not, however, show assemblages of features sufficiently diagnostic of any simple estuary type.

In Britain these complex estuaries fall into two distinct categories. One is a group of the six major Scottish estuaries: the Solway Firth, the Moray, Cromarty and Dornoch Firths, and the Firths of Tay and Forth. The hydrodynamics of these estuaries are similar to those of coastal plain estuaries, but their overall size and geomorphological complexity sets them apart.

A second group, of four estuaries in north-east England, are sites which reflect the influence of geological controls, glaciation and incision into relatively hard rock types during periods of relative sea-level change during the Quaternary. The Conwy Estuary in north Wales also has some features of complex estuaries, since it is partly channelled by rock, but for review purposes is included as a coastal plain site.

5.7.7 Barrier beaches

Barrier beaches are open coast systems which characteristically develop as soft shores in shallow water, where the dissipation of wave and current energy offshore leads to the development of bars and barriers. Abundant sediments are present in these coastal systems. Two British review sites are classified as barrier beach systems (Figure 5.10). Only one of these, the North Norfolk Coast, is, however, a classic barrier beach system in which extensive saltmarshes, creeks and tidal flats have developed behind a shingle and sand-dune barrier. The other barrier beach included in the Estuaries Review, Lindisfarne on the Northumberland coast, has also developed mostly in the shelter of an extensive dune and shingle system. This barrier has in turn been deposited in the lee of the limestone and volcanic outcrop that forms Holy Island, so the site also has some characteristics of a bar-built estuary.

5.7.8 Linear shore sites

The linear shore sites include those where there is little indentation of the coast and the coastal outline is convex, linear or only slightly concave. Seven review sites have been identified, including a cluster in south-east England at Dengie, Maplin, Southend and North Kent Marshes (Figure 5.11). Such broad areas of soft sediments are deposited in conditions of shallow seas and abundant sediments, where wave and tidal energy are dissipated out from the shore, as in the development of barrier islands. Note, however, that taken on a larger scale these Essex and Kent linear shores can be considered as component parts of the very extensive estuarine complex of the 'Greater Thames Estuary'. This extensive area of overall coastal plain type covers the complex of river mouths and intervening soft shores on the Essex and north Kent coasts.

5.7.9 Embayments

Embayments are formed where the line of the coast follows a concave sweep between rocky headlands. Soft sediments generally infill such embayments. In the Estuaries Review classification, 14 embayment coasts have been recognised. These are widely distributed around the coast of

Britain (Figure 5.12) and include, for example, Carmarthen Bay, Morecambe Bay and The Wash. At a local scale, each of the various rivers that discharge into these large embayments may

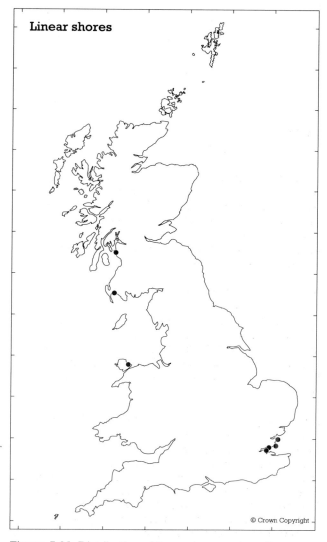

Figure 5.11 Distribution of linear shore review sites

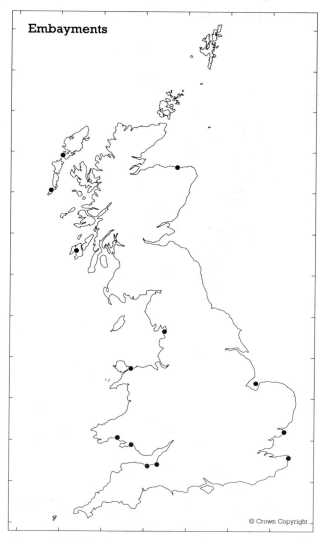

Figure 5.12 Distribution of embayment review sites

51

demonstrate characteristics of coastal plain estuaries. For the purposes of the Estuaries Review these sites have, however, been classified according to the characteristics of the overall system.

5.7.10 Overall distribution of estuary types

The broad geographical distributions of these nine estuary types is summarised in Table 5.1. This emphasises the very different patterns of estuary type in England, Scotland and Wales. Wales is notable chiefly for its preponderance of bar-built estuaries. Although Scotland also has bar-built estuaries, over half its estuaries are fjords and fjards, reflecting its recent glacial history. In contrast, over 80% of the estuaries in England are of just three categories: rias, coastal plain and bar-built estuaries, and well over half English estuaries are of the last two categories.

Table 5.1 The distribution by country of the different estuary types

Estuary type	England	Scotland	Wales
Fjord	0	6	0
Fjard	0	19	1
Ria	13	0	2
Coastal plain	29	1	5
Bar-built	24	10	13
Complex	4	6	0
Barrier beach	2	0	0
Linear shore	4	2	1
Embayment	6	4	3

5.8 Estuaries and tidal influence

Tidal range is an important factor in understanding estuarine processes and their distribution. The gross morphology of estuaries, described above, provides the basic framework within which present-day processes operate. Although morphology sets constraints on processes, these latter can, nevertheless, produce a wide variety of forms and even differences between estuaries which share a common origin. The most important control on estuarine processes is tidal range. This determines the tidal current and residual current velocities and therefore the rates and amounts of sediment movement.

Davies (1973) and Hayes (1975) have classified estuaries and coastal environments according to average spring tidal range: **microtidal** where the range is less than 2 m; **mesotidal** where it is between 2 m and 4 m; and **macrotidal** where it is more than 4 m.

The distribution of these three types of tidal estuary around Britain is shown in Figure 5.13. Variations in tidal range among the different estuary types are summarised in Table 5.2, which shows that over two-thirds of British estuaries are macrotidal.

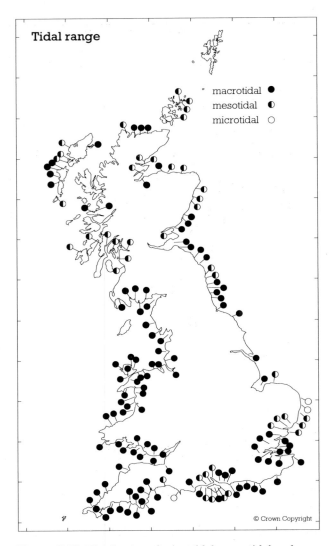

Tidal range

- macrotidal ●
- mesotidal ◑
- microtidal ○

© Crown Copyright

Figure 5.13 Distribution of microtidal, mesotidal and macrotidal review sites. Note that the three sites with exceptionally large tidal ranges (Severn Estuary, Bridgwater Bay and Blue Anchor Bay) are included in the macrotidal category.

Table 5.2 Numbers of estuaries of each estuary type in each tidal range category[a]

Estuary type	Macrotidal	Mesotidal	Microtidal
Fjord	1	5	0
Fjard	14	6	0
Ria	15	0	0
Coastal plain	25	10	0
Bar-built	29	13	5
Complex	7	3	0
Barrier beach	1	1	0
Linear shore	6	1	0
Embayment	8	4	1
Total	106	43	6

[a] The exceptionally large tidal ranges of the Severn Estuary, Bridgwater Bay, and Blue Anchor Bay are included in the macrotidal range

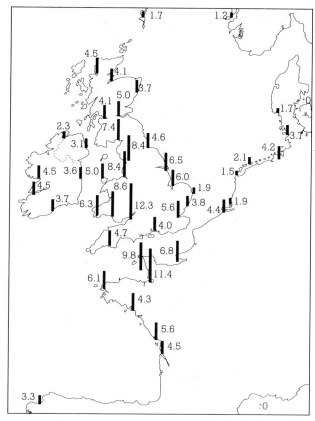

Figure 5.14 The average range, in metres, of spring tides in western Europe, from Pienkowski (1983).

Tidal ranges in Britain, and particularly those on the western coasts are larger than on most other parts of the west European coastlines (Figure 5.14). Three review sites, the Severn Estuary, Bridgwater Bay and Blue Anchor Bay in south-west England, have exceptionally large tidal ranges. The tidal range at Avonmouth on the Severn Estuary at mean spring tides is 12.3 m. This makes the Severn Estuary one of the three estuaries with the largest tidal ranges anywhere in the world, the others being the Bay of Fundy in eastern Canada and the Baie du Mont St. Michel in north-west France. This large estuary is thus of exceptional interest as one of the world's best examples of such an extreme tidal environment.

In macrotidal estuaries, strong tidal and residual currents may extend far inland. Estuaries with such a tidal range do not possess the ebb-flow deltas that occur in mesotidal estuaries. Instead the central channel near the estuary mouth is occupied by long linear sand bars parallel with the tidal flow. The estuarine shape is the distinctive trumpet-shaped flare typical of coastal plain estuaries around Britain (Pethick 1984). Macrotidal estuaries are represented in all estuary types (Table 5.2). Over half of the coastal plain and bar-built estuaries, the most common types, are macrotidal, as are most fjards, rias, linear coasts and complex estuaries.

Mesotidal estuaries are dominated by strong tidal currents, rather than the freshwater influence. The fairly limited tidal range, however, means that the tidal flow does not extend far upstream, and therefore most mesotidal estuaries are rather short and wide (see Pethick 1984). Mesotidal estuaries are represented in all of the types identified except rias, and most fjords are mesotidal (Table 5.2).

In microtidal estuaries, processes are dominated by freshwater discharge upstream of the estuary mouth and by wind-driven waves from outside the mouth. The resulting form of the estuary is a composite one. Wind-driven waves tend to produce spits and barrier islands which enclose bar-built estuaries. Microtidal estuaries tend to be wide and shallow. There are only six microtidal estuaries in Britain: Traigh-cill-a-Rubha, Breydon Water, Oulton Broad, Christchurch Harbour, Poole Harbour, Montrose Basin, and The Fleet and Portland Harbour.

The tidal range round Britain varies considerably due to the interaction of the tidal waves with each other and the confining coastlines (Figure 5.13). In some places, known as amphidromic points, the tidal waves completely cancel out, so the further an estuary is from an amphidromic point the greater its tidal range. The effects of this, coupled with the shape of the coastline, on resulting tidal ranges is shown for all review sites in Figure 5.15. All estuaries in Wales, western England and south-west Scotland are macrotidal. Around the rest of the Scottish coast, and on the east coast of England south to the North Norfolk Coast, estuaries are macrotidal and mesotidal. There is a wide variety of tidal ranges in Essex and Kent, but along the south coast of England almost all estuaries are macrotidal, with the exception of three (Christchurch Harbour, Poole Harbour and The Fleet) with restricted tidal openings and small tidal ranges.

5.9 Estuaries and geology

The geology of Britain is remarkably diverse both in rock types and structure, and some of the effects of geological controls on estuary types have been noted above. Some generalisations can also be made about the distribution of estuary types in relation to the geology of Britain (Figure 5.16). Fjords, fjards and rias are characteristic of the more resistant rocks of the north and west of Britain. The distribution of fjords and fjards also corresponds to the areas of more intense glaciation. The coastal plain and soft coast types of estuary have a much wider distribution on eastern, southern and some western coasts, but do not occur in the north-west. Their distribution reflects various factors: first, the generally weaker rocks and lower topography of the south and east; second, patterns of sediment availability, for example associated with glacial deposits in eastern Scotland, west Wales and East Anglia, weak coastal cliffs along parts of the south coast, and the presence or absence of onshore movement of sediments; and third, the pattern of relative sea-level change and the contrast between subsidence in the south and south-east and isostatic uplift in the north. Steers (1964, 1973, 1981) provides specific examples of the interaction of these factors.

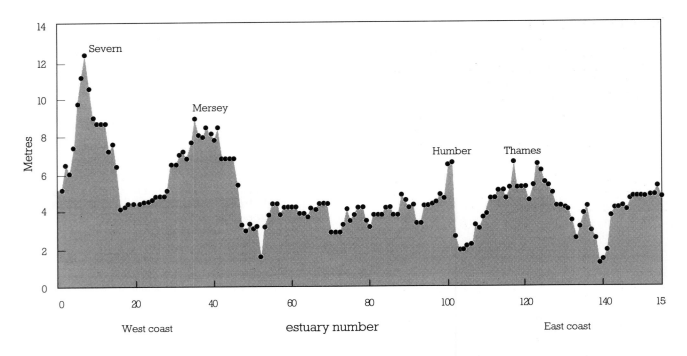

Figure 5.15 Mean spring tidal ranges of estuaries around the coastline of Britain, derived from Bolt & Mitchell (in press). Estuaries are numbered sequentially clockwise around the coast from Land's End (see Figure 5.2).

5.10 Conclusions

The coastline of Britain is notable for the diversity of its geomorphology, reflected in the wide range and distribution of the different estuary types, summarised in Table 5.2. These variations have evolved in response to a long history of glacial, river and marine processes acting upon the different rock types found in the coastal zone of Britain. In particular, the multiple effects of glaciation and sea-level change have left a strong imprint, not only from their direct erosional role, but also through their influence on the supply and transfer of sediments to the present coastline. Although much of the pattern and form of estuaries seen now has arisen since the Holocene transgression, their history is by no means confined to this recent period of geological time. A longer and varied history during the Quaternary is evident from numerous features on estuaries. These include the raised platforms, often overlain by raised beaches, on many of the estuaries of southwest Britain, and the terrace systems associated with rivers and estuaries in eastern Britain.

In essence, estuaries are dynamic systems, constantly adjusting over different timescales to changes of varying magnitude and duration in the coastal zone, but with the constraints imposed by, for example, geology, tides and climate.

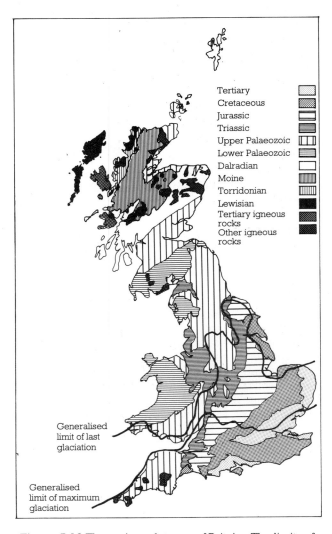

Figure 5.16 The main rock types of Britain. The limits of both the maximum glaciation and the last glaciation (Late Devensian) are shown.

54

5.11 References

BOLT, S., & MITCHELL, R. In press. Ecological effects of barrages. *In: The changing coastline*, ed. by J. Pethick. Estuarine and Coastal Sciences Association, Symposium 20.

BURD, F. 1989. *The saltmarsh survey of Great Britain.* Peterborough, Nature Conservancy Council. (Research & survey in nature conservation No. 17.)

DAVIDSON, N.C., & EVANS, P.R. 1989. The role and potential of man-made and man-modified wetlands in the enhancement of the survival of overwintering shorebirds. *Colonial Waterbirds, 9,* 176-188.

DAVIES, J.L. 1973. *Geographical variation in coastal development.* London, Longman.

DAY, J.W.jr., HALL, C.A., KEMP, W.M., & YANEZ-ARANCIBIA, A. 1989. *Estuarine ecology.* New York, John Wiley & Sons.

EMBLETON, C., & KING, C.A.M. 1975. *Glacial geomorphology.* London, Edward Arnold.

FAIRBRIDGE, R.W. 1980. The estuary: its definition and geodynamic role. *In: Chemistry and biogeochemistry of estuaries,* ed. by E. Olausson and I. Cato, 1-35. New York, Wiley.

HAYES, M.O. 1975. Morphology of sand accumulation in estuaries. *In: Estuarine research, Volume 2: Geology and engineering,* ed. by L.E. Cronin, 3-22. New York, Academic Press.

PETHICK, J. 1984. *An introduction to coastal geomorphology.* London, Edward Arnold.

PRITCHARD, D.W. 1967. Observations of circulation in coastal plain estuaries. *In: Estuaries,* ed. by G.H. Lauff, 3-5. Washington, D.C., American Association for the Advancement of Science. (AAAS Publication No. 83.)

RATCLIFFE, D.A. 1977. *A nature conservation review.* Cambridge, Cambridge University Press.

STEERS, J.A. 1964. *The coastline of England and Wales.* 2nd edition. Cambridge, Cambridge University Press.

STEERS, J.A. 1973. *The coastline of Scotland.* Cambridge, Cambridge University Press.

STEERS, J.A. 1981. *Coastal features of England and Wales.* Cambridge, Oleander Press.

SUGDEN, D.E., & JOHN, B.S. 1976. *Glaciers and landscape.* London, Edward Arnold.

6 The size of the British estuarine resource

Contents

6.1 Introduction

This chapter provides an analysis of the size, distribution and European context of the 155 estuaries defined and classified in Chapter 5 as forming the British estuarine resource. The locations of the estuaries covered by this report are shown in Figure 5.2. This chapter sets the scene for the more detailed distributional analyses of estuarine plant and animal habitats, communities and species in Chapter 8. Analysis of the areas of different habitats around the estuarine resource, where these are known, is presented in Chapter 8.1.

6.2 Measuring estuary areas and lengths

For each core site, areas and lengths of shorelines have been measured. Boundary setting criteria for review sites have been described in Chapter 5.3 and 5.4. The following measurements have been made, with areas in hectares and lengths in kilometres:

1 area (intertidal and subtidal) of the core site, below EHWS of the shoreline;

2 intertidal area of the core site;

3 length of shoreline of the core site, including shores of major islands, measured along EHWS; and

4 length of longest tidal channel, measured along mid-channel line from NTL to the defined estuary mouth.

Where a review site has an area of associated intertidal (AI) two additional measurements were taken:

5 area of associated intertidal (AI) from EHWS to MLW; and

6 length of shoreline of associated intertidal.

Measurements were made from 1:50,000 Second Series OS maps using the NCC's Intergraph Geographical Information Service (GIS). Measurements are listed for each review site in Appendix 2. These measurements provide a comprehensive picture of the scale of Britain's estuarine resource.

6.3 Shorelines

Estimates of the total coastline of Britain vary substantially depending on the measurement techniques and map scales used and the extent to which small islands are included. More detailed estimates of shoreline length and intertidal areas for each habitat, based on 1:10,000 map measurements, will become available once the NCC's Coastwatch project is completed in 1991. Current estimates vary from 14,611 km from Countryside Commission and Scottish Development Department sources (Gubbay 1988) and 14,500 km (Prater 1981) to 19,306 km from the NCC's Coastal Resources Database (CRD), although the latter did not include some upper parts of tidal river channels. CRD figures show that 30.6% of this shoreline is in England, only 8.4% in Wales, and 61.0% in Scotland. Much of the shoreline in Scotland is on islands with predominantly rocky shores: 61.6% of the Scottish shoreline is on islands (Gubbay 1988), although there are only 15 review sites on this part of the British coast (Figure 5.2).

Estuaries form a very substantial component of the coastal zone. The total areas and length of shorelines of British estuaries are summarised in Table 6.1. The parts of the British shoreline that are within review sites are shown in Figure 6.1. The total shoreline of estuaries up to Normal Tidal Limits is over 9,230 km (Table 5.1), almost half (47.8%) of the CRD estimate for the total coastline of Britain (Table 6.2).

Table 6.1 The size of the British estuarine resource[a]

	Core sites	Associated intertidal	Total
Total area (ha)	524,842	4,476	529,318
Intertidal area (ha)	303,443	4,476	307,919
EHWS shoreline (km)	9,091	140	9,231
Tidal channel (km)	2,451	–	2,451

[a] Measured from 1:50,000 Second Series OS maps

Figure 6.1 The parts of the British shoreline covered by the Estuaries Review. Shoreline shown includes tidal channels up to NTL.

Table 6.2 The proportion of the British coastline formed by review sites

	Estuaries	Total coastline	% estuarine
Intertidal area (ha)	307,919	370,157[b]	83.2
EHWS shoreline (km)	9,231	19,306[c]	47.8

[a] Review site totals from Table 6.1
[b] Source: Ordnance Survey basic scale mapping
[c] Source: NCC Coastal Resources Database

6.4 Total areas and intertidal areas

The total area of the intertidal and subtidal parts of review sites covers almost 530,000 ha (Table 6.1), of which 41.8% is subtidal and 58.2% is intertidal. The total intertidal area, which includes all mudflats, sandflats, shingle, rocks and saltmarshes below EHWS, is almost 308,000 ha, 98.5% of which is on core sites (Table 5.1). Estuaries hold a major part of Britain's intertidal shore area, and all major areas of intertidal soft shores have been included in the Estuaries Review. The Estuaries Review covers over 83% of the total intertidal area of the British coastline, as measured by the Ordnance Survey (Table 5.2). This may, however, be slightly too high a percentage since the OS measurement is only to Mean High Water whereas our measurements were made to EHWS. Two other recent estimates of intertidal areas are rather lower than those of the Estuaries Review, largely because of more restrictive boundaries to their measurements: the Coastal Resources Database estimated the total area of intertidal flats and saltmarshes as 273,963 ha and Prater (1981) measured intertidal flats in estuaries at 260,000 ha. Prater (1981) quotes an estimated 44,800 ha of saltmarshes around estuaries in the 1960s. This figure, added to Prater's total for intertidal flats, gives a total of 304,800 ha – close to the Estuaries Review measurements.

Even though estuaries form such a substantial part of Britain's coastal zone they form only a small part of the total land area: 2.3% of the 23,373,113 ha of the total area of British land (data from OS basic scale mapping). British estuaries also form 3% of the area of 178,929 km^{-2} of British territorial waters.

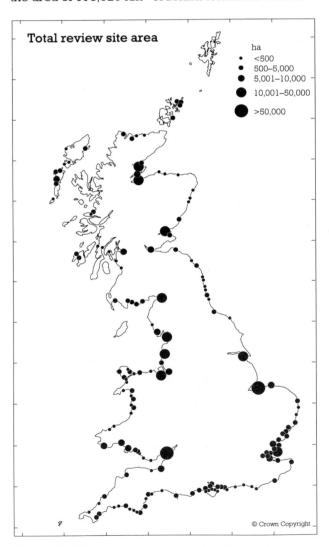

Figure 6.2 The total areas of estuaries. The measurements for each review site are listed in Appendix 2.

The distribution and areas of review sites are shown in Figure 6.2 for total areas and in Figure 6.3 for intertidal areas, and the numbers of estuaries of different sizes are summarised in Figure 6.4. Two review sites exceed 50,000 ha in total area: The Wash (66,654 ha) and the Severn Estuary (55,684 ha). Nine other review sites are between 10,000 and 50,000 ha. These are Maplin Sands and the Humber Estuary in eastern England, the Firth of Tay and the Moray and Dornoch Firths in eastern Scotland and, on the west coast of Britain, the Dee Estuary and North Wirral, the Ribble Estuary, Morecambe Bay and the Solway Firth.

The estuaries with the largest intertidal areas are Morecambe Bay (33,749 ha), The Wash (29,770 ha) and the Solway Firth (27,550 ha). Three other estuaries (Severn Estuary, Dee Estuary and North Wirral, and the Humber Estuary) each have more than 10,000 ha of intertidal habitat (Figure 6.3).

These few large estuaries account for a substantial part of the area of Britain's estuarine resource. The six intertidal sites exceeding 10,000 ha have between them 43% (132,204 ha) of the estuarine intertidal area. Similarly the 11 review sites with total areas exceeding 10,000 ha have 60.7% of the total estuarine area covered by the Estuaries Review. At the other end of the scale, however, many estuaries in Britain are small. 67 review sites (43.2%) each have a total area of less than 500 ha; 80 (61.5%) have intertidal areas of less than 500 ha. These small sites are widely distributed around the coasts of Britain (Figures 6.2 and 6.3). Although together they form only a small proportion of the total area of British estuaries – the 80 sites of less than 500 ha of intertidal area total less than 13,500 ha (4.3% of the total intertidal area) – these sites are an important component of the estuarine resource, and many have features of considerable wildlife importance, described in Chapter 8. Many small sites provide, for example, the very sheltered conditions which are mostly lacking from large estuaries but which are needed by some organisms.

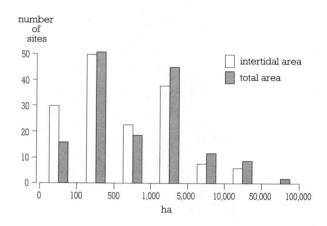

Figure 6.4 The size distribution of Estuaries Review sites measured as intertidal area and total area (ha)

6.5 Areas of different estuary types

Table 6.3 summarises the proportions of the British estuarine resource that are formed from estuaries of different geomorphological type, as classified in Chapter 5. Table 6.3 shows that although coastal plain estuaries are only the second most numerous

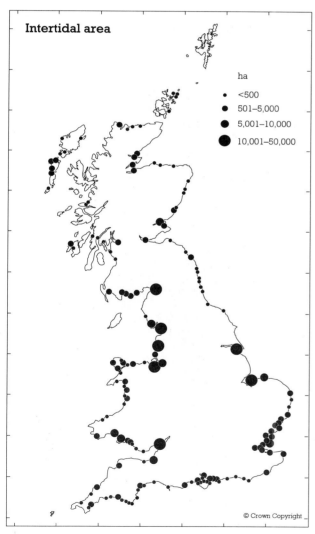

Figure 6.3 The intertidal areas of British estuaries. The measurements for each review site are listed in Appendix 2.

Table 6.3 The proportions of the British estuarine resource areas within estuaries of different geomorphological types

Estuary type	% of total area	% of intertidal area
Fjord	2	1
Fjard	5	6
Ria	3	2
Coastal plain	35	31
Bar-built	6	8
Complex	18	17
Barrier beach	2	3
Linear Shore	4	6
Embayment	25	26

type of estuary they form the largest part of the resource, containing over a third of the total estuarine area in Britain. Large areas of the resource are also contained in embayments and complex estuaries, notably the major firths in Scotland. Together these three types of estuary contain 77% of the total area and 74% of the intertidal area of British estuaries.

In contrast, although bar-built estuaries are numerically the most abundant type of British estuary they are small estuaries and contribute only 6% of the total area and 8% of the intertidal area. Other types of estuary, notably rias, fjords and fjards, also make only small contributions to the total areas of the resource, but such estuaries nevertheless have considerable nature conservation importance for the particular plants and animals they support.

To maintain the range of geomorphological interest on British estuaries, strategies for their conservation need to ensure the safeguard of all these types of estuary, both common and scarce.

6.6 British and European estuaries

The number and variety in form (see Chapter 5) and size of estuaries in Britain is unrivalled anywhere in Europe. British estuaries are important in a European context, not only for this diversity but also for the large total area of estuarine habitat that they provide. The area of British estuaries forms approximately 28% of the total estuarine (intertidal and subtidal) habitat of the North Sea shores and the Atlantic seaboard of western Europe of c. 1,895,000 ha (Figure 6.5).

This is the largest single national area of estuaries in Europe, since the single largest estuarine area in Europe – the international Wadden Sea – is spread between three countries. The Wadden Sea stretches along the coasts of The Netherlands, the Federal Republic of Germany, and Denmark and totals c. 764,000 ha of tidal flats, saltmarshes and subtidal channels that have developed in the shelter of a chain of barrier islands. Together the estuaries of Britain and the Wadden Sea account for over 70% of the estuarine area of western Europe. Elsewhere there are a number of major estuarine areas in the Delta region of the southern Netherlands, the Channel and Atlantic coasts of France and the Atlantic coasts of Ireland, Spain and Portugal. There are, however, only small numbers of estuaries in most of these countries, although some individual estuaries are large.

As well as being very extensive, the estuaries of Britain take on an added significance because of their location on the western extremity of Europe. The influence of the warm waters of the Gulf Stream keep Britain, particularly its western parts, relatively warm during the winter compared with the other shores of the North Sea. In January, south-west England averages 5°C warmer than the Wadden Sea (Figure 6.6). This means that freezing weather is less frequent and less severe in Britain than on most other major estuarine areas north of Spain (Pienkowski 1983).

In addition to the more clement winter weather the large tidal ranges in much of Britain, particularly in western Britain, compared with elsewhere in the North Sea (see Figure 5.14), ensure predictable exposure and covering of tidal flats regardless of weather conditions. In contrast the tidal flats on

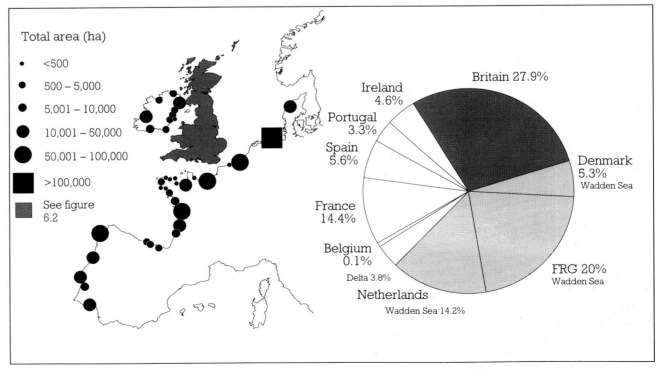

Figure 6.5 a) The distribution of estuarine areas, and b) national proportions of the total estuarine area, on the Atlantic and North Sea coasts of western Europe. Data were derived mostly from Carp (1980), Laursen & Frikke (1984), Prokosch (1984), Wolff & Smit (1984), Meire *et al.* (1989), and NCC's Estuaries Review. No data for Norway were available.

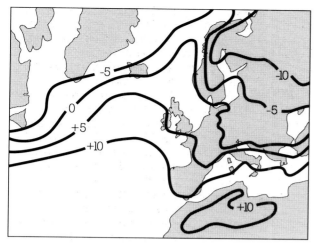

Figure 6.6 Average surface air temperatures in the North Atlantic and western Europe, 1931-1960, from Pienkowski (1983).

estuaries elsewhere in Europe with smaller tidal ranges are more likely to remain covered by the tide during periods of low atmospheric pressure and gales. As well as providing abundant habitat, therefore, British estuaries also provide very favourable conditions for some wildlife such as birds that feed on intertidal habitats (see Chapter 8.6).

6.7 References

CARP, E. 1980. *Directory of wetlands of international importance in the Western Palearctic.* Gland, Switzerland, United Nations Environment Programme & International Union for the Conservation of Nature and Natural Resources.

GUBBAY, S. 1988. *A coastal directory for marine nature conservation.* Ross-on-Wye, Marine Conservation Society.

LAURSEN, K., & FRIKKE, J. 1984. The Danish Wadden Sea. *In: Coastal waders and wildfowl in winter,* ed. by P.R. Evans, J.D. Goss-Custard and W.G. Hale, 214-223. Cambridge, Cambridge University Press.

MEIRE, P.M., SEYS, J., YSEBAERT, T., MEININGER, P.L., & BAPTIST, H.J.M. 1989. A changing Delta: effects of large coastal engineering works on feeding relationships as illustrated by waterbirds. *In: Hydro-ecological relations in the Delta waters of the south-west Netherlands,* ed. by J.C. Hooghart and C.W.S. Posthumus, 109-146. The Hague, TNO Committee on Hydrological Research.

PIENKOWSKI, M.W. 1983. Identification of the relative importance of sites by studies of movement and population turn-over. *In: Shorebirds and large waterbirds conservation,* ed. by P.R. Evans, H. Hafner and P. L'Hermite, 52-67. Brussels, Commission of the European Communities.

PRATER, A.J. 1981. *Estuary birds of Britain and Ireland.* Calton, T. & A.D. Poyser.

PROKOSCH, P. 1984. The German Wadden Sea. *In: Coastal waders and wildfowl in winter,* ed. by P.R. Evans, J.D. Goss-Custard and W.G. Hale, 224-237. Cambridge, Cambridge University Press.

WOLFF, W.J., & SMIT, C.J. 1984. The Dutch Wadden Sea. *In: Coastal waders and wildfowl in winter,* ed. by P.R. Evans, J.D. Goss-Custard and W.G. Hale, 238-252. Cambridge, Cambridge University Press.

7 Review methodology

Contents

Throughout the following chapters presenting the main result of this review we have, as far as possible, attempted a standardised approach to the description of features affecting estuarine wildlife conservation. The information contained in this report has been compiled from a great many different sources, people and organisations. Sources of information, the methods used for data collation, handling and analysis, and the presentation of the information in this report, are outlined below.

7.1 Sources and structure of information

7.1.1 Wildlife resources and conservation status

There has been very extensive research on many aspects of the wildlife of many British estuaries. We have used this existing information, from both published sources and the NCC's unpublished reports and records, in compiling and assessing the wildlife resource of British estuaries. We have not attempted to collect new field data in the timescale of the review, but in several parts of the review, notably in the estuary classification and the classification of aquatic estuarine communities, the comparative analysis of the data collated during the Estuaries Review had not previously been attempted. Sources of information are described in more detail in the appropriate chapters. Although we have attempted to cover all major sources of information, some reports and sources were not available to us during this phase of the review. Our analyses do, however, indicate for which sites and features there are gaps in our information.

7.1.2 Human activities

Our object is to describe the distribution patterns of human activities around the British estuarine resource. Although the locations of activities within the boundaries of a review site were often recorded (to facilitate the collection and analysis of activities data), this was not the object of this report.

Our intention in compiling information on what human activities occur on estuaries has been to provide comparable basic information for each review site on a comprehensive range of activities. To achieve this we have completed a standard questionnaire for each review site on a list of over 250 separate activities grouped into 19 broad categories. These activities are listed in Appendix 2.

For each activity we have aimed to identify its presence or absence on a review site. Where an activity is recorded as being present we have attempted to collect some additional numerical information, varying in type depending on the nature of the activity. The information can be on the number of locations of an activity (e.g. the number of dock sites or complexes) or individual features (e.g. the number of marina berths), and/or the area (in hectares) or proportion of review sites on which the activity is known to occur. This type of data has been collected in particular for activities such as recreation, fisheries and wildfowling. For some activities, for example coastal defences and angling, it has been more appropriate to use the length (in kilometres) or proportion of the shoreline of the review site affected.

Where an activity has resulted in the loss of, or substantial damage to, wildlife habitat, we have noted the size of any land-claim on the core site and its associated terrestrial and intertidal habitats, where known. Throughout this report we use 'land-claim' to describe the conversion of estuarine wildlife habitat for a variety of usually industrial, recreational or agricultural purposes, in preference to the more generally used 'reclamation'. Reclamation implies the reinstatement of land to its former purpose; estuarine land-claim is the irreversible transformation of an area from its natural state.

The status of each activity has been recorded in one or more of 10 categories: not available, none, proposed (current), proposed (defunct), consent application, consented, development, operational, ceased, and historical. Each occurrence in a category constitutes a record for a review site: an activity can occur in one or more categories on a site. Categories are defined below:

Not available: no information available to the review.

None: activity known not to occur on the review site.

Proposed (defunct): proposal for activity (often through a specific site development proposal) made within the last five years but known to be now withdrawn. The withdrawal may be by a recorded indication from the prospective developer, or by rejection of a planning application or public inquiry appeal. It is worth noting, however, that although a particular proposal may be defunct, similar proposals may arise in future.

Proposed (current): active proposal at the time of data collection. We have included here as wide a range of known proposals as possible, from the initial publicity for development plans to firm proposals under pre-application discussion or environmental impact assessment. Any proposal made within the last five years that is not definitely known to have been shelved is included in this category. Whilst not all such proposals will lead to a consent application where appropriate, the inclusion of all proposals is important here since it permits an assessment of the extent and distribution of likely future pressures on review sites.

Consent application: current proposal and subject of a planning application under the Town & Country Planning Acts, Parliamentary Private Bill, or the equivalent consent application for developments outside the local planning system.

Consented: activity or development given consent under appropriate legislation, but the activity not yet taking place or development construction not yet started.

Development: activity currently under construction but not yet in operation (usually a specific development site).

Operational: activity taking place at the time of data collection.

Ceased: activity has been operational at some time during the last five years, but no longer occurs.

Historical: activity has occurred on the review site in the past, but not during the last five years. For some activities recorded as operational, particularly those such as port facilities, industrial, recreational and infrastructure developments, construction took place historically and involved land-claim. For these the activity is recorded as operational but the land-claim associated with its construction is recorded as historical.

Activities information was collected between February and June 1989. Historical activities are thus those that occurred only in 1983 or earlier; activities are recorded as ceased if they stopped more recently than 1983.

It is important to recognise that the activities analyses in this report provide a 'snap-shot' of the status of estuarine human activities at the time of the survey. The status of many proposed activities changes rapidly so it is inevitable with any survey of this kind that the status of some individual proposals will have changed by the time this report is published. Some active proposals will have been dropped, others may have progressed to

consent applications or have been consented to and be operational. In addition some new proposals have been announced since the first half of 1989. Although major changes occurring since the review are mentioned where appropriate in Chapter 10, in this report we have not generally updated the activities data since its collection. Data held in this way provide a suitable basis for monitoring by comparison with future patterns of estuarine activities.

The primary sources of information on activities were the NCC's regional staff, particularly Assistant Regional Officers (AROs) with site casework responsibility for areas including review sites. The knowledge of AROs and the information held in the NCC's regional files have provided an unparalleled source of comparable and comprehensive information available within the review timescale. The NCC is a statutory consultee on planning applications that directly or indirectly affect Sites of Special Scientific Interest (SSSIs). In addition, the NCC issues consents under the Wildlife & Countryside Act 1981 for many types of operation to continue on the SSSI. Since part or all of many review sites are SSSIs (see Chapter 9), AROs were able to provide much of the information needed by the Estuaries Review. For some review sites additional information was obtained from other local sources. Some categories of information were not, however, generally available from NCC sources. For these we consulted published sources and, where possible, other organisations and individuals, although it has not been possible to include all such detailed information in this report.

Activities data were collected by a visit to each ARO during which a standard questionnaire for each site was completed, supplemented by maps, marking locations of features, and ancillary material extracted from files. For some review sites responsibility is divided between two or more AROs. For these sites a complete picture was built into a single questionnaire by combining information from all sources. Activities data were then entered into the Estuaries Review database described below.

7.2 The Estuaries Review database

To handle and analyse the large number of data points collected in the 18 month data collection and analysis phase of the Estuaries Review, we established a computer database using Advanced Revelation database software linked to a map-plotting routine developed by the NCC's Invertebrate Site Register. The 'Sites' part of the database is linked to the geomorphological classification and the area and length measurements for each site.

Linked to the Sites database are also a number of other databases (Figure 7.1) containing data on marine communities, protected sites designations, coastal habitats, birds and human activities. Coastal and bird parts of the Estuaries Review database are largely pre-existing databases that were already developed the NCC. These parts of the database remain under the overall control of their original database managers. Other parts of the database are developed and managed by the Estuaries Review.

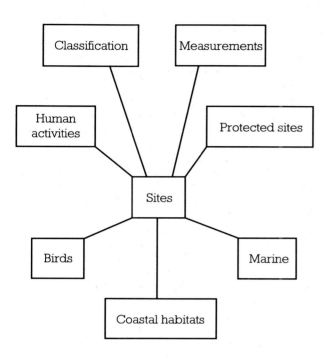

Figure 7.1 Schematic representation of the Estuaries Review database.

In the wildlife resource parts of the review the feature on British estuaries is then, as far as possible, set in its national and international context. This is followed by a description of the conservation of the feature, covering its current conservation designation and the main pressures and problems affecting its conservation. The descriptions of conservation status and the key patterns of activity affecting British estuaries follow similar patterns of presentation.

7.3 Analysis and data representation

For analysis and the preparation of this report the database was interrogated to provide listings and distribution maps of each feature, keyed to the review sites. These analyses have been supplemented for some topics by information not held on the database.

We have mostly followed a standard treatment and presentation to describe each feature on British estuaries. For each there is first a description of the feature and then an account of the size and distribution of the feature. For all distribution maps generated by the Estuaries Review we have produced a standard pattern with information plotted over the centre grid reference of each review site. Centre grid references are listed in Appendix 1. This approach facilitates comparisons of resource and activity distributions around the estuaries. It should be noted, however, that on large estuaries a symbol as plotted by centre grid reference may be some distance from the actual geographical location of the feature on that estuary. Within-site locations of key features are included in the site-by-site estuarine inventory currently in preparation by the Estuaries Review.

8 Britain's estuarine wildlife resource

Introduction

As already outlined in Chapter 7, estuaries support a wide range of wildlife that has evolved the capacity to cope with the fluctuating physical and chemical conditions of estuaries. Some plants and animals, for example many intertidal invertebrates, depend entirely on estuarine conditions for their survival throughout their lives. Others, particularly the more mobile organisms such as birds and fish, depend on estuaries for a part of their lifecycles. Nonetheless estuaries are important for their survival through critical periods.

This chapter describes the range and variety of wildlife on estuaries that together make estuarine wildlife such an important component of Britain's remaining conservation resource. Wildlife importance in Britain is currently assessed on the presence of both wildlife habitats and taxonomic groups. Hence the wildlife importance of an estuarine ecosystem is assessed on the importance of its various key component elements rather than on its importance as a whole ecosystem. This chapter follows current conservation practice in describing the estuarine wildlife resource according to these categories, and is divided as follows:

8.1 Estuarine habitats

8.2 Terrestrial and non-marine invertebrates

8.3 Aquatic estuarine communities

8.4 Fish

8.5 Amphibians and reptiles

8.6 Birds

8.7 Mammals

This approach does mean, however, that some facets of estuarine ecosystems are not afforded detailed separate coverage in this report. For example, intertidal macrobenthos is covered as a component of aquatic estuarine communities (Chapter 8.3) rather than in a separate section. This treatment is used because tidal flats and their macrobenthos have so far been included in estuarine conservation sites largely because of their significant role as feeding grounds for the large and important migrant and wintering bird populations (Chapter 8.6) which feed on the macrobenthos, rather than for the macrobenthos or other tidal flat features themselves.

Nationally important wildlife sites in Britain were identified by Ratcliffe (1977). Ratcliffe listed these as Nature Conservation Review (NCR) sites, further described in Chapter 9. Many of the NCR sites on coasts and estuaries are included by virtue of a range of different habitats: as described in Chapter 8.1, an estuary typically comprises typically a mosaic of several important wildlife habitats. Nevertheless the selection of sites worthy of conservation for their habitat features is made by habitat (e.g. saltmarsh or sand-dunes), so that many coastal and estuarine NCR sites include several different features of wildlife interest.

For each feature of wildlife interest the text follows a broadly similar pattern. A general description of the ecological and behavioural characteristics of the wildlife that are relevant to their conservation is followed by an analysis of the extent and distribution of the wildlife feature around the 155 Estuaries Review sites. As far as possible this estuarine resource is then set in its wider context both in terms of the British resource and its European and international significance. This resource description is followed by a description of the current approach to conserving the particular wildlife feature and an identification of the major pressures and threats as they affect that part of the wildlife resource. These two sections complement the overall analyses of conservation status in Chapter 9 and human activities in Chapter 10 by focussing on the particular needs and issues of each different component of the wildlife resource.

Inevitably some parts of this chapter are able to go into considerably more detail and to describe more of the key ecological needs of the wildlife than others. For example, there is less comprehensive information available on the distribution of aquatic estuarine communities, and much less is known of the ecological requirements of many individual terrestrial invertebrate species than is known of the distribution and requirements of estuarine bird populations. This is in part a reflection of the historical balance of effort directed at the conservation of the various features of estuarine ecosystems.

The Estuaries Review is restricted to looking at the wildlife of the 155 sites identified as estuarine in nature. It is important, however, to recognise that estuaries are not isolated from other coastal and wetland ecosystems. Although many estuaries form discrete areas separated from the next by very different landforms such as exposed rocky shores and cliffs, and although many plants and animals are concentrated on estuaries, estuaries form just part of the coastal zone. There are thus many links between the wildlife of estuaries and coastal systems outside them. Similarly, estuaries can be regarded as being towards one end of a spectrum of types of wetland ranging from the truly marine through inland freshwater bodies, rivers and fens to peatlands. Many of these wetlands face similar pressures and conservation problems to those described for estuaries. Overall analysis of all such wetland systems is, however, outside the scope of this report. Other current studies are directed towards broader coastal zone conservation, notably the Directory of the North Sea Coastal Margin (Doody *et al.* in prep.) and the report of the Irish Sea Study Group (Irish Sea Study Group 1990).

We have treated each section of this chapter as self-contained for bibliographic purposes: a reference list appears at the end of the section to which it refers rather than there being one very long reference list at the end of the chapter. We have also included a brief summary at the start of each of the longer sections.

A review of the diverse wildlife interest of estuaries has needed the help and knowledge of many habitat and taxonomic group specialists within the Nature Conservancy Council. Hence this chapter has been written by a number of specialists, with contributions and information from many more. Authors and contributors for each section are identified and acknowledged in Chapter 2.

References

DOODY, J.P., JOHNSTON, C., & SMITH, B. In prep. *Directory of the North Sea coastal margin.* A report to the Department of the Environment. Peterborough, Nature Conservancy Council.

IRISH SEA STUDY GROUP. 1990. *Irish Sea Study Group: nature conservation.* Liverpool, Irish Sea Study Group.

RATCLIFFE, D.A. 1977. *A nature conservation review.* Cambridge, Cambridge University Press.

8.1 Estuarine habitats

Contents

Summary

Even small estuaries are typically composed of a mosaic of between four and nine major habitat types of wildlife interest (subtidal, intertidal mudflats, intertidal sandflats, saltmarshes, shingles, rocky shores, lagoons, sand-dunes and grazing marshes/coastal grassland). Tidal flats occur on all, and subtidal areas and saltmarshes on almost all, estuaries.

Tidal flats are a major part of estuarine ecosystems. They vary from soft muds in the sheltered inner parts of estuaries to firm sandflats in outer parts. Mudflats especially support large numbers and biomass of characteristic estuarine invertebrate animals, notably crustacea, molluscs and worms on which fish and many of the nationally and internationally important waterfowl feed. There are over 265,000 ha of tidal flats – over 83% of the intertidal area of estuaries.

Major British tidal flat areas are in Morecambe Bay, The Wash, the Dee Estuary and North Wirral, the Humber Estuary, around the Thames Estuary, and in north-east Scotland.

Tidal flats are vulnerable to progressive land-claim,

bait and shellfish collecting, and the impacts of waste discharge and pollution. Maintaining healthy tidal flats is crucial to estuarine conservation since this habitat is the source of much of the richness of the estuarine ecosystem.

Saltmarsh vegetation develops in a series of characteristic zones on fine sediments on the upper shore in sheltered parts of estuaries. Saltmarshes are a major source of nutrients to an estuary.

Extensive saltmarshes with full zonation occur mostly only where there is ample sediment, but land-claim has now removed much of the upper zone vegetation from many saltmarshes.

Saltmarshes larger than 0.5 ha are found on 135 estuaries. They total over 42,250 ha – over 95% of the British saltmarsh resource and almost 14% of the total intertidal area on estuaries. Largest saltmarsh areas are in the Greater Thames estuaries of Essex and Kent, and in Liverpool Bay. Individual estuaries with the largest areas (more than 3,000 ha each) are The Wash, Morecambe Bay and the Solway Firth.

Saltmarsh plant communities are particularly diverse in southern and eastern Britain, where they include plants such as sea-purslane in low-mid marsh, and sea-lavender and shrubby sea-blite in mid-upper marsh.

Cord-grass swards now occur on 82 estuaries and dominate the lowest zones of saltmarsh especially in southern and western England. Overall cord-grass forms over 16% of the British saltmarsh area. It first appeared in Southampton Water in the late 19th century and has spread both naturally and by widespread planting to aid sea defence and land-claim. Cord-grass now appears to be dying back naturally in southern England, but elsewhere its spread is still causing loss of tidal flat feeding grounds for waterfowl.

Saltmarshes are grazed extensively by livestock. Grazed and ungrazed marshes each have conservation value for different types of estuarine wildlife. 39 estuaries have nationally important saltmarshes and 101 estuaries have saltmarshes within Sites of Special Scientific Interest.

Sand-dunes, an important and widespread coastal feature, are associated with 55 estuaries. They develop in more exposed parts of estuaries than saltmarshes.

Many form spits across estuary mouths and in some places have been a major force in shaping the estuary. Sand-dunes on barrier islands shelter the shore from waves, permitting estuarine intertidal habitats to develop in their lee.

Many sand-dunes are naturally mobile, particularly on their outer edges. On their landward side dune vegetation, especially marram grass, gradually binds the sand together, resulting in grassy swards,

wetter slacks and sometimes heath, scrub and woodland. Major areas of once-mobile dunes have been afforested, greatly reducing their wildlife value, which is most often enhanced by grazing and sand mobility. Housing, recreation (including caravan parks), roads, golf courses and intensive agriculture also affect the wildlife interest of estuarine sand-dunes.

There are seven nationally important **shingle** structures in Britain, five of them associated with estuaries. The protection afforded by these shingles, on the Moray Firth, Spey Estuary, North Norfolk Coast, Ore/Alde/Butley Estuary and The Fleet, has been a major influence in the development of these estuaries.

Shingle is an important estuarine feature for its geomorphology, characteristic vegetation and invertebrate animals.

About 83% of the area of British **saline lagoons** is associated with only 37 estuaries in England and Wales.

About half are natural lagoons behind shore barriers, often shingle. They support a highly specialised flora and fauna, often of very local distribution. Natural saline lagoons are very vulnerable to damage from sea defence and other construction work, and from changes in hydrology and water quality.

There are few **sea cliffs** on estuaries, but soft cliffs including those outside estuaries are often important sediment sources for estuaries such as the Humber Estuary and The Wash. They have an important but neglected invertebrate fauna.

Coastal grazing marshes (many of them originally saltmarsh) and other lowland wet grasslands are associated with at least 53 estuaries, especially in southern England where they are fast vanishing. Coastal grazing marshes have a wide range of salinities, which encourages the growth of a large variety of often rare or scarce plants, especially in the ditches.

Some lowland wet grasslands (especially around The Wash and Severn Estuary) are washlands created to prevent more widespread winter flooding. These are important waterfowl breeding and wintering areas.

Almost all the **nationally rare vascular plant** species of tidal flats, saltmarshes, shingle, sandy shores and sand-dunes are associated with estuaries. One or more rare plant species is found on 36 estuaries, mostly in southern and western England and Wales.

Ten nationally rare plants in Britain are entirely dependent on estuarine habitats. Estuaries and the maritime habitats surrounding them also support populations of four rare or scarce endemic plants.

8.1.1 Introduction

A vital consideration for the wildlife importance of estuaries is that estuaries consist of a complex mixture of many distinctive habitat types that are, to a varying extent, affected by proximity to the coast. ('Habitat' is used here in its broad sense of a land feature occupied by a characteristic group of organisms.) These habitats within the matrix that comprises each estuary do not exist in isolation. Rather there are physical, chemical and biological links between them, for example in their hydrology, in sediment transport, in the transfer of nutrients and in the way mobile animals move between them both seasonally and during single tidal cycles. This means that many organisms depend on more than one estuarine habitat during their lifetime, and many (notably fish, mammals and migratory birds) depend also on habitats far removed from estuaries.

Some of these habitats, notably tidal flats and saltmarshes, are characteristic of estuaries and, as described below, almost all the British resource of these features occurs within review sites. Others such as shingle and sand-dunes are more widespread coastal features but with many important examples on estuaries. Some habitats such as rocky shores and sea-cliffs by definition occur mostly on open coasts outside estuaries. Nevertheless some rock features do occur within estuaries, usually as small patches of shore or in the outer parts of review sites.

As Ratcliffe (1977) pointed out, the landward limits of coastal habitats are difficult to define since such a division has to be based chiefly on the strength of the effects of the sea rather than on distance. This applies equally to the subset of estuarine habitats described here. We focus chiefly on maritime and submaritime terrestrial habitats (see Ratcliffe 1977) as well as those falling below high water mark. We also give attention to coastal grazing marshes and other coastal wet grasslands since these are particularly associated with estuaries. Many are still strongly influenced by the sea, since they were originally saltmarsh claimed by man for more intensive agriculture. Others, particularly those adjacent to the upper, tidal but freshwater, parts of estuaries are under little direct influence of the saline conditions of the coast. In addition to all these habitats, a few other habitats of wildlife interest occur fringing a few British estuaries. These include lowland heath in places such as Poole Harbour and woodlands on the Stour Estuary in Essex and along some of the steep-sided rias of south-west England.

Most British estuaries consist of a mosaic of several habitats: at least 144 review sites (93% of the total) are composed of three or more of the nine major habitat types. Estuaries with many habitats are widely distributed around the British coastline (Figure 8.1.1). It is also important to recognise that it is not only physically large estuaries that are made up of such mosaics: even small estuaries generally have several estuarine habitats present

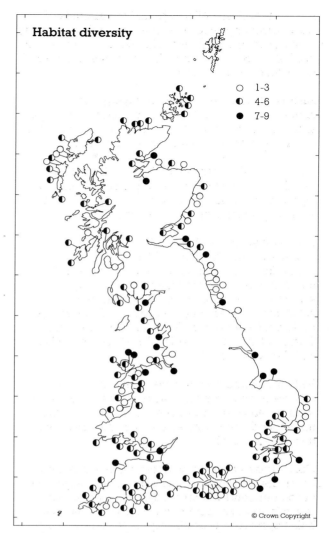

Figure 8.1.1 Estuaries are typically composed of a mosaic of habitats, as shown by the minimum number of main habitat types present on each review site. Nine habitat types are included: subtidal, intertidal mudflat, intertidal sandflat, shingle, rock, saltmarsh, lagoon, sand-dune and grazing marsh/coastal grassland. A few estuaries are also fringed by other habitats such as fen, woodland and heathland.

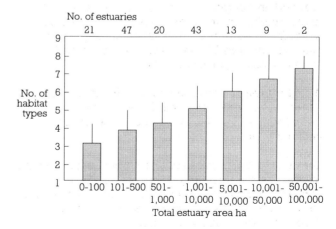

Figure 8.1.2 The average number of characteristic estuarine habitats (see Figure 8.1.1) on British estuaries of different sizes shows that both small and large estuaries consist of habitat mosaics, but that the number of habitats increases as estuaries become larger. The vertical bars show one standard deviation above the average value for each size category of estuary.

71

(Figure 8.1.2). Figure 8.1.2 does show, however, that there is a progressive increase in the diversity of habitats present on review sites as the size of the estuary increases. Even so, some very small estuaries are extremely diverse, with six or seven (of a possible nine) habitat types on and around several estuaries of less than 500 ha of intertidal and subtidal area.

The sections below describe the characteristics, distribution and conservation of the various habitats of British estuaries. The treatment of information is consistent with the current approach to wildlife conservation and is not intended as a detailed review of current knowledge of estuarine ecology. In addition to descriptions of each habitat, we have included here information on rare and scarce vascular plants since their distribution is defined in terms of estuarine and coastal habitats.

8.1.2 Subtidal habitats

Many of the characteristic habitats of estuaries occur both in zones exposed by the tide and subtidally, below low water mark. Subtidal areas are widespread, occurring within the defined boundaries of 146 review sites (94% of review sites) shown in Figure 8.1.3. Subtidal areas are effectively absent from only 10 review sites, chiefly the embayments and open coast sites such as Dengie Flat where there is little or no freshwater outflow and no major subtidal channels draining the intertidal flats. In practice most of even these sites are likely to retain small areas that are permanently inundated, in tidal channels and depressions in tidal flats. The characteristic plant and animal communities associated with these varied subtidal habitats, that include muddy and sandy bottoms, gravels and rocky shores subject to a variety of degrees of wave exposure and salinity, and their conservation, are described in detail in Chapter 8.3 (Aquatic estuarine communities). The distribution and significance of the key intertidal habitats of estuaries, mudflats and sandflats, are described in more detail below.

8.1.3 Rocky shores

Estuaries are characterised by their predominantly soft sediments and shores. Since rocky coastlines have been explicitly excluded from this review, rocky shores (i.e. intertidal areas of rocks) would not be expected to be a widespread feature of review sites. Nevertheless rocky shores are present within at least 52 (34%) of the estuaries covered by this review. Most of these rocky shores are on estuaries in the north and west of Britain; few are on the predominantly soft shores of eastern England (Figure 8.1.4). In most estuaries rocky shores form only a minor component of the habitat mosaic and appear mostly as small areas of outcrop on the shore or as rocky promontories sheltering bays of soft sediments. On a very few, such as at Blue Anchor Bay, areas of flat rocky shore form a major feature of the site. In places

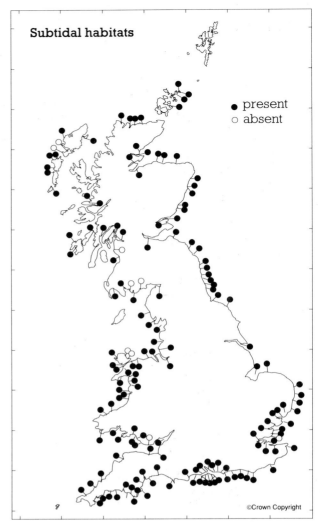

Figure 8.1.3 The presence of subtidal areas on review sites

such as here and the Severn Estuary, the rocky exposures on the shore are of considerable geological and geomorphological interest (see Chapter 9). Elsewhere rocks feature in estuaries chiefly on the outer fringes of the review sites and on rocky islands in the mouths of estuaries such as the Firth of Forth.

These intertidal rocky areas, as well as subtidal rocks and boulder shores, support a considerable variety of aquatic tidal communities, many of which are also characteristic of rocky shores outside estuaries (see Chapter 8.3), and contribute much to the overall diversity of aquatic estuarine communities within estuaries, although forming only small areas in comparison with soft substrates.

8.1.4 Tidal flats

Intertidal mudflats and sandflats form a major and vital part of the British estuarine resource. The varying tidal and river currents and often large volumes of sediment carried in suspension in the water column during periods of high tide result in river estuaries and other shallow shores usually being places of active change and key zones for

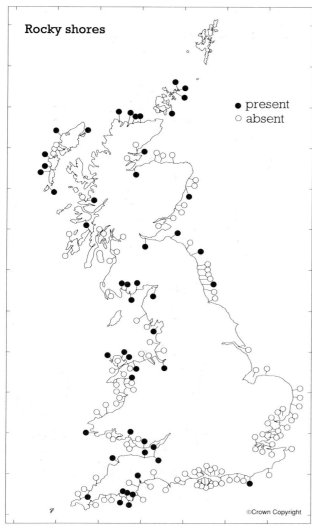

Figure 8.1.4 The presence of rocky shores on review sites

the formation of geomorphological features. Estuaries are therefore important in the accretion of sedimentary deposits that ultimately form much of the sedimentary rock of which the land is built.

The precise nature of the substrate in an estuary, its form and particle size, depends on a complex interaction between these physical factors in an ever-changing environment. In general the finest suspended sediments are deposited in the most sheltered places, so mudbanks generally form in the inner parts of estuaries. Closer to the mouth, in main river outflow channels and on more exposed shores, higher wave energy and/or faster tidal currents usually keep fine sediments in suspension. In these areas only the coarser sediments are deposited, resulting in sandflats. Such features can form substantial parts of high energy estuaries such as the Severn Estuary. There most of the intertidal flats in the main part of the estuary are highly mobile sandbanks. Movement of windborne sand on estuaries where there are extensive intertidal sandflats often leads to the development of sand-dune systems above the high water mark. These sand-dune habitats are described below in Section 8.1.6. Smaller estuaries are, however, generally

more sheltered and so a greater proportion of their intertidal flats are muddy.

Although many mudflats appear relatively stable in location and form, their continued presence intertidally depends on the maintenance of a dynamic equilibrium between the rate of deposition of sediments from the water column and the rate of erosion by tidal currents and wave action. Where deposition exceeds erosion tidal flats accrete. Higher tidal level flats become suitable for colonisation by pioneer saltmarsh plants which in turn generally increase accretion by trapping sediment amongst their roots and stems. This development of saltmarsh plant communities is described further in Section 8.1.5 below.

Tidal flats provide a substrate within which lives a very large biomass of macrobenthos, notably polychaete worms and gastropod and bivalve molluscs. These animals often live in very high densities and provide abundant food for estuarine fish when the flats are covered by the tide. When the flats are exposed they provide feeding grounds for the many species of migrant and wintering waterfowl for which British estuaries are so nationally and internationally important (see Chapter 8.6).

The characteristic macrobenthic fauna varies on different substrate types. For example, soft mudflats typically support high densities of the small gastropod mollusc *Hydrobia ulvae*, bivalve molluscs such as the clam *Mya arenaria*, the polychaete ragworm *Hediste (Nereis) diversicolor* and the amphipod crustacean *Corophium volutator*. On sandier mudflats the macrobenthic fauna is often dominated by bivalve molluscs such as the cockle *Cerastoderma edule* and Baltic tellin *Macoma balthica*. The polychaete lugworm *Arenicola marina* is also characteristic of these stable muddy sandflats. Substantial beds of mussels *Mytilus edulis* develop where there is sand or gravel or sometimes on sheltered mudflats. Such places generally support the highest biomass of any part of the tidal flats which forms an important food source for waterfowl, notably oystercatchers *Haematopus ostralegus* and eiders *Somateria mollissima*. Sandflats, however, because of their greater instability, generally support smaller numbers and a lower biomass of macrobenthos. These flats have their own typical fauna, notably several species of isopod and amphipod crustaceans that are capable of swimming strongly and so maintaining their position in the estuary in the face of strong wave and tide action.

The characteristic plant and animal communities of these various types of tidal flat are described further in Chapter 8.3 Aquatic estuarine communities.

British distribution of estuarine tidal flats

By definition every review site includes tidal flats since the presence of tidal flats was used as a key selection criterion for the sites included in the Estuaries Review.

For the purposes of this report the area of tidal flats on each review site was estimated by subtracting the area of saltmarsh (see Section 8.1.5) from the total intertidal area (Appendix 2). This will give a slight overestimate of the area of tidal flats for some review sites since it includes intertidal shingle and rock features. Since, however, extensive rocky shores are explicitly excluded from the review the overall error is small. These figures show that there is a total of 265,668 ha of tidal flats on British estuaries. Tidal flats are a very major feature of British estuaries, forming 86.3% of the intertidal area of review sites. They form the most abundant estuarine habitat (in terms of their area) and are a substantial feature of the British coastline as a whole, forming almost 72% of the total intertidal area of the coast (*cf.* Table 5.2).

As would be expected from the overall size of the estuarine resource (Chapter 6), British tidal flats form a large part of the tidal flat resource of north-west Europe. Elsewhere, the international Wadden Sea has the single largest area of tidal flats, with an area of 499,000 ha (Wolff & Smit 1984). Only the Federal Republic of Germany, with 319,000 ha of tidal flats in the Wadden Sea, has a larger national area of tidal flats than Britain. Even including the 26,400 ha of tidal flats remaining in the Dutch Delta area (Meire *et al.* 1989), The Netherlands with 156,400 ha has less than two-thirds the total area of tidal flats on British estuaries.

As with total estuary areas, most of the tidal flat area in Britain is concentrated in just a few large estuaries and embayments. The largest single expanse of intertidal flats, 30,500 ha (11.5% of the estuarine total), is in the embayment of Morecambe Bay. Elsewhere The Wash (25,540 ha) and the Solway Firth (24,630 ha) have very large areas of tidal flats. Only three other estuaries, the Severn Estuary, the Humber Estuary and the Dee Estuary and North Wirral, have in excess of 10,000 ha of tidal flats. Together these six estuaries contain 119,600 ha of tidal flats, almost half (45.8%) of the British estuarine resource.

Figure 8.1.5 shows that, in addition to these individual estuaries with very large tidal flat areas, several parts of the coastline have concentrations of estuaries with large tidal flats. These include south-east England, where the 10 constituent review sites of the 'Greater Thames estuary' (from the Colne Estuary to the Swale Estuary) have a total of 25,500 ha of tidal flats, making this one of the four largest continuous areas of tidal flats in Britain. Elsewhere the four large firths of north-east Scotland (Loch Fleet to the Moray Firth) have almost 12,300 ha, the 11 review sites around the Solent on the south coast of England over 5,100 ha, and those of the south coast of Dumfries and Galloway have over 6,700 ha of tidal flats.

Most of the tidal flats are concentrated on these few areas, but the remainder are scattered around the

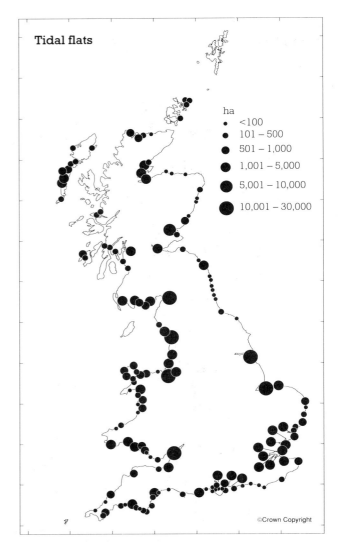

Figure 8.1.5 The distribution and size (ha) of intertidal flats on review sites

whole coastline on smaller estuaries (Figure 8.1.5). Many British estuaries have only a small area of tidal flats: 85 review sites (56% of the total) have intertidal flats of less than 500 ha. Nevertheless these smaller areas together contribute over 13,000 ha of tidal flats (5% of the total area of flats). Hence they form an important component of the resource since they are often largely mudflats of high productivity which support high densities of wintering waterfowl (see Section 8.6.2).

As well as the local conditions within different parts of an estuary that lead to the formation of intertidal flats from a variety of types sediment, there are also some broader-scale patterns. In general, coarse-grained sandflats tend to be prevalent in the north and west of Britain and fine-grained muds in the south and east (Ratcliffe 1977). The distribution of major sandflats and mudflats around review sites (Figures 8.1.6 and 8.1.7) reflects this trend. It should be noted that these figures show only the presence the relevant habitat. Figures 8.1.6 and 8.1.7 thus show wider distributions than those for the aquatic estuarine communities that occur within these habitats (Chapter 8.3), since a location for a community is shown only where there is

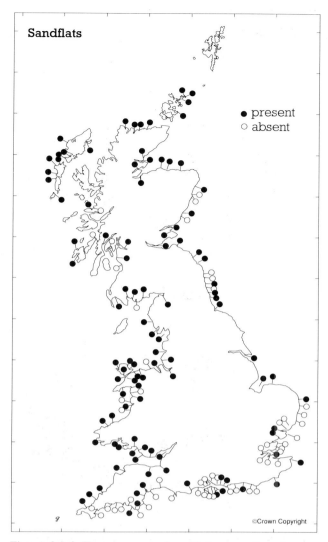

Figure 8.1.6 The presence of sandflats on review sites

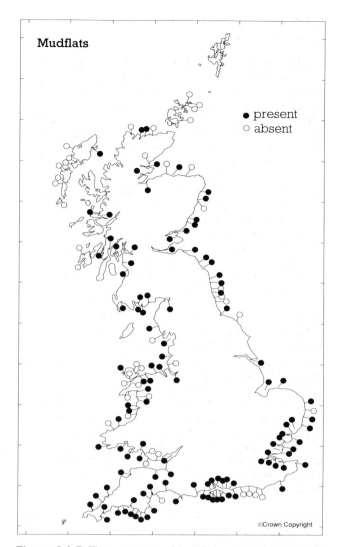

Figure 8.1.7 The presence of mudflats on review sites

documented evidence of the presence of the constituent plant and animal species. The large sandflats in places such as the Moray Firth and in the Outer Hebrides are often also of importance as a source of sand for the extensive sand-dune and machair systems that have developed on their landward edge. There are of course major exceptions to this general pattern of mudflat and sandflat distribution, for example the extensive mudflats of major north-western estuaries such as the Solway Firth and Morecambe Bay.

The abundant supplies of fine sediments and the sheltered conditions in the southern North Sea and south coast of Britain lead to the intertidal sediment on these estuaries being predominantly muddy and sometimes supporting extensive beds of eel-grass *Zostera* spp. and green algae *Enteromorpha* spp., the latter especially in nutrient-rich areas. Although most estuaries have small areas of different substrate types associated with a preponderance of either mudflats or sandflats, there are rather few British estuaries in which there is a wide range of intertidal sediments well represented: Ratcliffe (1977) notes particularly the Exe Estuary and the Dyfi Estuary.

Conservation of tidal flats

On the basis of their plant communities Ratcliffe (1977) divided coastlands into six physiographic categories. Of these, tidal flats are distinctive in supporting very little vegetation. Consequently within the Nature Conservation Review tidal flats were identified as of national importance chiefly in terms of the abundance of their macrobenthic fauna and the consequent ability of an area of tidal flats to support large populations of migrant and wintering waterfowl. In these terms areas of tidal flats attain particular importance if they are extensive, exposed at a variety of tidal heights and muddy and so support large waterfowl populations. All 50 coastland sites with a major element of tidal flats that were identified by Ratcliffe (1977) as being of national importance are within estuaries. Their distribution between only 48 review sites (Figure 8.1.8) reflects closely the distribution of large estuaries (*cf.* Figure 8.1.5) and especially those with fine sediments in south-east and southern England.

Since Ratcliffe (1977) was published, the increasingly comprehensive understanding of the numbers and distribution of migrant and wintering bird populations (see Chapter 8.6, e.g. Figures

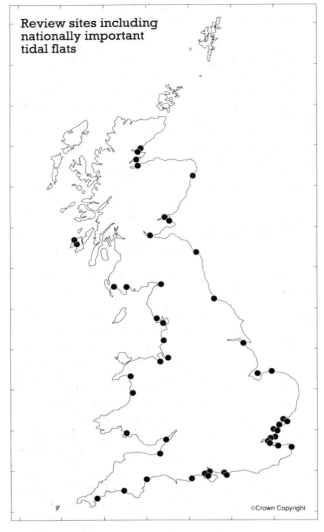

Figure 8.1.8 Review sites which include nationally important tidal flats listed by Ratcliffe (1977)

8.6.76 and 8.6.77) has led to the inclusion of part or all of further review sites within the SSSI series.

This approach to conserving tidal flats indirectly through their bird populations means that, unlike vegetated coastal habitats such as saltmarshes and sand-dunes, for each of which there is a series of nationally important sites identified as characteristic of the variety and diversity of its plant communities (see later), there is currently no such directly identified site series for tidal flats. Of course even the division into tidal and subtidal zones, although necessary in relation to administrative and legislative procedures, is rather artificial in estuaries, since many characteristic estuarine macrobenthic species live both intertidally and subtidally or move seasonally between the two.

Tidal flats are included in Britain's conservation effort not only because of their identification as bird feeding areas but also as an element of marine conservation. Here assessments are currently made chiefly on an individual marine community basis (see Chapter 8.3), although as yet rather few assessments have been made for individual communities on individual estuaries. Interestingly,

for mudflat and sandflat communities most, except for *Zostera* and *Ruppia* beds, have so far been assessed as of only local or regional, rather than national or international, significance. This contrasts with the overall national and international importance of many of the estuaries concerned, and of the overall British resource. Comprehensive marine community assessments, including those of tidal flats, are currently being made for Britain through the NCC's Marine Nature Conservation Review (MNCR). A review is also underway of the extent to which features of marine conservation significance are present within existing coastal and estuarine SSSIs.

Ratcliffe (1977) notes that coastlands are of great physiographic importance and that the series of nationally important coastal sites for the Nature Conservation Review was chosen in part for the range of features illustrating the dynamic processes involved in their formation and continuing development. Some NCR sites were at that time chosen to illustrate the relationships between the different physiographic features and habitats on an estuary. Nevertheless, earth science conservation currently treats the different types of geomorphological feature separately on estuaries. Hence only major shingle, sand-dune and some saltmarsh features are included in the Geological Conservation Review (GCR) (see Chapter 9). Ironically, despite being the key feature identifed in this review as characteristic of estuarine ecosystems, tidal flats themselves do not currently feature in the GCR coastal geomorphology series of SSSIs. The physiographic features surrounding estuaries often derive much of the sediment of which they are built from tidal flats. Although the surrounding saltmarshes, sand-dunes and shingle ridges are thus inextricably linked to tidal mudflats and sandflats through their sediment transport regimes, whole estuaries are not currently treated for conservation purposes as features based on their geomorphological type (see Chapter 5).

Pressures on tidal flats

Tidal flats as an estuarine habitat are vulnerable to many of the pressures affecting estuaries. Since they are a key wildlife habitat central to most estuaries their continued existence and health is pivotal to the maintenance of the British estuarine resource. Land-claim that leads directly to loss of tidal flat habitat is therefore a key pressure on British estuaries. As is described further in Chapter 10, land-claim generally occurs in a piecemeal way, although very large areas can be claimed at one time and for many different purposes.

In some British estuaries the overall impact of such piecemeal land-claim has been to entirely or almost entirely eradicate the mud and sandflats of the estuary. Examples include the Tees Estuary, where over 80% of the intertidal flats have been claimed for agriculture, industry and ports since 1720, and the Tyne Estuary, where no broad intertidal flats remain. On the Thaw in south Wales the whole river estuary has been claimed. There are many other estuaries on which some land-claim has affected tidal flats, and such pressures continue (see Chapter 10).

The area of intertidal flats can be eroded in a number of ways. As well as by direct land-claim, tidal flats can be reduced by sediment extraction from intertidal areas and by widening and dredging tidal channels. Such dredging, especially where it involves deepening of tidal channels, can have indirect consequences for adjacent tidal flats by increasing erosion as sediment is drawn down into the channel (see also Chapter 10). In a similarly indirect fashion land-claim involving saltmarsh above the level of tidal flats can also result in a gradual further loss of the flats. In places such as The Wash new saltmarsh accretes outside the new sea-wall on what was formerly the upper tidal flats (Hill & Randerson 1987), leading to a reduced tidal flat area on a steeper shore profile. A downshore spread of saltmarsh leading to overall loss of tidal flats has been accelerated on some estuaries (chiefly in south and west England and Wales) by the planting of cord-grass *Spartina anglica*, and also by its subsequent natural spread. On some estuaries *Spartina* is, however, now dying back to reveal bare mud again, albeit usually at an initially higher tidal level and without the abundant macrofauna of established mudflats. The impact of *Spartina* on British estuaries is further described in Section 8.1.5.

Areas of tidal flats can also be reduced by the manipulation of water levels in estuaries through the use of barriers and barrages. The impacts of barrages vary. The most immediately and comprehensively damaging to tidal flats are those 'leisure' barrages designed to provide for waterborne recreation, since these maintain constant high water conditions.

Barrages that lead to reductions in tidal amplitude, for example tidal power and storm surge barrages, also usually substantially alter the distribution and structure of tidal flats within an estuary. High tidal flats cease to be inundated and low tidal flats cease to be exposed. The immediate effect of barrage closure is thus a loss of tidal flat area within the estuary. In the longer term the area of tidal flats may become further reduced by the downshore development of saltmarsh below the new high water mark. Temporarily increased deposition in the less turbid waters, and a longer-term redistribution of sediment through changed erosion patterns and infilling of tidal creeks, may eventually lead to a stable new pattern of tidal flats. Behind barrages such flats are generally likely to become muddier at the expense of the extensive sandflats characteristic of high-energy coastal plain estuaries. Such changes are, however, proving difficult to predict and restabilisation may take many years (e.g. Hooghart & Posthumus 1989). In addition to such direct changes to tidal flat structure from barrages across estuary mouths, there is concern that barrages placed on tidal rivers upstream of tidal flats can alter the sediment budget by inhibiting sediment delivery into the estuary.

Overall loss of tidal flat area has serious implications for the organisms which depend on them. Since the number of birds using an estuary depends in part on its intertidal area (see Figure 8.6.31), reduction in the area of available feeding grounds is likely to lead to reduced bird populations. Indeed the reduction of intertidal flat areas through *Spartina* spread has been implicated in the decline in the British wintering population of dunlins (Goss-Custard & Moser 1988). Many land-claims disproportionately affect the upper tidal levels of estuarine flats, since land-claim episodes are generally excursions from the shore. Permeable barrages also affect these upper tidal levels, as well as the low level flats, since they act to damp down the tidal range such that the former high tidal levels then remain permanently exposed and low tidal levels permanently submerged.

The presence of high tidal level flats (areas which are only covered by the tide for short periods) are very important for the many migrant and wintering waterfowl which feed on tidal flats since these birds at times need to feed for most or all of the tidal cycle to gain their energy requirements. Removal of upper tidal flats restricts this feeding period on heavily man-modified estuaries. This increases the risk of the birds dying of starvation, especially during periods of severe winter weather when energy demands are high (Davidson & Clark 1985). At times, however, this shortfall in feeding time has apparently been buffered, on extensively land-claimed estuaries such as the Tees, by the incidental development of peripheral wetlands, on which birds can continue to feed during high water (Davidson & Evans 1986). In addition to its effects on birds, loss of high level tidal flats may also interfere with the life-cycles of major components of the intertidal macrofauna since this is where most successful spatfall occurs in some species prior to their dispersion into the intertidal flats throughout the estuary.

In addition to land-claim, some human activities can damage the quality of intertidal flats. Notable amongst these are some forms of collection of intertidal macrofauna, for example suction dredging for cockles *Cerastoderma edule* and lugworms *Arenicola marina* (reviewed by Fowler 1989). The sediment disturbance and filtering techniques from even shallow dredging for cockles can kill large numbers of undersized cockles and other macrofauna such as Baltic tellins *Macoma balthica* as well as destroying eel-grass *Zostera* in the dredged areas. Some deeper dredging, such as for clams *Mercenaria mercenaria* and lugworms, may be even more damaging to both the physical integrity of the tidal flats and the macrobenthic populations living in them (van den Heiligenberg 1987). Although some mobile species can recover quickly by migrating into the dredged areas, others, particularly those with slow or variable recruitment of young into the population, can take much longer. Hence dredging can reduce biomass and alter species composition of tidal flats.

Hand-digging lugworms and ragworms for bait can

have similar consequences to dredging on intertidal flats. Carried out intensively it has at times resulted in the local eradication of the target species and heavy mortality of other macrobenthos in the dug areas (van den Heiligenberg 1987).

Physical disturbance to tidal flats from activities such as digging and hydraulic dredging is also of concern in polluted estuaries, since such disturbance can release pollutants such as heavy metals and other toxins from anoxic layers of sediment (Howell 1985). This highlights one impact of pollution, which is a major factor affecting the quality of tidal flats.

Pollution stress from organic discharges and inputs is known to change the structure of benthic communities, which become dominated by a low diversity of small animals (Gray 1972). At severe pollution levels anoxic conditions develop and macrobenthos mostly dies; such places can support few fish and bird predators. Such eutrophication also leads to the growth of dense algal mats, which both physically prevent predators feeding and induce anoxic conditions in the underlying mud, so reducing macrobenthic populations (e.g. Hull 1987). Conversely under some less extreme conditions of eutrophication there is evidence of increased benthic production (e.g. Beukema & Cadee 1986) which may lead to temporary increases in some bird populations (van Impe 1985), although for most estuaries there is no clear point known at which such nutrient enrichment ceases to increase production.

Such organic enrichment is seldom, however, the whole pollutant picture on estuaries since organic waste discharges are often accompanied by persistent pollutants, notably polychlorinated biphenyls (PCBs) and heavy metals. Some come directly from industrial sources in estuaries and some enter and accumulate in estuaries from their river catchments, probably in enhanced quantities as a consequence of human activities such as mining in metalliferous strata. Such persistent pollutants become bioaccumulated as they pass from the water column and from sediment up through food chains. Some heavy metal pollutants can have a drastic effect on some estuarine organisms, a notable example being the widespread disruption of the reproductive biology of the dogwhelk *Nucella lapillus* by leachates from tributyl tin (TBT)-based antifouling paints used on boats (Spence *et al.* 1990).

Only in exceptional circumstances, however, are pollutant levels known to cause mortality of top predators feeding on tidal flats, an exception being mortality of dunlins and other waders in the Mersey Estuary in 1979 in which organic lead compounds were implicated (NERC 1983). Waders are, however, known to accumulate substantial heavy metal loads on polluted British estuaries such as the Tees (Evans & Moon 1981; Evans *et al.* 1987). Impacts on top predators are more likely to be chronic and may involve depression of lifetime breeding output, as recently found for tufted ducks

fed on mussels from a polluted Dutch estuary (Scholten & Foekema 1988 in Meire *et al.* 1989).

Overall then effective estuarine conservation depends on safeguarding the continued existence, quality and variety of tidal flats, particularly through the enhancement of degraded systems. The efforts to reduce pollutant levels on beaches and in estuaries, directed through approaches such as Water Quality Standards (WQS) for estuarine waters, will help restore the natural state of many of the still extensive and internationally important tidal flats of British estuaries.

Tidal flats have suffered more than most habitats even on estuaries from the view that estuaries are wastelands suitable for cheap waste disposal and the claiming of building land. The widely misused word 'reclamation', generally used in such proposals, implies that estuarine land-claim is designed to take back what was previously dry land. In the current post-glacial period of rising sea-levels it would seem, however, to be the sea rather than man that is undertaking the reclamation.

Some tidal flat land-claim proposals go further than simply treating intertidal land as wasteland of no intrinsic value. It is regrettable that a primary objective of some schemes, notably leisure barrages and associated waterside developments, appears to be that of covering up the tidal flats regardless of even their national and international importance to wildlife. Such tidal flats are apparently deemed an unsuitable setting for modern ideals of housing and leisure.

It is ironic that this 'stinking mud' attitude towards some of Britain's most important natural resources is strongest where man's activities themselves, by heavily polluting estuaries, have created the smelly anoxic conditions used to justify the destruction of the tidal flats.

8.1.5 Saltmarshes

Saltmarsh development

Saltmarshes develop wherever tidal waters are sufficiently quiescent to allow the deposition of fine sediments. Stabilisation of the sediment begins with the binding action of surface algae. Aeration of the 'soil' by the numerous mud-dwelling invertebrates and the interaction between these and plants such as *Enteromorpha*, which may become attached to loose invertebrate shells, encourages further sediment deposition. Above this zone, which usually exists at the lower levels of the shoreline, progressively more terrestrial types of vegetation occur, depending on the number of tidal inundations which cover the plants.

At the lowest levels, where immersion occurs on nearly every tide (i.e. approximately 700 times per year), higher plants, which are tolerant of high salinities and able to withstand physical movement by the incoming tide, become established. These

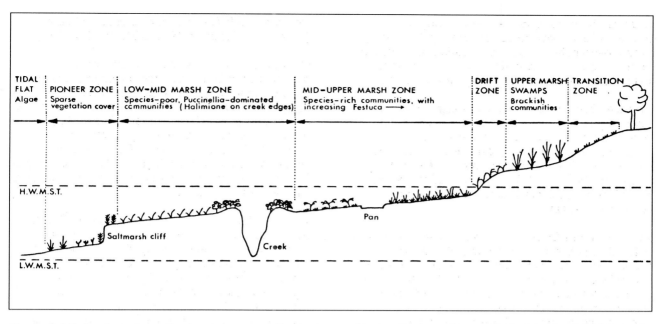

Figure 8.1.9 A saltmarsh profile showing a generalised scheme of 'natural' saltmarsh succession, from Burd (1989)

are represented by a very few species (eel-grass *Zostera* and tasselweed *Ruppia*) which are essentially aquatic in type and lie flat when the tide is out. Above this zone, at about the mean water level of the lower, neap tides, plants with a more terrestrial growth form predominate. Again these are dominated by a few salt-tolerant species such as the annuals glass-wort *Salicornia* spp. and sea-blite *Suaeda maritima* and the perennial cord-grass *Spartina anglica* (see below) whose seedlings require a number of days free from tidal movement to become rooted in the sediment. At this level the flats receive less than 600 tidal immersions per year. Chapman (1960) distinguishes between 'lower marshes' which have more than 360 submergences per year and 'higher marshes' with less than 360 submergences per year. In the former, the important point is that the maximum period of freedom from tidal inundation is nine days.

Once established, these plants help the deposition of sedimentation and, in the classic model (Chapman 1938, 1939) succession takes place. This results in the marsh level at any one point receiving progressively fewer tidal inundations as the process of sedimentation raises the marsh level. As this happens, the vegetation and its associated animals become more varied. This general picture is, however, very simplified, and true succession of this kind may only occur in estuaries where relatively rapid sedimentation takes place. Elsewhere in higher energy coastal environments, such as on more exposed high sandy beaches or in areas where sediment supply is restricted, such as Scottish sea-lochs, a spatial zonation of communities occurs, which changes only very slowly with time, if at all. Another important factor in the successional development is the nature of the anthropogenic management, which can extensively modify the community structure and wildlife value.

Given ideal conditions and with an ample supply of sediment, extensive saltmarshes can develop. These show, in the best examples, the full successional sequences from pioneer low-marsh through mid-marsh communities and transitions to other terrestrial vegetation such as grazing marsh, sand-dunes, fens and, in a very few cases, woodland. The extent of the transitional habitats, in particular, is dependent on the extent of enclosure for the development of agriculture, ports, houses, industry, roads and the like. Today very few of the larger marshes within estuaries show the complete sequence of vegetation as depicted in Figure 8.1.9.

Saltmarshes and estuaries

Saltmarshes play a fundamental role in the life of an estuary. Not only do they help to bring stability to its margins, but they also operate as a source of primary productivity. Estimates vary as to the contribution to the overall energy budget, but the rates of production may be very high. Carter (1989) quotes net values between 500 g and 1,500 g m^{-2} yr^{-1} carbon. Comparisons between the dry-weight production of plant material for a variety of saltmarshes was made by Hussey & Long (1982). These ranged from 153 to 2,722 g m^{-2} for the mean live weight and 63 to 1,534 g m^{-2} for mean dead weight. The lowest figures are for *Puccinellia maritima* marsh in the Netherlands, the highest for *Spartina foliosa* in California, USA (mean live weight), and *Spartina cyanosuriodes* in Georgia, USA.

The precise (relative) importance of this depends on other contributions, mainly from the algae of the tidal waters (the benthos) and the extent of detritus being brought in from the river or by the tides. The distribution of saltmarshes amongst Estuaries Review sites is shown in Figure 8.1.10. These data are derived from a national survey of the saltmarsh resource (Burd 1989) made between 1981 and

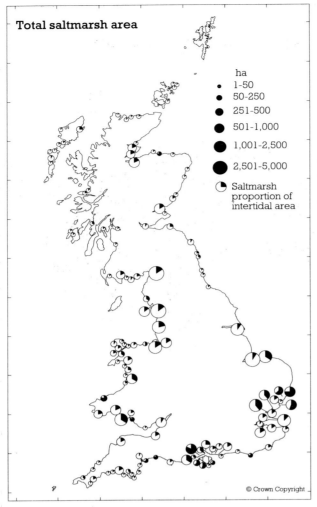

Total saltmarsh area

ha
- 1–50
- 50–250
- 251–500
- 501–1,000
- 1,001–2,500
- 2,501–5,000

◑ Saltmarsh proportion of intertidal area

© Crown Copyright

Figure 8.1.10 The distribution of saltmarsh habitat on review sites, derived from data collected by the NCC's Saltmarsh survey of Great Britain. For each review site the size of the symbol shows the area of saltmarsh and the filled segment shows the proportion of the total intertidal area of that site formed by saltmarsh.

1988, as part of a review of coastal habitats being undertaken by the NCC's Coastal Ecology Branch within the Chief Scientist Directorate.

Saltmarshes have been recorded in 135 of the 155 Estuaries Review sites. Their areas range from 1 ha in the Wansbeck Estuary to 4,228 ha in The Wash. Saltmarsh almost certainly occurs in the remaining 20 estuaries, though only as small pockets at the very edge of the sites and of less than 0.5 ha, the usual lower limit for inclusion in the *Saltmarsh survey of Great Britain* (Burd 1989).

The total area of saltmarsh within the 135 estuaries is 42,251 ha and represents 95.2% of the total Great Britain resource of 44,370 ha. This very high proportion is not surprising since it is the fundamental nature of estuaries – soft, shallow, sheltered, tidal shores – that provides the most favourable conditions for saltmarsh growth. Elsewhere, limited sediment supply and/or exposure restrict their growth to very localised and small areas such as at the heads of otherwise hard-shore sea-lochs.

The largest concentrations of saltmarsh occur around the Greater Thames estuary in Essex and Kent – 8,525 ha (19%) – and Liverpool Bay – 8,662 ha (20%) – where shallow offshore waters are able to deliver vast quantities of fine sediment to the coast. Individually, two sites, The Wash and Morecambe Bay, each have a large proportion of the total resource, with 4,228 ha (9.5%) and 3,753 ha (7.3%) respectively. The Solway Firth has almost 3,000 ha, and the North Norfolk Coast, Loughor Estuary, Ribble Estuary and Dee Estuary and North Wirral each have in excess of 2,000 ha of saltmarsh. In order to give some indication of the significance of this to the functioning of the estuaries, the ratio of saltmarsh to total intertidal area is shown in Figure 8.1.10 and for major sites in Table 8.1.1.

Table 8.1.1 The relative proportion of saltmarsh within the 10 review sites with the largest total intertidal areas

Site	Intertidal area (ha)	Saltmarsh area (ha)[a]	% saltmarsh
Morecambe Bay	33,749	3,253	9.6
The Wash	29,769	4,228	14.2
Solway Firth	27,550	2,925	10.6
Severn Estuary	16,890	933	5.5
Humber Estuary	13,521	1,419	10.5
Dee Estuary and North Wirral	12,981	2,108	16.2
Maplin Sands/ Crouch-Roach Estuary[*]	10,979	1,059	9.6
Ribble Estuary	10,674	2,184	20.5
Loughor Estuary	6,552	2,187	33.4
North Norfolk Coast	5,874	2,127	36.2

[a] Saltmarsh areas are derived from the Saltmarsh Survey of Great Britain (Burd 1991)

[*] The Saltmarsh Survey of Great Britain site boundaries overlap these two adjacent review sites

Review sites with the largest areas of saltmarsh are amongst those where there has been relatively little alteration of the estuary shape by man. On the North Norfolk Coast saltmarsh exists in close association with other coastal habitats, chiefly sand-dunes and shingle bars (see Figure 8.1.11). There has been relatively little enclosure and the plant communities span the full successional range from low-marsh to high-marsh and transitions into swamp vegetation and other habitats. The saltmarshes are old and structurally diverse with a rich flora and fauna. On the Loughor Estuary there has also been almost no land-claim. Here the landward boundary is natural sand-dune transition. In the Loughor Estuary the larger proportional area of saltmarsh is, however, partly related to the spread of *Spartina anglica*, which currently accounts for almost 20% of the saltmarsh area. Elsewhere, such as on the Dee Estuary, the saltmarshes are much younger, dating from about 1910 when the last major land-claims of the upper estuary took place. Some 25–30% of the estuary has been enclosed (Figure 8.1.12) and transitions to upper saltmarsh and other habitats, notably *Phragmites* swamp, are very restricted. Overall, although large, these saltmarshes are less

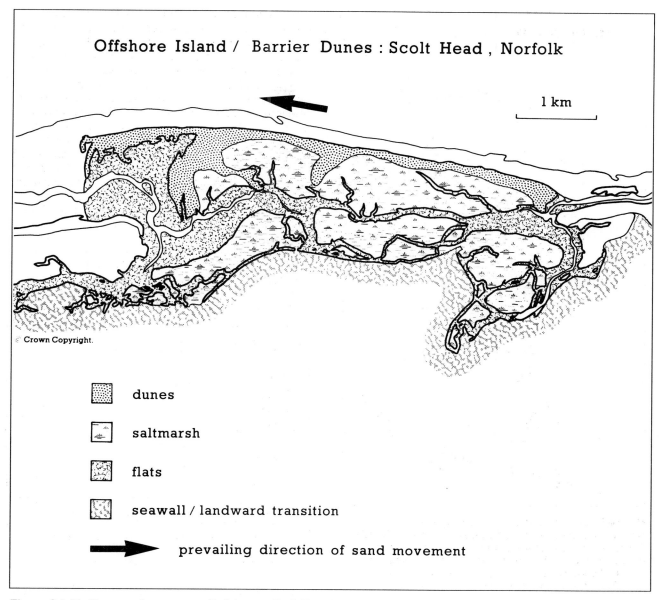

Figure 8.1.11 The complex pattern of habitats on Scolt Head Island on the North Norfolk Coast

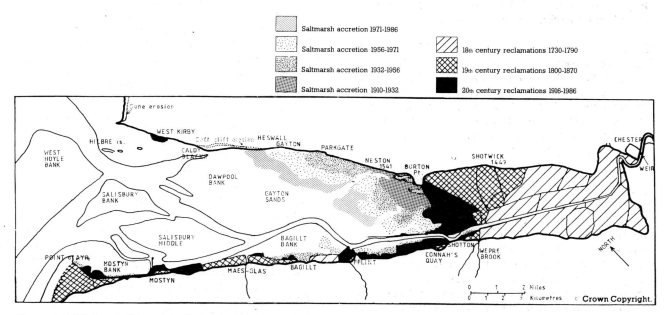

Figure 8.1.12 Land-claim and saltmarsh development on the Dee Estuary

Table 8.1.2 The relationship between National Vegetation Classification (NVC) plant communities and those of NCC's Saltmarsh Survey of Great Britain, after Burd (1989)

Saltmarsh Survey community	NVC communities	
1. *Spartina*	SM4	*Spartina maritima*
	SM5	*Spartina alternifolia*
	SM6	*Spartina anglica*
2a. *Salicornia/Suaeda*	SM7	*Arthrocnemum perenne*
	SM8	Annual *Salicornia*
	SM9	*Suaeda maritima*
2b. *Aster*	SM11	*Aster tripolium* var. *discoideus*
	SM12	Rayed *Aster tripolium*
3a. Puccinellia	SM10	Transitional low marsh vegetation
	SM13	*Puccinellia maritima*
	–	*P. maritima* sub-comm.
3b. *Halimione*	SM14	*Halimione portulacoides*
	–	*H. portulacoides* sub-comm.
	–	*Juncus maritimus* sub-comm.
	–	*P. maritima* sub-comm.
4a. *Limonium/Armeria*	SM13	*Puccinellia maritima*
	–	*Limonium/Armeria* sub-comm.
4b. *Puccinellia/Festuca*	SM13	*Puccinellia maritima*
	–	*Glaux maritima* sub-comm.
	–	*Plantago/Armeria* sub-comm.
	–	turf fucoid sub-comm.
	SM16	*Festuca rubra*
	–	tall *F. rubra* sub-comm.
	SM17	*Artemisia maritima*
4c. *Juncus gerardii*	SM16	*Festuca rubra*
	–	*P. maritima* sub-comm.
	–	*J. gerardii* sub-comm.
	–	*Festuca/Glaux* sub-comm.
	–	*Leontodon autumnalis* sub-comm.
	–	*Carex flacca* sub-comm.
4d. *Juncus maritimus*	SM15	*Juncus maritimus/Triglochin maritima*
	SM18	*Juncus maritimus*
	–	*J. maritimus/O. lachenalii* sub-comm.
	–	*Festuca arundinacea* sub-comm.
5a. *Agropyron (Elymus)*	SM24	*Elymus pycnanthus*
	SM18	*Elymus repens*
5b. *Suaeda fruticosa*	SM25	*Suaeda vera* drift line
	–	*E. pycnanthus* sub-comm.
	–	*H. portulacoides* sub-comm.
6. Upper marsh swamps	S4	*Phragmites australis*
	S19	*Eleocharis palustris*
	S20	*Scirpus lacustris* ssp. *tabernaemontani*
	S21	*Scirpus maritimus*
7i. Shingle/Dune transition	SM21	*Suaeda vera/Limonium binervosum* typical sub-comm.
	–	*Frankenia laevis* sub-comm.
	SM22	*H. portulacoides/F. laevis*
7ii. Freshwater transition	MG11	*F. rubra/A. stolonifera/P. anserina*
	–	*Lolium perenne* sub-comm.
	–	*Atriplex hastata* sub-comm.
	–	*Honkenya peploides* sub-comm.
7iii. Grassland transition	MG12	Coarse *Festuca arundinacea*
		Lolium perenne/Holcus lanatus sub-comm.
		Oenanthe lachenalii sub-comm.

biologically diverse than those of North Norfolk. They are younger, have resulted from a rapid expansion of *Spartina anglica* and are grazed – all factors which tend to reduce biological diversity.

The relatively smaller areas of saltmarsh on Maplin Sands, including the Crouch-Roach Estuary, and the Severn Estuary are probably the result of the exposed nature of much of the tidal flats. Elsewhere the saltmarsh area provides a significant proportion of the intertidal land. In terms of productivity, 1 ha of saltmarsh could provide 10,000 kg or 10 tonnes in one year (assuming a net dry weight production of approximately 1,000 g m^{-2} – a relatively conservative estimate of productivity) – making a significant contribution to the primary productivity of an estuary.

Plant communities of saltmarshes

The National Vegetation Classification (NVC) has identified communities, including transitions to other habitats, which are predominantly dependent on or associated with tidal regimes (Rodwell in press). A summary of these is given in Table 8.1.2 which also shows their relationship with the saltmarsh communities recorded in the *Saltmarsh survey of Great Britain* (Burd 1989).

The distribution of these community types nationally provides some indication of the factors which influence the type of marsh which develops. The following discussion highlights some of the more important features, namely climate and anthropogenic impacts. For a more complete description see Burd (1989), Adam (1978) and Rodwell (In press).

Climatic factors operate across Great Britain to produce communities with distinctive characteristics. South of a line running roughly from the Solway in the west to north-east Fife in the east several species which do not occur further north are either characteristic or major components of a number of important saltmarsh communities. Sea-purslane *Halimione portulacoides* is one of the more significant and forms sometimes extensive communities in the low-mid marsh zone. A high proportion, 55 %, of review sites in England and Wales have examples of these communities. They are well represented in the estuaries of the Humber, The Wash, the North Norfolk Coast, Essex and north Kent (Figure 8.1.13).

Other species have similar distributions to that of sea-purslane, for example common sea-lavender *Limonium vulgare*, sea-couch *Elymus pycnanthus*, sea wormwood *Artemisia maritima* and hard-grass *Parapholis strigosa* (Perring & Walters 1976). It is thought that the controlling factor may be temperature, although as described below anthropogenic factors also restrict their occurrence on individual sites.

Northern saltmarshes are characterised by the absence of the above species rather than their replacement by other plants with a northern

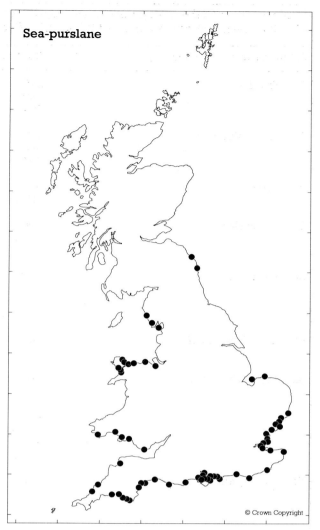

Figure 8.1.13 Distribution of sea-purslane *Halimione portulacoides* dominated communities on review sites in Britain

distribution. An exception is saltmarsh flat-sedge *Blysmus rufus* which can be dominant in the upper saltmarsh, notably on rocky or gravelly shores.

In the north and west there are more frequent transitions to non-tidal vegetation, notably grassland. In these regions the salinity of the regime is diluted by the high levels of rainfall, allowing non-halophytic plants to form a more significant feature of the vegetation. This is most clearly exemplified by the distribution of transitional grassland (Figure 8.1.14). The absence of extensive transitional communities, in the south and east particularly, is also a function of the extent of land-claim (see below).

Sites with communities transitional to sand-dunes are amongst the more important botanical examples of saltmarsh. In particular, on sites in south-east England, notably North Norfolk, there are species with an essentially southern and Mediterranean distribution. These include rare and scarce species such as shrubby sea-blite *Suaeda vera*, matted sea-lavender *Limonium bellidifolium* and sea-heath *Frankenia laevis*, the last species

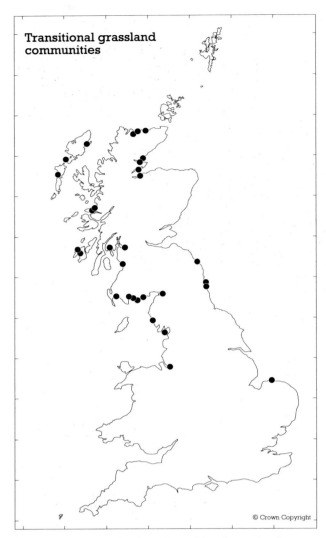

Figure 8.1.14 Distribution of transitional grassland communities on review sites in Britain

and the structure of the marsh is altered. At the most intensive grazing levels, experienced in north-west England (up to 6.5 sheep per ha year-round) (Gray 1972), 'lawns' of tightly grazed, species-poor, grass-dominated marsh are prevalent.

The significance of this for nature conservation interest is considerable, not only in relation to the diversity of saltmarsh plants, but also for the structure of the plant communities. In its turn this has important consequences for the associated animals, notably terrestrial invertebrates and birds.

Enclosure of saltmarsh by the erection of earth banks or other sea-walls has been an established practice for centuries at some sites, notably in The Wash, where some 32,000 ha of agricultural land have been created. Historically, as the sea receded, during periods of sea-level fall or when saltmarsh accretion rates exceeded rates of sea-level rise, saltmarsh expanded onto exposed mudflats. As the number of tidal inundations became less frequent the marshes were used more extensively for grazing. The erection of a summer earth bank extended the grazing period and stronger defences ultimately resulted in the complete exclusion of the tide.

As enclosure techniques improved, the saltmarsh was bunded at lower and lower levels and the resulting land area 'won' from the sea became extensive. In Essex and north Kent, as much as 4,340 ha of the current agricultural land was obtained in this way (Boorman & Ranwell 1977). This same pattern of historical land-claim has taken place in some of our major estuaries. Today many are much smaller versions of the originals; examples include the Ribble Estuary (Figure 8.1.15) and the Dee Estuary and North Wirral (Figure 8.1.12), which have been reduced in area by at least one third (see also Chapter 10.5).

The consequence for saltmarshes of these sometimes extensive incursions is to remove from the tidal regime the transitional and upper saltmarsh communities, which are usually biologically the most diverse. The implications for the remaining marshes are that they have proportionally more low marsh and pioneer communities in relation to the total marsh area.

Figure 8.1.16 shows the area of each of the saltmarsh survey communities for the 10 sites with the largest total saltmarsh area. This clearly shows the impact on the community mosaic across the marsh of the repeated reclamations in The Wash, where 80% of the saltmarsh is pioneer marsh or low-mid marsh. By comparison, in the Solway Firth, 80% of the remaining marsh is upper marsh. The overall implications of this for the balance of the community types is shown in Figure 8.1.17 where the areas are shown for two contrasting NCC regions. The shift in proportion of community type to the lower, species-poor end of the spectrum in areas where there has been extensive enclosure of saltmarsh is clearly shown.

occurring also at Merthyr Mawr (Ogmore Estuary) in south Wales.

Anthropogenic factors are also significant in helping to determine the type of saltmarsh vegetation that develops. Grazing and enclosure are the two most important, though the appearance of common cord-grass *Spartina anglica*, a plant which has been intimately associated with man on the south coast, has also played a major role.

Grazing by domestic stock has been a feature of saltmarshes for many centuries. Relatively low densities (2 sheep or 0.33 cattle per ha) and open range grazing are thought to be best from a nature conservation point of view (Beeftink 1977).

As grazing levels increase, however, common saltmarsh-grass *Puccinellia maritima* and red fescue *Festuca rubra*, which are nationally important and diagnostic species of a wide range of low-mid and mid-upper marsh communities respectively, are given a competitive advantage. At the same time, sensitive species such as common sea-lavender *Limonium vulgare* and sea-purslane *Halimione portulacoides* tend to be eliminated from the sward

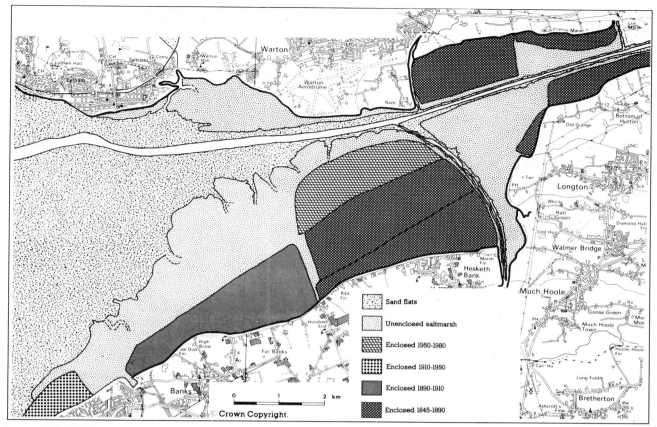

Figure 8.1.15 The pattern of enclosure of saltmarshes in the Ribble Estuary between 1845 and 1980

Legend (from map):
- Sand flats
- Unenclosed saltmarsh
- Enclosed 1950-1980
- Enclosed 1910-1950
- Enclosed 1890-1910
- Enclosed 1845-1890

© Crown Copyright.

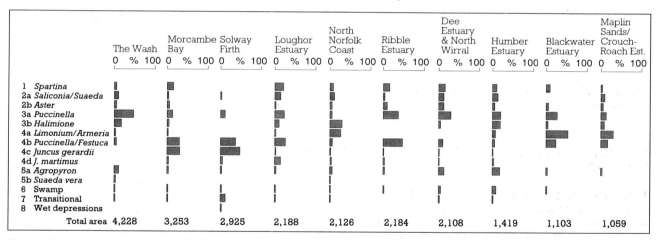

Figure 8.1.16 The proportional distribution of the 14 main saltmarsh community types on the review sites with the 10 largest saltmarsh areas. Different patterns of natural and man-induced changes are reflected in different diversity and proportions of communities.

The *Spartina* story

The history of *Spartina* is important and interesting in the context of both the development of saltmarsh vegetation and the conservation of winter bird feeding areas within estuaries. Prior to 1870 there was only one known species of cord-grass *Spartina* in Great Britain, small cord-grass *S. maritima*. This species, though never common, formed a significant community of the low marsh around The Wash, the Thames Basin and the Solent.

The accidental introduction of smooth cord-grass *Spartina alterniflora*, a native of America, to Southampton Water prior to 1870, and its subsequent crossing with the native plant, resulted in the appearance of a fertile amphidiploid, common cord-grass *S. anglica*, which is now the most frequent species encountered (see Marchant 1967 for a review of the origin of the species).

Since its appearance, the ability of *Spartina* to colonise open mudflats at a faster rate, and further seaward, than its rivals has been recognised as of potential benefit to man. As a consequence it was extensively planted throughout Britain (Hubbard & Stebbings 1967), in Europe, and even as far as China, as an aid to stabilisation of coastlines and a stimulus to enclosure and land-claim.

The benefit to nature conservation within estuaries is not so readily apparent. The rapid colonisation of

85

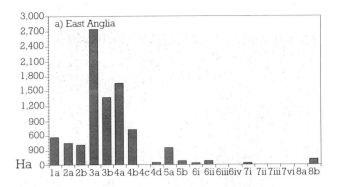

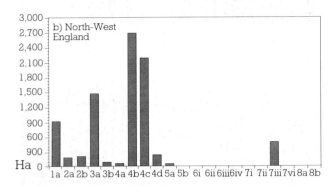

Figure 8.1.17 The distribution of major saltmarsh communities in two NCC regions with different extents of coast protection: a) East Anglia, with c. 60% of coastline protected by sea-walls and embankments; and b) North West England, with c. 30% of coastline protected by sea-walls and embankments, from Burd (1989). Names of main community types are listed in Figure 8.1.16.

Spartina over the extensive flats in sites with large wintering populations of waders and wildfowl which feed in the intertidal zone has been identified as a major concern (see Chapter 8.6). As a consequence, there have been several attempts to control the species by spraying with herbicide in sites of high wildlife interest, for example the Cefni Estuary in north Wales and Lindisfarne NNR in north-east England. These have met with some success although the current status of the species, which is expanding rapidly in north-west England and Wales, still poses a significant problem. Doody (1984) and, more recently, Gray & Benham (1990) give general discussions of the issue.

The impact of *S. anglica* on the native flora is also of some concern. Firstly, it appears that it may have helped the demise of the native *S. maritima*, though no causal link has been established. The latter is now much less widely distributed than formerly. Prior to 1930 it was recorded from 46 10-km squares, according to the Atlas of the British Flora. According to records since the 1930s, it had disappeared from 20 of these by the mid-1970s (Perring & Walters 1976). In addition, by taking over the mantle of the native pioneer species, *S. anglica* has altered the course of succession. Because of its invasive qualities it usually produces a mono-culture which has much less intrinsic value to wildlife than the normally occurring marsh.

Although succession to other communities does take place these are themselves usually restricted in their species composition, and the general principle of control or eradication is the recommended course of action on sites of high wildlife value (Doody 1990).

Figure 8.1.18 provides a summary of *Spartina* distribution in the mid-1980s, derived from the NCC's *Saltmarsh survey of Great Britain* (Burd 1989) and the area of *Spartina* on review sites. *Spartina* occurs on 82 (52.9%) review sites. *Spartina*-dominated communities have a southern and western distribution and occur in generally small areas on only seven Scottish estuaries. In total *Spartina* dominates 6,774 ha of saltmarsh, 15.3% of the total estuarine saltmarsh area in Britain. The largest areas of *Spartina* are on the estuaries of southern England, particularly Poole Harbour and around the Solent. On these estuaries *Spartina* covers a major part of the total saltmarsh area: over 80% of saltmarsh is *Spartina* in Poole Harbour, and

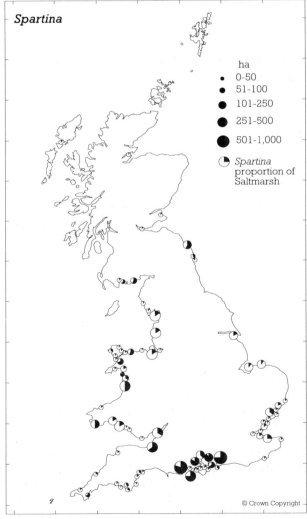

Figure 8.1.18 The distribution of *Spartina*-dominated saltmarsh on review sites, derived from data collected by the NCC's Saltmarsh survey of Great Britain. For each review site the size of the symbol shows the area of *Spartina* marsh and the filled segment shows the proportion of the total saltmarsh area of that site formed by *Spartina* marsh.

six of the 16 estuaries where *Spartina* covers over half of the saltmarsh area are on the Poole Harbour to Chichester Harbour coastline. These large areas and proportions of *Spartina* are there despite the phenomenom of 'die-back' that is being experienced on the south coast. This appears to be a natural process, although its cause is not fully understood. 'Die-back' is itself causing concern to those responsible for sea defence, as the demise of the saltmarsh can expose the toe of the sea-wall to greater wave attack. This is discussed in more detail below.

Large areas of *Spartina* occur also on the Severn Estuary and in Wales and north-west England (Figure 8.6.18). The present vigour of the species in north-west England and north Wales is giving some cause for concern. There extensive colonisation is taking place, notably in Morecambe Bay, although here as elsewhere in north-west England *Spartina* as yet forms only a relatively small proportion of the large saltmarsh area. In the Dee Estuary, which is at a later stage of development, much of the present large saltmarsh area has developed since 1910 as a result of rapid *Spartina* expansion (see Figure 8.1.12).

The importance of grazing management for saltmarshes

Grazing management has important consequences for the type of saltmarsh vegetation which develops, as has been discussed above. In summary, with little or no grazing by domestic stock (and in the absence of land-claim), saltmarshes:

a) are rich in a wide variety of saltmarsh plants, including species-rich communities transitional to other vegetation;

b) have a good structural diversity which provides important food for terrestrial invertebrates and habitat for breeding birds; and

c) provide winter feeding for small populations of grazing ducks and geese.

Figure 8.1.19a shows a saltmarsh in north Norfolk with high wildlife interest; species diversity, and hence structural diversity, result in high invertebrate interest and high breeding bird numbers.

As grazing pressure increases and species and structural diversity decrease, the saltmarsh becomes less important floristically and relatively more important for animals (mainly birds) grazing on the palatable grasses that are favoured. Thus at the higher grazing levels (Figure 8.1.19b) saltmarshes:

a) tend to have lower plant diversity, although some transitional communities may retain their species richness;

Figure 8.1.19 The appearance of grazed and ungrazed saltmarshes: a) high plant diversity ungrazed saltmarsh on the North Norfolk Coast; and b) low plant diversity heavily grazed saltmarsh in Morecambe Bay

b) have little or no structural diversity, resulting in a much reduced variety of terrestrial invertebrates and much lower densities of breeding birds; and

c) provide important winter feeding for large numbers of grazing ducks and geese.

For a more detailed discussion of the principles see Doody (1987).

The assessment of the conservation value of any particular saltmarsh has to take into account each of the above factors. In fact, 101 review sites (65.7% of the total) have saltmarshes within Sites of Special Scientific Interest. This is dealt with in more detail below.

Conservation importance and protected status of saltmarshes

Saltmarshes are important for a variety of nature conservation reasons. They are a rare and specialised habitat in their own right. Overall, there are only 44,370 ha of saltmarsh in Great Britain. This compares with approximately 1,300,000 ha of peatland and 350,000 ha of ancient semi-natural woodland (Burd 1989) – themselves rare in national terms. Many of the plants which occur there survive nowhere else and are specifically adapted to the high and often changing salinities of the soil and to regular tidal immersion.

Saltmarshes are among the most natural ecosystems remaining in Britain, especially where enclosure has not taken place and where grazing by domestic stock is either absent or present at a very low level. They support important and, in some cases, specially-adapted invertebrates which include a number of rare species (see Chapter 8.2). They are also home for a wide variety of breeding birds, and even where the communities are highly modified by domestic grazing they are still important in providing winter feeding grounds for sometimes internationally important numbers of waterfowl (described further in Chapter 8.6).

In addition to this they form an important and integral part of the life of an estuary, not only in relation to the interests described above but also as part of the functioning whole. As we have seen above, they sometimes make up a significant proportion of the estuarine system. By virtue of their high productivity, they can supply an important contribution to the primary sources of material for the complex food chains within an estuary (see Chapter 7).

The selection of sites within the SSSI series depends on a combination of features of conservation significance. Individual saltmarshes are selected primarily on the basis of their representation of the main types of geographical variation in the vegetation referred to above. In addition, the extent of the development of the full successional sequence from pioneer saltmarsh through the mid-upper levels and transitions to other habitats is an important factor. The presence of individual species (plants, invertebrate animals and breeding birds), including rare species, is a further consideration.

However, it is because of their importance to the functioning of the major estuarine systems and the survival of the large populations of winter feeding birds (wildfowl and waders – see Chapter 8.6) that a very high proportion – 83% in GB as a whole (Burd 1989) – of this habitat is protected as SSSI. This is not to denigrate the other interests, but their significance for birds is a much more obvious manifestation of the conservation value of saltmarshes.

Internationally, the largest area of saltmarsh is in the Wadden Sea where there is estimated to be a total of 35,000 ha. However, the total area of saltmarsh in Great Britain is greater than this. In addition, the sites are widely distributed and support communities which span the northern and southern elements of the European range of variation (Djkema 1984).

Site protection

Given these interests and the concentration of saltmarshes on review sites, it is perhaps not surprising that a high proportion of the saltmarshes within review sites are protected by designation as Sites of Special Scientific Interest. There are 101 Estuaries Review sites which include saltmarsh within the designated area.

Figure 8.1.20 shows the proportion of saltmarsh protected by SSSI status in Great Britain from information assembled between 1981-1988 (from Burd 1989). Of the 101 review sites with known saltmarshes, 39 have national importance as examples of saltmarsh habitat, i.e. they support a full and representative sequence of plant communities covering the range of variation in Great Britain. These places are named on Figure 8.1.21.

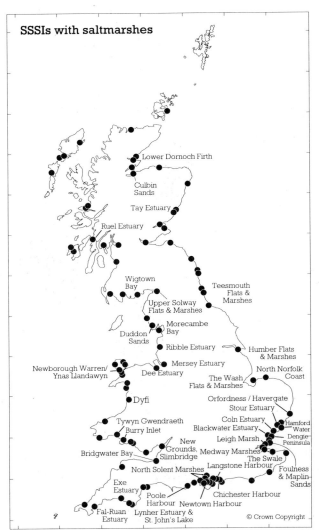

Figure 8.1.21 The presence of saltmarshes within SSSIs on review sites. Nationally important saltmarshes are names

Saltmarsh threats include the continuation of those activities which have historically caused substantial losses. These include enclosure (mainly for agriculture) and other 'land-claim' development,

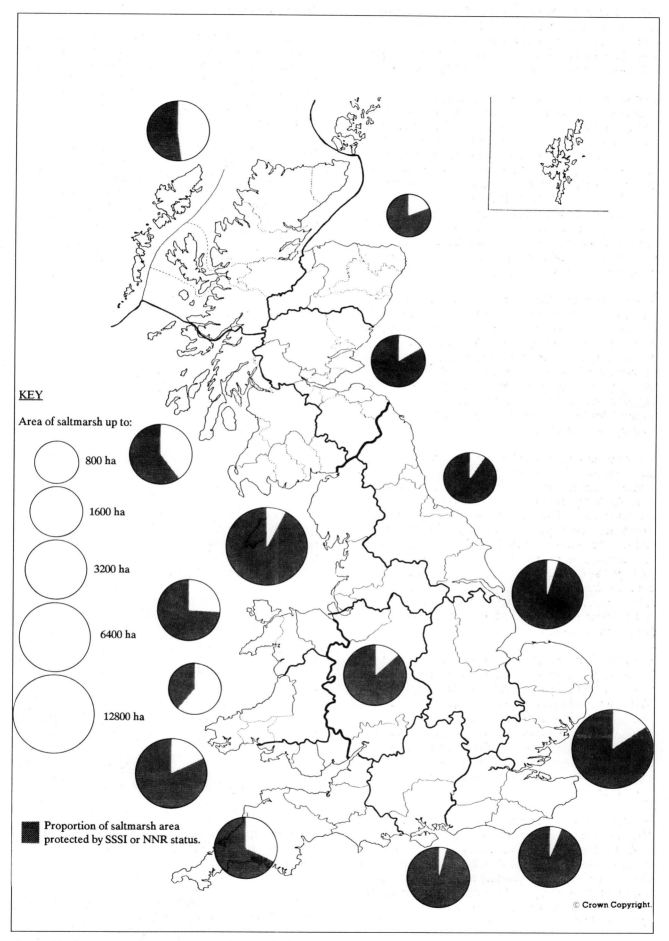

Figure 8.1.20 The proportion of saltmarsh that is protected as SSSI in Great Britain, arranged by NCC regions, from Burd (1989)

through tipping and the building of roads, marinas and housing. More recently, proposals for tidal barrages have given great cause for concern since, whilst a tidal regime will normally continue, the modifications of the high tide levels and duration would have substantial effects on the higher saltmarsh zones. Moderation of the tidal regime would almost certainly cause a reduction in tidal levels and the number of tides reaching the upper saltmarsh levels. Such a change in tidal regimes after barrage construction can have rapid, dramatic and long-term effects on saltmarsh vegetation structure, as found for post-barrage vegetation changes in the Delta region of the Netherlands (see e.g. Hooghart & Posthumus 1989).

The continuing expansion of *Spartina* in north-west England also poses a threat to some aspects of estuarine conservation. By contrast in south and south-east England decay of the marsh and erosion, brought about by *Spartina* die-back in the former and, it is thought, sea-level rise in the latter, are resulting in major losses in these areas. Conservation measures must take into account these factors.

Recreation, including wildfowling, does not have a direct adverse impact on the saltmarsh habitat. Other activities such as pollution through effluent discharge, fertiliser outwash and other, often toxic, materials are not known to have a long-lasting adverse effect on the habitat. Even oil pollution is not damaging to saltmarsh vegetation in the long-term if left to degrade naturally.

8.1.6 Sand-dunes

Introduction

Although sand-dunes are not so often intimately related to estuaries as are saltmarshes, sand-dunes are often found associated with them. In a number of places the extent of the sand and mudflats and saltmarshes which develop within an individual estuarine complex may largely depend on the presence of sand-dunes which afford protection from the higher energy environment to seaward. The two usual sand-dune formations which provide this protection are spits (to form 'bar-built' estuaries) and barrier islands (to form 'barrier-beach' estuaries), although sometimes more substantial hindshore dunes may occur (see Figure 8.1.22).

Sand-dunes normally develop in a higher energy environment than saltmarsh, an environment where by definition the larger-sized grains are moved by both the tide and the wind. The former deposits them on a high beach plain which, when large enough and exposed for long enough to enable it to dry out, makes material available to be driven on-land by wind. In this way, sometimes massive accumulations can occur, particularly on the west coasts, notably in northern Scotland, where prevailing and dominant winds reinforce each other.

The development of vegetation in this highly mobile environment is dependent on the establishment of specialist plants. As dunes develop above the strandline (the highest limit of the tidal range), plants such as marram *Ammophila arenaria* and lyme-grass *Elymus arenarius*, which can tolerate rapid sand accumulation, comprise the major dune-forming species.

Behind this zone, grassland or heathland may develop. The type of vegetation is dependent on the age of the dune surface and the original calcium carbonate content of the beach sand. Rich plant and animal communities can occur where calcium carbonate content is high and may include a number of species specifically associated with dunes such as sea-holly *Eryngium maritimum*. As sand deposition decreases and the dunes become more stable, species-rich calcareous grasslands more typical of inland habitat types sometimes develop, under the influence of grazing. These often include orchid populations of considerable variety and, in a few cases, rarity.

On dunes with silica sand which is low in calcium carbonate or where leaching has removed it from the surface soil, dune heath may develop. Whilst this may not support such a wide range of species, it is a rare habitat in its own right with a characteristic plant and animal association.

Details of the plant and animal communities and their importance are not given here; the most up-to-date description of the plant communities can be found in Rodwell (In press). The physical system is here considered to be the most important factor in relation to the conservation of Estuaries Review sites, and this is reviewed below.

Sand-dunes and estuaries

There are 30 British estuaries where sand-dune systems form a major component of the physical environment, and at least a further 25 sites have substantial sand-dunes associated with them. Their distribution is shown in Figure 8.1.23. Like saltmarshes the total area of sand-dunes in Britain is relatively small (c. 56,000 ha – Doody 1989) and, since many dune systems are on open coasts, the area associated with estuaries will be much less than this total. There are for example major dune systems in many parts of the Inner and Outer Hebrides, on the south Wales coast and on the Northumberland coast that are on open coasts rather than estuaries (Doody 1989). The precise contribution of estuaries to the British sand-dune resource will become clearer once the NCC's current Sand-dune survey of Great Britain is completed.

Sand-dunes are widespread along the coasts of western Europe (Olson & van der Maarel 1989), with major stretches of dunes along much of the coast of Denmark, the islands of the international Wadden Sea, the coasts of The Netherlands and Belgium, the Atlantic coast of France and also on parts of the Irish and Spanish coasts. Dune systems

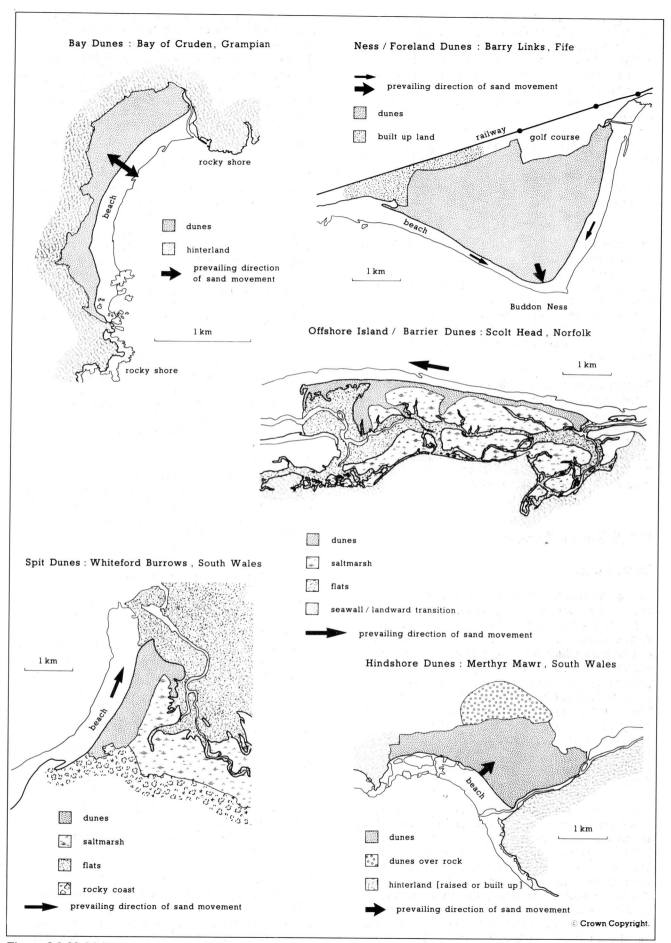

Bay Dunes : Bay of Cruden, Grampian

rocky shore

beach

- dunes
- hinterland
- prevailing direction of sand movement

1 km

rocky shore

Ness / Foreland Dunes : Barry Links, Fife

- prevailing direction of sand movement
- dunes
- built up land

railway   golf course

beach

1 km

Buddon Ness

Offshore Island / Barrier Dunes : Scolt Head, Norfolk

1 km

- dunes
- saltmarsh
- flats
- seawall / landward transition
- prevailing direction of sand movement

Spit Dunes : Whiteford Burrows, South Wales

1 km

beach

- dunes
- saltmarsh
- flats
- rocky coast
- prevailing direction of sand movement

Hindshore Dunes : Merthyr Mawr, South Wales

beach

1 km

- dunes
- dunes over rock
- hinterland [raised or built up]
- prevailing direction of sand movement

© Crown Copyright.

Figure 8.1.22 Major types of dune systems in Great Britain, from Ranwell & Boar (1986). All examples in this figure, except Bay of Cruden, are on review sites.

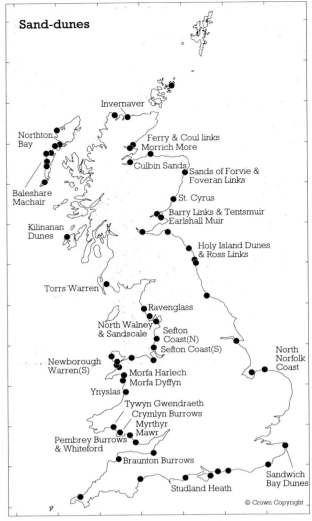

Sand-dunes

Invernaver

Northton Bay

Ferry & Coul links
Morrich More

Culbin Sands

Sands of Forvie & Foveran Links

Baleshare Machair

St. Cyrus

Barry Links & Tentsmuir
Earlshall Muir

Kilinanan Dunes

Holy Island Dunes & Ross Links

Torrs Warren

Ravenglass

North Walney & Sandscale

Sefton Coast(N)

Sefton Coast(S)

North Norfolk Coast

Newborough Warren(S)

Morfa Harlech
Morfa Dyffyn

Ynyslas

Tywyn Gwendraeth
Crymlyn Burrows
Myrthyr Mawr

Pembrey Burrows & Whiteford

Braunton Burrows

Sandwich Bay Dunes

Studland Heath

© Crown Copyright

Figure 8.1.23 The distribution of major sand-dunes on review sites. Nationally important dune systems are named.

are also extensive along the southern shore of the Baltic Sea.

In Britain sand-dunes are most frequently found on an estuary as a spit or spits enclosing the mouth of the estuary. For a few small estuaries, such as the Esk in Cumbria (see Figure 8.1.24) and Loch Fleet in the Highland Region, the dunes form a major component in the development of the estuary. At many more they serve to enhance the protection afforded by other structures such as cliffs or shingle. They can be quite substantial, such as the Studland Peninsula which restricts the entrance to Poole Harbour and encloses an arm of the former estuary (now known as 'Little Sea'), or small, such as Gibraltar Point which has only limited and local influence on the extensive embayment of The Wash (Figure 8.1.24).

More substantial hindshore dunes may also have had a major influence on the development of a few estuaries. At Braunton Burrows, for example, a substantial dune has effectively overwhelmed the tidal land of the Taw-Torridge Estuary. A narrow estuary now exists with a substantial area of grazing marsh behind. The third type of dune

which is found in close association with review sites is the 'barrier island'. These help protect the shore from wave attack and are often found in close association with shingle deposits. Estuarine conditions develop in their lee. The best example is Scolt Head Island on the North Norfolk Coast where complex interactions between sand-dunes, shingle and saltmarsh also occur (see Figure 8.1.11). The critical factor in each of these examples is that the enclosing sand-dune provides shelter for the otherwise exposed coast. Behind it, in the quiescent water, the deposition of sediment can take place and the typical mudflats and saltmarshes develop. It is difficult to be precise about the fundamental role of sand-dunes, as opposed to cliffs or other hard structures, whether natural or man-made, or, as we shall see below, shingle structures, in the development and survival of estuaries. However, the above examples show that, in many cases, there is an important geomorphological interrelationship.

Sand-dune stability

The ability of sand-dunes to retain sand in relatively stable formations depends on several factors. Most important is the way in which vegetation helps bind the sand grains to create vegetated dune and dune grassland. Where dunes form an important component of the protection afforded to an estuary, their stability may be considered to be of critical importance. In this context a brief review of the patterns of vegetation development is appropriate.

Marram and lyme-grass are the principle dune-forming species in Great Britain. Sand is blown landwards and collects around these plants and, in some cases, buries them. Dune plants are specially adapted to accomodate this and assemblages may include a range of specialist drought-tolerant species in these early stages. As the dunes grow, other species invade and a more or less closed sward develops. Inland, sand deposition decreases and the soil structure becomes more complex and stable. Plants specifically associated with sand-dunes decline in frequency and importance, and under certain circumstances scrub or even woodland may develop. These processes are described in a number of publications (see particularly Ranwell 1972). A simplified diagram of the processes is given in Figure 8.1.25.

To those concerned with the conservation of an estuary where dunes form an important component, the current status and likely future position of the dunes will be all-important. Thus a system which is highly mobile (i.e. consists of a high proportion of bare sand) may be considered to be a problem. However, in very few cases is this conclusion likely to be reached, given a full understanding of the relationship between the dunes and the estuary. It is likely that even if there is a catastrophic breakdown of the dune formation, it will be many months or even years before the effects are felt within the body of the estuary. Of more significance, particularly to the engineer or

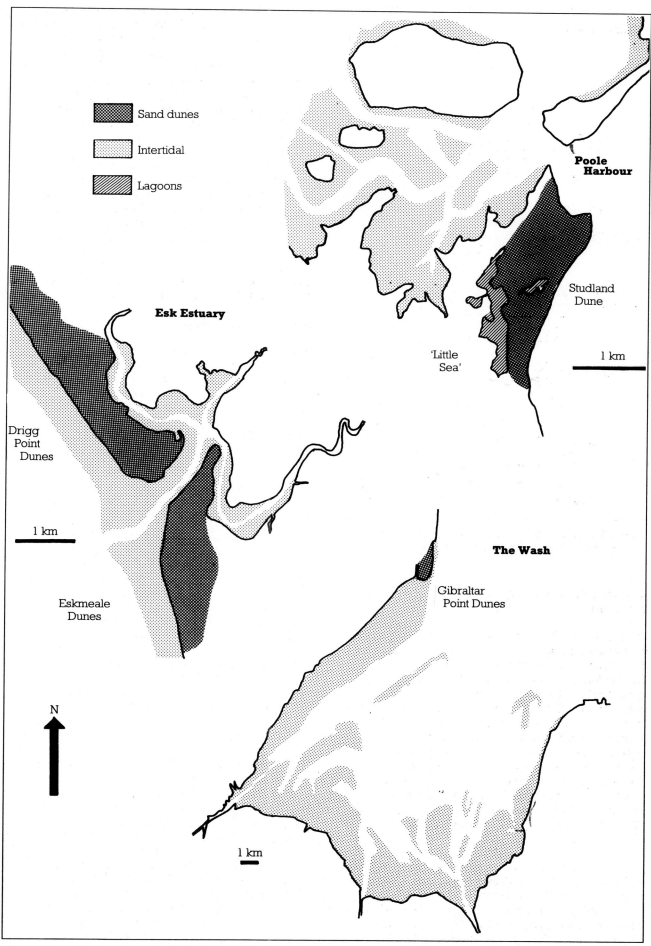

Figure 8.1.24 Examples of the scale of dune systems in relation to estuaries in Great Britain

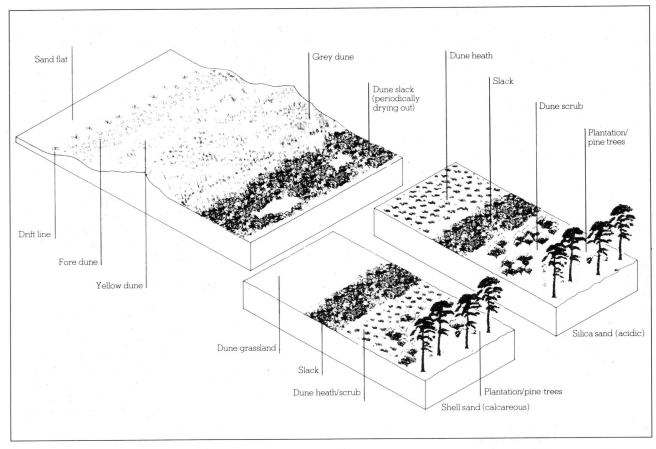

Figure 8.1.25 Schematic diagram showing main dune successions

local planning authority, is the threat from flooding if an enclosing or protecting sand spit is lost.

Until now, the almost universal but erroneous view, even amongst nature conservationists, has been that sand-dune mobility poses a threat to both the dunes and the land behind them. Sand stabilisation has, as a consequence, become a major preoccupation at many sites, not only in Great Britain but also throughout the world. This has involved large-scale afforestation with pines, as at Tentsmuir in Fife at the north of the Tay Estuary (see Figure 8.1.26), and the sites where techniques for slowing down sand movement and fixing dunes have been undertaken are legion. Of the 50 review sites with sand-dunes associated with them, no less than 31 have operational sand stabilisation activities. Sand fencing (11 sites), marram planting (20 sites) and the introduction of sea buckthorn *Hippophae rhamnoides* are amongst the more favoured options (see Ranwell & Boar 1986 for a recent analysis). This preoccupation has resulted in other, perhaps more damaging, changes taking place without their nature conservation significance being appreciated. Of these the most widespread is overstabilisation resulting in a loss of rich plant and animal communities. Rabbits may have played a critical role in the current status of sand-dunes, and the issues raised are discussed briefly below.

Sand-dunes and rabbits

Rabbits have probably been important agents in

the development of sand-dunes since Roman times. Prior to the advent of myxamotosis in 1953 they kept the vegetation short and introduced a degree of mobility in the system. Since then the drop in rabbit numbers, reduction in grazing of dunes by

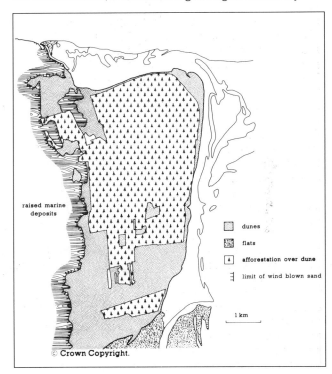

Figure 8.1.26 Dune afforestation at Tentsmuir (Tay Estuary and Eden Estuary), from Doody (1989)

94

domestic stock and the success of stabilisation programmes have all served to fix dune landscapes, particularly in England and Wales. Thus whilst erosion is seen as a continuing problem at a number of localities with high recreational pressure, many sites are becoming overgrown with coarse grasses and scrub, to the detriment of their species-rich dune grasslands and dune slacks. The reintroduction of grazing or other methods of control of the rank vegetation is essential if the dunes are to retain their often precious wildlife interest. It is ironic that this problem is prompting the reconsideration of closing dunes to sand movement. The issues are discussed in relation to Holland by Wanders (1989) and Great Britain by Doody (In press).

At first sight this approach might seem to be in conflict with the requirements of sea defence and the maintenance of shelter within estuaries. However, dunes are naturally mobile, and their formation is dependent on species adapted to the stresses imposed by this mobility. Allowing these natural forces to operate may in the long term provide a more cost-effective solution to the maintenance of the protection afforded to an estuary by a sand-dune. Crucial to this will be an understanding not only of the processes involved, but also of the ways in which the individual dune systems operate. This will require an extensive programme involving investigation of the relationship between dune development and the survival of the estuarine systems. This should result in a more complete understanding of the geomorphological setting in which estuaries and their associated habitats operate.

Conservation importance and protected status of sand-dunes

Sand-dunes are a rare and specialised habitat. They cover only approximately 56,000 ha in Great Britain. These are scattered widely but with particular concentrations in north-west Scotland. The machairs of the Western Isles, which, for the most part, are not associated with estuaries, form a large proportion of the total resource.

As with saltmarshes, at least in their early stages of formation they are relatively natural habitats. Modification by man, notably by their use as grazing for domestic stock, has created dune grassland. This is often rich in species, including those of calcareous grassland in addition to the more typical dune plants and animals.

Some dunes provide important breeding sites for birds, notably eiders *Somateria mollissima* in north-east Scotland and shelducks *Tadorna tadorna* throughout Britain (see Section 8.6.4). The beaches and bare mobile dune ridges can also be important nesting areas for gulls and terns. The dry, warm, open, sandy habitats provide favoured sites for some of our rarest reptiles, such as the smooth snake and sand lizard, and almost all Britain's natterjack toads breed in dune slacks associated with estuaries (see Chapter 8.5).

The selection of sand-dune sites for statutory designation as SSSIs is determined on the basis of the representation of the full sequence of vegetation types, from mobile foredunes, dune grassland (or heathland) and dune slacks and transitions to, for example, saltmarsh, shingle or, in a very few cases, scrub and native woodland. Size is an important consideration, as is freedom from massive human interference such as forestry. The presence of rare characteristic invertebrates, together with the rare amphibians and reptiles, also provides a justification for notification.

All of the national sites identified as forming an important component of the estuarine environment are designated in whole or in part as SSSIs. The majority of the other sites shown in Figure 8.1.23 are also designated as SSSIs.

Threats to sand-dunes

Historically the planting of forests of non-native pines has caused a major loss of natural sand-dune habitat, affecting some of the largest sites. Culbin Sands (Moray Firth), for example, was once the largest mobile dune system in Great Britain, but is now almost completely stabilised and covered in pine forest. Additional adverse impacts affecting important nature conservation sites in decreasing order of significance are:

1   housing and industrial development,

2   static caravans and other recreational building,

3   airfields and roads,

4   golf courses and general recreation,

5   Ministry of Defence use, and

6   intensive agriculture, including cultivation and grazing.

Paradoxically, whilst all of these have caused direct destruction of the sand-dunes upon which either buildings or other surface structures were placed, some may have helped to protect the body of the dune from more extensive damage. Principle amongst these is their use by the MoD for bombing practice which, because of the large safety zones involved, prevents other more damaging activities from taking place (see Boorman 1977 and Doody 1989). However, even here protection is not assured. The recent decision by Shell (UK) to let a contract to develop a pipe fabrication facility in one of the most ecologically sensitive parts of Morrich More (Dornoch Firth) – nearly three years after the Secretary of State for Scotland granted permission following a Public Inquiry where the NCC, amongst others, objected – is extremely regrettable.

Threats to sand-dunes today come in a variety of forms. They include a continuation and increase in the activities described above. In addition a continuation of the process of stabilisation is certain to reduce species diversity in the long term, unless remedial action is taken to either re-expose the dunes to a degree of mobility and/or reintroduce grazing. Recreation, whose effects stabilisation is often intended to ameliorate, is usually a localised problem. The techniques for dealing with this through remedial action and people-management are available and widely understood.

In the longer term, of much more significance is the prospect of an increase in the rate of sea-level rise. Where it occurs at present, it causes a steepening of the foreshore and increased wave attack at the base of the dune. When combined with extraction of offshore sediments, which may serve to exacerbate the foreshore steepening, serious wholesale erosion could take place.

Few dunes in Great Britain are today prograding (i.e creating new dunes to seaward of existing ones). Most appear to be fossilised in their present location or retreating landwards. Under attack from the sea and with major development landward (forests, recreational facilities, housing etc.), the natural response will be to try to defend the dune in its present location. However, as has already been indicated, dunes are naturally unstable and, if left to their own devices, exist in a dynamic equilibrium. The foreshore sand which builds up in the dunes forms a reservoir of material which can replenish the beach during storms and helps to buffer the coast from wave attack (see Carter & Stone 1989).

A much more informed and enlightened approach to sand-dune management is required if they are to continue to perform their sea defence, nature conservation and recreational roles. This must be based on a better understanding of the way they behave and in particular on the role they play as an integral part of an estuarine system. Given this better understanding, it may be recognised that mobility may be an important characteristic of dunes and that all 'erosion' is not necessarily 'bad'.

This approach will also require local authorities, who see their responsibilities to the recreational visitor on beaches and dune systems as paramount, to recognise the implications of some of their activities. For example, 'beach cleaning', which involves the removal of the strandline material, is practised to provide clean beaches for visitors in some areas. The link between the erosion of the dunes behind and this activity seems not to have been generally recognised.

At other sites, subtidal dredging for sand has not been directly linked with beach and foredune erosion nearby. However, given the predictions for sea-level rise, it would be prudent to look at the sediment budget, both within and outside estuaries, and review the system for granting extraction licences.

8.1.7 Shingle

Introduction

Shingle structures develop in high energy environments where the sea can move and pile up larger sized pebbles on shore above the normal tides. These pebbles may range from 2 mm up to 200 mm, though the normally encountered range on mobile shingle is 20 mm – 60 mm. The structures so formed include narrow fringing shorelines, and where successive beaches are piled against each other large systems can sometimes form, with predominantly terrestrial habitats. As far as estuaries are concerned, there are very few examples of a shingle structure being a significant determinant of the form and location of intertidal habitats. Individual examples (mostly shingle bars or spits) are discussed below. In some cases they are mixtures of shingle and sand-dune, the sand-dune normally forming over the shingle bar and obscuring it, making the relative importance of the two structures difficult to determine. However, the shingle structures identified in relation to Estuaries Review sites are those where exposed shingle forms a significant part of the site (Figure 8.1.27).

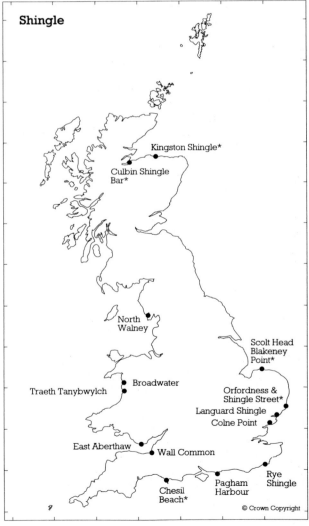

Figure 8.1.27 The distribution of major exposed shingle systems associated with review sites. Nationally important shingle sites are shown with an asterisk.

Shingle structures and estuaries

The relationship between shingle structures and estuaries is very important, where they coincide. The major coastal lagoon of The Fleet is wholly dependent for its existence on Chesil Beach. The long river estuary of the Ore/Alde/Butley has been progressively pushed southwards since the original opening was closed by the southern development in about 1500 AD of Orfordness shingle spit, now one of the most important shingle spits in Great Britain. The Blakeney Point spit provides conditions for sand-dune, mudflat and saltmarsh development, as does the Culbin Shingle Bar in north-east Scotland. Both protect the inner coastline from major wave attack and allow relatively sheltered conditions to exist in which important saltmarshes are a major factor in the survival of the associated estuarine habitat. There are seven shingle sites of national importance, five of which are associated with Estuaries Review sites – Orfordness (Ore/Alde/Butley Estuary), Culbin Shingle Bar (Moray Firth), Chesil Beach (The Fleet), the Kingston Shingles (Spey Estuary), and Blakeney Point (North Norfolk Coast) (Figure 8.1.27).

Stable shingle structures develop a variety of vegetation types. These include species, such as sea-kale *Crambe maritima*, specially adapted to the unstable and exposed nature of the storm beach associated with most shingle. Behind this, in the spray zone, maritime plants may occur and, sometimes, extensive lichen-rich vegetations. Acid grassland, heath or scrub may be found on the larger sites. In the highest energy environments none of these has a particular influence on the stability of the shingle since the forces acting upon them are much greater than any binding action of the plants. However, Carey & Oliver (1918) discussed the way in which shrubby sea-blite *Suaeda vera* helped build up the shingle at Blakeney Point.

In order to consider the conservation of these important shingle areas in relation to the Estuaries Review, it is most useful to look at some individual sites.

Chesil Beach

Chesil Beach is a 29 km bank of shingle which, over most of its length, encloses the largest lagoon in Great Britain (The Fleet). This shingle structure ranks among the four most important shingle sites in Great Britain, the others being Dungeness, Orfordness and the Culbin Shingle Bar.

Over much of its length the wide bank is devoid of vegetation; however, at the western end extensive stands of the specialist shingle plants sea-kale and sea-pea *Lathyrus japonicus* occur. Additional small patches of closed maritime vegetation, with thrift *Armeria maritima* and sea plantain *Plantago maritima*, occur on the more stable sections of the beach.

The biggest threat to this site is the extraction of shingle. Recent unlawful removal showed that,

despite statutory protection, damage can occur. More difficult to control is the legitimate artificial protection of the beach near Portland to prevent overtopping and flooding. There is little doubt, however, that too much interference would detract from the scientific value of the site as a unique shingle feature. The future of the site and The Fleet which it protects may lie in a more thorough knowledge of its origin and development. Several authors have considered this (see Steers 1946), although no firm conclusions have been reached about its origin.

Orfordness

In contrast to Chesil, this beach consists of a ness, with several beaches piled upon each other, which has slowly migrated southwards. In front of it a shingle spit (Orford Beach) has been extending rapidly along the coast since at least about 1530 AD, when the early maps showed the village of Orford as a thriving port (Anon 1966). Since then the River Ore's exit to the sea has been pushed progressively further south-west, until today it is some 6 km from the village (Figure 8.1.28).

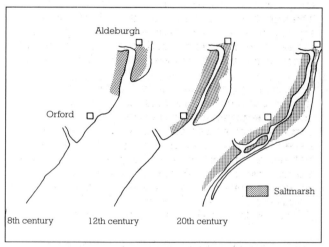

Figure 8.1.28 The historical development of Orfordness (Ore/Alde/Butley Estuary), from Beardall *et al.* (1988)

The area of the spit south of the land owned by the Ministry of Defence, designated as a National Nature Reserve, contains probably the finest undisturbed shingle vegetation in Great Britain. In addition to the specialist shingle plants, it has an acid shingle heath second only to Dungeness and a fine, extensive and probably unique example of maritime lichen-covered shingle.

Whilst the future of the National Nature Reserve seems assured, the area of the Ness to the north is not. Past use for a wide range of military activities, development of gravel extraction and public access have all taken their toll on the surface of the shingle and its vegetation. The management of the beach at Orfordness to raise the sea defences has also not been sympathetic to the origins and development of the site. Fuller & Randall (1988) suggest that, far from helping, these latter activities "have greatly restricted the width of the beach, threatening to worsen the situation...".

Culbin Shingle Bar

Culbin Shingle Bar acts much like the sand/shingle barrier islands already described, notably those on the North Norfolk Coast. Behind the protection afforded by the bar the high beach plain is sheltered and flats and saltmarshes occur. The extensive Culbin sand-dunes lie inland of this, and the bar is thought to be the latest of the series of ridges upon which the dunes have developed.

In the seventeenth century, the bar extended as a spit right across the mouth of the River Findhorn. The present bar represents the westernmost 55 ha of this spit, which is eroding at its eastern end, moving westwards. It remains one of the least disturbed sites in Great Britain and shows important coastal processes in action. The vegetation patterns and sequence in relation to the ages of individual shingle ridges are also significant. A detailed description of the site is provided by Fuller (1975).

Most other shingle structures occurring in association with Estuaries Review sites are of less conservation importance in their own right. Walney Island, however, is an important shingle bar with extensive dune cover, enclosing part of Morecambe Bay and the adjacent Duddon Estuary.

Conservation and protected shingle sites

The nature conservation importance of vegetated shingle structures lies in the development on them of plant communities unique to such structures. Notable amongst them are those maritime lichen-dominated communities and the mostly single-species stands of plants adapted to growing just above the most mobile parts of the shore. The larger sites are also of considerable geomorphological significance. All the sites shown on Figure 8.1.27 are designated as SSSIs. The biggest threat to these important sites is from disturbance of the surface shingle. The tracks from a single passage of a vehicle over long-established vegetated shingle will remain visible indefinitely. Extraction of material, whether for construction or sea defence, destroys the shingle surface and its vegetation. When coupled with unsympathetic sea-defence measures, these activities can affect the sites to a considerable degree. As with other sedimentary habitats, understanding of the origins and development of each site is essential if long-term damage is not to be caused, which might ultimately in its turn threaten the associated estuarine habitats.

The problem of the stability of Hurst Spit (Lymington Estuary) in Hampshire provides an important illustration of the problem. This narrow spit provides protection for a major part of the intertidal land of the Solent. Recent storms breached this and only rapid action by the sea-defence authority prevented a major rupture. However, the seeds of this problem may lie in the extraction of gravel taking place elsewhere in the system and preventing the natural replenishment of the spit.

8.1.8 Sea cliffs

Introduction

Sea cliffs are rarely intimately associated with estuaries. Their geographical location may, however, form an important element in the way in which estuaries develop, since they can provide shelter from wave action, as do shingle or sand bars. However, their importance more often lies in the way they provide material for deposition within the estuary through erosion. In this section, therefore, the general features of cliffs associated with estuaries are described.

Cliff formations in Great Britain represent a range of rock types, from the hard granites of north-east Scotland, through the limestones of south Wales and the chalk cliffs of the south coast to, perhaps most importantly, the boulder clay cliffs of Holderness and further south on the east coast. These last are particularly important since they often provide the source material for estuarine structures – the shingle bars and sand-dunes as well as fine sediments. The Holderness coast, for example, may be the main source of fine material for the Humber Estuary, Lincolnshire coast and The Wash (see below).

Vegetation on cliffs

Cliffs support a range of vegetation types which are important in their own right. Their value as seabird nesting areas is discussed in Section 8.6.4. Hard rock cliffs (including the harder limestones) often support important examples of species-rich calcareous grassland. The more acid rocks, notably in north Scotland, can have high quality heathland vegetation. The coastal nature of the communities is emphasised in two main ways, first by the direct effects of exposure to salt spray and secondly by the effects of exposure to high winds, notably in the north and west. In the south and east and along some parts of the sheltered west coast, by contrast, the warmth of the sea may soften the climate.

These factors combine to give a range of variation which provides for a zonation inland across the cliff which is related to the maritime influences. Superimposed on this is the influence of the underlying geology which in the more stable rock types allows heathland or calcareous grassland to develop. In the most exposed situations, where the cliffs are drenched in salt spray, there are communities very similar to those of upper saltmarshes. However, more usually a few coastal plants such as sea campion *Silene maritima* and thrift are present as a narrow zone to seaward of the more inland community types. The effects of exposure to the prevailing winds can be seen in the wind-pruned scrub and stunted woodland of parts of south-west England and south Wales, notably Pembrokeshire.

Geographically the ameliorating effects of the coastal situation on the vegetation can be seen in the south-east, where the chalk cliffs of Beachy Head support grasslands with a number of thermophilous plants. In the north and west, the warm, wet winds facilitate the development of lichen- and moss-rich communities in woodland, mostly associated with the sea-lochs in Scotland. Sea cliff communities are described in the NVC (Rodwell in press).

Vegetation of the softer, slumping cliffs in south, south-east and eastern England can be very different. By its very nature, it comprises more ephemeral communities. Maritime effects, notably of salt spray, are also reduced as the sites are mostly situated away from the prevailing westerly winds and absorb rather than reflect wave energy. In this way they make sediment available through erosion at the bottom of the cliff slope, helping to retain mobility of sediments on the cliff face. The rate at which this tallus is removed helps to determine the degree of stability in the soils above, resulting in a range of community types from closed scrub and woodland to open skeletal communities with a few ephemeral species.

The vegetation of cliffs and cliff tops has been modified by the long history of management of accessible areas mainly for agriculture, especially grazing of domestic stock. Whilst this continues in Scotland (with sheep), in much of England and Wales the move away from more pastoral agriculture to intensive arable farming has resulted in losses of important open cliff vegetation. This has occurred principally through the direct loss of cliff-top vegetation to ploughing and reseeding or conversion to arable land. However, the growth of rank grassland and scrub at the expense of species-rich grassland and heath has also been a major problem. Resolution of these issues is the subject of an NCC contract with Lancaster University, due to report in 1990. Reintroduction of grazing appears to be a major requirement if the value of some of the more important of the cliff and cliff-top grasslands is to be retained.

Coast protection

Coast protection is the second major issue affecting the soft coastlines of Great Britain. From a biological point of view the effects are important. The use of concrete sea-walls, groynes or other structures to protect the toe of the cliff from erosion has important consequences for the vegetation and its associated animals, notably invertebrates. The presence of the protection may have the desired effect of slowing down erosion. This may occur at such rate and to such an extent that cliff stability (the engineer's desired state) is reached. Given time, this stability will result in the development of

scrub and eventually woodland at the expense of the more open and, from a nature conservation point of view, often more interesting plant and animal communities.

The number of cliff sites protected as Sites of Special Scientific Interest and directly associated with Estuaries Review sites is small (see also the section on Geological Conservation Review Sites in Chapter 9). The future of these sites may not be directly related to the development of policies concerned with the conservation of estuaries. However, it is important to recognise that they do form part of the coastline and may in some instances be critical to estuary survival. Examples include the Naze in Suffolk and Hengistbury Head in Sussex, both of which are rapidly eroding and would expose the estuaries of Hamford Water and Christchurch Harbour respectively to wave attack if they disintegrate entirely. It is debatable from a nature conservation point of view whether this would be acceptable. In general, however, there is much advantage in allowing some of these natural processes to take place and for the coastline as a whole to re-adjust.

Protection of eroding cliff lines can be successful, though it often requires a considerable input of funds. In the long term it seems possible that the compartmentalisation of a coastline, where some areas are protected and some not, could lead to a greater likelihood of the catastrophic collapse of protected cliffs. Again a better understanding of the mechanisms of cliff retreat and the role of beaches in protecting them may be important. Insofar as estuaries are concerned, the contribution of sedimentary material from eroding cliffs to the sediment budget of an estuary also requires a better understanding if estuary conservation is to be fully integrated with other coastal uses.

8.1.9 Strandlines

A strandline is the accumulation at different high water levels along the upper shore of organic and inorganic material. Because of their position strandlines are mostly ephemeral, and where they persist on the sheltered shores of estuaries they tend to be composed mainly of litter and rotting organic matter. However on exposed shores standlines can be extensive. Here they can act as precursors to sand-dunes. On the few shores where sand-dunes are accreting progressively seaward (prograding), the species of the strandline, such as sea sandwort *Honkenya peploides*, prickly saltwort *Salsola kali* and sea rocket *Cakile maritima* form an important first stage in the process of trapping sand. Without these species the development of foredunes may be inhibited. This could have significant consequences for dune stability, particularly in areas of high recreational pressure. The practice of 'beach-cleaning' mentioned above is an important consideration, and recent proposals to extend this activity in north Wales give considerable cause for concern.

Deposits of litter at the upper tidal range can occur within estuaries and result in strandline communities developing. These may include species such as orache *Atriplex* spp., including grass-leaved orache *A. littoralis*, which may themselves act as precursors for other vegetation. In a very few sites sea wormwood *Artemisia maritima* may occur in this upper shoreline, and, whilst normally associated with upper saltmarsh, it is an important food plant for a wide variety of invertebrates, notably the rare Essex emerald moth *Thetidia smaragdaria*. No strandline conservation sites of importance have been identified separately on review sites.

8.1.10 Marine/maritime islands

There is virtually no direct relationship between marine/maritime islands and estuaries, except insofar as they may reinforce the general patterns of shelter afforded by other physical structures (cliffs, bars etc.). However, there are a few islands which exist within the body of some estuaries. It is important to recognise their existence, since policies relating to the conservation of an estuary as a whole may well influence what happens on these islands. Examples include Flat Holme and Steep Holme in the Severn, Hilbre Island in the Dee and the several islands in the Firth of Forth.

The importance of most of these areas is as habitat for birds, notably for breeding seabirds. Some of these birds rely on the associated estuary for their food. Some islands also support rare plants. Construction development of these areas may be the most serious threat, since they can provide firm foundations for proposed river or estuary crossings or barrages.

8.1.11 Saline lagoons

Introduction

Until recently Britain's saline lagoon resource was poorly understood. Between 1984 and 1989 the NCC commissioned surveys to document the distribution and abundance of saline lagoons in Britain. During this work 444 potential sites were examined of which 210 were investigated in detail. Barnes (1989a) and Sheader (1989), in their overview reports for the NCC, carried out a conservation appraisal of all the sites considered, and these reports form the basis of this section.

Coastal saline lagoons occur in Britain mainly on the east and south coasts. The exact number of saline lagoons in Britain is difficult to determine as definitions vary between workers. For this review, lagoons are defined as those sites which fit into the two categories defined below or which contain species of animals and plants specific to lagoonal or brackish habitats. Lagoons can have salinities varying from less than 1‰ to full-strength sea water or may even be hypersaline.

Types of saline lagoon

There are two main types of saline lagoons: natural saline lagoons, formed behind shingle or sand barriers, and artificially constructed coastal saline ponds.

Saline lagoons are natural physiographic features consisting of shallow open bodies of brackish or saline water, partially separated from an adjacent coastal sea by a barrier of sand or shingle. All or most of the water mass is retained in the lagoon at low tide. Sea water is exchanged directly by a natural or man-modified channel or via percolation through, or overtopping of, the sediment barrier (Barnes 1989a). Barnes (1989a) splits this category into eight types on the basis of lagoon location and physiomorphological characteristics.

Coastal saline ponds comprise of a variety of artificially or naturally formed brackish or saline water bodies, which do not fit into the 'natural saline lagoon' category defined by Barnes, but which nevertheless have physical characteristics and species composition similar to those of natural saline lagoons (Sheader 1989). Sheader (1989) further divides this major category into five types using similar principles to Barnes (1989a).

The numbers of each of the major types of British saline lagoons are shown in Figure 8.1.29. Most lagoons occur as silled ponds, where there is some degree of direct exchange of water with the sea and where water is retained a low tide by a sill at the mouth. Lagoons that are isolated from the sea in saltmarsh or grazing marsh and receive seawater input periodically or, to a lesser extent, by seepage, form the next commonest group. Percolation pools, where seawater exchange is through a shingle barrier separating the lagoon from the sea, are less common still, whilst sea inlet lagoons are the least common type, accounting for only a handful of sites.

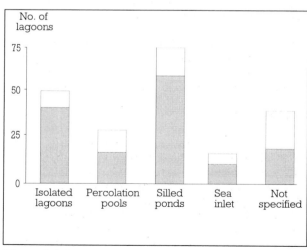

Figure 8.1.29 The numbers of British saline lagoons of different lagoon types. Shaded areas represent those on review sites.

The proportions of artificial, natural and mixed origin lagoons and ponds are shown in Figure 8.1.30. High proportions of all lagoon and pond types occur on Estuaries Review sites. Lagoons with an artificial origin are more common than natural lagoons and are formed as a result of a wide range of man's activities including sea-wall construction, the digging of borrow pits and the construction of drainage systems in low-lying land bordering estuaries.

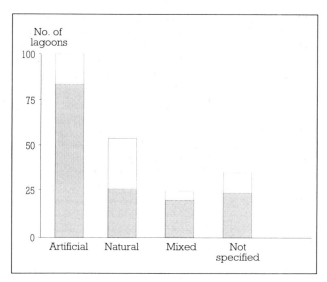

Figure 8.1.30 The numbers of British saline lagoons of different origins. Shaded areas represent those on review sites.

The distinction between 'natural' and 'artificial' saline lagoons is not, however, entirely clear-cut. Some of the different categories describe the same physical situation, the only distinction being that of natural or man-made origin. Most, if not all, naturally formed lagoons are modified by man. For example, The Fleet in Dorset is a good example of a natural lagoon formed by the isolation of a marine bay by the longshore shingle barrier of Chesil Beach (see also Section 8.1.7). However, the entrance channel to The Fleet has recently been considerably modified by man in order to rebuild a bridge. In addition the overall hydrography of The Fleet may have been modified by the earlier construction of Portland Harbour at its mouth.

Distribution

Saline lagoons are present on 37 Estuaries Review sites (Figure 8.1.31), with major concentrations around the Humber, the Thames Estuary and the Solent system. Only a limited amount of survey work has been carried out in Scotland, so it is unclear if the scarcity of lagoons on review sites in Scotland is as marked as it appears from the available data. The bulk of saline lagoons in Britain are very small (Figure 8.1.32), the majority being less than 10 ha in area and most as small as 1 ha or less. Taken together the total saline lagoon resource for Britain currently stands at around 770 ha. This does not including large sites such as The

Fleet, Poole Harbour and Christchurch Harbour. All these sites have been classified by some authorities as lagoonal in character, but for the purposes of the Estuaries Review they have been included within the classification of bar-built estuaries (see Chapter 5). By area, about 83% of the British saline lagoon resource can be found bordering Estuaries Review sites. If the three large sites are included as lagoons then the British resource increases to about 3,900 ha.

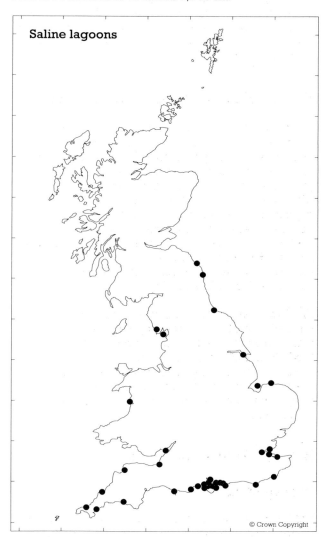

Figure 8.1.31 The distribution of review sites with saline lagoons

Barnes (1989b) and Sheader (1989) carried out a conservation appraisal of important coastal saline lagoon sites for the NCC. Natural lagoons and saline ponds were considered separately, but each site was assessed on a scoring system using an adaptation of the 14 criteria used by the NCC for appraising the conservation potential of sites. These criteria are defined in Chapter 8.3 (Aquatic estuarine communities).

For natural coastal lagoons, the best representatives of their type are listed in Table 8.1.3. Over half occur on Estuaries Review sites or form complete review sites.

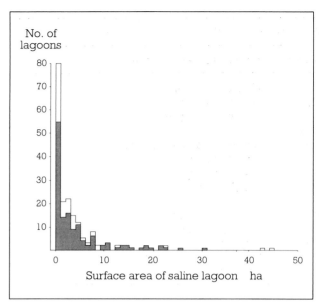

Figure 8.1.32 The size (surface area in ha) of British saline lagoons. Shaded areas show lagoons on review sites.

Sheader (1989) considered coastal saline ponds and used a slightly different scoring system from that used by Barnes (1989b) for natural coastal lagoons. Sheader (1989) also scored for the presence of species protected under the Wildlife & Countryside Act 1981, in addition to scoring for specialist lagoonal species. This difference however, does not alter the overall ranking of sites, but merely the number of points achieved by each site. Sheader separates the best saline lagoon sites into three categories: those of considerable conservation value; those strongly recommended for conservation; and those recommended for conservation. These sites are listed in Table 8.1.4. All of these sites except Fort Gilkicker Moat and Aldeburgh Lagoon directly abut Estuaries Review sites.

Lagoonal species

There are 38 known specialist lagoonal species in Britain. These are species defined as distinctly more characteristic of lagoon-like habitats than of fresh water, estuarine brackish water or the sea. These species are listed in Table 8.1.5. Five of these species are protected under Schedule 5 of the Wildlife & Countryside Act 1981. Of these five species, Ivell's sea anemone *Edwardsia ivelli* is only known from Widewater Lagoon, West Sussex, near the mouth of the Adur Estuary. This lagoon has degraded over recent years, probably owing to reduced water percolation through the coastal defence works and to reduced freshwater input resulting from isolation of this lagoon from the surrounding marshland. An extensive search of the lagoon in the summer of 1990 failed to find any specimens of this anemone and it is highly likely that this species is now extinct worldwide.

The starlet sea anemone *Nematostella vectensis* is restricted to southern Britain with major populations on review sites around the Solent and the Isle of Wight. Another protected lagoon species is the lagoon sandworm *Armandia cirrhosa*. This also has a southern distribution but is restricted in Britain to just one review site on the Solent. The lagoonal sand shrimp *Gammarus insensibilis* has a wider but also southern distribution and has been recorded from review sites stretching from around the Solent to the Humber on the North Sea coast. The other scheduled lagoonal species is the foxtail stonewort *Lamprothamnion papulosum*, an aquatic plant which is limited in distribution to just three review sites around the Solent and Isle of Wight.

Conservation of British saline lagoons

British saline lagoons occur on the coastal fringe, an area of land particularly susceptible to damage from the construction of coastal defences and other engineering works. New lagoon formation is now therefore very restricted owing to a lack of suitable sites. In the north Atlantic, coastal saline lagoons formed in macrotidal conditions are a relatively short-lived feature. The natural rate of formation of new lagoons will inevitably be insufficient to replace lagoons as they are lost through natural processes of succession to freshwater lakes, fen or carr, or are lost through man's activities. Natural coastal lagoons as a physiographic feature are a rare and diminishing resource.

Table 8.1.3 The most important natural saline lagoon sites in Britain (from Barnes 1989b). Sites marked with an asterisk are considered to be of national importance and the best examples of their type in Britain

Saline lagoon site	Estuaries Review site
1 Blakeney Spit Pools, Norfolk	North Norfolk Coast
2 Holkham Salts Hole, Norfolk	North Norfolk Coast
3 Broadwater, Norfolk	North Norfolk Coast
4 Benacre Broad, Suffolk*	–
5 Shingle Street/Bawdsey, Suffolk*	–
6 Widewater Lagoon, W. Sussex.	Adur Estuary
7 Bembridge Lagoons, Isle of Wight*	Bembridge Harbour
8 Christchurch Harbour, Dorset	Christchurch Harbour
9 Poole Harbour, Dorset*	Poole Harbour
10 The Fleet, Dorset*	The Fleet & Portland Harbour
11 Swanpool, Cornwall	–

Table 8.1.4 Important coastal saline lagoon sites in Britain (Sheader 1989).

	Saline lagoon site	Status	Estuaries Review site
1	Easington Lagoons, N. Humberside	**	Humber Estuary
2	S. Killingholme Lagoons, S. Humberside	**	Humber Estuary
3	Humberston Fitties, Lincolnshire	***	Humber Estuary
4	Aldburgh, Suffolk	***	–
5	Cliffe Marshes Lagoons, Kent	***	South Thames Marshes
6	Pagham Lagoons, W. Sussex	***	Pagham Harbour
7	Widewater Lagoon, W. Sussex	*	Adur Estuary
8	Birdham Pool, W. Sussex	*	Chichester Harbour
9	Fort Gilkicker Moat, Hampshire	***	–
10	Little Anglesey, Hampshire	**	Portsmouth Harbour
11	Shut Lake, Hampshire	*	Langstone Harbour
12	Keyhaven – Lymington Lagoons, Hampshire	***	Lymington Estuary
13	Brading Marshes system, Isle of Wight	***	Bembridge Harbour
14	Horsey Island Pool, Devon	*	Taw-Torridge Estuary

***	Of considerable conservation value
**	Strongly recommended for conservation
*	Recommended for conservation

Table 8.1.5 Specialist British lagoonal plant and animal species

Plants
  Chara canescens
  Chara baltica
  Chara connivens
  Lamprothamnium papulosum
  Tolypella n. nidifica
  Ruppia maritima
  Chaetomorpha linum

Cnidaria (Anemones and hydroids)
  Laomedea loveni
  Edwardsia ivelli
  Nematostella vectensis

Polychaeta (Polychaete worms - Annelida)
  Armandia cirrhosa
  Alkmaria romijni

Crustacea (Crustaceans)
  Sphaeroma hookeri
  Idotea chelipes
  Gammarus chevreuxi
  Gammarus insensibilis
  Corophium insidiosum
  Palaemonetes varians

Mollusca (Molluscs)
  Hydrobia ventrosa
  Hydrobia neglecta
  Onoba aculeus
  Littorina tenebrosa
  Tenellia adspersa
  Cerastoderma glaucum

Bryozoa (Bryozoans)
  Conopeum seurati
  Victorella pavida

Insecta (Insects)
  Sigara selecta
  Sigara stagnalis
  Sigara coccinna
  Agabus conspersus
  Berosus spinosus
  Coelambus parallelogrammus
  Dytiscus circumflexus
  Enochrus bicolor
  Enochrus melanocephalus
  Enochrus haliphilus
  Haliplus apicalis
  Ochthebius marinus
  Ochthebius punctatus
  Paracymus aeneus

Coastal saline ponds, however, although vulnerable to destruction by man, can be more easily conserved and may be created as new habitats. They are also important refuges for lagoonal species and, if suitably managed, form a habitat indistinguishable from naturally formed lagoonal habitat.

Both naturally and artificially formed lagoons, being small and shallow, are fragile and vulnerable. They are very susceptible to minor changes to their retaining barriers and salinity regimes and are particularly vulnerable to pollution, having only a limited ability to buffer changes in water quality. Many are potentially relatively easily claimed to form land, isolated from the sea to form freshwater lakes, or dredged to form harbours and marinas. Rising sea levels over the coming decades will place further pressures on coastal lagoons, and construction, or reconstruction, of sea-walls to combat this threat may cause an increased rate of loss of this habitat, unless such developments are carefully managed.

8.1.12 Coastal grazing marshes

Introduction

Grazing marshes are areas of flat low-lying grassland drained by complex networks of freshwater or brackish drainage ditches. These ditches control water levels, and provide supplies of drinking water for cattle and sheep and act as 'wet fences' to keep stock within the fields. Some of the best known grazing marshes are not coastal, for example the bulk of the Somerset Moors and the Pevensey Levels in East Sussex, but others have a degree of brackish influence stemming from their coastal location and many of these are closely associated with review sites. Figure 8.1.33 shows that coastal grazing marshes and other lowland wet grasslands are associated with at least 59 review sites. Most are in England, particularly in southern and eastern England, and the most extensive grazing marshes have been associated with review sites in south-east England. The few sites in Scotland are chiefly areas of wet machair grassland adjacent to review sites. They form part of the very extensive machair systems in these regions, most of which are not directly associated with review sites (Fuller *et al.* 1986).

Coastal grazing marshes generally originated through land-claim of estuarine saltmarsh by the construction of enclosing sea-walls, although sometimes they have developed to landward of natural barriers such as sand-dunes or shingle storm-beaches. Many grazing marshes have been in their present condition only since the introduction of pumped drainage, often post-war; previously they flooded regularly, either with fresh water or, occasionally, sea water. Most grazing marsh in its present state is probably less than 200 years old, yet this recently developed habitat contains many features of value for nature conservation.

Grazing marsh grasslands

The grasslands of coastal grazing marshes are typically dominated by the more common grasses of neutral soils, for example meadow fox-tail *Alopecurus pratensis*, crested dog's-tail *Cynosurus cristatus*, rye-grass *Lolium perenne* and meadow barley *Hordeum secalinum*. They contain few species in comparison with inland unimproved pastures and hay-meadows, although herbs such as hairy buttercup *Ranunculus sardous*, strawberry clover *Trifolium fragiferum* and grass vetchling *Lathyrus nissolia* may be frequent on coastal grazing marsh in southern and eastern England, and help to give these grasslands a distinctive, if not particularly striking, appearance.

Grasslands subject to brackish influence can support a number of species with predominantly coastal distributions in Britain, for example saltmarsh rush *Juncus gerardi*, slender spike-rush *Eleocharis uniglumis* and hard-grass *Parapholis strigosa*. Indeed, in south-eastern England coastal

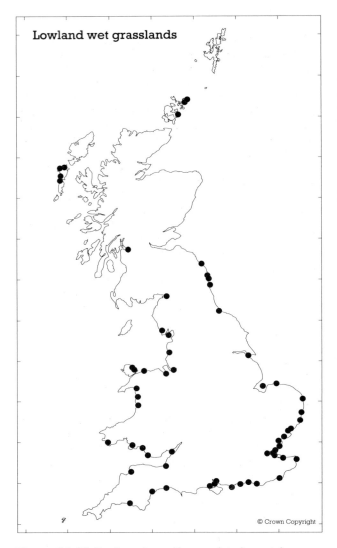

Figure 8.1.33 Review sites with associated coastal grazing marshes and other lowland wet grasslands

grazing marsh can support extensive areas of upper saltmarsh communities that are now either rare or absent from the adjoining tidally-influenced saltmarsh.

Grazing marsh grasslands (including the enclosing earth banks) support a large number of nationally rare or scarce plants which in Britain are very largely restricted to such habitats (see also Section 8.1.12). Examples are divided sedge *Carex divisa*, slender hare's-ear *Bupleurum tenuissimum*, sea clover *Trifolium squamosum*, sea barley *Hordeum marinum* and least lettuce *Lactuca saligna*. Stalked sea-purslane *Halimione pedunculata* was recently rediscovered in Britain, after an absence of 50 years, on saline grazing marsh in Essex (Leach 1988). Most rare plants associated with grazing marsh grasslands are 'continental' species having a markedly south-eastern distribution in Britain, and not surprisingly it is the grazing marshes of north Kent and Essex that are of greatest importance in this respect. These marshes are all associated with review sites.

Washlands

There are a number of 'washland' areas, notably in and around The Wash and the Severn Estuary, where this semi-natural habitat provides an important reservoir for winter flooding. The Ouse Washes and Nene Washes in Cambridgeshire are perhaps the best examples, where winter flooding of the surrounding fenlands, themselves reclaimed from the extensive wetlands of the fenland basin, is prevented by pumping water into a large area between two main drainage channels. This periodic winter flooding provides not only a wintering ground for large numbers of ducks and geese, but also summer habitat for a variety of breeding birds (Section 8.6.4). The unimproved grasslands of the 'washlands' are also used for a variety of agricultural purposes. The way in which these areas operate as a flood control mechanism may point to other ways of viewing the coastal grazing marsh resource, in the context of the possible impacts of global warming (Chapter 11).

The ditch systems

The wildlife interest of coastal grazing marshes is often chiefly to be found in their networks of drainage ditches. While water salinity is of overriding importance in determining species composition, position in the hydrosere and soil type are also significant. Ditches are prevented from reverting to dry land by the management efforts of water authorities, internal drainage boards and landowners. Their interventions create a spectrum of ditch sizes ranging from broad deep drains, in which the vegetation is removed usually annually and in which re-profiling is frequently undertaken, to small field ditches which are irregularly managed depending on the farmer's priorities. Ditch structure can also influence the plant communities and is probably even more important than size in helping to determine the composition of the invertebrate fauna (see Chapter 8.2).

Brackish ditches support quite different assemblages of plants from freshwater ditches further inland. In the most saline ditches the tasselweeds *Ruppia maritima* and *R. spiralis* can occur, and the fringing emergent vegetation resembles saltmarsh with plants such as sea-aster *Aster tripolium*, saltmarsh grass *Puccinellia maritima* and cord-grass *Spartina anglica*. Less saline ditches typically have sea club-rush *Scirpus maritimus* as the dominant emergent, along with a number of aquatic species, for example fennel pondweed *Potamogeton pectinatus*, spiked water-milfoil *Myriophyllum spicatum*, and two nationally scarce species, brackish water-crowfoot *Ranunculus baudotii* and soft hornwort *Ceratophyllum submersum*. The transition to fresh water may be either sharp or gradual, and is often marked by the abundance of dominance of common reed *Phragmites australis*. Inland from this transition are ditches supporting a varied and often very diverse assemblage of plant species, characterised by those more typically associated with freshwater

swamps and fens, for example greater pond-sedge *Carex riparia*, reed sweet-grass *Glyceria maxima* and branched bur-reed *Sparganium erectum*.

In south-eastern England, where natural transitions between saltmarsh and other habitats have invariably been lost (see Section 8.1.5.), the presence of relict grazing marsh ditch vegetation often provides the strongest evidence that such transitions ever existed in the past. For example, in Broadland there is a distributional sequence of aquatic and emergent plant communities that is very closely related to water salinity (Figure 8.1.34) (Doarks & Leach in prep.).

Conservation importance and protected status

Coastal grazing marshes are important for a variety of nature conservation reasons; in particular brackish marshes are valuable as representing a scarce resource in a national context and support plant and animal species (including many that are nationally rare or scarce) that in Britain show a distinct preference for this habitat type. Grazing marshes are also important for a wide variety of breeding birds, including several rare species afforded special protection under Schedule 1 of the Wildlife & Countryside Act, and provide winter feeding and roosting for sometimes internationally important numbers of waterfowl (see Chapter 8.6). Some extensive areas of grazing marsh lie within SSSIs and NNRs. So far many of these have been included primarily for their ornithological interest, and it is likely that further areas will need to be added to the SSSI series once botanical and entomological surveys have been completed.

In recent decades grazing marshes have come under increasing pressure from improved (deep) drainage and conversion to arable or intensive grassland management (see e.g. Williams & Hall 1987; Mountford & Sheail 1982, 1989), while some large areas have been lost to industrial and residential developments (Thornton & Kite 1990). This has given rise to a considerable reduction in the overall extent of grazing marsh in many parts of Britain, including an overall reduction of 60% on the Thames Estuary over the period 1935-1981 (see also Chapter 10).

Much of this habitat loss has affected the ditch systems as well as the grasslands: for example for one area in Broadland Driscoll (1983) found that 33.5% of drainage ditches had been lost due to infilling between 1973 and 1981, while many of those remaining had become floristically impoverished. Recent surveys have highlighted a widespread deterioration in the aquatic flora of grazing marshes in Broadland, with eutrophication of water supplies being the most probable cause (Doarks 1990). It is likely that similar changes have occurred on sites elsewhere in Britain, and the protection of surviving areas of high quality coastal grazing marsh is thus an urgent priority.

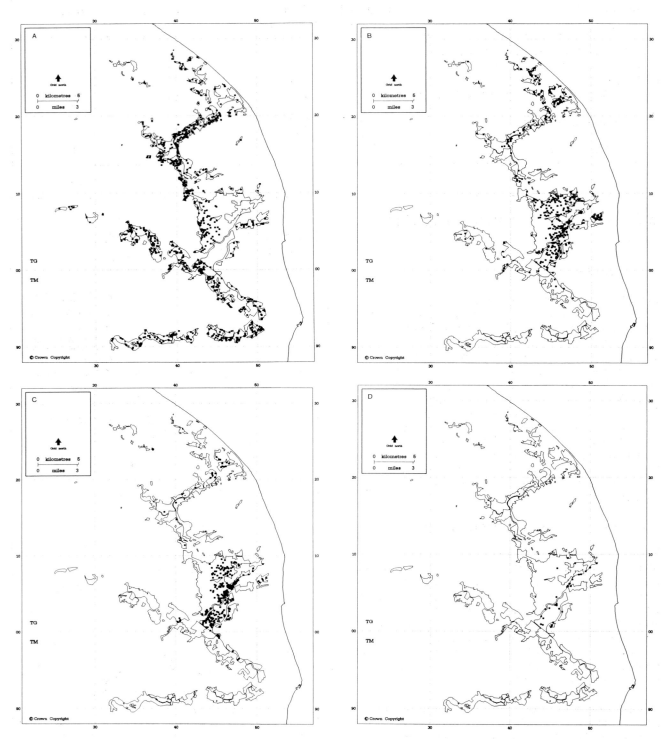

Figure 8.1.34 The distribution of selected ditch types on grazing marshes (mostly associated with the Breydon Water review site) in the Norfolk Broads, from Doarkes & Leach (In prep.). Ditch types depend on soil salinities and have varying degrees of proximity to the tidal rivers: a) freshwater ditches, characterised by the emergents *Carex riparia* and *Phragmites australis*, widespread in the upper tidal reaches; b) slightly saline ditches dominated by species-poor stands of *Phragmites australis*, widespread but mostly in marshes on the lower reaches; c) moderately saline ditches characterised by the emergent *Scirpus maritimus*, with a similar but less widespread distribution to b); d) highly saline ditches characterised by an emergent fringe of saltmarsh species such as *Juncus gerardi* and *Puccinellia maritima*, closely associated with the variable salinity lower parts of the estuary around Breydon Water.

Table 8.1.6 Numbers of nationally rare and nationally scarce vascular plant species of coastal habitats in Britain, and the percentages of rare species of each habitat found on estuaries

Habitat type	Nationally rare	% on estuaries	Nationally scarce	Total
Tidal flats, creeks and lower saltmarshes	7	86	10	17
Mid and upper saltmarshes	3	100	9	12
Shingle	3	67	4	7
Waste places, open areas and sandy shores	3	100	15	18
Rocks	5	60	4	9
Dunes and dune-slacks	5	100	11	16
Sea cliffs	9	33	3	12
Coastal grassland	13	23	9	22
Total	48	58	65	113

8.1.13 Rare and scarce vascular plants

Introduction

In addition to their importance for their characteristic mosaic of habitats and their various plant communities, Britain's estuaries are also of wildlife interest for a number of individual rare and scarce plant species. Nationally rare vascular plant species are those found in 15 or fewer 10-km squares in Great Britain, and nationally scarce those found in 16 to 100 10-km squares. Distributional data on nationally rare plants in relation to review sites have been extracted from records held on the NCC's Rare Plants Databank, obtained from national assessments made in 1984. Where major changes in status are known, some more recent information has also been incorporated.

Rare and scarce estuarine plants

There are at least 48 nationally rare and 65 nationally scarce species and subspecies occurring in coastal habitats in Great Britain. These species are located in eight main habitat types, which occur either on the intertidal parts of estuaries or the adjacent coastal land areas. The habitats and the numbers of the rarer species associated with them are listed in Table 8.1.6. Further details on all these species, their English names and their distribution patterns are listed in Appendix 5.

Not all of these rare coastal species occur on or adjacent to estuaries. Of the 48 nationally rare coastal species, 28 (58%) occur on one or more estuary in Britain. Estuaries with one or more nationally rare species are shown in Figure 8.1.35. Almost all species of tidal flats, saltmarsh, shingle, wastes, open areas, sand-dunes and dune-slacks are associated with estuaries. In contrast, most species of sea cliffs and coastal grassland are on coasts outside estuaries (Table 8.1.6). Estuarine tidal flats and creeks and lower saltmarshes alone have seven nationally rare plants (14.6% of coastal nationally rare species), and 10 nationally scarce species (15%). Similarly mid and upper

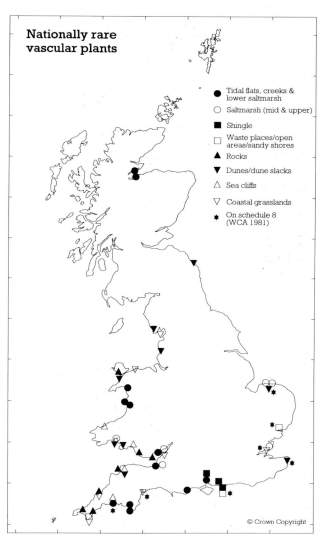

Figure 8.1.35 Review sites supporting one or more nationally rare plant species. Each symbol shows the habitat type occupied by one species on one review site. * indicates the presence of a species listed on Schedule 8 of the Wildlife & Countryside Act 1981.

saltmarshes on estuaries support three nationally rare and nine nationally scarce species. Since almost all tidal flats and saltmarshes in Britain are within estuaries (see Sections 8.1.4 and 8.1.5), these 29 species (25.7% of coastal rare and scarce

Table 8.1.7 British distribution of nationally rare and scarce vascular plant species of tidal flats and creeks and saltmarshes. Species names are listed in Appendix 5

British distribution	No. of species	
	Nationally rare	Nationally scarce
Northern	1	0
South-western	3	0
Southern	1	4
South-eastern	1	8
Eastern	1	1
Scattered	2	6
Total	9	19

species in Britain) are all substantially dependent on estuaries. These species are listed in Table 8.1.7; their national distributions are given in Perring & Walters (1982).

More than half of the localities for most tidal flat, saltmarsh, sand-dune, waste and open area species are also on review sites (Figure 8.1.36). In contrast, even for those species of rocky shore, cliff or coastal grassland that do occur on review sites, only a small proportion of localities are estuarine. Nevertheless all localities for one sea-cliff plant, sea

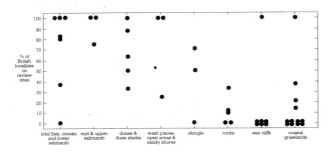

Figure 8.1.36 The extent of the dependence of nationally rare coastal species of vascular plants on estuaries differs between habitats and species. Each symbol shows the proportion of localities on review sites for a coastal species. Species names are listed in Appendix 5a.

stock *Matthiola sinuata*, and one coastal grassland plant, sand crocus *Romulea columnae*, are adjacent to review sites. In all, 10 nationally rare species are, in Britain, found only associated with review sites. These estuarine species are round-headed club-rush *Scirpus holoschoenus*, smooth cord-grass *Spartina alterniflora*, stalked sea-purslane *Halimione pedunculata*, matted sea-lavender *Limonium bellidifolium*, stinking goosefoot *Chenopodium vulvaria*, Welsh mudwort *Limosella australis*, childing pink *Petrorhagia nanteuilii*, Jersey cudweed *Gnaphalium luteo-album*, sea stock *Matthiola sinuata* and sand crocus *Romulea columnae*. They grow in six different types of habitat (Figure 8.1.36).

The majority of nationally rare coastal species are found in south-west, south and west Britain, whilst

nationally scarce species have a predominantly southern, south-eastern or scattered distribution (Appendix 5). The estuarine element of the flora also reflects these distribution patterns (see Table 8.1.7 and Figure 8.1.35). Figure 8.1.35 shows that nationally rare plants occur on 36 review sites (23% of British estuaries). 29 of these sites are in southern and western England and Wales, between Pagham Harbour (Sussex) and the Duddon Estuary (Cumbria); many of Britain's rare coastal species reach the northern and western limits of their largely southern and western European ranges here. Some British estuaries support several nationally rare species in different habitats, notably the Severn Estuary with four species on tidal flats and creeks, saltmarshes, rocks and coastal grassland.

Coastal species as part of the British flora

In Britain there are about 1,423 native species of vascular plants, 317 of which are nationally rare (Perring & Farrell 1983) and 307 of which are nationally scarce (NCC 1989). The 113 species of coastal habitats in these two categories represent 7.9% of the native British flora and 17.9% of the nationally rare and nationally scarce elements. The 17 rarer estuarine species contribute only 1.2% to the total flora, and 2.6% to the rarer element. However, it must be remembered that all these 16 species are confined to the very narrow range of niches offered to plants by estuaries and that they are only occasionally found in other related habitats, whereas species of other coastal habitats can often adapt to the more extensive inland conditions.

Endemic species

There are thought to be about 40 truly endemic species in Great Britain. These include several closely related species in the genera *Euphrasia* (eyebrights), *Sorbus* (whitebeams), *Taraxacum* (dandelions) and *Limonium* (sea-lavenders). Out of the 113 rare and scarce coastal species there are eight endemics, six of which occur at very few sites in Britain (Table 8.1.8). The sea-lavenders *Limonium paradoxum* and *L. recurvum* and Lundy cabbage *Rhynchosinapis wrightii* are each recorded from just one 10-km square. These three species are plants of cliffs and rocky places, but none, however, grows adjacent to British estuaries. Indeed none of the eight species is truly estuarine, most being characteristic of rocky outcrops or sandy shores.

What is of particular note is that there are three members of the sea-lavender genus *Limonium* amongst these endemics. *Limonium* has eight generally recognised species represented in Britain (although a recent taxonomic study has now indicated that there are many more – see Ingrouille & Stace (1986). Similarly coastal habitats support two out of the three British species of the cabbage genus *Rhynchosynapis*. The two subspecies of little robin *Geranium purpureum* are rare, but it is the

Table 8.1.8 Nationally rare and nationally scarce endemic species of coastal habitats in Britain

Species		No. of 10 km squares in GB	Review sites*
Epipactis dunensis	dune helleborine	9	25, 37, 39, 91
Geranium purpureum ssp. *forsteri*	little robin	2	129
Limonium paradoxum	sea-lavender	1	–
Limonium recurvum	sea-lavender	1	–
Limonium transwallianum	sea-lavender	2	–
Primula scotica	Scottish primrose	28	66, 67, 68
Rhynchosinapis monensis	Isle of Man cabbage	18	37, 37, 39, 40, 41, 47
Rhynchosinapis wrightii	Lundy cabbage	1	–

* See Appendix 1 for names and locations of review sites

endemic subspecies *fosteri* that is restricted to a handful of sites in Hampshire, centred on Langstone and Chichester Harbours.

The dune helleborine *Epipactis dunensis* is, as its name suggests, a plant of sand-dunes. It has a scattered but northerly distribution, being found on both the west and east coasts of Britain on Anglesey, in Lancashire and Northumberland and also at inland sites in Lincolnshire. Scottish primrose *Primula scotica* has an even more northerly distribution and is scattered along the extreme north coast of Scotland, with outliers on the north-east tip of Caithness and good populations on several of the Orkney Islands. It is restricted to a narrow zone of essentially maritime grassland and is rarely found more than 300 m from the sea, where it grows associated with three review sites.

The distribution on estuaries of the four endemic species of estuarine habitats is shown in Figure 8.1.37. It is notable that, in contrast to most nationally rare estuarine species, these endemics are chiefly northern and western in their distribution.

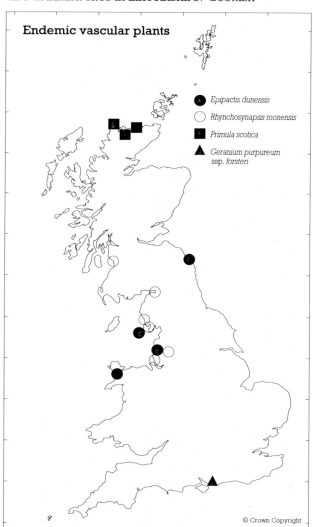

Figure 8.1.37 Distribution on review sites of endemic nationally rare estuarine vascular plant species

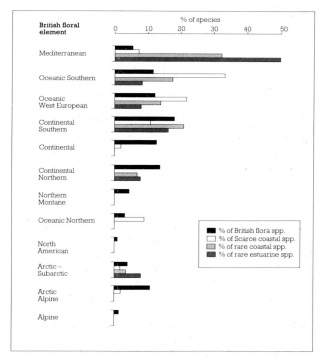

Figure 8.1.38 The biogeographical origins of coastal and estuarine rare and scarce plant species in comparison with those of the British vascular flora as a whole. The floral elements are from Matthews (1955)

Wider distribution and status

Matthews (1955) has reviewed the origins and distribution of the British vascular flora and has divided it into 12 biogeographical floral elements. These elements can be attributed from Matthews' lists for 82 of the rare and scarce coastal species. These species are associated with nine of the 12 elements. Over 89% of rare and 83% of scarce coastal species originate, however, from just four of these elements: Mediterranean, Oceanic Southern, Oceanic West European and Continental Southern. Similarly, 83% of the rare estuarine plants belong to these four elements, compared to only 48% of the British flora overall (see also Figure 8.1.38).

The presence of these largely southern and western biogeographical floral elements in higher proportions on coasts and estuaries than in the whole British flora is also reflected in the southern and western distribution in Britain of many of these rare estuarine species (Figure 8.1.35). So southern and western British estuaries are of particular significance for rare and scarce vascular plants. The continued presence of the habitats in which these species occur is thus essential for the maintenance of the diversity of particularly the southern and western biogeographical elements of the British flora.

Although northern and arctic elements of the British flora are generally poorly represented on coastal and estuarine habitats, there are clear exceptions. Several species, notably estuarine sedge *Carex recta* and oysterplant *Mertensia maritima*, belong to the Arctic-subarctic floral element (Figure 8.1.38). These have a generally northern and north-western British distribution.

Table 8.1.9 Wider distribution and status of British nationally rare species of tidal flats, creeks and saltmarshes

Species		Distribution	Status
Atriplex longipes	long-stalked orache	Denmark, Sweden, Poland, Finland and N Russia	rare
Corrigiola litoralis[*]	strapwort	throughout central Europe	not threatened
Carex recta	estuarine sedge	Faeroes, Norway Finland, North America	rare in Europe
Eleocharis parvula	dwarf spike-rush	central Fennoscandia south to Portugal central Yugoslavia and SE Russia	very local over much of its range
Halimione pedunculata	stalked sea-purslane	northern France east to Estonia and the Black Sea	rare
Limosella australis	Welsh mudwort	Africa, Australia, America	rare
Limonium bellidifolium	matted sea-lavender	Mediterranean, Black Sea, southern USSR and eastern England	rare
Scirpus holoschoenus	round-headed club-rush	widespread in Europe	not threatened
Scirpus triquetrus	triangular club-rush	west, central and southern Europe	not threatened
Spartina alterniflora	smooth cord-grass	France (accidentally introduced in GB from N. America pre-1836)	rare

* British site coastal, not estuarine

Table 8.1.10 Species of coastal habitats on Schedule 8 of The Wildlife and Countryside Act 1981

Species		Occurrence on review site*
Bupleurum baldense	small hare's-ear	–
Chenopodium vulvaria	stinking goosefoot	+
Corrigiola litoralis	strapwort	–
Gnaphalium luteo-album	Jersey cudweed	+
Lactuca saligna	least lettuce	+
Limonium paradoxum	sea-lavender	–
Limonium recurvum	sea-lavender	–
Ononis reclinata	small restharrow	–
Orobanche caryophyllacea	bedstraw broomrape	+
Petrorhagia nanteuilii	childing pink	+
Rhynchosinapis wrightii	Lundy cabbage	–
Romulea columnae	sand crocus	+
Scirpus triquetrus	triangular club-rush	+

* Each of these species occurs on a single review site

Figure 8.1.38 shows that there are particularly large proportions of the small Mediterranean element of the British flora present on coasts and estuaries. 37% of the 38 species listed by Matthews (1955) in this element are rare or scarce coastal species. Half the rare estuarine species for which origins are listed are Mediterranean.

Smith (1988) provides information on European status and distribution for nationally rare plants. This information is summarised in Table 8.1.9 for the 10 rare estuarine species of saltmarshes, tidal flats and creeks. Many of these rare species are of particular interest in the wider context. Few are widespread in Britain. Estuarine sedge *Carex recta* occurs at only six localities in Inverness, Ross, Sutherland and Caithness and dwarf spike-rush *Eleocharis parvula* in about seven places in Hampshire and Merioneth. Smooth cord-grass *Spartina alterniflora* has its only site in Southampton Water where it originally appeared in Britain. The two club-rush *Scirpus* species are both widespread in Europe, but restricted in Britain, *S. holoschoenus* growing in two confined patches in Devon and Somerset and *S. triquetus* being confined to the River Tamar (Plymouth Sound) on the borders of Cornwall and Devon. The latter species appears to be in danger of hybridizing out.

Long-stalked orache *Atriplex longipes* is a northern European species. It is an obligate halophyte, confined to tall saltmarsh vegetation bordering estuaries. There it grows on silty substrates in relatively undisturbed sites that are flooded by brackish water on high spring tides. It has so far been recorded from seven 10-km squares in Britain but as it is not readily distinguished from other oraches it may prove to be more widespread. Matted sea-lavender *Limonium bellidifolium* is confined in Britain to the North Norfolk Coast: outside Britain it is, however, more common throughout the Mediterranean. Stalked sea-purslane *Halimione pedunculata* and strapwort *Corrigiola litoralis* are confined to one native site each in Britain, although the site for strapwort – the muddy shingle margins the coastal lagoons at

Slapton Ley in Devon – is not estuarine.

Welsh mudwort *Limosella australis* is of particular note since it grows nowhere else in Europe. The plants growing on the two Welsh estuaries on which it occurs thus represent the entire European resource. Welsh mudwort has, however, a wide but disjunct world distribution, being known also from localities in Africa, Australia and America.

Conservation of rare and scarce plants

17 (14.3%) of the 113 vascular plant species that are nationally rare or nationally scarce occurring in coastal habitats in Britain are restricted to the saltmarshes, mudflats and creeks of estuaries. It follows that their continued presence as a significant part of the British flora depends on the continuing effective conservation of the estuaries on which they occur. The presence of eight coastal endemic species, four of which occur on a total of 12 review sites, is of particular importance in a European context (Walters 1978).

Specific national conservation measures exist for many British rare plants. The Wildlife & Countryside Act 1981 makes it illegal for any person to pick or destroy intentionally any of the 93 species listed on its Schedule 8. Thirteen of the nationally rare coastal species, eight of which occur on review sites, are on this Schedule (Table 8.1.10). The other five species are those of rocks and cliffs on open coasts. The presence of a viable population of any of these species is a sufficient criterion for designation of a site as an SSSI. All such sites on estuaries are within existing or proposed SSSIs.

Most of the 317 nationally rare plant species in the British Isles have at least one of their sites protected in an SSSI (Perring & Farrell 1983). All the species listed in the *British Red Data Book 1: vascular plants* (Perring & Farrell 1983) are candidate species for designating SSSIs, and the guidelines for the different categories of species are given in Nature Conservancy Council (1989).

The nationally scarce plants are often 'indicator' species and as such highlight the good examples of different habitats in Britain, for example old chalk grassland, ancient woodland and unpolluted estuaries. These species are also used in SSSI selection: if four or more of them occur together at a site, then this area should be considered for notification as an SSSI.

The presence of endemic species is also a guideline for notification, and it is recommended that the location of the largest population of an endemic in each Area of Search – usually a county (NCC 1989) – should be notified wherever practicable.

In addition to national measures, existing and proposed international conservation measures directly and indirectly provide safeguards for rare plants. A Council for the European Communities (CEC) Directive on the protection of natural and semi-natural habitats and of wild fauna and flora is currently in draft. Appendix 1 of this Directive covers endangered and vulnerable species, including three rare coastal and estuarine species: dune gentian *Gentianella uliginosa*, stalked sea-purslane *Halimione pedunculata* and shore dock *Rumex rupestris*. Dune gentian and shore dock depend in part on the habitats surrounding British estuaries; stalked sea-purslane occurs in Britain only adjacent to a review site. All three species are declining throughout much of their European range. The species are also under pressure in Britain: the populations of dune gentian at several of its eight known British localities are under threat; similarly populations of shore dock are under pressure, particularly from increasing recreational use of sandy beaches, since shore dock often grows at the top of the beach. The populations are also vulnerable to oil-spills along Britain's south-western coast, the most recent having occurred in May 1990 after a mid-channel collision.

Stalked sea-purslane was until recently considered extinct in Britain since it had not been seen growing since 1935. A single new colony was discovered, however, in 1987, growing in a narrow band of estuarine upper saltmarsh in Essex. This remains its only known British location.

In addition to the proposed measures in the EC 'habitats' directive for the direct safeguard of these rare species, international measures exist, notably the 'Ramsar' Convention on the Conservation of Wetlands especially as Waterfowl Habitat and the EEC Directive on the conservation of wild birds. These measures afford safeguard for estuarine habitats used by internationally important migrant waterfowl populations on many British estuaries and so also for the habitats on which many of the estuarine rare and scarce plants depend. These measures are described further in Chapters 8.6 and 9.

Rare plant species may be very restricted in their occurrence, but they serve to indicate good examples of natural and semi-natural habitat and ecological conditions which are themselves limited, either naturally or by human influence. They are often the first species to reflect change because of their sensitivity to environmental factors, and so can be used to give an early warning of change. The particular changes threatening coastal habitats in which these rare and scarce species occur are highlighted in sections 5-12 of this Chapter.

8.1.14 References

ADAM, P. 1978. Geographical variation in British saltmarsh vegetation. *Journal of Ecology, 66*, 339-366.

ANON. 1966. *Orford Ness. A selection of maps mainly by John Nordon.* Presented to James Alfred Steers. Cambridge, Heffer & Son.

BARNES, R.S.K. 1989a. The coastal lagoons of Britain: An overview and conservation appraisal. *Biological Conservation, 49*, 295-313.

BARNES, R.S.K. 1989b. The coastal lagoons of Britain: an overview. (Contractor: Department of Zoology, University of Cambridge.) *Nature Conservancy Council, CSD Report*, No. 933.

BEARDALL, C.H., DRYDEN, R.C., & HOLZER, T.J. 1988. *The Suffolk estuaries.* Saxmundham, Suffolk Wildlife Trust.

BEEFTINK, W.G. 1977. Saltmarshes. *In: The coastline*, ed. by R.S.K. Barnes. London, John Wiley & Sons.

BENHAM, P.E.M. 1990. *Spartina anglica* – a research review. Monks Wood, Institute of Terrestrial Ecology. (ITE Research Publication No. 2.)

BEUKEMA, J.J., & CADEE, G.C. 1986. Zoobenthos responses to eutrophication of the Dutch Wadden Sea. *Ophelia, 26*, 55-64.

BOORMAN, L.A., & RANWELL, D.S. 1977. *The ecology of Maplin Sands and the coastal zones of Suffolk, Essex and north Kent.* Cambridge, Institute of Terrestrial Ecology.

BOORMAN, L.A. 1977. Sand dunes. *In: The coastline*, ed. by R.S.K. Barnes. London, John Wiley & Sons.

BURD, F. 1989. *The saltmarsh survey of Great Britain: an inventory of British saltmarshes.* Peterborough, Nature Conservancy Council. (Research & survey in nature conservation No. 17).

CAREY, A.E., & OLIVER, F.W. 1918. *Tidal lands. A study of shore problems.* London, Blackie & Son.

CARTER, R.W.B., & STONE. 1989. Mechanisms associated with the erosion of sand dune cliffs. Magilligan, Northern Ireland. *Earth Surface Processes and Land Forms, 14*, 1-10

CARTER, R.W.G. 1989. *Coastal environments. An introduction to the physical, ecological and cultural systems of coastlines.* London, Academic Press.

CHAPMAN, V.J. 1938. Studies in saltmarsh ecology, Sections I-III. *Journal of Ecology*, 26, 144-178.

CHAPMAN, V.J. 1939. Studies in saltmarsh ecology, Sections IV-V. *Journal of Ecology*, 27, 160-201

CHAPMAN, V.J. 1960. *Saltmarshes and salt deserts of the world.* London, Leonard Hill.

DAVIDSON, N.C., & CLARK, N.A. 1985. The effects of severe weather in January and February 1985 on waders in Britain. *Wader Study Group Bulletin, 44*, 10-16.

DAVIDSON, N.C., & EVANS, P.R. 1986. The role and potential of man-made and man-modified wetlands in the enhancement of the survival of overwintering shorebirds. *Colonial Waterbirds, 9*, 176-188.

DOARKS, C., 1990. *Changes in the flora of grazing marsh dykes in Broadland, between 1972-74 and 1988-89.* Peterborough, Nature Conservancy Council. (England Field Unit Report (unpublished).)

DOARKS, C., & LEACH, S.J., In prep. *A classification of the grazing marsh dyke vegetation in Broadland.* Peterborough, Nature Conservancy Council. (England Field Unit Report, Project No 76 (unpublished).)

DOODY, J.P. 1984. Spartina anglica *in Great Britain.* Peterborough, Nature Conservancy Council. (Focus on nature conservation No. 5.)

DOODY, J.P. 1987. *Botanical and entomological implications of saltmarsh management in intertidal areas.* RSPB Symposium. Sandy, Royal Society for the Protection of Birds.

DOODY, J.P. 1989. Conservation and development of the coastal dunes in Great Britain. *In: Perspectives in coastal dune management*, ed. by F. van der Meulen, P.E. Jungerius and J.H. Visser. The Hague, SPB Academic Publishers.

DOODY, J.P. 1990. *Spartina*: friend or foe? – a conservation viewpoint. *In: 'Spartina anglica' – a research review*, ed. by A.J. Gray and P.E.M. Benham. Monks Wood, Institute of Terrestrial Ecology. (ITE Research Publication No. 2.)

DOODY, J.P. In press. Management for nature conservation. *Royal Society of Edinburgh. Proceedings, 96B.*

DIJKEMA, K.S. 1984. *Saltmarshes in Europe.* Strasbourg, Council of Europe.

DRISCOLL, R.J. 1983. Broadland dykes: the loss of an important wildlife habitat. *Transactions of the Norfolk and Norwich Naturalists Society, 26* (3), 120-172.

EVANS, P.R., & MOON, S. 1981. Heavy metals and shorebirds and their prey in north-east England. *In: Heavy metals in northern England: environmental and biological aspects*, ed. by P.J. Say and B.A. Whitton, 181-190. Durham, University of Durham.

EVANS, P.R., UTTLEY, J.D., DAVIDSON, N.C., & WARD, P. 1987. Shorebirds (S.Os Charadrii and Scolopaci) as agents of transfer of heavy metals within and between estuarine ecosystems. *In: Pollutant transport and fate in ecosystems*, ed. by P.J. Coughtrey, M.H. Martin and M.H. Unsworth. British Ecological Society Special Publication No. 6. Oxford, Blackwell Scientific Publications.

FOWLER, S.L. 1989. Nature conservation implications of damage to the seabed by commercial fishing operations. Nature Conservancy Council Contract Report No. 79 (unpublished).

FULLER, R.H., & RANDALL, R.E. 1988. The Orford shingles, Suffolk, U.K. – Classic conflicts in coastline management. *Biological Conservation, 46*, 95-114.

FULLER, R.M. 1975. The Culbin Shingle Bar and its vegetation. *Transactions of the Botanical Society of Edinburgh, 42*, 293-305.

FULLER, R.J., REED, T.M., WEBB, A., WILLIAMS, T.D., & PIENKOWSKI, M.W. 1986. Populations of breeding waders *Charadrii* and their habitats on the crofting lands of the Outer Hebrides, Scotland. *Biological Conservation*, 37, 333-361.

GOSS-CUSTARD, G.C., & MOSER, M.E. 1988. Rates of change in the numbers of dunlin, *Calidris alpina*, wintering in British estuaries in relation to the spread of *Spartina anglica*. *Journal of Applied Ecology, 25*, 95-109.

GRAY, A.J. 1972. The ecology of Morecambe Bay, V. The saltmarshes of Morecambe Bay. *Journal of Applied Ecology, 9*, 207-220.

GRAY, A.J. 1977. Reclaimed land. *In: The coastline*, ed. by R.S.K. Barnes. London, John Wiley & Sons.

GRAY, J.S. 1972. Effects of pollutants on marine ecosystems. *Netherlands Journal of Sea Research, 16*, 424-443.

HILL, M.I., & RANDERSON, P.F. 1987. Saltmarsh vegetation communities of the Wash and their recent development. *In: The Wash and its environment*, ed. by P. Doody and B. Barnett, 111-122. Peterborough, Nature Conservancy Council. (Research & survey in nature conservation No. 7.)

HOOGHART, J.C., & POSTHUMUS, C.W.S., eds. 1989. *Hydro-ecological relations in the Delta waters of the south-west Netherlands.* The Hague, TNO Committee on Hydrological Research.

HOWELL, R. 1985. The effect of bait-digging on the bioavailability of heavy metals from surficial intertidal marine sediments. *Marine Pollution Bulletin, 6*, 292-295.

HUBBARD, J.C.E., & STEBBINGS, R.E. 1967. Distribution, date of origin and acreage of *Spartina townsendii* (s.1.) marshes in Great Britain. *Botanical Society of the British Isles. Proceedings, 7*, 1-7.

HULL, S. 1987. Macroalgal mats and species abundance: a field experiment. *Estuarine & Coastal Shelf Science, 25,* 519-532.

HUSSEY, A., & LONG, S.P. 1982. Seasonal changes in weight of above and below ground and dead plant material in a saltmarsh at Colne Point, Essex. *Journal of Ecology, 70,* 757-771.

NGROUILLE, M.J., & STACE, C.L.A. 1986. The *Limonium binervosum* aggregate (Plumbaginaceae) in the British Isles. *Botanical Journal of the Linnean Society, 92,* 177-217.

LEACH, S.J. 1988. Rediscovery of *Halimione pedunculata* (L.) Aellen in Britain. *Watsonia, 17,* 170-171.

MARCHANT, C.J. 1967. Evolution in *Spartina* (Gramineae). I. The history and morphology of the genus in Britain. *Linnean Society. Journal, 60,* 1-24.

MATTHEWS, J.R. 1955. *Origin and distribution of the British flora.* London, Hutchinson's University Library.

MEIRE, P.M., SEYS, J., YSEBAERT, T., MEININGER, P.L., & BAPTIST, H.J.M. 1989. A changing Delta: effects of large coastal engineering works on feeding relationships as illustrated by waterbirds. *In: Hydro-ecological relations in the Delta waters of the south-west Netherlands,* ed. by J.C. Hooghart and C.W.S. Posthumus, 109-146. The Hague, TNO Committee on Hydrological Research.

MOUNTFORD, J.O., & SHEAIL, J. 1982. The impact of land drainage on wildlife in the Romney Marsh: the availability of base-line data. *Nature Conservancy Council, CSD Report,* No. 456.

MOUNTFORD, J.O., & SHEAIL, J. 1989. *The effects of agricultural land use change on the flora of three grazing marsh areas.* Peterborough, Nature Conservancy Council. (Focus on nature conservation No. 20.)

NATURAL ENVIRONMENT RESEARCH COUNCIL. 1983. Contaminants in top predators. *NERC Publications Series C,* No. 23.

NATURE CONSERVANCY COUNCIL. 1989. *Guidelines for the selection of biological SSSIs. Part C, Chapter 11: Vascular plants.* Peterborough, Nature Conservancy Council.

OLSON, J.S., & VAN DER MAAREL, E. 1989. Coastal dunes in Europe: a global view. *In: Perspectives in coastal dune management,* ed. by F. van der Meulen, P.E. Jungerius and J.H. Visser, 3-32. The Hague, SPB Academic Publishers.

PERRING, F.H., & FARRELL, L. 1983. *British Red Data Books 1: vascular plants.* 2nd ed. Lincoln, Royal Society for Nature Conservation.

PERRING, F.H., & WALTERS, S.M. 1976. *Atlas of the British flora.* Botanical Society of the British Isles.

PERRING, F.H., & WALTERS, S.M. 1982. *Atlas of the British Flora.* 3rd ed. Botanical Society of the British Isles.

RANWELL, D.S. 1972. *Ecology of saltmarshes and sand dunes.* London, Chapman & Hall.

RANWELL, D.S., & BOAR, R. 1986. *Coast dune management guide.* Monks Wood, NERC (Institute of Terrestrial Ecology).

RATCLIFFE, D.A., *ed.* 1977. *A nature conservation review.* Cambridge, Cambridge University Press.

RODWELL, J. In press. *British plant communities.* Cambridge, Cambridge University Press.

SHEADER, M.A. 1989. Coastal saline ponds of England and Wales: an overview. (Contractor: Department of Oceanography, University of Southampton). *Nature Conservancy Council, CSD Report,* No. 1009.

SMITH, A. 1988. European status of rare British vascular plants. *Nature Conservancy Council, Contract Surveys,* No. 33.

STEERS, J.A. 1946. *The coastline of England and Wales.* Cambridge, Cambridge University Press.

THORNTON, D., & KITE, D.J. 1990. Changes in the extent of the Thames estuary grazing marshes. London, Nature Conservancy Council.

VAN DEN HEILIGENBERG, T. 1987. Effects of mechanical and manual harvesting of lugworms *Arenicola marina* L. on the benthic fauna of tidal flats in the Dutch Wadden Sea. *Biological Conservation, 39,* 165-177.

VAN IMPE, J. 1985. Estuarine pollution as a probable cause of increase of estuarine birds. *Marine Pollution Bulletin, 16,* 271-276.

WALTERS, S.M. 1978. *In: Essays in plant taxonomy,* ed. by H.E. Street. London, Academic Press.

WANDERS, E. 1989. Perspectives in coastal dune management: towards a dynamic approach. *In: Perspectives in coastal dune management,* ed. by F. van der Meulen, P.D. Jungerius and J.H. Visser. The Hague, SPB Academic Publishers.

WOLFF, W.J., & SMIT, C.J. 1984. The Dutch Wadden Sea. *In: Coastal waders and wildfowl in winter,* ed. by P.R. Evans, J.D. Goss-Custard and W.G. Hale, 238-252. Cambridge, Cambridge University Press.

WILLIAMS, G., & HALL, M. 1987. The loss of coastal grazing marshes in south and east England, with special reference to east Essex, England. *Biological Conservation, 39,* 243-253.

8.2 Terrestrial and non-marine invertebrates

Contents

8.2.1 Introduction

A number of estuarine habitats support distinctive assemblages of terrestrial, semi-terrestrial and brackish water air-breathing invertebrates, here grouped under the general term 'terrestrial and non-marine invertebrates'. The aquatic intertidal and subtidal invertebrate fauna is treated separately in Chapter 8.3 (Aquatic estuarine communities).

General features of distribution

Individual vegetation types and successional stages of sand-dunes, saltmarshes, lagoons, reedbeds, vegetated shingle, grazing marshes and soft-rock cliffs all have characteristic faunas which also vary with the geographical position of the site. Usually there is a decline in species richness northwards, which is perhaps more pronounced on Britain's east coast than on the west. The number of species occurring in these habitats may total several thousand, many of which are non-fastidious species ranging widely over many different habitat types. Here it is only possible to give very limited examples to illustrate the particular microhabitats most crucial to species most typical of these types of habitat. Remarkably few, even of the typical species, are restricted purely to estuarine situations, most also occurring on similar habitats on non-estuarine sections of coast, or in saline or brackish water, or mobile, sandy conditions inland. Many species which also occur inland in southern Britain become more restricted to estuarine and coastal sites in the north.

Several microhabitats are of particular value for terrestrial and brackish-water invertebrates in estuarine situations. Their presence can give an indication of the potential of a site to support a significant fauna where there is a dearth of survey data.

Knowledge of the non-marine invertebrate fauna of British estuarine habitats is, however, extremely patchy. While certain elements of the fauna of most sand-dune sites around our coasts have been investigated in some detail, this cannot be said for other habitat types. The saltmarsh faunas of, for example, the Humber, Thames, Blackwater and Medway Estuaries, The Wash, the Swale Estuary and Rye Harbour are relatively well studied, whereas those of the Severn, Dee, Mersey, Ribble and Solway Estuaries are very poorly known. Within the NCC, available information on terrestrial invertebrates is collated by the Invertebrate Site Register (ISR) (see Section 8.2.12). Much of the information described in this chapter comes from ISR records, supplemented from other published sources. Endangered, rare, vulnerable and scarce insect species in Britain have been recently listed by Shirt (1987). The Red Data Book (RDB) status of such species is identified (e.g. by RDB2) where appropriate in the following text, and these status definitions are listed in Table 8.2.1.

Coping with the tide

Air-breathing invertebrates have to be able to cope with the rigours of a dynamic system in which the problems of respiration, osmotic/physiological stresses, and of being washed away, are great. Coastal terrestrial invertebrates have developed both physiological and behavioural mechanisms to overcome these difficulties, so allowing them to exploit the highly productive estuarine marshes. A simple mechanism is tolerance. Most arthropods of the supralittoral can tolerate several hours of immersion, with some species of spider and

Table 8.2.1 Status categories for threatened invertebrates in Britain, for Red Data Book (RDB) and other species, from Ball (1986) and Shirt (1987)

Status	Definition
Red Data Book	
RDB1 Endangered	Species in danger of extinction and whose survival is unlikely if the causal factors continue operating
RDB2 Vulnerable	Species believed likely to move into the endangered category in the near future if the causal factors continue operating
RDB3 Rare	Species with small populations that are not at present endangered or vulnerable, but are at risk
RDB4 Out of danger	Species formerly RDB1, 2 or 3 but now considered relatively secure
RDB5 Endemic	Species naturally occurring only in Britain. Such species may be also in RDB1-4
RDBk	Status uncertain
Nationally scarce	
Scarce A	Species known from 16-30 10-km squares
Scarce B	Species known from 31-100 10-km squares

Note The distribution of some species appears to qualify them for inclusion in the RDB lists, but their status is as yet too poorly known. These are usually given an RDBk status. For other species apparent RDB status has emerged after the preparation of the Red Data Book for insects. Such species are currently afforded provisional RDB status: pRDB.

carabid beetle able to survive 1-3 months provided the temperature is low (Heydemann 1979). The wolf spider *Pardosa agrestis* has a coastal form (originally described as a distinct species *P. purbeckensis*) which has long been known to cope with the rising tide by walking down a plant stem and clinging to its base until the tide retreats (Bristowe 1958). Similarly, the predatory bug *Halosalda lateralis*, when caught by the tide, clings to a nearby piece of vegetation and climbs down to its base to wait for the tide to recede. Although this species can tolerate submersion for 2-3 hours its true habitat is above the high-water mark (Southwood & Leston 1959). The tiny money spider *Erigone arctica* seeks shelter beneath a stone as the tide advances (Bristowe 1958).

A more complex adaptation to submersion by the tide involves synchronised patterns of locomotor activity, i.e. some animals are active only when not submerged. The behavioural mechanisms employed by a number of saltmarsh species are now known. For example the saltmarsh carabid beetle *Dicheirotrichus gustavi* has a circadian activity pattern which is suppressed by tidal submersion: it usually hunts nocturnally but not when the tide is high (Treherne & Foster 1977). The day-active saltmarsh mite *Bdella interrupta* has two peaks of locomotor activity on the marsh, their timing being governed by the tide. During periods of tidal submergence they have a periodicity of 12.5 hours, but this alters to 11.5 hours during periods of tidal emergence. This ensures that the mite is active only during daylight when the tide is out (Foster *et al.* 1979). The intertidal collembolan *Anurida maritima* has evolved the elegant strategy of maintaining an endogenous 12.4-hour circatidal rhythm, together with an exogenous rhythm of locomotor suppression during darkness. This rhythm is maintained throughout periods of immersion, so avoiding the need for a predictive mechanism for the timing of the next daylight low tide (Foster & Morton 1981).

Although posing behavioural and physiological problems, the tide is used to advantage by some terrestrial invertebrates. For example the intertidal aphid *Pemphigus trehemi* uses the shallowly flooding tide to disperse around saltmarshes (Foster & Treherne 1975).

8.2.2 Bare substrate

Firm intertidal and supralittoral sandy mud and sand, with sparse or no vegetation, is of importance for a number of groups of stenotypic invertebrates, including rare species. Adults of a number of families of beetles, most notably of the Heteroceridae and rove beetles of the genus *Bledius* (Staphylinidae), burrow into estuarine sandy or clay sediments, different species preferring different particle size distributions within their substrate. These species are algal or detrital grazers, while some burrowing ground beetles of the genus *Dyschirius* are specific predators on individual species *of Bledius*. Distribution maps of *Dyschirius* and *Bledius* species are under preparation in atlases being produced by the Biological Records Centre. The detritivorous larvae of a number of flies also burrow into similar sediments, extending much further into the intertidal than the beetles, and also occurring in much siltier sediments of large mudflats. Particularly significant are flies of the families Dolichopodidae (marsh flies), whose adults are predatory, Ephydridae (shore flies) and a few species of Tabanidae (horse flies), with adults of some species feeding on the blood of estuarine birds. A number of species of isopod and amphipod crustaceans, largely from marine groups, also burrow in sandy or clay sediments.

Bare or sparsely vegetated dry sandy substrates in sand-dunes are burrowed into by a considerable diversity of solitary wasps and bees, with different species nesting in flat and vertical sand faces, as well as by the larvae of three species of tiger beetles *Cicindela* spp., two of which are nationally scarce and confined to large dune areas in southern and western Britain. It is important that the substrate is sufficiently firm to support the burrows of these species as they are easily eliminated by excessive trampling.

Adults of a number of species of visually-hunting predatory insects and spiders need expanses of bare substrate over which to hunt. Sand and mud in different estuarine habitats support different faunas of these predators. Damp substrates support ground beetles (Carabidae) and shore bugs (Saldidae), e.g. *Saldula setulosa* (RDB2) – a species in Britain on the edge of its known range, known only from the sandy silt at the top of the littoral zone in Poole Harbour, where it is able to withstand submersion by high spring tides (Southwood & Leston 1959; Shirt 1987). There are also flies of the Dolichopodidae and Empididae (dance flies), as well as wolf spiders (Lycosidae). In dry, sandy substrates in dunes, these families are represented largely by different species, with the addition of flies of the Asiliidae (robber flies) and Therevidae (stiletto flies). The warm microclimate of patches of bare sandy ground is also needed by a number of thermophilic species in many orders of insect to maintain body temperature, this being the likely reason that a number of species become restricted to dune habitats in the northern part of their range in Britain.

Very small patches of bare substrate can be of great significance within otherwise vegetated habitat. Such microhabitats include the margins of salt pans and edges of creeks in saltmarsh, and the surface of lightly trampled paths, rabbit burrows, and small sand-blows in dunes. Large expanses of sandflat are needed specifically by relatively few species. The ground beetle *Bembidion pallidipenne* and the two maritime tiger beetles

Cicindela maritima and *C. hybrida* range very widely over extensive intertidal sandflats backed by dunes.

8.2.3 Vegetation structure

The structure of estuarine vegetation is almost as important as its plant species composition for determining the invertebrate assemblages that it supports. The extent of grazing of the vegetation is also significant in different ways for the invertebrates of sand-dunes and saltmarsh. On sand-dunes there are characteristic communities comprising species from most classes of terrestrial invertebrates associated with each stage of the early succession. This short vegetation is usually maintained by grazing, most commonly by rabbits but sometimes by domestic livestock. In the absence of grazing, coarser grasses and scrub eventually become dominant and the typical dune fauna becomes replaced by more generalist species common to many types of rough grassland.

In contrast, grazing on saltmarsh, particularly by sheep, is highly deleterious to the invertebrate fauna, there being relatively few species able to cope with the very short, even sward that this produces. This may contrast with the value of a saltmarsh to its avifauna, since grazed marsh may be very valuable as roosting or feeding grounds for wildfowl, although certainly tall marsh supports important breeding bird populations (see Chapter 8.6). The botanical species richness and structural diversity of an ungrazed saltmarsh produces a wider spectrum of terrestrial invertebrate niches, ranging from sites for web-spinning by spiders to habitat for specific phytophagous species on saltmarsh plants and in accumulations of plant litter at the roots of plants. Natural interfaces between saltmarsh vegetation and other terrestrial habitats, especially freshwater marsh, support a number of highly adapted species, notably among the two-winged flies.

8.2.4 Sand-dunes

The invertebrate assemblages of sand-dunes can be grouped according to habitat type characterised on the basis of floristic and structural diversity (Duffey 1968; see also Section 8.2.3). On young (yellow) dunes, the very open structure of the vegetation, with much bare sand between individual plants, is critical for the characteristic invertebrates. Species range from phytophagous insects associated with pioneer plants, such as the flea beetle *Psylliodes marcida* associated with sea-kale *Cakile maritima* and larvae of the noctuid moth *Photedes elymi* on lyme grass, to spider-hunting (pompilid) wasps such as *Episyron rufipes* searching among the marram, and scarabaeid beetles like *Aegilia arenaria* feeding underground on dry plant litter. Older dunes, with a slightly more closed cover of short vegetation, are important for numerous phytophagous ground and plant bugs, including the spectacular red and black

Corizus hyocyami and seed-eating ground beetles of the genera *Amara* and *Harpalus*, and the pseudoscorpion *Dactylochelifer latreillei,* a predator found in amongst tussocks of marram grass and under driftwood on the south and east coasts of Britain (Legg & Jones 1988). The shore wainscot moth *Mythimna littoralis* has larvae which feed nocturnally on marram grass and hide in the sand by day (Heath & Emmet 1983). The numerous rosette plants, such as plantains and storksbills, provide important cover for the ground-dwelling species.

Most species found commonly on sand-dunes are not restricted to this habitat. For example the wolf spider *Arctosa perita* is one of the most common and characteristic spiders of the yellow dune zone and yet it is found also inland in areas such as sand or shale/coal dust with a structurally similar substrate. Such distributions are fairly common and probably reflect microhabitat requirements, including plant architecture and release from competition (Duffey 1968).

A similarly intriguing disjunct distribution pattern exists for the sandhill rustic *Luperina nickerlii,* a noctuid moth with four phenotypically and ecologically distinct isolated populations (Figure 8.2.1), each a separate subspecies. One subspecies, *L.n. knilli,* is found only on crumbling cliffs on the Dingle Peninsula in Co. Kerry where its larvae probably feed on red fescue *Festuca rubra.* Two subspecies – *L.n. gueneei* on Anglesey and the north Wales coast, and *L.n. leechi* (known only from the shingle bar closing one coastal lagoon in south Cornwall) – have larvae which feed first on the sheaths and then on the rhizomes of sand couch *Elymus farctus.* They then pupate several centimetres deep in the sand. Adults of these two subspecies are found on sheltered sandhills where there is extensive growth of sand couch that is inundated only by the highest tides (Heath & Emmet 1983). The subspecies most recently confirmed as resident is *L.n. nickerlii,* found only on east coast saltmarshes from Kent to Suffolk (Emmet *et al.* 1985; unpublished information from B Skinner, D Agassiz and others). All sites known for the *gueneei* and *nickerlii* subspecies are on sand-dunes associated with three Welsh and eight east English review sites.

8.2.5 Saltmarsh

As with most estuarine habitats, the terrestrial invertebrates characteristic of saltmarsh are either phytophages of saltmarsh plants or rely upon the provision of suitable microhabitats within the system (see Section 8.2.3).

The scarce capsid bug *Orthotylus rubidus* feeds on saltwort *Salicornia* and is found in areas of saltmarshes and seepages subject to only occasional inundation, from Devon to Norfolk (Southwood & Leston 1959). Sea wormwood *Artemisia maritima* is host to a picture-winged fly *Paroxyna absinthii,* whose larvae feed on the flower

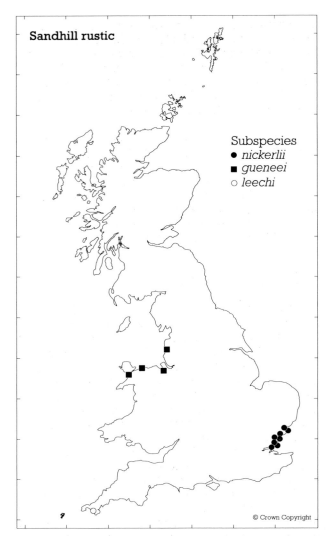

Figure 8.2.1 The British distribution of subspecies of the sandhill rustic moth *Luperina nickerlii,* derived from Heath & Emmet (1983) and records on the NCC's Invertebrate Site Register. Review sites with populations are shown as filled symbols; the open symbol is a population away from a review site.

heads (White 1988). It also hosts the larvae of the scarce pug moth *Eupithecia extensaria* (RDB3), a rare species confined to review site saltmarshes in Norfolk, Lincolnshire, Humberside and one site in Essex (Shirt 1987). Sea-lavender *Limonium* spp. supports a root-feeding weevil *Apion limonii* (Nb); a micro-moth *Goniodoma limoniella,* and the plume moth *Agdistis bennettii.* Sea aster *Aster tripolium* has a similarly characteristic suite of obligate herbivores including two aphids: the root-feeding *Pemphigus treherni* (Foster & Treherne 1975) and the stem-feeding *Macrosiphoniella asteris* (Heydemann 1979), a gall-forming picture-winged fly *Paroxyna plantaginis* (White 1988), and the noctuid moth *Cucullia asteris* which feeds on the flower heads. This moth is another example of a species occupying two distinct habitats: its other habitat is woodland, where the larvae feed on goldenrod *Solidago virgaurea.* There is evidence, however, of distinct behavioural differences between the two populations, with the saltmarsh populations tending to be more sluggish and to take longer to develop (Heath & Emmet 1983). The saltmarsh grasses also nourish a variety of moth species including sandhill rustic, Matthew's wainscot *Mythimna favicolor*, and the crescent striped *Apamea oblonga*, whose larvae feed at night on the roots and stem bases of *Puccinellia* and spend the day in small chambers among the roots or under stones (Heath & Emmet 1983).

A particular estuarine rarity – Fisher's estuarine moth *Gortyna borelii lunata* (RDB2) – is found only on one review site on the north Essex coast in a colony of its host plant, hog's fennel *Peucedanum officinale*. The larvae feed first on the leaf-axil and then descend and feed on the rootstock, making massive excavations and burrowing to a depth of 30 cm (Heath & Emmet 1983).

8.2.6 Reedbeds

The fauna of brackish-water reedbeds is distinct from that of freshwater reedbeds, and a discrete suite of species of noctuid moths, in particular species of wainscot moth *Mythimna* and others, have caterpillars feeding on and in the reed stems. These species are particularly common in some estuaries. Reeds in standing brackish water may prove more favourable for some phytophagous species, by isolating them from ground-dwelling predators which are more prevalent in tidal reedbeds or reedbeds over reed litter, each of which supports a distinctive fauna. The hoverfly *Sphaerophoria loewi*, a predator on aphids on reeds, seems also to be more common on reeds in standing water. Certain rare species of invertebrate also occur in fenland reedbeds, for example the reed-climbing ground beetle *Dromius longiceps*, which is largely restricted to coastal reedbeds and fens in East Anglia and the reedbeds of the upper Humber Estuary.

8.2.7 Shingle

Invertebrates associated with coastal and estuarine shingle tend either to be associated with the specialised flora of the shingle or to be dependent on the shelter provided by the shingle itself and the litter that accumulates on it.

Examples of species dependent on the specialist shingle flora include the darkling beetle *Omophlus rufitarsus*, known only from thrift *Armeria maritima* growing on shingle at The Fleet in Dorset, and the micro-moth *Aethes margarotana* (RDB2), the larvae of which feed on the roots of sea-holly *Eryngium maritimum*, itself a scarce plant. This moth was once known from a number of estuaries in southern England, but has declined and is now known only from Thorpness, outside the review site network (Shirt 1987). Another rare moth, *Pima boisduvaliella* (RDB3), has larvae that live in and feed on the pod of sea pea *Lathymus japonicum* (Shirt 1987). The rare jumping spider *Euophrys browningi* (pRDB3) lives amid litter in a few east coastal estuarine shingle systems, preferentially sheltering in cast-up whelk shells on the shingle.

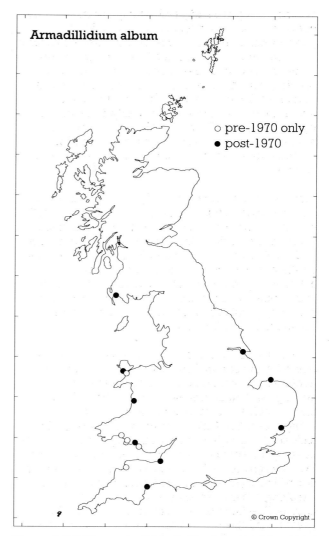

Figure 8.2.2 The review site distribution of the scarce woodlouse *Armadillidium album*. All records in Britain are associated with review sites.

It has the distinction also of being one of the few spiders endemic to Britain (Roberts 1985). The ground beetle *Aepus robini* lives amongst stable intertidal shingles in estuarine conditions.

8.2.8 Strandlines

Accumulations of various types of drift litter are home to various assemblages of terrestrial invertebrates, depending on the composition, humidity and state of decay of the drift material. The specialized woodlouse *Armadillidium album* lives beneath drift material in the upper drift lines of fore-dunes and saltmarshes (Harding & Sutton 1985). It can burrow up to 10 cm into the sand and seems to burrow when the drift material is washed away or buried (Duffey 1968). In Britain it is known only from 15 widely scattered review sites (Figure 8.2.2). Accumulations of seaweed at high-water mark support a wide diversity of specialist flies, with different species inhabiting fresh, rotting and dry weed. Several species of darkling beetles (Tenebrionidae), which are most frequent on

119

strandlines of dunes, as well as a large number of species of rove beetle (Staphylinidae), also live in rotting seaweed which can also support enormous numbers of wrack flies *Coelopa* upon which specialist predators feed. Dried out wrack high above average tidal strandlines is inhabited by the fly *Helcomyza ustulata*. One scarce beetle, *Aphodius plagiatus*, in a genus composed otherwise only of dung beetles, is associated with rotting fungi and accumulations of plant litter in dunes and saltmarsh. Species such as surface predators and nectar feeders, found also elsewhere in estuarine habitats, often either breed in strandline material or use it as shelter. Examples include the wolf spider *Arctosa fulvolineata* (RDB3), which lives and hunts amongst detritus and stones at the top of saltmarshes in East Anglia and around the Solent (Shirt 1987), and the spiders *Trichoncus hackmani* and *T. affinis* found on the south and east coast of England on shingle and in tidal litter (Roberts 1987).

Other species are associated with driftwood, either boring into saltwater-soaked timber, as does the wharf borer beetle *Nacerdes melanura*, sometimes a pest in wooden groynes, and the wood boring weevil *Pselactus spadix*, or deriving shelter under individual pieces of wood. Many predatory ground beetles (Carabidae) and rove beetles (Staphylinidae) are frequent under large pieces of wood, often also living under human jetsam on the strandline, such as fish-boxes and bits of old plastic. Particularly spectacular are the large ground beetles *Broscus cephalotes*, which construct long burrows in damp sand with the entrance under a piece of driftwood, feeding on sandhoppers *Talitrus* and *Orchestia*, and the yellow and black *Nebria complanata*. This sometimes occurs in large aggregations under flat pieces of timber such as old packing cases and is a species of very restricted distribution in Britain, occurring only on the strandlines of dunes along the south Wales and north Devon and Somerset coasts, including at least seven review sites (Figure 8.2.3).

8.2.9 Estuarine cliffs

Soft-rock and boulder clay cliffs, both along the coast and within estuarine situations, are the habitat of a number of burrowing invertebrates, again including rare species. Cliffs along the north bank of the Humber Estuary support a discrete colony of the rove beetle *Bledius dissimilis*, which is known otherwise only from similar cliffs on the Holderness coast and a single colony on an inland cliff in an old clay-pit. Solitary wasps and bees nest in estuarine cliffs, especially when they are warm and south-facing. In the south of England, such cliffs are particularly important in the conservation of some of the rarest of these species in the country. Cracks and fissures and accumulations of clay debris and drift material at the foot of actively slumping cliffs are home to a number of beetle, fly and spider species, including the large cream and chestnut brown ground beetle *Nebria livida*. This nocturnal species is now restricted to the boulder clay cliffs of the Yorkshire and Norfolk coasts and may have

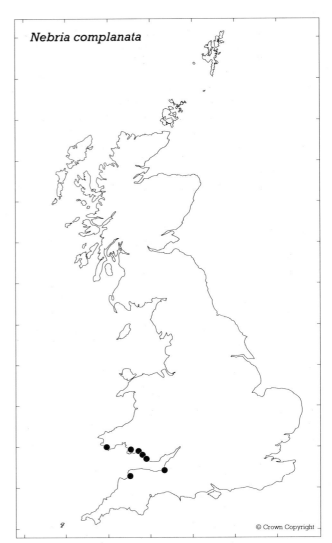

Figure 8.2.3 The review site distribution of the beetle *Nebria complanata*, which is restricted to strandlines in south Wales and south-west England.

been lost from truly estuarine situations. It is thought to be a 'Rhine relict' species – one that has become isolated in the British Isles since the last ice age. Freshwater seepages on such cliffs support scarce species of two-winged flies, most notably among the crane-flies (Tipulidae) and soldier flies (Stratiomyidae), especially where water trickles over bryophyte (moss) carpets.

8.2.10 Brackish and freshwater pools

Brackish still-water bodies associated with estuaries, such as saltmarsh pools and coastal lagoons, support highly characteristic groups of halophile species, notably among the water-beetles, e.g. *Berosus spinosus* (RDB3), and bugs (e.g. *Sigara stagnatilis* and the scarce *S. selecta* (Southwood & Leston 1959), caddis, two-winged flies (e.g. larvae of the snail-killing fly *Stratiomys longicornis* (RDB2) and the crane fly *Limonia bezzii* (RDB2) (Shirt 1987), molluscs and crustacea. These include a number of scarce and threatened species. Other invertebrates are associated with the characteristic vegetation of such water bodies, either feeding upon the plants themselves, or being dependent on their structural heterogeneity or upon the litter that builds up beneath them. The reed beetle *Macroplea mutica* is a species mainly of brackish water, feeding on the roots of *Potamogeton pectinatus*. This beetle is also reputed to feed on the roots of *Zostera*, although this has not been proved in this country. Others again live on wet mud and algal felts that occur at pool margins, while the dolichopodid flies *Dolichopus diadema* and *Machaerium maritimae* skim over the surface of saltmarsh pools.

The water-beetle *Ochthebius lenensis* (RDB2) is known only from brackish pools on the saltmarshes of the Dornoch and Moray Firths (Foster 1990). Other members of this genus show a similarly restricted distribution: *O. lejolisi* is found in saline pools on rocky shores and will not tolerate fresh water; *O. exaratus* is a thermophilous species and is found only in the coastal grazing levels of the south-east (Foster 1990). Such brackish-water bodies include natural lagoons and pools in saltmarsh, but now most commonly take the form of man-made sites such as ditches, drains and borrow pits, often behind a boundary sea-wall, where the saline influence may be entirely from seepage, as well as the ditches on estuarine grazing levels (see Section 8.2.11).

The interface between freshwater and brackish wetland supports a particularly rich assemblage of aquatic and semi-terrestrial species of fly and water-beetle. Such interfaces occur in freshwater outflows and seepages across saltmarshes and among the maze of ditches on grazing levels. Temporary freshwater pools in dune slacks also have a characteristic fauna, especially of water-beetles and micro-crustacea, the water-beetle *Dryops striatellus* being almost restricted to this habitat. The vegetation of dune-slack pools also supports a characteristic fauna of phytophagous species, including the spectacular chestnut and green leaf beetle *Chrysomela populi* feeding on *Salix herbacea* on which plant the parasitic wasp *Brachymeria minuta*, a parasite on fly larvae, is most often found.

Hypersaline pools, including saltmarsh salt pans, also have specialist faunas of terrestrially-derived as well as marine species. The water-beetle *Paracymus aeneus* is restricted to a single hypersaline lagoon behind the sea-wall at Bembridge Harbour on the Isle of Wight. (For a further description of saline lagoons see Section 8.1.11.)

8.2.11 Grazing marshes

Grazing marshes are a habitat of considerable conservation significance lying adjacent to estuaries, chiefly in the south and east of England. Their distribution and floristic interest are described in Section 8.1.12. Their invertebrate faunas, particularly those associated with ditches, are also of considerable conservation interest.

During the last decade the invertebrate fauna of many of the major grazing marsh areas have been surveyed, concentrating on the aquatic fauna although terrestrial invertebrates have also been examined on the Somerset Levels, the Gwent Levels, several marsh systems on the Thames Estuary, and on the North Kent Marshes (Stubbs *et al.* 1982; Drake *et al.* 1984; Drake 1986; Plant 1987; Eversham *et al.* 1989).

Grazing marsh faunas

Much of the focus of invertebrate interest lies in grazing marsh ditches and their banks. The unimproved grassland of the pasture itself sometimes also holds species of note, but none is exclusively associated with grasslands on coastal grazing marshes. These are essentially linear ponds which provide extensive margins and a variety of water depths. Their fauna is similar to that of natural ponds and fens. The dominant aquatic macroinvertebrates of such places are beetles (Coleoptera), bugs (Heteroptera), snails (Mollusca – Gastropoda) and fly (Diptera) larvae. The first three of these groups form a substantial proportion of the British species on coastal grazing marshes, and a ditch system can be home to over 50 species of water-beetle (Table 8.2.2). Other groups such as crustaceans, leeches, flatworms, caddis and mayflies are generally represented by only a few, although often abundant, species and so make a smaller contribution to the species richness. There is as yet little information on other, taxonomically difficult, groups such as mites, worms and smaller crustaceans. Comparable data for dragonflies (Odonata) are not available for all the grazing marsh areas in Table 8.2.1. Grazing marshes are, however, undoubtedly very important places for dragonflies since at least 12 species (of a British total of 44 species) occur on the Gwent Levels (Severn Estuary) and 14 species on the Essex grazing marshes.

The terrestrial fauna of grazing marshes appears dominated by two-winged flies, although this may reflect more the level of expertise of invertebrate surveyors than the true distribution of taxa. These dipteran faunas can be very diverse: for example 530 species of flies, including many whose larvae are aquatic or live in damp soil, were recorded in one survey on the Gwent Levels (Drake 1989). Some groups of flies were particularly well represented on the Gwent Levels: two surveys found about 40% of British species of snail-killing flies Sciomyzidae (27 species) and grass flies Chloropidae (59 species), about 25% of British shore-flies Ephydridae (32 species), hoverflies Syrphidae (59 species) and Dolichopodidae (67 species), and about 10% of the British non-biting midges Chironomidae (56 species) and dance-flies Empididae (46 species) (McLean 1982; Drake 1989).

Despite the large number of aquatic species recorded on grazing marshes, relatively few are ubiquitous even within one geographical area. For example, in more than 40% of samples in surveys of Essex and Suffolk grazing marshes only 18

Table 8.2.2 The numbers of taxa in the major aquatic invertebrate groups found on different areas of coastal grazing marshes compared with the total in Britain

	Gwent Levels	Somerset Levels	N Kent marshes	Essex marshes	Suffolk marshes	Britain
Leeches	9	8	6	8	8	16
Molluscs	25	19	12	24	26	71
Bugs	21	29	25	26	32	63
Beetles	99	64	53	88	80	254
Caddis	13	5	6	13	10	134
Larger crustaceans	8	7	10	14	13	20

species were found. There are thus considerable differences in the aquatic invertebrate assemblages on different grazing marsh systems. Even the most common species on each of six grazing marsh areas are dissimilar. Table 8.2.3 shows that only nine species (the snail *Lymnaea peregra*, the boatman *Hesperocorixa linnei*, and the beetles *Anacaena limbata*, *Haliplus ruficollis*, *Helophorus brevipalpis*, *Hydrobius fuscipes*, *Hydroporus palustris*, *Hygrotus inaequalis* and *Noterus clavicornis*) were widespread, occurring on four or more of the marsh areas. These are all generally ubiquitous species, common in most lowland water bodies.

Rare and scarce species

Many nationally rare and scarce invertebrates live on grazing marshes. In several NCC surveys of aquatic and terrestrial invertebrates (Palmer 1980; Stubbs *et al.* 1982; Drake *et al.* 1984; Drake 1986, 1988a, 1988b), Red Data Book (RDB) species (see Table 8.2.1) accounted for between 0.5-4.9% of all identified species, and nationally scarce species comprised between 11.2-17.1% of the identified species (Table 8.2.4). In addition, other records of rare species held by the NCC's Invertebrate Site Register (ISR) emphasise the conservation significance of grazing marshes for rare invertebrates.

For some rare species grazing marshes appear to provide their national stronghold. The geographical distributions of the RDB3 great silver water-beetle *Hydrophilus piceus* (RDB3), three scarce beetles *Peltodytes caesus*, *Limnoxenus niger* and *Berosus affinis*, and the soldier fly *Odontomyia ornata* (RDB2) closely follow that of the major

Table 8.2.4 Numbers and percentages of Red Data Book (RDB) and nationally scarce species (see Table 8.2.4) of invertebrates on grazing marshes, from various NCC surveys. Surveys of 'terrestrial' species were not made on the Suffolk and Essex marshes. The total named species includes only groups covered by Ball (1986) and Shirt (1987).

	Gwent Levels	Somerset Levels	N Kent marshes	Essex marshes	Suffolk marshes
Aquatic species					
RDB2 & pRDB2	1	1	0	3	4
RDB3	3	2	2	6	4
Scarce A	2	2	1	5	1
Scarce B	26	18	14	31	24
Total named species	222	150	128	211	201
% RDB	1.8	2.0	1.6	4.3	4.0
% scarce	12.6	13.3	11.7	17.1	12.4
'Terrestrial' species					
RDB1	1	0	1		
RDB2	5	1	7		
RDB3 & RDBk	9	0	11		
Scarce A	7	2	1		
Scarce B	59	26	43		
Total named species	576	217	388		
% RDB	2.6	0.5	4.9		
% scarce	11.5	12.9	11.3		

Table 8.2.3 The commonest invertebrate species on six coastal grazing marshes, derived from Palmer (1980), Drake (1986, 1988a, 1988b) and Drake *et al* (1984). The numbers of species included for the different areas varies between 22-26, depending on the analyses for each survey.

	Gwent Levels[a]	Somerset Levels[b]	North Kent marshes[c]	Essex coast[d]	Suffolk coast[e]	Lyth, Cumbria[f]
Triclads						
Polycelis spp.	+				+	
Molluscs						
Anisus vortex	+	+				
Bithnyia tentaculata	+				+	
Lymnaea palustris						+
L. peregra	+	+	+	+	+	+
Pisidium spp.						+
Planorbis planorbis	+	+			+	
Potamopyrgus jenkinsi			+	+	+	
Ephemeroptera						
Cloeon dipterum	+	+			+	+
Odonata						
Coenagrion puella	+					
Ischnura elegans			+	+	+	
Hemiptera						
Callicorixa praeusta			+			
Corixa affinis			+			
C. punctata			+			
Gerris lacustris	+					+
G. odontogaster				+		
Hesperocorixa linnei		+	+	+	+	
H. sahlbergi	+				+	
Hydrometra stagnorum						+
Iliocoris cimicoides	+	+	+			
Notonecta glauca		+			+	
N. viridis			+			
Plea minutissima		+	+			
Sigara dorsalis			+			
S. striata			+			
S. stagnalis			+	+		
Trichoptera						
Limnephilus affinis				+		
Diptera						
Dixella autumnalis					+	
Oplondotha viridula	+			+		
Coleoptera						
Agabus bipustulatus				+		+
A. sturmii					+	
Anaceana globulus						+
A. limbata	+	+		+	+	
Berosus affinis		+				
Cymbiodonta marginella				+		
Dytiscus circumflexus			+	+		
Enochrus halophilus				+		
Graptodytes pictus	+	+			+	
Gyrinus substriatus						+
Haliplus apicalis			+			
H. lineatocolis	+	+				+
H. ruficollis	+	+	+	+	+	
H. wehnkei						+

Table 8.2.3 (contd.)

	Gwent Levels[a]	Somerset Levels[b]	North Kent marshes[c]	Essex coast[d]	Suffolk coast[e]	Lyth, Cumbria[f]
Helophorus brevipalpis	+	+	+	+		+
H. grandis						+
H. minutus	+			+		
H. obscurus				+		+
Hydraena riparia						+
Hydrobius fuscipes		+		+	+	+
Hydroporus angustatus	+					
Hydroporus palustris	+	+			+	+
H. planus				+	+	
H. pubescens					+	
H. tesselatus						+
Hygrotus inaequalis	+	+	+	+	+	
Hyphydrus ovatus	+	+				
Laccobius bipunctatus	+	+			+	
Laccophilus minutus		+				
Noterus clavicornis	+	+	+	+	+	
Ochthebius minimus		+		+		
Porhydrus lineatus	+	+				
Rhantus frontalis				+		
Scirtes spp	+				+	
Crustacea						
Asellus aquaticus	+				+	+
A. meridianus				+		
Crangonyx pseudogracilis						+
Gammarus duebeni			+	+		
G. zaddachi			+			
Palamontes varians			+			

Grazing marsh areas are associated with review sites as follows:

[a] Severn Estuary
[b] Bridgwater Bay
[c] South Thames Marshes, Medway Estuary, Swale Estuary
[d] Colne Estuary, Blackwater Estuary, Dengie Flat, Crouch-Roach Estuary
[e] Orwell Estuary, Deben Estuary, Ore-Alde-Butley Estuary, Blyth Estuary
    Morecambe Bay

grazing marshes. The scarce diving beetle *Hydaticus transversalis* is now virtually restricted to the Gwent and Somerset Levels and Moors. The emerald dragonfly *Lestes dryas* (RDB2) has its stronghold in the ditches of the Essex grazing marshes. It has, however, recently been found in a few inland freshwater sites since its rediscovery (in 1983) after being considered extinct in Britain during the 1970s.

A much larger group of national rarities are amongst the more common or characteristic species of the grazing marshes but are not restricted to such places. They include the scarce soldier fly *Odontomyia tigrina*, the nationally scarce hairy dragonfly *Brachytron pratense*, the scarce blue damselfly *Coenagrion pulchellum*, the scarce diving beetle *Rhantus grapii* on the Somerset and Gwent Levels, and the scarce soldier fly *Stratiomys singularior*, the meniscus midge *Dixella attica* (RDB3), and the three scarce diving beetles *Agabus conspersus*, *Dytiscus circumflexus* and *Rhantus frontalis* on the Essex and Kent grazing marshes.

Environmental features influencing ditch invertebrate faunas

In areas of permanent pasture three factors dominate the structure and species richness of the invertebrate communities. These are the position of the ditch in the hydrosere, the soil type and the salt concentration.

Ditches are highly artificial systems with a rapid hydroseral succession leading to drier conditions of much less conservation significance than their wet state. The intervention of man keeps ditches at various stages of development from open water to fully clogged with vegetation (see also Section 8.1.12). There is a general trend for the more frequently maintained ditches to support a richer aquatic fauna that also contains more uncommon species than neglected ditches. This situation reflects the greater range of habitats available in a ditch with a mixed vegetation structure of emergent marginal plants as well as floating and submerged species. Emergent plants eventually dominate ditches that are not cleaned and may eradicate the open-water habitat and many of the invertebrate species associated with it. Associated with management intensity is water depth. In general, species richness and rarity decline rapidly in water shallower than 30 cm in freshwater ditches. Exceptions are, however, the brackish marshes of the Essex and Kent coasts where water may be only 15 cm deep yet still support an important fauna. This is largely because Essex and Kent grazing marshes have a large proportion of ephemeral, summer-dry ditches which support uncommon but mobile invertebrate species when they are flooded.

TWINSPAN (Two-way Indicator Species Analysis – Hill 1979) classifications of aquatic samples from the Somerset Levels and Moors and the Gwent Levels showed broad similarities in the features that characterised the main invertebrate communities (Drake *et al.* 1984; Drake 1986). Most samples were classified into a few large groups that reflected the hydroseral stage so that communities in wide deep ditches, smaller typical ditches with a varied vegetational structure, and those dominated by emergent vegetation in shallower water were distinguished in both TWINSPAN classifications. The coastal element of the fauna was, however, poorly represented in these western grazing marshes in comparison with the brackish Kent and East Anglian marshes where the coastal fauna is the dominant component.

Nearly all coastal grazing marshes where the invertebrates have been surveyed are on clay soils since these soils are largely derived from estuarine sediments. A few marshes on the Suffolk coast, however, notably around Sizewell (outside review sites) and on Morecambe Bay, are partly on peat. Inland, peat and alluvium occur more frequently and grazing marshes on these substrata support a range of species additional to those generally found on coastal levels.

Salinity has a pronounced effect on the aquatic invertebrate community structure. Not only do coastal specialists appear on marshes subject to brackish influence but there is also a marked decrease in species richness as a result of several major groups being poorly represented in such places. For example, on freshwater marshes there are typically more than 20 species of molluscs, over 10 species of dragonflies and up to nine species of leeches. In contrast in slightly brackish ditches leeches are usually absent, only two species of snail, *Lymnaea peregra* and *Potamopyrgus jenkinsi* are normally present, and the only frequently occurring dragonfly is the common damselfly *Ischnura elegans*, apart from the localised presence of the scarce emerald dragonfly on the East Anglian coast. Amongst other invertebrate groups several of the most abundant

and widespread species of freshwater ditches appear intolerant of even mildly brackish (oligohaline) water. At least 14 such species (the hoglouse *Asellus aquaticus*, the amphipod *Crangonyx pseudogracilis*, the mayflies *Cloeon dipterum* and *Caenis robusta*, the pond-skater *Gerris lacustris*, the saucer bug *Iliocoris cimicoides*, the caddis *Athripsodes aterrimus*, *Limnephilus lunata*, *L. flavicornis* and *L. marmoratus*, the china mark moth *Cataclysta lemnata*, and the beetles *Agabus sturmii*, *Anacaena globulus* and *Graptodytes pictus*) are, however, found in ditches carrying fresh water from the hinterland across otherwise brackish marshes.

Replacing these freshwater species in oligohaline ditches is a different, distinct, assemblage of coastal species, a large proportion of which is nationally scarce as a consequence of the scarcity of the habitat. Among the more frequently occurring species on the Kent, Essex and Suffolk grazing marshes are the amphipods *Gammarus duebeni* and *G. zaddachi*, the water-boatman *Sigara stagnalis*, the caddis *Limnephilus affinis* and the beetles *Agabus conspersus*, *Enochrus halophilus*, *Graptodytes bilineatus*, *Halipus apicalis*, *Limnoxenus niger* and *Berosus affinis*. Slightly brackish conditions may be essential to maintain healthy populations of some of these species found on the eastern grazing marshes, for example the water-boatmen *Sigara stagnalis* and *S. selecta* and the beetles *Agabus conspersus*, *Coelambus parallelogrammus*, *Halipus apicalis*, *Enochrus halophilus*, *E. bicolor*, *Ochthebius marinus*, *O. viridis* and most colonies of *Helophorus alternans*.

Many species that are characteristic of oligohaline water are, however, also found in smaller numbers at inland sites. Hence their distribution can be described as predominantly coastal although the ecological basis for such distributions has yet to be established. This predominantly coastal distribution occurs in, for example, the water-boatmen *Corixa affinis* and *Notonecta viridis,* the scarce emerald dragonfly, and the water-beetles *Graptodytes bilineatus*, *Dytiscus circumflexus*, *Gyrinus caspius* and *Ochthebius punctatus*.

An even more curious distribution occurs in the beetles *Limnoxenus niger*, *Berosus signaticollis* and *Helophorus alternans*. These species are locally frequent in brackish grazing marshes and saltmarshes but are also occasionally found inland at peaty sites.

In strongly brackish ditches, for example those immediately behind sea-walls where the ditches may contain more than 10% sea water, species richness is lower still. Large obligate halophile crustaceans, notably *Gammarus* spp. and the prawn *Palamonetes varians*, are frequently dominant. Other typically estuarine species such as *Sphaeroma* spp., *Neomysis intiger* and the mud snail *Hydrobia ulvae* can also occur in such ditches. Insects are poorly represented and, except for some chironomid larvae, are rarely numerous.

8.2.12 Conservation of terrestrial invertebrates

Compared with many other facets of conservation science, there has been a historical neglect of terrestrial invertebrate conservation in Britain. The current work on invertebrate conservation is aimed chiefly at assembling information on rare species and important sites so as to integrate practical conservation measures for invertebrates more fully into general conservation practice. A particular problem for invertebrate conservation is that it must not only address the often complex and widely differing conservation needs of species but also seek to conserve a great many species. Compared with many other groups of organisms, there are a very large number of terrestrial invertebrate species in Britain, for example, about 22,500 species of insects and about 7,500 species in other macro-invertebrate groups such as spiders, molluscs, woodlice, millipedes, centipedes and crustaceans (NCC 1989). Many of these species have specialised requirements which are as yet poorly understood. Lack of information is even more of a difficulty in the case of micro-invertebrate groups such as mites, of which there are about 2,000 British species currently known, and nematodes (about 1,000 species). So even basic distributional information is still needed for many invertebrates. Detailed ecological knowledge is even more sparse. This is in marked contrast to some other groups such as birds and vascular plants.

Many invertebrates have annual life cycles and so cannot survive even relatively brief periods when environmental conditions become unsuitable. This makes them susceptible to local extinctions. Furthermore many species, especially insects, have complex life-cycles in which one or more early stage has very different needs from those of the more mobile adult animals. For example the horsefly *Atylotus latistiatus* (RDB3) has larvae that inhabit estuarine mud, adult females which require a blood meal and males which feed on nectar from plants such as sea-lavender *Limonium* spp. This means that the conservation of habitat mosaics, both in terms of vegetation structure and different adjacent habitats, is of particular importance for invertebrates, whose needs may not always be served by the selection of a single habitat series as the basis of site safeguard (NCC 1989). Since estuaries are composed of such habitat mosaics (see Section 8.1.1), the general approach needed for the effective conservation of estuarine ecosystems is thus also entirely appropriate for terrestrial invertebrates.

All this means that the task of assessing the conservation needs of invertebrate species and assemblages is very substantial. The development of invertebrate conservation is being furthered through the NCC's Invertebrate Site Register (ISR), begun in 1980, which seeks to identify threatened species and sites with a significant terrestrial or semi-terrestrial invertebrate fauna. The ISR currently holds information on over 6,700 sites, and on about 15,000 species including 5,390 species of Red Data Book or nationally scarce status. Sites are graded as to their importance, proven or potential, for invertebrate conservation, based on the occurrence of characteristic faunas and the presence of scarcer stenotypic species. Information from the ISR is documented in a series of reports, detailing sites of known or suspected value in each county of Britain. Reviews of the national distribution, status, ecology and conservation needs of scarcer species have been prepared for most major taxonomic groups of invertebrates, enabling a more meaningful interpretation of information presented on individual sites. Reviews of the invertebrate faunas of individual habitat formations, including those associated with estuaries, are currently in preparation.

Several hundred ISR sites occur on review sites, with large estuaries frequently being divided into smaller habitat sub-units for analysis of their invertebrate fauna. Of these estuarine ISR sites, 52 sites have been graded "A" within the ISR (sites of national importance, equivalent to NCR on the basis of the invertebrate fauna), and a further 86 sites graded "B" (equivalent to SSSI). Analysis and grading are not yet complete for the whole of Britain, and for Scotland in particular need to be reassessed in the light of increasing knowledge of species' distribution and status.

In addition to the ISR, invertebrate conservation is supported by more intensive surveys of some habitats and areas, targeted at providing clearer information on the occurrence of invertebrates of special interest and of the effects of management practices on faunal abundance and composition. Such surveys currently include a study of East Anglian fens, including parts of the Norfolk Broads adjacent to the tidal rivers of Breydon Water. Several more detailed autecological studies into threatened species aim to both refine conservation management for these species and give insights into the fundamental principles of invertebrate conservation. The current study of the autecology of several rare moths includes the Essex emerald *Thetidia smaragdaria* which in 1987 had declined to a single known population of less than fifty caterpillars from one estuarine saltmarsh but for which there is now a captive breeding population (Waring 1990).

SSSIs may be selected purely for their invertebrate interest, particularly for the presence of threatened species and/or their diverse assemblages with strong habitat affiliation. In practice viable populations of most of the commoner or widespread invertebrate species are covered by sites selected for their habitat representation, so it is the rarer, more specialised species for which SSSIs are generally selected on invertebrate grounds (NCC 1989).

As well as its provisions for safeguarding wildlife through the SSSI series (see Chapter 9), the Wildlife & Countryside Act also provides special protection for a small number of terrestrial invertebrates listed in Schedule 5 of the Act. These include the Essex emerald moth, which was only the second species of insect to be afforded special legislative protection, under the Conservation of Wild Creatures & Wild Plants Act 1975.

Although it is as yet difficult to set Britain's terrestrial invertebrate fauna in an international context, some species are covered by international conventions, notably the Bern Convention, which lists invertebrates in its appendices, and the Ramsar Convention (see Chapter 9), which includes invertebrates amongst the wildlife features of wetlands appropriate for designation as wetlands of international importance.

8.2.13 Threats to terrestrial and non-marine invertebrates

The terrestrial invertebrate fauna of estuarine habitats is vulnerable to a variety of human influences but is also threatened in some instances by the natural succession of vegetation change. Pollution, particularly by spilled oil, may also pose a threat to intertidal and supralittoral invertebrates, but examples of damage to this fauna in pollution incidents have yet to be demonstrated.

The most significant threats to the fauna of sand-dunes come from the effects of human disturbance, usually from leisure activities. The thousands of trampling feet of holidaymakers, sand-sliding children and beach buggies have caused severe erosion of many dune systems and loss of vegetation cover and diversity. Many dunes have been irreversibly damaged by the siting of caravan sites and golf courses, and simple activities such as beach bonfires and barbecues may destroy the habitat of species dependent on driftwood. Perhaps this has been the fate of the staphalinid beetle *Cafius cicatricosus* (RDB1). This beetle was known from the strandline of several beaches on the British south coast, but it has not been found since 1908, at Southsea and Milton Creek (Hamps.) (Shirt 1987). In some heavily used areas, special beach-cleaning machines are now used and these effectively remove all strandline habitat important to the invertebrate species described above. Afforestation has also caused major losses of dune invertebrate habitat. The majority of dune systems that still support very rich dune faunas are now sites under some form of conservation protection, mostly as National or County Trust Nature Reserves, or are protected from leisure activity by their use as military areas, such as at Tywyn Point in Carmarthen Bay.

Compounding the habitat destruction and degradation caused by human agency, natural vegetation succession towards coarse grassland and scrub through lack of grazing has also reduced the area of useful invertebrate habitat on a number of protected sites.

Many of Britain's estuarine saltmarshes are very heavily grazed by sheep, considerably reducing their potential for terrestrial invertebrates. The introduction of grazing on previously ungrazed saltmarsh can be very damaging to its invertebrates. Removal of grazing on heavily grazed saltmarsh tends to lead to a dominance by low-diversity rank grassland, without the saltmarsh herb species on which many of the invertebrates depend. The invasion of cord-grass *Spartina anglica* into estuarine systems also has considerable potential for damaging invertebrate faunas, ultimately reducing saltmarsh vegetation diversity and isolating established saltmarsh faunas from tidal influence. Particularly damaging on saltmarsh has been the truncation of the natural vegetation succession by the construction of sea-walls at the landward end, with the loss of much of the most floriferous vegetation of the upper saltmarsh and any natural transition to other habitats. It is ironic that one of Britain's rarest moths, the Essex emerald *Thetidia smaragdaria*, should now survive in the wild on only a few individuals of its foodplant *Artemisia maritima*, growing on the very sea-walls that have in part led to the loss of its natural habitat.

In addition to the general threats to wildlife on grazing marshes, such as conversion to arable, silage production or intensive grazing, the heavy management of ditches, lowering of water tables, and eutrophication, there are some factors that particularly affect invertebrates. The most damaging operations are those that reduce the available range of sizes, water depths and vegetation structures of ditches , particularly in the botanically less interesting ditches towards the end of the hydrosere. These tend to receive less attention from conservationists, yet they support a range of invertebrates not found in more intensively managed ditches. This is especially true of oligohaline ditches, which are aesthetically and often botanically unappealing yet support large numbers of rarities such as the scarce emerald dragonfly.

As most terrestrial and freshwater invertebrates have annual life-cycles, they are vulnerable to even temporary loss of habitat. So, wide man-induced fluctuations in water level that lead temporarily to lethal conditions, such as freezing in winter or drying-out in summer, can locally damage populations. A large proportion of ditch species prefer the narrow zone at the margin of ditches so that re-profiling to produce steep smooth sides removes a valuable part of the habitat. Fencing both sides of ditches to exclude stock also prevents them from trampling down the profile of the margins, which would render them more favourable for aquatic invertebrates.

8.2.14 References

BALL, S.G. 1986. *Terrestrial and freshwater invertebrates with Red Data Book, notable or habitat indicator status.* Peterborough, Nature Conservancy Council. (Invertebrate Site Register report No. 66.)

BRISTOWE, W.S. 1958. *The world of spiders.* London, Collins. (New Naturalist Series.)

DRAKE, C.M. 1986. A survey of the aquatic invertebrates of the Gwent Levels. *Nature Conservancy Council, Contract Surveys,* No.1.

DRAKE, C.M. 1988a. *A survey of the aquatic invertebrates of the Essex grazing marshes.* Peterborough, Nature Conservancy Council. (England Field Unit Report No. 50a.)

DRAKE, C.M. 1988b. *A survey of the aquatic invertebrates of the Suffolk grazing marshes.* Peterborough, Nature Conservancy Council. (England Field Unit Report No. 50b.)

DRAKE, C.M. 1989. Diptera from the Gwent Levels, South Wales. *Entomologist's Monthly Magazine, 124,* 37-44.

DRAKE, C.M. FOSTER, A.P., & PALMER, M. 1984. A survey of the invertebrates of the Somerset Levels and Moors. *Nature Conservancy Council, CSD Report,* No. 572.

DUFFEY, E. 1968. An ecological analysis of the spider fauna of sand dunes. *Journal of Animal Ecology, 37,* 641-674.

EMMET, A.M., PYMAN, G.A., & CORKE, D. 1985. *The larger moths and butterflies of Essex.* London, Essex Field Club.

EVERSHAM, B.C., GREATOREX-DAVIES, J.N., & HARDING, P.T. 1989. Inner Thames Marshes SSSI, Rainham. Report on preliminary invertebrate survey at Wennington and Aveley marshes. Monks Wood, ITE. (Institute of Terrestrial Ecology Report, Project T13061a1.)

FOSTER, G.N. 1990. Maps of Hydraenidae. *Balfour-Browne Club Newsletter, 48,* 3-8.

FOSTER, W.A., & TREHERNE, J.E. 1975. The distribution of an intertidal aphid *Pemphigus treherni* Foster, on marine saltmarshes. *Oecologia, 21,* 141-155.

FOSTER, W.A., & MORTON, R.B., 1981. Synchronisation of activity rhythms with the tide in a saltmarsh collembolan *Anurida maritima. Oecologia, 50,* 265-270.

FOSTER, W.A., TREHERNE, J.E., EVANS, P.D., & RUSCOE, C.N.E. 1979. Short-term changes in activity rhythms in an intertidal arthropod (Acarina: *Bdella interupta* Evans). *Oecologia, 38,* 291-301.

HARDING, P.T., & SUTTON, S.L. 1985. *Woodlice in Britain and Ireland: distribution and habitat.* Monks Wood, Institute of Terrestrial Ecology.

HEATH, J.R., & EMMET, A.M., eds. 1983. *The moths and butterflies of Great Britain and Ireland. Volume 10.* Colchester, Harley Books.

HEYDEMANN, B. 1979. Responses of animals to spatial and temporal environmental heterogeneity within salt marshes. *In: Ecological processes in coastal environments,* ed by R.L. Jefferies and A.J. Davy, 145-163. Oxford, Blackwells.

HILL, M.O. 1979. *TWINSPAN – a FORTRAN program for arranging multivariate data in an ordered two-way table by classification of the individuals and attributes.* Ithaca, New York, Cornell University.

LEGG, G., & JONES, R.E. 1988. *Pseudoscorpions.* London, Linnean Society. (Synopsis of the British Fauna No. 40.)

MCLEAN, I.F.G. 1982. The Gwent Levels. A report on the terrestrial invertebrates recorded in July 1981. Peterborough, Nature Conservancy Council (unpublished report).

NATURE CONSERVANCY COUNCIL. 1989. *Guidelines for the selection of biological SSSIs.* Peterborough, Nature Conservancy Council.

PALMER, M. 1980. A survey of the aquatic fauna of the North Kent Marshes, 1980. Peterborough, Nature Conservancy Council (unpublished report).

PLANT, C.W. 1987. *The invertebrate fauna of Purfleet Army Range, Essex.* Wye, Nature Conservancy Council. (Report to NCC South-East England Region.)

ROBERTS, M.J. 1985. *The spiders of Great Britain and Ireland. Volume 1.* Colchester, Harley Books.

ROBERTS, M.J. 1987. *The spiders of Great Britain and Ireland. Volume 2.* Colchester, Harley Books.

SHIRT, D.B., ed. 1987. *British Red Data Books: 2. Insects.* Peterborough, Nature Conservancy Council.

SOUTHWOOD, T.R.E., & LESTON, D. 1959. *Land and water bugs of the British Isles.* London, Frederick Warne & Co.

STUBBS, A.E., MCLEAN, I.F.G, & SHEPPARD, D. 1982. The North Kent Marshes. A report on the terrestrial invertebrates recorded in July and September 1980. Peterborough, Nature Conservancy Council (unpublished report).

TREHERNE, J.E., & FOSTER, W.A. 1977. Diel activity of an intertidal beetle, *Dicheirotrichus gustavi* Crotch. *Journal of Animal Ecology, 46,* 127-138.

WARING, P. 1990. Conserving Britain's rarest moths. *British Wildlife, 1,* 266-284.

WHITE, I.M. 1988. Tephritid flies. Diptera, Tephritidae. *Handbook for the identification of British insects. Volume 10, Part 5a.* London, British Museum (Natural History).

8.3 Aquatic estuarine communities

Contents

Summary

Britain's shallow seas support a rich and varied mosaic of plant and animal communities, the species composition being determined by factors such as substrate type, salinity and degree of wave and tidal exposure. In the intertidal and subtidal parts of estuaries conditions range from exposed marine systems at the mouths of river estuaries and on open coast estuaries, to tidal and predominantly freshwater conditions in the upper reaches. A classification of aquatic estuarine communities, based on the NCC's Marine Nature Conservation Review (MNCR) classification, has been developed for the Estuaries Review and has been used in the description of communities on 102 estuaries.

Seventeen hard shore communities and 16 soft shore communities occur in estuaries. Individual hard shore community types typically occur only intertidally or subtidally, but 63% of soft shore communities occur in both situations. Many hard shore communities are also those characteristic of non-estuarine marine areas. Most are restricted to the outer parts of only a few estuaries: only two hard shore communities occur on more than 20% of Estuaries Review sites.

One is a **sheltered rocky shore community**, typically with dense growth of knotted wrack, found mostly in the outer parts of rias, fjords and fjards in south-west England and northern Scotland.

Rocky shore communities are most diverse on estuaries in south-west England and south Wales, and scattered sites in Scotland. They are largely absent from eastern England, where soft sediments predominate.

Soft shore community types are more widespread, with five communities being found on more than 20% of estuaries. These include an **exposed sand community** dominated by small crustaceans and polychaete worms in outer parts of estuaries; **mussel beds**, widespread around Britain in both intertidal and shallow subtidal parts of estuaries; and **beds of marine grasses** associated with the lower intertidal mud and muddy sand areas within estuaries.

The other two soft shore communities are particularly widespread, occurring on over 80% of assessed estuaries throughout Britain: a **muddy sand community** in areas of variable or normal salinity, and a **mud community** in more sheltered areas of variable or reduced salinity. Muddy sand is dominated by lugworms, although intertidally cockles, Baltic tellins and several polychaete worms are also abundant. Mud in intertidal and shallow subtidal parts of estuaries is dominated by clams and worms, typically ragworms. Small snails and crustaceans are also abundant.

Estuaries of major marine conservation interest are currently those with many different aquatic communities, but some individual scarce communities are also significant.

These include the **maerl beds** (maerl is a delicate coral-like alga) of the Fal Estuary, Helford Estuary and Milford Haven; a **sand or muddy sand community** dominated by razor shells on a few sites in south-west England and Wales and the Outer Hebrides; and the rich fauna of a **muddy gravel community** in outer estuaries and marine inlets of south and south-west Britain.

The aquatic estuarine communities of many intertidal parts of estuaries are covered by conservation designations such as Sites of Special Scientific Interest (SSSIs) but few subtidal areas are yet afforded such protection either statutorily through designation of Marine Nature Reserves, or non-statutorily, e.g. Marine Conservation Areas (MCAs).

8.3.1 Introduction

The seas around Great Britain support the highest diversity of marine habitats, communities and species of anywhere on the European Atlantic coast. The extensive soft sediment shores and near-shore subtidal areas included in the Estuaries Review form a significant part of the British marine resource (3% of the area within British Territorial Waters – see also Chapter 6). Many of the aquatic estuarine habitats, communities and species inhabiting these areas are of significant marine nature conservation importance.

This Chapter reviews the aquatic estuarine communities that have been recorded from Estuaries Review sites and discusses, as far as is currently possible, their individual distributions and conservation importance on a national and international basis. The description of these communities has, in itself, only been possible through the development for this review of a classification of British aquatic estuarine communities. The development of the classification has proved complex, since each estuary has a differing set of characteristics, based on geomorphology, bathymetry, freshwater input and substrata, that affect community structure. Furthermore there is an absence of sharp boundaries between many of the aquatic communities and there are gross variations in community structure over Great Britain as a whole. These gross variations result from changes in component species around the country, reflecting the presence of different marine biogeographic regions.

The resulting classification defines communities using physical and chemical characteristics and species of macroscopic non-mobile flora and fauna, i.e. predominantly the algae and invertebrates of the system. Where relevant there is also reference to other parts of these communities, notably fish and birds. In general, however, these organisms high in the food web are not covered in this section. The importance of British estuaries for fish and birds are described further in Chapter 8.4 and Chapter 8.6 respectively. For conservation purposes, those invertebrate groups that are largely terrestrial or freshwater in habit are assessed independently from marine systems. Such terrestrial and non-marine invertebrates on estuaries are described in Chapter 8.2.

The classification covers the range of aquatic estuarine communities which are typical of open coasts with negligible freshwater inflow, to those typical of river estuaries with marked gradients in salinity caused by the dilution of sea water by fresh water inflows. Estuaries contain aquatic communities in both their intertidal and subtidal zones which differ from those found on the open coast. At their mouths the communities can be exceptionally species-rich. However the fauna of estuaries with variable salinity is generally poor in numbers of species (Barnes 1974), although it is often rich in numbers and biomass of individuals (Chapter 4). This is partly due to the inability of many freshwater species to inhabit saline conditions and of many marine species to withstand anything but full salinity (Figure 8.3.1). Salinity, although important, is not the only feature which can affect the distribution of marine organisms. In certain situations the degree of shelter and water turbidity, and the uniformity of the substratum, can also be very important. Different community types are defined within the Estuaries Review classification using these different physical characteristics.

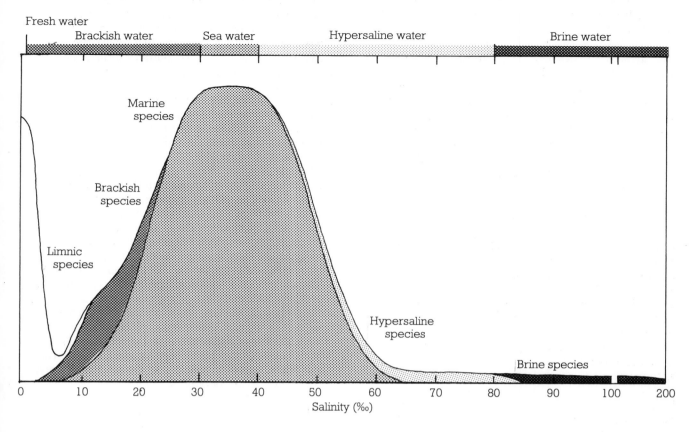

Figure 8.3.1 Quantitative relations between aquatic invertebrate species occupying fresh, brackish, sea, hypersaline or brine water. For each salinity (0‰ – 200‰), the relative number of species is indicated by the vertical extension of the respective areas (derived from Kinne 1971).

The species which can tolerate variable or lowered salinity estuarine conditions can be grouped into recognisable and characteristic species assemblages or communities. The term 'community', used above and throughout this part of the review, is not intended to imply any interdependence between the individual species, although spatial and resource competition can occur.

Although aquatic estuarine communities occur in all 155 review sites around Britain, detailed information for all of them was not available to us during the preparation of this chapter. The community distributions described below are based on marine biological information from 102 of the sites (Figure 8.3.2). Data for several additional sites has subsequently become available, but too late for incorporation. It should be recognised, therefore, that the distributions described below are likely in many cases to be minima and do not necessarily document the full distribution of each community around review sites. Nevertheless these analyses do serve our primary purpose of describing the broad patterns of distribution of aquatic estuarine communities around the British estuarine resource. In reading the descriptions that follow it should be noted that we have included the presence of a community on a review site only where surveys have documented the presence of

the plant and animal species characteristic of that community, and not just from the known presence of a particular substrate. Hence the distributions of the broad types of estuarine habitat (subtidal, rocky intertidal shores and tidal flats) described in Chapter 8.1 are generally known to be more widespread than the known distribution of the communities described in this chapter. The current extensive survey work underway for the NCC's Marine Nature Conservation Review will extend this comparable information base for more review sites and communities.

Many communities, particularly those of soft substrata, occur both in the intertidal and subtidal whilst others occur exclusively in the subtidal. In all, Table 8.3.1 shows that 69% of soft substrata communities occur both above and below low water mark. This is in marked contrast to the communities of hard substrata such as rocky shores (Table 8.3.2). These communities almost all occur either exclusively in the intertidal or in the subtidal, with only 11% occurring in both parts of the estuary. In this chapter intertidal rock communities have been distinguished from subtidal rock communities by the use of the word *shore* in the community name, i.e. sheltered rocky *shore* community compared to (the subtidal) variable salinity rock community.

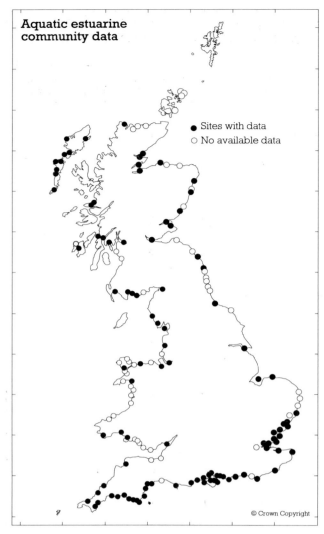

Aquatic estuarine community data

● Sites with data
○ No available data

© Crown Copyright

Figure 8.3.2 The 102 Estuaries Review sites for which aquatic estuarine communities could be assessed for this report. Note that the known presence of a broad habitat type alone was not adequate for the assessment of communities. Collection and collation of community information continues as part of the NCC's Marine Nature Conservation Review.

Details of how habitats and communities are classified are given in Appendix 6. The criteria which are applied to produce marine conservation assessments are outline in Section 8.3.6 and considered in more detail in Appendix 8.

8.3.2 Description of aquatic estuarine habitats and communities

Background to marine classifications

A classification system is useful in helping to categorise the marine environment as a series of habitats and associated communities and in the preparation of inventories of the resource. The results can be used to assist in the development of an overall marine conservation strategy allowing conservation assessments to be made for, and

between, different areas. A classification also aids the identification of rare or particularly threatened examples of marine communities and species and so enables attempts to be made to conserve these examples, whether by voluntary or legislative procedures.

Since the start of this century there have been several notable attempts to produce a classification system which could be used to describe marine communities in the north-east Atlantic using physical and biological features. Petersen (1913, 1915) made a start on the classification of sediments and his approach was followed and expanded by workers such as Ford (1923), Spark (1929), Thorson (1957) and Holme (1966). Jones (1950) and Glemarec (1973) also classified sediment communities but on a different basis from the 'characteristic species' approach used by Petersen and his followers. Borgensen (1905) used a classic phytosociological approach to describe hard substratum algal communities and this is the approach followed by other botanists, such as Den Hartog (1959) and Tittley et al. (1985). The rocky shore studies of Ballantine (1961) and Lewis (1964) did not attempt a comprehensive classification but their work, together with that of the phytosociology school and of Stephenson & Stephenson (1972), greatly helps us to separate different types of rocky shore communities. Hiscock & Mitchell (1980) and Erwin (1983) tackled subtidal habitats and associated communities, particularly those of rocky substrata, not closely following any previous workers. Augier (1982) has come closest, so far, to classifying marine habitats and communities on the basis of both environmental factors and the plants and animals present. Augier's work is, however, based on the Mediterranean, and although many of these studies are still considered classic pieces of research, no overall detailed classification system for Britain, covering the communities which occur on both hard and soft substrata, has yet emerged. The NCC is, however, undertaking research which will lead to the development of just such a classification system (see below).

In practice, the production of a classification system for marine habitats and communities is problematical, but the advantages to be obtained from developing such a system outweigh any potential disadvantages. The difficulty of gathering marine data on a standardised and therefore directly comparable basis is a major complication. For instance, whereas sediments can be sampled quantitatively and the organisms present in them are amenable to counting, those on rock live in a very heterogeneous habitat where quantification is difficult, and the particularly short time available during SCUBA dives forces the use of semi-quantitative techniques. Even more fundamental are the problems of placing into a clear framework the infinite variations displayed by community composition and habitat features, such as substrate composition, wave exposure and exposure to tidal currents. The marine classification system must also meet the requirements for which it was developed, which, for the NCC, are usually the

Table 8.3.1 Summary of the major marine communities which occur on soft substrata at Estuaries Review sites. Communities have been ranked by salinity tolerance(s) and by their occurrence in the intertidal and subtidal zones.

Community name [1]	Typical substratum and characteristic situation	Intertidal	Subtidal	Normal salinity	Variable salinity	Reduced salinity
CLEAN SAND COMMUNITY	Coarse sand, moderately exposed to wave action. Primarily occurs on clean well-sorted sandy beaches.	●	●	●		
SAND/MUDDY SAND COMMUNITY	Sand, or muddy sand, sheltered from wave action and tidal currents. Occurs on the open coast and in estuaries.	●	●	●		
GRAVEL/SHELL GRAVEL COMMUNITY	Gravel or shell gravel.		●	●		
MAERL COMMUNITY	Gravel or shell gravel in weak, to very strong, tidal currents.		●	●		
BEDS OF THE HORSE MUSSEL *MODIOLUS MODIOLUS*	Occurs in moderately strong tidal currents on a wide range of substrata, predominantly muddy gravels or mud.		●	●		
ALGAL COMMUNITY ON SEDIMENT SURFACE	Associated with a wide variety of sediments in a wide range of tidal currents from weak to moderately strong.		●	●		
MUDDY 'OFFSHORE' SAND COMMUNITY	Muddy sand sheltered from wave action and tidal currents.		●	●		
EUROPEAN OYSTER *OSTREA EDULIS* BEDS	Associated with a wide range of substrata.	●	●	●	●	
EXPOSED SAND COMMUNITY	Coarse and medium sand exposed to wave action.	●	●	●	●	
COMMON MUSSEL *MYTILUS EDULIS* BEDS	Sand, gravel or pebbles, sheltered from wave action but exposed to tidal currents. An open coast and estuarine community.	●	●	●	●	
CURRENT-SWEPT SAND COMMUNITY	Coarse sand or muddy gravel moderately exposed to tidal currents. It occurs on the open coast and estuaries, in areas subject to tidal scouring or turbulence.	●	●	●	●	
MUDDY GRAVEL COMMUNITY	Muddy gravel sheltered from wave action and tidal currents. It occurs in the outer parts of estuaries.	●	●	●	●	
NORMAL/VARIABLE SALINITY MUDDY SAND COMMUNITY	Muddy sand sheltered from wave action and tidal currents. An open coast and estuarine community.	●	●	●	●	
EELGRASS *ZOSTERA* SPP. BEDS[2]	Fine gravel, sand or mud sheltered from wave action and significant tidal currents. An open coast and estuarine community.	●	●	●	●	●
VARIABLE/REDUCED SALINITY MUD COMMUNITY	Mud, or occasionally muddy sand, sheltered, or extremely sheltered, from wave action with negligible tidal currents. Occurs in estuaries.	●	●		●	●
REDUCED SALINITY MUD COMMUNITY	Mud in extreme shelter at the top of estuaries, at the limit of marine influence. Species diversity extremely reduced.	●	●			●

[1] For information on other community names which have been used in the classification systems found in the literature see Appendix 7
[2] Individual species of *Zostera* have different habitat and salinity preferences. Data presented are for the genus as a whole.

Table 8.3.2 Summary of the major marine communities which occur on hard substrata at Estuaries Review sites. Communities have been ranked by salinity tolerance(s) and by their occurrence in the intertidal and subtidal zones.

Community name [1]	Typical substratum and characteristic situation	Intertidal	Subtidal	Normal salinity	Variable salinity	Reduced salinity
EXPOSED ROCKY SHORE COMMUNITY	Open coast rocky shore exposed to wave action.	●		●		
MODERATELY EXPOSED ROCKY SHORE COMMUNITY	Open coast rocky shore exposed to moderate wave action.	●		●		
SHELTERED ROCKY SHORE COMMUNITY	Open coast rocky shore sheltered from wave action which can also occur at the mouth of estuaries.	●		●		
SABELLARIA REEF COMMUNITY	A predominantly open coast community which occurs on hard substrata in areas subject to sand scour and moderately strong tidal currents.	●	●	●		
EXPOSED ROCK COMMUNITY	Rock exposed to wave action. An open coast community.		●	●		
SHELTERED ROCK COMMUNITY	Rock sheltered from wave action. An open coast community which can occur in estuaries but in areas of normal salinity.		●	●		
HYDROZOAN/BRYOZOAN TURF COMMUNITY	Boulders, cobbles and coarse sediment. An open coast community which occurs in areas subject to moderately strong tidal currents.		●	●		
SLIPPER LIMPET *CREPIDULA FORNICATA* BEDS	Cobbles, pebbles, coarse gravel and shells in areas swept by moderately strong, or strong, tidal currents. A south coast community which can occur on the open coast and in estuaries.		●	●	●	
ARTIFICIAL SUBSTRATA COMMUNITY	Artificial substrata in areas swept by moderately strong tidal currents.		●	●	●	
CURRENT-EXPOSED SHELTERED ROCKY SHORE COMMUNITY	The lower parts of rocky shores subject to significant tidal currents.	●			●	
VARIABLE SALINITY ROCKY SHORE COMMUNITY	Rocky shore sheltered, to extremely sheltered, from wave action. An estuarine community. Species diversity reduced.	●			●	
VARIABLE SALINITY CLAY COMMUNITY	Clay sheltered from wave action, usually in strong tidal currents.	●	●		●	
VARIABLE SALINITY ROCK COMMUNITY	Rocky substrate which is sheltered, or very sheltered, from wave action. Tidal currents very variable, ranging from weak to very strong. An estuarine community. Species diversity reduced		●		●	
VARIABLE (MAINLY REDUCED) SALINITY ROCKY SHORE COMMUNITY	Rocky shore sheltered, to extremely sheltered, from wave action. Occurs in estuaries, predominantly in the middle or upper reaches. Species diversity very reduced.	●			●	●
VARIABLE (MAINLY REDUCED) SALINITY ROCK COMMUNITY	Rocky substrata sheltered, to extremely sheltered, from wave action in predominantly the middle or upper reaches of estuaries. Species diversity very reduced.		●		●	●

Table 8.3.2 (contd.)

Community name [1]	Typical substratum and characteristic situation	Intertidal	Subtidal	Normal salinity	Variable salinity	Reduced salinity
REDUCED SALINITY ROCKY SHORE COMMUNITY	Rocky shore extremely sheltered from wave action at the top of estuaries, at the limit of marine influence. Species diversity extremely reduced.	●				●
REDUCED SALINITY ROCK COMMUNITY	Rocky substrata extremely sheltered from wave action at the top of estuaries, at the limit of marine influence. Species diversity extremely reduced.		●			●

[1] For information on other community names which have been used in the classification systems found in the literature see Appendix 7

description and conservation evaluation of nearshore marine and estuarine areas. Various, usually descriptive, methods have been used and a description of the strategy and methods used in marine work by the NCC can be found in Hiscock (In prep.).

The development of survey strategy and methods, and of a system for the classification of marine habitats and associated communities, has been undertaken as a part of the NCC's Marine Nature Conservation Review (MNCR). The classification will fulfil a similar role to that of the National Vegetation Classification (Rodwell in press) which is now of central importance in the selection of terrestrial sites of botanical nature conservation importance.

The MNCR was initiated in 1987 and was designed to extend knowledge of British marine ecosystems, identify sites of marine nature conservation importance by virtue of the importance of the habitats, communities and species present, and provide a broad base of information to support the more general measures required to combat the adverse effects of development and pollution. The MNCR has utilised information and ideas from some of the studies mentioned earlier, especially those of Borgensen (1905), Petersen (1915), Jones (1950), Den Hartog (1959), Bishop & Holme (1980) and Augier (1982), and has used them to develop a hierarchical and robust classification system. There have been earlier systems, such as the classification developed by the NCC and the Royal Society for Nature Conservation and the initial classification developed by Coordination of Information on the Environment (CORINE). These, however, enable marine descriptions to be made only for intertidal or very shallow submerged areas and have the additional drawback that they have been based on vegetation characteristics alone. These classification systems were clearly inadequate for use with the MNCR as they could not deal with the broad spectrum of habitats and communities known to occur in the marine environment. A new system was required.

The MNCR classification system is based on a

catalogue of definitive terms for describing marine sites and habitats. A complementary scheme for the identification of the community types associated with major site and habitat groupings is now being developed, the definitions of community types being based predominantly on the macrofaunal and macroalgal species present. Details of the MNCR marine ecosystem classification system are given in Appendix 6. This classification system is currently being developed and has been tested on work for the Irish Sea Study Group, a major study describing the ecology of the Irish Sea (O'Connor 1990). Additional studies, such as the Directory of the North Sea Coastal Margin, will help to develop and expand the range of habitats and communities covered.

The MNCR system has so far been developed only for fully marine situations and does not yet take account of occurrences of greatly lowered salinity, except where this is a localised effect of, for instance, a stream crossing a beach; a 'stand-alone' classification of habitats and communities associated with variable or reduced salinity has yet to be formulated. It has been necessary, however, to describe these communities specifically for the Estuaries Review for the reasons mentioned above. The community descriptions in this section are, therefore, of a preliminary nature and represent only the rudiments of an MNCR aquatic estuarine habitat and community classification system proper; the 'community' approach and salinity divisions used may change considerably as more research and survey work is carried out. Nevertheless it provides a functional system which makes it possible for the first time to discuss the distribution, abundance and conservation importance of aquatic estuarine habitats and communities on a Great Britain basis.

The Estuaries Review aquatic estuarine habitat and community classification

The aquatic estuarine habitat and community classification is structured according to the MNCR classification (Appendix 6) and thus, in effect, extends the MNCR system into estuarine or reduced salinity conditions. The classification produced for the Estuaries Review covers the habitats and communities present in estuaries *sensu stricto* and also those present in the open coast (full salinity) sites.

The classification was developed using the information from a wide range of survey reports and papers held on a computer database and drew particularly upon data held by the NCC, in particular the MNCR, and, to a lesser extent, on data held by outside bodies. The database was used to produce listings of species and/or communities by carrying out searches for particular features such as salinity range, substratum type or species composition. The results of the searches were then combined with information obtained from the literature to produce a basic but satisfactory initial classification system.

In the short timescale of this phase of the Estuaries Review, it was usually possible to consult only one major report, paper or symposium volume for each review site. For some sites no sources of suitable material were obtained in time for inclusion in the review, while for others no suitable studies have yet been carried out (Figure 8.3.2). However, more than enough information was obtained to make the general statements required for the purposes of this project; the information covers 102 (66%) of the 155 review sites – most of the remainder are small sites. The community abundances and distribution maps in this chapter are therefore far from complete; a recorded absence from a particular site may reflect the restricted amount of literature consulted rather than the true distribution of the community concerned. Details of the database are given in Appendix 7. Communities have been described purely in terms of their macrofaunal and macroalgal species as this represents the bulk of available data; data based on the smaller faunal and algal species exist but have not been included in this preliminary classification.

One major problem encountered in the classification of estuaries is how to divide up the variable salinity regime which occurs in estuaries. Several systems were considered, including the Venice system (a classification based on salinity gradients and most applicable to large estuaries), and studies conducted by a number of workers, including Den Hartog (1959), Remane (1971) and Wilkinson (1980), were consulted. Wilkinson (1980) noted that the Venice system was not universally applicable; one major problem is that each estuary is hydrographically individual, and so precisely similar algal distributions in relation to hydrographically correlated factors would not be expected in every estuary. After consideration, the classifications based on precise salinity gradients were rejected in favour of a simpler system revolving around a much broader division into normal (less than 40‰ but greater than 30‰), variable (less than 30‰ but greater than 18‰) or reduced (less than 18‰) salinity. This more basic approach is appropriate in view of the extreme variability of survey data and the fact that the bulk of marine ecological data on macrofauna and

macroalgae are not easily incorporated into a more precise classification system; very few surveys have exact and repeatable salinity measurements attached to them. In addition, the majority of Britain's estuaries are comparatively small, containing well-mixed or slightly stratified waters (Gameson 1973). In these conditions, variations in freshwater inflow may have a profound, probably seasonal, influence on local salinity levels, and thus it will always be extremely difficult to formulate a British estuarine classification system based on a salinity gradient of measurable, discrete units. In fact, such a system would have little utility.

8.3.3 Aquatic estuarine communities and their distribution

Thirty-three different major aquatic estuarine communities are identified as occurring at Estuaries Review sites (Table 8.3.1, Table 8.3.2). 20 of these communities have been recorded from the intertidal areas of review sites and 26 communities from the subtidal regions. 13 of the communities occur in both the intertidal and subtidal zones. In the intertidal zone nine communities occur in more than one salinity division. In the subtidal zone this number increases to 11 communities. Such a separation into intertidal and subtidal communities is usual in marine research as it recognises the different environmental conditions experienced by intertidal species from those encountered by species permanently submerged in fully saline or brackish water, in the subtidal zone. The communities have not been separated on the basis of intertidal or subtidal zones within the text descriptions, for reasons of economy of space.

The communities, and their associated habitats, have been named for the purposes of the Estuaries Review using key environmental features, e.g. 'exposed sandy shore community' or 'reduced salinity rocky shore community'. This has been necessary as some of the communities have not been named before. It also avoids the problems encountered in the past, particularly with sediment communities, when researchers named communities after a characteristic species, e.g. *Macoma* community (Petersen 1913), or the *Arenicola* community (Bishop & Holme 1980). The species involved may not in fact occur in every example of that community type but the use of the species name in the community title implies it. It also erroneously implies that the species may be the most important one in the community. In addition, species undergo taxonomic name changes which makes their use in community names undesirable, e.g. the *Tellina* community described by Bishop & Holme (1980) was named after a bivalve, *Tellina tenuis*, which has since been renamed *Angulus tenuis*. Details of the other community names which can be applied are given in Appendix 7 (Table A7.1).

In the following section the major estuarine communities are described in terms of salinity, exposure to wave action and currents, substrata composition and characteristic species and/or taxa. Only major community types have been covered in this preliminary classification. Minor communities will be incorporated as the classification is developed.

The communities have been divided into those which occur on soft substrata followed by the less widespread communities found on hard substrata. Technical terms have been kept to the necessary minimum in the text. The variation in species composition within each community is described, using examples, but only a limited number of characteristic or important species have been mentioned in each community description; many more species will in reality be present. The distribution of the communities, whether fully or partially known, is described and provisional community conservation assessments are given, but only where these have been made in the original source material (see earlier). Differences between the provisional conservation assessments made for a given community, in different review sites, are explained within the appropriate community description sections. The basis on which these conservation assessments are made is described further in Section 8.3.6. It is important to remember throughout the following sections that a conservation status refers only to that particular marine community and may not therefore be a guide to the overall marine nature conservation importance of the estuary on which the community occurs.

Where feasible, maps are provided to illustrate the documented distribution of the communities. As more information is analysed, or becomes available from new marine surveys, the distribution of community types will change; however the maps do provide an overall, but *provisional*, indication of the distribution of each community. In a similar way care should be taken over the interpretation of tables showing the relative abundance of communities (Table 8.3.3, Table 8.3.4) and those showing the relative conservation importance of communities (Figure 8.3.37, Figure 8.3.38). Both assessments will be subject to change as more data become available.

Communities on soft substrata

Sediments are a major feature of British estuaries and, by area, dominate the range of habitats available for colonisation by aquatic estuarine organisms. Nationally the estuaries and open coast sites included in this review account for most of the Great Britain resource of intertidal soft substrata. The inclusion of sites with extensive areas of sediment was one of the guiding principles of the review and accounts for the site selection criteria which were employed; the selection criteria have already been described in Chapter 5.

Coastal plain and bar-built estuaries are predominantly infilled by post-glaciation sediment; hard substrata are rare, occurring mainly in the

form of small boulders, cobbles or pebbles. In these systems sediments form an essential part of the dynamic estuarine system, e.g. sediment forms the bars of bar-built estuaries. In other types of inlets, such as rias, fjards and fjords, sediment areas are not so common and areas of rock are present.

The commonest types of estuarine soft substrata are sands and muds and this fact is reflected in the high abundance of the communities which colonise these habitats. Together, the normal/variable salinity muddy sand community, and the variable/reduced salinity mud community, account for the bulk of the estuarine soft substratum types, both in terms of area and frequency of occurrence. Such estuarine communities are physiologically 'stressed' by a lowered salinity regime and so the species which may occur are fairly predictable. In the more fully marine situations, where low salinity is not a 'stress' on the communities, species composition is much more varied and less easy to predict. Included here are the less common communities such as the sand/muddy sand community, the muddy gravel community and the muddy 'offshore' sand community.

The interest of soft substrata communities is not purely marine. The biomass of sediment communities, particularly estuarine ones, may be exceedingly high, providing an essential source of food for many species of migrant and wintering waders and wildfowl.

Gravel/shell gravel community

In lower shore fully marine gravel/shell gravel, a community can develop which includes burrowing echinoderms such as the heart urchins *Spatangus purpureus* and *Echinocardium flavescens* and a range of bivalve molluscs, including *Nucula hanleyi*, *Glycymeris glycymeris* and *Dosinia exoleta*. The community is predominantly an open coast one and has rarely been recorded from review sites (Figure 8.3.3). It has been described in the intertidal zone from the Yealm Estuary in Devon and a particularly rich example of the community has been recorded from around the jetty in Kentra Bay, on the west coast of Scotland. The Intertidal Survey Unit (Bishop & Holme 1980) noted that in northern Britain the community is found more frequently on the open coast, where it is often associated with maerl gravel. The community can also occur in the subtidal zone, predominantly in the shallow waters between the Isle of Skye and mainland Scotland. Although no provisional conservation assessments have been made for this community it should be noted that the Yealm Estuary site was provisionally graded by Powell *et al.* (1978) as of national marine biological importance.

A similar community, including the bivalve *Spisula solida*, occurs in current-exposed coarse sands and gravels and was described by Bishop and Holme (1980). This may be a poorly developed example of the gravel/shell gravel community and has been included here until more information becomes

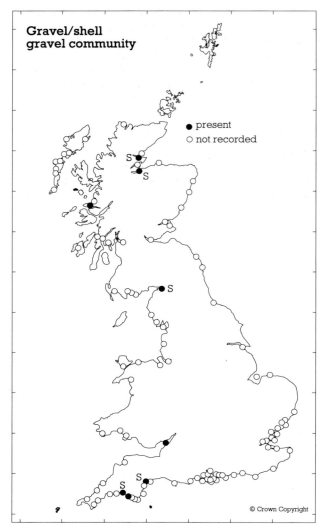

Figure 8.3.3 Provisional assessment of the distribution of the gravel/shell gravel community on in the 102 review sites for which marine data were examined. (S denotes sites with the *Spisula* variant of this community.)

available. The *Spisula* community variant has been recorded from a number of estuaries in the west of Britain (Figure 8.3.3). In the intertidal zone it has been documented from the Exe Estuary and Plymouth Sound (Powell *et al.* 1978), and in the subtidal from the Solway Firth (Perkins 1973), the Severn Estuary (Warwick & Davies 1977) and the mouths of the Dornoch and Moray Firths (Hunter & Rendall 1986). The Solway example is poorly developed, while in the Severn Estuary the community dominates the large sand banks formed by the strong tidal streams resulting from the exceptionally large tidal range. No provisional community conservation assessments have been made although the Exe Estuary was considered by Bishop & Holme (1980) to be overall of national marine biological importance.

Overall the gravel/shell gravel community is one of the rarer soft substrata communities to occur in estuaries. Records indicate that it occurs in only 8% of review sites for which marine data have been examined (Table 8.3.3).

Beds of the calcareous alga maerl *Phymatolithon calcareum and Lithothamnion corallioides*

Maerl beds occur subtidally on gravel/shell gravel in areas of normal salinity that are exposed to a reasonable degree of tidal current. The general distribution is one of open or enclosed coasts with an absence from inlets with lowered salinity. Maerl are calcium-depositing red algae, similar to the *Corallinacea* which form pinkish-red growths over rock surfaces. As maerl grows, it can form unattached, delicate, pinkish purple twig-like structures which, grouped together, form 'beds' on the gravel surface, or it can smother small pebbles to produce a 'hedgehog-like' effect. The community associated with maerl is most similar to the muddy gravel community (see below) but additional species may frequently be found in association. These species include a number of fish, polychaetes and foliose and filamentous red algae, including ephemeral species such as *Scinaia turgida*.

Within Estuaries Review sites, maerl beds have been recorded only from some of the ria systems in

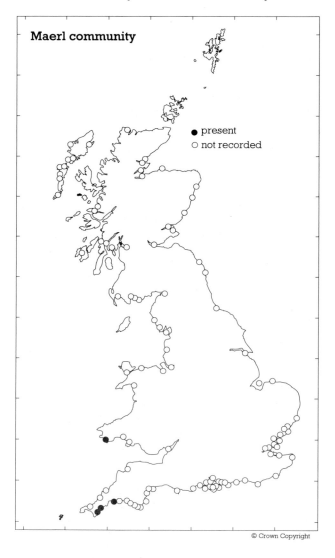

Figure 8.3.4 Provisional assessment of the distribution of the maerl community on the 102 review sites for which marine data were examined

Table 8.3.3 The documented abundance of some of the major aquatic estuarine communities on soft substrata in review sites, ranked in order of decreasing frequency of occurrence. Information is also provided for each community on the number of review sites for which provisional conservation assessments have been made. Care should be taken in interpretation of this table; the relative abundance of some communities will change as more data become available. Insufficient data are available on the reduced salinity mud community for its inclusion in the table. NA indicates that no conservation assessments have yet been made.

Community name	Abundance[1] of Community (%)	Abundance[1] of review sites for which conservation assessments have been made (%)
Variable/reduced salinity mud community	84	20
Normal/variable salinity muddy sand community	79	18
Beds of *Zostera* spp.	36	8
Common mussel *Mytilus edulis* beds	29	6
Exposed sand community	22	6
European oyster *Ostrea edulis* beds	18	NA
Clean sand community	16	NA
Algal community on sediment surface	12	NA
Current-swept sand community	12	NA
Sand/muddy sand community	11	6
Muddy gravel community	8	6
Gravel/shell gravel community	8	NA
Horse mussel *Modiolus modiolus* beds	5	1
Maerl community	4	3
Muddy 'offshore' sand community	3	2

[1] Abundance expressed as a percentage of the total number of sites *for which marine data have been examined*, at which the community occurs.

south-west Britain (Figure 8.3.4). The community is rare, occurring in only 4% of the review sites. Maerl is present in the Fowey Estuary (Hiscock in prep.) but only develops into 'beds' in the Helford Estuary (Rostron 1987), on St Mawes Bank in the Fal Estuary (Rostron 1985) and near Stack Rock in Milford Haven (Little & Hiscock 1987). Maerl is delicate and the community is therefore very susceptible to damage resulting from man's activities, particularly those which would either crush the maerl or alter the hydrodynamic regime of the inlet, causing the dispersal or silting-up of the beds. The most extensive and best developed maerl bed is found in the Fal Estuary, covering some 150 ha of seabed, and possessing two species of maerl, compared with just one in Milford Haven. The northern species of maerl, *Lithothamnion glaciale*, has not been recorded from review sites.

Maerl is regarded as of high conservation interest, owing to its limited distribution, fragility and the species-rich communities which it supports; this is reflected in the provisional community conservation ratings which have been applied (see Figure 8.3.37). The Fal Estuary maerl bed has been designated as a Voluntary Marine Nature Reserve (formerly the Roseland Marine

Conservation Area), a designation which was also applied, in 1988, to the Helford Estuary. Furthermore, Bishop & Holme (1980) concluded that, overall, the Helford Estuary could be considered of international marine biological importance for its sediment communities, while the Fal Estuary is of national marine biological importance.

Exposed sand community

The community occurs predominantly on normal salinity shores, generally consisting of coarse or medium sands that are exposed to wave action on the open coast or to tidal currents. The latter situation can occur inside estuaries along the sides of sand banks beside low-water channels; the steep slope of the sand allows it to dry out and, together with sediment mobility, precludes the development of any other community type. Such a situation may be exposed to lowered salinity levels. Conditions of wave or tidal exposure result in very mobile sediments which can be inhabited by only a limited number of very mobile species of invertebrates. The community is dominated by crustaceans, mainly small amphipod species such as *Haustorius arenarius* and *Pontocrates norvegicus*, and polychaete worm species such as *Nephtys cirrosa*,

Malacoceros fuliginosus and *Paraonis fulgens*. No species of bivalve molluscs are present as the wave exposure is too great. Under exposed conditions few species are present in the sand, but where the exposure is slightly less the number of species increases, although the dominance by Crustacea and Polychaetes is maintained.

The subtidal community is very similar to that in the intertidal zone. Additional species include sandeels *Ammodytes* spp. in the sediment and hermit crabs *Pagurus bernhardus* on the surface of the sediment.

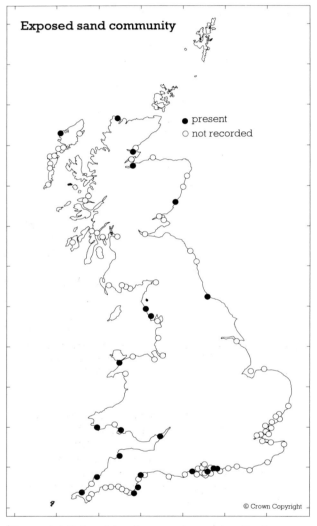

Figure 8.3.5 Provisional assessment of the distribution of the exposed sand community on the 102 review sites for which marine data were examined

The community has been documented as present at 22% of Estuaries Review sites distributed throughout Britain (Figure 8.3.5). The communities so far assessed have been of mainly low marine biological conservation interest (Figure 8.3.37). Of note, however, is the community present in West Angle Bay in Milford Haven. The Intertidal Survey Unit concluded that this was the best example of this community in south-west Wales (Bishop & Holme 1980). They also noted that the example of

the community on the sediment flats by West Ryde (Wootton Creek review site) was the best developed example in Hampshire.

Under certain circumstances a variant of this community occurs where the polychaete *Ophelia bicornis* is characteristically present. *Ophelia* occurs in Britain only in the Exe Estuary in Devon (Dixon 1986), the Loughor Estuary in south Wales (Moore 1989) and in Langstone Harbour (Dixon & Moore 1987). The highly restricted distribution of this community variant is reflected in the comparatively higher community assessment ratings which have been made for these examples (Figure 8.3.37).

Clean sand community

The clean sand community occurs on normal salinity beaches, consisting of clean sand under moderate exposure to wave action, but where there is sufficient protection to allow colonisation by some species of bivalve molluscs. The community also occurs in the subtidal zone. The bivalve mollusc *Angulus tenuis* and a slightly

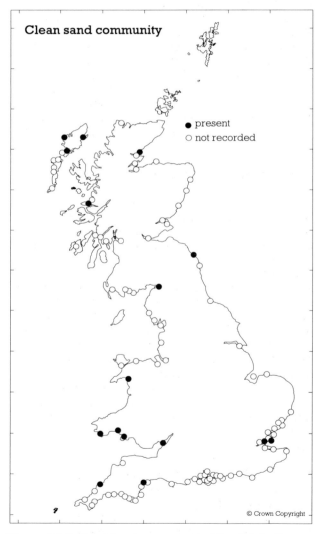

Figure 8.3.6 Provisional assessment of the distribution of the clean sand community on the 102 review sites for which marine data were examined

larger species of bivalve, *Donax vitattus*, may occur, depending on the fluctuating success of spatfall, along with other species typically found on wave exposed shores and belonging to the exposed sandy shore community described above. The clean sand community is best developed at mid- to low-tide levels on clean sandy beaches in land-locked bays, and the species are mostly tolerant of slightly brackish conditions, although the community as a whole does not penetrate far into estuaries owing to its dependence on sand with a low silt and clay fraction.

The community is one of the commoner sediment communities to occur on Estuaries Review sites (Figure 8.3.6); information from the literature documents the presence of the community in 16% of review sites (Table 8.3.3). The community occurs throughout Britain on moderately exposed beaches in, for example, the Outer Hebrides (Powell *et al.* 1979a), and inside inlets at the edges of, or on, sand banks, such as in Loch Fleet (Wells & Boyle 1975) and the Solway Firth (Perkins 1973). A well developed example of this community occurs in the Loughor Estuary (Powell *et al.* 1979b), while a variant of the typical community is present on Pendine Sands in south Wales (Bishop & Holme 1980). In the smaller, well drained inlets in west Wales the community occupies the low, beach-like area in the middle of the estuary, penetration further up the estuary being restricted by lowered salinity (Cook & Rees 1978). Too few assessments have been made of the conservation importance of this community to enable an overall appraisal to be given here.

Common mussel *Mytilus edulis* beds

In some areas the surface of sediments, consisting primarily of sand, gravel or pebbles, may become dominated by partial, or complete, cover of the bivalve *Mytilus edulis*, the common mussel. Mussel beds occur in both the intertidal and subtidal zones, in normal or variable salinity, in areas exposed to water currents. Species which commonly occur on mussel beds include barnacles, the periwinkles *Littorina saxatilis* and *Littorina littorea* and the brown fucoid algae, *Fucus vesiculosus* and *Fucus serratus*. Subtidally the mussels may provide anchorage points for a number of species of small hydroids and Bryozoa, the variety of which will be greater in more fully marine situations. Rich interstitial communities can develop between the individual mussels, while large populations of the starfish *Asterias rubens*, which feed on the mussels, may also be present.

Mussel beds are recorded at a large number of review sites (29%) distributed throughout Great Britain (Figure 8.3.7). The examples which have been assessed so far are regarded as predominantly of low marine conservation importance. There are exceptions, however, such as the mussel bed communities present in the Loughor Estuary. Moore (1989) considered the rich and diverse mussel community at Whiteford

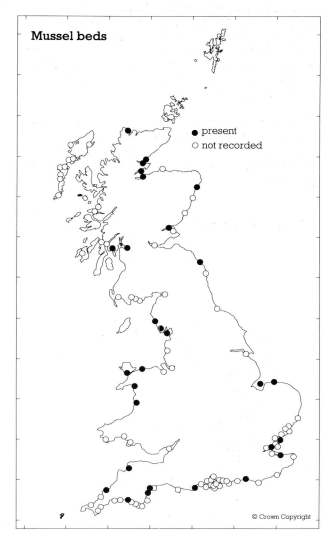

Figure 8.3.7 Provisional assessment of the distribution of common mussel *Mytilus edulis* beds on the 102 review sites for which marine data were examined

Point, especially on the lower shore, to be of high marine biological importance. It should also be noted that in certain situations mussel beds contribute to the value of estuarine systems which have been given high provisional marine conservation ratings, such as the Exe Estuary (Bishop & Holme 1980).

Horse mussel *Modiolus modiolus* beds

On muddy gravels with shells, or on mud with shells, in subtidal areas exposed to strong water currents, horse mussel communities can occur. These are dominated by the horse mussel *Modiolus modiolus* accompanied by a characteristic assemblage of species including hydroids, sponges and bivalves, notably the queen scallop *Aequipecten opercularis*.

Horse mussel beds have been recorded from a limited number (5%) of review sites distributed throughout Britain (Table 8.3.3). The distribution is illustrated in Figure 8.3.8 In some locations, notably the Firth of Forth, the populations are just outside the seaward review site boundaries but

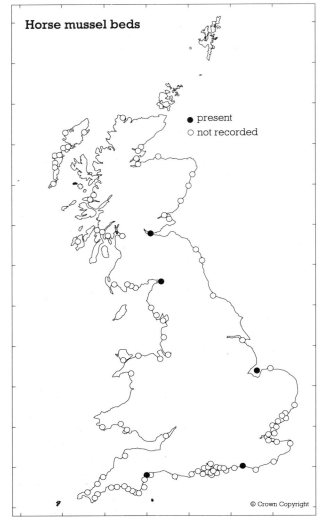

Figure 8.3.8 Provisional assessment of the distribution of horse mussel *Modiolus modiolus* beds on the 102 review sites for which marine data were examined

have been included here as they are such an important feature of the estuarine systems. In inlets most of the horse mussel beds are poorly developed, as in the mouth of the Exe Estuary (Dixon 1986) and in The Wash (Fowler 1987). The *Modiolus* populations form scattered clumps on the seabed. The only example of a *Modiolus* bed on the same scale as the large epifaunal beds which are so characteristic of this species in many Scottish lochs, occurs near the bridges in the Firth of Forth where Elliott and Kingston (1987) reported densities of up to 1,312 m^{-2}. The *Modiolus* communities present in Estuaries Review sites have accordingly been considered as of comparatively low provisional marine biological importance.

European oyster *Ostrea edulis* beds

Beds of the familiar European oyster *Ostrea edulis* can develop on the lower shore or in the subtidal zone on a wide range of substrata from mud and muddy gravels to bedrock and spat collectors. The community usually develops under sheltered conditions and its occurrence may be highly dependent on local fishery activities, which result in the re-laying or artificial 'seeding' of areas.

Oyster beds are distributed predominantly in the southern waters of Britain (Figure 8.3.9), especially in sheltered south east and south coast inlets, and have been recorded from 18% of review sites.

There is little information on the marine nature conservation importance of oyster populations.

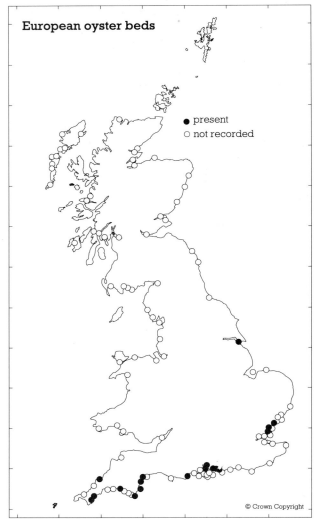

Figure 8.3.9 Provisional assessment of the distribution of European oyster *Ostrea edulis* beds on the 102 review sites for which marine data were examined

Populations have, however, been reduced steadily this century by introduced pests, diseases, overfishing and declining water quality.

Algal community on sediment surface

A distinctive algal community may develop on the surface of sediments in the shallow subtidal zone in areas which are usually exposed to water currents. The community consists primarily of the kelp *Laminaria saccharina* and the bootlace-like alga, *Chorda filum*. In southern regions of Great Britain the alien invasive alga, *Sargassum muticum* or 'Japweed', may be especially common. A wide variety of other smaller algae frequently occur. The community often exists in association with a variety of other sediment surface or infaunal communities.

The community has been documented as present on 12% of review sites. This is certainly an underestimate of the distribution of the community, as detailed in Figure 8.3.10, and probably results from the community not being recognised as distinct by past workers. The marine biological importance of the community is very much dependent on whether or not it occurs in association with other communities. The basic community of *Laminaria saccharina* and *Chorda filum* is of comparatively low (local) interest. In some situations, however, it can be of national importance, such as in the mouth of the Helford Estuary, where it occurs in association with a rich variety of algae on pebbles, gravel and shells (Rostron 1987). Under other conditions the community may develop on sediments which have a rich infaunal community, such as in Salcombe and Kingsbridge Estuary (Hiscock 1986). This may raise the conservation importance of the community complex of which it forms a part to the level of regional marine biological importance.

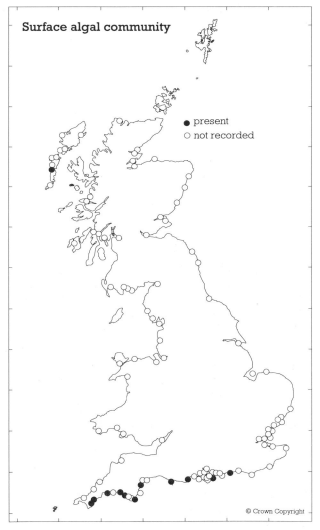

Figure 8.3.10 Provisional assessment of the distribution of the algal (*Laminaria saccharina/Chorda filum*) community on the 102 review sites for which marine data were examined

Current-swept sand community

Current-swept sands can be colonised by high densities of the tube-dwelling polychaete worm, *Lanice conchilega*. The community mainly occurs on the lower shore of sandy beaches or subtidally in areas which are subject to tidal scouring or turbulence. This community, termed the *Lanice* community by Bishop & Holme (1980), is only considered a distinct community where *Lanice conchilega* occurs at high densities. In lower densities *Lanice* occurs as a component of other communities, notably the clean sand community, the common mussel community, the sand/muddy sand community or the normal/variable salinity muddy sand community. The *Lanice* community is not mentioned in other literature, but has been included here to maintain compatibility with the MNCR classification system.

The community has been recorded from 12% of the review sites examined (Table 8.3.3). This is almost certainly an under-representation of the distribution, resulting from the fact that, previously, few workers have recognised this as a community in its own right. It probably occurs throughout Britain, where conditions are suitable, and not predominantly in the south, as indicated in Figure 8.3.11. It has been recorded in the intertidal zone, from the fjard systems in the Outer Hebrides to ria systems in south-west Britain. Very extensive intertidal beds are present in The Wash (R Mitchell pers. comm.). A rich population is present on Pilsey Sand in Chichester Harbour (Bishop & Holme 1980). Subtidally it has been recorded from inlets such as The Wash (Fowler 1987). It is inappropriate, in view of the under-recording of this community, to talk in detail about provisional marine biological importance. However, it should be noted that the community does occur in inlets which, as a whole, have been given high provisional conservation ratings, such as the Fal and Exe Estuaries (Bishop & Holme 1980).

Sand/muddy sand community

The community is found in normal salinity clean or slightly muddy sand. Slight variations in substratum composition will have a profound influence on species composition and abundance. Such sensitivity to substratum composition results in extremely diverse combinations of species which, for simplicity, have been grouped within the broad heading of 'sand/muddy sand community'. Well developed examples of the community can occur under relatively sheltered conditions where they may be associated with beds of eelgrass *Zostera marina*. The community occurs from the lower shore down to depths of 65 to 70 m. The razor shell *Ensis siliqua* is the predominant bivalve in the intertidal zone and may co-dominate this community, under moderately exposed conditions, with the burrowing echinoderm, *Echinocardium cordatum*. Under more sheltered conditions a wider range of species may be present, including polychaete worm species such as *Chaetopterus*

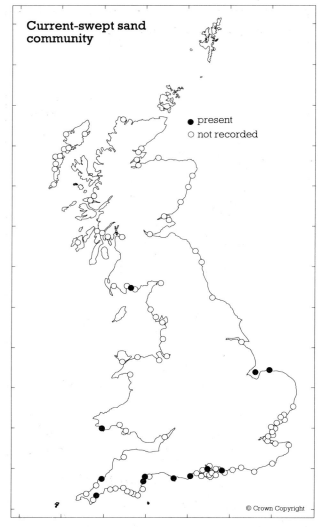

Figure 8.3.11 Provisional assessment of the distribution of the current-swept sand community on the 102 review sites for which marine data were examined

recorded as present. Bishop & Holme (1980) comment that these two bivalves have not been recorded from any other examples of this community.

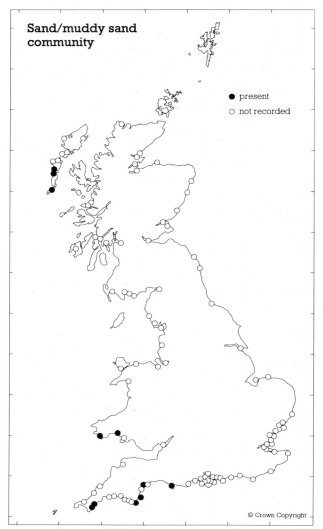

Figure 8.3.12 Provisional assessment of the distribution of the sand/muddy sand community on the 102 review sites for which marine data were examined

variopedatus, *Magelona papillicornis* and *Notomastus latericeus*; bivalve mollusc species such as *Cerastoderma edule*, *Gari fervensis*, *Lutraria lutraria* and *Angulus squalidus*; and a small assortment of 'brittlestar' starfish, burrowing anemones and burrowing holothurian 'sea cucumbers'. In the subtidal zone the community can be very similar except that the razor shell *Ensis siliqua* is replaced by the bivalve mollusc species *Chamelea gallina*.

The community has been recorded from 11% of sites investigated (Table 8.3.3), and occurs throughout Britain, predominantly in the west. The distribution stretches from the Outer Hebrides (Powell *et al.* 1979a) southwards as far as the ria systems of south-west Britain (Figure 8.3.12). Rich examples are recorded from Bagh Nam Faoilean in the Outer Hebrides (Powell *et al.* 1979a), from Mill Bay in the Salcombe and Kingsbridge Estuary (Powell *et al.* 1978), and from Treath on the Helford Estuary (Powell *et al.* 1978). At Small Mouth on The Fleet an unusual variant of this community was described by Bishop & Holme (1980) in which the bivalves *Pandora albida* and *Loripes lucinalis* were

In terms of provisional marine biological importance the community is of comparatively high marine biological interest owing to its sparse distribution and the fact that it can develop rich infaunal communities. This is reflected in Figure 8.3.37 showing the provisional marine conservation assessments which have been made for the community. Examples of such communities of high conservation interest include those present in Plymouth Sound (Hiscock & Moore 1986), Milford Haven (Bishop & Holme 1980; Little & Hiscock 1987) and in the Salcombe and Kingsbridge Estuary (Bishop & Holme 1980; Hiscock 1986).

Muddy gravel community

This community occurs on muddy gravel, sometimes with sand, in the outer parts of estuaries and marine inlets on the lower shore and in the subtidal zone. Once again, like the sand/muddy sand community, considerable species variation may occur within this broad community type. The bivalve mollusc species *Venerupis senegalensis*, which is frequently, but not necessarily, present may sometimes occur in large numbers in muddy gravels with the bivalve *Mya truncata* and, in less muddy conditions, with the razor shell *Ensis arcuatus*. Under more brackish conditions another bivalve species *Mya arenaria* may also be present. In not too stony conditions a number of sedentary polychaete worms may occur including *Amphitrite edwardsi*, *Neoamphitrite figulus*, *Megalomma vesiculosum*, *Myxicola infundibulum* and *Sabella pavonina*. Species of the Sipunculan *Golfingia* may be present and the anemone *Cereus pedunculatus* may be common attached to stones below the surface of the sediment. In the subtidal zone the community is very similar except that, in Southampton Water and the northern shore of the East Solent, the bivalve mollusc *Venerupis senegalensis* may be partially replaced by the alien species of bivalve *Mercenaria mercenaria* (R Mitchell pers. comm.). Also the polychaete species *Sabella pavonina* may on occasion be highly abundant, forming the dominant element in the community.

The community has only been recorded from comparatively few review sites (8%), all of which are located in south or south-west Britain (Figure 8.3.13). Examples include Milford Haven, where the community is present in Angle Bay and around Lawrenny (Powell *et al.* 1979b), the Helford Estuary, around Helford Passage and Treath (Powell *et al.* 1978), the Salcombe and Kingsbridge Estuary (Powell *et al.* 1978), the Fal Estuary (Powell *et al.* 1978) and in the East Solent where *Mercenaria mercenaria* replaces *Venerupis senegalensis* as described above (Holme & Bishop 1980). Examples of where the polychaete *Sabella pavonina* dominates the community occur in a small number of review sites, notably Poole Harbour (Dyrynda 1987; Howard & Moore 1989), The Fleet and Portland Harbour (Howard, Howson & Moore 1988) and The Wash (Fowler 1987). Sparsely developed examples of this community occur at Hurst Spit (Lymington Estuary review site) and at North Haven Point in Poole Harbour (Holme & Bishop 1980). The community is of comparatively high marine biological importance owing to its restricted distribution and the rich infaunal communities which can develop. This is reflected in Figure 8.3.37 which illustrates diagrammatically that the community is primarily of regional interest.

Muddy 'offshore' sand community

This community typically occurs in subtidal ('offshore') muddy sand, although a modified version occurs in more sheltered conditions where deposits are rich in organic material (Jones 1950). Considerable species variation may occur within this broad community type, and, as this community has such a restricted distribution, each example could almost be considered as a distinct

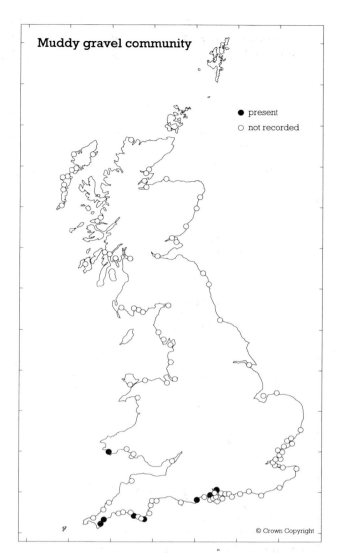

Figure 8.3.13 Provisional assessment of the distribution of the muddy gravel community on the 102 review sites for which marine data were examined

community type in its own right. They have, however, been grouped together under this broad heading for simplicity. Overall a range of species can occur including bivalve molluscs ranging from small species like *Abra alba* to large species like *Arctica islandica*, polychaetes such as *Nephtys incisa* and *Pectinariidae* spp., and the burrowing echinoderm species *Echinocardium cordatum*, *Leptosynapta inhaerens* and *Amphiura brachiata*. On the sediment surface the brittlestar *Ophiura ophiura*, the mollusc *Philine aperta*, and the seapen *Virgularia mirabilis* may also be present. The latter may be co-dominant with the echinoderm *Amphiura brachiata*, mentioned above.

The community is one of the rarest sediment communities to occur on review sites; information in the literature suggests that it is present on only 3% of the sites so far investigated (Figure 8.3.14). The *Virgularia mirabilis* co-dominated community variant has been recorded from a sheltered location in Portland Harbour and was provisionally graded by Howard, Howson and Moore (1988) as of national marine nature conservation importance. Other locations shown in Figure 8.3.14 may be of poorly developed examples or variants of this community.

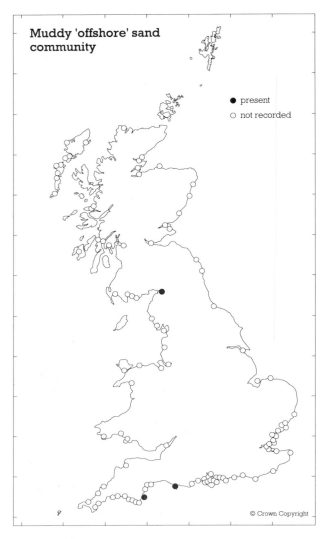

Figure 8.3.14 Provisional assessment of the distribution of the muddy 'offshore' sand community on the 102 review sites for which marine data were examined

Normal/variable salinity muddy sand community

This community is typically dominated by lugworms *Arenicola marina*. Populations of *Arenicola marina* reach their optimum development in the intermediate conditions of muddy sand, but do occur elsewhere in a wide range of sediments from almost pure mud to clean sand. The community occurs in both the intertidal and subtidal zones and has been recorded in the Baltic down to depths of 35 m (Luksenas 1969). Also present in the intertidal zone are a range of polychaete and bivalve mollusc species, including some of the species which occur in the clean sand community, although species such as the bivalve *Angulus tenuis* and some of the small crustaceans may be less common or absent. Typical species include the polychaetes *Pygospio elegans*, *Nephtys*

hombergi, *Scoloplos armiger*, and *Spiophanes bombyx* and the bivalves *Cerastoderma edule* and *Macoma balthica*. The small gastropod snail *Hydrobia ulvae* often occurs on the upper surface of the sediment and on the eelgrasses *Zostera noltii* and *Zostera angustifolia*, which may occur in this community in the upper parts of estuaries. The subtidal community is similar to that present on the shore except that certain species are not present. In particular the bivalve species *Macoma balthica* and *Cerastoderma edule* are generally accepted to be restricted to the intertidal zone (Tebble 1976). Under rare conditions the eelgrasses *Zostera noltii* and *Zostera angustifolia* may occur in the very shallow subtidal zone, but they too are considered as predominantly shore species (see below).

The community is the second commonest soft substrata community to be recorded from Estuaries Review sites. It is present in 79% of the sites investigated so far (Table 8.3.3). It is probably present in more sites than are indicated in Figure 8.3.15, and the community distribution will expand as more information is analysed. The community occurs throughout Britain, although it is absent from estuaries which do not have sediment shores around the mouth and from small estuaries with high freshwater flow. Either set of conditions will preclude the development of this community within the inlet. The community is particularly widespread on sediment flats in the south-east of England (Kay & Knights 1975) and it may occur in association with beds of *Spartina anglica* (Millard & Evans 1984). In conservation terms the community, although widespread, is not of merely local interest (Figure 8.3.37). In some situations it forms part of review site systems which have been highly rated in marine biological terms, such as Bagh Nam Faoilean (Bishop & Holme 1980).

Eelgrass *Zostera* spp. beds

Zostera beds can occur on the surface of sediment inhabited by the sand/muddy sand community, the normal/variable salinity muddy sand community or the variable/reduced salinity mud community. Twelve species of *Zostera* occur in the temperate seas of the world but only three species occur around the coast of Britain (Clapham, Tutin & Moore 1987). The largest of these three species is the eelgrass or grass-wrack, *Zostera marina*, a rhizomatous perennial grass with leaves of up to 1 m in length (Campbell 1976). It occurs on fine gravel, sand or mud, from low-water spring tides down to 4 m, mainly in the sea and fully marine inlets and only rarely in lower salinity estuarine conditions. The two other species, which are commoner in review sites with lowered salinity levels, are the narrow-leaved eelgrass, *Zostera angustifolia*, and the dwarf eelgrass, *Zostera noltii*. *Zostera angustifolia* is smaller than *Zostera marina* and more tolerant of lowered salinity, occurring on mudflats in estuaries and in shallow water, from mid-tide mark down to low water or, rarely, down to 4 m. *Zostera noltii* is smaller still, with leaves only 15 cm long. It occurs in a similar habitat and under similar conditions to *Zostera angustifolia* (Clapham,

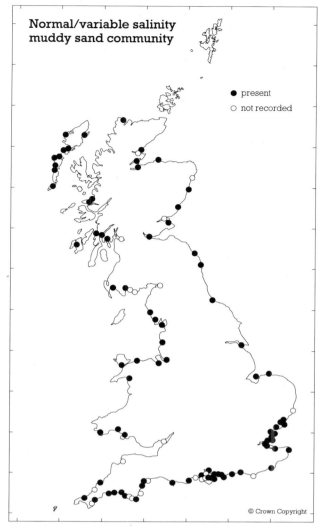

Figure 8.3.15 Provisional assessment of the distribution of the normal/variable salinity muddy sand community on the 102 review sites for which marine data were examined

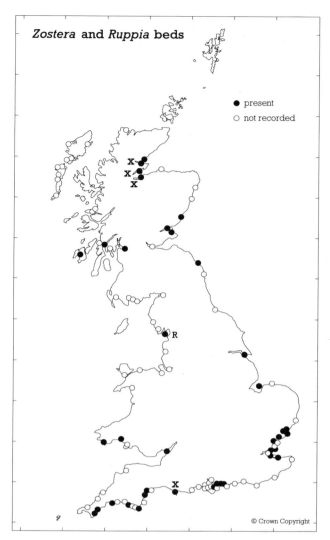

Figure 8.3.16 Provisional assessment of the distribution of beds of *Zostera* spp. and *Ruppia* spp. on the 102 review sites for which marine data were examined. R denotes a site where only *Ruppia maritima* occurs; X denotes sites where both *Ruppia* spp. and *Zostera* spp. occur.

Tutin & Moore 1987). The general distribution of the genus *Zostera*, and for comparative purposes the genus *Ruppia* (a group of brackish water grasses), is given in Figure 8.3.16. but it should be noted that, given the different habitat preferences outlined above, this represents a vast over-simplification of the situation.

Zostera beds occur on 36% of review sites (Table 8.3.3), and good examples can be found in Langstone Harbour (Tubbs 1975a), Portsmouth Harbour (Tubbs 1975b), The Fleet (Holme 1983), the outer Thames Estuary (Wyer, Boorman & Waters 1977) and at Lindisfarne on the Northumberland coast (Connor 1989). The beds in Langstone Harbour are particularly extensive and consist predominantly of *Zostera angustifolia* with small amounts of *Zostera noltii* and, in the subtidal zone, *Zostera marina* (Tubbs 1975a). Beds of *Ruppia* spp. frequently occur in association with *Zostera* beds, and notable examples occur in The Fleet (Holme 1983) and in the Dornoch and Moray Firths (Fox, Yost & Gilbert 1986; Sphere Environmental Consultants Ltd 1981) on the east

coast of Scotland. *Ruppia maritima* is the most widespread species of this genus, while the rarer *Ruppia cirrhosa* is restricted to a few scattered sites such as The Fleet in southern England (Holme 1983).

Zostera beds are particularly important as an invertebrate habitat, nursery areas for species of fish and as an invaluable food source for winter migrant birds, such as brent geese and wigeon. The conservation importance rating of *Zostera* beds takes this into account with most examples being of regional importance and some of national and international importance (Figure 8.3.37).

Variable/reduced salinity mud community

The community occurs in intertidal and shallow subtidal muds in harbours and estuaries, often in conditions of reduced salinity. The bivalve mollusc *Scrobicularia plana* is widespread in suitable intertidal habitats and, under similar conditions of reduced salinity but on more gravelly substrata, the bivalve *Mya arenaria* may occur, often in large numbers. Accompanying polychaete species include the ragworm *Hediste diversicolor*, and *Ampharete grubei* and *Melinna palmata*, in addition to those of the normal/variable salinity muddy sand community. Particularly dense populations of cockles *Cerastoderma edule* can occur under these conditions of lowered salinity. The eelgrass *Zostera noltii* may be present where the substratum is not too soft, and the snail *Hydrobia ulvae* is often common on the surface of the mud and the *Zostera*. Subtidally the community is very similar to that described from the shore except that certain species, notably *Scrobicularia plana*, are absent in the subtidal zone (Tebble 1976). In the intertidal and subtidal zones of Southampton Water the bivalve mollusc *Mya arenaria* may be replaced by the alien bivalve species *Mercenaria mercenaria* (Mitchell 1974).

This community is the most common soft substrata community to occur at review sites, being recorded from 84% of those investigated so far (Table 8.3.3). The community occurs throughout Britain (Figure 8.3.17) but is absent from locations where suitable fine sediment or freshwater influence are not present. Such sites include some of the fjard systems in the Outer Hebrides. The bivalve *Scrobicularia plana*, which is characteristic of this community in England and Wales, appears to be less common in Scotland where it approaches its northern limit. The community, although widespread, is not of merely low marine nature conservation interest, as communities of higher, regional, importance have been described from a wide number of review sites, including the Dart Estuary (Moore 1988b), the Exe Estuary (Dixon 1986) and Oitir Mhor (Bishop & Holme 1980). Nationally important communities have been described from the Loughor Estuary (Moore 1989) in south Wales and from Newton Harbour on the Isle of Wight (Howard, Moore & Dixon 1988).

Reduced salinity mud community

In extremely sheltered conditions and at the top of estuaries, near the limit of marine influence, an extremely species-poor mud community can develop. The intertidal mud can be dominated by vast numbers of oligochaete or tubificid worms, and the surface of the mud usually has a green covering of blue-green algae and diatoms. The bivalve *Scrobicularia plana* may penetrate this far up the estuary as, occasionally, may other marine species including the ragworm *Hediste diversicolor*. Also present may be a species of isopod crustacean, *Cyathura carinata*. In the subtidal zone a similar situation may occur where the mud is dominated by oligochaetes and tubificids. Eels *Anguilla anguilla* and flounders *Platichthys flesus* may also be present, as may salinity-tolerant species of freshwater invertebrates.

The community has been poorly documented but is thought to be widespread and present at the marine limit of many British estuaries. The

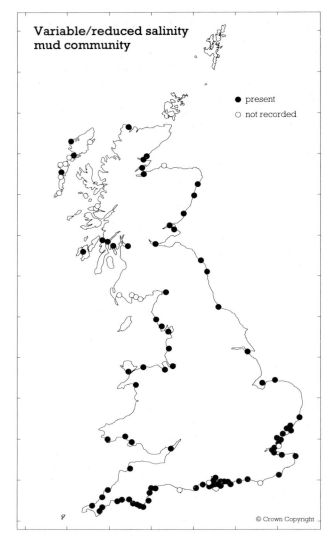

Figure 8.3.17 Provisional assessment of the distribution of the variable/reduced salinity mud community on the 102 review sites for which marine data were examined

community has been described from the Clyde (Wilkinson, Fuller & Rendall 1986) and from the Great Ouse and Nene Estuaries feeding The Wash (Dyer & Grist 1987) and was noted as present in Christchurch Harbour and in the Taw and Torridge Estuary in south-west Britain (D Laffoley *in lit.*).

No information is available concerning the provisional marine biological interest of this community. It is interesting to note, however, that Dyer & Grist (1987), in their study of the benthos of the Great Ouse and Nene Estuaries, recorded a species of oligochaete worm new to Britain in this community.

Communities on hard substrata

Hard substrata in the form of natural rocky shores are a comparatively uncommon feature of estuaries in Great Britain; expanses of rocky shore do not occur on all review sites. Where natural rock outcrops occur is very much dependent on the general geomorphological features of review sites (Chapter 5) and, in particular, on the location of post-glaciation sedimentation.

Rias, fjords and fjards are the most important types of inlet for rocky substrata; sediment deposition is generally restricted and rock is a common substratum in both the intertidal and subtidal zones. Coastal plain estuaries and bar-built estuaries have very little rocky substrata, and what is present is primarily in the form of boulders, cobbles or pebbles. In some locations, where there is a general lack of natural rocky substrata, marine organisms will settle on deposits of empty or live mollusc shells or on artificial hard substrata like piers, pilings and pipelines. This is the case at many review sites including the sheltered inlets of the large east coast firths such as the Dornoch, Cromarty and Beauly (Terry & Sell 1986). Subtidal rocky substrata are less common than intertidal rocky substrata at many review sites and are a major feature only of ria and fjord systems; they occur elsewhere mainly in the form of rock ridges or sills, or as part of the seabed where sediment deposition is at a minimum. The infrequent occurrence of subtidal rock on review sites is in part explained by the fact that a number of review sites drain almost completely during the tidal cycle.

The individual algal and animal species which occur on hard substrata have their own ecological requirements, and so typical vertical zonations occur both in the intertidal and subtidal zones. Such zonations are far less apparent in soft substrata communities, where the sediment slope is far less pronounced and where far fewer species of algae are present. The exact combination of algal and animal species which occurs on hard substrata is dependent on a number of factors including exposure to wave action and tidal currents and, more importantly in Estuaries Review sites, the salinity of the water. As with soft substrata conditions, the species composition of 'stressed' salinity communities is easier to predict than that of communities in fully marine situations. Accordingly, the open coast or fully marine community descriptions given below are a considerable over-simplification, and some, in particular the sheltered rock community, could justifiably be split further into a number of distinct community types.

Review sites contain examples of hard substrata from full salinity, wave-exposed conditions, to reduced salinity, extremely sheltered conditions. Many of the more exposed communities can be found elsewhere, outside review sites. These communities are best assessed in relation to the open coast, and not just in relation to Estuaries Review sites. The generally lower marine conservation interest of these exposed communities as found in Estuaries Review sites, should not, therefore, be taken as an expression of their overall conservation status in Britain. Well developed, high conservation interest examples of these communities occur elsewhere on the open coast. For Estuaries Review sites the communities of higher marine conservation interest are those in sheltered conditions, which reflects the fact that review sites generally hold a large proportion of the British sheltered hard substrata resource.

Exposed rocky shore community

Included here are rocky shores which are exposed to wave action. This type of shore is wide, owing to the sweeping of waves over the rocks, with a broad splash zone at the top of the shore, below the limit of terrestrial vegetation. A characteristic species at the top of the shore is the gastropod mollusc *Littorina neritoides*, whose small size enables it to live in crevices and cracks and thus avoid the dislodging effect of the waves. Also in the top shore zone other species occur, such as lichens (especially *Verrucaria maura*) and the alga *Porphyra*. The middle of the shore is dominated by a variable mixture of barnacles (predominantly *Chthamalus stellatus* and *Chthamalus montagui*), mussels *Mytilus edulis*, limpets *Patella* spp. and red algae (Rhodophycota) and the lower shore by the kelp *Alaria esculenta* and, in areas of slightly less exposure to wave action, another species of kelp, *Laminaria digitata*. Algae belonging to the group called Corallinacea may be particularly common on the lower shore. These algae, which deposit calcium during growth, form a distinctive thin, pink, crust-like cover on the rock surface. Some species, such as *Alaria esculenta*, are essentially limited in distribution to wave-exposed conditions, while other species, such as the gastropod mollusc *Littorina neritoides* mentioned above, although not restricted in distribution to this situation, do occur there in characteristic abundances and associations.

Lewis (1964), in his classic work on the ecology of rock shores, describes a number of patterns of zonation of the animals and algae which occur on exposed shores. Variations on the exposed rocky shore theme include the presence of the brown boot-lace alga *Himanthalia elongata* and Rhodophycota on the lower part of the shore, the addition of the marine lichen *Lichina pygmaea* on the upper shore and the invasion of the mid-shore by the mussel *Mytilus edulis* and Rhodophycota.

Exposed rocky shores are comparatively uncommon within review sites as they are primarily an open coast feature. They have been recorded from 13% of the sites investigated (Table 8.3.4), the bulk of sites occurring in the south-west of Britain (Figure 8.3.18). Exposed rocky shores have been described from headlands at mouths of ria systems in the south-west, headlands in the Outer Hebrides and outside the mouths of firths on the east coast of Scotland (lying outside review sites and so not shown in Figure 8.3.18). The rocky shores present at these sites are described by the various authors as 'exposed' shores but in reality they are on the less-exposed side of this category.

The exposed rocky shores that have been described are generally of low 'local' marine nature conservation interest with a single example of a nationally important site recorded from the mouth of the Salcombe and Kingsbridge Estuary by Hiscock (1986). Powell *et al.* (1979a) stated that the exposed to moderately exposed rocky shores outside the Laxdale Estuary, in the Outer Hebrides,

Table 8.3.4 The documented abundance of some of the major aquatic estuarine communities on hard substrata on review sites, ranked in order of decreasing frequency of occurrence. Information is also provided for each community on the number of review sites for which provisional conservation assessments have been made. Care should be taken in interpretation of this table; the relative abundance of some communities will change as more data become available. Insufficient data are available on the reduced salinity rock community for its inclusion in the table. NA indicates that no conservation assessments have yet been made.

Community name[1]	Abundance[1] of community (%)	Abundance[1] of review sites for which conservation assessments have been made (%)
Variable (mainly reduced) salinity rocky shore community	36	11
Sheltered rocky shore community	31	13
Moderately exposed rocky shore community	19	11
Exposed rocky shore community	13	10
Variable salinity rocky shore community	11	5
Variable salinity rock community	11	8
Hydrozoan/bryozoan turf community	10	5
Artificial substrata community	10	9
Variable salinity clay community	10	NA
Exposed rock community	9	9
Sheltered rock community	8	7
Sabellaria spp. reef community	6	NA
Slipper limpet *Crepidula fornicata*[2] beds	6	NA
Reduced salinity rocky shore community	4	1
Variable (mainly reduced) salinity rock community	3	2
Current-exposed sheltered rocky shore community	2	2

[1] Abundance expressed as a percentage of the total number of sites *for which marine data have been examined*, at which the community occurs.

[2] Abundance of community has been calculated on the distribution of extensive beds of *Crepidula fornicata*.

were of a type not seen elsewhere in the islands. Powell *et al.* (1979a) considered these shores, together with other features within Broad Bay, to be of national marine nature conservation importance.

The overall low conservation ratings applied to this community arise because much better examples of open coast communities are present elsewhere, on stretches of rocky coast not included in this review.

Moderately exposed rocky shore community

This community occurs on rocky shores that are only moderately exposed to wave action, and differs from the communities of exposed rocky shores by the general absence of species such as kelp *Alaria esculenta*, and by the addition of species such as the brown algae *Fucus vesiculosus* in the mid-shore and *Fucus serratus* on the lower shore. As a result of lessened wave activity, the shore may be vertically less extensive than exposed shores, with a comparatively reduced splash zone. On the upper shore the gastropod *Littorina neritoides* is

present along with the related gastropod species *Littorina saxatilis*; two brown algae species, invariably *Pelvetia canaliculata* and sometimes *Fucus spiralis*, are also significant additions in this zone. *Littorina saxatilis* is larger than *Littorina neritoides* and, as a more 'open surface' species, is generally limited to shores that are not too wave-exposed. The mid-shore is dominated by a mixture of limpets *Patella* spp., barnacles (predominantly *Semibalanus balanoides*) and/or brown algae, the composition of which depends upon the extent to which the brown algae have replaced the mussel *Mytilus edulis* and barnacle communities typical in this zone on exposed rocky shores. Under conditions where there is a poorly developed barnacle zone and a poorly developed fucoid algal zone on the mid-shore, the mid-shore may be colonised by a variety of gastropod species, including limpets and topshells, and by *Fucus spiralis*. A number of moderately exposed rocky shore community variations have been recognised by Lewis (1964).

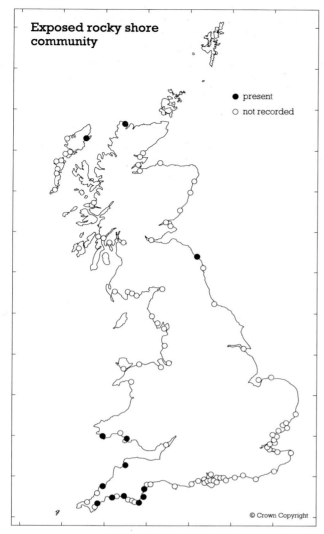

Figure 8.3.18 Provisional assessment of the distribution of the exposed rocky shore community on the 102 review sites for which marine data were examined

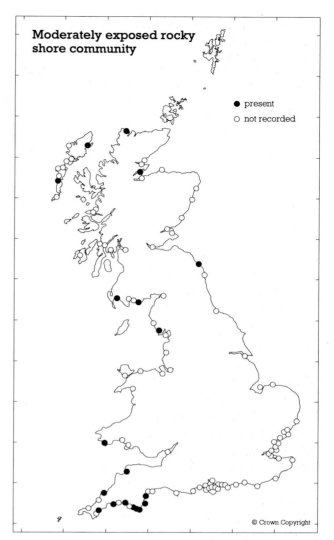

Figure 8.3.19 Provisional assessment of the distribution of the moderately exposed rocky shore community on the 102 review sites for which marine data were examined

Moderately exposed rocky shores have been recorded from 19% of the sites investigated, with just over half the sites described from the south-west of Britain (Table 8.3.4, Figure 8.3.19). Like exposed rocky shores, moderately exposed examples have been described from the mouths of rias in southern Britain, and from the mouths of fjards and fjords in northern areas. Most of the examples are of 'local' marine conservation interest but examples do occur of regional or even national importance (Figure 8.3.38). Regional examples have been described from Lindisfarne and Budle Bay (Connor 1989), Falmouth (Rostron 1985), the Avon Estuary (Moore 1988a), Milford Haven (Little & Hiscock 1987) and Plymouth Sound (Hiscock & Moore 1986), while nationally important examples have been described from Lindisfarne and Budle Bay (Connor 1989), and the Salcombe and Kingsbridge Estuary (Hiscock 1986). Powell *et al.* (1979a) considered the moderately exposed rocky shores present outside the Laxdale Estuary and in Bagh Nam Faoilean, both in the Outer Hebrides, to be parts of nationally important sites.

Sheltered rocky shore community

Under wave-sheltered conditions the width of the black band of *Verrucaria* lichen, at the top of the shore, is markedly reduced, bringing the familiar yellow and orange terrestrial-fringe lichens into almost direct contact with the upper shore algal species *Pelvetia canaliculata*. Typical sheltered shore species, such as the alga *Ascophyllum nodosum*, occur on the mid-shore and the kelp, *Laminaria saccharina*, is present on the lower shore. In extreme shelter *Fucus spiralis*, which is usually present, may be absent, leaving an isolated band of the alga *Pelvetia canaliculata* at the top of the shore. Further information, including representations of some of the patterns of zonation, is given in Lewis (1964).

In general, variations within this community arise from incompleteness of the algal cover on the shore, or differing proportions of the shore being occupied by the various species of fucoid algae. Thus in a situation where there is some wave action, or where stones and shingle are present, the brown fucoid algae *Fucus vesiculosus* and *Fucus serratus* predominate. Under more sheltered conditions and on a firmer substratum, however, it is *Ascophyllum nodosum* which dominates along with the characteristic red filamentous epiphitic alga *Polysiphonia lanosa*.

Sheltered rocky shores are the second commonest type of hard substratum community, being recorded from 31% of the sites investigated (Table 8.3.4). They are mostly restricted to ria, fjord and fjard systems and accordingly have a predominantly south-westerly or northerly distribution (Figure 8.3.20). Examples occur along the south coast in a small number of coastal plain sites; communities develop in these sites on artificial substrata or boulders and pebbles, rather than on natural bedrock shores.

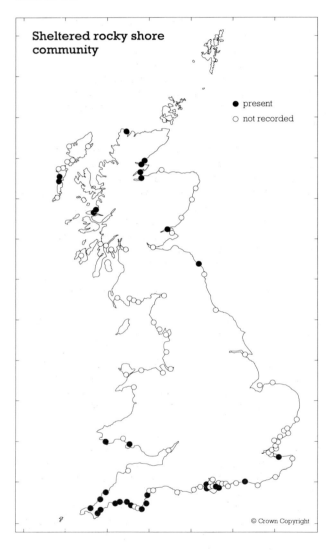

Figure 8.3.20 Provisional assessment of the distribution of the sheltered rocky shore community on the 102 review sites for which marine data were examined

Sheltered rocky shores are predominantly of local or regional marine conservation interest (Figure 8.3.38), although a few examples of national importance occur, including Bagh Nam Faoilean in the Outer Hebrides (Powell *et al.* 1979a). Shores in Milford Haven (Little & Hiscock 1987), Oitir Mhor (Powell *et al.* 1979a), Plymouth Sound (Hiscock & Moore 1986), Salcombe and Kingsbridge Estuary (Hiscock 1986) and in the Yealm Estuary (Hiscock & Moore 1986) were all considered to be of regional marine conservation importance. The site in the Outer Hebrides, Oitir Mhor, is of note due to the fact that here, under very sheltered conditions, a free-living form of the brown alga *Ascophyllum nodosum* develops. This is the only review site at which the *mackii* variant of *Ascophyllum* occurs, although *mackaii* itself is widespread in Scotland with extensive beds known elsewhere.

Variable salinity rocky shore community

This community occurs in situations where there is measurable and variable dilution of sea water. The community is similar to the sheltered rocky shore community of full salinity situations, except that the overall species diversity is reduced and some full salinity species, such as the lower shore kelp species, *Laminaria digitata* and *Laminaria saccharina*, are absent. The place of the kelp species is taken by brown algae, such as the sheltered shore species *Ascophyllum nodosum*, and by the fucoid alga *Fucus serratus*. These algal species are also found on the mid-shore. In both mid- and lower-shore situations the algae may be associated with barnacles (in particular *Semibalanus balanoides* and *Elminius modestus*) or limpets *Patella* spp..

Additional species which, although not purely estuarine in distribution, may occur in particular abundance include the small red algae *Catenella caespitosa* and *Bostrychia scorpioides*, the hydrozoans *Laomedia flexuosa* and *Clava multicornis*, the bryozoan *Bowerbankia imbricata*, and estuarine amphipod crustaceans such as *Echinogammarus marinus*. The individual abundance of these and the dominant algal species may vary from estuary to estuary owing to factors such as variability of river flow rates and differences in water turbidity.

The community occurs at review sites only where there is intertidal rock exposed to variable salinities. The community therefore has a restricted distribution and has only been recorded from 11% of the review sites investigated (Table 8.3.4, Figure 8.3.21). Most of the sites are rias in south-west Britain and the community is surprisingly absent from fjord and fjard systems, although this is probably a reflection of lack of records rather than the true distribution. The community is mainly of low conservation interest (Figure 8.3.38) although there are examples displaying regional marine conservation interest, such as at Falmouth (Rostron 1985), or national marine conservation interest, such as the rocky shores present in the Salcombe and Kingsbridge Estuary (Hiscock 1986). In the Camel Estuary (Gill & Mercer 1989) a variant of this community occurs where the rock is covered by growths of green algae *Enteromorpha* spp.. This may be partly related to the fact that under certain conditions sediment loading in the water column

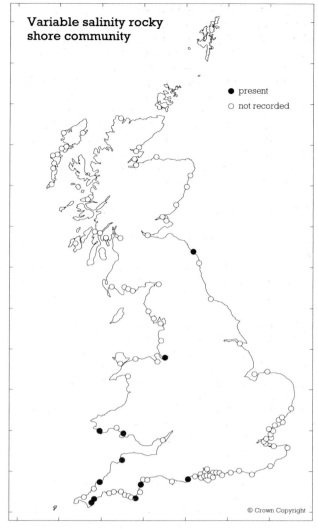

Figure 8.3.21 Provisional assessment of the distribution of the variable salinity rocky shore community on the 102 review sites for which marine data were examined

prevents the normal community from establishing: when turbidity decreases, opportunistic species, such as the one above, can colonise these areas. It may arise also partly because in estuaries which are completely flushed by fresh water at low tide, fucoids may be replaced below the low water mark by *Enteromorpha* spp. (Wilkinson 1980). *Enteromorpha* spp. is also known to be linked to nitrification; vast growths of these algae periodically occur in south coast inlets, indicating elevated nitrogen levels in the water.

Variable (mainly reduced) salinity rocky shore community

In conditions exposed to salinity levels which vary but which are predominantly low, a very species-poor rocky shore community occurs. Such a community is characterised as much by the large number of species which are absent as by the very few species which are present. The exact location of this community in estuaries depends very much on the topography of individual inlets; it predominantly occurs towards the upper reaches

but this is dependent on a number of factors including the degree of freshwater down-flow into the estuary. The black lichen *Verrucaria maura* is still present on the upper and mid-shore, and lower shore levels may be dominated by two species of brown fucoid algae, either *Fucus ceranoides* (in areas where fresh water flows over the shore) or *Fucus vesiculosus* (in areas of more generally reduced salinity). The upper shore fucoid algae species, such as *Pelvetia canaliculata*, are replaced by algal species which are more tolerant of variable salinity, such as *Blidingia* and *Rhizoclonium*. Such a modified shore zonation reflects the vertical salinity gradient which may be present at high tide this far up the estuary; sea water is denser than fresh water; hence at high tide the lower shore area is exposed to higher salinity levels than the upper shore (Wilkinson 1980).

Additional characteristic species which may occur include the estuarine barnacle *Balanus improvisus*, the estuarine isopod crustacean *Sphaeroma rugicorda* and occasionally the hydroid *Cordylophora caspia*. Considerable variation in exact species composition may occur because of local conditions such as river flow rate and water turbidity.

This community is the commonest hard substrata community, being recorded from 36% of the review sites investigated (Table 8.3.4, Figure 8.3.22). The community has been considered to be of local marine conservation interest (Figure 8.3.38), although on occasion, such as in the Dart (Moore 1988b), assessments have been made which suggest that the community warrants designation as of national importance.

Reduced salinity rocky shore community

In very reduced salinity in estuaries, at or close to the limit of tidal influence, an extremely impoverished rocky shore community develops. Most marine species are unable to tolerate such lowered salinity levels and rock surfaces are mostly colonised by blue-green algae and diatoms; filamentous green algae may be present.

The community has been recorded from very few review sites (Figure 8.3.23, Table 8.3.4), which suggests either a lack of hard intertidal substrata near tidal limits or under-recording. Examples are known from the tidal limits of rivers feeding the Firth of Forth (Wilkinson, Scanlan & Tittley 1987) and from the upper reaches of ria systems, notably the Taw and Torridge Estuary (D Laffoley *in lit.*), and the Tamar (Plymouth Sound), in south-west Britain (Hiscock & Moore 1986). No assessments have been made of the marine nature conservation significance of this community.

Sabellaria reef community

On bedrock and boulders a distinctive community can occur consisting of aggregates of tubes belonging to the polychaete worms *Sabellaria*

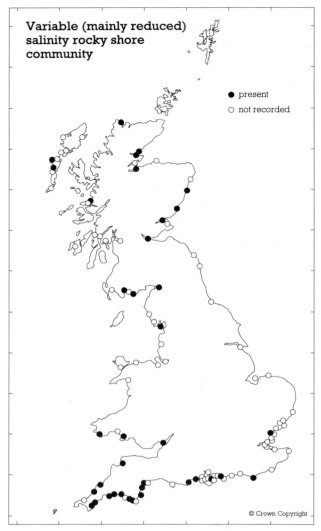

Figure 8.3.22 Provisional assessment of the distribution of the variable (mainly reduced) salinity rocky shore community on the 102 review sites for which marine data were examined

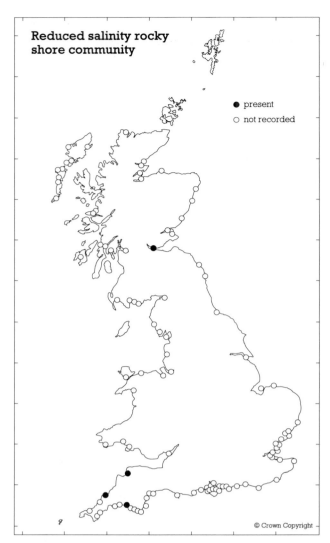

Figure 8.3.23 Provisional assessment of the distribution of the reduced salinity rocky shore community on the 102 review sites for which marine data were examined

alveolata or *Sabellaria spinulosa*. These aggregates vary from a thin patchy cover on the rocks to more substantial reef-like structures and can occur in areas subject to tidal scour with a high level of suspended material in the water. Both species can occur in the intertidal and subtidal zones; *Sabellaria spinulosa* has been reported to occur chiefly on the North Sea coast (Gubbay 1988).

Sabellaria reefs usually occur on the open coast and have only been recorded from 6% of the review sites investigated (Table 8.3.4, Figure 8.3.24). *Sabellaria spinulosa* has been recorded from Lindisfarne and Budle Bay (Connor 1989) but develops into larger aggregates only in the subtidal zone of The Wash (Fowler 1987). This species has undergone a dramatic decline over the years and is now either absent, or present only in very reduced numbers, in the Dee Estuary (Wallace 1982; McMillan 1982), the Humber Estuary, Morecambe Bay and the Thames Estuary (Rees *et al.* 1988). This decline has been attributed by some researchers to the destruction of the reefs by trawling for brown shrimps *Crangon crangon* and pink shrimps *Pandalus montagui*. *Sabellaria* is a

prime source of food for shrimps, and declines in shrimp fisheries in the Humber and Morecambe Bay, and elsewhere, followed the eventual destruction of the reefs (Rees *et al.* 1988). No marine nature conservation assessment has been made of well developed reefs formed by this species; the community in The Wash is now the only extensive example of *Sabellaria spinulosa* reef known from the literature examined for this section of the review.

Sabellaria alveolata reefs have been recorded from the intertidal of two review sites, the Exe Estuary (Dixon 1986) and the Taw and Torridge Estuary (Little 1990). Good examples of intertidal reefs have mainly been recorded outside review sites, such as at Duckpool, on the north coast of Devon, and on the shores of Cumbria (Covey & Davies 1989), and less well developed examples from the northern shore of the Outer Solway (Covey 1990). In the subtidal zone it is known from the Solway Firth (Perkins 1973) but forms extensive reefs only on one site in Britain, the subtidal zone of the Severn Estuary (University College Cardiff Consultants Ltd 1989), where it occurs along with

154

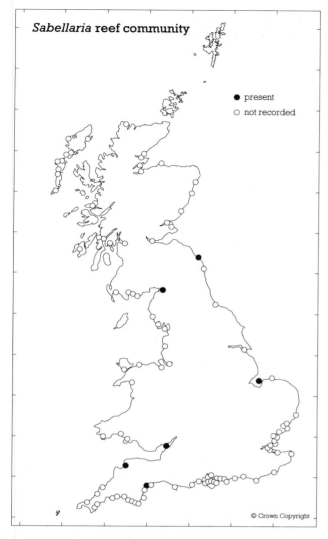

Figure 8.3.24 Provisional assessment of the distribution of the *Sabellaria* reef community on the 102 review sites for which marine data were examined

which is rich in species of sponges. It usually occurs on the lower part of the shore and may include rare and unusual species.

The community is rare and has only been recorded from two review sites (Table 8.3.4, Figure 8.3.25). The community is of high marine conservation interest. Covey & Davies (1989) describe a low shore community in Morecambe Bay which was dominated by the sponges *Halichondria panicea* and *Hymeniacidon perleve*, the latter species being present in well developed 'pipe forms'. They considered the community to be of regional importance. A richer community which was densely colonised by a variety of sponges, ascidians and anemones was described from the Yar Estuary on the Isle of Wight by Johnston (1989). She considered the community to be of national marine conservation interest owing to, amongst other things, the presence of a sponge *Suberites massa* which has been recorded from only three other sites in Britain, namely the dock walls at Southampton and Poole and the narrows at the entrance to The Fleet.

individuals of *Sabellaria spinulosa*. No marine nature conservation assessments have been made of the well developed reefs formed by this species on review sites, although the examples of the intertidal reefs on the open coast in Cumbria were considered by Covey and Davies (1989) to be of national importance. Regionally important examples of *Sabellaria alveolata* reefs are described by Covey (1990) on the open coast of the northern shore of the Outer Solway. *Sabellaria alveolata* approaches the northern limit of its distribution range on the Solway and only poorly developed reefs are constructed. The extensive reefs present in the Severn Estuary are clearly unique and, with the reefs of *Sabellaria spinulosa* in The Wash, are the only good examples of the *Sabellaria* community to be found within the review sites.

Current-exposed sheltered rocky shore community

Under conditions of normal or variable salinity, in areas swept by tidal currents but sheltered from wave action, a fragile community can develop

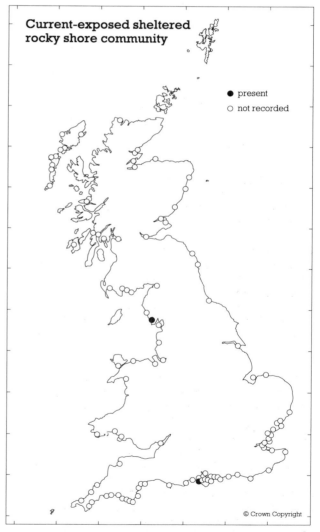

Figure 8.3.25 Provisional assessment of the distribution of the current-exposed sheltered rocky shore community on the 102 review sites for which marine data were examined

Exposed rock community

The community occurs in full salinity on subtidal rocky substrata exposed to wave action. The algal or infralittoral zone is colonised by a kelp forest consisting predominantly of the species *Laminaria hyperborea*, along with a variety of smaller foliose red algae. Below depths which can support algae is the animal-dominated or circalittoral zone. In wave-exposed conditions this is colonised by a variety of erect sponges, hydroids, erect bryozoans, anemones and cup corals. The exact species composition may be very variable depending on local conditions and a range of minor habitats may be present ranging from subtidal cliffs and caves to fissured rock.

The exposed rock community has been recorded from only 9% of review sites investigated (Table 8.3.4), reflecting the infrequent occurrence of subtidal rock throughout review sites in general. The exposed rock community has been recorded from the mouths of a number of ria systems in south-west Britain (Figure 8.3.26), such as the Camel Estuary (Gill & Mercer 1989), Milford Haven (Little & Hiscock 1987), Falmouth (Rostron 1985) and Plymouth Sound (Hiscock & Moore 1986).

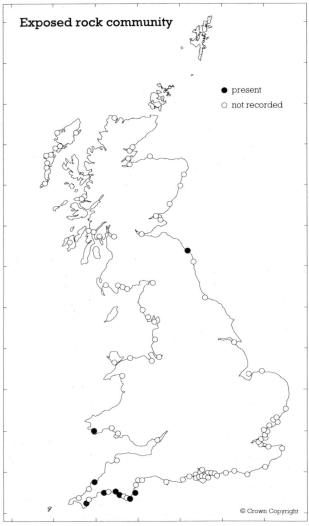

Figure 8.3.26 Provisional assessment of the distribution of the exposed rock community on the 102 review sites for which marine data were examined

Hiscock (pers. comm.) considers the infralittoral and especially the circalittoral community at the entrance to Plymouth Sound to be of high conservation importance. The community, which is uncommon on review sites, is best assessed in relation to open coast sites. The comparatively low marine conservation importance indicated in Figure 8.3.38 should not be taken as a reflection of this community's true conservation status; the community is essentially an open coast one, and well developed, high conservation interest sites occur in the rocky subtidal zone outside the areas considered for this review.

Sheltered rock community

The sheltered rock community develops in full salinity areas where there is subtidal rocky substrata which is sheltered from wave activity. The infralittoral (algal) zone may be dominated by the kelp species *Laminaria saccharina* and by a variety of foliose, or filamentous, red or brown algae. Particular smaller species of algae may form brown crusts on the rock surfaces. The circalittoral, animal-dominated, zone may have dense growths of encrusting sponges and bryozoans, with large solitary sea squirts which can often be abundant. Considerable variation in species composition may occur, depending on local conditions.

The sheltered rock community has been recorded from only 8% of review sites (Table 8.3.4), being almost completely restricted to ria systems in south-west Britain, although it is likely that the distribution is wider than that depicted in Figure 8.3.27. The community is of comparatively high marine conservation interest (Figure 8.3.38), being mainly of regional interest but with examples of both national and local interest. Nationally important examples have been recorded from Milford Haven (Little & Hiscock 1987) and from Plymouth Sound (Hiscock & Moore 1986), whilst regionally important examples include the sheltered rock communities present in The Fleet and Portland Harbour (Howard, Howson & Moore 1988), Falmouth (Rostron 1985), and the Yealm Estuary (Hiscock & Moore 1986).

Hydrozoan/bryozoan turf community

In subtidal conditions of moderately strong tidal currents a community may develop which is termed a 'hydrozoan/bryozoan turf'. The community is dominated by species of hydroids or bryozoans (hence the community name) and often develops on the upper surfaces of deposits of cobbles, pebbles and shells and on larger objects such as boulders. The community may develop in association with a number of other species or may have been recorded previously as part of subtidal community complexes. Species present range from foliose forms, such as the bryozoans *Flustra foliacea* and *Securiflustra securifrons,* to the more 'bushy' species, such as the hydroid *Abietinaria abietina* and the bryozoan *Eucratea loricata.*

The community has been recorded from 10% of the review sites investigated (Table 8.3.4), although

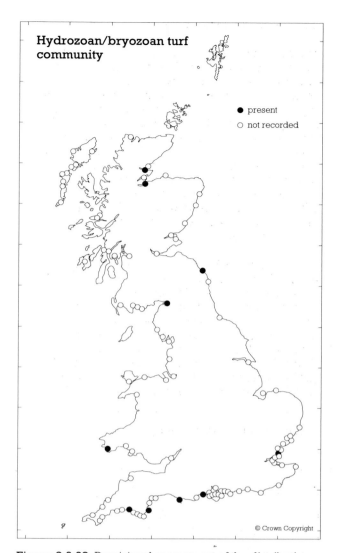

Figure 8.3.27 Provisional assessment of the distribution of the sheltered rock community on the 102 review sites for which marine data were examined

Figure 8.3.28 Provisional assessment of the distribution of the hydrozoan/bryozoan turf community on the 102 review sites for which marine data were examined

this figure is probably an underestimate; on occasions it has been difficult to decide from previous studies if a species-poor example of this community is present in some of the marine situations. The community has been recorded from enclosed coast sites throughout Great Britain (Figure 8.3.28). There does not appear to be any factor linking it to a particular classification of estuary; the only common theme is that it occurs in current-swept locations. Examples have been recorded from The Wash (Fowler 1987), Portland Harbour (Howard, Howson & Moore 1988) and from the current-swept middle reaches of the Dornoch and Moray Firths (Hunter & Rendall 1986). The community is of mainly local marine conservation importance (Figure 8.3.38), although examples of regional importance do occur, for example in the Dart Estuary (Moore 1988b).

Slipper limpet *Crepidula fornicata* beds

The slipper limpet *Crepidula fornicata* is an alien species of mollusc which was accidentally introduced into Britain with oysters imported from America. The species has spread around the south

coast of Britain and under certain conditions forms extensive beds in the subtidal zone. These beds support a variety of species of hydroids, bryozoans, tunicates and sponges. The *Crepidula* beds may in turn provide a settlement point for the European oyster *Ostrea edulis* or *vice versa*, and thus co-dominated *Crepidula/Ostrea* beds may develop. *Crepidula* is, however, normally regarded as a pest of oyster beds as it smothers the available hard substrata leaving less opportunity for oyster settlement.

Crepidula fornicata, as a species, has been recorded from 19% of review sites investigated (Figure 8.3.29, Table 8.3.4). It forms 'beds' in only 6% of review sites, but elsewhere well developed beds dominate, for example, the central part of the west Solent (Dixon & Moore 1987). The distribution of the community is of interest as it shows the species to be limited to southern regions of Britain, the most northerly review site locations on the west and east coasts being Milford Haven and the Blackwater Estuary respectively. Very few marine nature conservation assessments have been made of *Crepidula* beds within review sites, although a

Figure 8.3.29 Provisional assessment of the distribution of the slipper limpet *Crepidula fornicata* on the 102 review sites for which marine data were examined. The locations of extensive beds of this species are denoted by 'B'.

review of assessments made for communities which include *Crepidula* indicated mainly local importance.

Artificial substrata community

Under conditions of full or variable salinity, and in conditions of moderately strong tidal currents, a subtidal community can develop on artificial substrata. In estuaries the artificial substrata are most often jetty piles, piers, large mooring buoys or pipelines. The community is quite often very different from that of nearby natural substrata and is dominated by species of sponges and ascidians. Sponge species include *Halichondria* spp., *Haliclona oculata* and *Hymeniacidon perleve*, and ascidian species *Ascidiella aspersa*, *Ascidia mentula* and *Ciona intestinalis*. The anemone *Metridium senile*, the feather star *Antedon bifida*, the introduced sea squirt *Style clava* and a variety of bryozoans and hydroids may also be present.

The community has been recorded from 10% of the review sites investigated (Table 8.3.4) and has a

distribution essentially restricted to ria systems in south-west Britain (Figure 8.3.30); it is likely that this distribution will be expanded as further survey work is carried out. The presence of artificial substrata in a review site was taken as insufficient evidence to prove the presence of community at that site. Figure 8.3.30 therefore reflects the distribution of the community and not the distribution of artificial substrata within review sites. The community is predominantly of local or regional marine conservation interest (Figure 8.3.38). Examples assessed as of regional importance have been described from Milford Haven (Little & Hiscock 1987) and from The Fleet and Portland Harbour (Howard, Howson & Moore 1988).

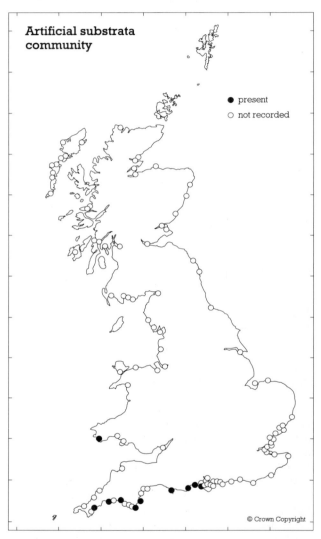

Figure 8.3.30 Provisional assessment of the distribution of the artificial substrata community on the 102 review sites for which marine data were examined.

Variable salinity rock community

The variable salinity rock community occurs in the subtidal zone in areas which are sheltered or very sheltered from wave action. Lowered salinity is physiologically stressful to many marine organisms and thus reduces the species diversity of the community. The community is, however, still very variable. Algae present include the kelp species *Laminaria saccharina* and a variety of predominantly green and red algal species. Sponges, such as *Halichondria panicea*, may dominate the community under some conditions whilst in other circumstances the rock surface may be covered by high densities of the sea squirt *Dendrodoa grossularia*. Under certain conditions the sponge *Dysidea fragilis* may occur, growing in a massive form contrasting with the encrusting open coast form, and the branching sponge *Haliclona oculata* may also be present. A variety of other species may occur including hydroids, bryozoans, anemones such as *Actinothoe sphyrodeta*, *Urticina felina* and *Metridium senile*, and common mussels *Mytilus edulis*. The barnacle *Balanus crenatus* can often dominate rock surfaces, and species which are normally considered to occur in the intertidal zone, such as the gastropod *Littorina littorea*, the brown alga *Fucus serratus* and the barnacle *Elminius modestus*, can extend into the subtidal zone.

The variable salinity rock community has a predominantly south-west distribution (Figure 8.3.31) and has been recorded from 11% of review sites investigated (Table 8.3.4). The community is usually of regional importance and very occasionally of national importance (Figure 8.3.38). Regionally important examples of this community have been recorded from, for example, the Camel Estuary (Gill & Mercer 1989), the Yealm Estuary (Hiscock & Moore 1986), the Teign Estuary (Frid 1989) and the Dart Estuary (Moore 1988), whilst nationally important examples are known from Plymouth Sound (Hiscock & Moore 1986) and Milford Haven (Little & Hiscock 1987).

Variable salinity clay community

In inlets, predominantly in areas of variable salinity, subtidal clay exposures can occur which may be colonised by a species-poor community. The impoverishment of the community is due largely to the unsuitability of clay for attachment or burrowing. The exposures frequently occur in areas subject to strong tidal currents; the currents account for the lack of sediment cover and the formation of the exposures in the first place. The community also occurs in the intertidal zone and is often associated with peat deposits and fossil forests, as at Brancaster on the North Norfolk Coast and in Southampton Water (R Mitchell pers. comm.). The community is characterised by the frequent presence of two species of burrowing bivalve, *Pholas dactylus* and the introduced species *Petricola pholadiformis*.

Exposures of clay occur in a number of review sites, mainly located on the central southern coast of Britain (Figure 8.3.32), although examples do occur in The Wash (R Covey pers. comm.), on the North Norfolk Coast (R Mitchell pers. comm.) and in the Blyth Estuary (Suffolk)(C Beardall pers. comm.) The majority of outcrops occur in the Solent system, as at the mouth of Chichester Harbour (Holme & Bishop 1980), around the mouth of Newton Harbour

Figure 8.3.31 Provisional assessment of the distribution of the variable salinity rock community on the 102 review sites for which marine data were examined

(Dixon & Moore 1987) and in Southampton Water (R Mitchell pers. comm.). The community has been recorded from 10% of review sites (Table 8.3.4). No assessments have been made of the marine nature conservation importance of the clay community. Clay is, however, an unusual habitat and is restricted to only a few sites, suggesting that the impoverished community it supports is of some conservation interest.

Variable (mainly reduced) salinity rock community

The community occurs in enclosed coast sites, mainly in the middle to upper reaches of estuaries, where there is subtidal rock which is sheltered or very sheltered from wave action. The variations in salinity result in low species diversity within the community, with only a limited number of species able to tolerate the physiologically stressful environmental conditions. The water is usually, but not necessarily, turbid. The community which develops is either a species-poor hydrozoan/bryozoan turf or consists of single-species stands. Characteristic species include the

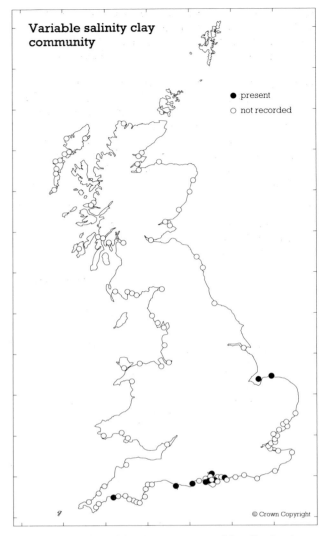

Figure 8.3.32 Provisional assessment of the distribution of the variable salinity clay community on the 102 review sites for which marine data were examined

Figure 8.3.33 Provisional assessment of the distribution of the variable (mainly reduced) salinity rock community on the 102 review sites for which marine data were examined

hydroids *Cordylophora caspia*, *Hartlaubella gelatinosa* and *Coryne muscoides*, the erect bryozoan *Bowerbankia pustulosa* and the encrusting bryozoan *Electra crustulenta*. Barnacles are also present, such as *Elminius modestus*, *Balanus improvisus* and *Balanus crenatus*.

The community is very uncommon; it has been documented as present in only 3% of review sites (Figure 8.3.33, Table 8.3.4). Data on this community are limited and few assessments have been made of its marine conservation interest. An example which was assessed as of national importance was found in the Tamar (Plymouth Sound review site) by Hiscock & Moore (1986), whilst another possible example, present in the upper reaches of Christchurch Harbour, was assessed by Dixon (1988) as of local interest.

Reduced salinity rock community

The reduced salinity rock community occurs in the subtidal, on rocky substrata at the head of estuaries, at or near the limit of marine influence. The reduced salinity conditions mean that species

diversity is highly reduced. Data are sparse but green algae, such as species of *Vaucheria*, *Blidingia* and *Cladophora*, are important in this situation (Wilkinson 1980). Blue-green algae, predominantly species of *Rivularia* and *Nostoc*, may be in evidence covering rock surfaces.

Information on the occurrence of this community is very limited and is insufficient to enable any comment to be made on its distribution or conservation interest.

8.3.4 Tidal freshwater habitats and communities

In the upper reaches of river discharge estuaries there is usually a tidal freshwater zone. The communities of these areas appear less well known than either the marine-influenced parts of estuaries or the non-tidal freshwater parts of rivers.

The extent of tidal freshwater conditions on an

160

individual site depends on a combination of the amount of inflowing water, the rate of delivery of fresh water and the nature of the tidal regime. Some of these alter on a weekly or seasonal cycle and result in great variability in the position and extent of freshwater tidal conditions at an individual site (Chapter 4.5). Seawater incursions may occasionally occur far upstream on spring tides and strong currents may develop in larger water courses at low water. Only a few species are able to tolerate these conditions, just as only a few can tolerate the conditions found in aquatic estuarine communities in reduced salinity at the tops of estuaries. Fringing vegetation of these tidally influenced river channels is similar to those of the adjacent freshwater grazing marsh ditches (see Section 8.1.12).

The actual transition to fresh water is often marked by an abundance of common reed *Phragmites australis*, which can also tolerate brackish conditions, for example in the extensive reed beds on the Firth of Forth. Inland from this transition banks and ditches support an often very diverse assemblage of plant species, characterised by those more typically associated with freshwater rivers, swamps and fens.

More work is required on the interface between full freshwater conditions and reduced salinity (estuarine) conditions in order to establish the true identity of the communities present and to discover more about their nature conservation significance and distributions on a local and national scale.

8.3.5 The diversity of aquatic estuarine communities

Estuaries usually contain a wide range of aquatic estuarine communities as a result of, for example, their salinity variations and habitat heterogeneity. The previous sections have described each community separately and have provided information, when known, on the marine nature conservation importance of each one. The overall nature conservation importance of the aquatic communities on a given estuary site does not, however, depend as much on these individual assessments as on the diversity and quality of communities within an estuarine ecosystem as a whole.

Provisional maps indicating the diversity of communities on soft and hard substrata are given in Figures 8.3.34 and 8.3.35. A reasonable range of communities on soft substrata are present on most review sites, with the highest diversity being in south-west England (Figure 8.3.34). Comparatively lower diversity occurs on the central, south-east and east coasts of England. A similar pattern of community diversity occurs with those communities described for hard substrata (Figure 8.3.35). The highest diversity of communities on hard substrata occurs in south Wales and south-west England, reaching peak values amongst the sites so far assessed in the larger sites such as

Milford Haven and Plymouth Sound. South-east and east coast sites are predominantly of a sedimentary nature and accordingly have a very low diversity of communities on hard substrata.

The overall pattern of aquatic community diversity on Estuaries Review sites is given in Figure 8.3.36. This reinforces the individual patterns described for soft and hard substrata, revealing a marked trend of decreasing diversity from the ria systems of south-west England and south Wales to the coastal plain estuaries of east and south-east England.

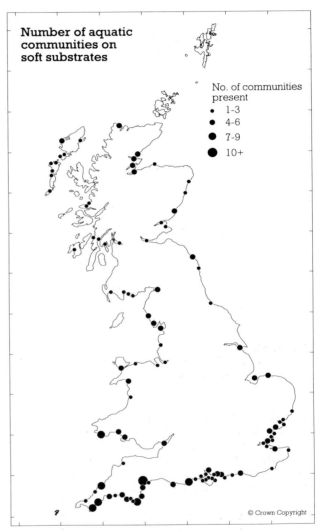

Figure 8.3.34 Provisional assessment of the diversity of aquatic estuarine communities on soft substrata on the 102 review sites for which marine data were examined

8.3.6 Conservation of aquatic estuarine communities

As an initial step towards identifying a series of key sites showing all the representative and important features within the range of estuarine ecosystems in Britain, the aquatic estuarine habitats and communities of review sites have been defined and assessed individually, as described above. This process, and the community descriptions, follow that of the NCC's Marine Nature Conservation

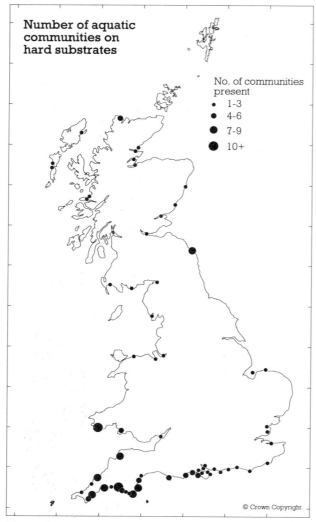

Figure 8.3.35 Provisional assessment of the diversity of aquatic estuarine communities on hard substrata on the 102 review sites for which marine data were examined

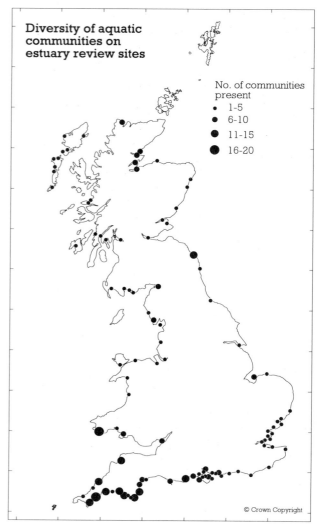

Figure 8.3.36 Provisional assessment of the diversity of aquatic estuarine communities on the 102 review sites for which marine data were examined

Review which is undertaking key site assessment of the whole British marine nature conservation resource. Formerly the key site selection process was based on a consensus of expert opinion. Site evaluation criteria were subsequently introduced to provide a structured framework, allowing better integration and appraisal of the information available (NCC/NERC 1979; Mitchell 1987). The marine site evaluation criteria are similar in concept to those used as guidelines in the selection of terrestrial biological SSSIs and described in NCC (1989).

In Britain a number of criteria have become accepted by which the nature conservation value of terrestrial sites can be judged (Ratcliffe 1977). Ray (1976) cited the use of the Ratcliffe criteria in his International Union for Conservation of Nature and Natural Resources (IUCN) report on critical marine habitats and, at the same time, the NCC adapted the terrestrial comparative site evaluation criteria for selecting key marine sites around Britain (Mitchell 1977, 1979; NCC/NERC 1979). It is intended that the criteria-based approach will lead to the selection of a 'representative' range of marine Sites of Special Scientific Interest, reducing the bias towards high diversity, 'high interest', sites

by ensuring the inclusion of an adequate number of areas of typically low diversity, including those which are naturally degraded (Mitchell 1987). Originally only 10 comparative marine site assessment criteria were put forward (NCC/NERC 1979) but these were expanded to the 14 criteria cited in Mitchell (1987). These recommended criteria fall into two main types, 'ecological/ scientific' criteria, and 'practical/pragmatic' criteria, although there is inevitably some blurring of this distinction. The 14 marine criteria are listed below and brief definitions, together with notes on particular applications, are given in Appendix 8.

Ecological/scientific	*Practical/pragmatic*
1 Naturalness	7 Situation
2 Representativeness	8 Recorded history
3 Rarity	9 Research and education potential
4 Diversity	
5 Fragility	10 Restoration potential
6 Size	
11 Intrinsic appeal	
12 Vulnerability	
13 Urgency	
14 Feasibility	

162

In using the criteria to evaluate sites and communities the 'ecological/scientific' criteria are applied first, to produce a short-list from which the potential conservation areas are selected on 'practical/pragmatic' considerations (Mitchell 1987). The ordering of the criteria within these categories is considered to be an appropriate sequence for their application.

In order to provide a structured means of assessing the 'international', 'national', 'regional' and 'local' importance of the habitats and communities present at a particular location, a series of definitions have been developed which express the marine conservation importance in relation to north-east Atlantic marine ecosystems. These definitions of 'international', 'national', 'regional' and 'local' conservation importance are outlined in Hiscock & Mitchell (1989) and brief definitions are given in Appendix 8. The definitions are used to qualify the first six scientific site selection criteria, especially 'representativeness' and 'rarity'.

The criteria-based approach has been successfully applied in the provisional assessment of the scientific interest and nature conservation importance of marine areas as a whole. They have also been applied to produce provisional conservation importance ratings for specific habitats, communities and species. The information to support a more thorough assessment of these will not be available until completion of relevant parts of the MNCR. Between 1973 and 1987 the criteria and definitions given above were developed and used on over 180 research projects commissioned, supported or undertaken by the NCC. These projects ranged from surveys of large areas of coastline (e.g. the partially completed Intertidal Survey of Great Britain: 1976 to 1981; the South-west Britain Sublittoral Survey: 1977 to 1981, and the Survey of Harbours, Rias and Estuaries in Southern Britain: 1985 to 1989) to much smaller studies of particular sites such as islands, lochs or marine inlets. They are currently used by the MNCR, together with other sources of information, to evaluate the results of marine surveys carried out throughout Great Britain.

The provisional conservation assessments of the various aquatic communities described in Section 8.3.3 originate from over one-third of the NCC-commissioned reports resulting from the research projects discussed above. Whilst the Estuaries Review community classification was produced from the results of a wide range of studies conducted both by the NCC and by external organisations and individuals, conservation assessments have been provided primarily from the NCC-commissioned research. It was not possible within the Estuaries Review timescale to evaluate other 'non-NCC' data sources for review sites and produce additional comparative evaluations of the conservation importance of their communities.

Provisional conservation status ratings are summarised for selected individual soft substrata communities in Figure 8.3.37 and for individual hard substrata communities in Figure 8.3.38. It is noticeable that, especially for communities on hard substrata, most have been afforded local or regional conservation importance, with relatively few examples of communities of national or international significance. In the case of hard substrata communities this, as mentioned above, arises in part because the best known examples are outside estuaries. This cannot be so for soft substrata since most of the extensive soft shores in Britain are within review sites (Chapter 6). This apparent paradox between the overall very great conservation significance of British estuarine wildlife and these aquatic community ratings arises largely because the ratings have been applied to

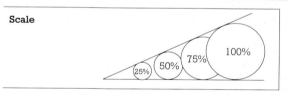

Figure 8.3.37 Diagrammatic representation of the provisional conservation importance of selected soft substrata communities on review sites, ranked in order of abundance (see Table 8.3.3). The symbol size shows the percentage of sites of each community which have been assessed as of international, national, regional or local interest (see Appendix 8). The figure can be taken only as a guide to the conservation importance of the communities that have been assessed so far and the overall conservation importance of individual communities may change as more examples are assessed. In addition, the conservation importance of individual communities shown in the figure cannot be extrapolated to similar 'un-assessed' communities in the field: each new example has to be assessed on its individual merits using the 14 criteria listed in Appendix 8.

Community name	Provisional community conservation assessment		
	International National	Regional	Local
Variable (mainly reduced) salinity rocky shore community	·		⬤
Sheltered rocky shore community	●	⬤	⬤
Moderately exposed rocky shore community	●	●	⬤
Variable salinity rock community	·	⬤	⬤
Variable salinity rocky shore community	●		⬤
Hydrozoan/bryozoan turf community		●	⬤
Artificial substrata community		●	⬤
Exposed rock community		·	⬤
Sheltered rock community	●	⬤	⬤

Scale

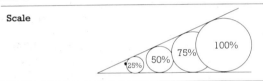

25% 50% 75% 100%

Figure 8.3.38 Diagrammatic representation of the provisional conservation importance of selected hard substrata communities on review sites, ranked in order of abundance (see Table 8.3.4). The symbol size shows the percentage of sites of each community which have been assessed as of international, national, regional or local interest (see Appendix 8). The figure can be taken only as a guide to the conservation importance of the communities that have been assessed so far and the overall conservation importance of individual communities may change as more examples are assessed. In addition, the conservation importance of individual communities shown in the figure cannot be extrapolated to similar 'un-assessed' communities in the field: each new example has to be assessed on its individual merits using the 14 criteria listed in Appendix 8.

individual communities. Hence one estuary is made up of a mosaic of aquatic estuarine communities (Figure 8.3.36) which, although each regarded independently as of relatively low significance, together can form a site of major marine interest.

Many assessments have already been made of the marine nature conservation importance of these individual communities (Section 8.3.3). The next level of conservation assessment, that of the

identification of key estuaries and other parts of the coast that are of major marine conservation importance, is in progress as part of the work of the MNCR. However, even at this early stage of their work, it is becoming clear that a number of review sites are of national or international importance for the aquatic estuarine habitats, communities and species that they support. Such sites are indicated where appropriate in Section 8.3.3 and include both larger, more diverse estuarine ecosystems, smaller sites containing classic examples of particular communities, and sites possessing an example of a community that is of great importance on a national or international basis.

Pressures on aquatic estuarine communities

The aquatic estuarine habitats, communities and species present on Estuaries Review sites can be damaged or destroyed as a result of a wide range of human activities. These activities are considered in brief below and also in Chapter 10.

Many human activities have only a low-level or temporary effect on the aquatic estuarine communities. Some, such as bait digging, only become of concern for those communities when carried out continually or at high intensity. Others cause substantial damage to the nature conservation interest of a site and so are of considerable concern, wherever and whenever they occur. One of the most significant activities in this respect is the loss of estuarine area through land-claim. Land-claim primarily affects the intertidal communities causing a loss of area for colonisation, which in turn can affect the abundances of bird populations dependent on these communities for food. Large land-claim schemes may, in addition, alter the hydrodynamic regime of an individual inlet causing the diversion of tidal currents and (potentially) increased scour of previously current-sheltered areas.

Another activity which results in increased scour and lowered marine community diversity is the canalisation of of the upper reaches of estuaries with substantial flood banks. Such activity results in a decrease in the width of the estuary and (potential) loss of meanders, together with markedly increased rate of water flow. This results in the community structure being dominated by a few communities that prefer higher flow rates. The erection of coast protection barriers in the lower reaches of the estuary also causes a loss of estuarine habitats, predominantly the upper parts of the intertidal zone.

Barrages and barriers constructed for a variety of purposes will, at the very least, restrict tidal amplitude, effectively raising the low water mark. In extreme cases, such as with leisure barrages, the tidal influence is entirely removed so that low water is effectively raised to equal high water. Barrages can accordingly have a profound effect on the aquatic estuarine communities, resulting, in extreme cases, in the loss of all intertidal communities and the loss or redistribution of subtidal communities which are favoured by higher rates of water flow.

Spoil dumping and dredging for aggregates are other potentially damaging operations but these mostly occur outside review sites. There are notable exceptions such as the dredging for maerl that occurs in the Fal Estuary and the dumping of spoil from dredging activities which has, in the past, occurred inside the Salcombe and Kingsbridge Estuary. Such operations result in either the complete removal of areas of benthic community or the smothering of areas of the seabed. The communities affected may then take many years to re-establish. Dumping and dredging also release fine suspended material into the water which can affect organisms over a wider area by clogging the gills of fish and the water-filtering apparatus of filter-feeding organisms (Mitchell 1990).

Water quality may also affect marine communities. Extensive growths of green algae caused by eutrophication can smother intertidal sediment communities and, at the worst, kill or displace many species of algae and fauna. The effects are particularly evident in inlets with low water exchange rates with the open sea, e.g. Portsmouth and Langstone Harbours. The eutrophication of estuarine waters is currently a matter of some discussion and, following the announcement of new water quality criteria to be introduced in 1992, the NCC is carrying out work to establish criteria that will meet nature conservation objectives in estuaries.

Conservation designations covering aquatic estuarine systems

Conservation of marine wildlife on review sites is complex, whether it aims to protect individual communities or the estuarine system as a whole. Many intertidal areas, notably tidal flats on British estuaries, are identified as of national importance and are incorporated within SSSIs that generally cover a mosaic of estuarine habitats (see Chapter 8.1). These areas are usually selected for the habitat and macrobenthic food they provide for wintering and breeding birds, especially waterfowl, rather than for the aquatic estuarine communities themselves.

However, there are many marine areas of nature conservation importance which are outside the scope of SSSI notification. There are currently two main ways in which the marine interest of these subtidal areas may be afforded protection. One involves the statutory designation of a Marine Nature Reserve. The other is through the non-statutory, but nevertheless still formal, designation of a Marine Consultation Area. Both are considered below and, in relation to other forms of statutory and non-statutory protection, in Sections 9.3.7 and 9.3.8.

The Wildlife & Countryside Act 1981 makes provision for the designation of Marine Nature Reserves (MNRs) in order to conserve marine flora, fauna, geological or physiographical features of interest or to provide opportunities for the study of, or research into, these features. A Marine Nature Reserve can be designated out to the three mile limit and, by an Order in Council, out to the twelve mile limit. In practice, however, only nearshore and comparatively small sites have been put forward for designation or have been designated. The designation of an area as an MNR by the appropriate Secretary of State can only occur after all objections concerning the site have been resolved by consultation with interested parties. The argument for this process is that MNRs are difficult to police and therefore without the consent and co-operation of all interested parties the protection would be ineffective. The implementation of the MNR designation has accordingly proved to be both very complex and lengthy. Only two MNRs have been designated to date, Lundy in the Bristol Channel and Skomer off west Wales. Neither is close to a review site but amongst proposed sites is the Menai Strait in North Wales, which covers part or all of five Estuaries Review sites (see Section 9.3.7).

Marine Consultation areas (MCAs) are a form of non-statutory but formal protection for the marine environment. MCAs are areas identified by the NCC as "deserving of special distinction in respect to quality and sensitivity of their marine environment, and where the scientific information available fully substantiates their nature conservation importance". Twenty-nine MCAs have been identified so far and all are in rocky shore sea-lochs in north-west Scotland. Only one, Loch Indaal, is on a review site. The white paper on the environment, *This common inheritance* (HMSO 1990), states that the Government are considering whether the MCA scheme in Scotland should be extended to England and Wales. If this does occur then it is highly likely that a number of estuaries and inlets in England and Wales would be afforded a degree of increased protection under this designation.

8.3.7 Conclusions

Britain's shallow seas support a wide variety of marine life in a mosaic of plant and animal communities, the species composition being determined by factors such as substratum type, salinity and degree of wave and tidal exposure. In the intertidal and subtidal parts of review sites this ranges from exposed marine areas at the mouths of estuaries and open coast review sites to tidal, predominantly freshwater, conditions in the upper reaches.

Many of the communities described in this chapter generally only occur on British estuaries. A number of these communities are of interest at a regional level and some are of marine nature conservation importance on a national or international level. Accordingly the diversity and quality of these communities at a given site contributes to our understanding of Britain's estuaries as a resource of national and international value.

In recent years, an increasing frequency of damage to the aquatic habitats, communities and species on review sites has been evident. This has ranged from a significant loss of estuarine area from activities involving land-claim and other coastal developments, to damage or destruction of subtidal communities from activities such as spoil dumping, water quality problems or dredging activities. In addition, there are ever-increasing pressures on the coastal fringe for recreation and associated developments, all of which have some degree of impact on the aquatic estuarine communities. Rising sea level over future decades will impose additional problems, squeezing the intertidal communities into an ever-decreasing area between immovable landward barriers and the sea itself (see Chapter 11).

It is important that planners and developers take account of the national and international value of these communities and that research is continued to identify further areas of marine nature conservation importance. Consideration should be given to increase the statutory protection of intertidal and subtidal estuarine aquatic communities as a whole.

8.3.8 References

AUGIER, H. 1982. *Inventory and classification of marine benthic biocenoses of the Mediterranean.* Strasbourg, Council of Europe. (Nature and Environment Series No. 25.)

BALLANTINE, W.J. 1961. A biologically-defined exposure scale for the comparative description of rocky shores. *Field Studies, 1*(3), 1-19.

BARNES, R.S.K. 1974. *Estuarine biology.* London, Edward Arnold. (Studies in Biology No.49.)

BISHOP, G.M., & HOLME, N.A. 1980. Survey of the littoral zone of the coast of Great Britain. Final report – Part 1: The sediment shores – an assessment of their conservation value. (Contractor: Scottish Marine Biological Association/Marine Biological Association.) *Nature Conservancy Council, CST Report,* No. 326.

BORGENSEN, F.C. 1905. The algae vegetation of the Faroese coasts with remarks on the phytogeography. *In: Botany of the Faeroes based upon Danish investigations. Part III: Appendix I – XXVIII.,* ed. by E. Warming. London, John Weldon and Co.

CAMPBELL, A.C. 1976. *The Hamlyn guide to the seashore and shallow seas of Britain and Europe.* London, Hamlyn.

CLAPHAM, A.R., TUTIN, T.G., & MOORE, D.M. 1987. *The flora of the British Isles.* Cambridge, Cambridge University Press.

CONNOR, D. 1989. Marine biological survey of Berwick to Beadnell including the Farne Islands. *Nature Conservancy Council, CSD Report,* No. 902.

COOK, W., & REES, E.I.S. 1978. Survey of the macroinvertebrate populations in the Glaslyn/Dwyryd estuary. (Contractor: Marine Science Laboratories, University College of North Wales.) *Nature Conservancy Council, CSD Report,* No. 222.

COVEY, R., & DAVIES, J. 1989. Littoral survey of South Cumbria (Barrow-in-Furness to St Bees Head). *Nature Conservancy Council, CSD Report,* No. 985.

COVEY, R. 1990. Littoral survey of the north coast of the Outer Solway (Mull of Galloway to Auchencairn). *Nature Conservancy Council, CSD Report.*

DIXON, I.M.T. 1986. Surveys of harbours, rias and estuaries in southern Britain. The Exe Estuary. (Contractor: Oil Pollution Research Unit, Field Studies Council.) *Nature Conservancy Council, CSD Report,* No. 670.

DIXON, I.M.T. 1988. Surveys of harbours, rias and estuaries in southern Britain. Christchurch Harbour. (Contractor: Oil Pollution Research Unit, Field Studies Council.) *Nature Conservancy Council, CSD Report,* No. 815.

DIXON, I.M.T., & MOORE, J. 1987. Surveys of harbours, rias and estuaries in southern Britain. The Solent System. (Contractor: Oil Pollution Research Unit, Field Studies Council.) *Nature Conservancy Council, CSD Report,* No. 723.

DYER, M., & GRIST, N. 1987. The ecology of the Great Ouse and Nene Estuaries. *In: The Wash and its environment,* ed. by P. Doody and B. Barnett, 138-147. Peterborough, Nature Conservancy Council. (Research & survey in nature conservation No. 7.)

DYRYNDA, P.E.J. 1987. Poole Harbour subtidal survey – VI. Baseline assessment. (Contractor: Swansea University.) *Nature Conservancy Council, CSD Report,* No. 704.

ELLIOT, M., & KINGSTON, P.F. 1987. The sublittoral benthic fauna of the estuary of the Firth of Forth, Scotland. *Royal Society of Edinburgh. Proceedings, 93B,* 449-466.

ERWIN, D.G. 1983. The community concept. *In: Sublittoral ecology: the ecology of the shallow sublittoral benthos,* ed. by R. Earll and D.G. Erwin, 144-164. Oxford, Clarendon Press.

FOWLER, S. 1987. The subtidal ecology of The Wash basin. *In: The Wash and its environment.* ed. by P. Doody and B. Barnett, 148-153. Peterborough, Nature Conservancy Council. (Research & survey in nature conservation No. 7.)

FORD, E. 1923. Animal communities of the level sea-bottom in the waters adjacent to Plymouth. *Marine Biological Association of the United Kingdom. Journal, 13,* 164.

FRID, C. 1989. Surveys of harbours, rias and estuaries in southern Britain. The Teign estuary. (Contractor: Oil Pollution Research Unit, Field Studies Council.) *Nature Conservancy Council, CSD Report*, No. 920.

FOX, A.D., YOST, L., & GILBERT, D. 1986. *A preliminary appraisal of the intertidal sea-grass resource in the Moray Firth.* Edinburgh, Nature Conservancy Council, South East Region, Scotland.

GAMESON, A.L.H. 1973. Estuaries of the United Kingdom. *In: Mathematical and hydraulic modelling of estuarine pollution*, ed. by A.L.H. Gameson, 3-13. London, HMSO.

GILL, C., & MERCER, T. 1989. Surveys of harbours, rias and estuaries in southern Britain. The Camel estuary. (Contractor: Oil Pollution Research Unit, Field Studies Council.) *Nature Conservancy Council, CSD Report*, No. 953.

GLEMAREC, M. 1973. The benthic communities of the European North Atlantic continental shelf. *Oceanographic and Marine Biology (London). Annual Review, 11*, 263-289.

GUBBAY, S. 1988. *A coastal directory for marine nature conservation.* Ross-on-Wye, Marine Conservation Society.

HARTOG, C. Den. 1959. The epilithic algal communities occurring along the coast of the Netherlands. *Wentia, 1*, 1-241.

HISCOCK, K. In prep. *Marine Nature Conservation Review: field survey methods.* Peterborough, Nature Conservancy Council.

HISCOCK, K. 1986. Surveys of harbours, rias and estuaries in southern Britain. Salcombe and Kingsbridge Estuary. (Contractor: Oil Pollution Research Unit, Field Studies Council.) *Nature Conservancy Council, CSD Report,* No. 668.

HISCOCK, K., & MITCHELL, R. 1980. The description and classification of sublittoral epibenthic ecosystems. *In: The shore environment, Volume 2: Ecosystems*, ed. by J.H. Price, D.E.G. Irvine and W.F. Farnham, 323-370. London, Academic Press.

HISCOCK, K., & MITCHELL, R. 1989. Practical methods of field assessment and conservation evaluation of nearshore/estuarine areas. *In: Developments in estuarine and coastal study techniques*, ed. by J. McManus and M. Elliott, 53-55. Denmark, Olsen & Olsen. (EBSA symposium No. 17.)

HISCOCK, K., & MOORE, J. 1986. Surveys of harbours, rias and estuaries in southern Britain. Plymouth area including the Yealm. (Contractor: Oil Pollution Research Unit, Field Studies Council.) *Nature Conservancy Council, CSD Report*, No. 752.

HISCOCK, S. In prep. Surveys of harbours, rias and estuaries in southern Britain. The Fowey Estuary. (Contractor: Oil Pollution Research Unit, Field Studies Council.) *Nature Conservancy Council, CSD Report.*

HMSO. 1990. *This common inheritance. Britain's environmental strategy.* Cm. 1200. London, HMSO.

HOLME, N.A. 1966 The bottom fauna of the English Channel. II. *Marine Biological Association of the United Kingdom, Journal, 65*, 1051-1072.

HOLME, N.A., & BISHOP, G.M. 1980. Survey of the littoral zone of the coast of Great Britain. 5: Report on the sediment shores of Dorset, Hampshire and the Isle of Wight. (Contractor: Scottish Marine Biological Association/Marine Biological Association.) *Nature Conservancy Council, CST Report*, No. 280.

HOLME, N.T.H. 1983. The distribution of *Zostera* and *Ruppia* in the Fleet. (Contractor: Alconbury Environmental Consultants.) *Nature Conservancy Council, CSD Report*, No. 500.

HOWARD, S., HOWSON, C., & MOORE, J. 1988. Surveys of harbours, rias and estuaries in southern Britain. Portland and Weymouth Harbours. (Contractor: Oil Pollution Research Unit, Field Studies Council.) *Nature Conservancy Council, CSD Report*, No. 851.

HOWARD, S., & MOORE, J. 1989. Surveys of harbours, rias and estuaries in southern Britain. Poole Harbour. (Contractor: Oil Pollution Research Unit, Field Studies Council.) *Nature Conservancy Council, CSD Report*, No. 896.

HOWARD, S., MOORE, J., & DIXON, I.M.T. 1988. Surveys of harbours, rias and estuaries in southern Britain. Newton and Bembridge Harbours. (Contractor: Oil Pollution Research Unit, Field Studies Council.) *Nature Conservancy Council, CSD Report*, No. 852.

HUNTER, J., & RENDALL, D. 1986. The sub-littoral fauna of the Inverness, Cromarty and Dornoch Firths. *Royal Society of Edinburgh. Proceedings, 91B*, 263-274.

JOHNSTON, C.M. 1989. Surveys of harbours, rias and estuaries in southern Britain: minor south coast inlets. *Nature Conservancy Council, CSD Report*, No. 978.

JONES, N.S. 1950. Marine bottom communities. *Biological Reviews, 25*, 283-313.

KAY, D.G., & KNIGHTS, R.D. 1975. The macro-invertebrate fauna of the intertidal soft sediments of south-east England. *Marine Biological Association of the United Kingdom. Journal, 55*, 811-832.

KINNE, O. 1971. 4. Salinity, 4.3 animals, 4.31 invertebrates. *In: Marine ecology*, ed. by O. Kinne, 822-995. London, Wiley-Interscience.

LEWIS, J.R. 1964. *The ecology of rocky shores.* London, English Universities Press.

LITTLE, A.E. 1990. Surveys of harbours, rias and estuaries in southern Britain. Taw and Torridge estuary. (Contractor: Field Studies Council Research Centre.) *Nature Conservancy Council, CSD Report*, No. 1002.

LITTLE, A.E., & HISCOCK, K. 1987. Surveys of harbours, rias and estuaries in southern Britain. Milford Haven and the estuary of the River Cleddau. (Contractor: Oil Pollution Research Unit, Field Studies Council.) *Nature Conservancy Council, CSD Report*, No. 735.

LUKSENAS, J.K. 1969. Biocenoses and trophic groups of bottom invertebrates in the southern parts of the Baltic sea. *Oceanology, 9*, 108-114.

McMILLAN, N.F. 1982. The mollusca of Hilbre. *In: The Cheshire island. Its history and natural history.* ed. by J.D. Craggs, 144-153. Liverpool University Press.

MILLARD, A.V., & EVANS, P.R. 1984. Colonization of mudflats by *Spartina anglica*; some effects on invertebrate and shorebird populations at Lindisfarne. *In: Spartina anglica in Great Britain, 10 November 1982,* ed. by P. Doody, 41-48. Peterborough, Nature Conservancy Council (Focus on Nature Conservation, No.5).

MITCHELL, R. 1974. Aspects of the ecology of the Lamellibranch *Mercenaria mercenaria* (L.) in British Waters. *Hydrobiological Bulletin (Amsterdam), 8*, 124-138.

MITCHELL, R. 1977. Marine wildlife conservation. *In: Progress in underwater science*, ed. by K. Hiscock and A.D. Baume, 65-81. London, Pentech Press.

MITCHELL, R. 1979. Marine wildlife conservation in the coastal zone. *In: Monitoring the marine environment*, ed. by D. Nichols, 181-193. London, Institute of Biology.

MITCHELL, R. 1987. *Conservation of marine benthic biocenoses in the North Sea and the Baltic.* Strasbourg, Council of Europe. (Nature and Environment Series No. 37.)

MITCHELL, R. 1990. Sensitive zones: the implications for nature conservation of dredging and dumping in the marine environment. *In: Proceedings of the international seminar on the environmental aspects of dredging activities. 27 November to 1 December.* Nantes, France, 317-329.

MOORE, J. 1988a. Surveys of harbours, rias and estuaries in southern Britain. Avon and Erme Estuaries. (Contractor: Oil Pollution Research Unit, Field Studies Council.) *Nature Conservancy Council, CSD Report*, No. 854.

MOORE, J. 1988b. Surveys of harbours, rias and estuaries in southern Britain. Dart Estuary including the Range. (Contractor: Oil Pollution Research Unit, Field Studies Council.) *Nature Conservancy Council, CSD Report*, No. 818.

MOORE, J. 1989. Surveys of harbours, rias and estuaries in southern Britain. Loughor Estuary, incorporating the Burry Inlet. (Contractor: Field Studies Council Research Unit.) *Nature Conservancy Council, CSD Report*, No. 1004.

NATURE CONSERVANCY COUNCIL. 1989. *Guidelines for the selection of biological SSSIs.* Peterborough, Nature Conservancy Council.

NATURE CONSERVANCY COUNCIL & NATURAL ENVIRONMENT RESEARCH COUNCIL. 1979. *Nature conservation in the marine environment.* Peterborough, Nature Conservancy Council.

O'CONNOR, F.B., *ed.* 1990. *The Irish Sea. An environmental review. Part one: nature conservation.* Liverpool, Liverpool University Press.

PERKINS, E.J. 1973. *The marine fauna and flora of the Solway Firth.* Dumfries, The Dumfriesshire and Galloway Natural History and Antiquarian Society.

PETERSEN, C.G.J. 1913. Valuation of the sea. II: The animal communities of the sea bottom and their importance for marine zoogeography. *Danish Biological Station. Report, 21*, 3-43.

PETERSEN, C.G.J. 1915. On the animal communities of the seabottom in the Skaggerack, the Christiana fjord and the Danish waters. *Danish Biological Station. Report, 23*, 3-28.

POWELL, H.T., HOLME, N.A., KNIGHT, S.J.T., & HARVEY, R. 1978. Survey of the littoral zone of the coast of Great Britain. 2: Report on the shores of Devon and Cornwall. (Contractor: Marine Biological Association/Scottish Marine Biological Association.) *Nature Conservancy Council, CST Report*, No. 209.

POWELL, H.T., HOLME, N.A., KNIGHT, S.J.T., HARVEY, R., BISHOP, G., & BARTROP, J. 1979a. Survey of the littoral zone of the coast of Great Britain. 3: Report on the shores of the Outer Hebrides. (Contractor: Marine Biological Association/Scottish Marine Biological Association.) *Nature Conservancy Council, CST Report*, No. 272.

POWELL, H.T., HOLME, N.A., KNIGHT, S.J.T., HARVEY, R., BISHOP, G., & BARTROP, J. 1979b. Survey of the littoral zone of the coast of Great Britain. 4: Report on the shores of south-west Wales. (Contractor: Marine Biological Association/Scottish Marine Biological Association.) *Nature Conservancy Council, CST Report*, No. 269.

RATCLIFFE, D.A., *ed.* 1977. *A nature conservation review.* Cambridge, Cambridge University Press.

RAY, G.C. 1976. *Critical marine habitats.* Gland, Switzerland, International Union for Conservation of Nature and Natural Resources. (IUCN publication No. 37.)

REES, H.L., RILEY, J.D., FRANKLIN, A., & GREEN, G.S.J. 1988. Fish and shellfish in the Humber estuary. *In: The Humber ecosystem, Proceedings of a one-day conference in support of European Year of the Environment, 17 March 1988,* ed. by A.M.C. Edwards, 51-65. University of Hull.

REMANE, A. 1971. Ecology of brackish water. *In: Biology of brackish water*, ed. by A. Remane and C. Schlieper, 1-210. New York, John Wiley & Sons, Inc.

RODWELL, J. In press. *British plant communities.* Cambridge, Cambridge University Press.

ROSTRON, D. 1985. Surveys of harbours, rias and estuaries in southern Britain. Falmouth. (Contractor: Oil Pollution Research Unit, Field Studies Council.) *Nature Conservancy Council, CSD Report*, No. 623.

ROSTRON, D. 1987. Surveys of harbours, rias and estuaries in southern Britain. The Helford River. (Contractor: Oil Pollution Research Unit, Field Studies Council.) *Nature Conservancy Council, CSD Report*, No. 850.

SPARK, R. 1929. Preliminary survey of the results of quantitative bottom investigations in Iceland and Faroe waters, 1926-27. *Rapport et proces-verbaux des reunions. Conseil permanent international pour l'exploration de la mer, 57*, 1.

SPHERE ENVIRONMENTAL CONSULTANTS LTD. 1981. *The Beatrice Project: environmental monitoring programme in the Moray Firth. Zostera spp. and other plant communities, Nigg Bay 1981.* A report for the British National Oil Corporation.

STEPHENSON, T.A., & STEPHENSON, A. 1972. *Life between tide marks on rocky shores.* San Francisco, W.H. Freeman and Company.

TEBBLE, N. 1976. *British bivalve seashells.* London, British Museum (Natural History).

TERRY, L.A., & SELL, D. 1986. Rocky shores in the Moray Firth. *Royal Society of Edinburgh. Proceedings, 91B*, 169-191.

THORSON, G. 1957. Bottom communities (sublittoral or shallow shelf). *Memoires of the Geological Society of America (Washington), 67*, 461-534.

TITTLEY, I., FARNHAM, W.F., FLETCHER, R.L., MORRELL, S., & BISHOP, G. 1985. Sublittoral seaweed assemblages of some north Atlantic Islands. *Progress in Underwater Science, 10*, 39-52.

TUBBS, C.R. 1975a. *Langstone Harbour, Hampshire: a review of its ecology and conservation objectives.* Nature Conservancy Council. (Unpublished report.)

TUBBS, C.R. 1975b. *Portsmouth Harbour site of scientific interest. An ecological appraisal.* Nature Conservancy Council. (Unpublished report.)

UNIVERSITY COLLEGE CARDIFF CONSULTANTS LTD. 1989. *Distribution of subtidal benthos associated with sediments.* A report for the Severn Tidal Power Group (unpublished).

WALLACE, I.D. 1982. The marine invertebrate fauna of Hilbre. *In: Hilbre: the Cheshire island*, ed. by J.D. Craggs, 117-143. Liverpool University Press.

WARWICK, R.M., & DAVIES, J.R. 1977. The distribution of sublittoral macrofauna communities in the Bristol Channel in relation to the substrate. *Estuarine and Coastal Marine Science, 5*, 267-288.

WELLS, J.B.J., & BOYLE, P.R. 1975. *Loch Fleet littoral invertebrate survey. 22-28 March, 1975.* (Contractor: University of Aberdeen.) Peterborough, Nature Conservancy Council.

WILKINSON, M. 1980. Estuarine benthic algae and their environment: a review. *In: The shore environment. Volume 2: Ecosystems*, ed. by J.H. Price, D.E.G Irvine and W.F. Farnham, 425-486. London, Academic Press.

WILKINSON, M., FULLER, I., & RENDALL, D. 1986. The attached algae of the Clyde and Garnock Estuaries. *Royal Society of Edinburgh. Proceedings, 90B*, 143-150.

WILKINSON, M., SCANLAN, C.M., & TITTLEY, I. 1987. The attached algal flora of the estuary and Firth of Forth, Scotland. *Royal Society of Edinburgh. Proceedings, 93B*, 343-354.

WYER, D.W., BOORMAN, L.A., & WATERS, R. 1977. Studies on the distribution of *Zostera* in the Outer Thames Estuary. *Aquaculture, 12*, 215-227.

8.4 Fish

Contents

8.4.1 Introduction

Over 350 species of fishes have been recorded in and around the British Isles (Maitland 1974). 122 of these species are known to inhabit British inshore marine waters and of these 118 species have been recorded from the intake screens of 12 coastal power stations (Henderson 1988). However, only 18 species of fish are recognised by Maitland (1974) as occurring regularly in estuarine waters or are considered to be true estuarine species (Table 8.4.1). This Chapter concentrates on these 18 species. In addition, however, a number of freshwater species colonise the upper reaches of many estuaries whilst the lower, fully marine, areas are penetrated by numerous species of truly marine fish during high tide. Marine fish also enter and remain within estuaries for extended periods of time, often in very large numbers and particularly when immature (Claridge, Potter & Hardisty 1986).

The 18 species of fish that regularly use estuaries during some part of their life-cycle can be divided into three species groups: **estuarine**, **anadromous** and **catadromous**. True **estuarine** fish, as the name implies, are those that are generally dependent on estuarine conditions in order to complete their life-cycle. Some other species, however, are dependent on estuaries as migration

Table 8.4.1 Native British fish which are dependent on estuaries at some stage of their life-cycle or migrate through estuarine waters (based on Maitland 1974 and NCC 1989a)

Common name	Scientific name	Life-style
Sea lamprey	*Petromyzon marinus*	anadromous
River lamprey	*Lampetra fluviatilis*	anadromous
Sturgeon	*Acipenser sturio*	estuarine/anadromous
Allis shad	*Alosa alosa*	estuarine/anadromous
Twaite shad	*Alosa fallax*	estuarine/anadromous
Salmon	*Salmo salar*	anadromous
Trout (brown, sea, etc.)	*Salmo trutta*	(anadromous)
Humpback salmon*	*Oncorhynchus gorbuscha*	anadromous
Houting	*Coregonus oxyrinchus*	estuarine/anadromous
Smelt	*Osmerus eperlanus*	estuarine/anadromous
Eel	*Anguilla anguilla*	catadromous
Three-spined stickleback	*Gasterosteus aculeatus*	(estuarine)
Sea bass	*Dicentrarchus labrax*	estuarine
Common goby	*Pomatoschistus microps*	estuarine
Thick-lipped grey mullet	*Chelon labrosus*	estuarine
Thin-lipped grey mullet	*Liza ramada*	estuarine
Golden mullet	*Liza aurata*	estuarine
Flounder	*Platichthys flesus*	catadromous/estuarine

* The humpback salmon is an introduced species

Anadromous = ascending rivers from the sea to breed
Catadromous = descending rivers to the sea to breed
Parentheses indicate occurrence in fresh water as well as in these circumstances

routes to and from the freshwater reaches or sea. **Anadromous** species are those that migrate from the sea into the freshwater parts of rivers to breed. **Catadromous** species do the reverse, migrating to the sea to breed. On a gross scale this division works well, but for some species variations in habitat preference occur with changes in latitude. For example, flounders *Platichthys flesus* show an increasing liking for freshwater environments in higher latitudes, whilst in contrast three-spined sticklebacks *Gasterosteus aculeatus* become more common in marine habitats towards the north of the British Isles (Wheeler 1977).

The nomenclature used throughout this section follows that defined by Howson (1987) in the Marine Conservation Society's Species Directory to British Marine Flora and Fauna.

8.4.2 Estuarine fish

Britain has very few truly estuarine fish species. Of the approximately 350 fish species recorded for Britain, only five (1.4%) are considered to be true estuarine species – species that generally require estuarine conditions in order to complete their life-cycle. Maitland (1974) lists these five species as the sea bass *Dicentrarchus labrax*, the common goby *Pomatoschistus microps*, the thick-lipped grey mullet *Chelon labrosus*, the thin-lipped grey mullet *Liza ramada* and the golden mullet *Liza aurata*. A further seven species are classified by Maitland (1974) as estuarine but these species also occur in fresh water or are also catadromous or anadromous. These additional species are the flounder *Platichthys flesus*, the sturgeon *Acipenser sturio*, the allis shad *Alosa alosa*, the twaite shad *Alosa fallax*, the houting *Coregonus oxyrinchus*, smelt *Osmerus eperlanus* and the three-spined stickleback. All 18 regularly occurring estuarine species are illustrated in Figures 8.4.1, 8.4.2 and 8.4.3.

The sea bass (Figure 8.4.1a) is a large, silvery, spiny-finned fish. It is an indigenous, widespread and common species in estuaries, particularly in southern and western Britain, although it is also abundant on off-shore reefs such as the Eddystone (Wheeler 1979). Adults can grow up to 30-50 cm long (Maitland 1972). Estuaries are particularly important to sea bass (Kelly 1988b), especially for juvenile fish and as spawning and nursery grounds, with the late postlarvae (essentially very juvenile fish) congregating around the saltwater/freshwater boundary at the top end of many Estuaries Review sites (Sabriye, Reay & Coombs 1988).

The common goby (Figure 8.4.1b) is an extremely abundant shallow-water small goby and is the only British species of this genus to be found regularly in fresh and estuarine waters. It occurs especially in estuaries and in intertidal sandy-bottomed pools on muddy saltings. Along the Essex coast it is extremely abundant in such habitats and Wheeler (1960) notes that reports of gobies on the north Kent marshes in the late 1950s probably refer to this species. As an abundant estuarine species it

has a significant impact, both as predator and prey, on the ecosystems of British estuaries (Rogers 1988). It breeds prolifically throughout the summer months, hollowing out a small 'nest' under a pebble or shell, and occurs in huge numbers in many inlets including, for example, the sheltered, shallow East Anglian waters of the Crouch-Roach, Blackwater and Colne Estuaries, and, during the autumn, in Hamford Water (Wheeler 1979).

Several other species of goby occur irregularly in brackish waters. These are generally restricted to the lower reaches of estuaries, as is, for instance, the sand goby *Pomatoschistus minutus* (Wheeler 1979). Sand gobies spend the summer and autumn in estuaries, migrating out to the sea during the winter. Large populations can be found in, for example, the Ythan Estuary in eastern Scotland (Jaquet & Raffaelli 1988).

Three species of mullet occur in British estuaries: the thick-lipped grey mullet (Figure 8.4.1c), the thin-lipped grey mullet (Figure 8.4.1d) and the golden mullet (Figure 8.4.1e). (A fourth species of mullet, *Mugil cephalus*, has now been recorded in Britain but only from the Camel Estuary, as a result of the capture of just a single fish weighing only 0.27 g (J.Reay pers. comm.).) All three species are indigenous but only the thick-lipped grey mullet is considered widespread and common (Maitland 1972). Thick-lipped grey mullet are distributed throughout European seas but become less common in Scottish waters and rarer still further north (Wheeler 1979). The thin-lipped grey mullet has a more restricted distribution, only extending as far north as Scotland. The golden mullet has not been recorded from Scotland but is present in England and Wales. Like the golden mullet, the thin-lipped grey mullet is, in general, fairly local and uncommon, occurring in coastal as well as estuarine waters. Both species seem to be mainly restricted to coasts between south Wales and Essex (J Reay pers. comm.). In some locations, such as The Fleet in southern England, golden mullet can be commoner than the other two species (Bass 1986). Generally, however, within estuaries the thin-lipped grey mullet is more common, penetrating as far as the freshwater reaches (Wheeler 1979). Thick-lipped grey mullet are, by contrast, generally more abundant in the lower, more marine reaches, favouring in particular the high salinity harbours on the south coast (J Reay pers. comm.).

Maitland (1974) classified seven other species (Figure 8.4.2) as facultative estuarine fish: species that also occur in fresh water or are catadromous or anadromous. These fish spend most of their life-cycles within the estuarine and/or freshwater reaches and display migratory behaviour, moving down to the sea or up river to breed.

Such facultative estuarine fish include the flounder (Figure 8.4.2a). The flounder is the only flatfish to be found in fresh water and in abundance in the upper reaches of British and European estuaries. Superficially, flounder resemble plaice

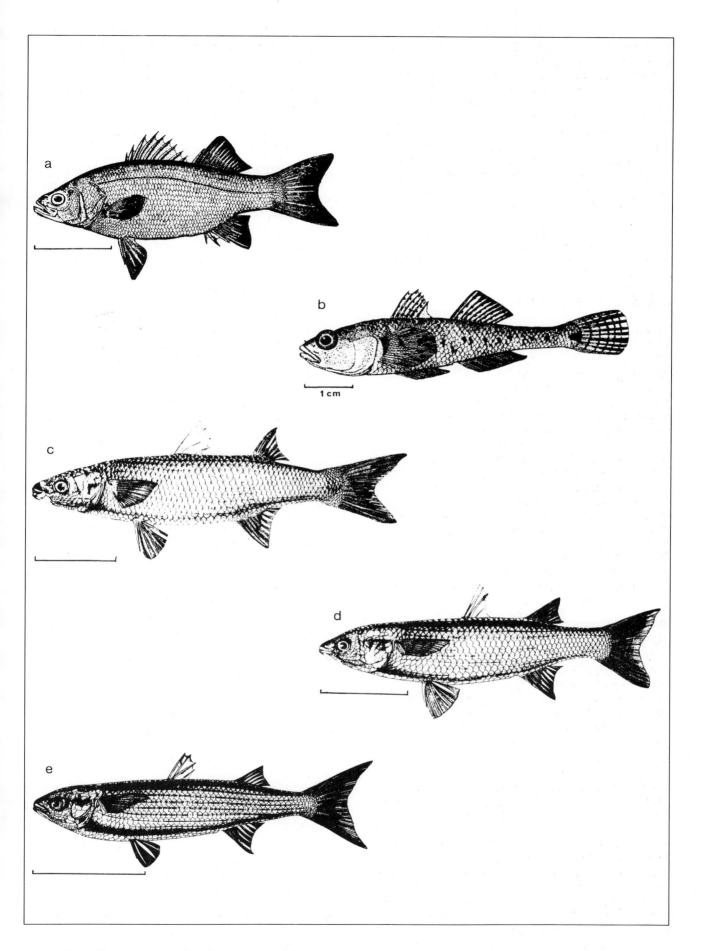

Figure 8.4.1 True estuarine fish, after Maitland (1972). a) Sea bass *Dicentrarchus labrax*; b) common goby *Pomatoschistus microps*; c) thick-lipped grey mullet *Chelon labrosus*; d) thin-lipped grey mullet *Liza ramada*, and e) golden mullet *Liza aurata*. Scale bars show the average length of adult fish. Unless otherwise stated the scale bar represents 10 cm.

Pleuronectes platessa but lack the bright orange spots. They are coloured dull olive brown on the back and white ventrally and have a line of small prickles along the bases of the fins (Wheeler 1979). It is an indigenous species, widespread and common throughout Britain in estuaries, sandy rivers and lakes which are easily accessible from the sea. It is catadromous, migrating to the open sea to breed. The juvenile fish are extremely common close inshore and enter estuaries at an early age, using the incoming tides to help them upstream (Wheeler 1979). The return of the flounder to the Thames Estuary is just one illustration of the improving water quality of this river. Between the 1920s and 1968 no flounder were caught in the Thames. By the end of the 1960s flounder were starting to be caught above London and the numbers present increased, resulting now in a resident population (Wheeler 1979).

The sturgeon (Figure 8.4.2b) is one of a number of species in the group that displays anadromous behaviour, migrating up river to breed. It is a large and distinctive fish which can reach lengths of 150 to 250 cm (Maitland 1972) and which is perhaps best known as the 'Royal fish' and for the 'caviar' eggs laid by the female. Exceptional specimens have been recorded reaching lengths of up to 500 cm, making the sturgeon one of the largest species of fish to occur in British waters (Newdick 1979). The sturgeon is now an endangered species in western Europe and the nearest breeding population is in the River Gironde in France. It is a vagrant in British estuaries and is rare, since 1960 being recorded at only a handful of Estuaries Review sites, including the Severn, Thames and Fal Estuaries in England and Wales and the Moray Firth in Scotland.

Two species of shad occur in British estuaries, the allis shad (Figure 8.4.2c) and the twaite shad (Figure 8.4.2d). Both species are anadromous and indigenous, occurring in estuaries and the lower reaches of rivers. The allis shad is the bigger of the two species, growing up to 60 cm in length. It is much rarer than the twaite shad, being mainly restricted to parts of the west coast of England and Scotland and, to a lesser extent, to some south coast estuaries (Newdick 1979). Maitland (1972) described the allis shad as fairly local and rare. There are suggestions that the current restricted distribution may be due to pollution of rivers and disruption of traditional migration routes (Wheeler 1979). Maitland (1972) indicates that since 1960 the allis shad has been recorded from only two Estuaries Review sites, the Severn Estuary and the top end of Southampton Water, although these data may now be out of date, given Wheeler's (1979) report of allis shad in the Thames and Newdick's (1979) suggestion that it may still be present in the Firth of Forth. The twaite shad is, however, more widespread, with a wide distribution in European seas. In Britain it is present around most of the coastline, although more frequently on the west coast (Newdick 1979). The twaite shad ascends rivers in late spring to spawn in the lower reaches

of fresh water still within tidal influence, the adults subsequently returning to the estuary later in the year (Aprahamian 1988). The allis shad displays similar behaviour but breeds far up in the freshwater reaches and not in areas of tidal influence (Wheeler 1979).

Houting (Figure 8.4.2e), another anadromous species, is indigenous but very local and very rare. Adult fish reach lengths of 25 to 35 cm. After a decline in its numbers in recent years it can best be described as a vagrant in British estuaries. It is likely to be found only in estuaries on the North Sea coast (Newdick 1979). Breeding takes place between December and January but it has never been known to occur in the British Isles (Maitland 1972), and in general little appears to be known about this species in Britain.

A more widespread anadromous species is the smelt – a close relative of the salmon family. It is a relatively small fish with a small fleshy fin on the back between the dorsal fin and tail fin (Figure 8.4.2f), and like salmon and trout it is migratory. An unusual characteristic of smelt is its strong scent of cucumber. Smelt are fairly widespread and common, occurring in rivers, the lower reaches of estuaries and inshore waters (Maitland 1972; Newdick 1979). Smelt breed in fresh water or at the extreme tops of estuaries, at the upper limit of tidal influence (Wheeler 1979). Estuaries are particularly important to smelt, not just as feeding sites but also as larval or juvenile nursery areas (Dadswell 1988). Like the flounder, smelt were absent from the Thames in the earlier part of this century, possibly due to pollution. It had previously been common, but it was not until the late 1960s that smelt were caught once more in the river. Now, once again, the species is common in the estuary and, as an 'indicator' species, clearly demonstrates the success of the various authorities in controlling pollution (Wheeler 1979; Andrews 1988).

The three-spined stickleback (Figure 8.4.2g) is a species which generally occurs in estuaries and a variety of freshwater habitats. As mentioned above (Section 8.4.1), in higher latitudes this species becomes increasingly common in marine habitats, predominantly seashore pools. In Scotland it occurs in the open sea and has occasionally been captured far out to sea. Changes in salinity are seemingly of little importance but it is more sensitive to low levels of dissolved oxygen and is therefore absent from badly polluted rivers and estuaries. It has been recorded from a large number of Estuaries Review sites including the Fal, Thames, Humber and Severn Estuaries, The Wash and the Dornoch, Cromarty and Moray Firths.

8.4.3 Anadromous fish

Britain has four species of fish that are anadromous, migrating up river from the sea to breed. These are the sea lamprey *Petromyzon marinus*, the river lamprey *Lampetra fluviatilis*, salmon *Salmo salar* and

174

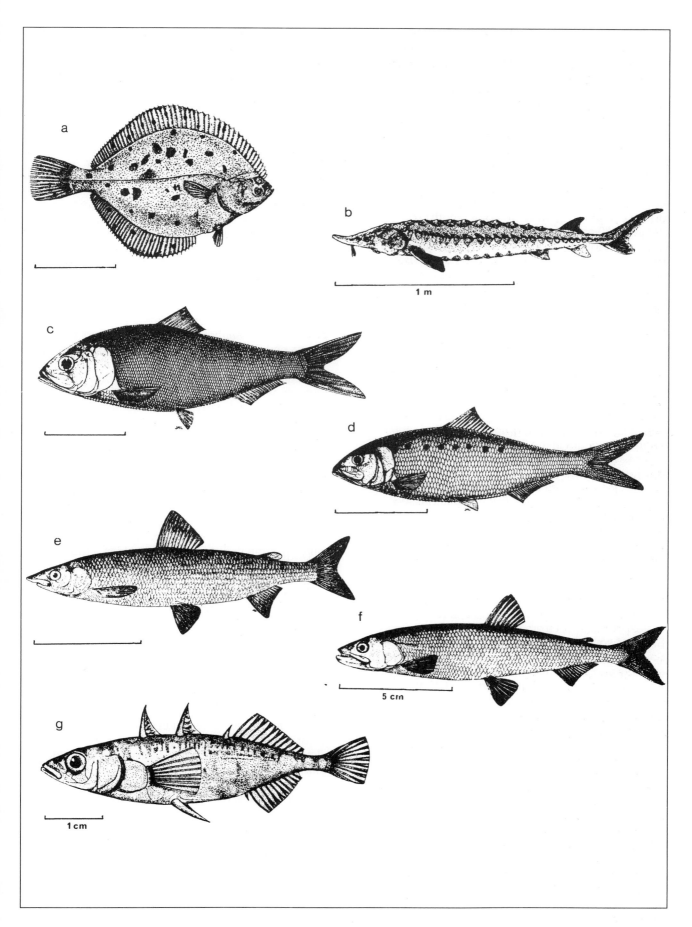

Figure 8.4.2 Fish species that are estuarine and catadromous, or estuarine and anadromous, after Maitland (1972). a) Flounder *Platichthys flesus*; b) sturgeon *Acipenser sturio*; c) allis shad *Alosa alosa*; d) twaite shad *Alosa fallax*; e) houting *Coregonus oxyrinchus*; f) smelt *Osmerus eperlanus*, and g) three-spined stickleback *Gasterosteus aculeatus*. Scale bars show the average length of adult fish. Unless otherwise stated the scale bar represents 10 cm.

the humpback salmon *Oncorhynchus gorbuscha*. Brown and sea trout *Salmo trutta* are also partly freshwater, and a further five species (sturgeon, allis and twaite shads, houting and smelt) are anadromous as well as estuarine in nature (see Section 8.4.2).

Lampreys are jawless fish which obtain nourishment by sucking the blood from bony fish. They attach themselves to fish by way of a sucker disc on the underside of the head which is well armed with teeth. The sea lamprey (Figure 8.4.3a) is the larger of the two species which occur in British estuaries, growing to adult lengths of between 60 and 90 cm. The river lamprey or lampern (Figure 8.4.3b) is smaller, reaching between 30 to 50 cm in length when adult. Both species occur in estuaries and easily accessible lakes, rivers and streams (Maitland 1972). The sea lamprey is fairly widespread, occurring all around almost the entire coastline but more frequently in England and Wales than in Scotland, whilst the river lamprey is widespread and generally common but scarce in northern Scotland (Newdick 1979). The sea lamprey spawns in fresh water, migrating up river from the sea to do so. River lampreys undertake a similar migration which, in the Severn Estuary, occurs between mid-November and mid-February (Hardisty & Huggins 1975). A similar migration occurs in the Thames (Wheeler 1979). The onset of the main migration occurs after the first heavy rainfall of the autumn when river levels start to rise. The sea lamprey, although fairly widespread, is now a rare fish in industrialised lowland regions, owing to widespread pollution and disruption to migration routes from the construction of weirs, dams and other structures (Lelek 1987). Similarly the river lamprey is also less common than formerly, for the same reasons.

The salmon (Figure 8.4.3c) is almost certainly the best known of all British fishes. It is indigenous, widespread (apart from the coastline of eastern England south from the Humber Estuary to the Solent) and common, inhabiting clear stony rivers, streams and lakes. Its distribution range covers the whole of the northern European coast, from northern Spain up to Iceland, and the Atlantic coast of North America. Salmon spawn in the head-waters of rivers. The eggs are laid in winter in small gravel hollows or 'redds' and hatch in the spring. The young fish remain in the river for one to three years, descend to the sea for up to four years and then return to spawn in the river where they originally hatched.

Salmon favour clean water and are now, with increasing implementation of pollution controls, returning to previously polluted rivers such as the Thames. Indirect pollution through the atmosphere and more intensive agricultural practices have increased but, so far, do not seem to have had any large effect on the distribution of salmon populations. In Scotland salmon occur in all Scottish river systems but local distribution within some rivers in the central industrial belt is limited by pollution and weirs (Williamson 1988). Direct industrial pollution is decreasing in Scotland. For example, in the Clyde Estuary, Curran & Henderson (1988) have described how the gradual improvement in dissolved oxygen levels has resulted in the return of significant numbers of salmon to the River Gryfe and its tributary around 1978, and to the Clyde itself in 1983.

Within the last decade research using radio tracking devices has revealed much new information about how salmon move through estuaries. Such studies have been undertaken at a number of sites including the Ribble (Priede *et al.* 1988), the Dee in Aberdeenshire (Hawkins *et al.* 1988) and the Fowey in Cornwall (Solomon & Potter 1988). Results from the Fowey Estuary indicated, for example, that most salmon entered the fresh water at the top of the estuary on flood tides and at night (Potter 1988).

The humpback salmon (Figure 8.4.3d) is much rarer than the salmon *Salmo salar*. It is not truly native since its occurrence in Britain results from introductions made from rivers in north-west Russia (Shearer & Trewavas 1960) and it is only an occasional and rare vagrant. Like the salmon it favours clear stony rivers and streams. Maitland (1972) indicates that since 1960 this species has been recorded from only one review site, the Cromarty Firth. There is no record of it breeding in the British Isles (Maitland 1977).

The trout *Salmo trutta* (Figure 8.4.3e) is another well known species and is also, like salmon, exploited commercially, mostly for sport fishing. It is widely distributed in northern Europe and is widespread and common in Britain, being found in almost all types of unpolluted freshwater bodies where spawning grounds are available but where there are not too many predators. Trout exist in two types, a migratory type, the sea trout, and a non-migratory type, the brown trout. These types are not genetically or morphologically distinct and are not recognised as distinct subspecies.

8.4.4 Catadromous fish

Only two species of fish in Britain are catadromous, migrating to the sea to breed. These are the flounder described above (Section 8.4.2) and the eel *Anguilla anguilla*.

The eel (Figure 8.4.3f) is an abundant fish in Europe, although most widespread in the countries bordering the Atlantic Ocean and the Baltic, North and Mediterranean Seas (Wheeler 1979). In Britain it is indigenous, widespread and common with substantial numbers living in estuaries and on the sea coast. Eels which inhabit British estuaries and rivers breed at sea, in the Atlantic Ocean, south-east of Bermuda. The postlarvae cross the Atlantic, mainly by ocean currents, and change into transparent elvers in British coastal waters. The elvers then migrate into estuaries and up river during late winter and early spring (Wheeler 1979).

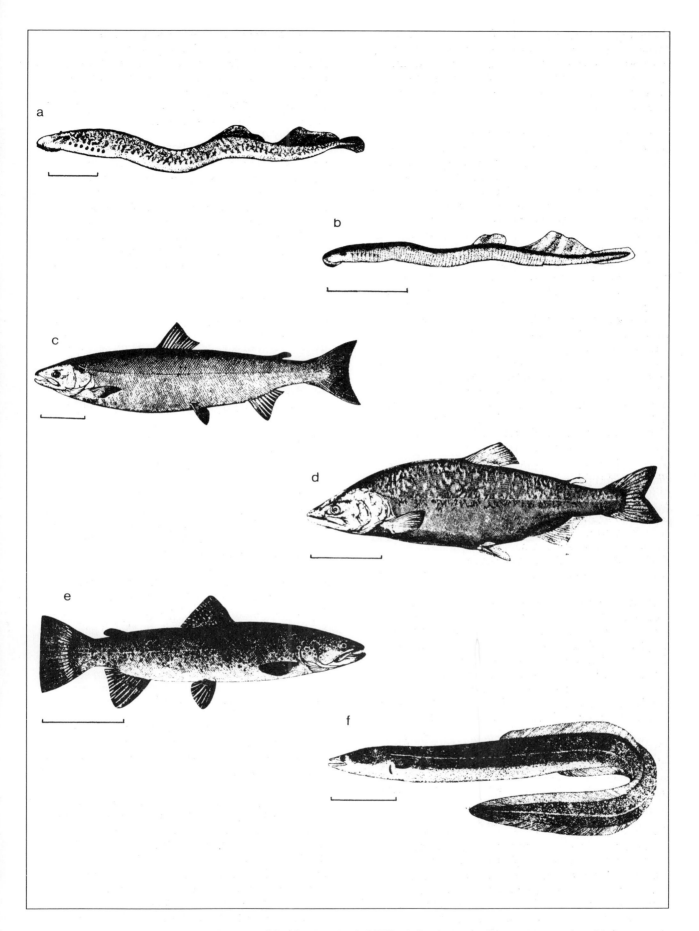

Figure 8.4.3 Anadromous and catadromous fish, after Maitland (1972). a) Sea lamprey *Petromyzon marinus*; b) river lamprey *Lampetra fluviatilis*; c) salmon *Salmo salar*; d) humpback salmon *Oncorhynchus gorbuscha*; e) brown and sea trout *Salmo trutta*, and f) eel *Anguilla anguilla*. Scale bars show the average length of adult fish. Unless otherwise stated the scale bar represents 10 cm.

8.4.5 Other fish species

The 18 fish species described above are just a fraction of the actual number of species that can be found in marine inlets and estuaries. Much information on the full range of species present has been derived from fisheries operations, individual studies and from fish caught on the intake screens of coastal power stations.

Henderson (1988), for example, records 118 species from the intake screens of 12 coastal power stations. Species caught include commercially important ones such as cod *Gadus morhua*, whiting *Merlangius merlangus*, plaice *Pleuronectes platessa*, dab *Limanda limanda*, Dover sole *Solea solea* and herring *Clupea harengus* (Turnpenny 1988). Research in the Firth of Forth has shown that at least 34 species of fish use the estuary throughout, or at some time during, the year (Elliott, O'Reilly & Taylor 1990). Species present include commercially important ones, such as those listed above, as well as more unusual species like the angler fish *Lophius piscatorius*, five-bearded rockling *Ciliata mustela*, pogge *Agonus cataphractus* and lumpsucker *Cyclopterus lumpus*.

Studies undertaken in the shallow creeks of estuaries in west Wales and south-west England show that, in addition to grey mullet and flounders, large numbers of sand smelts *Atherina boyeri*, sandeels and clupeids also inhabit these areas (Kelley 1988a). Sand smelt also occur elsewhere and The Fleet in southern England supports a local breeding population (Henderson & Bamber 1986). More widespread are sandeels which can be found in estuaries wherever there are sandbanks. There are bait fisheries for sandeels in, for example, the Camel and Fowey Estuaries (J.Reay pers. comm.). The main species involved is *Ammodytes tobianus*, but in the Camel Estuary, for example, Raitt's sandeel *Ammodytes marinus*, Corbin's sandeel *Hyperoplus immaculatus* and the greater sandeel *Hyperoplus lanceolatus* have all been recorded (J Reay pers. comm.).

Dipper (1987) records a number of fully marine species that are tolerant of reduced salinities and that live in or enter estuaries to feed. These species include the brill *Scophthalmus rhombus* and turbot *Scophthalmus maximus*, the black goby *Gobius niger*, the leopard-spotted goby *Thorogobius ephippiatus* and the broad-snouted pipefish *Syngnathus typhle*. The young of the red gurnard *Aspitrigla cuculus* are often found in estuaries whilst adults of a more exotic species, the sting ray *Dasyatis pastinaca*, can be found in south coast estuaries but only during the summer and autumn when this species moves north into the English Channel.

8.4.6 Spawning grounds and nursery areas

The sheltered waters provided by estuaries and

marine inlets in Britain are particularly important as spawning and nursery areas for a number of species and are vitally important to a restricted number of 'estuarine-dependent' species. These estuaries are important not only for a number of the estuarine, anadromous and catadromous species described earlier (Section 8.4.2) but also for some more fully marine species in the extreme lower reaches of inlets. In addition, marine fish will also enter estuaries and inlets when young, to feed and to obtain protection from the effects of adverse weather in the open sea.

For example, in the Tamar Estuary in Plymouth, juvenile Dover sole use the estuary as a nursery area. They enter the estuary during April and May when they are only 10 mm long and remain there for two summers. When they leave the Tamar they are 150 to 200 mm in length. During their time in the estuary individual fish appear to inhabit and restrict themselves to a single mudflat, with only limited movement of fish between adjacent mudflat areas (Coggan & Dando 1988). Such sedentary populations are very susceptible to localised disturbance or the destruction of mudflat areas. Dover sole will also spawn in estuaries, and in the Humber spawning has been reported upstream of Spurn Head (Riley 1979).

The Humber Estuary also acts as a significant nursery area for other commercially important species, notably plaice and cod (Rees *et al.* 1988). The juvenile cod are winter visitors to the Humber and are survivors of spawning which occurs off Flamborough Head in February.

Other commercially important species that use estuaries as nursery areas or spawning grounds include sea bass and herring.

Significant numbers of young sea bass occur in 32 Estuaries Review sites (Figure 8.4.4) in England and Wales (MAFF pers. comm.). These sites include The Fleet, rias such as Plymouth Sound in south-west England, and the shallow sedimentary inlets around the south and east of Britain such as Portsmouth and Langstone Harbours and the estuaries of the Medway and Swale. Dwindling stock numbers in the last ten years have prompted the introduction of new legislation in 1990 to conserve stocks (see Section 8.4.9).

Herring use the extreme outer parts of estuaries and inlets, particularly in Scotland, as nursery areas or spawning grounds. Herring used to spawn in the Firth of Forth and were commercially exploited up to the early 1940s. The fishery was based on a population of spring-spawning herring, spawning inside the firth. This important local fishery reached its peak in 1938 when a total catch of over 18,000 tonnes was taken. In 1946 the fishery failed and there has been no subsequent recovery (Howard, McKay & Newton 1987).

The Fleet in southern England is important as a spawning and nursery area for a number of fish species including sand smelt. Sand smelt also use

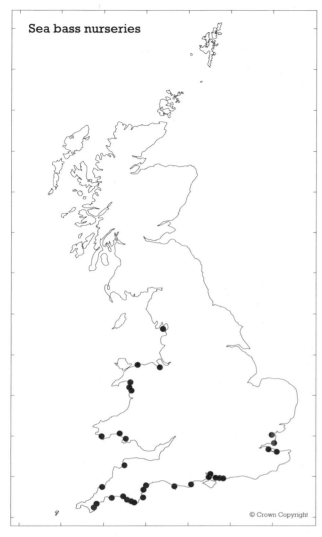

Sea bass nurseries

© Crown Copyright

Figure 8.4.4 Major sea bass *Dicentrarchus labrax* nursery areas in England and Wales (MAFF pers. comm.)

The Fleet for the first year or two of adult life before passing into the open sea. Studies suggest that there is probably minimal mixing with other localised populations (Henderson & Bamber 1986). Such populations dependent on individual inlets, are vulnerable and highly susceptible to disturbance.

8.4.7 Commercial and non-commercial fisheries

A number of fish species that occur in estuaries are of considerable economic importance and many have established fisheries. Information obtained during the Estuaries Review shows that, for example, netting for fish occurs in most of the larger review sites but, on a commercial basis, only on about 15% of sites. Netting is predominantly for salmon and sea trout but is also used for species such as bass, mullet, flounder, dabs and sole. Fixed nets and other devices are also used for catching (predominantly) salmon, although the extent of such operations appears now to be less extensive than formerly. Occasional trawling of

nets occurs in a handful of estuaries, mainly for bottom-living species such as flounder, sole and dabs, but other species are also caught, including herring and species of grey mullet. Apart from angling on a non-commercial basis, fyke netting for eels is the most widespread fishery, known to occur on over 20% of review sites. In many estuaries it is carried out at a comparatively low level and on a non-commercial or semi-commercial basis. On some sites however, and in particular the Severn Estuary, this fishing practice rivals even salmon fishing in terms of financial reward (Severn-Trent Water Authority pers. comm.).

Wheeler (1979) provides an excellent account of the fisheries of the tidal Thames, from historical times to the present day. In the Thames the theme has been one of controlled commercial exploitation of native stocks providing employment for the fishing community and providing food for the populations of the local communities and London. Within the last century most of these fisheries have been badly affected by pollution stemming from the development of London and by interference with the river's flow. Traditional fisheries in the upper reaches for smelt, salmon, lampreys and shad were ruined, whilst the mid-reach fisheries for flounder, eel and whitebait were seriously affected. Those fisheries that continued were forced to move downstream, away from the most polluted areas, to the mouth of the Thames.

In the Humber Estuary there are currently commercial fisheries for marine species such as sole, plaice, roker, cod, dogfish and eel, although as elsewhere they are mostly part-time concerns (Rees *et al.* 1988). Many other species are of lesser importance and are considered to be of value at a local rather than national level. A summary of the value of the 18 British estuarine fish is given in Table 8.4.2, which indicates whether species are primarily of scientific, angling, recreational or commercial value.

Many of the economically important species are under pressure from fishing operations, whether sporting or commercial, and through disturbance to the estuarine habitat and pollution. Legislation operates to control many fisheries and ensure continued viability of stocks. Two commercially important species are considered in detail below: the sea bass and the salmon.

Sea bass are under growing pressure from both anglers and commercial fishermen, its value to the latter being increased by high prices and improvements in capture and location techniques (Kelley 1988b). Accordingly much work has been carried out on this species by the Ministry of Agriculture, Fisheries and Food (MAFF) and Kelley (e.g. 1988b), most recently in response to a long-term downward trend in stock abundance. MAFF's strategy for managing the bass resource is to reduce the mortality of juvenile fish so as to improve yields to the industry and sustain the spawning stock. Studies have been undertaken

Table 8.4.2 Value of British estuarine fish (based on Maitland 1974)

Common name	Scientific name	Britain	International*
Sea lamprey	*Petromyzon marinus*	Scientific	Commercial
River lamprey	*Lampetra fluviatilis*	Scientific	Commercial
Sturgeon	*Acipenser sturio*	Scientific	Commercial
Allis shad	*Alosa alosa*	Angling	
Twaite shad	*Alosa fallax*	Angling	Commercial
Salmon	*Salmo salar*	Angling & commercial	
Trout (brown, sea, etc.)	*Salmo trutta*	Angling & commercial	
Humpback salmon	*Oncorhynchus gorbuscha*	Scientific	Commercial
Houting	*Coregonus oxyrinchus*	Scientific	Commercial
Smelt	*Osmerus eperlanus*	Scientific	Commercial
Eel	*Anguilla anguilla*	Angling & commercial	
Three-spined stickleback	*Gasterosteus aculeatus*	Recreation	
Sea bass	*Dicentrarchus labrax*	Angling	
Common goby	*Pomatoschistus microps*	Recreation	
Thick-lipped grey mullet	*Chelon labrosus*	Angling	Commercial
Thin-lipped grey mullet	*Liza ramada*	Angling	Commercial
Golden mullet	*Liza aurata*	Angling	Commercial
Flounder	*Platichthys flesus*	Angling & commercial	

* Value stated only when different from that in Britain

throughout England and Wales, especially in nursery areas, where juvenile bass are particularly vulnerable to capture. These studies have shown, for example, that in the Solent seasonal movements take place. Juvenile bass move to the west through the Solent in summer and autumn, travelling as far as Christchurch and Poole Bays before returning east in the following spring (Pawson 1988). Similar winter migrations have been reported in the Severn Estuary (Hardisty & Huggins 1975) and the Thames Estuary (Wheeler 1979).

Legislation has been introduced in 1990 to protect sea bass nursery areas. This legislation also indirectly protects the nursery areas of other estuarine and marine species in response to reductions in stock abundance. 34 estuaries and inlets, covering 32 Estuaries Review sites, have been identified (Figure 8.4.4) and are now protected under Section 5 of the 1967 Sea Fish (Conservation) Act. Within these areas regulations will be introduced to prohibit certain fishing methods for all or specific months of the year. A year-round ban on fishing, not just for sea bass but for all sea fish, will operate in The Fleet, Plymouth Sound and the Medway Estuary. Within the other sites identified, fishing will be prohibited between May and October. It is hoped that such action will result in a recovery of stocks of sea bass and other species.

Salmon are another economically important species and in many places have provided local fishermen with a living, not just in Scotland but also further south. In the Severn Estuary for example, the annual salmon catch 60 years ago was in the order of 25,000 to 30,000 fish per season. A salmon fishery still exists, but today's catches are much smaller, the total averaging between 3,000 and 4,000 fish for all types of commercial fishing (Severn-Trent Water Authority pers. comm.).

In Scotland there are no public rights of salmon fishing. Instead, exclusive salmon fishery rights for each stretch of river and shore are under private ownership. The salmon themselves do not belong to anyone until caught and, once caught, belong to whoever catches them. The salmon rights are heritable property and can be bought, sold or leased independently of adjacent land, although a minor exception to this occurs in Orkney and Shetland. For whoever owns the local fishing rights salmon fishing can be very lucrative, with very high prices paid for fishing permits on the best runs. There is also an indirect but significant input into the local economy, resulting from anglers' incidental requirements for board and lodging. On a national Scottish basis a study of the economic value of the sporting salmon fishery in three areas of Scotland estimated the total annual value to be in the region of £34 million (Edinburgh University Tourism and Recreation Unit 1984).

Since 1952 there has been a decline in the abundance of spring salmon caught (Figure 8.4.5). In 1987 the total number of salmon and grilse caught in Scotland was 268,779, the lowest reported number since records began in 1952 (Department of Agriculture and Fisheries 1988). (A grilse is a fish that has returned to the river after spending only one year at sea.) In England and Wales the commercial catch for 1987 was 24% below the average for the previous five years (Russell & Buckley 1989). Williamson (1988) has suggested that the decline in abundance may be due to the significant exploitation of Scottish-origin fish in Greenland, north-east England, (probably) off the coast of Ireland and in the Faroe Islands.

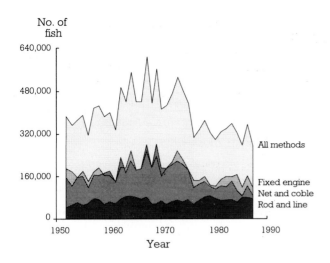

Figure 8.4.5 The total number of salmon and grilse caught in Scotland, 1950-1988, from DAFS (1988)

Much of the commercial salmon fishing is carried out using fixed nets set at right-angles to the shores outside river mouths. These nets are designed to catch salmon as they move along close to the shore before migrating through estuaries and moving further up-river to spawn. Within some estuaries there are also commercial salmon fisheries using various other netting techniques. Salmon fishing in the upper parts of estuaries is, as on freshwater rivers, restricted to rod and line sport fishing. There is currently debate over the extent to which the diminishing fish stocks are a consequence of river-mouth netting. Around some estuaries netting rights are now being acquired and rendered inactive by the Atlantic Salmon Trust, with the aim of maintaining up-river salmon stocks for sport fishing.

8.4.8 Threats to estuarine fish

Fish species that occur in estuaries and are dependent on them for part of their life-cycle, whether as a migration route or as spawning or nursery grounds, are very vulnerable to disturbance and exploitation. Disturbance may take the form of pollution of the water mass, disruption of water flow, loss of estuarine area to land/water-based developments or recreational activities. Populations in estuaries are also susceptible to exploitation in the form of commercial or non-commerical fishing, and where stocks, especially those dependent on a single estuary, are over-exploited subsequent declines in populations can occur.

Pollution comes mostly from domestic, agricultural or industrial wastes and includes thermal pollution from power stations and industry. In relation to estuarine fish populations pollution can be either toxic, eliminating all fish species present, or selective, killing off sensitive species or altering the environment to favour only a few species (Maitland 1974). Estuarine fish and those with marine

affinities are particularly threatened by water pollution. It is normally the lowest reaches of rivers and estuaries that are most seriously polluted. Resident species will be affected, as will those anadromous or catadromous species that must pass through the lower reaches to complete their life-cycles. The flesh of salmon may become discoloured, as in the River Don, or individual fish may contain high levels of pesticides, like the eels in the River Lossie (Brown 1990). Such effects, whilst not necessarily killing the fish, may have severe consequences for predators and species further up the food chain. Implementation of pollution controls over the last few decades has, however, resulted in fish returning to previously grossly polluted British estuaries and rivers.

Overall changes to water bodies, such as eutrophication, are also potentially damaging to resident fish populations. Eutrophication, the nutrient enrichment of the water mass, usually from the surrounding land, results in increased growth rates of fish, increased fish parasite populations and the selective loss of certain fish species from affected water bodies. For example, one of the consequences of eutrophication is lowered oxygen levels in the water which results in some species being more favoured than others. In the lower reaches of estuaries dinoflagellate blooms can also be devastating on local marine faunas (G Potts pers. comm.).

The disruption of estuarine water masses by the construction of weirs, dams or barrages is another serious threat to the local fish populations. Such structures can result in anadromous or catadromous fish being unable to complete their life-cycles successfully. Some dams and weirs now have fish passes to ensure the continued successful migration of species, and much work has been conducted to investigate the success and mortality rates of fish passing through the turbines of tidal barrages (e.g. Davies 1988). The construction of these structures also has, however, a more widespread effect on local fish populations, transforming shallow tidal areas into deeper water areas, with associated changes in the tidal regime. Barrages alter the tidal range and can cause changes in the turbidity of the water, the distribution of water currents and the degree of exposure of the estuary to prevailing winds. Weirs and dams result in a partial to complete loss of tidal influence and a reduction of the estuarine area available to the fish.

Land-claim can also be a threat to estuarine fish, although it may less serious than some of the pressures already described. Major land-claim projects will, however, result in large-scale loss of intertidal and subtidal estuarine habitats. These areas may be vital to some species as nursery areas, spawning grounds or feeding areas. On a large scale, land-claim will also alter the hydrodynamic regime of the inlet and this may result in the loss of sheltered areas and the favouring of species that prefer higher rates of water flow. The dredging of navigation channels in harbours and estuaries may also be a problem as this operation releases fine suspended matter into the water column which can clog the gills of fish.

Power stations are another threat, not only from thermal discharges but also because the intake screens destroy very large numbers of small fish each year. This threat could be alleviated by better design of the intake screens to ensure that they are less destructive and by better siting of the screens to avoid fish migration routes (G Potts pers. comm.).

Individual fish species may also be under threat from more insidious sources. For example, concern has recently been expressed over the genetic purity of wild Scottish salmon and the problems that may develop if interbreeding occurs between native stocks and escaped fish-farmed salmon. Escaped fish may also disturb the native stocks. Concern is based on the fact that breeding activity may be disrupted in rivers and that there is a possibility of fish-farmed salmon disrupting the natural behaviour of native salmon at sea when the native stocks prepare to move up-river (NCC 1989b).

8.4.9 Conservation of estuarine fish

The term 'conservation', in relation to fish species that inhabit estuaries, can be interpreted in a number of different ways. Most of the discussion on fish conservation in the past has been based on species that are considered to be commercially important. Recently, however, other aspects have been receiving attention, such as the amenity and recreational value of fish and the conservation, in the true sense of the word, of rare or endangered species.

Four out of the 18 species of fish that occur regularly in estuaries are considered by Maitland (1974) to be rare or of restricted distribution and so are of particular nature conservation interest. These species are the sturgeon, allis shad, twaite shad and the houting. Until recently none of these species was protected under the Wildlife & Countryside Act 1981, but the allis shad has now been added to Schedule 5 of the Act.

The Berne Convention on the Conservation of

European Wildlife and Natural Habitats 1979 (see Chapter 9) covers fish. Appendix III of the Berne Convention lists these six estuarine species as rare:

> Salmon *Salmo salar*
>
> Sea lamprey *Petromyzon marinus*
>
> River lamprey *Lampetra fluviatilis*
>
> Twaite shad *Alosa fallax*
>
> Allis shad *Alosa alosa*
>
> Common goby *Pomatoschistus microps*

The sturgeon *Acipenser sturio* is listed under Appendix I and II of the Convention on International Trade in Endangered Species of Wild Fauna and Flora (CITES).

It is not entirely clear, however, what actually constitutes a 'rare' British marine fish. Work is currently underway at the Marine Biological Association of the United Kingdom, under contract to the Nature Conservancy Council, to rectify this situation by collating all records of fish reported as rare or uncommon. A provisional list is given in Table 8.4.3. Such information will be invaluable in the conservation of these species, although any measures will have to be taken in conjunction with the protection of estuaries as a whole and the management of the more damaging of man's activities.

In general the main hope for the future, in terms of the general conservation of estuarine fish, would seem to lie in persuading those concerned in sport and other fisheries' management to maintain a responsible attitude towards our native fish stocks (Maitland 1974). In addition, those concerned with all aspects of estuarine and general water use need to be stimulated into taking account of the value of these native fish populations.

Practical steps that could be taken to help conserve some of these rarer species range from maintaining free access to streams where anadromous species such as the sea lamprey are known to occur, to making further improvements in water quality in estuaries (Lelek 1987). Water quality has been a major factor in the decline of many species and improvements would assist not only populations of commoner estuarine, catadromous and anadromous species, but also species such as the sturgeon, the allis shad and the twaite shad.

Table 8.4.3 Rare estuarine fish (based on Swaby & Potts in press)

Common Name	Scientific name	IUCN category of threat	Abundance	Distribution
Sturgeon	*Acipenser sturio*	endangered	scarce	localised
Allis shad	*Alosa alosa*	vulnerable	scarce	localised
Twaite shad	*Alosa fallax*	vulnerable	scarce	localised
Houting	*Coregonus oxyrinchus*	endangered	scarce	single pop[n]

8.4.10 Conclusions

Overall, estuaries play a crucial role for many species of fish, by providing the necessary migration routes, spawning and breeding areas, or by providing an environment in which the limited number of true estuarine species can spend almost the wholes lives and in which a larger number of less estuarine-dependent species spend part of their lives.

The pressures on estuaries and their fish populations is likely to continue and to be augmented by other complications as the demand for water by industrial, domestic and recreational concerns increases (Maitland 1974). It is only through careful planning and the management of exploited stocks that we will be able to ensure the continued diversity, abundance and viability of British estuarine fish populations.

8.4.11 References

ANDREWS, M.J. 1988. Monitoring for change – a Thames experience. *In: Fish in estuaries: abstracts*. Southampton University, Fisheries Society of the British Isles.

APRAHAMIAN, M.W. 1988. The biology of the twaite shad *Alosa fallax fallax* (Lacepede) in the Severn estuary. *Journal of Fish Biology, 33A*, 141-152.

BASS, J. 1986. Fishes of The Fleet. *Porcupine Newsletter, 3*, 147-148.

BROWN, A.E. 1990. *The rivers and lochs of Scotland, a contribution to Operation Brightwater*. Peterborough, Nature Conservancy Council and Scottish Conservation Projects.

CLARIDGE, P.N., POTTER, I C., & HARDISTY, M.W. 1986. Seasonal changes in movements, abundance, size composition and diversity of the fish fauna of the Severn estuary. *Marine Biological Association of the United Kingdom. Journal, 66*, 229-258.

COGGAN, R.A., & DANDO, P.R. 1988. Movements of juvenile Dover sole, (*Solea solea* L.) in the Tamar estuary, south west England. *Journal of Fish Biology, 33A*, 177-184.

CURRAN, J.C., & HENDERSON, A.R. 1988. The oxygen requirements of a polluted estuary for the establishment of a migratory salmon, *Salmo salar* L., population. *Journal of Fish Biology, 33A*, 63-70.

DADSWELL, M.J. 1988. Diadromous fishes in estuaries – an overview. *In: Fish in estuaries: abstracts*. Southampton University, Fisheries Society of the British Isles.

DAVIES, J.K. 1988. A review of information relating to fish passage through turbines: implications to tidal power schemes. *Journal of Fish Biology, 33A*, 111-126.

DEPARTMENT OF AGRICULTURE, FISHERIES & FOOD. 1988. *Statistical bulletin. Scottish salmon and sea trout catches: 1978*. Edinburgh, DAFS.

DIPPER, F. 1987. *British sea fishes*. London, Underwater World Publications.

EDINBURGH UNIVERSITY TOURISM AND RECREATIONAL UNIT. 1984. *A study of the economic value of sporting salmon fisheries in three areas of Scotland*. Edinburgh, Edinburgh University.

ELLIOTT, M., O'REILLY, M.G., & TAYLER, C.J.L. 1990. The Forth estuary: a nursery and overwintering area for North Sea fishes. *Hydrobiologia, 195*, 89-103.

HARDISTY, M.W., & HUGGINS, R.J. 1975. A survey of the fish population of the middle Severn estuary based on power station sampling. *International Journal of Environmental Studies, 7*, 227-242.

HAWKINS, A.D., SMITH, G.W., JOHNSTONE, A.D.F., WEBB, J., & LAUGHTON, R. 1988. Temperature gradients in the estuary of the Aberdeenshire Dee, and their significance for the entry of adult atlantic salmon. *In: Fish in estuaries: abstracts*. Southampton University, Fisheries Society of the British Isles.

HENDERSON, P.A. 1988. The structure of estuarine fish communities. *In: Fish in estuaries: poster presentation*. Southampton University, Fisheries Society of the British Isles.

HENDERSON, P., & BAMBER, R. 1986. Sand smelt in The Fleet. *Porcupine Newsletter, 3*, 149-151.

HOWARD, F.G., McKAY, D.W., & NEWTON, A.W. 1987. Fisheries of the Forth, Scotland. *Proceedings of the Royal Society of Edinburgh, 93B*, 479-494.

HOWSON, C., ed. 1987. *Species directory to British marine flora and fauna*. Ross-on-Wye, Marine Conservation Society.

JAQUET, N., & RAFFAELLI, D. 1988. The ecological role of the sand goby (*Pomatoschistus minutus*) in an estuarine food web. *In: Fish in estuaries: abstracts*. Southampton University, Fisheries Society of the British Isles.

KELLEY, D. 1988a. Species present in shallow creeks of estuaries in W.Wales and S.W.England. *In: Fish in estuaries: poster presentation*. Southampton University, Fisheries Society of the British Isles.

KELLEY, D. 1988b. The importance of estuaries for sea-bass, *Dicentrarchus labrax* (L.). *Journal of Fish Biology, 33A*, 25-34.

LELEK, A. 1987. *The freshwater fishes of Europe. Volume 9: threatened fishes of Europe*. Wiesbaden, AULA-Verlag.

MAITLAND, P.S. 1972. *A key to the freshwater fishes of the British Isles with notes on their distribution and ecology*. Ambleside, Freshwater Biological Association. (Scientific Publication No 27.)

MAITLAND, P.S. 1974. The conservation of freshwater fishes in the British Isles. *Biological Conservation, 6,* 7-14.

MAITLAND, P.S. 1977. Freshwater fish in Scotland in the 18th, 19th and 20th centuries. *Biological Conservation, 12,* 265-278.

NATURE CONSERVANCY COUNCIL. 1989a. *Guidelines for the selection of biological SSSIs.* Peterborough, Nature Conservancy Council.

NATURE CONSERVANCY COUNCIL. 1989b. *Fishfarming and the safeguard of the natural marine environment of Scotland.* Edinburgh, Nature Conservancy Council.

NEWDICK, J. 1979. *The complete freshwater fishes of the British Isles.* London, Adam & Charles Black.

PAWSON, M.G. 1988. The abundance, distribution and integrity of the juvenile bass population in the Solent, its harbours and Southampton Water. *In: Fish in estuaries: abstracts.* Southampton University, Fisheries Society of the British Isles.

POTTER, E.C.E. 1988. Movements of Atlantic salmon *Salmo salar* L., in an estuary in south-west England. *Journal of Fish Biology, 33A,* 153-160.

PRIEDE, I.G., SOLBE, J.F., NOTT, J.E., O'GRADY, K., & CRAGG-HINE, D. 1988. Behaviour of adult atlantic salmon (*Salmo salar* L.) in the estuary of the R. Ribble in relation to variations in dissolved oxygen and tidal flow. *Journal of Fish Biology, 33A,* 133-140.

REES, H.L., RILEY, J.D., FRANKLIN, A., & GREEN, G.S.J. 1988. Fish and shellfish in the Humber Estuary. *In: The Humber ecosystem. Proceedings of a conference in support of the European year of the environment,* 51-65. Hull, Humber Estuary Committee.

RILEY, J.D. 1979. The biology of young fish in the Humber. *In: The Humber estuary,* 20-24. NERC Publication, Series C, No 20.

ROGERS, S.I. 1988. The seasonal partitioning of energy in an estuarine fish, the common goby, *Pomatoschistus microps* Kroyer. *Journal of Fish Biology, 33A,* 45-50.

RUSSELL, I.C., & BUCKLEY, A. 1989. *Salmonid and freshwater fisheries statistics of England and Wales, 1987.* Lowestoft, MAFF Fisheries Laboratory. (Fisheries Research Report No.16.)

SABRIYE, A.S., REAY, P.J., & COOMBS, S.H. 1988. Sea-bass larvae in coastal and estuarine plankton. *Journal of Fish Biology, 33A,* 231-234.

SHEARER, W.M., & TREWAVAS, E. 1960. A Pacific salmon (*Oncorhynchus gorbuscha*) in Scottish waters. *Nature, London, 188,* 868.

SOLOMON, D.J., & POTTER, E.C.E. 1988. First results with a new estuary fish tracking system. *Journal of Fish Biology, 33A,* 127-132.

SWABY, S.E., & POTTS, G.W. 1990. Rare British marine fishes – identification and conservation. *Fisheries Society. Journal,* in press.

TURNPENNY, A.W.H. 1988. Fish impingement at estuarine power stations and its significance to commercial fishing. *Journal of Fish Biology, 33A,* 103-110.

WHEELER, A. 1960. The 'common goby' in the London area. *London Naturalist, 39,* 18.

WHEELER, A. 1977. The origin and distribution of the freshwater fishes of the British Isles. *Journal of Biogeography, 4,* 1-24.

WHEELER, A. 1979. *The tidal Thames. The history of a river and its fishes.* London, Routledge & Kegan Paul.

WILLIAMSON, R.B. 1988. Salmon fisheries of Scotland. (Unpublished ms.)

12 species of native amphibians and reptiles occur in Britain. Most are widespread but three species, the natterjack toad *Bufo calamita*, the sand lizard *Lacerta agilis* and the smooth snake *Coronella austriaca*, are much more restricted in their population size and distribution.

Natterjack toads are particularly associated with estuaries in Britain and of an estimated adult population of a few tens of thousands approximately 95-96% occur on coastal areas adjacent to estuaries (A S Cooke pers. comm.). The great majority (at least 81%) of the British population lives in the extensive dune and marsh systems associated with the estuaries of the Solway, Esk, Duddon, Ribble and Alt in south-west Scotland and north-west England (Figure 8.5.1). Elsewhere there is a small population on Morecambe Bay, and there are small populations, each amounting to no more than 2% of the total, on the Dee in north-west England and the Humber and North Norfolk Coast. Those on the North Norfolk Coast have been reintroduced there. Away from estuaries natterjack toads occur only on a coastal dune system in East Anglia and two heathlands in southern and eastern England (NCC 1986).

Sand lizards now number only a few thousand adults and are restricted chiefly to mature heathland in southern England, including the heathlands surrounding Poole Harbour. Elsewhere in Britain there is a small isolated population in the Merseyside dunes within 2 km of the shores of the Ribble and Alt estuaries, with an estimated 5% of the British population. The smooth snake is now restricted to mature southern England heathlands including those surrounding Poole Harbour.

The ranges of all three species have contracted substantially during the last century largely as a consequence of the destruction of and damage to their heathland and sand-dune habitats by afforestation, urbanisation, agricultural land-claim, military activities, mineral extraction and leisure and recreational pursuits. The combined effects have been considerable: there are historical records of about 70 heathland populations of natterjack toads of which only one or two survive. The populations in the north-west England coastal systems have fared better; these habitats have been subject to less change and, especially further north, are of crucial importance to natterjack toads in Britain.

The endangered status of the natterjack toad, sand lizard and smooth snake was recognised when they were afforded special protection under the Conservation of Wild Creatures & Wild Plants Act 1975 and the Wildlife & Countryside Act 1981. It is illegal to disturb, catch, kill, possess or sell these species without an appropriate licence.

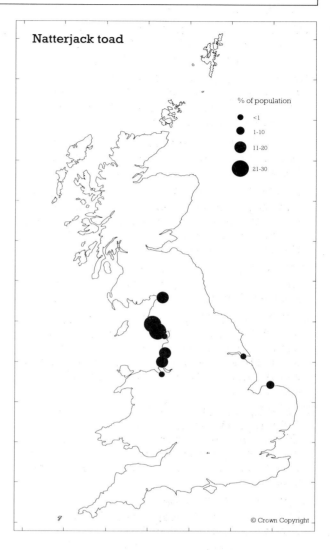

Figure 8.5.1 The distribution of natterjack toads *Bufo calamita* on Estuaries Review sites

Reference

NATURE CONSERVANCY COUNCIL. 1986. *The conservation of endangered amphibians and reptiles.* Peterborough.

Contents

Summary

British estuaries are of major national and international importance for migrant and wintering waterfowl. Many species depend wholly or largely on British estuaries for crucial periods of the year. Three groups of birds are particularly striking and abundant: waders and wildfowl (together known as waterfowl), and seabirds.

Many waterfowl that breed across vast areas of arctic, sub-arctic and temperate regions crowd onto British estuaries in winter. Many others use them as vital staging areas before flying south to overwinter in Europe and Africa and then back north to their breeding grounds in spring. Some waders and seabirds breed at high densities on saltmarshes and the habitats surrounding estuaries.

Estuarine birds can be highly mobile, and depend on a network of sites or parts of sites during their annual cycles. Their use of a particular estuary varies from bird to bird, from species to species and from year to year.

Migrant and wintering waterfowl

Wintering waterfowl depend on the mosaic of habitats within estuaries. Many waders and some wildfowl feed on the intertidal mudflats, sandflats and saltmarshes, and sometimes during high tide on surrounding pools and pastures. Many roost on undisturbed saltmarshes and shingle banks and other surrounding terrestrial habitats. Other wildfowl feed on surrounding marshes and farmland, returning to roost on the estuary.

In January over 1,740,000 waterfowl are present on estuaries – 62% of the British wintering population, and over 10% of the relevant international populations. 581,000 of these are wildfowl (38% of the British and almost 4% of north-west European populations); and almost 1,159,000 are waders – a massive 90% of the British and over 15% of the East Atlantic flyway populations.

Waterfowl are widely distributed around estuaries. Major concentrations are on The Wash (over 180,000 birds), Morecambe Bay (over 140,000 birds) and the estuaries of Essex and north Kent (almost 229,000 birds – over 13% of the British estuarine population). Just 25 estuaries (each with more than 20,000 waterfowl) hold 83% of the estuarine population in midwinter. Estuaries with smaller populations together support over 3% (waders) and 2% (wildfowl) of international populations.

Twenty-six wildfowl species and 18 wader species occur regularly in winter on estuaries. Almost three-quarters of the waders are dunlins, knots and oystercatchers, and over half the wildfowl are wigeon, dark-bellied brent geese and shelduck.

In January estuaries support more than half of 18 British waterfowl populations and more than 10% of 21 international waterfowl populations.

Estuaries are of particular international importance for knots (67% of the international population), redshanks (55%), bar-tailed godwits (50%), *alpina* subspecies dunlins (27%) and oystercatchers (26%). Amongst wildfowl, estuaries support over 75% of the small Svalbard-breeding population of light-bellied brent geese, and major proportions of international populations of dark-bellied brent geese (over 50%) and barnacle geese (100% of the Svalbard population, 70% of the Greenland population).

Five wader species and three wildfowl species (redshank, curlew, oystercatcher, dunlin, ringed plover, mallard, shelduck and wigeon) are particularly widespread on estuaries. In contrast, most goose populations are restricted to less than one-quarter of estuaries.

Estuaries are important for waterfowl not just as wintering sites but also as refuges in cold weather, as moulting sites and as migration staging areas. At these times many other populations and individuals depend on British estuaries. During migration many more waterfowl use British estuaries than are present at any one time – at least 15-20% of the international wader population in autumn and in spring. Maintenance of late spring staging areas is particularly critical as birds are then rapidly storing energy and nutrient reserves for long-distance migration and for survival on their breeding grounds.

The key implications for estuarine conservation of these winter and migratory waterfowl numbers and distributions are that –

– British estuaries overall are of major national and international importance for waterfowl assemblages, and for many individual species.

– Although many waterfowl are widely dispersed around estuaries, many are almost entirely dependent on them for their winter and migratory survival, and for some species a few particular sites are crucial.

– Wintering waterfowl depend on habitats on both small and large estuaries.

– Movements and population turnover, especially during migration, mean that a much greater proportion of the international population of each species depends on estuaries than is present at any one time.

– Estuaries are used as a network, and different parts of the network are important for different species and populations, and at different times.

Estuaries support a variety of other wintering birds, notably divers, grebes and sea-ducks (especially in north-east Scotland), gulls, birds of prey (especially hen harrier, peregrine and merlin) and passerines, for example Lapland buntings and twites.

Breeding birds

Estuaries are of particular conservation importance for their breeding bird assemblages, typically dominated by waders or locally by seabirds.

Saltmarshes around Britain support some very high densities of **breeding waders** – sometimes over 100 pairs per square kilometre. Some grasslands associated with estuaries also support large populations, but generally total densities, and densities of individual species such as redshank, are higher on saltmarshes than on nearby coastal grasslands.

British estuarine populations of redshanks and ringed plovers are particularly important in a national and international context. 7% of the international population of redshanks and 19% of ringed plovers breed around estuaries.

Britain is of major international importance for **breeding seabirds**, supporting over half the European Community population of each of 14 species. Gulls and terns breed on at least 75 estuaries. Most estuarine breeding seabirds are on upper saltmarshes, sand-dunes and shingle, and estuaries support over 1% of the international breeding population of six species. Estuaries support almost three-quarters of the scarce British breeding population of little terns.

The conservation of estuarine birds depends on safeguarding remaining areas of estuarine habitats. The dependence of birds on site networks means that they are particularly vulnerable to piecemeal habitat loss. The loss of one part can destroy the integrity of the network. Maintaining the health of all parts of an estuary is also vital, since breeding and wintering birds depend on the habitat mosaic and are vulnerable to pollution and recreational disturbance.

8.6.1 Introduction

Birds are one of the most striking features of estuarine wildlife. Three groups of birds are particularly abundant on estuaries: waders (sometimes also called shorebirds), wildfowl (including grebes, ducks, geese, swans and coots) and seabirds (especially gulls and terns). Migrant waders and wildfowl, together called waterfowl, congregate in large numbers on estuaries during their non-breeding seasons. Here the abundance of invertebrate animals in the mudflats and sandflats provides food for many species of waders and some wildfowl, and grasses and seeds on both intertidal areas and the surrounding sub-maritime habitats provide food for wildfowl. The open nature of estuaries and the relative inaccessibility of many parts of them provide security from attack by predators and safe undisturbed roosting sites for waders when their feeding grounds are covered by the tide, and for wildfowl at night.

The large number and size of British estuaries and their location in the east Atlantic leads to their providing particularly favourable conditions for waterfowl (see Chapter 5). British estuaries are of major national and international importance for many of these species. Many waterfowl breeding throughout the tundras and other arctic habitats use Britain as a wintering ground or as a migration staging area before flying further south to overwinter in southern Europe and on the western seaboard of Africa. These waders, ducks, geese and swans visiting Britain breed across a vast area of the northern hemisphere from as far west as the central Canadian arctic (105° W) and east to central Siberia (110°E). Other species, particularly some ducks, that reach Britain in winter breed further south over a large area of temperate and boreal Europe and western Asia (Figure 8.6.1).

The short summers and limited natural productivity impose constraints on the breeding densities of arctic-breeding birds, and most waders and wildfowl nest at low densities over extensive areas of the arctic. For example, Meltofte (1985) found a maximum breeding density of 16.6 pairs km^{-2} for waders in high arctic Greenland and northern Canada. By contrast, in winter these waders are highly concentrated on estuaries such as those in Britain and often occur in flocks of tens of thousands. Densities on British estuaries are exceptionally high and exceed 500 birds km^{-2} km on many estuaries. The wintering population on a single estuary can therefore represent the breeding birds from a vast area of the arctic. Similarly, high densities of wildfowl occur in winter on many British estuaries yet these species too breed at very low densities in the arctic. There were, for example, only 16 breeding pairs of Greenland white-fronted geese *Anser albifrons* in a 750 km^2 area of prime breeding habitat in west Greenland – a density of 0.02 pairs km^{-2} (Stroud 1981).

Many estuarine birds are highly mobile; they depend on a network of estuaries during their annual cycle and the ways in which they use estuaries are complex. Their use of estuaries emphasises the importance of conserving networks of such sites on both a national and international basis, since the loss of one site in the network may critically affect the success with which migrant birds can move between their breeding and wintering grounds. So international conventions and directives, notably the Convention on Wetlands of International Importance especially as Waterfowl Habitat (the 'Ramsar Convention') and EEC Directive 79/409/EEC on the Conservation of Wild

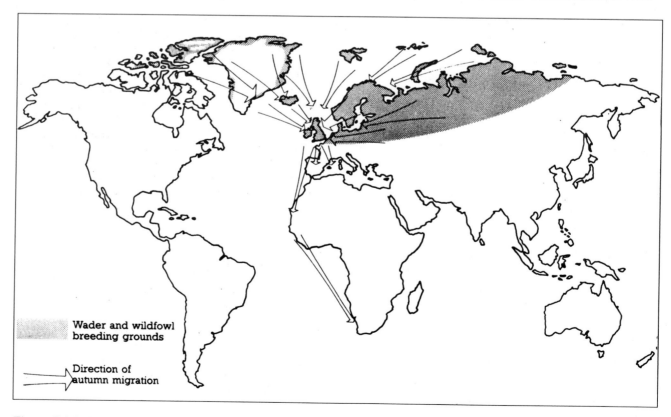

Figure 8.6.1 Breeding range of waders and wildfowl that use Britain as a wintering area and migration staging area. Arrows show generalised migration routes of birds returning from their breeding grounds in autumn.

Birds, play a particularly significant part in the conservation of estuarine birds and the protection of their habitats. The implementation of these international measures is described in Sections 9.2.6 and 9.2.7.

The saltmarshes, shingle ridges, sand-dunes and grasslands around estuaries provide important breeding habitats for waders, wildfowl and seabirds, and for some of these species British estuaries are internationally important. Some species of wader breed at very high densities around parts of British estuaries (Fuller et al. 1986), much higher densities than for arctic-breeding waders. The areas of suitable breeding habitat in Britain – as elsewhere in western Europe – are, however, much smaller than in the arctic. Some birds breeding on estuaries (for example some ringed plovers Charadrius hiaticula) remain close to their breeding areas throughout the year (e.g. Pienkowski 1980). Other waders and terns migrate further south and west after breeding to overwinter in southern and western Europe and western Africa.

This chapter describes the ways in which British estuaries are used by birds, the species involved, their distribution and abundance in both national and international terms, and the conservation significance of estuaries for them. It focuses first on general features of the use of British estuaries by migrant and wintering waterfowl. This provides an important contextual basis for understanding the analysis of the winter distribution and size of the waterfowl and other wintering bird assemblages, and for deciding the approaches to their conservation. The significance of British estuaries for breeding waterfowl and seabirds is then assessed and the chapter finishes with a description of the approaches to estuarine bird conservation and the main conservation issues affecting the use by birds of Britain's estuaries.

8.6.2 Migrant and wintering waterfowl

Background

A great deal is known about the distribution, behaviour and ecology of migrant and wintering waterfowl, through extensive research and surveys in Britain and elsewhere throughout their range. The origins and destinations of waders and wildfowl have been discovered, particularly since the mid 1960s, by the extensive catching, ringing (with individually numbered metal leg-rings), releasing and subsequent reporting of many thousands of birds. This work has been undertaken extensively on their wintering grounds in Britain and elsewhere, on their migration staging areas and, to a lesser extent, on their breeding grounds. More recently the use of a variety of colour-marks (especially temporary plumage dyes, temporary coloured leg-flags and permanent colour-rings) has become widespread in Europe and elsewhere, as a

means of identifying the origins of birds without the need to recapture them and as an aid to the detailed behavioural studies that have revealed much of importance in the conservation of waterfowl (e.g. Townshend 1985). Since waterfowl are so mobile the success of many of these studies has depended on national and international co-operation on a wide scale, often arranged through the Wader Study Group (e.g. Pienkowski & Pienkowski 1983; Piersma et al. 1987a).

The distribution of waders and wildfowl during their non-breeding seasons has been established through regular co-ordinated counting of birds, involving the co-operation of a large number of voluntary counters simultaneously visiting estuaries and other wetlands, usually monthly (e.g. Prater 1981; Owen et al. 1986; Salmon et al. 1989). In addition there are a large number of more detailed studies of individual estuaries and species, that have provided much vital information on how waders and wildfowl use estuaries.

Sources and treatment of information

The major source of comparable information on non-breeding waders and wildfowl on different British estuaries is the monthly counts undertaken by the Birds of Estuaries Enquiry (BoEE), begun in 1969 and organised by the British Trust for Ornithology, with funding from the NCC, RSPB and recently from the Department for the Environment for Northern Ireland. This enquiry gives information on the distribution of estuarine waders and permits monitoring of population trends.

Counts of wildfowl made during BoEE counts are incorporated into the National Wildfowl Counts (NWC). This programme was established by the Nature Conservancy (the fore-runner of the NCC) and has been operated since 1947 by the Wildfowl and Wetlands Trust, funded by the NCC. NWC counts are made monthly between September and March and cover over 1,900 sites in Britain and Northern Ireland. In addition special censuses are made of some goose species that feed away from wetlands during the day. National Wildfowl Counts provide information for some review sites not covered by the BoEE. The results of the NWC are analysed in detail in Owen et al. (1986).

The results of the first five years of BoEE which provide information on both wintering birds and those present in autumn and spring, are described in detail by Prater (1981), and more recent results are summarised in annually-produced reports, the most recent being Salmon et al. (1989). Waders, wildfowl and some other estuarine birds are included in BoEE counts which regularly cover 112 British sites listed by Moser (1987). The BoEE provides a long-term and comprehensive picture of estuarine bird populations unparalleled anywhere else in the world.

The Estuaries Review includes some sites not covered by the regular wildfowl and wader counts. Information on these sites is less comprehensive.

In 1984-1985 over 90% of the non-cliff shores outside estuaries (*sensu* Moser 1987) were surveyed for waders in midwinter by the Winter Shorebird Count, which was undertaken as an extension of the BoEE and co-sponsored by the Wader Study Group (Moser & Summers 1987). This survey aimed to provide an estimate of the total coastal wintering populations of waders and to provide contextual information about estuarine waders. Some of these 'non-estuarine' sites that fall within review sites have subsequently been counted regularly as part of BoEE.

Review site coverage

Taking all these sources together, midwinter numbers could be calculated for 138 review sites (89%) for waders and 116 review sites (75%) for wildfowl. Site coverage is shown in Figures 8.6.2 and 8.6.3. In total there is coverage for waders and/or wildfowl for 142 review sites. Sites not covered for waders are scattered round the coast of Britain and are chiefly small sites with little intertidal area. In a few instances a site has been excluded from the Estuaries Review analysis when the only relevant count comes from a Winter

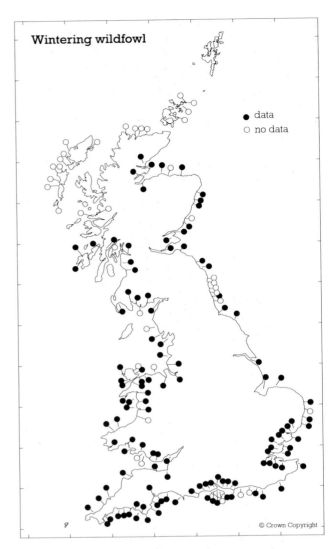

Figure 8.6.3 Review sites for which there are data on numbers of wintering wildfowl

Shorebird Count that also covered a long stretch of open coast outside the review site. Most review sites for which there are no data for wildfowl are those in north and west Scotland that have received only Winter Shorebird Count coverage for waders.

National and international population sizes

The numbers for each species and review site are set into their national and international context by comparison with estimates of the total British and international numbers of the appropriate biogeographical populations. A biogeographical population is described as a more or less discrete group of birds which live in a particular area (or group of areas in the case of a migratory population), interbreed freely within the group and rarely breed or exchange with individuals of other groups (Mayr 1970). In most cases a biogeographical population relates directly to a species or subspecies, but for some geese that overwinter in Britain there are several distinct biogeographical populations within a subspecies (see Owen *et al.* 1986; Stroud *et al.* 1990). This approach fits with the accepted approach to conservation planning embodied in the Ramsar

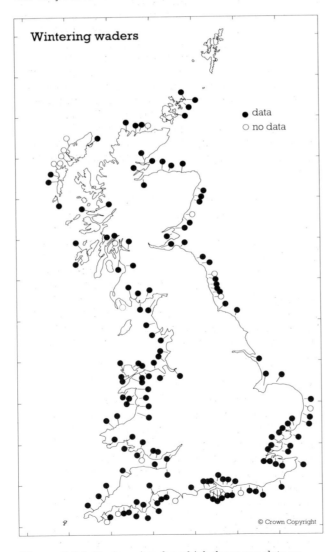

Figure 8.6.2 Review sites for which there are data on numbers of wintering waders

Convention. Note however that in some cases the BoEE/NWC data do not permit full separation into biogeographical populations, particularly where there are small numbers of birds present away from their main wintering areas. In these instances the biogeographical populations are summed in the general analysis for consistency of treatment, and are later described in more detail based on additional biological studies.

The most recent comprehensive estimates of the British populations of waders in January are given

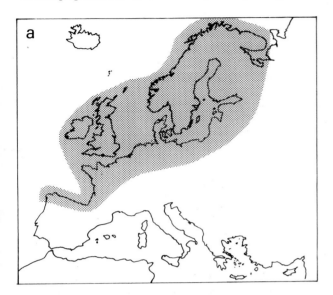

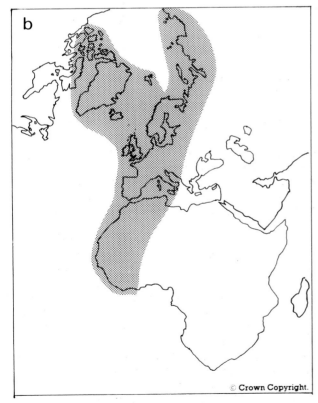

Figure 8.6.4 The wintering distribution of international populations of waterfowl used for comparison with the estuarine populations. a) North-west Europe for wildfowl, derived from Owen *et al.* (1986) and Pirot *et al.* (1989), and b) the East Atlantic Flyway for waders, from Smit & Piersma (1989).

by Moser (1987) for the period 1981 to 1985. Similar estimates of British wildfowl populations are given for 1977-1981 by Owen *et al.* (1986).

International population estimates come from data co-ordinated by the International Waterfowl and Wetlands Research Bureau (IWRB). Wildfowl population sizes are derived, for the western palearctic and Sahelian Africa, largely from January counts made during the International Waterfowl Census, recently updated by Pirot *et al.* (1989). International wader population estimates have also been recently updated by Smit & Piersma (1989). The relevant international wintering populations are those of north-west Europe for wildfowl and the East Atlantic Flyway for waders (Figure 8.6.4).

Choice of data to describe wintering populations

The total populations of waders and wildfowl used for individual site conservation assessments are generally the mean of the peak totals counted during the course of the winter (November – March for waders, September – March for wildfowl) (Prater 1981; Salmon *et al.* 1989). These values are usually calculated over the most recent five winters, to allow for annual variations in population size, and give a good general assessment of numbers at that site. For species that are mobile, i.e. most waders and wildfowl, the sum of the mean peaks is, however, usually greater than the total population of the birds. This is because birds move between estuaries and so can be counted in different months on different sites. The importance of this population turnover is further discussed below. Because of this turnover, peak means are, however, inappropriate for analysing the proportions of the biogeographical populations occurring on review sites.

As the basis for describing the distribution and significance of wintering waterfowl on British estuaries we have therefore used the numbers present in January. For sites for which there are BoEE/NWC counts we have calculated a five-year January mean for the most recent years of data available to us – 1983-1987. To these have been added the Winter Shorebird Count data for other review sites, collected mostly in midwinter 1984/85. The population sizes so calculated thus represent the best estimate of the size and distribution of the midwinter population.

Use of January counts for this assessment has several advantages, in addition to permitting the incorporation of Winter Shorebird Count data. January is usually the month in which peak numbers of many species of waders and wildfowl occur in Britain, although some do occur in greater numbers during migration periods (see Salmon *et al.* 1989). January is also the month in which greatest coverage of sites is achieved in Britain (Salmon *et al.* 1989). It coincides also with the International Waterfowl Counts, and so permits direct comparison of the populations on British estuaries with the international population estimates (Pirot *et al.* 1989; Smit & Piersma 1989).

Furthermore, January is the period of the winter in which there is least population movement (except when a period of severe weather causes birds to move – see later) since most waterfowl have by then reached their winter quarters but have not yet begun their return spring migration. Note however that the January distributions and numbers described below provide a minimum indication of the numbers of birds using an estuary and are not directly applicable to the conservation assessment of nationally and internationally important sites (see Stroud et al. 1990).

It is important to note that the estimates of national and international population totals are made only periodically and so are held fixed for periods of several years. This has important advantages in establishing medium-order stability in conservation assessments of waterfowl populations. However, since many high arctic waterfowl, especially species such as brent geese, have very variable breeding success, actual numbers may fluctuate round the average value. The calculation of a five-year mean does, however, help to smooth out these fluctuations. For populations undergoing a long-term decline or increase in numbers it means that the best estimate for the biogeographical population lags behind the true population. So in some instances the observed population may apparently exceed the total national or international population. Calculated percentages of total populations should therefore be treated as approximate and indicative.

Assessing autumn and spring populations

Assessing the patterns of usage of British estuaries during autumn and spring from BoEE/NWC counts is more difficult than for winter for a variety of reasons. Firstly, coverage of sites is more restricted during these periods. Secondly, several biogeographical populations behaving in different ways may be present on an estuary at the same time, but are not usually distinguishable in total counts. In autumn some birds arrive on estuaries in Britain and elsewhere in western Europe and then spend several weeks or months there moulting their body and wing feathers. At the same time other populations from different breeding grounds depend more briefly on the same estuaries without moulting, before migrating further south to southern European and African wintering grounds. For such birds these sites provide vital feeding areas that permit them to store the fat and protein reserves essential for their onward migration to more southerly wintering areas. At these times the rate of turnover can be very rapid so that a single monthly count does not adequately represent the total usage of the site.

Spring, when there is rapid turnover of birds returning from southern wintering grounds joining those that may have overwintered in Britain, presents a similar problem. Many spring migrant waterfowl also spend only two to three weeks on such staging areas so that monthly counts, as in autumn, cannot elucidate site use; such single snapshot counts underestimate the numbers using a site. Nevertheless such staging sites provide vital feeding grounds that enable these birds to accumulate sufficient nutrient reserves to return to their breeding grounds and breed successfully. Accordingly we describe the use of British estuaries outside the midwinter period from the evidence of the more detailed studies of moult and migration that have been carried out in some places (e.g. Steventon 1977; Ferns 1980a, 1980b, 1981a, 1981b; Moser & Carrier 1983; Prys-Jones et al. 1988).

The use of BoEE/NWC counts for assessing bird populations on review sites

BoEE/NWC counts provide the most comprehensive and comparable information for describing the distribution and abundance of British estuarine waterfowl but their interpretation requires an understanding of their limitations in relation to the behaviour of the birds. Counts are made usually during the period of high tide, when waders are either aggregated on their roost sites or arriving at or leaving the sites, since at this time the birds are most readily counted. At low tide birds are dispersed widely over often extensive tidal flats and cannot readily be counted accurately, particularly on large estuaries. The counts therefore provide a reliable assessment of the numbers of birds roosting in the area. Whilst in many instances waders roost close to their feeding grounds, some, however, can move considerable distances to roost (Furness 1973; Davidson & Evans 1985; Mitchell et al. 1988), even into adjacent estuaries. So high tide counts may not always represent the numbers that feed on the same estuary.

The feeding distribution and numbers of waterfowl present during low water are becoming known for an increasing number of British estuaries, but not yet widely enough for a comparative assessment of review sites. Furthermore such data have often been collected for only one year, or at most a few years, frequently as part of environmental impact studies for proposed developments. Low-water count distributions cannot yet provide the long-term picture needed for adequate site assessment for these mobile birds with their variable breeding success.

High-tide counts provide a good assessment of the numbers of those wildfowl species that both feed and roost on the same estuary. Some species, especially swans and geese, feed during daylight on farmland away from the estuary, returning there only to roost at night. Since high-tide counts are made during daylight they can underestimate the numbers of wildfowl using the estuary, and for these species special counts are made. Numbers of wildfowl counted on estuaries should therefore be regarded as minima.

Boundaries of review sites have been set on a geographical basis and have been designed to permit the assessment of a wide variety of wildlife features and human activities rather than just the bird populations. In most cases BoEE sites (Moser 1987) fall within review sites. Boundaries of BoEE sites are, however, generally more limited than review site boundaries since they are determined by the location of roost sites and not the location of the intertidal feeding areas. For some review sites this means that only part, usually the lower reaches, is covered by BoEE counts. Since the counts are designed to cover the places where there are waterfowl present, and since generally few waterfowl occur on the narrow upper tidal river channels, this is unlikely to affect the counts substantially. Some review sites, e.g. the Moray Firth and the Firth of Forth, are covered by several BoEE sites: counts for these have been summed to provide a total coincident with the relevant review site boundaries. Detailed studies on the mobility of waders using these estuaries (Symonds et al. 1984; Symonds & Langslow 1986) have shown that the notional line between contiguous intertidal areas, used to delimit Estuaries Review sites, coincides with natural boundaries for some species, although some other studies link several of these areas together, as for example on the Dornoch, Cromarty and Moray Firths (see Figure 8.6.18).

In some parts of Britain, areas of freshwater wetlands adjacent to the upper parts of review sites are used extensively by wintering wildfowl. Such places include the Ouse and Nene Washes (The Wash) and Amberley Wild Brooks (Arun Estuary). These wintering bird populations are not directly associated with estuaries at any time and they have been excluded from the calculations of waterfowl population sizes, since their inclusion would greatly distort the apparent population sizes and densities on some estuaries.

The 1% criterion as an indicator of population importance

In some of the analyses we have described patterns of population dispersal in relation to populations comprising at least 1% of the estuarine, national or international populations. The 1% criterion has proved valuable as a basis for evaluating the international importance of a site for birds since it has been found to provide an appropriate degree of protection for many populations and is useful in the definition of ecologically coherent sites (Atkinson-Willes et al. 1982; Fuller & Langslow 1986). The criterion has gained wide acceptance throughout the world and is used by the Contracting Parties of the Ramsar Convention as a criterion for identifying wetlands of international importance (Atkinson-Willes et al. 1982). However, the 1% measure works well only for those populations which tend to congregate. This means that it is a particularly effective criterion for those species such as whooper swan and brent goose that depend on just a few traditional wintering areas. It is important to remember that, although we describe the distribution of many waders and wildfowl as being widespread around estuaries, estuaries form only 2.3% of the total area of Britain (see Chapter 6), so that all waterfowl

species that are substantially dependent on estuaries have a highly restricted distribution in national and international terms. Nevertheless this analysis shows later that, even for some of the waterfowl that are more widely dispersed around British estuaries, a 1% site assessment criterion alone is inadequate to identify the location of all sites important to a wintering population.

This 1% assessment is, however, only one aspect of the assessment of the significance of an estuary for its wildlife importance (see Stroud et al. 1989), and it generally provides a minimum assessment the importance of a site. All sites supporting 1% or more of a population at any one time are undoubtedly of national or international importance. With supplementary understanding of the ways in which birds use these sites (see below) these sites generally assume even greater importance and others attain such significance (see e.g. Stroud et al. 1990; Ridgill & Fox 1990). Even as a direct numeric assessment there are, however, complications with the use of this 1% criterion alone, as is discussed below.

Stroud et al. (1990) point out that the 1% level is fairly conservative for both national and international assessments. For example, human populations are an extreme example of a numerous species that forms dense concentrations, with a British population of about 56,000,000 and hence a 1% level of 560,000. On the 1% basis the only cities qualifying as 'nationally important' would be London, Birmingham, Sheffield, Manchester and Liverpool. Glasgow could be included if its satellite towns (e.g. Paisley) were included. Only London would be defined as 'internationally important'.

The 1% levels quoted in this review generally underestimate the importance of individual sites since they are expressed in relation to January population sizes only, rather than to the values for the average peak wintering populations used in site conservation assessment. Even so a 1% value based on peak monthly counts is still conservative since the turnover of individuals present on an estuary means that the total proportion of an international population using it can be very much higher than the number of individuals present at any one time (see e.g. Smit & Piersma 1989). The effects of population turnover are described further below. It important to recognise that the analyses in this report are designed to describe the ways in which wintering waterfowl use British estuaries, and do not provide the definitive assessment of their individual conservation importance for birds. The approach to such conservation assessments is set out in NCC (1989) and Stroud et al. (1990).

Reliable use of 1% values in assessing demographic patterns and site importance depends on there being good estimates of the total national and biogeographical populations. The BoEE programme of co-ordinated monthly counts provides this detailed information for Britain and forms a part of extensive co-ordinated counts in western Europe that provide good estimates for north-west European wildfowl populations and waders on the East Atlantic Flyway (Pirot *et al.* 1989; Smit & Piersma 1989), and, recently, in the New World, particularly in South America (Morrison & Ross 1989). However, for most other parts of the world such necessary and detailed information on the status of migratory bird populations is incomplete or non-existent (Parish *et al.* 1987; Summers *et al.* 1987; Parish 1989).

A further complication of using only a 1% population level in site assessment is the variations in the preference shown by birds for different sites. When populations are small, birds select first those sites that most fully provide for their requirements and where their chances of survival are highest (Pienkowski & Evans 1985). As populations increase, however, not all birds are able to use these favoured sites and an increasing number use less suitable sites elsewhere. Hence the proportion of the population on the most preferred sites declines as the overall population increases.

The clearest demonstration of this phenomenon is for grey plover *Pluvialis squatarola*. The numbers of grey plovers wintering on British estuaries, and the range of sites used, have greatly increased in recent years, such that the index of British midwinter population size is now almost four times larger than in 1973 (Salmon *et al.* 1989). Moser (1988) showed that there seems to be a limit to the numbers of grey plovers that can use any one site. Thus at many preferred sites, where carrying capacity has apparently been reached, the midwinter population is no longer increasing. As a consequence of the overall increase in numbers, the *proportion* of the population using these preferred sites (some of which are small estuaries) has declined. As Moser (1988) points out, this trend means that even an area such as the north-west Solent (Beaulieu River and Lymington Estuary review sites), which is one of the most preferred sites for grey plovers in Britain, would cease to be 'nationally important' in numerical terms (on the arbitrary 1% criterion) once the national population levels rose to 30,000, although the area probably held 5% of the national population when there were only 5,000 grey plovers wintering in Britain.

Moser (1988) proposed a refinement to the 1% criterion to take into account the ranking of sites on their degree of preference by different species, where such data exist. Even less-preferred sites are, however, important for arctic-breeding bird populations with variable breeding success, since there is a need to support a population when it is at a high level so as to ensure that there will still be adequate breeding populations after a sequence of years of poor breeding success (Stroud *et al.* 1990).

Overall then a 1% criterion provides an effective initial tool in the identification of important wetlands for wintering waterfowl, particularly where a more detailed understanding of the behaviour and ecology of waterfowl using a site is lacking. Assessment of the overall conservation importance of a wetland must, however, also take into account other factors, such as the favourability of the site and its population turnover, and various additional values of the site such as its use when birds are moulting their feathers, and when accumulating nutrient reserves before or during migrations (Piersma *et al.* 1987a; Smit & Piersma 1989). The role that British estuaries play in relation to these features is described further in the following part of this review.

General features of the use of British estuaries by waterfowl

The annual cycle of migrant waterfowl

The severe winter weather and general absence of available food mean that waders and wildfowl that breed in the arctic and also in some more southerly

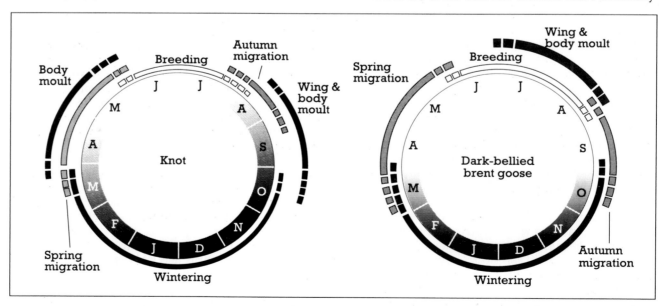

Figure 8.6.5 Summaries of the annual cycles of high-arctic breeding waders and wildfowl, typified by *islandica* race knot (derived from Davidson & Wilson 1990) and dark-bellied brent goose (derived from Owen *et al.* 1986). Shaded parts of the year show when birds depend on review sites.

latitudes cannot spend the whole of the year where they breed. Indeed high-arctic breeders spend a very short time on their breeding grounds – often only the six to eight weeks between their arrival in early June and departure in mid-July to early August. In the other 10 months of the year they move great distances to and from their wintering grounds in places such as British estuaries, where they spend more than half the year. The annual cycle of typical high-arctic waders and wildfowl is summarised in Figure 8.6.5.

In the short period on their breeding grounds, arctic-breeding waterfowl must lay eggs, incubate them and, if successful, care for their precocial young until they have fledged, and also accumulate sufficient energy reserves to fly south towards their wintering areas. In general, adult waders leave their breeding grounds rather earlier than their young, since the juvenile birds have to grow a full set of flight feathers and also store reserves for their first migration. In contrast adult geese stay with their young throughout the autumn and subsequent winter.

Migrations to and from arctic breeding areas often involve birds making flights of several thousand kilometres over inhospitable terrain such as mountains, oceans, high-altitude ice-caps, snow-covered land and other areas lacking suitable feeding grounds. To do this, waders and wildfowl store large amounts of fat and muscle protein that provide the fuel and the power for non-stop flights. These are often of over 3,000 km and last several days (e.g. Davidson 1984; Davidson & Evans 1988; Piersma & Jukema 1990).

Many species stop at one or more migration staging areas, where they pause usually for only one or two weeks to replace nutrient and energy reserves used during the previous migratory flight *en route* to their wintering grounds. By early August many wader populations have left their breeding grounds and have reached estuaries in Britain and elsewhere in the southern North Sea, where they moult their wing feathers and body plumage. Other wader populations again pause for only a few days in western Europe to store further fat reserves and then fly on to western African shores before moulting. In contrast to waders, both arctic-breeding wildfowl and those of lower latitudes undergo a rapid moult in late summer before leaving their breeding grounds. During this period many wildfowl become flightless (Owen *et al.* 1986). Waders remain able to fly but their flying performance may be impaired (see e.g. Pienkowski *et al.* 1976).

Wing moult in waders takes about two to three months and by early October most birds have completed their moult. Some remain on the same estuaries to overwinter; others move to wintering grounds elsewhere in Britain and western Europe. Likewise most wildfowl begin to arrive on their British wintering grounds from mid-September onwards. Some remain on one estuary throughout the winter, but others are known to move between

a network of estuaries during the course of the winter (e.g. Pienkowski & Pienkowski 1983; Pienkowski & Evans 1984, 1985).

Most waders and wildfowl begin to prepare for their return migration to their breeding grounds in March, when they begin to accumulate fat and protein reserves. To do so some remain in the same places in which they overwintered; others move in March to early-spring staging areas which provide particularly favourable feeding conditions for rapid acquisition of nutrient reserves. Many of the waders that overwinter on the west coast of Africa begin to return to west European staging areas at this time (Ens *et al.* 1989). By April and early May many of the waterfowl breeding in boreal regions are returning to their breeding grounds. High-arctic breeders remain on staging areas, some moving further north in early May to late spring staging areas in Iceland and northern Scandinavia (e.g. Wilson 1981; Davidson *et al.* 1986c). There they replenish nutrient reserves for further migratory flight. During spring, waders also moult their body feathers from a wintering plumage into an often more brightly coloured breeding plumage.

Waders particularly show a great variety of migration strategies in moving between wintering and breeding grounds (Burger & Olla 1984; Piersma 1987). These range from making a large number of small 'hops' – a strategy dependent on availability of suitable feeding in many places and one in which the birds need to store only small reserves of fat as fuel for the short flights – to the behaviour of species such as knots *Calidris canutus* and bar-tailed godwits *Limosa lapponica* that 'jump' between a very few staging areas and store large amounts of fat for long flights (Piersma 1987). In some birds this pre-migratory accumulation of fat and muscle protein results in a doubling of their body weight.

This variety of migration strategies means that the significance of a particular British estuary during spring or autumn differs considerably between the members of a waterfowl assemblage present on the site. Different individuals of the same species may even have different migration strategies (see e.g. Pienkowski & Evans 1984). Furthermore individuals may also require a different series of sites in different years (see e.g. Townshend 1985; Pienkowski 1990).

High-arctic waterfowl mostly leave their final spring staging areas in late May and early June, arriving on their breeding grounds a few days later. Such timing appears generally to have evolved to coincide with the period of snow-melt on the breeding grounds, so that food is available when, or soon after, the birds arrive (Green *et al.* 1977; Meltofte 1985).

Not all individuals return to the breeding grounds in late spring, and some non-breeding individuals of many species, especially waders, remain on estuaries in western Europe and West Africa.

These summering birds are largely juveniles or sub-adults in species that do not usually breed at one year old (e.g. Prater 1981; Smit & Wolff 1981). Their survival is thus a crucial component of the conservation of the populations.

Long-term population trends and variations in breeding success

The numbers of each waterfowl species reaching its wintering grounds in Britain and elsewhere depends on the survival of the adult birds during their migrations and breeding season, on how many young they have managed to rear successfully and on the success of these young birds in making their first migration to their wintering grounds. Numbers, particularly of those species that breed in the high arctic, can vary substantially from year to year.

From detailed studies of individually-marked birds, Evans & Pienkowski (1984) showed that the annual survival of adult waders is very high, averaging over 80%, and that generally at least half the mortality occurred on their wintering grounds. So despite flying such long distances over inhospitable terrain, mortality on migration and breeding grounds is generally small, although Evans & Pienkowski did detect some years in which migration and summer mortality in high-arctic breeders were unusually high. This fits with observations that in occasional years there is high adult mortality of these species when severe weather occurs after the birds have started to breed (Morrison 1975; Meltofte 1985; Boyd in press). Similarly high annual survival of adult waterfowl has been found in detailed studies of many species (Owen et al. 1986).

There is much more variation in the numbers of juveniles reaching western Europe. In part this is because many inexperienced young birds die in early autumn during their first migratory flight from their natal area (Pienkowski & Evans 1985; Owen & Black 1989). Once they have reached their wintering grounds the mortality of first-year waterfowl is often only slightly higher than that of adults. Migratory mortality is, however, superimposed on the often considerable variation in the numbers of young reared successfully to fledging. This has been particularly well studied in arctic-breeding swans and geese since they remain in family parties throughout the winter. So the numbers of young raised by each breeding pair can be readily counted when the birds are on their wintering grounds. This permits the use of age-related plumage differences to assess overall proportions of juveniles in flocks.

There are large variations in the annual breeding success of geese breeding in many different arctic and sub-arctic areas. The breeding success of dark-bellied brent geese *Branta bernicla bernicla* that nest on the Taymyr peninsula in northern Siberia has been particularly well studied, and found to vary greatly – between over 50% of the winter population being juveniles in some years to almost no juveniles in others. There is much current debate over the causes of these variations in breeding success, centring on the contributions to breeding success of the accumulation of sufficient nutrient reserves on spring staging areas, the weather conditions on the breeding grounds, and the impact of predation of eggs and young by arctic foxes *Alopex lagopus* (Ebbinge 1985, 1987, 1989; Summers 1986; Boyd 1987; Dhondt 1987; de Boer & Drent 1989). It has been suggested that in years when lemming populations are low but fox populations remain high the foxes change their diet to eat more waterfowl eggs and chicks (Summers 1986).

There is also a striking link between the breeding success of brent geese and waders such as curlew sandpipers *Calidris ferruginea* and *canutus* subspecies knots that are believed to breed in the same areas of Siberia (Summers & Underhill 1987; Underhill et al. 1989). Waders such as knots breeding in the nearctic also vary greatly in their breeding success but the annual success is not correlated between the two areas (Underhill et al. 1989; Davidson & Wilson 1991).

Whatever the underlying causes of these variations in breeding success, they result in sometimes large annual variations in the numbers of waterfowl occurring during autumn migration and in winter on estuaries in Britain and elsewhere in western Europe. As described above these variations in wintering population size affect the ways in which the distribution of populations and their conservation significance are described.

Breeding failures can also contribute to longer-term changes in population size. A series of poor breeding seasons in the early 1970s, attributed to late springs and severely cold summer weather on their breeding grounds, appears to have contributed to the prolonged decline in the total population size of the knots that breed in Greenland and northern Canada (Boyd 1991). The total wintering population of this subspecies has not recovered substantially in numbers since the mid-1970s (Davidson & Wilson 1991).

A number of other waterfowl populations wintering in western Europe and Africa have also been undergoing long-term changes. These are summarised by Pirot et al. (1989) and Smit & Piersma (1989). In some cases it is difficult to identify the effects of improvements in international counting coverage, In comparison with counts from the early 1970s – summarised by Prater (1976) – Smit & Piersma (1989) found increases that they considered to be at least in part due to real changes in population size in the west European wintering populations of several wader species. These are oystercatcher *Haematopus ostralegus*, grey plover, bar-tailed godwit and ringed plover. Smit & Piersma found decreases in dunlin *Calidris alpina*, knot and, to a small extent, redshank *Tringa totanus*. These overall changes are apparent in Britain in increases in the population indices of oystercatcher and grey plover and decreases in the indices of knot and dunlin, as derived from the BoEE (Figure 8.6.6).

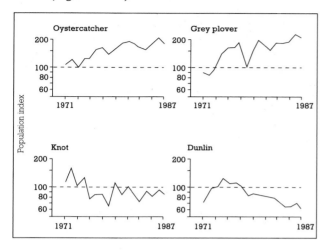

Figure 8.6.6 Indices of wintering population size of increasing and declining waders in Britain, from Smit & Piersma (1989), with data derived from Salmon *et al.* (1987). The indices were set at an arbitrary value of 100 (shown by the dashed horizontal lines) for 1973.

There can be many causes of changes in population sizes, which may arise from conditions on breeding grounds, wintering grounds and/or migration staging areas. The changes in different wader populations seem to arise for different reasons. In oystercatchers an expansion of breeding range and diversification of habitat use is implicated (Sharrock 1976; Piersma 1986). The reasons for the increase in grey plover and bar-tailed godwit populations are not clear, although for grey plovers Tubbs (In press) suggests that the cessation in 1954 of formerly heavy shooting pressure in Britain may be a contributor. The decline in nearctic knot, as described above, seems to have arisen through adult mortality and poor breeding success in the early 1970s, but the reasons for the failure of the population to recover its numbers since then are not clear.

The decline in dunlin numbers has been particularly marked in Britain but has also occurred elsewhere in Europe. Goss-Custard & Moser (1988) have shown that loss of feeding grounds in wintering areas is implicated in this decline. They showed that declines have been largest where the spread of cord-grass *Spartina anglica*, which largely prevents dunlins from feeding within its dense sward, has been most extensive. (This species of *Spartina* resulted from the hybridisation of native and introduced species – see Section 8.1.5.) Long-term population changes can improve understanding of the significance of British estuaries for wintering waterfowl. A larger proportion of the total wintering population of knots now occurs on British estuaries than when the population was high in the early 1970s (Davidson & Wilson 1991), a further indicator of the likely preferred nature of British estuaries as wintering sites.

Pirot *et al.* (1989) report stable or increasing

population sizes for many wildfowl overwintering in north-west Europe but a decrease in pochard *Aythya ferina* numbers. The various biogeographical populations of geese have increased mostly significantly during the last few decades – see the example of dark-bellied brent geese in Figure 8.6.7. For many, including these brent geese, these increases are recoveries to formerly much larger populations rather than increases from healthy populations. These population increases have been attributed by Ebbinge (1985) and Madsen (1987, 1989) largely to reductions in mortality, brought about by restrictions on shooting in many parts of Europe, and to changes in agricultural practices which have provided better winter foraging. Several geese such as dark-bellied brent geese *Branta bernicla bernicla* have moved from saltmarshes and grazing marshes to feed increasingly in recent years on arable farmland. This seems to have arisen in part because the area of available saltmarsh has become increasingly restricted (see Chapter 10) and partly from the conversion of coastal grasslands, formerly used extensively by geese, to arable.

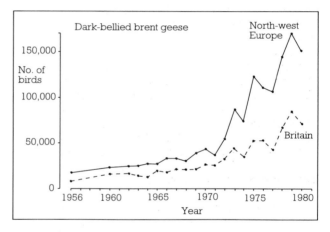

Figure 8.6.7 The increase in the total population of wintering dark-bellied brent geese in Britain and north-west Europe, from Owen *et al.* (1986)

One small goose population has not increased since the relaxation of shooting pressure. The Svalbard population of the light-bellied brent goose *Branta bernicla hrota*, many of which overwinter in Britain at Lindisfarne, still numbers only less than 4,000 birds. Madsen *et al.* (1989) suggest that it may now be under pressure from competition on its breeding grounds from an expanding population of barnacle geese *Branta leucopsis* (Prestrud 1989), but the reasons for the decline are complex (see Stroud *et al.* 1990).

An understanding of population sizes and dynamics is important in developing conservation measures for waterfowl, particularly since annual population sizes may vary substantially. Small populations and/or those that depend on just a few estuaries are clearly vulnerable to loss or damage to their habitats. Substantially larger populations may, however, be more vulnerable than they seem. Baker & Strauch (1988) and Baker (1991) have recently found that most shorebird populations are much less genetically variable than those of other bird taxa. This means that the effective genotypic population size can be very substantially smaller than the observed number of birds, and that even apparently large and less vulnerable populations may face substantial risks from genetic bottlenecks leading to extinctions. Maintenance of population sizes and geographical ranges is therefore vital for the future conservation of these species.

Autumn migration on British estuaries

In addition to the arrival of birds returning to overwinter on British estuaries, these places have an added importance in autumn as staging and moulting areas for other waterfowl populations that overwinter further south.

Migration routes and timings in waders

The first waders returning to British estuaries in late July are adults. These are mostly birds whose breeding attempts have failed. Numbers of adults of most species then increase rapidly in August and September as those adults that have successfully reared young return. Juveniles generally arrive later than most adults, in August and September (e.g. Branson & Minton 1976; Insley & Young 1981; Townshend 1985).

Many arctic-breeding waders reach Britain, and other estuaries in western Europe, after pausing to refuel at migration staging areas such as Iceland (Wilson 1981); most of those breeding further south probably move directly from their breeding grounds to the estuaries. It is difficult to disentangle the patterns of use of British estuaries during autumn since there is often more than one age-class and population of a species present on one estuary at any given time.

This mixing of populations is particularly complex in dunlins where adults and juveniles of three different subspecies (four biogeographic populations) use British estuaries in autumn (Cramp & Simmons 1983). The small Greenland-breeding *arctica* population passes through British estuaries, *en route* for West African wintering grounds, in small numbers in August. This is also the main period of arrival of the nominate *alpina* dunlins from northern USSR and northern Scandinavia. Adult *alpina* dunlins remain on these estuaries to moult during the next few months (see below). After moulting some remain on the same estuary to overwinter, while others disperse either locally or to estuaries elsewhere in Britain. The large Icelandic population of *schinzii* dunlins begins passing through Britain in early to mid-July, pausing on many British estuaries to replenish nutrient reserves for flight onward to north and west African wintering grounds. The presence of the much smaller Baltic and British-breeding population of *schinzii* dunlins is generally masked by the presence of large numbers of Icelandic birds, but ringing recoveries have shown that these temperate *schinzii* begin to pass through British

estuaries in early July, with females arriving rather earlier than males (Pienkowski & Dick 1975). As a further complication, some *schinzii* dunlins begin to moult their wing feathers on south coast British estuaries such as Portsmouth, Chichester and Langstone Harbours (Steventon 1977), before flying further south to complete their moult. Juveniles of each population pass through British estuaries later than the adults. Thus the composition of the dunlin population (summarised in Figure 8.6.8) that is present in autumn on British estuaries is complex and rapidly changing. To elucidate the ways in which wader populations use estuaries in autumn requires detailed studies on a site, involving catching, ringing and measuring birds to identify their origins and destinations.

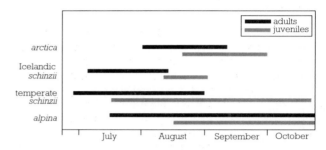

Figure 8.6.8 Periods of presence of different biogeographical populations of dunlins on British estuaries in autumn, derived from Pienkowski & Dick (1975). Solid bars are adults and shaded bars are juveniles. *Alpina* dunlins remain to overwinter in Britain; other populations migrate further south.

There are similarly complex patterns of use by other waders using British estuaries in autumn. For example ringed plovers on British estuaries in autumn include moulting birds from the populations breeding locally, and from elsewhere in Britain, the southern North Sea and the Baltic. These birds generally remain to overwinter in Britain. In addition there are passage populations of arctic and subarctic breeding birds from Iceland, Greenland and northern Scandinavia. Some of these birds may have already started moulting before leaving their breeding grounds. These populations move further south to overwinter in north and west Africa after storing large reserves of fat (Clapham 1978; Insley & Young 1981; Cramp & Simmons 1983; Davidson et al. 1986b).

Similarly, the autumn redshank population includes moulting birds from three biogeographic populations (*robusta* from Iceland, *totanus* from Britain and *totanus* from Scandinavia and continental western Europe). The moulting birds remain to overwinter in Britain, but others from Britain and Europe move further south to moult and overwinter in Africa (Cramp & Simmons 1983, Davidson et al. 1986b).

In other species such as knot and curlew *Numenius arquata* the autumn populations on British estuaries are much less complex and consist almost entirely of one biogeographic population. Knots belong almost entirely to the nearctic *islandica* race. Knots in Britain in autumn moult chiefly on a few major estuaries, notably The Wash, the Dee and North Wirral, the Ribble Estuary and Morecambe Bay, some before dispersing to overwinter elsewhere on British estuaries. Curlews in Britain in autumn are a moulting population of birds that have bred in Scandinavia, the southern Baltic and as far west as Belgium (Bainbridge & Minton 1978; Davidson *et al.* 1986b).

Several other waders, notably whimbrel *Numenius phaeopus*, greenshank *Tringa nebularia* and ruff *Philomachus pugnax*, occur on British estuaries almost exclusively during passage in autumn and spring (Prater 1981).

Juvenile waders generally leave their breeding grounds after the adults have departed and so must make their first migrations without any of the advantages accruing from making the flight with adults. Juvenile waders may not inherit a precise migration destination for this autumn flight; Pienkowski & Evans (1985) have suggested that instead juveniles leave their natal area with a general direction and a minimum distance to travel before alighting at a potential staging site. This pattern of autumn migration would explain why juveniles disperse more widely and appear on many estuarine and non-estuarine sites in which adults are scarce or absent (Pienkowski & Evans 1985; OAG Munster 1987).

In some biogeographic populations using the East Atlantic Flyway large numbers of adults occur in Britain only in exceptional circumstances, even during migration times. Examples are the Siberian-breeding curlew sandpipers and *canutus* knots. However in some years many birds, particularly juveniles, appear in Britain in autumn, often mostly on the east coast. These appear to be mainly birds that have overshot their normal staging areas further east (such as the Wadden Sea), often apparently assisted by strong easterly winds at the time of migration (Stanley & Minton 1972; Dick *et al.* 1987; Kirby *et al.* 1989). Influxes of curlew sandpipers seem to occur in years when breeding productivity is high (Kirby *et al.* 1989) and the birds are then more widespread on British estuaries and not restricted to the 39 review sites on which they regularly occur in small numbers (Figure 8.6.9).

Establishment of autumn migration patterns in waders

The pattern of migration established by a juvenile wader during its first autumn and winter appears to be very important. Townshend (1985) has shown that the migration phenology followed by juvenile grey plovers determines the migration and wintering areas they use later in their lifetime. Some first-year grey plovers arriving at Teesmouth in autumn managed to remain there along with the adult population throughout the winter. These birds returned to overwinter at Teesmouth as adults in subsequent years. In contrast, some first-year grey plovers were competitively excluded by

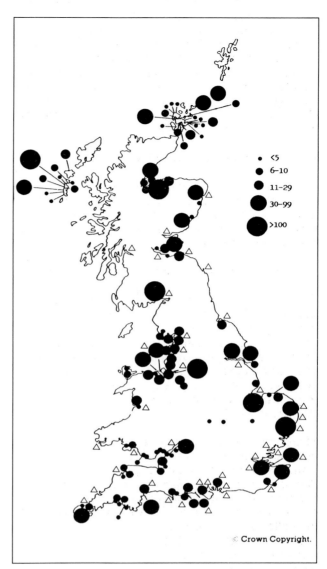

Figure 8.6.9 Autumn peak counts of curlew sandpipers in Britain in 1988, from Kirby *et al.* (1989). Note that most localities are estuarine. Sites in which there are regularly small numbers (average peak autumn count <35 birds) are marked with a triangle.

adults from the feeding grounds. These birds left Teesmouth in the autumn and early winter, and some are known to have flown further south and attempted to overwinter in France. In subsequent years such birds used Teesmouth only briefly as a migration staging area in autumn. These findings also illustrate the migration staging site fidelity shown by many individual waders and species (e.g. Pienkowski & Evans 1984).

Autumn wader distributions on British estuaries

The distribution of many species of waders on British estuaries is much the same in autumn as it is in winter, although some species, such as knot, are particularly concentrated on a few sites, mainly because these are used as moulting areas (Prater 1981). The species assemblage of waders on British estuaries in August, the period of peak migration for many species, is illustrated in Figure

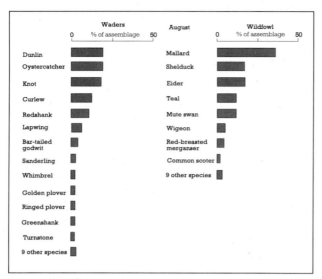

Figure 8.6.10 August wader and wildfowl species assemblages on review sites, derived from Prater (1981)

8.6.10. This can only give a broad picture of the abundance and diversity of waders using British estuaries as moulting and migration staging areas, because of the continual changes in population structure at this time of year, as described above. The total population counted in August is approximately 835,000 waders (11% of the East Atlantic Flyway population), rather smaller than the January population of about 1,160,000 waders (see later). The total numbers using British estuaries will, however, be much more than the August population, since many birds stay for only a few days or weeks on British estuaries before migrating further south. This population turnover means that many more individuals use British estuaries at some point in autumn. Studies of turnover (see Smit & Piersma 1989, and below) indicate that actual numbers of a migrant population using an estuary are at least 1.5 times the number present at any one time. Thus the total number of waders using British estuaries in autumn may be in excess of 1,250,000 birds (at least 17% of the East Atlantic Flyway population – Table 8.6.1).

Comparison with the midwinter population (Figure 8.6.33) shows some broad similarities with the August population, which is dominated, although to a lesser extent than in midwinter, by dunlins, knots and oystercatchers. Together these three species form over 55% of the August assemblage. The approximately 160,000 knots are all juveniles and moulting *islandica* adults and were about 30% of the international population of this species in the early 1970s. Almost all the remainder of this population moults on the Wadden Sea (Davidson & Wilson 1991). Much of the population occurs on four major estuaries: The Wash, Morecambe Bay, the Ribble Estuary, and the Dee Estuary and North Wirral (Prater 1981; Davidson & Wilson 1990). Oystercatchers and dunlins are much more widespread around British estuaries (Prater 1981). The assemblage in autumn is more diverse than in midwinter, with 13 species each forming more than 1% of the assemblage. Two of these species, whimbrel and greenshank, are almost entirely migratory on British estuaries. In other species at least part of the autumn population remains to overwinter.

Table 8.6.1 Totals of waders, wildfowl and waterfowl[1] on British estuaries in January 1983-1987. Data are from BoEE/NWC counts.

a) All review sites

	No. of sites	No. of birds	% British population[2]	% International population[3]
Waders	138	1,158,943	90.1	15.4[4]
Wildfowl	116	581,238	37.9	3.7
Waterfowl	142	1,740,181	61.7	10.2

b) Sites with large populations[5]

	No. of sites	No. of birds	% British estuarine population	% British population[2]	% International population[3]
Waders	27	924,451	79.8	71.9	12.2
Wildfowl	21	376,764	64.8	24.6	2.3
Waterfowl	24	1,447,419	83.2	51.3	8.5

[1] Waterfowl = waders and wildfowl combined
[2] British populations: waders 1,286,130 (Moser 1987); wildfowl 1,533,750 (Stroud *et al.* 1990)
[3] International populations: waders (East Atlantic Flyway) 7,547,000 (Smit & Piersma 1989); wildfowl (north-west Europe) 16,231,000 (Pirot *et al.* 1989)
[4] % on European Atlantic coast, of 3,207,900 birds (Smit & Piersma 1989) = 36.1%
[5] Waders >10,000 birds; wildfowl >10,000 birds; waterfowl >20,000 birds

Migration routes and timings in wildfowl

Wildfowl have rather different autumn migratory patterns from waders, since they generally moult on their breeding grounds before returning to western European estuaries. In addition, for geese and swans there is no difference in the timing of migration of adults and juveniles since they migrate as family parties which remain together during the subsequent winter (e.g. Evans 1979a; Owen 1982, 1984). Arctic and subarctic-breeding geese from Iceland and Greenland do not generally reach Britain until late September and October, with the Greenland populations of species such as the white-fronted goose and barnacle goose staging in Iceland. Many Siberian-breeding geese and swans reach areas of Denmark, West Germany and the Netherlands in autumn, some after staging in Norway and the Baltic. Movement to Britain generally occurs gradually in early winter, with the exact timing and numbers of birds reaching Britain dependent on the severity of winter weather (Owen *et al.* 1986). In some instances, however, autumn staging sites in Britain are of major importance to wildfowl. Substantially the whole population of Greenland barnacle geese *Branta leucopsis* arrives in October at one review site, Loch Gruinart on Islay in the Inner Hebrides (Easterbee *et al.* 1987). Here they feed for a few weeks before dispersing throughout their wintering range in Ireland and western Scotland, when a slightly smaller proportion of the population depends on estuaries.

Most ducks also move to their wintering grounds only in very late autumn and early winter, after they have moulted in autumn, generally near their breeding grounds. Arrivals on British estuaries occur mostly from late October onwards. Very few of the arctic and northern-breeding species move further south than France to overwinter, so in marked contrast to waders there is little staging and onward migration of waterfowl on British estuaries. A notable exception is the shelduck *Tadorna tadorna* which undertakes a moult migration in late summer, with some birds moving to Bridgwater Bay and many others moving from Britain to Helgoland in the German Bight (Patterson 1982) – see below.

The total number of wildfowl on British estuaries in early autumn is less than 50,000 and the assemblage is dominated by locally-breeding ducks such as mallard *Anas platyrhynchos*, shelduck and eider *Somateria mollissima* (Figure 8.6.10), since few of the main wintering populations have reached Britain by then.

Moult

Bird's feathers fulfil vital functions of insulation and flight, but, with use, feathers wear and become less effective as insulators and less efficient aerodynamically. Birds therefore generally replace their feathers on a regular basis, although the pattern of timing in the annual cycle differs between populations and markedly between waders and wildfowl. Safe and undisturbed moulting areas, which for many migratory waterfowl are found on estuaries, are vital for these species.

Moult in waders

The main annual moult in waders wintering in northern temperate areas occurs in late summer and autumn, when adults moult their body feathers from a breeding plumage to a wintering plumage, and also moult their wing and tail feathers. A second annual moult, of body feathers only, takes place during spring migration, when waders change to their breeding plumage. A typical annual cycle of moult is shown in Figure 8.6.11.

Figure 8.6.11 The annual moult cycle of grey plovers, summarising annual changes in appearance and timing of body moult and wing moult (labelled as 'primary moult score'), from Smit & Piersma (1989)

For many populations the autumn moult takes place on estuaries in Britain and elsewhere in western Europe between August and October. As described above, in some more southerly wintering populations of waders such as ringed plovers, wing moult may be started on staging areas in western Europe, then suspended whilst the birds migrate further and completed on the wintering grounds. Active wing moult in waders involves the simultaneous dropping and regrowth of several flight feathers and so may interfere with efficient flight (see e.g. Boere 1976; Pienkowski *et al.* 1976; Smit & Piersma 1989). Very few populations migrate during active moult. The different migration patterns and timings mean that wing moult takes place earlier on northern estuaries than in African wintering quarters, so that it is complete on estuaries in Britain and elsewhere around the North Sea by late October. Moult starts later, generally in September, in west Africa and takes longer, with new wing feathers not completely grown until December. A recent summary of moult timing and duration at different latitudes is given by Smit & Piersma (1989) and shown in Figure 8.6.12.

Many moulting waders concentrate in autumn on a few major estuaries in western Europe. The largest population is in the Wadden Sea, with other major

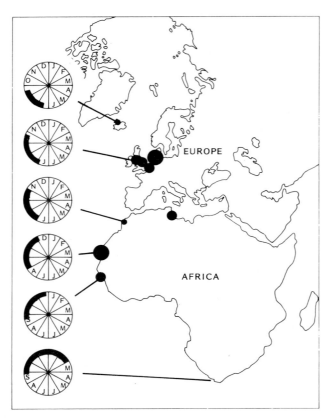

Figure 8.6.12 Latitudinal variation in the timing and duration of the wing moult of adult coastal waders and the location of the largest moulting sites, from Smit & Piersma (1989). Large symbols show sites with >1,000,000 birds, medium symbols sites with >100,000 birds, and small symbols show some other sites.

concentrations in The Wash, Morecambe Bay, the Dee Estuary and North Wirral and the Ribble Estuary, and in the Dutch Delta (Boere 1976; Prater 1981; Smit & Piersma 1989). It is generally considered that waders when moulting congregate on large estuaries because they provide an abundant food resource at an energetically costly time, and because there the birds are safe from disturbance at a time when flight is impaired (Boere 1976; Prater 1981). Nevertheless small moulting populations, particularly of more abundant waders such as dunlins, redshanks, oystercatchers and curlews, are widespread on smaller estuaries around Britain (e.g. Steventon 1977; Goodyer & Evans 1980; Insley & Young 1981; Pienkowski & Pienkowski 1983; Davidson & Evans 1985). It is not possible to assess the proportion of different moulting wader populations in autumn on these smaller British estuaries, since moulting and passage birds cannot be distinguished in BoEE counts. Such an overall analysis requires analysis of the age and moult status of birds caught for ringing.

Moult, especially the moult of wing feathers, has been generally regarded as an energetically costly process for many birds including waders and wildfowl (e.g. Hanson 1962; Payne 1972; Boere 1976). Masman et al. (1986) have recently shown, however, that the energetic costs of moult depend on diet, and that carnivorous birds, such as most

waders during their non-breeding seasons, may need little additional food above their normal daily intake. Despite this Smit & Piersma (1989) point out that there are some indirect additional energetic costs of moulting, notably a reduction in insulation that increases the costs of thermo-regulation when the ambient temperature is low and increased energy costs of flight using incompletely replaced wings.

Moult in wildfowl

Moulting wildfowl do not face these problems of flight energetics since during their main annual moult in late summer they become flightless, moulting all their flight feathers simultaneously. In this post-breeding moult, wildfowl replace their body and flight feathers at sites usually on or near their breeding grounds, and before their migration to their wintering grounds. Some species do move from breeding areas and undergo a moult migration (Salomonsen 1968). For example non-breeding pink-footed geese *Anser brachyrhynchus* migrate from Iceland to east Greenland to moult, before returning to Iceland to rejoin the breeding adults and their young before migrating to Britain (Taylor 1953). Another more recently developed moult migration involving a British estuary is the movement of non-breeding and immature feral Canada geese *Branta canadensis* to the Beauly Firth (the inner part of the Moray Firth review site). This moult migration has developed since 1947. It involves mostly birds from Yorkshire and, more recently, a few from further south in the Midlands (Dennis 1964; Owen et al. 1986).

Another moult migration for which British estuaries are of considerable significance is made by shelducks. This involves both breeding and non-breeding birds, most of which move in mid-July from all parts of north-west Europe to the Helgoland Bight in the West German part of the Wadden Sea. The flightless moulting flock here exceeds 100,000 birds. Several British estuaries have now been discovered to support smaller moulting flocks (Figure 8.6.13); there are no known moulting sites outside estuaries. The best known estuary is Bridgwater Bay, which can support up to 2,000 birds believed to be mostly Irish breeders. Elsewhere there are up to 3,000 birds on the Firth of Forth which certainly include locally-breeding birds, up to 1,500 birds on The Wash, a few hundred on the Humber Estuary, and a small flock on the Dee Estuary and North Wirral (Owen et al. 1986). These flocks on British estuaries probably represent at least 10% of the British wintering population and up to 3% of the international population. Furthermore Owen et al. (1986) consider that the use of British estuaries by moulting shelducks is spreading.

Most ducks moult their body feathers into an inconspicuous 'eclipse' plumage, and then again into winter plumage as their wing moult is completed. This rapid and extensive moult coupled with the vegetarian diet of many species makes moulting a costly process for wildfowl

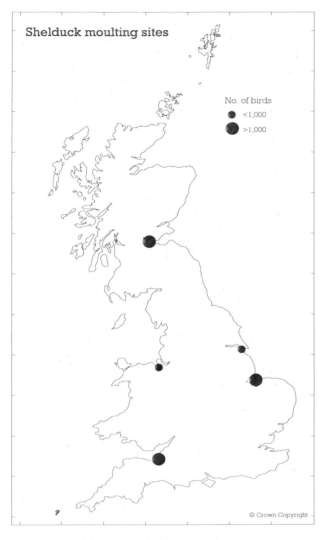

Figure 8.6.13 Autumn moulting sites for shelducks on British estuaries

(Ankney 1979, 1984; Masman *et al.* 1986). Unlike waders, wildfowl do not, however, moult their body feathers again in spring before breeding. The presence of these moulting flocks accounts for the large proportion (17%) contributed by shelducks to the autumn wildfowl assemblage on British estuaries (Figure 8.6.10). After moult shelducks gradually disperse back to wintering areas during November and December.

Movements and site networks during the non-breeding season

The use of migratory staging sites in autumn has been described above. There is increasing evidence, derived from analysis of reports of ringed birds, systematic counts and observations of colour-marked birds, that in waders several further migrations occur within the general wintering area. The pattern of these movements can be complex, as an individual wader can depend on a network of several estuaries. In those birds that move, the first migration is in late autumn, or sometimes as late as midwinter, from a moulting site to a wintering site. Some remain, however, all winter on their British moulting sites, such as The Wash. Others move just

once after moulting to spend all winter on one British estuary (see e.g. Evans & Pienkowski 1984; Pienkowski & Evans 1985; Townshend 1985). Yet others, particularly of some wader species, are more mobile and depend on a network of sites during the course of the winter.

These movement patterns are described and their significance reviewed by Pienkowski & Pienkowski (1983), Evans & Pienkowski (1984) and Pienkowski & Evans (1985). Some of these movement patterns of waders involving British estuaries are described below.

Dunlins

The movements of *alpina* dunlins (the population which overwinters in western Europe) are described in detail by Pienkowski & Pienkowski (1983) and Pienkowski & Evans (1984). They are summarised in Figures 8.6.14 – 16. Figure 8.6.14 shows a complex pattern of dispersal in late autumn of birds moving from moulting to wintering areas, involving movements into Britain from elsewhere, particularly the Wadden Sea and Dutch Delta, movements between estuaries in different parts of Britain, and movements out of Britain to estuaries further west in Ireland and further south in France, Spain and Portugal. Some British estuaries such as

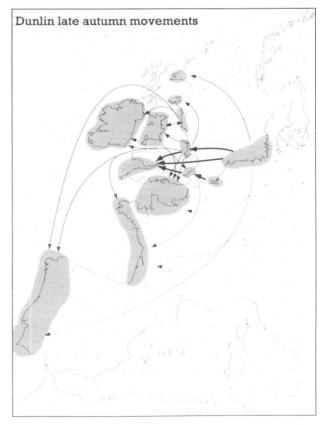

Figure 8.6.14 Late autumn movements of dunlins *Calidris a. alpina* within their wintering range (from Pienkowski & Pienkowski 1983) show that a complex network of sites is used by these internationally important populations. Arrows show known movements during a single autumn between different regions of the wintering area, shown shaded. Lines show links between sites, but are not intended to show actual migration routes..

The Wash are major net 'exporters' of dunlins at this time of year. Dispersal from moulting sites also involves northward movements in Britain from The Wash to as far north as the Moray Firth (Figure 8.6.14).

Another important feature of these autumn migrations is the movement to the same wintering estuaries of birds from different moulting sites; there is thus considerable intermixing of the populations at different times of year.

There is usually much less movement in the midwinter period between November and February. Nevertheless some dunlins move from estuaries in eastern England to others on the Irish Sea coast, and others move southwards to France and Iberia (Figure 8.6.15). In addition, counts of marked birds, particularly at small estuaries in Britain, have found that some movements occur throughout the winter. There are however no major influxes in midwinter into some sites such as the Firth of Forth (Symonds et al. 1984).

In late winter and early spring dunlins start moving to staging areas where they begin to moult and accumulate nutrient reserves before migrating to their wintering grounds. For alpina dunlins this generally involves a movement northwards and eastwards in March and early April from southern Europe to estuaries in eastern Britain, and

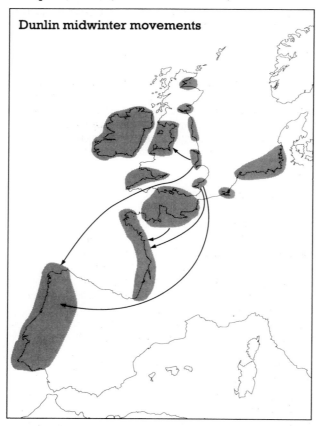

Figure 8.6.15 Midwinter movements of dunlins Calidris a. alpina within their wintering range (from Pienkowski & Pienkowski 1983). Arrows show known movements during a single winter between different regions of the wintering area, shown shaded. Lines show links between sites, but are not intended to show actual migration routes.

elsewhere on the southern North Sea, and from Britain to the Wadden Sea (Figure 8.6.16). Some others, however, move southwards (i.e. away from their breeding grounds) down the east coast of Britain from estuaries such as the Firth of Forth.

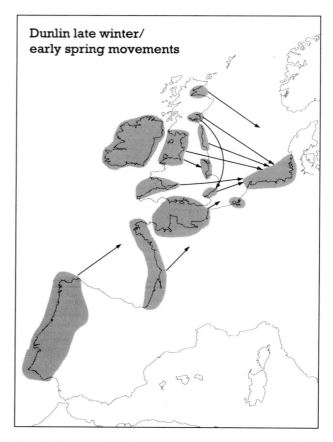

Figure 8.6.16 Late winter and early spring movements of dunlins Calidris a. alpina within their wintering range (from Pienkowski & Pienkowski 1983) show northward and westward movement between estuaries. Arrows show known movements during a single winter between different regions of the wintering area, shown shaded. Lines show links between sites, but are not intended to show actual migration routes.

Grey plovers

Other species have different movement patterns. More limited information from marked grey plovers shows that in late autumn and early winter some are known to move from moulting areas in The Wash and the Wadden Sea to the Medway and Stour Estuaries, from The Wash to the Severn Estuary and Taw-Torridge Estuary in south-west England, and from the Wadden Sea to Teesmouth (Figure 8.6.17). Grey plovers differ from dunlins in their movement pattern in that they do not seem to move northwards from moulting areas to wintering sites (Pienkowski & Evans 1984). Other adult grey plovers reach Teesmouth later in the winter, in late December and January, probably also from the Wadden Sea, and these displace some juveniles from Teesmouth further south to France. Other adults appear in February and may be starting to return towards their breeding grounds (Townshend 1985). In spring some grey plovers, like dunlins, return from Teesmouth to stage in the

Wadden Sea before returning to their Siberian breeding grounds.

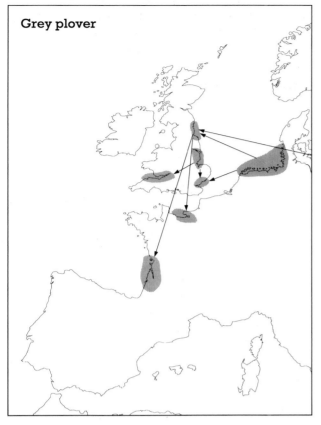

Grey plover

Figure 8.6.17 Autumn and winter movements of grey plovers within their wintering range (from Pienkowski & Evans 1984). Arrows show known movements during a single winter between different regions of the wintering area, shown shaded. Lines show links between sites, but are not intended to show actual migration routes.

Knots

Knots use a more restricted number of estuaries during the non-breeding season than do most other species (see also Figure 8.6.47). Even so Dugan (1981) found that individual knots moved up the coastline of eastern Britain from their major moulting area on The Wash, reaching the Humber Estuary, Tees Estuary, Northumberland coast and the Firth of Forth. Timings suggested that individual birds may have used a network of more than one of these east coast estuaries during a single winter. Knots also disperse from The Wash to west coast estuaries including the Dee Estuary and North Wirral, the Ribble Estuary and the Clyde Estuary, as well as south to estuaries in north Kent (Dugan 1981; Cooper 1984). At the same time there is a movement into eastern British estuaries in November and December of knots that have moulted in the Wadden Sea (Dugan 1981; Prokosch 1988).

Implications for survival of dependence on site networks

From these and other studies it is clear that many individual waders appear to follow the same movement patterns in different years, or predictably different patterns in different years. There is considerable evidence of strong wintering site fidelity in many species with internationally important wintering populations on British estuaries, including dunlin, sanderling *Calidris alba*, turnstone *Arenaria interpres*, ringed plover, grey plover, bar-tailed godwit and curlew (Evans & Pienkowski 1984). This strong site fidelity, coupled with evidence that shorebirds are best able to compete for food in the places to which they regularly return (Townshend 1985) and that for some species, such as grey plovers, many preferred wintering sites are at their capacity to support birds (Moser 1988), means that waterfowl using an estuary during the non-breeding season can be very vulnerable to loss of or damage to that site.

Loss of habitat on any one site in a network may threaten the survival of birds using it, since these birds will then be forced to try to find alternative areas for feeding so as to survive. But there is evidence that they are then at a competitive disadvantage with birds already regularly using and familiar with a site (Townshend 1985; Davidson & Evans 1985). The implications are particularly great with mobile species since a much higher proportion of a mobile waterfowl population will be affected than is present at any one time, and the loss of one site may threaten the survival of birds using much of the estuarine resource both in Britain and throughout their flyways.

Local movements during winter

As well as these large-scale movements between estuaries in the wintering area, waders are known to move extensively within estuaries and estuarine complexes during the winter. Understanding such movements is important in determining the conservation needs and approach for wintering waterfowl.

Movements to roosting sites

In some instances the movement is related to the tidal cycle and the location and availability of secure roosting sites. Many waders move considerable distances from feeding grounds to roosting sites on the Firth of Forth (Furness 1973; Symonds *et al.* 1984). In Essex oystercatchers are known to move from feeding on the Stour Estuary to roosting on the nearby Orwell Estuary (Davidson & Evans 1985). An extreme example is the change in roosting pattern of waders on the Dee Estuary and North Wirral. Since the mid 1970s the number of roosting waders on the Dee has declined by almost 60%, largely a reflection of major decreases in the numbers of roosting bar-tailed godwits, knots and dunlins. Mitchell *et al.* (1988) have found that many of the bar-tailed godwits and knots have continued to feed on the Dee but now fly over 20 km to roost on the Alt Estuary across Liverpool Bay. The declines in roosting numbers on the Dee have been attributed to increases in the amount of human disturbance to birds roosting on the shoreline. Numbers of waders roosting on the Alt have increased dramatically since 1978/79 (Kirby *et al.* 1988), and numbers that remain to feed there are sometimes but not always substantial. Kirby *et al.'s* (1988) analyses suggest that the estuaries of the Alt, Ribble, Dee and probably also the Mersey should be considered as a single intertidal complex in terms of their use by knots, bar-tailed godwits and dunlins.

Movements between feeding areas

A similar picture of high mobility of knots, bar-tailed godwits and dunlins during winter has been found within another major British estuarine

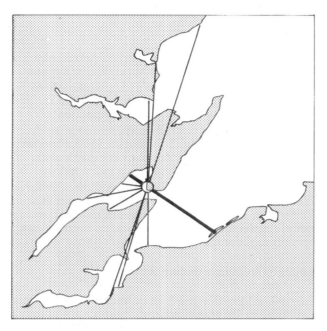

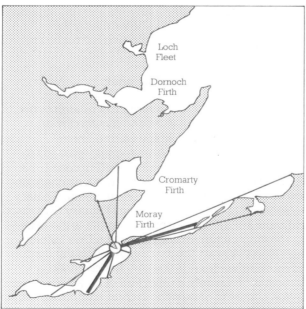

Figure 8.6.18 Movements in winter of knots caught and marked on roost sites in the Cromarty Firth and Moray Firth in November, derived from Symonds & Langslow (1986). Thick lines link the marking site with locations of more than 10% of subsequent sightings, and thin lines with locations of less than 10% of sightings.

complex, the Moray, Cromarty and Dornoch Firths and Loch Fleet in north-east Scotland (Symonds & Langslow 1986). For example knots marked when roosting in the Moray Firth and the Cromarty Firth in November were found widely distributed around all four review sites later in the winter, and a few also moved outside the estuaries onto open coasts (Figure 8.6.18). Symonds & Langslow (1986) found that turnstones, curlews, ringed plovers, oystercatchers and redshanks remained much more loyal to selected feeding areas. Wintering wigeon *Anas penelope* on the Moray Firth, like these waders, move very little between feeding sites (Mudge 1989).

These interspecific differences in the extent of mobility around large wintering sites appear to be general, since Symonds *et al.* (1984) found similarly high mobility around the various feeding areas within the Firth of Forth in knots, dunlins and bar-tailed godwits, but little movement in turnstones, grey plovers, oystercatchers and redshanks. Minton (1975) found similar mobility patterns for most of these species in The Wash. Dunlins move extensively between different feeding areas even on some much smaller estuaries such as the Tees (Davidson & Evans 1986a) and the Orwell (Davidson & Evans 1985).

Some intraspecific variation in mobility does, however, seem to exist at least in dunlins, since Clark (1983) found considerable site fidelity in parts of the dunlin population on the Severn Estuary, and Minton (1975) found that there was little movement of dunlins around The Wash in winter. This may, however, be related to differences in the scale of the movements, in that dunlins have a degree of mobility intermediate between the highly mobile knots and bar-tailed godwits and more sedentary species such as ringed plovers and oystercatchers.

In some waders different individuals have markedly different patterns of winter mobility. This is particularly so for sanderlings. Some wintering sanderlings in the population centred on Teesmouth remain all winter within the estuary and the coastal sandy beaches immediately nearby. In addition to these 'residents' there are 'transients' that move along tens of kilometres of coastline (Evans *et al.* 1980). This mixed pattern seems to be typical of wintering sanderling populations, since it has also been found by Myers *et al.* (1988) in both North and South America.

Conservation implications of local movements

There is considerable significance for the conservation of wintering waterfowl populations in these mobility patterns. First the conservation approach needs to allow both for species and populations that depend on a localised feeding and roosting area and for those whose feeding depends on widely distributed feeding areas around estuaries and estuary complexes. Since the preferred winter feeding strategy of some species such as knot, bar-tailed godwit and dunlin is to move around many or all feeding areas on such estuaries, the conservation approach must seek to avoid piecemeal loss of some parts of these intertidal feeding grounds.

Second, some estuaries must be considered as part of a linked estuarine complex. Identification of these movement patterns requires detailed marking and observation studies of the kinds described above, which have as yet not been carried out on all estuarine complexes in Britain. The evidence of the intraspecific consistency of movement patterns of wintering waterfowl shows however that such linkages are likely to exist between all such estuarine complexes, some of which, for example the 'Greater Thames Estuary' of the Essex and Kent coasts, can be very large. The linking of such complexes forms part of the approach embodied in the designation of a network of sites of international importance under the Ramsar Convention and EC Wild Birds Directive (see Stroud et al. 1990).

Cold weather movements

It is clear that in mobile species such as migratory waders and wildfowl a site does not have to be of numerical importance at all times of the year, or even in every year, to be of major importance to the survival of the population (Stroud et al. 1990). Severe winter weather poses particular problems since the energetic costs of thermo-regulation are greatly increased during periods of low temperatures and strong winds (e.g. Dugan et al. 1981; Davidson & Morrison 1989). To meet these increased costs birds must either draw on energy reserves stored prophylactically or find more food (Davidson 1981). Yet at these times their food usually becomes less available or completely inaccessible through changes in the behaviour of the prey (Evans 1979b; Pienkowski 1983a) or the freezing-over of the feeding grounds (e.g. Swennen & Duiven 1983). At these times waterfowl can adopt one of two alternative options: either remain where they are at the start of the cold spell, and draw on stored fat and protein reserves (e.g. Davidson 1981; Clark 1983; Pienkowski et al. 1984), or move to more clement areas. The effects of severe hot weather and wind which can affect waterfowl wintering in Africa are not an issue for British estuaries.

British estuaries as cold weather refugia

In severe weather estuaries and coasts become of increased importance as refuges for waterfowl since the buffering effect of sea temperature and salinity usually means that estuaries and coasts freeze over far less than inland and freshwater wetlands. British estuaries take on additional importance as severe weather refugia in western Europe since they are relatively milder than those of continental Europe in periods of severe weather (see Pienkowski & Evans 1984, and Chapter 6). In addition the interactions of wind and tide, that can exacerbate the impact of cold weather on estuaries

with small tidal ranges, such as the Wadden Sea, affect British estuaries much less (Pienkowski & Pienkowski 1983; Pienkowski & Evans 1985). Severe weather can result in almost all the intertidal areas of major continental European estuaries, such as the Wadden Sea, freezing over so that waterfowl are unable to feed for days or even weeks (Swennen & Duiven 1983). At these times there can be greatly increased mortality of waders, especially oystercatchers on the Wadden Sea (Swennen & Duiven 1983) and the Dutch Delta (P Meininger pers. comm.).

Increased mortality of estuarine waders does also occur during periods of prolonged severe winter weather in Britain, despite the precautions of reserve storage or movement to milder areas (Dobinson & Richards 1964; Davidson 1982a; Davidson & Evans 1982; Clark & Davidson 1986). Severe weather mortality often affects redshanks and oystercatchers most seriously, although it is not clear why these species should suffer consistently greater mortality than other waders. Other waders, notably dunlins and grey plovers, can also be affected (e.g. Davidson & Clark 1985; Clark & Davidson 1986) and Davidson (1982b) found evidence from ringing recoveries of increased mortality in seven out of ten wader species during two periods of severe winter weather at Teesmouth.

The geographical pattern of severe weather and its effects on wildfowl differ considerably between years and cold spells (Davidson & Clark 1985; Clark & Davidson 1986). Hence the locations of effective estuarine refugia from severe weather also differ, although in general the more southern and western estuaries remain milder during spells of severe weather.

There are two types of movement related to severe weather. The most obvious is a movement directly in response to the onset of severe weather. Many of the regular westward and southward movements of post-moulting waterfowl described above are, however, also likely to have evolved as a response to the avoidance of areas in which severe weather is most likely later in the winter (Pienkowski & Evans 1984, 1985).

Responses of waders to cold weather

An analysis from ringing recoveries of the cold weather movements of waders and other waterfowl (Baillie et al. 1986) confirmed that most waders remain on their usual wintering grounds in severe weather and draw on their reserves of fat and protein to balance their energetic and nutritional budget (Davidson 1981). Baillie et al. (1986) found that some lapwings Vanellus vanellus, curlews and snipe Gallinago gallinago moved south out of Britain to France and Iberia in response to cold weather, and many lapwings and golden plovers Pluvialis apricaria are known to move from their inland feeding areas to estuaries and coasts in Britain (Dobinson & Richards 1964; Davidson 1981).

Although most estuarine waders in Britain remain on their wintering areas if cold weather begins, some do move from the more severely affected continental estuaries, many flying to Britain. For example van Eerden (1977) reported a movement of redshanks and oystercatchers out of the Dutch Wadden Sea at the start of cold weather, Davidson (1982c) reported a similarly timed movement of some redshanks from Teesmouth, and major influxes of dunlins into the Orwell Estuary in Suffolk coincided with the onset of particularly severe weather in continental Europe (Davidson & Evans 1985). Another severe weather influx on the eastern English coast is the arrival of some individual grey plovers at Teesmouth in midwinter only in years when there is severe weather in the Wadden Sea (Townshend 1982). In such years these birds return to regular sites, despite their irregular pattern of appearance.

Responses of wildfowl to cold weather

Wildfowl show a similarly complex pattern of movement in response to severe weather. Those wintering on freshwater habitats are particularly vulnerable to freezing conditions. Many then move to coasts and estuaries, and as with waders which areas the birds move to depends on the distribution of the most severe weather. For example Fox & Salmon (1988) reported major movements of pochard *Aythya ferina* to maritime habitats, especially the inner part of the Thames Estuary, during severe weather in January 1979. In severe weather in 1981/82 populations increased substantially on estuaries widespread around Britain, including Poole Harbour, the Severn Estuary, Hamford Water, Teesmouth and the Firth of Forth, although overall the movements involved less of the population than in 1979. Fox & Salmon (1988) considered this to be because in 1981/82 the very severe weather caused even many estuaries to freeze. Pintail *Anas acuta* are also very mobile and move westwards onto estuaries on the Irish Sea coast of Britain and further west into Ireland in response to severe weather, shelducks move from the Wadden Sea and northern Britain to estuaries in southern Britain and France (Baillie *et al.* 1986), and Ridgill & Fox (1990) have found evidence of movements in response to cold weather in seven common species of wildfowl.

Some geese also move in response to severe weather: most pink-footed geese move south from Scotland into the coastal regions of north-west England (Baillie *et al.* 1986; Owen *et al.* 1986). The winter distribution of the small vulnerable population of Svalbard light-bellied brent geese *Branta bernicla hrota* is strongly linked to winter weather conditions on their wintering grounds in Denmark (Madsen 1984). A larger proportion of the world population moves to its only major British wintering ground at Lindisfarne when winter weather is severe in Denmark, and the relationship is particularly strong in response to January temperatures.

Conservation implications of cold weather refugia on British estuaries

British estuaries are of major importance as severe weather refugia for many waterfowl, an importance that is additional to their very major international importance as waterfowl wintering areas during mild winters. This means that estuaries can assume a critical importance for the survival during severe weather of very much larger parts of waterfowl populations than are present at any time during mild weather. Even though such places may function as cold weather refugia, they often serve this purpose for only a few days or weeks and only in some winters. Ridgill & Fox (1990) point out that some sites assume national and international importance only during their critical function as cold weather refugia, and that such importance fails to show up through the application of the 1% criterion based on five-year average count values. This highlights the need to consider additional features of waterfowl usage of estuaries in identifying and developing conservation measures for waterfowl populations, in line with the requirements of international conservation measures.

It should be noted that the winter distribution analysis made below is based on the five-winter period from January 1983 to January 1987, when winters were generally mild. The population sizes and distributions described are therefore the baseline of importance which is considerably added to in severe winters.

It is often considered that it is the western British estuaries that are of increased importance during severe weather. Whilst they are of undoubted importance, particularly to birds moving from northern and eastern Britain, eastern British estuaries are also of significance, as refugia for waterfowl from continental European coasts. Other populations that use Britain in mild winters depend on cold weather refugia further south and west in Europe. Furthermore, the geographical location of the estuaries that provide effective refugia differs between spells of severe weather, depending on which parts of Britain are most affected by the severe weather. Since some waterfowl die during severe weather even with the precautions of energy reserves and refugia to which they move, it follows that without suitable feeding grounds in milder areas winter mortality would be much higher. Effective conservation of these mobile populations thus requires the maintenance of a network of estuaries throughout Britain so as to provide refugia wherever a cold spell strikes.

Peripheral feeding areas

In addition to these large-scale responses to severe weather, many waders using a single estuary alter their feeding behaviour in response to weather conditions and food availability. Waders that feed in intertidal habitats are time-limited by the period of exposure of the feeding grounds by the tide, in some cases interacting also with the daylight period. When energy requirements increase, as for example in severe weather, the birds may need to increase their feeding period beyond the duration of exposure of their tidal feeding grounds. These birds then move to feed on habitats peripheral to the estuary. Pasture-feeding during high tide occurs widely in redshanks, oystercatchers and curlews around estuaries in various parts of Britain, from the Ythan Estuary in north-east Scotland to the Exe Estuary in south-west England.

On the heavily-industrialised Tees Estuary, where land-claim has restricted the period of tidal exposure of the main mudflats, Davidson & Evans (1986a) found that many waders fed on a variety of brackish-water and grassland habitats during high tide. Greatest use of this suite of peripheral habitats was by redshank and dunlin, and on some occasions by knot, curlew and grey plover. There was considerable interspecific variation in habitat choice (Figure 8.6.19). Choice of site, and the proportion of the populations involved, depended

on both tidal and weather conditions, but curlews feed mostly on pastures, redshanks and grey plovers on sheltered brackish areas, and dunlins and knots on unsheltered high-level tidal flats. There were also seasonal differences related to weather conditions: most species fed more in sheltered areas in mid and late winter, during periods of high winds and low temperatures (Davidson & Evans 1986a).

Under some weather conditions some waders, particularly redshanks, dunlins and curlews, chose to leave the main mudflat feeding areas even when they were available as feeding grounds. These birds then fed on the peripheral areas during the low-tide period. Redshanks in particular moved from exposed mudflats to feed in sheltered creeks and pools when winds were very strong (Davidson & Evans 1986a).

Some parts of the wintering populations of waders depended more heavily than others on the peripheral feeding areas. For example at Teesmouth many juvenile grey plovers and dunlins fed on peripheral wetlands (Davidson & Evans 1986a). Curlews have a winter feeding distribution in which it was mainly males, which have shorter bills, that fed on peripheral pastures during the low-water period (Townshend 1981). These were joined over high water by some females that had been feeding on the main mudflats before they were covered by the tide. Townshend attributed this pattern to the main prey of curlews on the mudflats (the ragworm *Hediste diversicolor*) moving deeper into the mud in winter and so becoming less accessible to the short-billed males. These birds then shifted to feeding on earthworms on pastures, to be joined by the longer-billed females needing to extend their feeding time beyond the period of exposure of the main mudflats. In periods of severe weather, however, all curlews were forced to move back onto the mudflats as the pastures froze over.

Waterfowl are at risk from death by starvation during severe winter weather (e.g. Davidson 1982b; Davidson & Evans 1982). Even on estuaries where some additional feeding is possible, such as Teesmouth, winter mortality of several waders was higher in severe winters (Evans & Pienkowski 1984). Hence mortality in severe weather is likely to increase if those birds that remain on estuaries (rather than moving to milder areas) are unable to extend their feeding onto other areas when the main intertidal flats are covered, or cannot find sheltered feeding areas during periods of low temperatures and high winds (Dugan *et al.* 1981; Davidson & Evans 1986a).

Particularly for those estuaries where the intertidal feeding grounds have been restricted by land-claim and other developments (see Chapter 10), the effective conservation of waterfowl populations at times of stress such as severe weather may depend on the maintenance of a suite of peripheral habitats, as well as tidal flats. The varying habitat

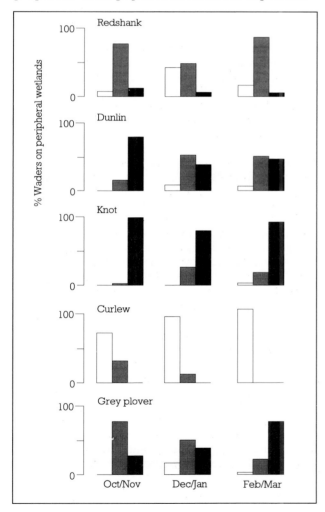

Figure 8.6.19 There are both seasonal and interspecific variations in the choice of habitats used by waders at Teesmouth for feeding when high tide has covered their main feeding grounds. The clear bar shows pasture, light stipple is sheltered pools and tidal flats, and heavy stipple is exposed tidal flats. From Davidson & Evans (1986a).

preferences of different species, ages and sexes under different weather conditions means that a variety of habitats are often needed to buffer waterfowl populations against the risks faced during severe weather, as well as at other times.

Population turnover

As mentioned briefly in describing autumn migration, many waders and wildfowl move extensively between estuaries during their non-breeding season. It is not usual for all of a population to move at once so there is generally a turnover of individuals using one estuary. If the number of arriving birds equals the number of those departing then the total number present in a simple count will appear unchanged. If the numbers arriving and leaving differ the presence of turnover can be detected. Sequential counts will, however, reveal only the net change in numbers and not the total number of individual birds involved. During migration periods in both spring and autumn there may be continual arrivals and departures of birds over a period of weeks with each individual remaining for a shorter time than the whole period over which birds of that population are present. Where several biogeographic populations, or sub-populations, with different migration strategies are involved the picture is particularly complicated, and even in winter there can be substantial population turnover. For example the turnover of shelducks using Teesmouth in winter was such that the total number of individuals using the estuary over the winter was several times the peak number present on any one day (Evans & Pienkowski 1982).

An understanding of turnover is valuable in two ways when implementing effective conservation of migrant waterfowl. Firstly, it helps in assessing the significance of particular estuaries in the migrations and annual cycles of waterfowl. Secondly, since turnover means that even peak counts will underestimate the proportion of a biogeographic population using an estuary, it is needed to qualify the data used to assess the basic 1% criterion used in the identification of estuaries of national and international importance. Turnover data, where available, are taken into account in conservation site assessments as well as in the formal guidelines for the identification of Ramsar sites (Stroud et al. 1990).

Assessing population turnover

A minimum assessment of turnover and the numbers of individual birds using an estuary can be made by summing all the increases in numbers between successive population counts during a season. Turnover is best assessed, however, from studies of individually marked birds that are resighted or recaptured during their staging time at a site. Unfortunately these studies are complex and time-consuming and have as yet been made at only a few estuaries and for only a few species.

Most studies of turnover have been on wintering or spring migrant waders (e.g Dugan 1981; Symonds & Langslow 1981, 1985; Pienkowski 1983; Moser & Carrier 1983; Kersten et al. 1983; Kersten & Smit 1984; Symonds et al. 1984; Davidson & Evans 1986b; Prokosch 1988; Smit & Piersma 1989). As well as assessing the total numbers of birds using an estuary, turnover studies yield information on the average stopover period for the migrant – information valuable in understanding the scheduling of migrations and the use of sites within the migratory network. The general findings on turnover are described below.

The extent of population turnover

Turnover studies have shown that the extent of turnover can differ in the same species at different estuaries on a migratory route, and between different species using an estuary at the same time. Thus at least twice the number of ringed plovers used the Solway Firth in spring than the number present on the peak count, but there was almost no turnover in the migrant turnstone population over the same period (Moser & Carrier 1983).

Kersten & Smit (1984), studying waders migrating north towards Britain and elsewhere in western Europe, found that the turnover of ringed plovers earlier in spring on the Sidi Moussa estuary in Morocco, like that of redshanks and dunlins, resulted in about 1.5 times the number of individual birds using the site than were present in early March. The average length of stay of ringed plovers at Sidi Moussa was only 6.3 days. Redshanks (8.5 days) and dunlins (12.2 days) stayed rather longer.

Turnover of between one and three times the maximum daily population seems general for waders on spring staging sites, since Prokosch (1988) reported over twice the number of grey plovers using the Wadden Sea in spring as were present in peak numbers. More knots and bar-tailed godwits also passed through the Wadden Sea than were present at any one time, although measures of turnover were not possible.

Even more rapid turnover in spring can, however, occur. Cronau (1988) reports that little stints *Calidris minuta* stayed an average of only 3.5 days during April and May at a wetland in Turkey, and estimated a turnover of at least eight times the number of individual little stints present in the peak count.

Arrivals and departures from late spring staging areas are often highly synchronous. For example nearctic-breeding knots from wintering grounds on British estuaries and the Wadden Sea pause for two weeks in May at Balsfjord in northern Norway. These birds almost all arrive over a period of five days and leave in late May over just three or four days (Davidson et al. 1986c; Uttley et al. 1987). Observations of colour-marked birds in 1985 suggested little turnover. Recaptures of ringed birds confirmed that the total numbers of individuals using Balsfjord in May was less than 1.5

times the peak count (Davidson & Evans 1986b). So even here in such a highly synchronised population there is a small amount of turnover, and this is supported by counts and observations there and elsewhere in northern Norway in later years (Uttley *et al.* 1987; Strann in press).

The significance of population turnover in assessing estuary usage by waders is illustrated in Figure 8.6.20, with the example of the use of the Sidi Moussa estuary in Morocco by dunlins (largely the *schinzii* population) in early spring. This provide a clearer illustration of turnover than is yet available for waterfowl in migrating through Britain and many of the birds involved are likely to use British estuaries as their next staging site. The Moroccan example is derived from studies in 1981 and 1982 by Kersten *et al.* (1983), Kersten & Smit (1984) and Smit & Piersma (1989). Counts through the period from early March to late April found that the maximum population present on any day was 7,000 birds in early March. Counts during the two months showed a decline in numbers followed by an increase in early April and then a further decline. Analysis of these counts, and also observations of the proportions of marked birds in flocks, gave a cumulative count total over this period of 12,000 birds, almost twice the number present at any one time (Figure 8.6.20).

These analyses also permitted assessment of the turnover rate for the whole migration period from late February to early March at three times the number of birds present in early March. Thus about 21,000 individual dunlins used the estuary during their spring migration, almost double the number derived from even cumulative counts. In this case it means also that Sidi Moussa qualifies as of international importance for dunlins, since 1% of the population is 14,000 birds, although this was not apparent from counts since the population on any day was never more that one-third of the total using the site (Smit & Piersma 1989).

The extent of turnover for different species and estuaries will depend on the role of each site as a staging area in the migrations of waterfowl. The functions of these staging areas in spring are described further below. Detailed studies of migrant populations have all shown some degree of turnover. Hence any assessment of an estuary for conservation purposes should treat population counts as an indicator of minimum usage and importance. In general a larger, and sometimes a very much larger, proportion of each waterfowl population than is apparent at any one time depends on each estuary in the network used during the non-breeding season. This is particularly so for those sites which act as spring and autumn staging for migrants, but also applies to wintering sites. Overall the implication is that many estuaries which fall below the 1% criterion on the basis of peak monthly counts alone, in reality support more than 1% of the relevant populations during the course of a year and so will qualify as nationally or internationally important.

Spring migration

Most waders and wildfowl return to their breeding grounds between early March and May, depending on latitude. Breeding waterfowl generally reach temperate breeding areas such as Britain and western Europe beginning in March, some returning direct from the estuaries on which they have overwintered. At the same time populations breeding in arctic and sub-arctic regions such as Iceland and northern Scandinavia begin the return migration from African wintering areas. The timing of the spring migration of waders is summarised by Pienkowski & Evans (1984), but migration routes and migration strategies are generally poorly known (Piersma *et al.* 1987a).

Waders show a variety of strategies for making their spring migrations. These range from birds such as some turnstones that make their migration in a series of short hops, and so use several spring staging areas, to others such as *schinzii* dunlins and redshanks which fly longer distances between staging areas, with each individual using only a few staging areas. At the extreme are migrants such as knots and bar-tailed godwits that make very long jumps, generally using just one or two staging areas between wintering and breeding grounds (Piersma 1987).

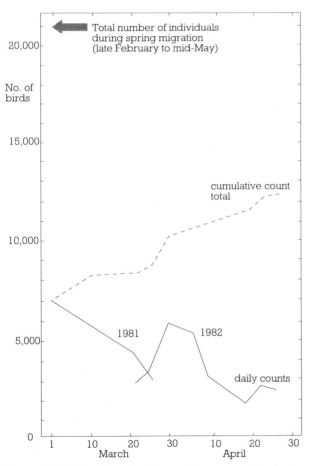

Figure 8.6.20 Spring migration and turnover of dunlins at Sidi Moussa, Morocco, in 1981 and 1982, derived from Smit & Piersma (1989). The figure shows that many more individual birds used the estuary than were present at any one time.

British estuaries are vital staging areas for many spring migrant waterfowl populations. At the same time as more southerly wintering populations are arriving in Britain some of the British wintering populations of species such as *alpina* dunlins (Pienkowski & Pienkowski 1983, and Figure 8.6.16), *islandica* knots (Davidson & Wilson 1991) and dark-bellied brent geese (Owen *et al.* 1986) move east and south-east to the Wadden Sea. Britain and the Wadden Sea support the largest populations of spring migrant waterfowl in Europe (Prater 1981). The picture of use of a single Britain estuary is often complex, since there is continual change in the species and population composition of the assemblage due to differences in migration timing like those described above. In addition, there is also generally a substantial turnover of individuals within a population.

With such rapid spring movements, monthly BoEE/NWC counts can give only a general representation of the size and distribution of spring migrant populations and can miss populations that pass rapidly through British estuaries, since many individuals stay for only a few days or weeks (see Turnover above). Understanding the complexities of the spring migration systems of waterfowl has required more detailed studies involving more frequent counts at staging areas, coupled with catching and observations of marked birds, to determine how individuals move along the flyway during a single migration.

There has been recent progress in clarifying spring migration patterns along the East Atlantic Flyway from detailed studies made at individual staging areas such as the Solway Firth (Moser & Carrier 1983), Mauritania (Ens *et al.* 1989), Morocco (Kersten & Smit 1984), the Wadden Sea (Prokosch 1988), Iceland (Morrison & Wilson 1972) and northern Norway (Davidson & Evans 1986b). In addition the collection of much information has depended on the organisation of international spring migration projects, often co-ordinated by the Wader Study Group (Dick 1979; Ferns 1980a, 1980b, 1981a, 1981b, 1981c; Pienkowski & Pienkowski 1983; Moser *et al.* 1985; Davidson & Piersma 1986). In Britain co-ordinated studies have concentrated particularly on establishing spring migration patterns on west coast estuaries (see Moser *et al.* 1985), although their findings are not yet fully available and the spring migration usage and importance of individual British estuaries, and of these estuaries for most species, cannot yet be described.

The general spring waterfowl species assemblages on British estuaries are summarised in Figures 8.6.21 and 8.6.22, derived from BoEE/NWC counts.

The spring wildfowl assemblage

About 70,000 wildfowl use British estuaries in April. The species composition (Figure 8.6.21) shows an assemblage dominated by shelduck (38% of the total population). These are birds returning to breed around British estuaries, and the 27,000 birds in April must be most of the estimated British breeding population of 15,000 pairs (Stroud *et al.* 1990). The remainder of the assemblage is a mixture of some other species such as eider returning to breed around estuaries, with small remaining populations of late migrant arctic breeders such as dark-bellied brent geese and long-tailed ducks *Clangula hyemalis*. The majority of arctic-breeding ducks and geese have, however, already left Britain by April and moved to spring staging areas such as the Wadden Sea and Iceland (Owen *et al.* 1986). Long-tailed ducks form a larger proportion of the wildfowl assemblage than at other times of year. These birds are mostly in the firths of north-east Scotland, where there is a marked spring passage (Prater 1981).

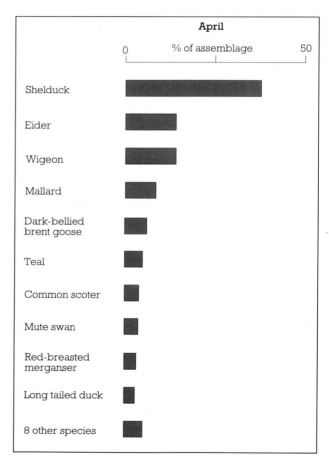

Figure 8.6.21 The spring (April) species assemblage of wildfowl on British estuaries, derived from Prater (1981)

The spring wader assemblage

As would be expected from the general patterns of migration and turnover of waders in spring, there are marked differences in the species composition of the wader assemblage on British estuaries in April and May (Figure 8.6.22).

In April, as at other times of year (Figures 8.6.10 and 8.6.33), the assemblage is dominated by dunlin, knot and oystercatcher. The wader population in April is a mixture of high-arctic breeders such as knots, *alpina* dunlins and bar-tailed godwits, and species such as redshanks, curlews and *schinzii* dunlins returning through Britain to breed at lower latitudes.

By May most individuals of some high-arctic breeders such as knots have left Britain for staging areas further north (Davidson & Wilson 1990). The assemblage is dominated by dunlins even more than at other times of year, and almost half the waders on British estuaries in May are dunlins, although the total population of dunlins present (*c.* 150,000 birds) is smaller than in April. Dunlins in May are predominantly the arctic-breeding *alpina* population, along with some late migrant Icelandic breeders and the small *arctica* population that breeds in Greenland. Other high-arctic breeders form a significant part of the May assemblage, notably the *c.* 30,000 sanderlings which form almost 10% of the assemblage. Some migrants heading for more temperate breeding grounds from southern wintering areas, notably whimbrels (8% of the assemblage), are passing through Britain at this time. Golden plovers also form a larger part of the spring assemblage in spring than at other times of year. The May assemblage is more diverse, with 11 species each forming more than 1% of the population, compared with nine species in April.

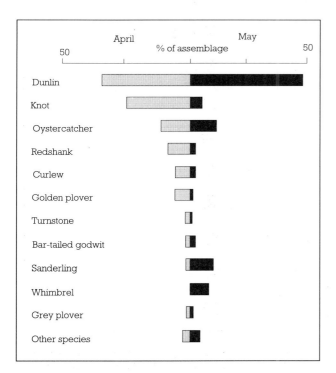

Figure 8.6.22 The spring (April and May) species assemblage of waders on British estuaries, derived from Prater (1981)

Population size in spring

The total population of waders present in April and May is lower than in midwinter: *c.* 510,000 in April and 310,000 in May, compared with 1,160,000 in midwinter. These totals alone correspond to 7% and 4% respectively of the East Atlantic Flyway population. The rapid turnover of populations and individuals in spring (see above) means, however, that many more individuals depend on British estuaries in spring than the population counted on any one date in either April or May. It is not possible to determine precisely the total population

involved since detailed turnover studies have not been made sufficiently widely. Turnover studies from elsewhere suggest that between 1.5 and three times the number of individuals may be involved. Based on the April population alone this suggests that between 765,000 and 1,530,000 waders used British estuaries in spring, so that in excess of 20% of the international flyway population may depend on British estuaries in spring.

Estuarine distribution of waders in spring

Although Prater (1981) indicated that estuaries on the west coast of Britain were particularly important as staging areas for spring migrant waders, it is now clear that many east coast estuaries also support important spring migrant populations. In eastern Britain most major staging areas are in the southern part of the region, notably the Essex coast, The Wash and the Humber Estuary. Nevertheless estuaries further north in eastern Britain, such as Teesmouth (Goodyer & Evans 1980; Davidson & Evans 1988) and the Moray Firth (Swann & Mudge 1989), also support passage populations of several wader species.

Populations of most wader species are concentrated on fewer estuaries during spring passage than in midwinter (Prater 1981). This generally more restricted distribution was further confirmed for estuaries in western Britain by Moser *et al.* (1985) who reported that sanderlings and ringed plovers concentrated in spring on a few large estuaries, and that there was no observable migration through many of the smaller west-coast estuaries. Figure 8.6.23 illustrates the spring distribution of four common migrant waders during the late 1970s. Large numbers of sanderlings staged on just five estuaries (Dee and North Wirral, Alt, Ribble, Morecambe Bay, and Duddon). More frequent counts in the early 1980s have shown an apparent shift in spring distribution with lower peak counts on the Dee and the Duddon Estuaries, but larger numbers on the Solway Firth (Clark *et al.* 1982; Moser *et al.* 1985).

Detailed marking studies on sanderlings at Teesmouth (Evans 1980) have found several components to the spring migrant population. Some from the wintering population leave in March and April and are known to move to Iceland later in the spring. These birds presumably breed in Greenland and Canada. Others pass through Teesmouth in early May, and yet others leave in late May (Davidson & Evans 1988). The destinations of these birds are less clear, but may be Siberia, since none of these spring passage birds has been seen in Iceland (P R Evans pers. comm.).

Ringed plovers occurred in large numbers in May 1984 on just four west coast estuaries: Severn, Ribble, Morecambe Bay and Solway Firth (Moser *et al.* 1985). Small numbers also occurred on all of the 18 review sites for which counts were made, although in some cases these may have been only locally-breeding birds. Figure 8.6.23 shows ringed

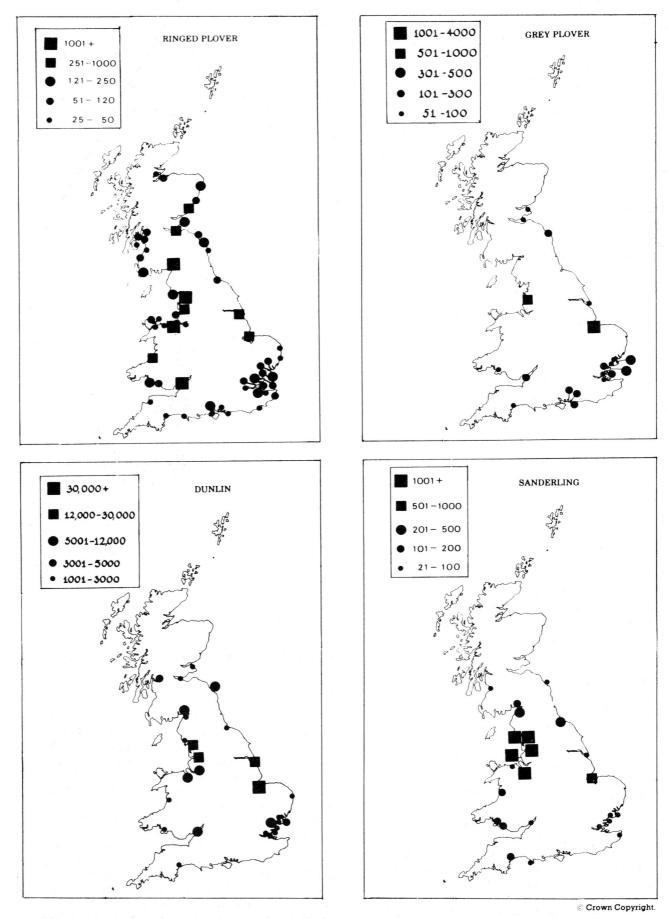

Figure 8.6.23 Spring distribution of ringed plovers, grey plovers, sanderlings and dunlins on British estuaries, from Prater (1981)

plovers to be amongst the most widespread of waders in spring.

Dunlins are also widespread in April and May (Figure 8.6.23) but again are concentrated onto major estuaries. In contrast to ringed plovers and sanderlings, there are some major staging areas in eastern Britain, with the largest population being on The Wash. East coast passage involves both the *schinzii* population heading for Iceland and *alpina* dunlins *en route* to northern Scandinavia and the USSR. Most dunlins staging in western Britain in spring belong to the Icelandic breeding population; there is a general movement of the wintering *alpina* population east and south-east in later winter and early spring to staging areas in eastern Britain and the Wadden Sea (Figure 8.6.16).

Grey plovers, which also breed in the Siberian arctic, are also concentrated chiefly on a few eastern British estuaries by May (Figure 8.6.23) and, like dunlins, are known to move east from eastern Britain to use the Wadden Sea as a spring staging area (Pienkowski & Evans 1984; Townshend 1985).

Likewise, many of the British wintering knots move in March to the Wadden Sea. Smaller numbers remain in Britain, chiefly on the major west coast estuaries of the Dee, Ribble and Morecambe Bay, with a few thousand on The Wash. All these birds leave their early spring staging areas in Britain and the southern North Sea during the first week of May and fly to late spring staging areas in Iceland or northern Norway. There is mixing of birds from all parts of the wintering area and early spring staging sites on the late spring sites (Davidson *et al.* 1986c; Davidson & Wilson 1991).

Moser *et al.* (1985) also cite examples of ringed plovers flying from early spring staging areas in western Britain to spend late spring at Teesmouth in eastern Britain. Thus although many waders heading for Iceland, Greenland and Canada use estuaries in western Britain in early spring, and many heading for Scandinavia and Siberia pass through eastern Britain, the division is by no means clear-cut.

Patterns of spring estuary use by waders

Colour-marking studies have helped to reveal the place of British estuaries in individual waders' use of the network of estuaries along the East Atlantic Flyway and their movements within Britain. International collaboration on dye-marking studies in spring 1985 showed that *schinzii* dunlins from the wintering population in the Banc d'Arguin (Mauritania), and from Portugal and western France, used British estuarine staging areas in spring (Figure 8.6.24). Most of these migrants used estuaries on the west coast of Britain from the Taw-Torridge Estuary in north Devon to as far north as the Outer Hebrides. Dunlins marked on the British west coast were subsequently seen in western Iceland later in the same spring. No dunlins were found to move between estuaries in western Britain

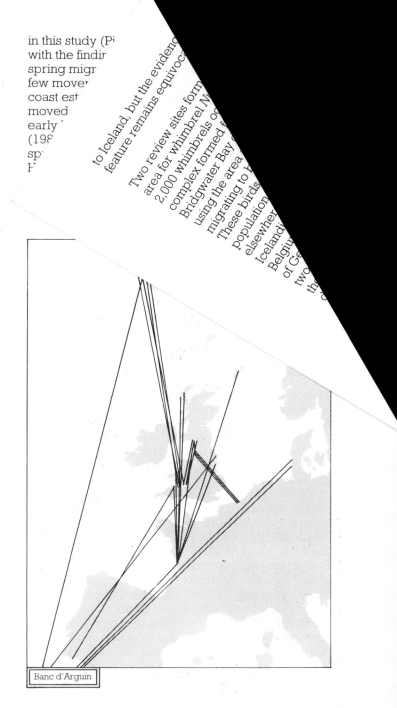

Figure 8.6.24 Movements to and through Europe of individual *schinzii* dunlins within a single spring migration period in 1984 or 1985. From Piersma *et al.* (1987a) with additional information from Moser *et al.* (1985).

Moser *et al.* (1985) found a similar pattern of dependence on a single British spring staging site by individual ringed plovers, sanderlings and turnstones, with at most a few individuals moving to a second British site, usually, but not always, further north. For ringed plovers and sanderlings this is similar to the earlier interpretation of counts and caught birds, but the pattern differs for turnstones (Ferns 1980a, 1980b, 1981a). Ferns describes a complex pattern for turnstones with some evidence that birds moved north in a series of small steps, often staging briefly at a sequence of sites. Some turnstones have been thought to pause in the Outer Hebrides as a final British staging area before flying

...e for this as a regular
...l (Prys-Jones *et al.* 1988).

...an important spring staging
...*menius phaeopus*. About
...cur around the estuarine
...rom the Severn Estuary and
...during late April and early May,
...as a final staging area before
...reed in Iceland (Ferns *et al.* 1979).
...form about 1% of the Icelandic
...and few whimbrels occur in spring
...e in Britain (Prater 1981). Most of the
...c breeding population migrates through
...m, The Netherlands and the Federal Republic
...rmany in spring. Whimbrels roost at night in
...places, one in Bridgwater Bay and the other on
...e Welsh shore of the Severn Estuary. During the
...ay they disperse to feed on pastures on the Gwent
Levels adjacent to the Severn Estuary and the
Somerset Levels stretching inland from Bridgwater
Bay.

Fidelity to spring staging sites

In most instances individual waders return to the
same spring staging areas on the same migration
schedule in successive years (e.g. Goodyer &
Evans 1980; Uttley *et al.* 1987; Prokosch 1988;
Evans & Townshend 1989). They are thus
dependent on the continued availability of these
places to enable them to complete their migration.
In a few circumstances waders use alternative
staging areas in different years. One instance of
this has been well documented in Siberian knots,
which usually make a long non-stop migration from
the Banc d'Arguin to the West German Wadden
Sea in early May. In most years only a few knots
appear at other estuaries along their migration
route, in Portugal, France and The Netherlands. In
a few years, however, a much larger number of
knots appear at these 'emergency staging areas',
particularly in western France. Knots that do
appear at these places generally have low masses
and stay a shorter time than their usual spring
staging period; they seem to move on to their
normal staging area in the Wadden Sea (Piersma *et
al.* 1987b). Their appearance at emergency sites is
linked to adverse weather conditions during their
migration northwards, which force the birds to
pause and replenish their energy reserves before
completing their migration (Smit & Piersma 1989).
Although it is not apparent from general counts, the
continued availability of these alternative staging
sites is thus critical in the long term for the survival
of a large part of the populations of long-distance
migrants.

Less explicable is the use of alternative spring
staging areas by the other subspecies of knot, the
islandica population, most of which overwinters in
Britain. In late spring about two-thirds of the world
population of these birds stage in west Iceland, with
the remaining third using two fjords, Balsfjord and
Porsangerfjord, in northern Norway (Davidson *et al.*
1986; Davidson & Wilson 1990). Numbers of knots

in Balsfjord vary considerably from year to year
and Strann (1991) suggests that this relates to the
ice conditions in early May in Porsangerfjord, about
200 km further north than Balsfjord. Porsangerfjord
usually holds the larger staging population. In
years when spring is late, intertidal feeding
grounds in Porsangerfjord remain ice-covered
throughout May and under these circumstances it
seems that a larger proportion of the population
may return south to Balsfjord to stage before flying
to their breeding grounds.

Even more unexpected is the apparent use by
some *islandica* knots of a late spring staging area in
Norway in one year and Iceland in the next year,
revealed only by detailed marking studies (Uttley
et al. 1987). This implies that these birds must
leave their early spring staging area in a quite
different direction in different years, unlike the use
of 'emergency staging areas' which lie on the same
migration route. Evidently much remains to be
understood about spring migration strategies of
waterfowl and how this relates to their use of British
estuaries.

Staging areas and nutrient reserve storage

Flight is an energetically costly activity. During
flight energy is expended at a rate between seven
and 10 times that of resting (Masman & Klaassen
1987). To fuel their migratory flights birds store
reserves of fat, since fat has a high energy content
for its mass and so is an economical way of
carrying energy reserves. In general the size of
reserves stored is related to the distance to be
flown to the next staging area, and in some small
waders can amount to half the total body mass just
before departure on migration (Davidson 1984).
Waders and wildfowl also increase the size of their
pectoral muscles. This is to enable them to
generate enough power from their muscles to fly
efficiently with the large amounts of extra weight
stored as fat (Davidson & Evans 1988). Recent
studies on waders using the East Atlantic Flyway
have shown that the 50-60% of the increase in mass
before departure in long-distance migrants is fat
and the remainder is muscle protein (Smit &
Piersma 1989).

In addition to the reserves of fat and protein
needed for migratory flight, arctic-breeding
waterfowl carry reserves of fat and protein that
contribute to egg production and provide nutrients
and energy for the incubating bird in early spring
when food availability is poor (see Ankney 1984;
Mainguy & Thomas 1985; Murphy & Boag 1989).
Waterfowl breeding further south generally carry
smaller reserves into the breeding attempt and rely
more on readily available food supplies on the
breeding grounds. It has recently been
established that arctic-breeding waders, like
wildfowl, carry reserves of fat and protein to their
breeding grounds and that these are sufficient to
make a substantial contribution to egg formation
(Davidson & Evans 1988).

Waterfowl arriving on arctic breeding grounds in late May and early June can face very hostile conditions of severe weather. This makes high energy demands for thermo-regulation at the same time that most feeding areas remain inaccessible under a blanket of snow. To survive these conditions at the start of the breeding season waders need to draw on some of these reserves (Davidson & Morrison 1989; Morrison & Davidson 1990). Even so the weather can be sufficiently severe in some years to cause the death through starvation of many adults (Morrison 1975). Even if adults survive such severe weather they may later be forced to abandon their breeding attempt for lack of reserves. Thus it is very important for the survival and breeding of these species that they are able to accumulate sufficient nutrient reserves before they migrate to their breeding grounds.

Likewise the food obtained by geese on spring staging areas is important in determining the size of the clutch of eggs subsequently laid by the female on her arctic breeding grounds (e.g. Ankney & MacInnes 1978; Thomas 1983; Ankney 1984). Similarly the feeding conditions and reserves accumulated by dark-bellied brent geese on their spring staging areas in the Wadden Sea are important in determining their subsequent reproductive success (Ebbinge et al. 1982; Prokosch 1984): geese that departed in spring below a certain mass had a high probability of returning with no young in the following winter.

Arctic-breeding birds have a very short summer period in which to breed. Hence they must arrive on their breeding grounds, with sufficient nutrient reserves, immediately before conditions are suitable before breeding (Green et al. 1977; Meltofte 1985). Arrival too early can lead to death during severe weather or a serious depletion of reserves precluding egg laying. Arrival too late can mean that chicks cannot be hatched and fledged in time to take advantage of the peak abundance of food or to migrate south before the onset of winter. The use of spring staging areas reflects these needs; birds must arrive on staging areas and store sufficient nutrient reserves on the correct schedule so as to be able to leave their last staging area at precisely the optimum time to reach their breeding grounds. There generally appears to be more leeway in timing during the early stages of the return to the breeding grounds, and rates of accumulation of fat reserves are often lower on early spring staging sites than on late spring staging sites (e.g. Davidson & Wilson 1991).

Waterfowl sometimes change their diet and their foraging habitats during spring staging (e.g. Madsen 1985; Prins & Ydenberg 1985). These changes seems to be associated with the demands of accumulating large nutrient reserves before migration. The rate of spring accumulation of fat can depend on foraging habitat: greater snow geese staging in the Gulf of St. Lawrence in Canada gain fat faster when feeding on their traditional feeding grounds of freshwater marshes than on

brackish marshes recently invaded by cord-grass Spartina (Gauthier et al. 1984). Changes in staging area habitat may therefore affect the ability of migrant waterfowl to store sufficient nutrient reserves for their migration and breeding.

Although rates of mass gain can be very rapid – often in excess of 5% of body mass per day (e.g. Davidson 1984; Piersma & van Brederode in press) – at least in waders they may not always be maximal. There is some evidence that waders can accelerate their rate of mass gain to compensate for delays in the migration schedule, such as weather-induced delays in movement between staging areas or arrival with lower than normal reserves as a consequence of adverse weather encountered during the migration (e.g. Piersma 1987; Piersma & Jukema 1990; Evans et al. In press). The precision of the amount of reserves accumulated, and of migration timing, is greatest on the late spring sites (Davidson & Wilson 1991). Smit & Piersma (1989) comment that feeding conditions on these final staging areas may be the most critical for migrants since they offer the last opportunity to bring reserves to the level needed for successful migration and breeding. Nevertheless the loss of any staging area in the sequence used may jeopardise the ability of waterfowl to make a successful migration to or from their breeding grounds, either because alternative areas have insufficient food supplies to permit the necessary reserve accumulation, or because the additional distance flown to other staging areas may delay the subsequent larger replenishing of reserves and so prevent birds reaching breeding grounds in time.

Staging areas with abundantly available food and free from disturbance allow the birds rapidly to accumulate reserves and are thus essential for the breeding strategy of migrant waterfowl, even though each site may be used for only very short periods of the year, or even sometimes only in some years. Hence many more staging areas, like cold weather refugia, may support nationally and internationally important populations of wildfowl than are currently apparent from 1% criteria based on average peak monthly counts.

The ability to ingest food in excess of daily requirements, so letting birds store fat and protein reserves, is also vital in early winter. Such reserves are used by waterfowl as an insurance against inability to find sufficient food during severe weather later in the winter (Hanson 1962; Pienkowski et al. 1979; Davidson 1981; Dugan et al. 1981). The size of fat and protein reserves stored by waders in Britain generally reflects the severity of the winter weather on each estuary (Pienkowski et al. 1979; Davidson et al. 1986a). Both the winter distribution of the birds and their reserve accumulation are adapted to ensure survival in winter. So the winter distributions described below reflect the presence of wintering sites where early winter reserve storage can be sufficient to ensure survival during severe late winter weather (e.g.

Davidson 1982c), just as successful migration and breeding depends on the presence of staging areas with abundant food supplies.

Wintering waterfowl distribution

General patterns of waterfowl distribution

British estuaries support very large numbers of wintering waterfowl. Total populations are summarised in Table 8.6.1. In January there are over 1,740,000 waterfowl present on review sites. This is almost 61% of the British wintering population and over 10% of the relevant international waterfowl populations (East Atlantic Flyway for waders, north-west Europe for wildfowl). The total waterfowl population on British estuaries divides between just over 581,000 wildfowl (38% of the British and 6% of the north-west European wintering population) and almost 1,159,000 waders: a massive 90% of the British coastal population and over 15% of the East Atlantic Flyway population. Over 36% of the waders wintering on the Atlantic coast of Europe are on British estuaries (Table 8.6.1). British estuaries are thus of very major national and international significance for their wintering waterfowl.

Total waterfowl distribution

Waterfowl are widely distributed around British estuaries. Some are present on each of the 142 review sites for which there are data on January numbers of waders and/or wildfowl (Figure 8.6.25). There are review sites in most parts of Britain with large numbers of wintering waterfowl, although sites in western and northern Scotland, and in south-west England generally, support regular midwinter populations of less than 10,000 birds. The largest midwinter populations are on The Wash (over 180,000 birds) and Morecambe Bay (over 140,000 birds). Five other review sites support in excess of 50,000 waterfowl in January: the Severn Estuary, the Dee Estuary and North Wirral, the Ribble Estuary, the Solway Firth and the Humber Estuary. Elsewhere there are major concentrations of waterfowl on the estuaries around the Solent in Sussex and Hampshire, in the firths of north-east Scotland and the complex of estuaries of the Suffolk, Essex and north Kent coasts. Taken together the stretch of almost continuous estuarine habitat from the Colne Estuary south to the Swale Estuary (effectively a 'Greater Thames Estuary') supports a substantial proportion of the wintering waterfowl populations in Britain: almost 229,000 birds (13.1% of the British estuarine waterfowl population).

Altogether 25 review sites each support more than 20,000 waterfowl. These sites hold the bulk of the estuarine wintering population: a total of 1,444,419 birds (83.2% of the January estuarine population (Table 8.6.1). Most review sites support much smaller populations than this; over half the review sites (84 sites) have wintering waterfowl populations of less than 5,000 birds, and 31 of these each support less than 500 birds. Taken together,

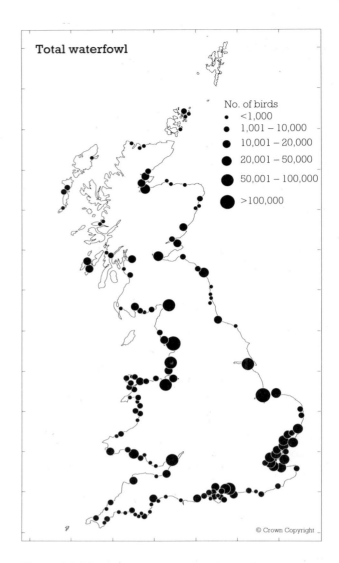

Figure 8.6.25 The distribution of total waterfowl populations on review sites in January

however, all these sites with small populations make an important contribution to the waterfowl populations since almost 17% of the estuarine wintering population is on sites with less than 20,000 birds. As described above, however, although these are sites with small populations, they are often of additional significance as preferred feeding areas, migration staging areas and cold weather refugia.

Total wader distribution

The distribution of waders and wildfowl around review sites is broadly similar (Figures 8.6.26 & 8.6.27). By far the most numerically important estuaries for wintering waders are The Wash and Morecambe Bay, with almost 133,000 and 130,000 birds respectively. Other review sites important for their total populations are the three with more than 50,000 wintering waders: The Dee Estuary and North Wirral, the Solway Estuary and the Humber Estuary. There are a further 22 review sites each supporting January populations of more than 10,000 waders. Taken together these 27 review sites hold almost 925,000 waders, almost 80% of the British estuarine population. The 'Greater Thames

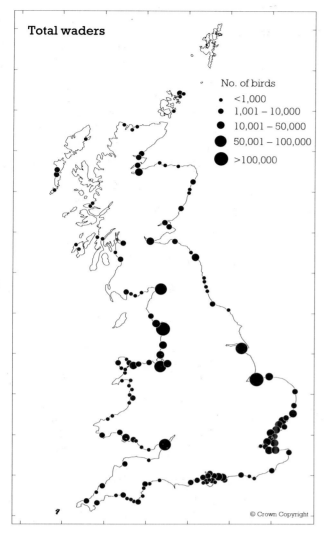

Figure 8.6.26 The distribution of wader populations on review sites in January

more than 20,000 wildfowl. Again the 'Greater Thames Estuary' is of major significance with over 89,000 wildfowl (15% of the British estuarine population) in January. 95 estuaries that each supports less than 10,000 wildfowl, taken together these have a total of 204,500 wildfowl, 2.2% of the international wintering population.

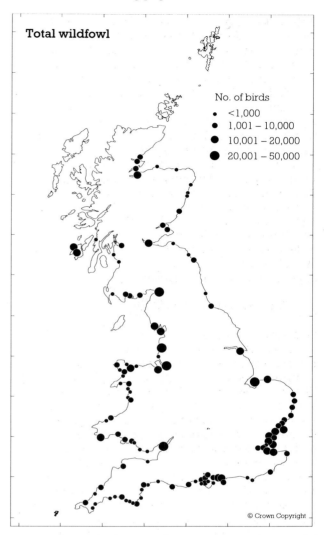

Figure 8.6.27 The distribution of wildfowl populations on review sites in January

Estuary' is of major significance for wintering waders, with over 139,000 birds (12% of the British estuarine population). As for the total waterfowl populations, however, many review sites each have small populations of waders (42 sites each have less than 500 waders in January – Figure 8.6.28) but nevertheless sites each supporting less than 10,000 waders make a substantial contribution to the wintering wader population, with a total of over 234,000 birds (over 3% of the East Atlantic Flyway population) on these 111 sites.

Total wildfowl distribution

Wildfowl are more dispersed than waders, with only 23 review sites supporting more than 10,000 wildfowl each. These sites together support less than two-thirds of the British estuarine population. Many wildfowl in Britain are less dependent on estuaries than are waders – only about 38% of the British wintering population uses review sites in January. Nevertheless several review sites are of major significance for wildfowl, and five review sites (Severn Estuary, Mersey Estuary, Ribble Estuary, Solway Firth and The Wash) each support

Waterfowl distributions in Europe

Outside Britain there are few estuarine areas on the East Atlantic Flyway that support large numbers of wintering waders in midwinter (Figure 8.6.29). On the Atlantic coast of Europe the international Wadden Sea of Denmark, the Federal Republic of Germany and The Netherlands is by far the largest area of estuarine habitat in Europe, with about 4,000 km² of tidal flats (Chapter 6), but the Wadden Sea has a midwinter population of 780,000 waders (Smit & Piersma 1989), only two-thirds of the British population. Elsewhere the Dutch Delta area is of major significance with 250,000 waders in January. Further south several parts of the African coast support very large numbers of wintering waders.

The Gulf de Gabes in the western Mediterranean has 267,000 waders. Of even greater significance are several parts of the West African coast, notably the coastline of the Democratic Republic of Guinea (400,000 waders) and the Archipelago dos Bijagos in Guinea-Bissau (980,000 waders). By far the most numerically important site on the East Atlantic Flyway in midwinter is the Banc d'Arguin in Mauritania, which supports an estimated 2,038,000 waders (27% of the flyway population) (Smit & Piersma 1989).

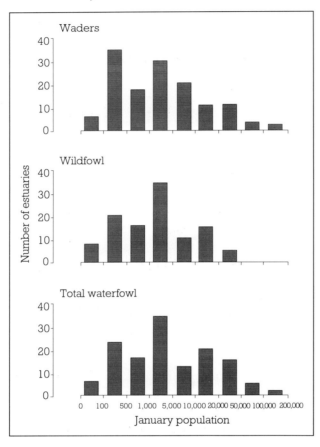

Figure 8.6.28 The frequency of January wader, wildfowl and total waterfowl populations of different sizes on review sites.

Most wintering wildfowl in north-west Europe outside Britain are in the coastal wetlands of Denmark, the Federal Republic of Germany and The Netherlands, where the Wadden Sea is again of major significance, with over 500,000 wildfowl in midwinter (Pirot *et al.* 1989).

Correlates of population size and density

Figures 8.6.26 and 8.6.27 show that there are broadly similar patterns of distribution of waders and wildfowl around British estuaries. This link between the distributions of the two groups is further supported by Figure 8.6.30, which shows a highly statistically significant correlation between the numbers of waders and the numbers of wildfowl on each review site. Thus estuaries with large wintering populations of wildfowl also have large wader populations. Although this correlation

explains over 60% of the variations in numbers, individual estuaries do diverge considerably from the average regression line. This is not surprising since waders and wildfowl tend to use estuaries in different ways, and have different food requirements. Furthermore there are many different species involved, each of which has different habitat and food needs. Nevertheless Figure 8.6.30 suggests an underlying common factor influencing waterfowl distribution around Britain.

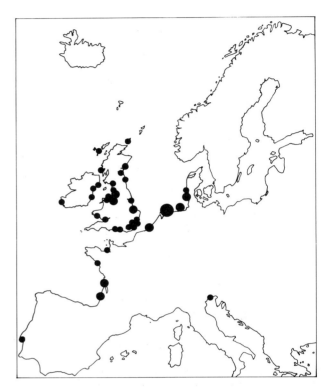

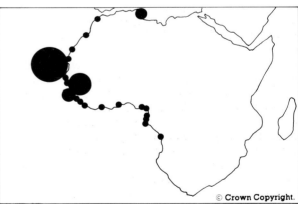

Figure 8.6.29 Main coastal wintering areas for waders on the East Atlantic Flyway (derived from Smit & Piersma 1989). Only areas supporting more than 20,000 waders in midwinter are shown, with symbols scaled according to population size.

A major determinant of wildfowl and wader population sizes on an estuary is its size. There are strong correlations between estuary size, both when measured as intertidal area and as total (intertidal and subtidal) area, and the January

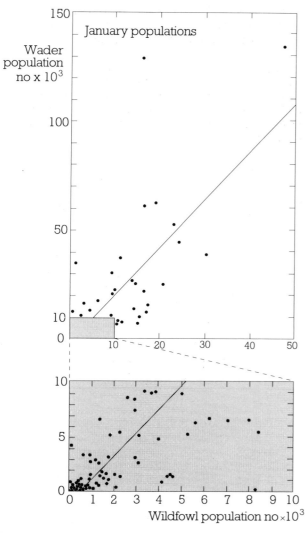

Figure 8.6.30 Estuaries that support large numbers of wintering wildfowl also support large numbers of wintering waders. Each symbol is a review site and the solid line shows the highly significant least-squares regression $Y = 2.163X - 145.6$, $r = 0.781$, $n = 112$, $P<0.001$.

wader, wildfowl and total waterfowl populations (Figure 8.6.31). The area of estuary accounts for between 49% and 62% of the between-site variation in bird numbers. The correlations account for slightly more of the variation in numbers of wintering waders than wildfowl, as might be expected since many waders are more closely tied to estuaries than are some wintering wildfowl. These are strong correlates, considering that on some estuaries densities will be distorted by the movement of roosting birds to feed on other estuaries, and because some wildfowl only roost on estuaries.

If the density of birds is the same on estuaries of different sizes then the slopes of the least-squares regressions shown in Figure 8.6.31 will be unity. These statistical analyses show, however, that in all cases the slopes of the regressions are significantly ($P<0.01$) less than unity. This means that the densities of waders, wildfowl and total waterfowl are higher on small estuaries than on large estuaries. The differences are substantial. For

example the average density of waders on an estuary with an intertidal area of 20,000 ha is 1.55 birds ha^{-1} but for a 200 ha estuary is 4.2 birds ha^{-1}, a density 2.7 times higher. The difference for wildfowl is slightly less marked, with the equivalent figures being 1.02 birds ha^{-1} and 2.29 birds ha^{-1}, a density 2.2 times larger on the smaller estuary. These figures also emphasise that densities of waders are higher than those of wildfowl throughout the size range of British estuaries.

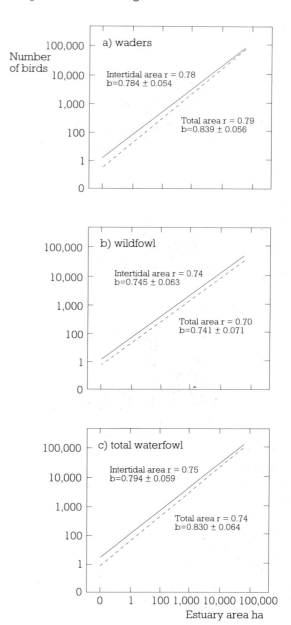

Figure 8.6.31 Relationships between review site area (total area and intertidal area) and the January populations of a) waders, b) wildfowl, and c) total waterfowl. Solid lines show the least-squares regressions for intertidal area and dashed lines are for total area. For each regression the correlation coefficient (r) and the regression coefficient (b ± 1 standing error) are given. All correlations are highly significant ($P<0.001$).

These strong correlations do however mask a very considerable variation in waterfowl densities on different estuaries of similar sizes – see for example Figure 8.6.32. This arises because some estuaries provide particularly good conditions for some species or assemblages for a variety of reasons such as location, diversity of habitats, weather conditions or food supply (e.g. Goss-Custard *et al.* 1977; Pienkowski & Evans 1984; Moser 1987). In addition different estuaries provide the most favourable conditions for different species assemblages.

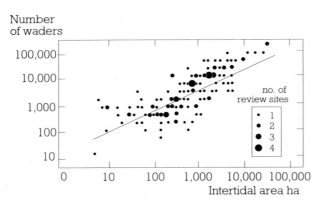

Figure 8.6.32 The relationship between intertidal area and January wader populations on review sites. The solid line is the least-squares regression, from Figure 8.6.31, and each symbol is a review site. Note that for review sites of a given size the wader population can vary up to one-hundredfold.

A similar pattern of increasing population size of individual wader species with increasing estuary size was found by Prater (1981) for estuaries in eastern England. From Prater's analysis it appears that most individual wader species occur at higher densities on smaller estuaries. Prater also found that the densities of total wader populations on eastern English estuaries were highest on small

estuaries, which he attributed chiefly to the likely inclusion in large estuaries of more areas unsuitable for feeding.

Mudge (1989) has recently shown similar strong correlations between numbers of mallard, wigeon and teal and site area for a smaller number of estuaries, or parts of estuaries, in Britain. Mudge's analyses also found slopes consistently much less than unity for these regressions. Hence individual waterfowl species, as well as the total populations of the species assemblages, occur at lower densities on larger sites.

Since in general the highest densities of waterfowl occur on the most favourable estuaries, these results show that small estuaries can be of very considerable importance to wintering waterfowl even though individually they may support only relatively small populations. This has important consequences for approaches to conserving these populations since it emphasises that numerical importance should not be used as the only measure for identifying key sites for waterfowl during their non-breeding seasons.

Waterfowl assemblages on British estuaries

26 species of wildfowl and 18 species of waders regularly occur on British estuaries in winter. These species, and their population sizes, are listed in Tables 8.6.2 and 8.6.3. Many of these species occur together on estuaries and often roost together as mixed species flocks, although they may use the estuary in different ways as each species has particular feeding requirements.

Table 8.6.2 Populations of wader species on review sites in January. Data are average populations for January 1983-1987, from BoEE/NWC counts.

Species	No. of review sites[1]	Review site population	British population[2]	% British population	International population[3]	%International population
Oystercatcher	133	227,732	279,500	81.5	874,000	26.1
Avocet	13	474	500	94.8	67,000	0.7
Ringed plover	124	7,926	23,040	34.4	48,000	16.5
Golden plover	90	20,352	200,000	10.2	1,000,000	2.0
Grey plover	98	24,399	21,250	114.8[4]	168,000	14.5
Lapwing	116	66,021	1,000,000	6.6	2,000,000	3.3
Knot	80	232,081	222,830	104.2[4]	345,000	67.3
Sanderling	59	5,842	13,710	42.6	123,000	4.7
Purple sandpiper	31	1,234	16,140	7.6	50,000	2.5
Dunlin	130	380,332	433,000	87.8	1,373,000	27.4
Ruff	22	99	1,500	6.6	1,000,000	<0.1
Snipe	93	2,483	–		1,000,000	0.2
Black-tailed godwit	40	4,146	4,770	86.9	66,000	6.3
Bar-tailed godwit	99	56,919	60,810	93.6	115,000	49.5
Curlew	134	52,894	91,200	58.0	348,000	15.2
Spotted redshank	15	39	200	19.5	6,500	0.6
Redshank	136	60,388	75,400	80.1	109,000	55.4
Greenshank	38	164	400	41.0	19,000	0.9
Turnstone	114	12,710	44,480	28.6	67,000	19.0

[1] Of 138 review sites with data
[2] From Moser (1987), Prater (1989), and Stroud *et al.* (1990)
[3] From Smit & Piersma (1989)
[4] Current estuarine population exceeds most recent British population estimate – see text

Table 8.6.3 Populations of wildfowl species on review sites in January. Data are average populations for January 1983-1987, from BoEE/NWC counts.

Species	No. of review sites[1]	Review site population	British population[2]	% British population	International population[3]	% International population
Mute swan	94	3,112	18,000	17.3	180,000	1.7
Bewick's swan	23	738	7,000	10.5	17,000	4.3
Whooper swan	26	616	6,000	10.3	17,000	3.6
Pink-footed goose[4]	18	33,671	110,000	30.6	110,000	30.6
European white-fronted goose	26	6,069	6,000	101.1[5]	300,000	2.0
Greenland white-fronted goose	3	157	10,000	1.6	22,000	0.7
Grey-lag goose	41	11,803	100,000	11.8	100,000	11.8
Barnacle goose[4]	17	17,539	37,000	47.4	42,000	41.8
Light-bellied brent goose[4]	17	2,417	3,000	80.6	4,000	75.0
Dark-bellied brent goose	58	90,995	90,000	101.1[5]	170,000	53.5
Shelduck	102	70,613	75,000	94.2	250,000	28.2
Wigeon	102	166,836	250,000	66.7	750,000	22.2
Gadwall	46	673	6,000	11.2	12,000	5.6
Teal	98	42,899	100,000	42.9	400,000	10.7
Mallard	107	59,373	500,000	11.9	5,000,000	1.2
Pintail	73	21,493	25,000	86.0	70,000	30.7
Shoveler	57	1,384	9,000	15.4	40,000	3.5
Pochard	62	5,254	50,000	10.5	350,000	1.5
Tufted duck	74	5,871	60,000	9.8	750,000	0.8
Scaup	51	3,489	4,000	87.2	150,000	2.3
Eider	56	13,061	50,000	26.1	3,000,000	0.4
Long-tailed duck	24	748	20,000	3.7	2,000,000	<0.1
Common scoter	26	3,871	35,000	11.0	800,000	0.5
Velvet scoter	10	111	3,000	0.4	250,000	<0.1
Goldeneye	96	5,940	15,000	39.6	300,000	2.0
Smew	33	103	50	–	15,000	0.7
Red-breasted merganser	82	4,515	10,000	45.2	40,000	11.3
Goosander	33	1,767	5,500	32.1	10,000	17.7

[1] Of 116 review sites with data
[2] From Owen *et al.* (1986), and Stroud *et al.* (1990)
[3] From Pirot *et al.* (1989)
[4] Biogeographic populations are combined for this analysis – see text
[5] Current estuarine population exceeds most recent British population estimate – see text

The wintering wader assemblage

The numerical species composition of the midwinter wader and wildfowl populations on British estuaries (Figure 8.6.33) shows that the wader assemblage is dominated by three abundant species – dunlin, knot and oystercatcher – which together form 72.5% of the wader population. Five other wader species each form more than 1% of the assemblage. Comparison with the species composition of coastal waders on the whole East Atlantic Flyway (Figure 8.6.33) shows that some species including knot, oystercatcher and lapwing form a much larger proportion of the wader assemblage on British estuaries than on the flyway as a whole. In contrast estuaries elsewhere on the flyway, especially in west Africa, are used by populations of some other important flyway species such as curlew sandpiper and little stint. These are species that occur in Britain almost entirely only during migration.

The wintering wildfowl assemblage

The wintering wildfowl assemblage on British estuaries is, like the wader assemblage, dominated numerically by only a few species, notably wigeon *Anas penelope*, dark-bellied brent goose and shelduck, which together form over 56% of the total waterfowl population. A further 11 species each contribute more than 1% of the population.

Comparison with the north-west European waterfowl assemblage (Figure 8.6.33) shows that several species, including wigeon, dark-bellied brent goose, shelduck, teal *Anas crecca* and pintail, form substantially larger proportions of the estuarine assemblage in Britain than in north-west Europe as a whole.

Interspecific differences in estuarine dependence

The species of waders and wildfowl in these assemblages depend in varying degrees on estuaries in winter. The proportions of the British populations of waders and wildfowl that are found on estuaries in January are shown in Figure 8.6.34. For several species of waders, including grey plover, knot, avocet *Recurvirostra avosetta*, bar-tailed godwits and black-tailed godwits *Limosa limosa*, dunlin, oystercatcher and redshank, the wintering populations are almost entirely restricted to estuaries, with over 80% of the British population of each species on review sites. Note that these figures are approximate because of short-term population fluctuations since the last comprehensive national population estimates. For two species, grey plover and knot, this results in the estuarine population apparently exceeding the national 'total'. In the case of grey plovers this arises because the wintering population has been increasing rapidly in recent years (Moser 1988).

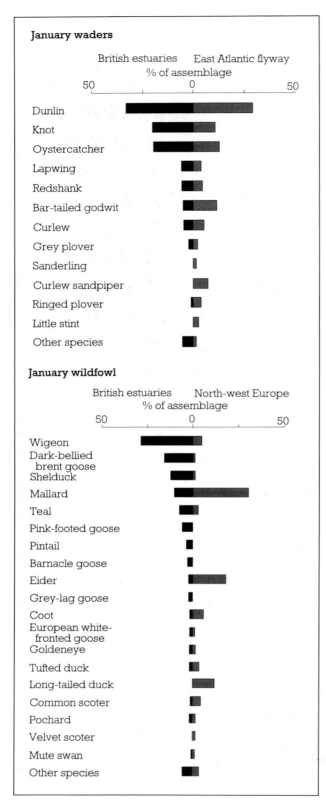

Figure 8.6.33 Species composition of January wader and wildfowl populations on British estuaries in comparison with their international populations – East Atlantic Flyway for waders, derived from Smit & Piersma (1989); north-west Europe for wildfowl, derived from Pirot et al. (1989)

Likewise the British knot population has increased slightly in recent years after a major decline during

the 1970s (Salmon *et al.* 1989; Davidson & Wilson 1991).

Only small proportions of the British populations of some other waders such as lapwings and sanderlings occur on estuaries, despite being numerous there (Figure 8.6.34). Sanderlings, turnstones, ringed plovers and purple sandpipers *Calidris maritima* are predominantly birds of open sandy and rocky coasts in winter (Moser & Summers 1987). Others such as lapwings and golden plovers mostly overwinter on inland pasture and arable fields, except during periods of severe weather.

Wildfowl have a similarly varying proportion of their wintering population on estuaries. Rather few species of wildfowl are substantially restricted to estuaries in midwinter: only eight wildfowl populations have more than half of their British wintering populations on review sites (Figure 8.6.34). These are four goose populations (dark-bellied and light-bellied brent geese, barnacle geese and European white-fronted geese *Anser albifrons albifrons*) and four species of duck (shelduck, scaup *Aythya marila*, pintail and wigeon). Note however that many barnacle geese and dark-bellied brent geese and wigeon feed on pasture and arable farmland in the environs of estuaries rather than on the estuaries themselves, returning to the estuaries chiefly for roosting. Other species in the varied estuarine wildfowl assemblage overwinter chiefly elsewhere, either on freshwater wetlands (e.g. mallard, pochard and tufted duck *Aythya fuligula*) or marine coastal areas (e.g. eider *Somateria mollissima*, long-tailed duck and common scoter *Melanitta nigra*). Despite most of their populations overwintering elsewhere, some of these wildfowl, notably mallard and teal *Anas crecca*, form an important component of the estuarine assemblage because of their nationally large populations (Figure 8.6.33).

Proportions of international wintering populations dependent on review sites

Populations comprising more than 1% of the relevant biogeographical population are generally considered to be of international significance on these simple numerical grounds. There are also additional reasons for international importance (see earlier, and Stroud *et al.* 1990). Fourteen species of waders and 21 species of wildfowl occur on review sites in midwinter in numbers exceeding 1% of their international population (Figure 8.6.35), even with the conservatism of using 1% of the January populations (see above).

British estuaries are of major international significance for some species. A total of 67% of nearctic knots depend on British estuaries in midwinter, along with 55% of the East Atlantic Flyway population of redshanks, almost 50% of bar-tailed godwits, 27% of *alpina* dunlins, and 26% of oystercatchers. In addition British estuaries support more than 10% of a further four wader

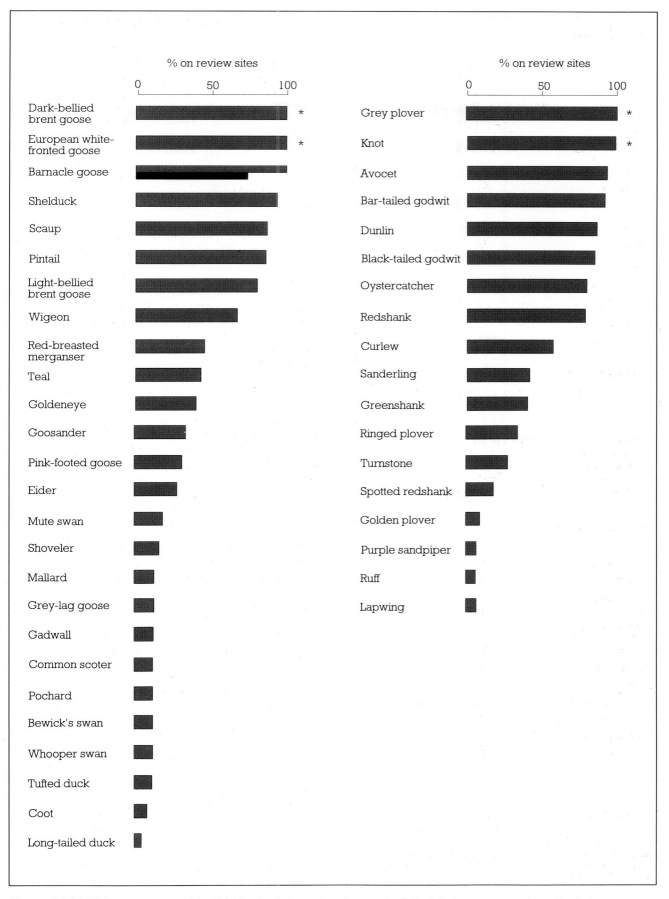

Figure 8.6.34 The percentages of the British populations of waders and wildfowl that occur on review sites in January. Total British population sizes are from Owen *et al.* (1986) and Stroud *et al.* (1990) for wildfowl, and from Moser (1987) for waders. For species marked * the current review site population exceeds the estimated British population – see text for explanation. For barnacle goose the shaded portion is the Svalbard population and the black portion is the Greenland population.

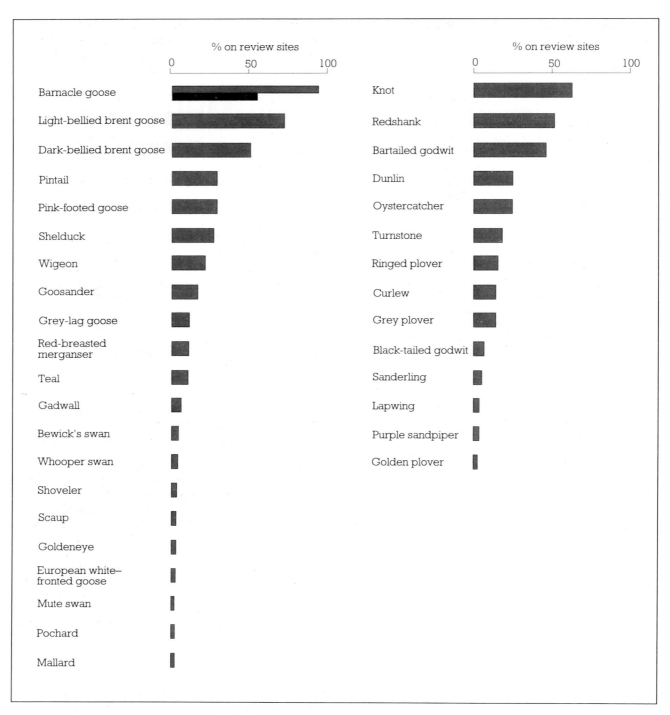

Figure 8.6.35 The percentage of international populations of waders and wildfowl that occur on review sites in January. Only species with >1% of the international population are shown. For barnacle goose the shaded portion is the Svalbard population and the black portion is the Greenland population.

species (turnstone, ringed plover, curlew and grey plover).

British estuaries are of great international importance for some wildfowl, especially barnacle and brent geese. Over 80% of light-bellied brent geese (which come almost entirely from the very small Svalbard breeding population) occur on British estuaries, chiefly at Lindisfarne in Northumberland. The precise proportion varies between years depending on how many birds move across the North Sea from their early winter Danish feeding grounds (Owen *et al.* 1986). In

addition there are over 50% of dark-bellied brent geese and 100% of the Svalbard breeding population and *c.* 70% of the Greenland breeding population of barnacle geese on review sites. Other wildfowl with major international populations overwintering on review sites are pintail, pink-footed goose and shelduck, each with about one-quarter of the international population on such sites, and British estuaries support 10-25% of five other wildfowl species: wigeon, goosander *Mergus merganser*, grey-lag goose *Anser anser*, red-breasted merganser *Mergus serrator*, and teal.

Distribution of waterfowl within the British estuarine resource

The general dispersion pattern

Some waterfowl are very widely dispersed around British estuaries; others have a much more restricted distribution. This variation in dispersion has important consequences for the effective conservation of estuarine waterfowl assemblages, since some species critically depend on the safeguarding of relatively few key sites, whilst the wintering populations of others depend on a much wider range of estuaries.

The dispersion of wintering waterfowl on review sites is summarised in Figure 8.6.36. Many wader species are particularly widespread, and redshanks, curlews, oystercatchers and dunlins can be found in winter on over 90% of British estuaries, including many small sites as well as the major estuaries. Others are less ubiquitous, but nevertheless altogether 12 of the 19 regularly occurring wintering waders each use over half the review sites. In comparison, most waterfowl have a more restricted distribution. This is particularly so for geese, many of which depend on just a few traditional wintering areas. The only widespread estuarine goose is the dark-bellied brent goose, but even this population occurs regularly on only half the review sites. Only 10 of the 24 regularly occurring estuarine wildfowl use more than half the

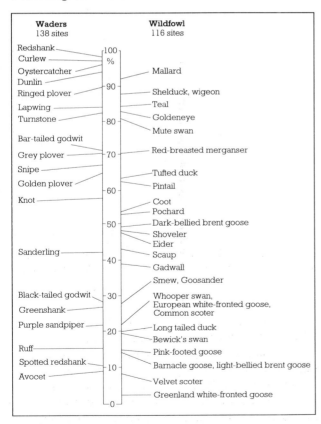

Figure 8.6.36 The interspecific variation in dispersal of waders and wildfowl on review sites in January, shown as the number of review sites on which the population regularly occurs expressed as a percentage of the number of sites for which there are data (138 review sites for waders, 116 for wildfowl)

review sites, and only the commonest wildfowl species, the mallard, uses more than 90% of the sites. The estuarine specialists, shelduck and wigeon, are also widespread.

The populations of each species are not, however, evenly distributed around the review sites on which they occur, and Moser (1987) has shown that in most species a large proportion of the wintering population occurs on just a few estuaries.

Examples of wildfowl distributions

Within this general dispersion pattern around British estuaries, different species are distributed very differently. This is illustrated in Figures 8.6.37 to 8.6.46 for a range of waterfowl species whose distributions in January are described below. These provide examples of different types of distribution pattern and are not intended to give a comprehensive description for each waterfowl species present on estuaries. Such species descriptions can be found in Prater (1981) for waders and Owen *et al.* (1986) for wildfowl.

Shelduck

Shelduck are one of the most widely distributed and characteristic waterfowl of estuaries, with 94% of the British population wintering on review sites, where they feed chiefly on a variety of small invertebrates on chiefly soft intertidal mudflats. Most wintering shelducks in Britain breed around British estuaries, although some probably come from breeding areas around the southern North Sea (Prater 1981). Although they are common (in waterfowl terms) throughout Britain they are particularly abundant on the east coast of Britain from the Eden Estuary southwards, on the south coast between Poole Harbour and Pagham Harbour and in north-west England (Figure 8.6.37). The largest January population (over 12,000 birds) is on The Wash, but elsewhere midwinter numbers are less than 5,000 birds on any estuary.

Scaup

Other ducks are predominantly estuarine in Britain in winter but have a much more restricted distribution. Scaup breed in Iceland and the USSR and reach peak numbers in Britain in January, although the British total population is relatively small compared with those of The Netherlands and the Baltic. Scaup feed in shallow estuarine waters on mussels *Mytilus edulis* and other bivalves such as cockles and Baltic tellins *Macoma balthica* (Owen *et al.* 1986). In the 1970s scaup were concentrated mostly close to sewage outfalls (Campbell 1978) or where distilleries discharged their grain waste. These areas had clearly enriched benthic communities which provided invertebrate food. Prater (1981) shows the largest population, sometimes up to 40,000 birds, in the Firth of Forth in the late 1960s. The sewage discharge there has since been reduced (Campbell 1984), and the population in the estuarine Firth of Forth is now very small (Figure 8.6.38). The national population

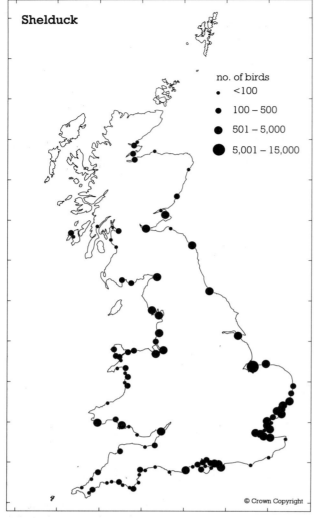

Figure 8.6.37 The January distribution of shelduck on review sites. Data are mostly from BoEE/NWC counts for 1983-1987.

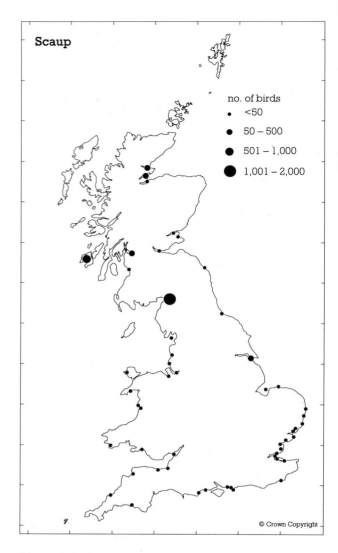

Figure 8.6.38 The January distribution of scaup on review sites. Data are mostly from BoEE/NWC counts for 1983-1987.

has also declined overall. The largest wintering group, although at about 1,700 birds much smaller than in the past, is now in the Solway Firth. Elsewhere wintering populations exceed 50 birds on only five estuaries – on Islay, associated with domestic sewage discharge and to a lesser extent distillery discharges, in the Clyde Estuary, the Dornoch and Cromarty Firths and the Humber Estuary – although even smaller numbers are widespread around the British coastline (Figure 8.6.38).

Eider

Some other waterfowl also have a northern distribution in Britain. An example is the eider (Figure 8.6.39), which winters in large concentrations (>1,000 birds) only north from Morecambe Bay in the west and Lindisfarne in the east, although again much smaller numbers are scattered widely on estuaries throughout Britain. Eiders, almost entirely from the British breeding population, are not restricted to estuaries in winter, but review sites support over one-quarter of the British wintering population (Table 8.6.3), and

eiders form a large component of the waterfowl assemblage on some northern estuaries.

Barnacle goose

Many wintering populations of geese are even more restricted in their wintering distribution, the most restricted being the barnacle goose. Two biogeographic populations of barnacle geese overwinter in Britain (Figure 8.6.40). The Svalbard population stages in autumn on Bear Island (Owen & Gullestad 1984), about 650 km south of the breeding grounds, and then flies non-stop the 2,500 km to the Solway Firth where the whole breeding population of about 12,100 birds overwinters.

The Greenland population breeds in east Greenland and reaches the islands of western Scotland, particularly Islay, in late October via a staging area in southern Iceland (Owen et al. 1986). Substantially the entire world population uses the Loch Gruinart review site as an autumn arrival and staging area before dispersing more widely to other parts of the wintering range (Easterbee et al. 1987). About 20,000 of the 27,000 British

230

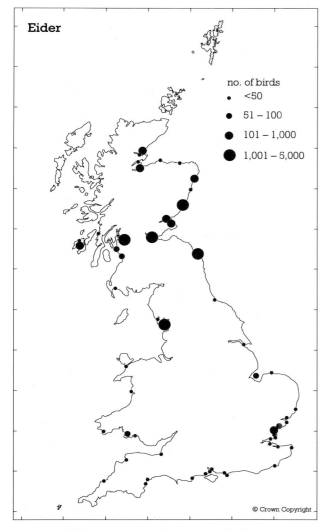

Figure 8.6.39 The January distribution of eider on review sites. Data are mostly from BoEE/NWC counts for 1983-1987.

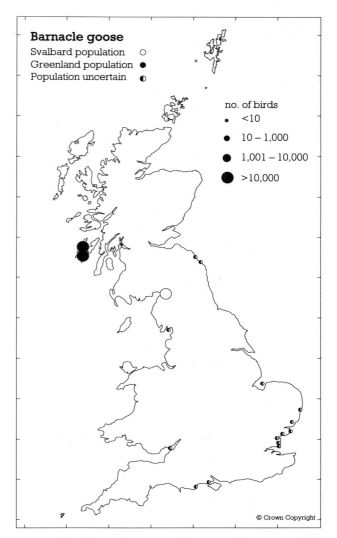

Figure 8.6.40 The January distribution of barnacle geese on review sites. Filled symbols are the Greenland breeding population, the open symbol is the Svalbard breeding population and half-filled symbols are birds of unknown origin. Data are mostly from BoEE/NWC counts for 1983-1987 with additional data from special goose counts.

population occurs on the two review sites on Islay, where they roost at night before spreading out to feed on nearby grasslands during the day. Very small numbers of barnacle geese occur in midwinter on a few other British estuaries (Figure 8.6.40). Their origins are uncertain but those in north-east England and Morecambe Bay are probably from the Svalbard populations whilst those on several estuaries in East Anglia may have moved from The Netherlands, where a third biogeographical population, from Siberia, overwinters (Owen *et al.* 1986). The few birds in southern and western England may be from feral flocks.

Dark-bellied brent goose

In contrast to these northern estuarine distributions, other geese depend heavily on estuaries in southern Britain. As for most other geese, the population of dark-bellied brent geese has increased very greatly since the 1950s. These birds feed on eel-grass *Zostera* on tidal flats and, increasingly, on pastures and arable farmland surrounding estuaries. The population decreased

greatly in the 1930s, a decline generally attributed to a concurrent substantial disease-related decline in the abundance of *Zostera*, and has been increasing rapidly since the 1970s, possible as a consequence of the easing of hunting pressure in Europe. Since the 1930s the wintering distribution has become more southerly (Owen *et al.* 1986). The population overwintering in Britain breeds in northern Siberia, particularly on the Taymyr Peninsula, and reaches Britain via staging areas in the Wadden Sea.

Birds begin reaching Britain between September and November, when they congregate particularly on the tidal flats of Maplin Sands and Southend-on-Sea, before dispersing to estuaries in southern and eastern England (St. Joseph 1979). There are three main wintering areas: The Wash and North Norfolk Coast, the south coast from Pagham Harbour to the Exe Estuary and the estuaries of Essex and Kent. In recent years the Essex estuaries have declined in relative importance whilst the proportions wintering in Norfolk and on the south coast have increased (Owen *et al.* 1986). The Wash holds the largest single part of the wintering population: 17,750 birds (almost 20% of the British population – Table 8.6.3). Away from their main wintering areas small numbers of dark-bellied brent geese overwinter on a number of south-coast and west-coast estuaries as far north as Morecambe Bay, with an average of 500 birds now occurring on the Loughor Estuary, and as far north as Lindisfarne in eastern England (Figure 8.6.41). Before the 1930s Lindisfarne was a major wintering ground for this population.

Light-bellied brent goose

The small (*c.* 3,000 birds) Svalbard-breeding population of light-bellied brent geese has not, unlike that of other arctic-breeding geese, increased greatly in recent years (Madsen 1987). It underwent a serious decline in the early 20th century, largely as a consequence of autumn shooting in Denmark and human disturbance in Svalbard (Madsen 1984; Owen *et al.* 1986). The absence of any subsequent increase is probably due to a number of factors, including high levels of nest predation and possibly also competition on their breeding grounds with the rapidly increasing Svalbard population of barnacle geese (Madsen *et al.* 1989). Many of these light-bellied brent geese overwinter in Denmark on just a few sites and some move to Lindisfarne in midwinter. The number reaching Lindisfarne generally depends on the severity of the winter weather in Denmark (Madsen 1984), but in recent years there has been a regular wintering flock at Lindisfarne, reinforced by influxes in severe weather. Between 1983 and 1987 an average maximum of three-quarters of the world population was at Lindisfarne (Table 8.6.3). Small numbers of light-bellied brent geese do occur elsewhere in two areas of Britain (Figure 8.6.41). Those in eastern Scotland, as far north as the Moray Firth (where many used to overwinter), are probably wanderers from the Svalbard population. There are also small numbers on eight review sites in south-western England and Wales. These may belong to the Greenland and Canadian breeding population which overwinters almost entirely in Ireland (Owen *et al.* 1986; O'Brien & Healy 1990). If they are all from the nearctic population these approximately 130 birds may be about 1% of the Irish-wintering population of that race in recent years.

Examples of wader distributions

Waders, like wildfowl, have major differences between species in their winter distributions. At the two extremes of distribution patterns are avocet (Figure 8.6.42) and dunlin (Figure 8.6.43).

Avocet

The wintering population of avocets is small but, like the breeding population (see later), is increasing rapidly. This has been documented

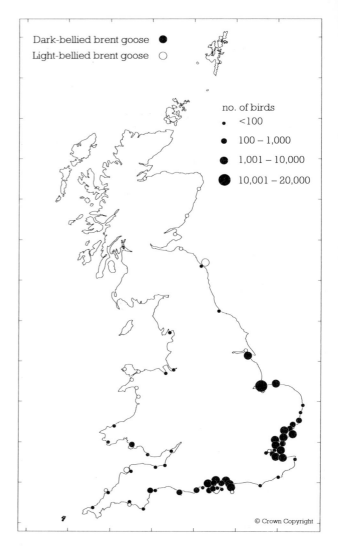

Figure 8.6.41 The January distribution of dark-bellied brent geese (filled symbols) and light-bellied brent geese (open symbols) on review sites. Data are mostly from BoEE/NWC counts for 1983-1987.

recently by Cadbury *et al.* (1989). Avocets in winter are restricted to 13 review sites in southern and eastern England. Overwintering began in the early 1950s in Plymouth Sound and subsequently in the Exe Estuary, expanding in the mid-1960s to Pagham and Poole Harbours and soon afterwards also close to their breeding grounds in the Ore-Alde-Butley Estuary in Suffolk. More recently, small numbers have begun to overwinter in Essex and Kent and winter counts in 1988/89 indicate a wintering population now exceeding 700 birds, about 1% of the East Atlantic Flyway population (Figure 8.6.42).

Dunlin

In contrast to avocets, the 380,300 dunlins wintering on British estuaries are widespread throughout Britain (Figure 8.6.43). In midwinter they are absent from only a few very small estuaries with little intertidal mud, scattered around Britain. Dunlins are the most abundant wader in Britain, but even so are relatively scarce compared with many

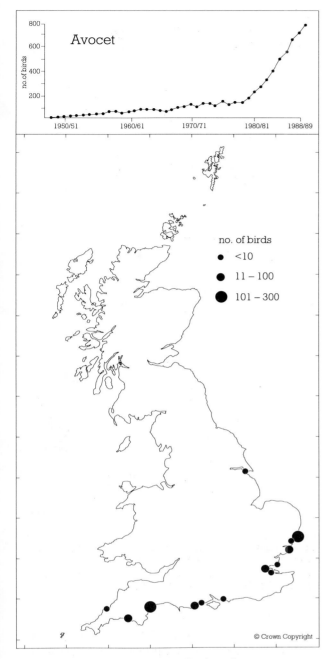

Figure 8.6.42 The January distribution of avocets on review sites. Data are mostly from BoEE/NWC counts for 1983-1987. The graph shows the increase in the British wintering population since 1950, from Cadbury *et al.* (1989).

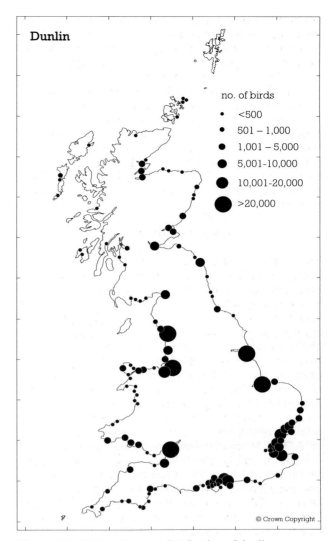

Figure 8.6.43 The January distribution of dunlins on review sites. Data are mostly from BoEE/NWC counts for 1983-1987.

wintering British birds, since they depend almost entirely on estuaries, as do many other wintering waterfowl (Figure 8.6.34). Wintering dunlins belong almost exclusively to the *alpina* population that breeds in northern Scandinavia and the USSR and overwinters in western Europe (Cramp & Simmons 1983), and British estuaries support over 27% of the East Atlantic Flyway population (Table 8.6.2). Dunlins occur in large numbers on many British estuaries but are most abundant on large estuaries such as Morecambe Bay (over 26,000 birds), The Wash (over 24,000 birds) the Mersey Estuary (over 22,000 birds) and the Humber Estuary (21,000 birds), but the largest midwinter

population is on the Severn Estuary where the over 34,000 dunlins in January comprise 2.5% of the international population. Elsewhere there are major concentrations of dunlins on Suffolk, Essex and north Kent estuaries, where there are in excess of 93,500 birds (almost 7.5% of the international population) between the Blyth and Swale Estuaries, and the Hampshire and Sussex estuaries from Pagham Harbour to the Lymington Estuary, where there are over 50,000 dunlins (3.7% of the international population) in January.

The distribution of dunlins, although still widespread, is that of a population that has declined substantially since the 1970s, a decline attributed by Goss-Custard & Moser (1988) to losses of feeding grounds, seemingly through the encroachment of *Spartina anglica* and its subsequent effects on mudflat character. This decline is a man-influenced change, since *Spartina* arose through hybridisation with an introduced species and was subsequently deliberately planted in many estuaries for sea-defence and land-claim purposes (see Chapter 8.1 and Chapter 10).

Knot

Knots wintering in Britain are the *islandica* population that breeds in high-arctic Greenland and Canada. Knots make some of the longest non-stop flights of any waders, reaching Britain in autumn via staging areas in western Iceland. Some reach Britain in early winter after moulting on the Wadden Sea. In spring they return via early spring staging areas chiefly in north-west England and the Wadden Sea. Birds from each of these sites fly to late spring staging areas in either Iceland or northern Norway, from where they fly up to 3,500 km direct to their high-arctic breeding grounds (Alerstam *et al.* 1986; Davidson & Evans 1986b; Davidson *et al.* 1986c). Knots are amongst the most highly migratory of waders. Some breed on the northernmost areas of land in the world within 600 miles of the North Pole in northern Canada, and some from the Siberian breeding population reach as far south as the southern tip of Africa in winter (Dick *et al.* 1987). The Siberian-breeding population (the *canutus* subspecies) migrates chiefly through the Wadden Sea in spring and autumn and overwinters in West Africa (Dick *et al.* 1987). None is thought to overwinter in Britain, although some Siberian knots do occur on migration, especially in eastern Britain in autumn.

The migrations and distribution of *islandica* knots have been recently reviewed by Davidson & Wilson (1991). These birds overwinter chiefly in Britain, the Wadden Sea, the Dutch Delta, and as far south as western France. Like *alpina* dunlins, this knot population has declined by about 40% since the early 1970s, but this seems to be largely because of a series of poor breeding seasons and adult mortality in the 1970s (Davidson & Wilson 1991; Boyd 1991).

Knots are heavily dependent on British estuaries in winter and over 67% of the international population occurs here in January (Table 8.6.2). Since the population decline, Britain has supported a larger proportion of the wintering population than previously. Knots overwinter in large numbers on rather fewer British estuaries than dunlins (Figure 8.6.44), but are very mobile and some move between a network of these sites during the course of the winter (Dugan 1981).

Knots occur chiefly on large estuaries, where they aggregate into flocks of many thousands of birds to feed mostly on small bivalve molluscs such as *Macoma balthica*. They occur in midwinter chiefly in four areas: the Essex and north Kent coasts, The Wash and the Humber Estuary, north-west England from the Dee Estuary to the Solway Firth, and east Scotland (Figure 8.6.44). The Wash is the major wintering site for knots: there are over 71,000 birds there in midwinter. This is over 20% of the world population of *islandica* knots. Elsewhere the largest wintering populations are on the Humber Estuary (25,700 birds: 7.4% of the international population) and the Alt Estuary (24,800 birds: 7.1% of the international population). The population on the Alt Estuary may not accurately reflect the distribution

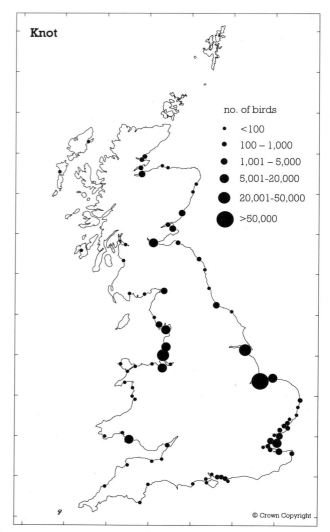

Figure 8.6.44 The January distribution of knots on review sites. Data are from BoEE/NWC counts for 1983-1987.

of feeding birds since, as described above, many knots now fly from feeding in the Dee Estuary to roost undisturbed on the Alt Estuary (Mitchell *et al.* 1988). In total this mobile Liverpool Bay population (from the Dee, Mersey, Alt and Ribble Estuaries) is an important part of the international distribution, amounting to over 48,700 birds (14.1% of the international population).

Bar-tailed godwit

Bar-tailed godwits have a broadly similar distribution to that of knots (Figure 8.6.45), with small numbers scattered around many estuaries throughout Britain. Bar-tailed godwits are characteristic of muddy sand habitats on estuaries, where they feed chiefly on lugworms *Arenicola* and ragworms *Nereis* and *Hediste*. These muddy sand habitats are widespread on fairly exposed review sites such as those in western Scotland (see also Chapter 8.3), and this is reflected in the distribution of the birds. Britain supports almost 50% of the midwinter population overwintering in Europe (Table 8.6.2). These birds are thought to come from breeding populations in northern Scandinavia and the western USSR (Smit & Piersma 1989).

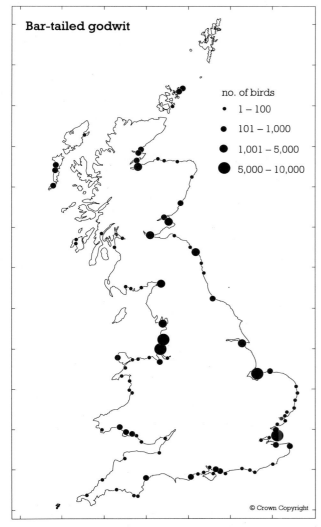

Bar-tailed godwit

no. of birds
- 1 – 100
- 101 – 1,000
- 1,001 – 5,000
- 5,000 – 10,000

© Crown Copyright

Figure 8.6.45 The January distribution of bar-tailed godwits on review sites. Data are from BoEE/NWC counts for 1983-1987.

Although they are widely distributed in Britain, just four review sites together support over 50% (almost 29,000 birds) of the British estuarine population. These are the Alt and Ribble Estuaries, The Wash and Maplin Sands.

Black-tailed godwit

In contrast to the bar-tailed godwit, the distribution of the closely related black-tailed godwit is much more restricted, and it occurs in largest numbers on different estuaries from its congener (Figure 8.6.46). Wintering black-tailed godwits come from the Icelandic-breeding population which winters in Britain, Ireland and south along the Atlantic seaboard to Morocco (Smit & Piersma 1989). Increasing numbers of black-tailed godwits have overwintered in Britain since the 1940s (Prater 1981) and most of the small (c. 5,000 birds) British wintering population occurs on estuaries, where the birds generally feed on much softer mud areas than bar-tailed godwits (Cramp & Simmons 1983). The stronghold of wintering black-tailed godwits is the Stour Estuary in Suffolk/Essex, where the January population exceeds 700 birds and is of

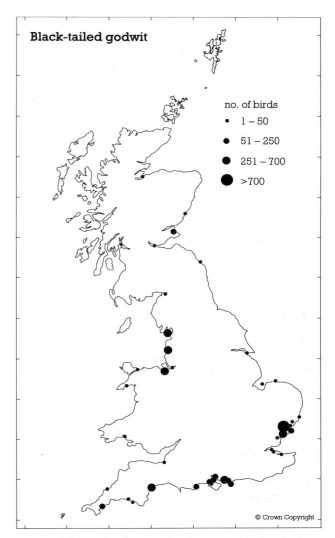

Black-tailed godwit

no. of birds
- 1 – 50
- 51 – 250
- 251 – 700
- >700

© Crown Copyright

Figure 8.6.45 The January distribution of black-tailed godwits on review sites. Data are from BoEE/NWC counts for 1983-1987.

international significance. The Suffolk and Essex estuaries are a major wintering area. Elsewhere black-tailed godwits winter around the Hampshire and Sussex estuaries, on the Exe Estuary, on the large estuaries of north-west England, and on the Eden Estuary in eastern Scotland. Elsewhere they are very scarce or absent (Figure 8.6.46).

Overall implications of waterfowl dispersion patterns

The dispersion pattern of all regularly occurring waders and wildfowl is further analysed in Figure 8.6.47. Here the British estuarine wintering population for each species is divided into two components: the proportion on major wintering sites (here defined as sites in which the January population exceeds 1% of the British estuarine wintering population), and the proportion on other sites each with less than 1% of this wintering population.

Several important distributional features emerge from this analysis. For wildfowl the number of sites each with more than 1% of the January estuarine

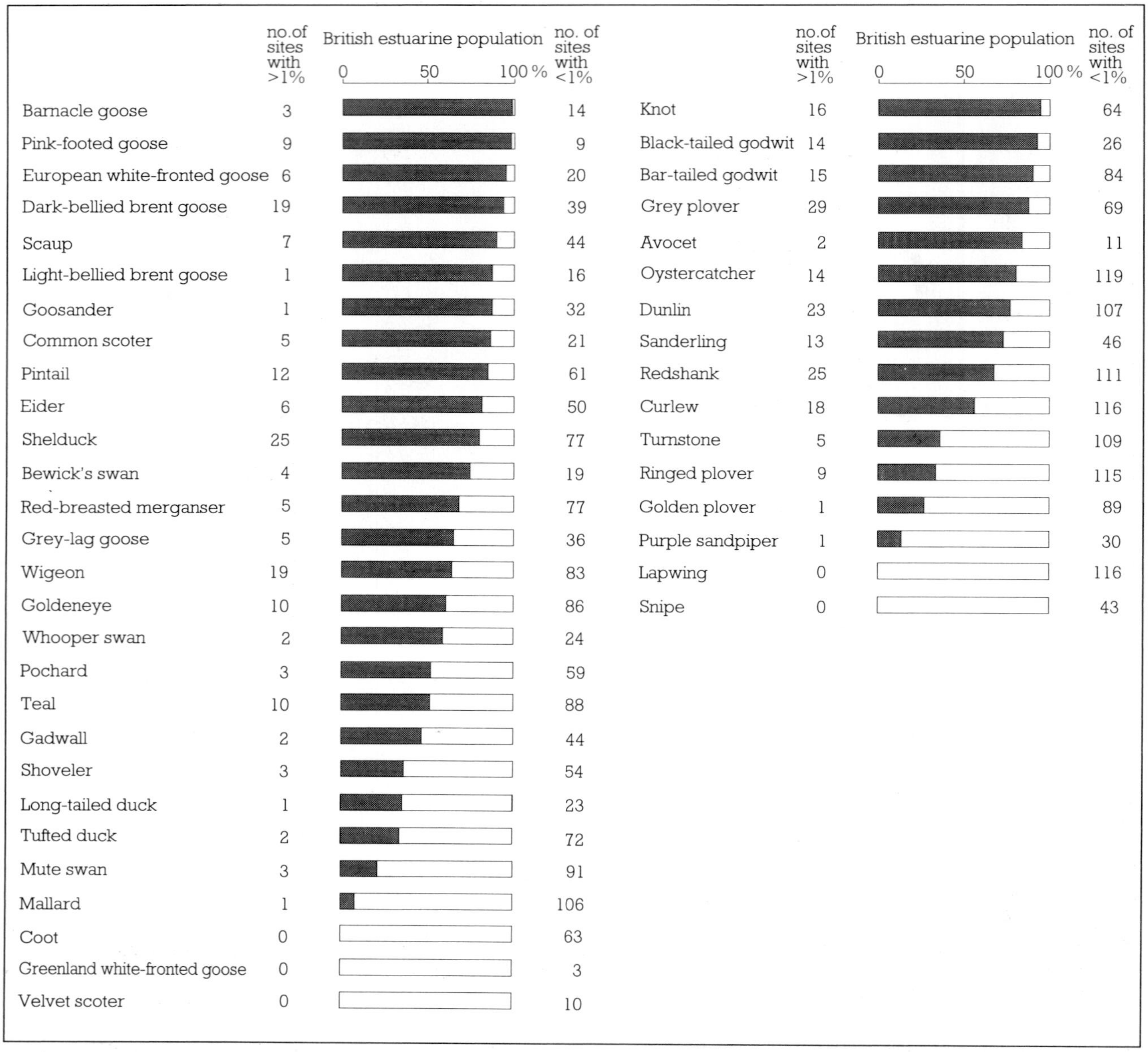

	no. of sites with >1%	British estuarine population 0 50 100%	no. of sites with <1%		no. of sites with >1%	British estuarine population 0 50 100%	no. of sites with <1%
Barnacle goose	3		14	Knot	16		64
Pink-footed goose	9		9	Black-tailed godwit	14		26
European white-fronted goose	6		20	Bar-tailed godwit	15		84
Dark-bellied brent goose	19		39	Grey plover	29		69
Scaup	7		44	Avocet	2		11
Light-bellied brent goose	1		16	Oystercatcher	14		119
Goosander	1		32	Dunlin	23		107
Common scoter	5		21	Sanderling	13		46
Pintail	12		61	Redshank	25		111
Eider	6		50	Curlew	18		116
Shelduck	25		77	Turnstone	5		109
Bewick's swan	4		19	Ringed plover	9		115
Red-breasted merganser	5		77	Golden plover	1		89
Grey-lag goose	5		36	Purple sandpiper	1		30
Wigeon	19		83	Lapwing	0		116
Goldeneye	10		86	Snipe	0		43
Whooper swan	2		24				
Pochard	3		59				
Teal	10		88				
Gadwall	2		44				
Shoveler	3		54				
Long-tailed duck	1		23				
Tufted duck	2		72				
Mute swan	3		91				
Mallard	1		106				
Coot	0		63				
Greenland white-fronted goose	0		3				
Velvet scoter	0		10				

Figure 8.6.47 The proportions of British estuarine populations of waders and wildfowl that occur in January on review sites each holding >1% of the British wintering population (shaded portion) and <1% (unshaded portion)

population is generally small, and only dark-bellied brent goose, shelduck and wigeon occur on more than 15 review sites in such numbers. Nevertheless for many species of wildfowl these sites support a very large part of the British estuarine wintering population: over 80% of the January numbers of 11 species or populations occur on just a few major sites each. Most other wildfowl occur on at least a few sites in populations exceeding 1% of the British estuarine population but have a substantial proportion distributed around a large number of other review sites. At the extreme, a few species have few or no populations exceeding 1% of the January British estuarine population. Most of these are common and widespread wildfowl such as mallard, tufted duck, mute swan *Cygnus olor* and coot *Fulica atra*; others such as velvet scoter *Melanitta fusca* and Greenland white-fronted goose predominantly use non-estuarine wintering habitats.

The patterns for waders are similar to those of wildfowl in that different species vary, from some, notably knot and the two godwit species, with almost their entire estuarine wintering populations on major sites each supporting more than 1% of the population, to widespread, often non-estuarine, species such as golden plover, lapwing and snipe with little or none of their populations on such major sites. The number of major (i.e. >1% of the population) sites used by many waders is much higher than for wildfowl: six of the 16 commonly occurring wader species each occur on more than 15 major sites, compared with only three of 28 wildfowl species. It is notable that even those widespread waders whose wintering populations are mostly non-estuarine (turnstone, ringed plover, purple sandpiper and sanderling) have more than 1% of their wintering population on some review sites. This is most marked in sanderlings with 13 major sites holding 71.5% of the wintering population (Figure 8.6.47).

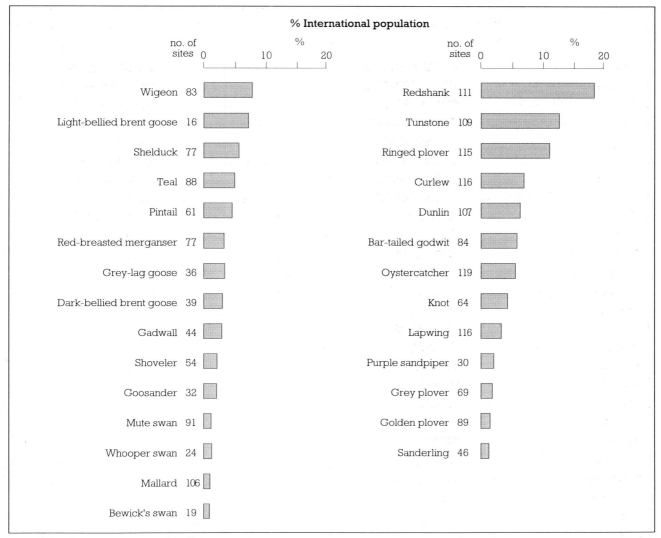

Figure 8.6.48 The percentages of international populations of waders and wildfowl in January on review sites each holding <1% of the British population of that species or biogeographic population. Only species where such sites support more than 1% of the international population are shown.

An important consequence of the widespread estuarine distribution of many wintering waders and wildfowl is illustrated in Figure 8.6.48, which shows that in excess of 1% of the international wintering population of 15 species of wildfowl and 13 species of waders are dispersed around the many estuaries that each hold only a small part of the wintering population. For many species, especially waders, this internationally important component of the wintering population is distributed on over 100 of the 155 review sites. This emphasises the value of the network of sites formed by Britain's estuaries, and also stresses the cumulative importance of the individually small estuaries.

For some species of waterfowl the percentage of the international wintering population on estuaries with only small numbers each is surprisingly large. A total of 17.9% of the East Atlantic Flyway population of redshanks is dispersed around 111 British review sites each supporting less than 600 birds. 12.3% of the international turnstone population is on 109 sites each with less than 127 birds, and 11.0% of ringed plovers are on 115 sites each holding fewer than 80 birds. Even in knots,

which are well known for their concentration into large flocks on just a few wintering sites (Cramp & Simmons 1983), 4.4% of the flyway population uses 64 review sites, each with less than 2,300 birds. More than 5% of the international population of four other waders (curlew, dunlin, bar-tailed godwit and oystercatcher) occurs on between 84 and 119 review sites, each with a small population of that species.

Generally smaller proportions of international wildfowl populations are dispersed around review sites in small numbers. Most importantly, more than 5% of the international populations of three estuarine specialist wildfowl (wigeon, light-bellied brent goose and shelduck) depend on review sites with small populations, the largest being 7.8% of the north-west European wigeon population distributed around 83 review sites, each with less than 1,080 birds.

The spectacularly large flocks of wintering waders and wildfowl on major British estuaries, such as the Dee Estuary, the Solway Firth, the Humber Estuary, The Wash and Morecambe Bay, are well-known to be of very great national and international importance in wildlife conservation. It is clear from this analysis that the network of estuaries throughout Britain, including the small estuaries each with relatively small waterfowl populations, are also an important and vital component of the world's estuarine wildlife resource. Indeed some of the small estuaries, with their high densities of birds, may be the preferred wintering grounds for many species (see e.g. Moser 1988) and may thus be crucial to the long-term survival of these populations.

8.6.3 Other estuarine wintering birds

Several other groups of wintering birds occur on or close to British estuaries during their non-breeding seasons. These include seabirds, other waterbirds, raptors and passerines.

Seabirds

Many seabirds such as auks winter in coastal and inshore waters around Britain, but generally occur in areas outside the outer limits of the review sites. Distributions in the North Sea are reviewed by Tasker *et al.* (1987) and Tasker & Pienkowski (1987).

Some species, particularly seaducks such as common and velvet scoters and long-tailed ducks, occur both within review sites (with their distributions described above) and in outer parts of large firths such as the Moray Firth. These populations are of considerable national significance, with about 50% of the British population (3% of the north-west European population) of common scoters in the Dornoch/Firth Moray Firth area in midwinter. The largest long-tailed duck flock in the North Sea also occurs in this area, in and around six review sites (Loch Fleet, Dornoch, Cromarty and Moray Firths, Lossie Estuary and Spey Estuary), and has a total of about 20,000 wintering sea-ducks (Mudge & Allen 1980).

Other inshore species that are under-represented in BoEE/NWC counts, but which occur in the outer parts of review sites, are divers, chiefly red-throated divers *Gavia stellata* and a few black-throated divers *Gavia arctica* and great northern divers *Gavia immer*. Red-throated divers are widespread along the North Sea coast of Britain in winter and occur also around estuaries in North Wales and parts of north-west England and Scotland (Lack 1986; Moser *et al.* 1986). The estimated early winter population is about 20,000 birds, of which about three-quarters are on the North Sea coast. Major concentrations are in the outer parts of the Moray Firth complex, with up to 1,500 birds at times (Barrett & Barrett 1985) and up to 1,000 divers in the outer parts of the 'Greater Thames Estuary' (Tasker & Pienkowski 1987).

Grebes and other waterbirds

Some other waterbirds, such as grebes, regularly occur in estuaries in small numbers in winter. Like divers they are frequent in the outer parts of estuaries and so may be under-represented in counts. The commonest are the little grebe *Tachybaptus ruficollis* and great-crested grebe *Podiceps cristatus*, although both overwinter chiefly on inland freshwater sites. Prater (1981) reports about 1,500-2,000 little grebes on estuaries (about 10% of the British population). Great-crested grebes now breed widely on fresh water in Britain and Europe. In winter some move to estuaries and sheltered coasts, particularly in severe weather, and the 1,800 birds on estuaries reported by Prater (1981) is probably an underestimate. There are concentrations of wintering great-crested grebes on estuaries in north Wales and north-west England, the Firth of Forth, The Wash and the sheltered estuaries of Essex and around The Solent (Prater 1981).

Three other species of grebes occur in smaller numbers. About 200 red-necked grebes *Podiceps grisegena* overwinter in Britain, chiefly in estuarine and other coastal waters, with more moving from continental Europe in severe weather. The largest concentration is in the Firth of Forth, with up to 40 birds, and there are much smaller numbers scattered around the English coast at Lindisfarne, The Wash and North Norfolk Coast, Southampton Water and elsewhere (Prater 1981; Chandler 1986a). About 400 Slavonian grebes *Podiceps auritus* overwinter on sheltered coasts scattered around Britain. Wintering birds may come partly from the small British breeding population as well as from major breeding areas such as Iceland and Scandinavia. Many of the wintering population are on estuaries, with more than 10 wintering regularly on each of several widely scattered sites including the Dornoch Firth, Firth of Forth, Blackwater Estuary, Poole Harbour and Exe Estuary. Small numbers are also found in the estuaries of The Solent (Prater 1981; Chandler 1986b). There are just over 100 black-necked grebes *Podiceps nigricollis* overwintering in Britain, again mostly estuarine but with a more southerly and westerly distribution than the other two scarce grebes. The main estuary appears to be Langstone Harbour, with a few elsewhere in The Solent, Poole Harbour, The Fleet, the Teign Estuary, the Loughor Estuary and around Anglesey.

In winter cormorants *Phalacrocorax carbo* occur chiefly on coastal waters including estuaries around much of the coast of Britain. Dunnet (1986) estimates a British wintering population of 20,000-25,000 birds, of which there are at least 9,000 (36-45%) wintering on estuaries (Prater 1981).

Gulls

Most gulls are widespread throughout Britain in winter in both inland and coastal habitats (Prater 1981; Lack 1986). In addition to these widely distributed species small numbers of the arctic and subarctic-breeding Iceland gull *Larus glaucoides* and glaucous gull *Larus hyperboreus* occur on Britain's estuaries and coasts, particularly in northern and eastern Britain (Hume 1986a, 1986b). Small but apparently increasing numbers of the more pelagic little gull *Larus minutus* also occur in winter around coasts in Britain, notably around the estuaries of Liverpool Bay (Prater 1981), although they are less frequent on estuaries in winter than in autumn when juveniles are dispersing widely and occur on coastal lagoons and pools (Hutchinson 1986).

There has been no recent comprehensive assessment of the numbers and distribution of gulls on estuaries, but Prater (1981) found that the commonest estuarine gull in winter was the black-headed gull *Larus ridibundus*, which feeds on the intertidal flats alongside waders during the day (e.g. Curtis & Thompson 1985), as well as roosting on estuaries at night. Many black-headed gulls also feed on coastal grazing marshes and other grasslands in winter. Prater (1981) reported four estuaries with an average peak of over 20,000 black-headed gulls: the Severn Estuary, The Wash, the Clyde Estuary and the Solway Firth. Another five estuaries supported in excess of 10,000 birds. Many birds move from inland to estuaries during severe cold weather. Other widespread gull species (common gull *Larus canus*, herring gull *Larus argentatus*, lesser black-backed gull *Larus fuscus* and greater black-backed gull *Larus marinus*) chiefly use estuaries during winter as safe night-time roosts (Prater 1981). Several estuaries throughout Britain provide roosting areas for over 100,000 gulls in winter. These include the Thames Estuary, The Wash, the Mersey Estuary, Morecambe Bay and the Solway Firth.

Raptors

Two other groups of birds – raptors and some passerines – are characteristic of estuaries in winter. Several species of raptors hunt widely over saltmarshes and coastal grazing marshes. Between 200 and 300 hen harriers *Circus cyaneus* overwinter in Britain from breeding populations in Britain and continental Europe (Clarke 1986). Most are coastal and estuarine and gather in communal roosts in reed beds or marshes adjacent to estuaries such as The Wash and North Norfolk Coast, from which they radiate out to hunt during daylight. Although the wintering population is scattered widely around Britain there is an increasing population along the east coast of England from the Humber south to Kent (Clarke 1986). Short-eared owls *Asio flammeus* are widespread in England and southern Scotland in winter (Glue 1986) and some hunt over coastal saltmarshes and grazing marshes.

Two falcons, the merlin *Falco columbarius* and the peregrine *Falco peregrinus*, are particularly characteristic members of the winter bird assemblage on estuaries, as are sparrowhawks *Accipiter nisus* on some estuaries. Both overwinter widely throughout Britain (Bibby 1986; Ratcliffe 1986), in the case of the peregrine largely in western and northern Britain, but many move from

upland breeding areas to prey on the large concentrations of wintering waterfowl on estuaries throughout Britain. The recovery of raptor populations in Britain since the major declines due the effects of pesticides in the 1960s means that numbers hunting on estuaries may have increased recently, although only small numbers of raptors may still be involved. For example at Teesmouth the estuary is hunted regularly by one merlin, with occasional visits from a peregrine and a sparrowhawk (Townshend 1984).

As top predators in estuarine systems, raptors depend on a variety of other bird species for food during winter. Merlins and sparrowhawks on estuaries feed on both small passerines and small waders such as dunlin, ringed plover and redshank; peregrines take larger waders and ducks such as teal and wigeon as well as other birds such as wood pigeons *Columba palumbus* (Cramp & Simmons 1983). Although raptor numbers may be small, Townshend (1984) suggested that they could take between 10% and 20% of the midwinter dunlin population on the Tees Estuary. Similarly, on Tyninghame Bay Whitfield (1985) estimated that raptors, mostly sparrowhawks but also peregrines and merlins, ate 15% of redshanks, 19% of ringed plovers and 4% of dunlins wintering there. Even larger proportions of a wintering population of redshanks were eaten by raptors, mostly sparrowhawks, on a nearby stretch of narrow rocky and sandy shore.

Passerines

Large flocks of some passerines, chiefly finches and buntings, congregate on estuaries in winter to feed on the abundant seed stock on upper saltmarshes, and along strand-lines. These flocks include some widespread species such as linnet *Carduelis cannabina*, greenfinch *Carduelis chloris* and chaffinch *Fringilla coelebs* and others that are largely restricted to coasts and estuaries. Lapland buntings *Calcarius lapponicus* and shorelarks *Eremophila alpestris* are largely restricted to the coasts of eastern Britain in winter. Snow buntings *Plectrophenax nivalis* also have a wintering bias to eastern coasts but some also overwinter in the uplands of Scotland and northern England (Lambert 1986a). Snow buntings feed on both saltmarshes and sandy shores and so are not restricted on the coast to estuaries, although large flocks of several hundred birds are characteristic of the outer parts of many estuaries in eastern Britain. Shorelarks come from a breeding population in northern Scandinavia and the USSR, and the small wintering population (*c.* 300 birds) is largely restricted to a few estuaries in eastern Britain including the Firth of Forth, Tyninghame Bay, Lindisfarne, the Tees Estuary, the Humber Estuary, The Wash, the North Norfolk Coast and several estuaries in Essex and Kent (Lambert 1986b). On estuaries they depend on areas of developing saltmarsh, where they feed chiefly on glasswort *Salicornia* seed during low tide, and on adjacent dune systems, where they feed at high tide (Lambert 1986b).

Lapland buntings are more widespread on the east coast from the Firth of Forth south to north Kent (Lambert 1986c), where they feed, often in association with skylarks *Alauda arvensis*, on coastal arable and pasture fields and on saltmarshes. Lambert (1986c) estimated the wintering population at 200-500 birds, but Davies (1987) has recently found a wintering population of over 500 Lapland buntings on saltmarshes of The Wash, substantially increasing the total wintering population and making The Wash the most important estuary for Lapland buntings in Britain. Davies (1987) suggests that these birds come from the Norwegian-breeding population. Wintering populations of skylarks can be very large on estuaries and Davies (1987) estimated 26,000-32,000 birds on the saltmarshes of The Wash, although these still form a small proportion of the estimated 25 million skylarks wintering in Britain (Green 1986).

Twites *Carduelis flavirostris* are also mainly coastal and estuarine in winter, although Lambert (1986d) shows a scattered distribution elsewhere in Scotland and northern England. Their main wintering strongholds are, however, the extensive saltmarshes of The Wash and the Essex estuaries. Davies (1987) estimated that up to 17,000 twites overwinter on The Wash and showed from ringing recoveries that these come from the isolated breeding population of the southern Pennines. In some winters the Wash birds probably comprise almost all this breeding population (Davies 1988). Numbers vary between years, however, and the birds may move elsewhere, perhaps across the southern North Sea, in years when the seed production by saltmarsh plants is low.

Passerines and raptors further enhance the varied and abundant assemblages of wintering waders, wildfowl and other waterbirds which contribute very substantially to the great national and international significance of Britain's estuaries for wildlife. Indeed, raptors as well as waterfowl are two (the other being seabirds – see Section 8.6.4) of the three groups of birds for which Britain is most internationally important.

8.6.4 Breeding Birds

Introduction

Breeding birds are an important and vulnerable feature of the conservation interest of estuaries. The mosaic of habitats surrounding estuaries provides suitable nesting sites for important numbers of various bird species, notably waders and seabirds. For many waders, especially, estuaries support nationally and internationally important breeding populations. The abundant macrobenthic fauna in the intertidal mudflats nearby provide rich feeding grounds for both adults and young of waders and wildfowl, for example shelduck. The major breeding habitats associated with British estuaries are coastal wet grasslands, beaches and shingle systems, sand-dunes and saltmarshes.

Important assemblages of breeding birds occur on saltmarshes and the shingle, machair and lowland grasslands associated with estuaries. Such assemblages, with their complex behavioural and ecological links, are of particular scientific and conservation importance, in addition to that of the individual species involved (Stroud *et al.* 1990). Estuarine breeding assemblages are characteristically dominated by their breeding wader populations. Typical assemblages on lowland wet grasslands include redshank, lapwing, snipe *Gallinago gallinago* and curlew, with more rarely ruff and black-tailed godwit. On coastal grasslands the association often includes oystercatcher and ringed plover and, on the machair of the Outer Hebrides, ringed plover and dunlin. The rich breeding wader assemblages of the Outer Hebrides are described in detail by Fuller *et al.* (1986). A typical saltmarsh assemblage includes redshank, lapwing, oystercatcher and ringed plover.

Assemblages of estuarine breeding waders also often include other birds; for example, on wet grasslands, breeding waders are often associated with passerines including yellow wagtail *Motacilla flava*, skylark, meadow pipit *Anthus pratensis* and reed bunting *Emberiza schoeniclus*, and wildfowl such as mallard, pochard, and sometimes garganey *Anas querquedula* and shoveler *Anas clypeata* (e.g. Mitchell 1983; Williams *et al.* 1983; Everett 1987). Similarly Fuller (1982) showed that among the particularly abundant saltmarsh breeding species were (in addition to waders) skylark, reed bunting meadow pipit and mallard, and also sometimes yellow wagtail and colonial gulls and terns. Estuarine shingle systems are characterised by breeding ringed plover, oystercatcher and little tern *Sterna albifrons*, as well as colonies of gulls and terns in some places.

Although the breeding assemblages on estuaries, particularly on saltmarshes and shingle, are often species-poor compared with those of such habitats as woodland and farmland (Green 1987), breeding populations can be very large, especially when they involve colonial-breeding seabirds.

The precise habitat requirements vary between species. Most species depend, however, on the continuity of a generally similar breeding habitat and are affected similarly by damaging changes such as the drainage of wet grasslands and excessive human recreational disturbance of breeding bird assemblages on beaches. The distribution, abundance and conservation needs of the characteristic and important breeding birds of British estuaries are described below.

Breeding waders

Background and data sources

The major wader breeding habitats associated with British estuaries are shingle systems and beaches, sand-dunes and saltmarshes. In addition, avocets are particularly associated with brackish lagoons. The coastal grazing marshes and other wet grasslands close to the upper reaches of tidal estuaries also support substantial breeding wader populations. The assemblages of breeding waders on and adjacent to estuaries are a major component of the national and international conservation importance of estuaries. The Wader Study Group's compilation of information on population sizes of breeding waders in Europe (Piersma 1986), published with the support of the NCC and The Netherlands national conservation authorities, and other national compilations encouraged by the Wader Study Group (Dominguez *et al.* 1987; Hromadkova 1987; Bartovsky *et al.* 1987; Tinarelli & Bacetti 1989; Nankinov 1989), have emphasised the major international importance of Britain for temperate breeding wader populations.

Several extensive surveys of breeding waders in the last 10 years have shown that important breeding areas for breeding waders are distributed throughout Britain. The widespread and continuing loss of wet grasslands through land drainage, agricultural intensification and conversion to arable cultivation has, however, fragmented and much reduced the area of suitable breeding habitat for waders. An extensive survey in 1982 assessed the breeding populations of five wader species (lapwing, snipe, curlew, redshank and oystercatcher) on almost 1,300 lowland wet grassland sites in England and Wales (Smith 1983), and a related survey covered Scottish agricultural land in 1982 and 1983 (Galbraith *et al.* 1984). The breeding wader populations of saltmarshes have received less comprehensive survey coverage. The most widespread survey was made for the NCC in 1985 (Allport *et al.* 1986). This covered 77 sample plots on saltmarshes throughout mainland Britain and on Mull, including plots on 34 review sites. A national census of ringed plovers *Charadrius hiaticula* was carried out by the British Trust for Ornithology in 1973/74 (Prater 1976b) and repeated in 1984 (Prater 1989).

Other surveys have covered one or more wader breeding habitats on a smaller geographical scale. Among the more comprehensive was the extensive survey of the very important breeding populations of waders on the machair and associated land of the Outer Hebrides, undertaken jointly by the Wader Study Group and the NCC (Fuller *et al.* 1986). Review sites in Orkney were covered as part of a survey of wetland areas (Campbell *et al.* 1988). Other regional surveys covering counties or estuaries include Greenhalgh (1969, 1971, 1975), Williams *et al.* (1983), Murfitt & Weaver (1983), Mitchell (1983) and Holzer *et al.* (1989). Other such surveys have revealed major concentrations of breeding waders on machair and associated habitats in other places such as Coll and Tiree, where they are not directly associated with estuaries (Stroud 1990).

The distribution and size of the various breeding populations in Britain are described below using data extracted from these surveys. Wherever possible data are from surveys conducted in the 1980s so as to minimise any differences due to historical changes in the size of the breeding populations. For saltmarshes, comparable data on densities of breeding pairs are available for sample areas on 36 review sites from Allport *et al.* (1986), Campbell *et al.* (1988) and Roberts (1988). Maximum densities for each review site have been used in comparisons. Similar maximum breeding densities for wet grasslands have been derived from the data collected during Smith's (1983) survey and from the Outer Hebrides and Orkney surveys (Fuller *et al.* 1986; Campbell *et al.* 1988). The latter two surveys covered a wider range of habitats than just wet grassland: the Hebrides surveys covered both wet and dry machair grassland and associated habitats including dunes (Fuller *et al.* 1986). Altogether there are data on grassland-breeding waders for 55 review sites. Review sites for which there are data on grassland and/or saltmarsh-breeding waders are shown in Figure 8.6.49. As the grassland surveys covered most or all suitable habitat in each area, population sizes have also been calculated for each review site. For ringed plovers only population sizes are available, except for sites on the Outer Hebrides

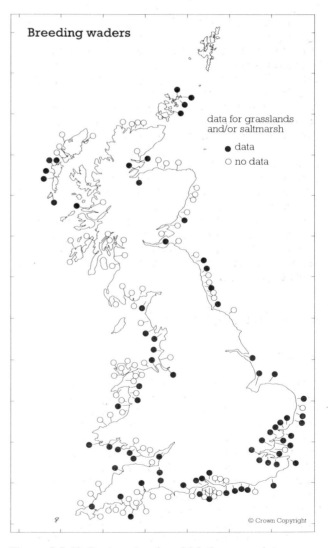

Figure 8.6.49 Review sites for which there are data on breeding waders on wet grasslands and/or saltmarshes

Table 8.6.4 The frequency of occurrence of breeding waders on review sites in Britain

	Saltmarshes No.	%	Wet grasslands No.	%
Estuaries with data	36		55	
Redshank	31	86.1	44	80.0
Oystercatcher	28	77.8	31	56.4
Lapwing	17	47.2	46	83.4
Curlew	7	19.4	10	18.5
Snipe	1	2.8	32	58.2
Dunlin	5	13.9	5	9.1
All species	**31**	**86.1**	**47**	**85.6**

and Orkney. Sources for scarce or rare species of breeding waders are described separately.

Total British population estimates were made by Reed (1985) and set in their European context by Piersma (1986). These, modified and updated where appropriate by Stroud *et al.* (1990), have been used to assess the national and international importance of British estuaries for breeding waders.

The frequency of occurrence of common breeding waders on British estuaries is summarised in Table 8.6.4, and population estimates for waders breeding on wet grasslands adjacent to estuaries are given in Table 8.6.5.

Redshank

Redshanks are one of the most characteristic and widespread of waders breeding on British estuaries. They breed predominantly on saltmarshes and wet grasslands, occurring on saltmarshes on 86.1% of review sites studied and on grasslands on 80.0% of review sites (Table 8.6.4). Redshanks were the most widespread breeding wader found by Allport *et al.* (1986) and they occur on estuarine saltmarshes throughout Britain, except that they are largely absent from south-west England (Figure 8.6.50). Breeding densities are highest in eastern Britain and on marshes where there is medium grazing pressure (Allport *et al.* 1986). Where there is little or no grazing, vegetation grows too high to provide suitable habitat, and at high grazing pressure many nests are destroyed by trampling and the absence of cover leads to high predation levels. Redshanks nest chiefly on upper saltmarshes where the risk of tidal inundation is low and usually where there is considerable diversity of saltmarsh vegetation (Allport *et al.* 1986; Cadbury *et al.* 1987).

Redshanks breed at very high densities on some saltmarshes and on many are the most abundant breeding wader. Allport *et al.* (1986) found highest densities on part of the west side of the Wash (115 pairs km^{-2}), with densities exceeding 100 pairs km^{-2} on parts of the Colne (Essex), Beaulieu (Hampshire), and Morecambe Bay. Figure 8.6.50 shows that major areas for saltmarsh-breeding redshanks are in Lancashire, The Wash and North Norfolk, Suffolk and Essex, and Hampshire. Saltmarsh densities are generally lower in Wales

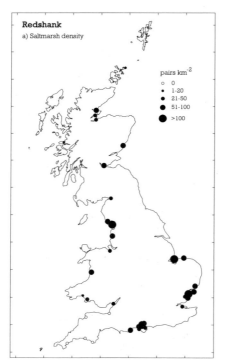
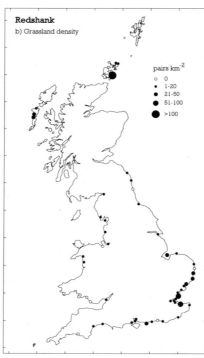
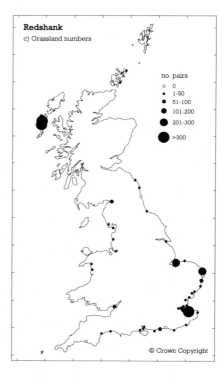

Figure 8.6.50 The distribution of redshanks breeding on review sites. a) Maximum densities (pairs km^{-2}) on estuarine saltmarshes; b) maximum densities (pairs km^{-2}) on wet grasslands adjacent to estuaries; and c) total numbers of pairs on wet grasslands.

242

Table 8.6.5 Breeding populations of waders on grasslands adjacent to estuaries in Britain. Grasslands are wet grasslands and coastal grazing marshes in England and Wales, and machair and associated habitats in Orkney and the Outer Hebrides.

Species	Estuarine popn. (pairs)	% Outer Hebrides	% Ouse & Nene Washes	% Norfolk Broads
Redshank	2,194	27.5	13.3	12.6
Oystercatcher	1,143	64.6	2.0	10.3
Lapwing	4,170	23.5	12.6	16.0
Curlew	57	0	0	0
Snipe[a]	1,037	13.1	71.1	5.0
Total waders	9,239	36.2	13.5	12.2

Sources: NCC/BTO/RSPB Survey of Breeding Waders in Wet Grasslands, WSG/NCC surveys of breeding waders in the Outer Hebrides, and Campbell *et al.*(1988)

[a] Surveyed as number of displaying males

and Scotland. Cadbury *et al.* (1987) made a preliminary estimate of 17,500 pairs of saltmarsh-breeding redshanks based on the area of saltmarshes in Britain.

Redshanks are widespread breeders in grasslands adjacent to estuaries, although densities in England and Wales are consistently lower than those on saltmarshes on the same estuaries (Figure 8.6.51). Redshanks are either absent or breed only in densities of less than 50 pairs km^{-2} on estuarine grasslands in western and northern England and in Wales, but densities are consistently higher in East Anglia and Kent (Figure 8.6.50). Highest densities occur on the Ouse and Nene Washes adjacent to the upper tidal reaches of The Wash, the marshes of the Norfolk Broads and the Swale in Kent (53.7 pairs km^{-2}). Densities are high also on the machair grasslands of the Outer Hebrides, and also in parts of Orkney adjacent to estuaries, although there the area of wet grassland is small and hence total populations are low (Figure 8.6.50).

Although densities are generally low on estuarine grasslands, the large areas of grasslands in the Outer Hebrides, Norfolk Broads, Ouse and Nene Washes and the Swale Estuary mean that these areas support substantial numbers of breeding redshanks. Together they have 53.4% of the total of 2,194 pairs of redshanks breeding on estuarine wet grasslands on review sites for which there are data (Table 8.6.5). Away from these areas adjacent to estuaries the only other lowland wet grasslands in England and Wales with comparable numbers are the Derwent Ings in Yorkshire and the Somerset Levels, with a joint total of 8.7% of the England and Wales population. Wet grasslands adjacent to estuaries are very important for breeding redshanks, supporting 68.8% of the breeding pairs (1,525 pairs) found on all wet grassland in England and Wales. Similarly areas of machair adjacent to estuaries support 23.2% (604 pairs) of redshanks breeding in the Uists.

Since data are not available for some review sites,

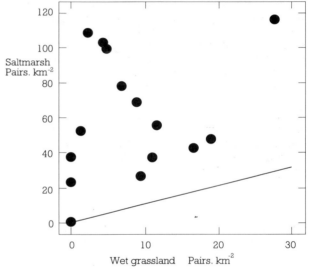

Figure 8.6.51 The densities of breeding redshanks on estuarine saltmarshes are consistently much higher than the densities breeding on wet grasslands on the same estuaries. The solid line shows equal densities in the two habitats.

notably mainland estuaries in Scotland, the total British estuarine breeding population is difficult to assess but must be in excess of 19,700 pairs. Britain, Norway and The Netherlands are the strongholds of breeding redshanks in Europe, together supporting over 70% of the breeding population of the nominate *totanus* subspecies (Piersma 1986). 12% of *totanus* redshanks breed in Britain (Stroud *et al.* 1990). Hence a minimum of 60.6% of the British-breeding population and 7.3% of the north-west and central European population breeds on or adjacent to British estuaries. Smith's (1983) survey showed redshanks in England and Wales to have been largely restricted to a few, mostly coastal, sites and to have declined as an inland-breeding species in the last few decades. Subsequent monitoring has found further declines in the redshank populations of wet grasslands (Smith 1988), so in future saltmarshes and associated estuarine grasslands are likely to become even more important for breeding redshanks.

Oystercatcher

Oystercatchers are the second most common breeding wader in Britain with a total population of 38,000 pairs (17% of the north-west and central European population) (Stroud *et al.* 1990). Most of the rest of the European population breeds in Norway and The Netherlands (Piersma 1986). Although many oystercatchers are coastal breeders they also breed in increasing numbers inland in Scotland and in northern England, and even on rooftops in Aberdeen. Coastal pairs breed in a variety of habitats, chiefly sand and shingle beaches, saltmarshes and grasslands. There are no recent comprehensive data on the distribution and population sizes on sand and shingle, but oystercatchers nest widely on saltmarshes on estuaries throughout Britain, occurring on 77.8% of review sites for which there are data. Breeding on coastal and adjacent wet grasslands is less frequent, but even so oystercatchers nested on grasslands on over half the review sites for which there are data (Table 8.6.4). The distribution and densities of breeding pairs (Figure 8.6.52) shows that densities on grassland are generally low (<20 pairs km^{-2}) in England and Wales and that oystercatchers are largely absent from grasslands in western England and Wales. Grassland breeding in England is most frequent in East Anglia (on 76% of review sites between Norfolk and Kent). Although over 60% of grassland-breeding oystercatchers in England and Wales are adjacent to estuaries, the total number of breeding pairs (342) is small.

In contrast to the low breeding densities on English and Welsh grasslands, densities in Scotland are much higher (Figure 8.6.52), reaching up to 83 pairs km^{-2} on the small wetlands adjacent to Orkney review sites, and 103 pairs km^{-2} on the machair grasslands of the Uists. The Uists are an important breeding area for oystercatchers, with 740 pairs (1.9% of the British breeding population) occurring adjacent to review sites alone. Elsewhere the major grassland sites in terms of size of total breeding population are the Solway and the wet grasslands of the Norfolk Broads (Figure 8.6.52).

Oystercatchers breed widely on saltmarshes around Britain, but as on grasslands they are scarce or absent from south-west England and Wales (Figure 8.6.52). Elsewhere they were found breeding on all 21 review sites surveyed except for Kentra Bay in north-west Scotland. Highest densities were on the Solway (72 pairs km^{-2}), with other dense populations on the Duddon Estuary and Morecambe Bay in north-west England, the firths of north-east Scotland, around the Solent and on the North Norfolk Coast. Densities on saltmarsh were consistently higher than on adjacent grasslands on the same estuaries.

Although coastal-breeding oystercatchers are often considered to be largely associated with shingle beaches, Figure 8.6.52 shows them to be widespread breeders on other habitats in Britain. Those nesting on beaches are, like ringed plovers, vulnerable to human disturbance where there is public access. This may account for the scarcity in some areas of oystercatchers breeding on shingle rather than saltmarshes and grasslands. For example the Ore/Alde/Butley (Suffolk) has the extensive shingle systems of Orfordness, but

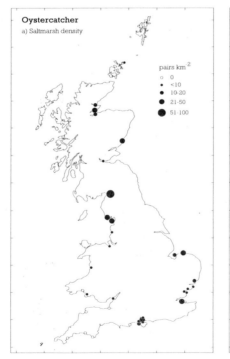
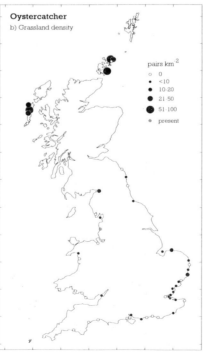
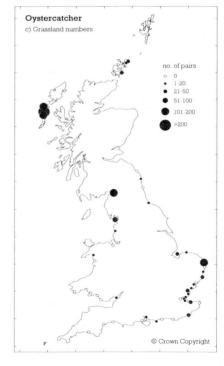

Figure 8.6.52 The distribution of oystercatchers breeding on review sites. a) Maximum densities (pairs km^{-2}) on estuarine saltmarshes; b) maximum densities (pairs km^{-2}) on wet grasslands adjacent to estuaries; and c) total numbers of pairs on wet grasslands.

although 47% of oystercatchers breeding on Suffolk estuaries were on this estuary, only 18% nested on shingle compared to 47% on saltmarsh and 34% on grassland (Holzer *et al.* 1989).

Lapwing

Lapwings are the most abundant breeding wader in Europe and breed in large numbers over much of northern Europe (Piersma 1986). Britain supports the largest breeding population in Europe: an estimated 215,000 pairs, 25% of the north-west and central European population (Stroud *et al.* 1990). Lapwings nest widely throughout Britain and in particularly high densities on low-intensity farmland and traditionally-managed grasslands (e.g. Galbraith *et al.* 1984; Baines 1989). Smith (1983) found a pronounced coastal bias in the distribution of wet grassland-breeding lapwings in England and Wales, and lapwings bred on grasslands on a higher percentage (83.4%) of review sites than any other species (Table 8.6.5). As for other breeding waders, lapwings are scarce or absent from grasslands on most estuaries in south-west England and Wales (Figure 8.6.53). On wet grasslands adjacent to estuaries densities are highest in East Anglia and Kent (up to 75 pairs km⁻² on the South Thames Marshes), Pagham Harbour (79 pairs km⁻²) and the Mersey (59 pairs km⁻²). Lapwings breed abundantly also on the machair grasslands of the Uists, where the 978 pairs recorded on machair and associated habitats adjacent to review sites was 22.5% of the total lapwing population of the area (Fuller *et al.* 1986). In total, 4,170 pairs (1.9% of the British population) of lapwings bred on grasslands adjacent to review sites for which there are data (Table 8.6.5). In addition to the Uists other

major breeding sites are the The Wash (Ouse and Nene Washes), Breydon Water (the Norfolk Broads) and the Swale Estuary. These four areas support 64.8% of the lapwings breeding on grasslands adjacent to estuaries.

Although lapwings breed on saltmarshes they are less widespread there than on grasslands, occurring on saltmarsh on 47.2% of review sites surveyed (Table 8.6.4). On only seven of these 17 review sites does the breeding density exceed 20 pairs km⁻²; these are mostly in western England and eastern Scotland (Figure 8.6.53). In addition to their almost complete absence as a breeding bird on the estuarine saltmarshes of south-west England and Wales, breeding lapwings were also absent from East Anglian saltmarshes. Despite this more restricted distribution on saltmarshes, breeding densities are higher there than on the adjacent grasslands on three (Beaulieu, Duddon and Solway) of the five estuaries for which there are comparable data (Figure 8.6.54).

Curlew

The estimated 35,500 pairs of curlews breeding in Britain breed mainly in upland areas, preferring moist, poorly drained moors and heaths and low-intensity farmed grasslands (Baines 1989). The British population is about 28% of the European population; curlews breed abundantly elsewhere only in Eire, Sweden and Finland (Piersma 1986). In Britain curlews have a largely western and northern distribution, although they are scarce in north-west Scotland and have spread extensively into lowland areas during the 20th century (Sharrock 1976).

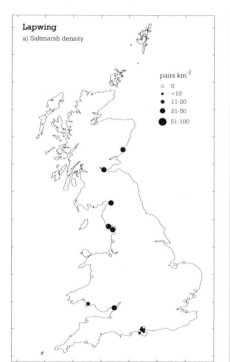 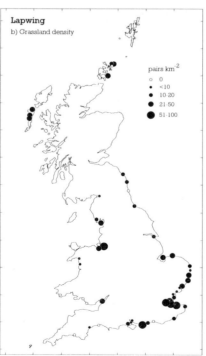 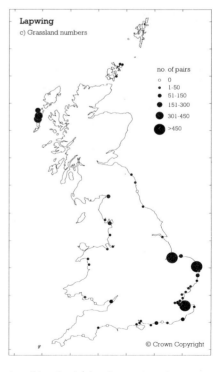

Figure 8.6.53 The distribution of lapwings breeding on review sites. a) Maximum densities (pairs km⁻²) on estuarine saltmarshes; b) maximum densities (pairs km⁻²) on wet grasslands adjacent to estuaries; and c) total numbers of pairs on wet grasslands.

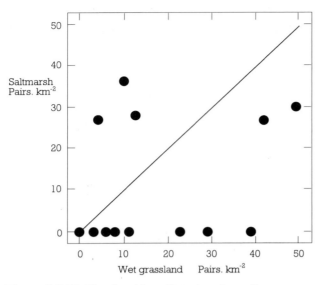

Figure 8.6.54 The densities of lapwings breeding on estuarine saltmarshes compared with those breeding on wet grasslands on the same estuaries. The solid line shows equal densities in the two habitats.

Curlews are an uncommon breeding bird on estuaries in Britain, occurring on only 18.5% of review sites for which there are grassland data, and 19.4% of surveyed saltmarsh review sites (Table 8.6.4). Curlews breed on estuarine saltmarshes only in north-west England, between Morecambe Bay and the Solway, and in eastern Scotland and always at low density (<10 pairs km^{-2}) (Figure 8.6.55). Grassland-breeding curlews occur on scattered sites in England and Wales and on Orkney, again at low densities and in small numbers (Figure 8.6.55). Highest breeding densities are on small wetlands adjacent to review sites in Orkney (up to 45 pairs km^{-2}).

Snipe

There are an estimated 30,000 British breeding pairs of snipe (4% of the European population), although this figure must be treated with caution, since snipe are a particularly difficult species to census. Snipe nest mostly in wet grasslands, bogs and fens. They are particularly vulnerable to the drainage, agricultural intensification and

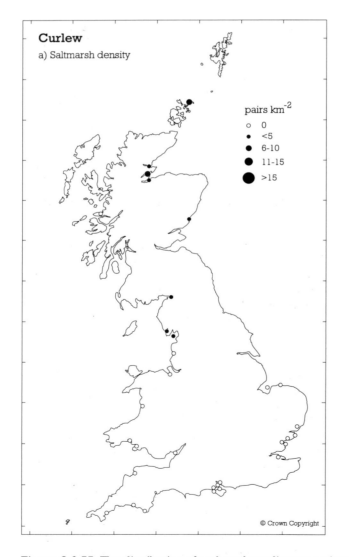

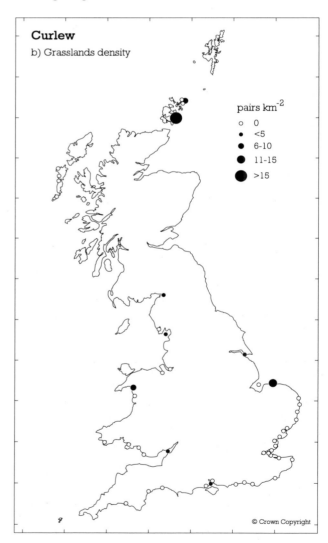

Figure 8.6.55 The distribution of curlews breeding on review sites. a) Maximum densities (pairs km^{-2}) on estuarine saltmarshes; and b) maximum densities (pairs km^{-2}) on wet grasslands adjacent to estuaries.

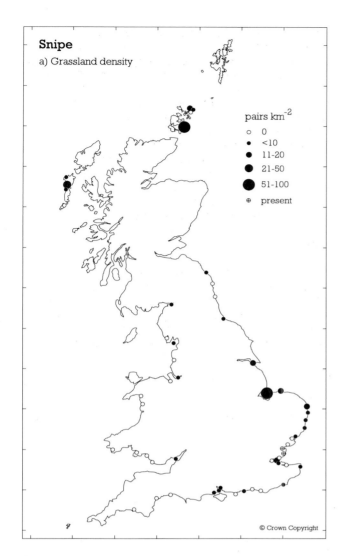

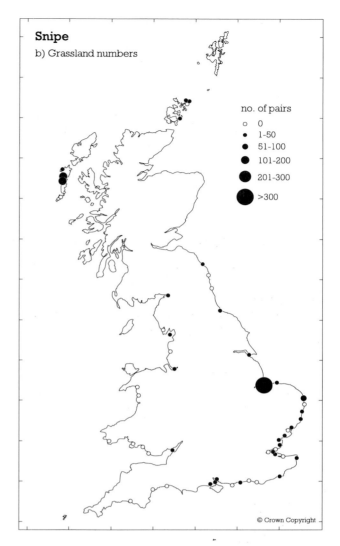

Figure 8.6.56 The distribution of snipe breeding on review sites. a) Maximum densities (pairs km^{-2}) on wet grasslands adjacent to estuaries; and b) total numbers of pairs on wet grasslands.

conversion to arable of lowland wet grasslands (Smith 1983; Stroud *et al.* 1990). The extensive losses of these traditional breeding habitats have resulted in a major population decline in England and Wales in recent years (Smith 1983). There is evidence that the decline is continuing (Smith 1988).

During the surveys of saltmarsh-breeding waders, snipe were found breeding on only one estuarine saltmarsh, at Aberlady Bay on the Firth of Forth. They are more widespread on wet grassland adjacent to estuaries, breeding there on 32 review sites (58.2% of sites for which there are data) (Table 8.6.4). These estuarine grasslands hold 52.4% of the 1,979 pairs of snipe estimated to be breeding on lowland wet grasslands in England and Wales (Smith 1983). Like most other breeding waders, snipe are absent or breed only at very low densities (<10 pairs km^{-2}) over most of England and Wales (Figure 8.6.56). Highest nesting densities (up to 60 pairs km^{-2}) were on the The Wash (Ouse and Nene Washes), adjacent to Oitir Mhor in the Outer Hebrides (42 pairs km^{-2}) and in a small wetland adjacent to Deer Sound in Orkney (83 pairs km^{-2}). By far the most important review

site for breeding snipe is the Ouse and Nene Washes, where the 737 breeding pairs recorded in Smith's (1983) survey are over 70% of the snipe breeding on grassland adjacent to surveyed review sites. A further 13% breeds on the machair adjacent to the Uists review sites.

Dunlin

Dunlins breed widely in arctic and subarctic regions but are a much scarcer breeding bird in temperate areas. The approximately 9,150 pairs of dunlins breeding in Britain are 82% of the *schinzii* race that breeds in temperate Europe (Piersma 1986; Stroud *et al.* 1990). This population is believed to overwinter in west and north Africa and has been greatly reduced in range and numbers elsewhere in western Europe (Jonsson 1986). Dunlins breed widely in upland Britain, but the main concentrations are on the peatlands of Lewis, Caithness and Sutherland, and the machair of the Outer Hebrides (Fuller *et al.* 1986; Stroud *et al.* 1987, 1990).

On estuaries, Allport *et al.* (1986) found dunlins breed at low density (maximum 6 pairs km^{-2}) on

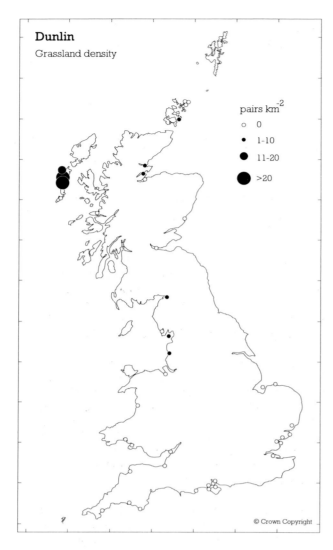

Figure 8.6.57 The distribution and density (maximum pairs km⁻²) of dunlins breeding on saltmarshes and wet grasslands adjacent to review sites

saltmarshes on only five estuaries (13.9% of review sites surveyed). All are in north-west England/south-west Scotland (Ribble Estuary to the Solway) and north-east Scotland (Dornoch and Cromarty Firths). The only estuaries in Britain with substantial numbers of breeding dunlins are Bagh nan Faoilean, Oitir Mhor and Vallay/Oronsay in the Outer Hebrides (Figure 8.6.57). Here dunlins breed at much higher densities (up to 46 pairs km⁻²) on saltmarshes and damp machair grasslands adjacent to the review sites. Overall densities in the Outer Hebrides were 53 pairs km⁻² on saltmarsh and even higher (66 pairs km⁻²) on damp machair (Fuller *et al.* 1986). The estimated 602 pairs adjacent to the Outer Hebrides review sites are 18% of the total breeding on the Outer Hebrides, 6.6% of the British breeding population and 5.4% of the European population of temperate-breeding *schinzii* dunlins.

Ringed plover

Britain supports 64% of the small temperate-breeding population of the nominate *hiaticula* race of ringed plovers. There are also subarctic

hiaticula birds breeding in Iceland, and a further arctic population in Greenland and northern Canada (Piersma 1986). National surveys in Britain in 1973/74 (Prater 1976b) and 1984 (Prater 1989) found that whilst most breeding ringed plovers are coastal, there is a small but increasing inland breeding population, especially in England and Wales. The main coastal-breeding habitats in most of Britain are shingle and sand beaches, with breeding success in some areas being higher on shingle (Pienkowski & Pienkowski 1989). 48.2% of coastal-breeding ringed plovers in the 1984 survey were on beaches. The other major coastal habitat for breeding ringed plovers is the machair grassland of the Outer Hebrides, with 27.5% of the coastal population (Prater 1989).

Estuaries provide breeding habitat for about half of the ringed plovers breeding in Britain. The 1984 survey (Prater 1989) found a total of 2,509 pairs of ringed plovers breeding on a minimum of 78 review sites (50.3%) distributed around much of the British coast (Figure 8.6.58). Ringed plovers are absent, or present only in low numbers, in south-west England, Wales and the north-west Scottish mainland, although in Scotland this finding may have been partly due to incomplete survey coverage (Prater 1989).

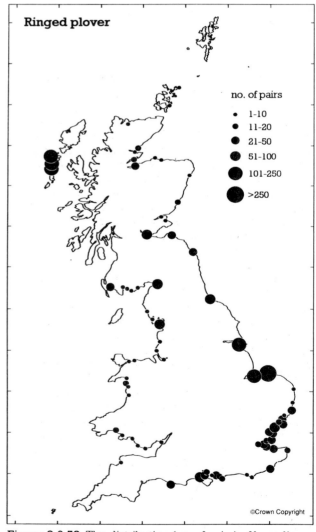

Figure 8.6.58 The distribution (no. of pairs) of breeding ringed plovers on review sites

Major breeding areas on estuaries are the machair grasslands adjacent to the sounds and open shores of the Uists, and the eastern English coast including the Humber Estuary, The Wash and North Norfolk Coast. The Uist review sites together support a total of 487 pairs (19.4% of the coastal population) and the extensive shingle and dune systems of the North Norfolk Coast support 433 pairs (17.3%). In all, these three east coast and four Uist review sites have 1,206 breeding pairs, or 48.1% of the British estuarine population. Only six other estuaries (Firth of Forth, Tees, Colne, Lymington, Morecambe Bay and Solway Firth) support more than 50 breeding pairs each. In total 43% of coastal-breeding ringed plovers, and 29.8% of the total British breeding population, occur on estuaries. Overall British estuaries are of major international importance for breeding ringed plovers, with 19.2% of the north-west and central European *hiaticula* population.

Breeding ringed plovers are very vulnerable to human disturbance where there is public access to the beaches on which they breed, and where such pressure is high few pairs nest successfully (Pienkowski 1984). Prater (1989) notes that most of the large breeding populations in eastern and southern England are now restricted to protected areas such as nature reserves, and anticipates that such localisation of the breeding population will continue.

Avocet

Avocets ceased to breed regularly in Britain in the early 19th century. They began to recolonise the East Anglian coast in the early 1940s when a few pairs started breeding at Minsmere in Suffolk and on Havergate Island in the Ore/Alde/Butley Estuary further south in Suffolk. Since then the breeding population has steadily increased and expanded its range (Figure 8.6.59) (Cadbury *et al.* 1989). In 1988 the breeding population totalled 385 pairs (2% of the north-west and central European population) (Stroud *et al.* 1990). Most of the European population breeds on the coasts of the Wadden Sea (Piersma 1986).

In 1988 avocets bred at 18 localities, all of which are on the English east coast between The Wash and north Kent. About 75% of British breeding avocets are on nine review sites in this region. Away from estuaries the only major breeding site is the coastal brackish lagoon system at Minsmere, where 95 pairs bred in 1989. Other major colonies are the up to 132 pairs at Havergate Island (Ore/Alde/Butley), and those at Titchwell and Cley (North Norfolk Coast) and Elmley (Swale). Most avocets breed on brackish lagoons adjacent to estuaries, and breeding adults feed on the nearby mudflats. A few pairs have now begun breeding on coastal wet grasslands (C Beardall pers. comm.).

Other breeding waders

In addition to the eight breeding wader species described above, four other scarce breeding waders occur adjacent to review sites. Black-tailed

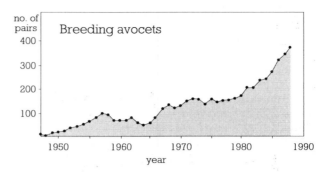

Figure 8.6.59 The increasing size of the breeding population of avocets in Britain since recolonisation in 1947 (from Cadbury *et al.* 1989)

godwits *Limosa limosa* formerly bred widely in wet grasslands in East Anglia and Yorkshire but ceased regular breeding there in the 1830s, probably owing to loss of habitat and persecution by shooting and egg-collecting (Cottier & Lea 1969). Breeding began regularly again in 1952 on the Ouse Washes (The Wash) and this remains the stronghold of breeding black-tailed godwits in Britain. Small numbers breed adjacent to at least two other review sites in eastern England. The total British breeding population remains small (in 1986 it was up to 47 pairs); all are associated with review sites. The British population is less than 1% of the European breeding population, where the stronghold of the nominate race is in the Netherlands (Piersma 1986).

Like the black-tailed godwit, the ruff *Philomachus pugnax* ceased to breed regularly in Britain in the late 19th century, as a result of drainage of its wet grassland breeding areas. Breeding began regularly again on the Ouse Washes in the 1960s (Cottier & Lea 1969) and since then the number of females believed to be breeding in Britain has fluctuated between 0 and 32, and is usually less than 10 (Stroud *et al.* 1990). Ruffs in Britain breed on coastal grazing marshes and on upper saltmarsh, and most of the British population is associated with two review sites in eastern England.

Most European whimbrels *Numenius phaeopus* breed in the subarctic of Iceland and northern Scandinavia (Piersma 1986). Whimbrels are a scarce breeding species in Britain and are restricted to northern Scotland, with most of the population of about 465 pairs on the moorland and maritime heaths of Shetland (Stroud *et al.* 1990). Between 5-10 pairs (1-2% of the British population) of whimbrels breed on coastal grasslands adjacent to one north-east Scotland review site.

Temminck's stints *Calidris temminckii* are a very rare breeding bird in Britain, with regular breeding by up to nine birds in Scotland since 1971 (Stroud *et al.* 1990). Since 1987 up to six adults have nested adjacent to one northern Scottish review site. The adults feed on the nearby mudflats of the estuary.

Total estuarine-breeding wader populations

The overall density of all breeding waders on estuaries is shown in Figure 8.6.60. This emphasises that estuaries with high densities of waders breeding on saltmarsh are widely distributed around Britain. Eight estuaries have areas of saltmarsh with waders breeding at a density in excess of 100 pairs km^{-2}, including estuaries on south, east and west coasts from Beaulieu in the south, with the highest density of 160 pairs km^{-2} at Montrose Basin in the north. Allport *et al.* (1986) derived a 'weighted wealth index' for saltmarshes with breeding wader populations, based on the density of breeding pairs, the species diversity and the relative size of the national breeding populations. They found that the 15 estuaries with the highest conservation importance for saltmarsh waders were likewise widely distributed throughout Britain, from the Dornoch Firth south to the Isle of Wight (Newtown Estuary), with the highest indices on the Solway Firth, Beaulieu River, Morecambe Bay and Duddon Estuary. Four of the 15 estuaries were, however, in north-west England and another five in eastern Scotland.

The pattern for grassland-breeding populations is different. Highest breeding densities occur in two widely separated parts of Britain: in south-east England, notably at Elmley on the Swale Estuary (117 pairs km^{-2}) and at Pagham Harbour (116 pairs km^{-2}); and in northern Scotland. Here there are exceptionally high densities (a maximum of over 300 pairs km^{-2}) on small wet grassland areas in Orkney, and total densities exceeding 100 pairs km^{-2} on machair adjacent to each of three Uist review sites (Figure 8.6.60). The exceptional importance of the machair of the Outer Hebrides is emphasised by the high total numbers of breeding waders in these areas (Figure 8.6.60): breeding populations adjacent to each of two review sites (Bagh nam Faiolean and Oithir Mhor) exceed 1,000 pairs, numbers only rivalled by the populations breeding on the Ouse and Nene Washes and on the extensive wet grasslands of the Norfolk Broads (Breydon Water). Total wader densities are, however, consistently higher on saltmarshes than on the adjacent grasslands of the same estuaries (Figure 8.6.61), and in the case of at least one species (redshank) the estimated total saltmarsh-breeding population appears to be about eight times larger than that on grasslands adjacent to estuaries. Population sizes on saltmarsh cannot yet be calculated for other breeding waders so the numerical importance of the two types of breeding habitat cannot be assessed. Likewise total numbers of breeding waders on estuarine shingle cannot be assessed as there are comprehensive data only for ringed plovers.

In some parts of Britain, notably southern England, estuaries and their adjacent habitats support almost all the breeding waders of the region. In Suffolk most of the breeding redshanks and oystercatchers are estuarine. Even in such a widespread species as the lapwing, 12% of the Suffolk population bred on estuaries (Holzer *et al.* 1989). In Sussex 81% of redshank and 64% of snipe were associated with estuaries (Mitchell 1983). Such trends towards coastal breeding may become even more widespread as inland breeding habitats continue to disappear.

Twelve wader species breed regularly on estuaries in Britain and an average of 3.8 species

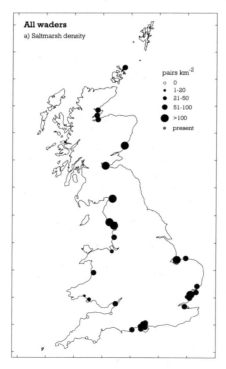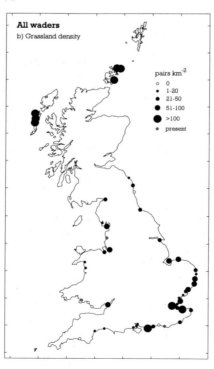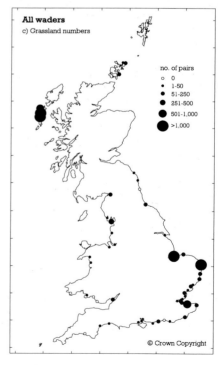

© Crown Copyright

Figure 8.6.60. The distribution of total waders breeding on review sites. a) Maximum densities (pairs km^{-2}) on estuarine saltmarshes; b) maximum densities (pairs km^{-2}) on wet grasslands adjacent to estuaries; and c) total numbers of pairs on wet grasslands.

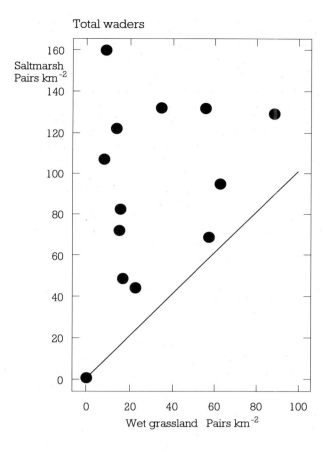

Figure 8.6.61 The total breeding populations of waders are consistently higher on saltmarshes than on grasslands adjacent to the same estuaries

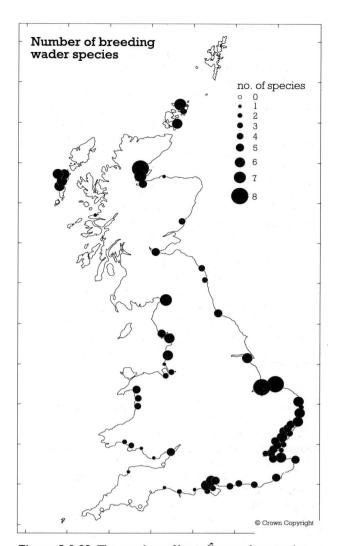

© Crown Copyright

Figure 8.6.62 The number of breeding wader species on review sites

per estuary breed on the 76 review sites for which there are reliable data. For at least four of these species (redshank, dunlin, ringed plover and avocet) the network of British estuaries provides breeding habitat for a population of international importance, since populations are in excess of 1% of the north-west and central European breeding population (Stroud *et al.* 1990). Even with incomplete data, minimum estimates of the British estuarine breeding population are: redshank – 7.3% of the north-west and central European population, dunlin – 5.4%, ringed plover – 19.2% and avocet – 1.5%.

No single review site supports breeding populations of all 12 of the breeding wader species, but three sites (Dornoch Firth, The Wash and the North Norfolk Coast) each have assemblages of eight species (Figure 8.6.62). Diverse estuarine assemblages also occur consistently in East Anglia and south-east England, in north-west England, the Outer Hebrides and Orkney. In general only small numbers of wader species breed on review sites in Wales, north-east England and south-east Scotland. Breeding waders are largely absent from south-west England (Figure 8.6.61).

Although these assemblages of breeding waders on an estuary, or on a particular habitat within an

estuary, often mean that different species regularly breed in association with each other, no two species have precisely the same habitat preferences even when all are nesting at high densities (e.g. Fuller *et al.* 1986). Hence sites favoured by one species may support only low densities of another. For example there is no correlation between the peak densities of breeding oystercatchers and redshanks on saltmarshes on the 34 review sites for which there are comparable data, or between lapwings and redshanks on the same sites (Figure 8.6.63). Waders generally breed in higher densities where conditions are most favourable for the successful rearing of young, so the absence of density correlations between species means that different parts of the network of breeding habitats on British estuaries are most important for different species. This is apparent also from the differences in distribution patterns around Britain (Figures 8.6.50 – 8.6.58). Effective conservation of estuarine breeding waders in Britain must therefore take into account the distribution, density and habitat preferences of each species, as well as the diversity and density of the wader assemblages.

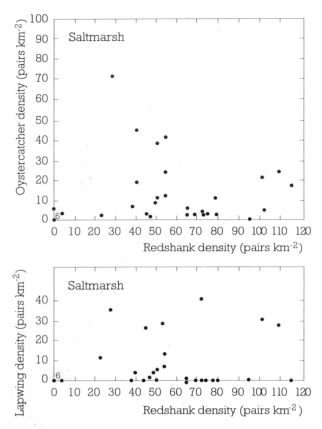

Figure 8.6.63 There is no correlation between the density of breeding redshanks and that of oystercatchers or lapwings on saltmarshes on the same estuaries

Breeding seabirds

General estuarine distribution

Britain is of major international importance for breeding seabirds. It holds more than half the European Community population of 14 species of seabirds and more than half the world population of four of these (Lloyd *et al.* in press). Many species are colonial nesters that breed in the safety of the steep cliffs and slopes of the islands and mainland coasts of northern and western Britain. These safe breeding sites are within range of rich coastal and offshore feeding grounds. Other coastal species, particularly terns, nest on shingle beaches and other flat sites such as island plateaux. Some gulls are predominantly coastal breeders in a variety of habitats, although some, such as the lesser black-backed gull *Larus fuscus* and common gull *Larus canus,* also nest in large inland colonies.

Although many of Britain's seabirds breed on the exposed rocky coasts and islands of northern and western Britain, information collected between 1985-1988 from the NCC/Seabird Group Seabird Colony Register shows that in the mid-1980s 75 estuaries (48.4% of review sites) had one or more pairs of breeding seabirds. These estuaries are widely distributed around the British coast (Figure 8.6.64), although this and Figure 8.6.65 show that there are only a few generally small colonies on the estuaries of Wales and south-west England. Many of these are small colonies of roof-nesting gulls,

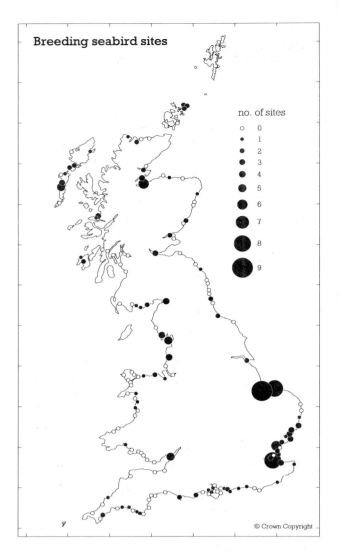

Figure 8.6.64 The number of locations with one or more pairs of breeding seabirds on each review site

chiefly herring gulls *Larus argentatus*, in towns adjacent to estuaries. Some other colonies in western and northern Britain comprise small numbers of cliff-nesting species on cliffs and rocky islets at the outer edges of the review sites. Nevertheless some British estuaries, notably Morecambe Bay, the Ribble, the North Norfolk Coast, parts of Suffolk, Essex and Kent and the Solent, support very large breeding seabird populations (Figure 8.6.65).

British estuarine breeding seabird populations are summarised in Table 8.6.6. Sixteen species breed on British estuaries and for some of these British estuaries are of considerable importance. For six of these species (black-headed gull *Larus ridibundus,* lesser black-backed gull, herring gull, Sandwich tern *Sterna sandvicensis,* common tern *S. hirundo* and little tern *S. albifrons*) the network of British estuaries supports breeding populations in excess of 1% of the west and central European breeding population. A further two species (common gull and arctic tern *S. paradisaea*) breed in numbers in excess of 1% of their British coastal breeding population. Numbers of common gulls are, however, very small. The distributions of

252

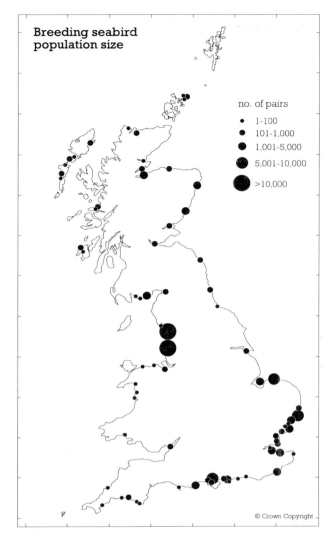

Breeding seabird population size

no. of pairs
- 1-100
- 101-1,000
- 1,001-5,000
- 5,001-10,000
- >10,000

© Crown Copyright

Figure 8.6.65 The total number of breeding seabirds (number of pairs) on review sites

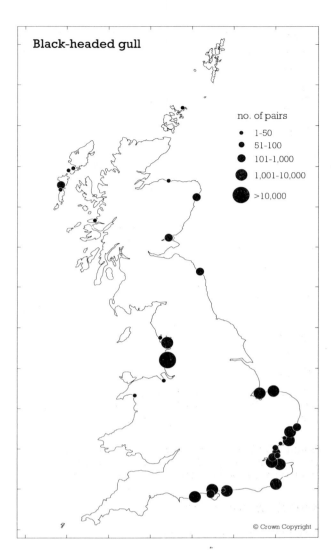

Black-headed gull

no. of pairs
- 1-50
- 51-100
- 101-1,000
- 1,001-10,000
- >10,000

© Crown Copyright

Figure 8.6.66 The distribution of breeding pairs of black-headed gulls on review sites

Table 8.6.6 British estuarine breeding populations of seabirds in 1985-88

Species	British estuarine popn. (pairs)	% British coastal popn.	% W & Central European popn.
Fulmar	2,092	0.4	0.4[a]
Cormorant	52	0.8	+
Shag	25	+	+
Arctic skua	1	+	+
Black-headed gull	49,957	93.1	4.2
Common gull	216	1.4	+
Lesser black-backed gull	18,560	30.1	10.5
Herring gull	17,683	13.2	1.9
Greater black-backed gull	165	0.9	+
Kittiwake	1,134	0.2	c. 0.1
Sandwich tern	6,446	46.2	13.8
Common tern	4,410	37.2	4.6
Arctic tern	1,100	1.4	0.6[**]
Little tern	1,783	73.7	12.9
Razorbill	19[*]	+	+
Black guillemot	40[*]	+	+

Sources: Lloyd *et al.* in press; NCC/Seabird Group Seabird Colony Register
+   Less than 0.1%
[a]   Excludes Iceland
[*]   No. of individuals
[**]   Excludes Iceland and the Faeroes

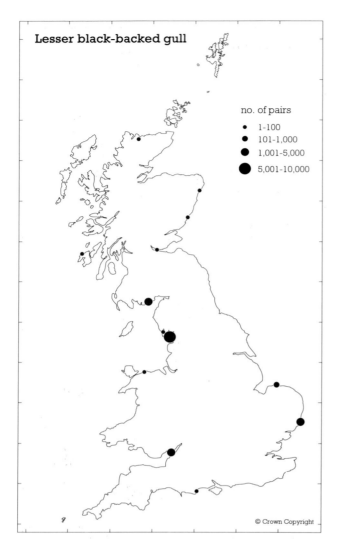

Figure 8.6.67 The distribution of breeding pairs of lesser black-backed gulls on review sites

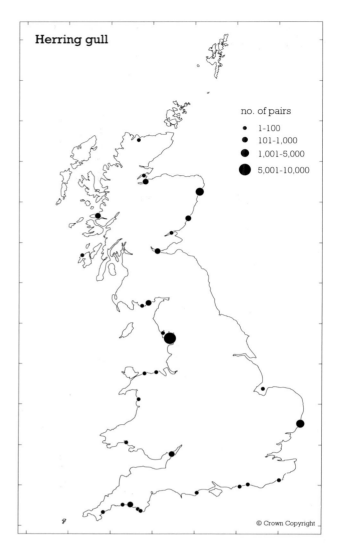

Figure 8.6.68 The distribution of breeding pairs of herring gulls on review sites

breeding seabird species for which British estuaries are important are shown in Figures 8.6.66 – 8.6.72 and are described below.

Black-headed gull

Almost 50,000 black-headed gulls nest on 35 review sites (Figure 8.6.66). Large estuarine colonies are typically found on saltmarshes and dune systems. Most are in east and south-east England, notably on The Wash, the North Norfolk Coast, the Suffolk, Essex and Kent coasts, the Rother Estuary and in parts of The Solent and in Poole Harbour. In western Britain the only estuarine colonies of over 1,000 pairs are on Morecambe Bay and the Ribble Estuary. One of the largest colonies, numbering 10,480 pairs in 1973, was on the Esk Estuary in north-west England (Gribble 1976), but this has since undergone a dramatic decline and became extinct in 1985. There is little evidence of the displacement of these breeding birds to Morecambe Bay, but many birds have moved elsewhere, primarily northwards and inland. The largest colony on the British coast is

now on the Ribble Estuary: 20,000 pairs. This colony alone holds over 37% of the British coastal-breeding total and 1.7% of the west and central European-breeding population. Elsewhere the largest estuarine colony is currently the 7,000 pairs breeding on the Beaulieu River in Hampshire. Here, as typically elsewhere, black-headed gulls breed as part of a mixed-species colony with several tern species and sometimes other gulls.

Lesser black-backed gull

30% of the British coastal-breeding population is estuarine, but lesser black-backed gulls have a breeding distribution restricted to 13 review sites. Only five sites hold more than 100 breeding pairs (Figure 8.6.67). Most of the estuarine population breeds in a colony of c. 10,000 pairs (5.7% of the western and central European population) on Walney Island on Morecambe Bay, along with various tern species and similar numbers of herring gulls. Here, and at the smaller colony on Orfordness in Suffolk (Ore/Alde/Butley Estuary), breeding numbers have greatly increased in recent years.

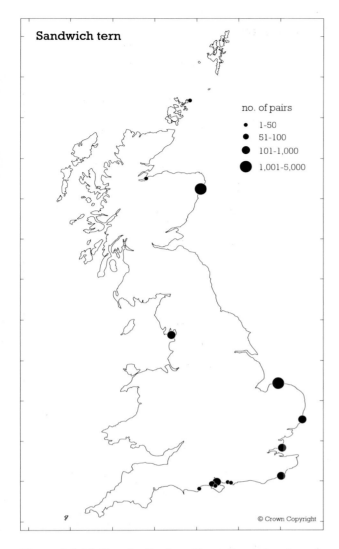

Figure 8.6.69 The distribution of breeding pairs of Sandwich terns on review sites

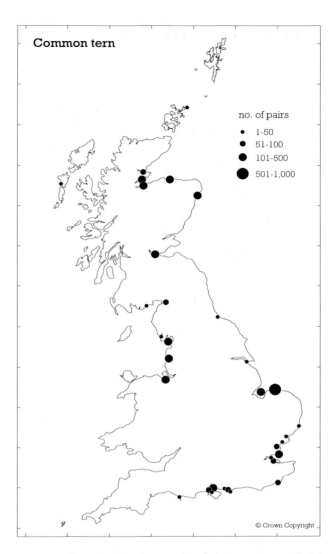

Figure 8.6.70 The distribution of breeding pairs of common terns on review sites

Herring gull

Although herring gulls often breed in mixed colonies with lesser black-backed gulls and the total numbers breeding on estuaries are similar, herring gulls are more widespread and breed on 29 review sites. These are mostly in northern and western Britain (Figure 8.6.68). Total numbers on British estuaries form a smaller proportion (13.2%) of the British coastal-breeding population, but, as for the lesser black-backed gull, the main breeding colony of c. 10,000 pairs is on Morecambe Bay and this site alone supports c. 1% of the international population. The only other colonies exceeding 1,000 pairs are on shingle and dune systems, on the Ythan Estuary in north-east Scotland and Orfordness (Ore/Alde/Butley Estuary). Elsewhere small colonies are on roofs, cliffs and rocky islands.

Sandwich tern

Britain is important as a breeding area for Sandwich terns, with the British breeding population totalling about 15,000 pairs – more than any other European country and about 32% of the European population (Table 8.6.6). Over 65% of the British-breeding population occurs in just six main colonies, four of which are on three review sites (Figure 8.6.69). Sandwich terns breed on shingle ridges and islands, usually amongst common or arctic terns. The largest colonies are on the Ythan Estuary (1,080 pairs) and the North Norfolk Coast (4,090 pairs) and Morecambe Bay (550 pairs). Smaller concentrations are restricted to 11 other estuaries, most of which are in south-east and southern England. Altogether estuaries are important for Sandwich terns, supporting 46.2% of the British coastal-breeding population and almost 14% of the European population.

Common tern

Common terns are more widespread than Sandwich terns and their estuarine colonies are scattered on 35 estuaries around most parts of Britain. They are largely absent, however, from north-west Scotland, south-west England and Wales (Figure 8.6.70). Common terns mostly breed near the coast on shingle and sand-dune systems, saltmarshes and islands. Although they breed widely in Europe, 37% of British common terns breed on estuaries, and these comprise 4.6% of the European population.

Arctic tern

The arctic tern is a circumpolar breeding species. Britain has about 44% of the European breeding population. In Britain most breed in Orkney and Shetland, and most of the British breeding range is in the north of the country (Figure 8.6.71). Arctic terns breed mostly on low, often rocky, islands as well as sand and shingle. They are less strongly associated with estuaries than are other British terns, with only about 1.4% of the British coastal population present on 22 review sites. All but two sites are in Scotland – there are small numbers breeding on Morecambe Bay and the North Norfolk Coast, in mixed colonies of terns.

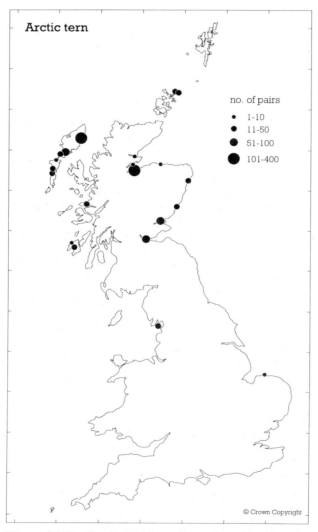

Figure 8.6.71 The distribution of breeding pairs of arctic terns on review sites

Recently there have been repeated breeding failures in the main British populations on the Shetlands, which have been attributed to the failure of the terns' main food supply, sand-eels *Ammodytes* spp. (Heubeck 1989; Monaghan *et al.* 1989).

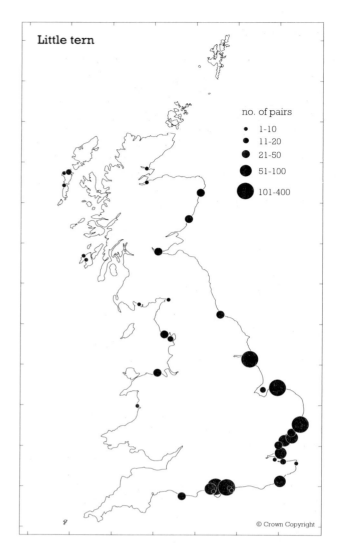

Figure 8.6.72 The distribution of breeding pairs of little terns on review sites

Little tern

Breeding colonies of little terns are widely scattered around the coasts of Britain on shingle and sand ridges, beaches and islands. The British-breeding population of about 2,500 pairs is internationally important and most (*c.* 74%) of the British population is on estuaries. The breeding population on British estuaries amounts to almost 13% of the European population (Table 8.6.6). Although this estuarine-breeding population is spread over most parts of Britain there are few little terns in western Britain, apart from small breeding colonies in north Wales and north-west England and north and west Scotland. The stronghold of the British population is in eastern and southern England (Figure 8.6.72). The largest colonies are on the Humber, North Norfolk Coast, the Suffolk and Essex estuaries and the harbours and estuaries of the Solent. The extensive shingle and sand-dune systems of the North Norfolk Coast are particularly important, with a breeding population amounting to over 20% of the British and 2.6% of the European population. The Humber Estuary also has a breeding population of more than 1% of the European population.

Other seabirds

Most other seabirds breeding on review sites are cliff- and rock-nesting species, with a few pairs on the outer parts of some of the rockier firths and bays. These colonies are insignificant compared with the large and internationally important populations elsewhere on the coasts of Britain (Table 8.6.6). Kittiwakes breeding on estuaries are, however, worthy of note. Although the populations are small (0.2% of the British coastal population), two small breeding colonies are located, unusually, on the artificial habitat of window ledges of buildings on the Tyne Estuary in north-east England. One has been the subject of intensive long-term population studies (Coulson & Thomas 1985).

Other breeding birds

Besides seabirds and waders, several other species of breeding birds are characteristic of estuaries and their surroundings or breed in substantial numbers in such areas.

Reedbed-breeding species

One group comprises species characteristic of reedbeds. Large reedbeds are now scarce in Britain. Major concentrations are on Anglesey, the south coast of England and in East Anglia. The only extensive coastal reedbeds in Scotland are on the Tay Estuary. Many of the remaining reedbeds are small, with only 15 exceeding 40 ha (Everett 1989). Many reedbeds are associated with estuaries. Some, such as at Blacktoft Sands on the Humber, and on the north shore of the Tay, are on tidal estuaries; others, such as on the Norfolk Broads, are on lowland river floodplains, adjacent or close to tidal rivers; and some are on coastal floodplains protected by sea defences from natural incursion by the sea. Some of these, such as at Leighton Moss on Morecambe Bay, are adjacent to estuaries.

Some breeding species, notably the reed warbler *Acrocephalus scirpaceus,* are common and widespread and particularly associated with reedbeds. Other warbler species, such as the common sedge warbler *A. schoenobaenus* and much rarer Savi's warbler *Locustella luscinoides* and Cetti's warbler *Cettia cetti*, often include reedbeds in their breeding territories (Everett 1989). Reedbeds are also important for warblers in autumn as places in which they accumulate fat reserves before migration. Bearded tits *Panurus biarmicus* are almost entirely confined to reedbeds as breeding sites. Yearly numbers are greatly affected by severe winter weather, and bearded tits presently have a largely coastal-breeding range from Yorkshire to Dorset, including many of the major reedbeds associated with estuaries in these regions (Batten *et al.* in press).

Raptors

In the 19th century marsh harriers *Circus aeruginosus* nested widely in British reedbeds but then became very scarce until an increase in the breeding population to over 75 nests in 1988 (Day 1988; Batten *et al.* in press). Most now breed in the reedbeds of East Anglia and these are important in a British context and in maintaining the geographic range of the species, although the overall population is small in comparison with elsewhere in western Europe (1-2% of the western European breeding population). The small population of Montagu's harriers *C. pygargus* that formerly bred in reedbeds in eastern and southern Britain now, however, breeds in arable crops (Elliot 1988). In contrast to the increasing populations of bearded tits and marsh harriers, bitterns *Botaurus stellaris* are in serious decline: in 1987 only about 20 males were present at 12 sites, and bitterns are largely confined to just three main sites in Lancashire and East Anglia (Everett 1989; Batten *et al.* in press). Unlike the other reedbed specialists, bitterns avoid tidal reedbeds and so are less closely associated with estuaries, although their three main remaining sites include Titchwell on the North Norfolk Coast and Leighton Moss beside Morecambe Bay.

Wildfowl

One species of British wildfowl, the shelduck, is particularly associated with estuaries for breeding. Shelducks breed widely around the coasts of Britain wherever there are suitable sandy or muddy shores close to nesting habitats. Shelducks nest in a wide variety of places, usually under cover, in old buildings, haystacks, banks and often in old rabbit burrows in sand-dunes (Owen *et al.* 1986). Most nests are on dunes and grazing marshes adjacent to sheltered estuaries (Sharrock 1976). Shelducks often nest colonially in places such as dune systems, although studies on the Firth of Forth have found that their breeding success in colonies may be much lower than in pairs nesting in isolation (Pienkowski & Evans 1982). Soon after hatching broods are led to nearby saltmarshes and intertidal mudflats to feed. Where these are close to colonies broods often aggregate into creches, although their survival is better on linear shores and where creches are not found (Evans & Pienkowski 1982).

Shelducks breed in north-west Europe, parts of the Mediterranean and the Middle East. Although the size of the north-west European breeding population is not known, the wintering population there and in the western Mediterranean is estimated at 265,000 birds (Pirot *et al.* 1989). By comparison an estimated 15,000 pairs of shelducks breed in Britain (Stroud *et al.* 1990). Britain is therefore of considerable international importance as a breeding area for shelducks, supporting at least 11% of the European population and, since not all shelducks present will breed, probably considerably more than this figure. Most of the British-breeding population utilises estuaries, and at least 135 review sites (87%) throughout Britain are used by breeding shelducks (Figure 8.6.73). Information from 29 review sites (from Allport *et al.* 1986; Roberts 1988) shows that densities present on saltmarshes are generally less than 20 pairs km⁻², and that highest densities are on Morecambe Bay and the Duddon Estuary where densities can be up to 102 pairs km⁻² (Figure 8.6.73). Nevertheless, Evans & Pienkowski (1982) found that most of the production of young may be from low density populations breeding on linear shores outside estuaries: a good example of where density is not a good measure of importance.

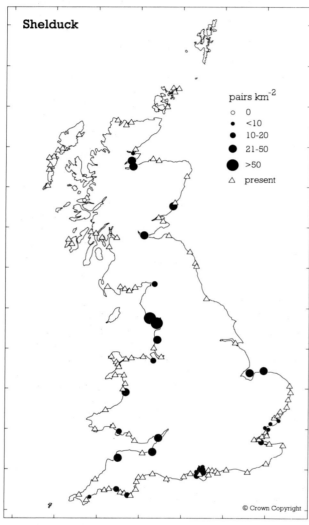

Figure 8.6.73 The distribution of shelducks breeding on review sites. Densities are shown as maximum estimated breeding pairs km⁻², and presence records are from Sharrock (1976).

In Britain, eider ducks *Somateria mollissima* also breed extensively on estuaries, almost exclusively in Scotland (Figure 8.6.74). Eiders are a very numerous species with an estimated wintering population of 3,000,000 birds in the western palaearctic (Stroud *et al.* 1990). The British-breeding population is much smaller, currently 20,000 pairs (Stroud *et al.* 1990). Eiders are common in west Scotland, Orkney and Shetland but the largest colonies are on the east Scottish coast, particularly on estuaries such as the Ythan, where *c.* 2,000 pairs bred in the 1970s, and on the Fife and Kincardine coasts, including the Eden and Tay Estuaries and Montrose Basin (holding up to 3,000 pairs).

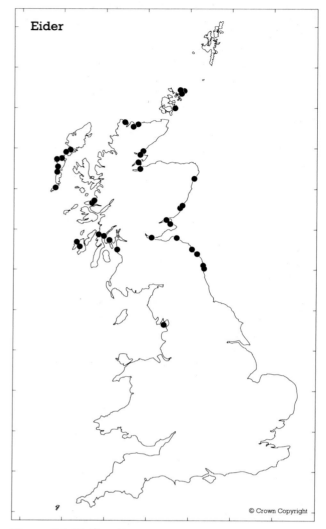

Figure 8.6.74 The distribution of breeding eiders on review sites, derived from Sharrock (1976)

8.6.5 Conservation of British estuarine birds

Estuarine birds comprise a major feature of estuarine wildlife. Most are at the top of their food chains and provide sensitive indicators of the health of estuaries, since they are vulnerable to the accumulation of pollutants and depend on areas safe from human disturbance where they can breed, feed and roost. Britain's estuaries are host to large and important populations of many breeding, migrant and wintering bird species. The dependence of these birds on estuarine ecosystems for their survival is recognised in international treaties to which Britain is a party (see Chapter 9). Much of the conservation of estuarine habitats and wildlife is currently initiated as a result of the identification of areas as of international importance for birds.

Whilst the general approach to the conservation of birds in Britain, through the selection and notification of SSSIs, is similar to that for other wildlife, the high mobility of birds, especially those such as the migrant and wintering waterfowl that use estuaries, adds a further dimension to the safeguarding of birds during each part of their life (NCC 1989). Furthermore the mobility of birds results in their dependence on a complex mosaic of habitats for their survival, in both the short term such as during a tidal cycle, and the longer term such as during migration and whilst on wintering grounds. In addition established distribution patterns can be modified by environmental stresses such as severe winter weather, so that some sites vital for a bird's survival may be used for only very short periods. This means that site selection needs to be based on population sizes as well as distribution patterns.

Birds, including many important estuarine bird species, are mobile on an international scale as well as a national one, as described in Section 8.6.2. This has led to birds becoming the subject of several international government agreements on wildlife conservation. Two are particularly significant. The first is *the Convention on the conservation of wetlands especially as waterfowl habitat*, often known as the 'Ramsar Convention', for which signatory states place wetland sites on a list of Wetlands of International Importance. The other is the Council of the European Communities' Directive 79/409/EEC on the Conservation of Wild Birds, which requires member states to undertake special protection measures for all migratory and some other vulnerable bird species. Among these measures is the designation of Special Protection Areas. Both these international agreements are of particular relevance to estuarine conservation.

The Ramsar Convention concerns the conservation of wetlands and their waterfowl populations. The EEC Wild Birds Directive places emphasis on the need to conserve habitats as a means of maintaining populations of all species of birds, and also focuses particularly on two main categories of birds. These are vulnerable species (listed in Annex 1 of the Directive) and all other regularly occurring migratory species. The Directive identifies the need to protect migratory species on their breeding, moulting and wintering areas and the staging posts along their migrations, and places particular emphasis on the protection of wetlands, particularly wetlands of international importance. Hence for the conservation of estuarine birds, particularly migrant and wintering populations, the EEC Wild Birds Directive and the Ramsar Convention are usually linked in the designation of sites. The operation and functioning of these and other international measures in Britain has recently been reviewed by Stroud *et al.* (1990), and their application to estuarine wildlife is described further in Chapter 9.

The functioning of the 1% of population size threshold for selection of sites has been outlined in Section 8.6.2. The 1% level has become widely accepted as a basis of the site selection component of bird conservation, since it covers both the rare and the more common, but localised, species. It forms an important element of both national and international site selection criteria (NCC 1989). As described in Section 8.6.2, use of a 1% criterion needs to be linked, however, with other approaches designed to ensure safeguarding of, for example, important bird assemblages and sites where large numbers of birds occur, such as breeding colonies. Thus a wetland is considered as internationally important under the Ramsar Convention if it regularly supports 20,000 waterfowl, or 1% of the individuals in a biogeographic population, or substantial numbers of individuals from particular groups of waterfowl indicative of wetland values, productivity or diversity. Recent guidelines also explicitly recognise the need to consider population turnover, and Ridgill & Fox (1990) emphasise the need to incorporate, in the national and international site network, sites that usually support lower numbers of waterfowl but which are critical for the survival of many more birds during periods of severe weather.

The descriptions in this review of the use of estuaries by birds have highlighted the many ways in which populations link habitats within the estuarine complex. Examples include the species that nest in one habitat such as grassland or sand-dunes and feed in another such as mudflats, and wintering populations that move between mudflats, saltmarshes, grasslands and shingle ridges during a tidal cycle of feeding and roosting. This interdependence highlights the need to conserve entire estuaries since loss of an area of habitat can have substantially graver consequences for the birds which depend on it as part of their mosaic than appears from the size of the area (e.g. Davidson & Evans 1985). The aim of safeguarding the entire estuarine complex is incorporated in international measures such as Article 2.1 of the Ramsar Convention. This recognises that the boundaries of wetlands designated under the convention may incorporate riparian and coastal zones adjacent to the wetlands and islands or bodies of marine water deeper than 6 m at low tide lying within the wetlands, especially where these have importance as waterfowl habitat.

In addition to safeguarding populations through the establishment of SPAs, the EEC Directive on Wild Birds also places an obligation (under Article 4.2) on Britain as an EEC member state to implement special protection measures elsewhere so that bird habitats in the wider countryside, outside the specially designated Ramsar/SPA sites, can be safeguarded. This follows from the requirement of the Directive that international conservation measures cover both the maintenance of the traditional geographic ranges of birds and the sustenance of levels of productivity. Furthermore the EEC Directive on Wild Birds indicates the need for special conservation measures for all species of birds to ensure their survival and reproduction in their area of distribution.

In considering the conservation measures appropriate for estuarine birds it is important to recognise that although many species appear widespread and abundant, where they occur, many are largely restricted to estuarine areas. In reality the populations of these estuarine species are generally small in comparison with those of many other birds. For example, estimated British wintering populations include 37 million starlings *Sturnus vulgaris*, 30 million chaffinches, 20 million dunnocks *Prunella modularis* and 25 million skylarks (Lack 1986). In comparison, the most abundant wintering wader in Britain is the lapwing, with a population of 1 million, and the most abundant predominantly estuarine wader is the dunlin, with a midwinter population of 433,000. No other wader and only one duck – the very widespread mallard – exceeds a wintering population of 300,000 birds in winter.

For many waterfowl even international populations are much smaller than this, and are much less than 100,000 for many waterfowl for which Britain has an international responsibility (Tables 8.6.3. and 8.6.4). Hence conservation of estuarine birds concerns generally scarce and localised species. Nevertheless considerable proportions of the populations of some species are scattered around sites which individually fall below the 1% criterion for importance (Figures 8.6.47 and 8.6.48), and so the wider countryside approaches embodied in Britain's international obligations are also relevant to the conservation of estuarine birds.

Conservation of breeding birds

The saltmarshes on estuaries and the grasslands, shingle and dunes associated with estuaries provide breeding habitat for breeding wader assemblages of major national and international importance, although estuaries are not the only key places in Britain for some of these species. Of particular significance are the over 60% of British redshanks and 30% of ringed plovers breeding on estuaries, and the large and diverse assemblages of breeding waders and other birds on many estuaries throughout Britain especially those adjacent to the review sites in the Outer Hebrides, the Norfolk Broads and the Ouse and Nene Washes alongside the tidal rivers of The Wash. Many of the breeding waders and other birds of saltmarshes and grazing marshes that occur in nationally and internationally important numbers on estuaries are, however, widespread in their breeding distribution.

Thirty-three estuarine sites containing saltmarsh and other coastal grassland bird habitats, and a further seven seasonally flooded neutral grasslands, are included within the designated and proposed Ramsar/SPA site network as internationally important ornithological sites. Machair areas adjacent to five review sites on the Outer Hebrides and Orkney are also included in the international site network because of their breeding bird populations (Stroud et al. 1990).

The saltmarshes, sand-dunes and shingle banks of estuaries are of considerable national and international conservation importance for their breeding seabirds. For seabirds the very large proportion of Britain's little tern population that breeds on estuaries is of particular national and international significance. British estuaries also support more than 10% of the western and central European breeding populations of lesser black-backed gulls and sandwich terns. Many of the largest gull and tern colonies in Britain, for example at Walney Island on Morecambe Bay, Blakeney Point and Scolt Head on the North Norfolk Coast, Orfordness on the Ore/Alde/Butley in Suffolk, and the Sands of Forvie on the Ythan estuary, are on estuaries.

Eighteen estuarine sites within the proposed Ramsar/SPA site network contain major seabird colonies (Stroud et al. 1990). In all 55 estuaries included in the proposed Ramsar/SPA site network contain saltmarsh and grassland-breeding bird assemblages and/or seabird colonies (Figure 8.6.75). (Note that in some places, for example the Stour and Orwell Estuaries in Suffolk, two or more review sites together form a single Ramsar/SPA site and that, because of resource constraints, the precise boundaries have yet to be determined for some proposed Ramsar/SPA sites (Stroud et al. 1990).) Sixteen review sites feature among the internationally important sites with both grassland/saltmarsh-breeding species and assemblages, and seabird colonies (Figure 8.6.75). All review sites that fall wholly or partly within the proposed Ramsar/SPA site network are shown in Chapter 9.

Although many seabird colonies are occupied consistently for long periods of years, some species, particularly terns, sometimes abandon formerly traditional breeding sites and move elsewhere. Such moves may be induced by local food shortages or by excessive disturbance to the breeding colony. (The presence of good inshore and coastal feeding grounds close to a safe breeding colony is important for successful breeding.)

Many seabird colonies, especially estuarine colonies on mainland sand-dunes and shingle systems, are very vulnerable to predation from ground predators such as foxes and human disturbance from beach recreation such as bathing and dog-walking. Shingle and beach-breeding waders such as oystercatchers and ringed plovers are also at risk from predation and human disturbance, particularly in areas where beach recreation is extensive such as in much of southern Britain. Many colonies are now closed to public access during the breeding season so as to minimise disturbance, and this protection has probably been instrumental in the increases in the breeding populations of some species such as Sandwich and little terns during the last few decades (e.g. Thomas 1982). There is a trend, however, for increasingly large proportions of the breeding populations of shingle-nesters to become concentrated in these fewer sites, as noted by Prater (1989) for ringed plovers in eastern and southern England.

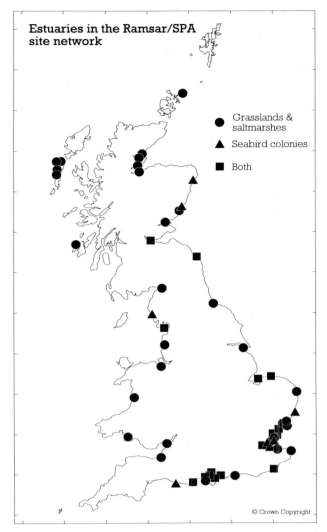

Figure 8.6.75 Estuaries with sites included in the Ramsar/SPA site network for their presence of seabird colonies and/or saltmarsh and grassland breeding bird habitat. Note that some Ramsar/SPA sites cover more than one review site.

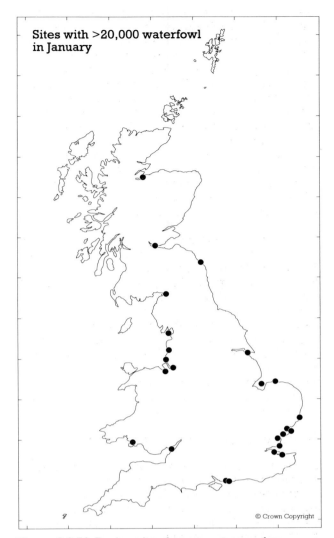

Figure 8.6.76 Review sites that support more than 20,000 waterfowl in January

There are very much higher overall breeding densities of waders (Figure 8.6.62), and of individual species such as redshanks (Figure 8.6.51), on saltmarshes than on wet grasslands. This implies that the very widespread and extensive past conversion of saltmarsh to coastal grazing marsh on estuaries, for example on the Ribble Estuary and The Wash (Doody 1987), has already resulted in major reductions in the total British breeding populations of redshanks and other waders.

The subsequent destruction of these coastal grazing marshes and lowland wet grasslands, through drainage and arablisation and agricultural intensification, is of major concern for the internationally important assemblages of breeding birds on such habitats. Change from low intensity traditional agricultural practices also reduces the suitability of wet grassland for breeding waterfowl. Reductions have been both extensive and recent.

For example, Williams *et al.* (1983) have documented a 49.5% reduction in the area of grazing marshes in north Kent (South Thames Marshes, Medway and Swale Estuaries) between 1935 and 1982. Major losses are not restricted to Britain (e.g. Beintema 1983; Nairn *et al.* 1988). Reduction and fragmentation of these habitats in Britain in the second half of this century has coincided with marked declines in grassland breeding populations of waders such as snipe and redshank (Mitchell 1983; Smith 1983). Changes to lowland grasslands and coastal grazing marshes are still occurring and there is recent evidence that the declines in lowland grassland breeding populations of redshank and snipe are continuing (Smith 1988; Holzer *et al.* 1989). Sympathetic farming and management of these habitats in Environmentally Sensitive Areas (ESAs) such as the Norfolk Broads, on SSSIs under management agreements with the NCC and on nature reserves, are, however, proving beneficial in some areas (e.g. Everett 1987; Stroud 1989; D Henshilwood in litt.).

261

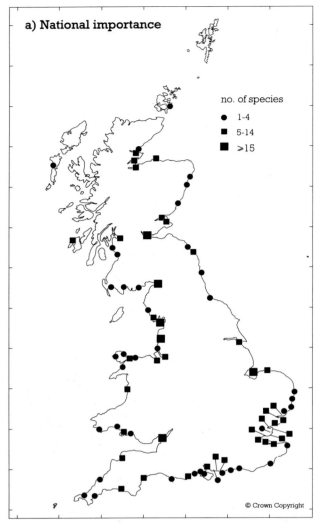

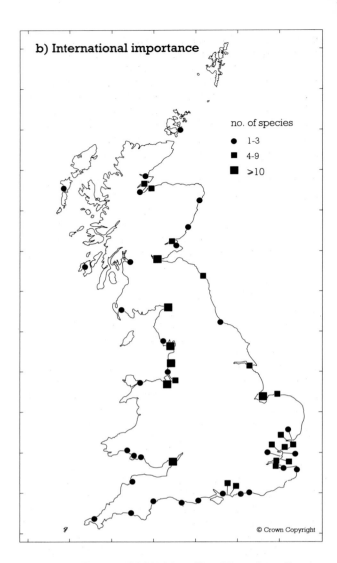

Figure 8.6.77 Numbers of individual species of a) national importance, and b) international importance, on review sites, derived from Prater (1981)

Conservation of migrant and wintering birds

The very considerable importance of Britain's estuaries for migrant and wintering birds is reflected by the fact that 68 review sites are currently included in the proposed Ramsar/SPA site network as sites containing migrant and wintering estuarine bird habitats (Stroud *et al.* 1990). Many review sites individually qualify as internationally important for several different reasons in respect of the Ramsar Convention and the EEC Wild Birds Directive. For example, 24 review sites each support in excess of 20,000 waterfowl in just January, qualifying by virtue of this alone as wetlands of international importance (Figure 8.6.76). As described above the January totals under-represent the total number of individuals using each site, so additional review sites qualify when such turnover is taken into account in conservation assessments, as for example by average peak monthly counts (e.g. Prater 1981; Salmon *et al.* 1989). Many more review sites qualify as nationally and internationally important for supporting in excess of 1% of a relevant

population: Prater (1981) identifies 82 review sites that each support nationally important populations of one or more migrant waterfowl species or subspecies (Figure 8.6.77). Fifty-four of these support internationally important populations of individual species of waterfowl (Figure 8.6.77), with many estuaries supporting nationally and internationally important numbers of 10 or more biogeographic populations.

The high mobility of individual birds and their dependence for survival during the non-breeding season on a network of different estuaries have also to be taken into account in fulfilling the international obligations to safeguard these populations. The movements of waterfowl around estuarine complexes is recognised in the setting of boundaries to Ramsar/SPA sites, some of which link several review sites where there is evidence of short-term movements between them of the bird populations which depend on them. The high proportions of some of these populations that overwinter on review sites other than those identified by the 1% criterion as individually important (Figures 8.6.47 and 8.6.48), and the known use by individuals of networks of sites during migration, moult and overwintering, mean that fulfilling international conservation obligations requires conservation measures to be applied to these wider estuarine areas, as well as to the sites supporting large populations, if the size and geographical range of populations are to be maintained, as embodied in the EEC Wild Birds Directive. This is particularly important in view of the evidence presented in Section 8.6.2 that many small estuaries may be the preferred sites for many waterfowl in winter, and that these sites provide the most favourable conditions for survival.

An example of the extent to which migrant and wintering waterfowl treat British estuaries as a single network is shown in Figure 8.6.78. This shows some of the known movements between review sites made by individual dunlins, based on reports of ringed birds and observations of colour-marked birds. This illustrates that the great majority of British estuaries are already known to be involved in the network upon which the internationally important populations of dunlins depend. It is important to note, however, that the pattern shown in this illustration represents a minimum of movements, since it is based on a selection of records and is dependent on where large numbers of birds have been caught and ringed. Thus absence of a link can represent lack of knowledge rather than lack of movement of dunlins. For example, very large numbers have been ringed on The Wash, and this is reflected in the many links between The Wash and other estuaries. Similarly, the relative paucity of links in northern and western Britain is more a reflection of the smaller numbers of birds marked there, coupled with the remoteness of the estuaries leading to fewer reports, rather than the absence of links. Even with these limitations, however, the figure demonstrates links between 93 (60%) of the 155 review sites.

The complex pattern of use and the distribution of estuarine birds means that many are vulnerable to the piecemeal loss of estuarine habitat resulting from land-claim for a wide variety of purposes (see Chapter 10). Such land-claim episodes have been widespread in the past and have resulted in very substantial reductions in the remaining available habitat on some estuaries such as The Wash (e.g. Doody 1987) and the Tees Estuary (Evans & Pienkowski 1983; Davidson & Evans 1986a). There are, however, many current activities on British estuaries that are causing further loss or severe degradation of estuarine habitats, and many further such episodes are proposed (Chapter 10). Some affect the intertidal and subtidal parts of estuaries, others the surrounding maritime and submaritime habitats. Each can affect waterfowl populations because of their complex patterns of use of the estuarine habitat mosaic. Those species that are highly concentrated onto a small number of estuaries are at high risk from habitat loss on those few sites; more widespread species are also at risk, however, because land-claim is simultaneously affecting many different estuaries. This piecemeal loss of habitat is of particular concern since it results in a continued decline in the area of remaining habitat and there is evidence that habitat loss is implicated in the recent decline of at least

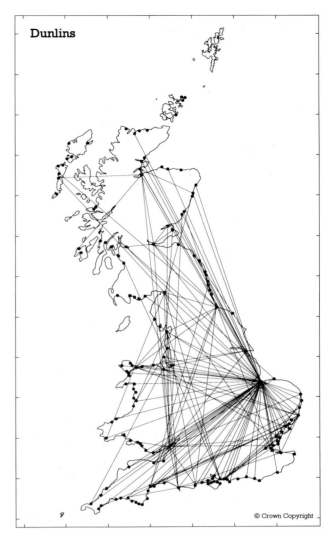

Figure 8.6.78 An example of a waterfowl site network within Britain: some of the known links between review sites for individual dunlins, from reports of ringed and colour-marked birds. Each line joins two review sites between which there is at least one reported individual movement. Information is taken largely from studies on The Wash (Cooper 1984; Branson 1989), Suffolk and Essex coasts (Davidson, Evans & Pienkowski 1986), Humber Estuary (Edwards 1988), Firth of Forth (Symonds & Langslow 1981), Moray Firth (Symonds & Langslow 1985), Severn Estuary (Clark 1983), and from reports listed in *Wader Study Group Bulletins*. Note that the pattern of known movements partly reflects the distribution of these studies.

one wader species, the dunlin, overwintering in Britain (Goss-Custard & Moser 1988).

Declines in populations of estuarine waterfowl are not restricted to Britain and Europe. Howe *et al.* (1989) report substantial declines in the migrant populations of whimbrels, short-billed dowitchers *Limnodromus griseus* and sanderlings in eastern North America, which may be a consequence of the major wetland losses that have occurred in North and South America.

The actual impact on bird populations of any particular loss of habitat is seldom in direct proportion to its area, as a consequence of the fact that more individuals use an area than are present at any one time (e.g. Evans & Pienkowski 1983; Davidson & Evans 1985). Thus even a small loss in a particularly sensitive place can have a major impact on waterfowl populations.

Loss of habitat takes on a further significance if the area is used as a cold weather refugium, or as a migration staging area. Loss of, or damage to, migration staging areas can be particularly critical since loss of these ecological bottlenecks may seriously affect the chances of waterfowl populations reaching their breeding grounds or breeding successfully (Smit & Piersma 1989).

One consequence of habitat loss is the focussing of all use of estuaries by wildlife and man into smaller areas, so increasing pressure on those remaining areas. A number of pressures can affect waterfowl using remaining areas of estuarine habitats. Human disturbance to feeding waterfowl can reduce the amount of time birds are able to feed in preferred feeding areas, so reducing their food intake. Such disturbance can be from a specific human activity such as wildfowling at night (Mudge 1989) or from a wide variety of causes during the day (e.g. Belanger & Bedard 1989). Similar effects of disturbance, affecting the distribution of waterfowl, occur also on inland waters, associated chiefly with watersports (e.g. Tuite et al. 1984). Effects of disturbance can be cumulative from different sources. For example, wildlife conservation on many estuaries has involved the establishment of wildfowl refuge areas in which wildfowling is not permitted. However, in one such refuge, at Budle Bay, Lindisfarne, disturbance from increasingly large numbers of bait-diggers has in recent years prevented birds from using the refuge area for feeding.

Human disturbance can also affect roosting birds. This can be a particular problem during severe weather when birds already face an energy deficit from high energy expenditure and low food availability. At such times disturbance causing birds to fly – an energetically very costly activity – will increase their rate of nutrient reserve loss. Disturbance to roosting birds can be severe and is implicated in the movement of waders tens of kilometres from the Dee Estuary to roost on the Alt Estuary in north-west England (Mitchell et al. 1988).

In spring waterfowl at migration staging areas need to accumulate fat and protein reserves rapidly if birds are to reach their arctic breeding grounds in time to breed and with sufficient reserves to both survive and assist in egg formation (e.g. Davidson & Evans 1988; Davidson & Morrison 1989). Disturbance that affects this reserve accumulation on spring staging areas is of particular concern. Belanger & Bedard (1990) have documented just such an instance where human disturbance caused significant energetic consequences for staging snow geese.

Pollution has a variety of impacts on estuarine waterfowl, depending on its nature and magnitude.

For example organic pollutants can cause serious eutrophication and oxygen depletion in the water at some times of year in estuaries. This enrichment, whilst causing general ecological deterioration of an estuary, can, however, increase the biomass of some macroinvertebrates that provide food for estuarine waterfowl. This may permit the numbers of birds using the area to increase (e.g. van Impe 1985), although such heavy pollution of systems can result in a reduction in the diversity of the estuarine system. Conversely reductions in organic pollutant levels can increase the range of plants and animals able to tolerate the estuarine conditions but may alter the overall species composition and size of the wintering waterfowl assemblages using the area (e.g. Campbell 1978, 1984; Furness et al. 1986).

Heavy metal pollution often accompanies organic enrichment in polluted estuaries. Heavy metals are known to accumulate in substantial concentrations in waterfowl on polluted estuaries in Britain (NERC 1983; Evans et al. 1987), but their effects appear to be generally chronic rather than rapidly fatal. One instance of high mortality attributed to heavy metal pollution was caused by poisoning by alkyl lead compounds in the Mersey Estuary (Bull et al. 1983). Waterfowl can also ingest fatally high levels of lead in the form of spent lead pellets from wildfowling (Mudge 1983).

Oil pollution generally causes fewer problems for estuarine birds than for seabirds in inshore waters, but oil spills within the confines of an estuary can be very serious, particularly outside the waterfowl breeding season. At such times oiling of many wildfowl and waders can occur, as in the Medway Estuary in the 1970s and the Firth of Forth in 1978 (Campbell et al. 1978). More recent incidents in the Mersey Estuary and the Humber Estuary have, largely by chance, avoided serious direct impacts on waterfowl.

The continued maintenance of the nationally and internationally important bird populations of estuaries thus depends on ensuring the effective conservation of all the remaining areas of estuarine habitat and at least the maintenance of the quality of these areas as waterfowl feeding, roosting, migration staging, moulting and breeding grounds.

8.6.6 References

ALERSTAM, T., HJORT, C., HOGSTEDT, G., JONSSON, P.E., KARLSSON, J., & LARSSON, B. 1986. Spring migration of birds across the Greenland inland ice. Meddelelser om Gronland, Bioscience, 21, 1-38.

ALLPORT, G., O'BRIEN, M., & CADBURY, C.J. 1986. Survey of Redshank and other breeding birds on saltmarshes in Britain 1985. Nature Conservancy Council, CSD Report, No. 649.

ANKNEY, C.D. 1979. Does the wing molt cause nutritional stress in Lesser Snow Geese? Auk, 96, 68-72.

ANKNEY, C.D. 1984. Nutrient reserve dynamics of breeding and molting Brant. *Auk, 101*, 361-370.

ANKNEY, C.D., & MACINNES, C.D. 1978. Nutrient reserves and reproductive performance of female Lesser Snow Geese. *Auk, 95*, 459-471.

ATKINSON-WILLES, G.L., SCOTT, D.A., & PRATER, A.J. 1982. Criteria for selecting wetlands of international importance. *In: Proceedings of the conference on the conservation of wetlands of international importance especially as waterfowl habitat. Cagliari, Italy, 24-29 November 1980*, 1017-1042. Supplemento alla Ricerche de Biologia della Selvaggina, 81.

BAILLIE, S.M., CLARK, N.A., & OGILVIE, M.A. 1986. Cold weather movements of waterfowl and waders: an analysis of ringing recoveries. *Nature Conservancy Council, CSD Report*, No. 650.

BAKER, A.J., & STRAUCH, J.G. Jr. 1988. Genetic variation and differentiation in shorebirds. *Proceedings of the XIX International Ornithological Congress, Ottawa, 1986*, 1639-1645.

BAKER, A.J. 1991. Molecular perspectives on population differentiation and speciation in calidridine sandpipers, with special reference to Knots. *In: Recent advances in understanding Knot migrations*, ed. by T. Piersma & N.C. Davidson. *Wader Study Group Bulletin, Supplement.*

BAINBRIDGE, I.P., & MINTON, C.D.T. 1978. Migration and mortality of Curlew in Britain and Ireland. *Bird Study, 25*, 39-50.

BAINES, D. 1989. The effects of improvement of upland, marginal grasslands on the breeding success of Lapwings *Vanellus vanellus* and other waders. *Ibis, 131*, 497-506.

BARTOVSKY, V., KLETECKI, E., RADOVIC, D., STRIPCEVIC, M., & SUSIC, G. 1987. Breeding waders in Yugoslavia. *Wader Study Group Bulletin, 51*, 33-37.

BARRETT, J., & BARRETT, C.F. 1985. Divers in the Moray Firth, Scotland. *Scottish Birds, 13*, 149-154.

BATTEN, L., BIBBY, C.J., CLEMENT, P., ELLIOTT,G., & PORTER, R.F., eds. In press. *Red Data Birds in Britain*. Nature Conservancy Council/Royal Society for the Protection of Birds. London, T. & A.D. Poyser.

BEINTEMA, A. 1983. Wet meadows in temperate Europe, threatened by agriculture. *In: Shorebirds and large waterbirds conservation*, ed. by P.R.Evans, H. Hafner and P. L'Hermite, 26-33. Brussels, Commission of the European Community.

BELANGER, L., & BEDARD, J. 1989. Responses of staging Greater Snow Geese to human disturbance. *Journal of Wildlife Management, 53*, 713-719.

BELANGER, L., & BEDARD, J. 1990. Energetic cost of man-induced disturbance to staging snow geese. *Journal of Wildlife Management, 54*, 36-41.

BIBBY, C.J. 1986. Merlin. *In: The atlas of wintering birds in Britain and Ireland*, compiled by P. Lack, 150-151. Calton, T. & A.D. Poyser.

BOERE, G.C. 1976. The significance of the Dutch Waddenzee in the annual life cycle of arctic, subarctic and boreal waders. Part 1. The function as a moulting area. *Ardea, 64*, 210-291.

BOYD, H. 1987. Do June temperatures affect the breeding success of dark-bellied Brent Geese *Branta b. bernicla*? *Bird Study, 34*, 155-159.

BOYD, H. 1991. British Knot numbers and arctic summer conditions. *In: Recent advances in understanding Knot migrations*, ed. by T. Piersma & N.C. Davidson. *Wader Study Group Bulletin, Supplement.*

BRANSON, N.J.B.A., & MINTON, C.D.T. 1976. Moult, measurements and migrations of the Grey Plover. *Bird Study, 23*, 257-266.

BULL, K.R., EVERY, W.J., FREESTONE, P., HALL, J.R., OSBORNE, D., COOKE, A.S. & STOWE, T. 1983. Alkyl lead pollution and bird mortalities on the Mersey Estuary, UK, 1979-1981. *Environmental Pollution, Series A, 31*, 239-259.

BURGER, J., & OLLA, B.L., eds. 1984. *Behavior of marine animals. Volume 6, Shorebirds*. New York, Plenum Press.

CADBURY, C.J., GREEN, R.E., & ALLPORT, G. 1987. Redshanks and other breeding waders of British saltmarshes. *RSPB Conservation Review, 1*, 37-40.

CADBURY, C.J., HILL, D., PARTRIDGE, J., & SORENSEN, J. 1989. The history of the Avocet population and its management in England since recolonisation. *RSPB Conservation Review, 3*, 9-13.

CAMPBELL, L.H. 1978. Patterns of distribution and behaviour of flocks of seaducks wintering at Leith and Musselburgh, Scotland. *Biological Conservation, 14*, 111-123.

CAMPBELL, L.H. 1984. The impact of changes in sewage treatment on seaducks wintering in the Firth of Forth, Scotland. *Biological Conservation, 28*, 173-180.

CAMPBELL, L.H., STANDRING, K.Y., & CADBURY, C.J. 1978. Firth of Forth Oil Pollution Incident, February 1978. *Marine Pollution Bulletin, 9, 335-339.*

CAMPBELL, L.H., CHRISTER, W.G., STENNING, J.M., DAVEY, P.R., & MEEK, E.H. 1988. Wetland and marginal moorland in Orkney. *Nature Conservancy Council, CSD Report*, No. 891.

CHANDLER, R.J. 1986a. Red-necked Grebe. *In: The atlas of wintering birds in Britain and Ireland*, compiled by P. Lack, 44-45. Calton, T. & A.D. Poyser.

CHANDLER, R.J. 1986b. Slavonian Grebe. *In: The atlas of wintering birds in Britain and Ireland*, compiled by P. Lack, 46-47. Calton, T. & A.D. Poyser.

CLAPHAM, C. 1978. The Ringed Plover populations of Morecambe Bay. *Bird Study, 25,* 175-180.

CLARK, N.A. 1983. *The ecology of Dunlin (Calidris alpina L.) wintering on the Severn Estuary.* Ph.D. Thesis, University of Edinburgh.

CLARK, N.A., & DAVIDSON, N.C. 1986. WSG project on the effects of severe weather on waders: sixth progress report. *Wader Study Group Bulletin, 46,* 7-8.

CLARKE, N.A., TURNER, B.S., & YOUNG, J.F. 1982. Spring passage of sanderlings *Calidris alba* in the Solway Firth. *Wader Study Group Bulletin, 36,* 10-11.

CLARKE, R.G. 1986. Hen Harrier. *In: The atlas of wintering birds in Britain and Ireland,* compiled by P. Lack, 136-137. Calton, T. & A.D. Poyser.

COTTIER, E.J., & LEA, D. 1969. Black-tailed Godwits, Ruffs and Black Terns breeding on the Ouse Washes. *British Birds, 62,* 259-270.

COOPER, R. 1984. Summary of results of Wash-wader dye-marking in winters 1980/81, 1981/82, 1982/83. *Wash Wader Ringing Group Report 1981-82,* 12-17.

COULSON,J.G., & THOMAS, C. 1985. Differences in the breeding performance of kittiwake gulls. *In: Behavioural ecology. Ecological consequences of adaptive behaviour,* ed. by R.M. Sibly and R.H. Smith, 489-503. Oxford, Blackwell. (Symposium of British Ecological Society.)

CRONAU, J.P. 1988. Migration and turnover rates of dunlin and little stint in the Cukurova Deltas. *In: South Turkey Project. A survey of waders and waterfowl in the Cukurova deltas, spring 1987,* ed. by T.M. van der Have, V.M. van den Berk, J.P. Cronau and M.J. Langeveld. WIWO Report No. 22. Zeist, The Netherlands, WIWO.

CURTIS, D.J., & THOMPSON, D.B.A. 1985. Spacing and foraging of Black-headed Gulls *Larus ridibundus* in an estuary. *Ornis Scandinavica, 16,* 145-252.

CRAMP, S., & SIMMONS, K.E.L., eds. 1983. *The birds of the western palearctic, Volume 3.* Oxford, Oxford University Press.

DAVIDSON, N.C. 1981. Survival of shorebirds during severe weather: the role of nutritional reserves. *In: Feeding and survival strategies of estuarine organisms,* ed. by N.V. Jones and W.J. Wolff, 231-249. New York, Plenum Press.

DAVIDSON, N.C. 1982a. The effects of severe weather in 1978/79 and 1981/82 on shorebirds at Teesmouth: a preliminary view. *Wader Study Group Bulletin, 34,* 8-10.

DAVIDSON, N.C. 1982b. Increases in wader mortality at Teesmouth detected from ringing recoveries. *Wader Study Group Bulletin, 36,* 9.

DAVIDSON, N.C. 1982c. Changes in the body condition of Redshanks during mild winters: an inability to regulate reserves? *Ringing & Migration, 4,* 51-63.

DAVIDSON, N.C. 1984. How valid are flight range estimates for waders? *Ringing & Migration, 5,* 49-64.

DAVIDSON, N.C., & CLARK, N.A. 1985. The effects of severe weather in January and February 1985 on waders in Britain. *Wader Study Group Bulletin, 44,* 10-16.

DAVIDSON, N.C., & EVANS, P.R. 1982. Mortality of redshanks and oystercatchers from starvation during severe weather. *Bird Study, 29,* 183-188.

DAVIDSON, N.C., & EVANS, P.R. 1985. Implications for nature conservation of the proposed Felixstowe Dock expansion. Report to Nature Conservancy Council (unpublished).

DAVIDSON, N.C., & EVANS, P.R. 1986a. The role and potential of man-made and man-modified wetlands in the enhancement of the survival of overwintering shorebirds. *Colonial Waterbirds, 9,* 176-188.

DAVIDSON, N.C., & EVANS, P.R., eds. 1986b. *The ecology of migrant knots in North Norway during May 1985.* Report SRG86/1. University of Durham, Department of Zoology (unpublished).

DAVIDSON, N.C., EVANS, P.R., & UTTLEY, J.D. 1986a. Geographical variation of protein reserves in birds: the pectoral muscle mass of Dunlins *Calidris alpina* in winter. *Journal of Zoology, London, 208,* 125-133.

DAVIDSON, N.C., EVANS, P.R., & PIENKOWSKI, M.W. 1986b. Origins and destinations of waders using the coasts of Suffolk and Essex. *Ringing & Migration, 7,* 37-49.

DAVIDSON, N.C., STRANN, K.-B., CROCKFORD, N.J., EVANS, P.R., RICHARDSON, J., STANDEN, L.J., TOWNSHEND, D.J., UTTLEY, J.D., WILSON, J.R., & WOOD, A.G. 1986c. The origins of Knots *Calidris canutus* in arctic Norway in spring. *Ornis Scandinavica, 17,* 175-179.

DAVIDSON, N.C., & PIERSMA, T. 1986. International wader migration studies along the East Atlantic Flyway: preliminary results from spring 1986. *Wader Study Group Bulletin, 47,* 2-3.

DAVIDSON, N.C., & EVANS, P.R. 1989. Pre-breeding accumulation of fat and muscle protein by arctic-breeding shorebirds. *Proceedings of the XIX International Ornithological Congress,* 342-352.

DAVIDSON, N.C., & MORRISON, R.I.G. 1989. *Pre-breeding shorebirds at Alert, Ellesmere Island, Canada, 1986-88.* Canadian Wildlife Service/Nature Conservancy Council Report 1989/1.

DAVIDSON, N.C., & WILSON, J.R. 1991. The migration system of the nearctic Knot *Calidris canutus islandica. In: Recent advances in understanding knot migrations,* ed. by T. Piersma and N.C. Davidson. *Wader Study Group Bulletin, Supplement.*

DAVIES, M. 1987. Twite and other wintering passerines on the Wash saltmarshes. *In: The Wash and its environment*, ed. by P. Doody and B. Barnett, 123-132. Peterborough, Nature Conservancy Council. (Research & survey in nature conservation No. 7.)

DAVIES, M. 1988. The importance of Britain's Twites. *RSPB Conservation Review, 2*, 91-94.

DAY, J. 1988. Marsh Harriers in Britain. *RSPB Conservation Review, 2*, 20-21.

DE BOER, W.F., & DRENT, R.H. 1989. A matter of eating or being eaten? The breeding performance of arctic geese and its implications for waders. *Wader Study Group Bulletin, 55*, 11-17.

DENNIS, R.H. 1964. Capture of moulting Canada Geese on the Beauly Firth. *Wildfowl Trust Annual Report, 15*, 71-74.

DHONDT, A. 1987. Cycles of lemmings and Brent Geese *Branta b. bernicla*: a comment on the hypothesis of Roselaar and Summers. *Bird Study, 34*, 151-154.

DICK, W.J.A. 1979. Results of the WSG project on the spring migration of Siberian Knot *Calidris canutus* 1979. *Wader Study Group Bulletin, 27*, 8-13.

DICK, W.J.A., PIERSMA, T., & PROKOSCH, P. 1987. Spring migration of the Siberian Knot *Calidris canutus canutus*: results of a co-operative Wader Study Group project. *Ornis Scandinavica, 64*, 22-47.

DOBINSON, H.M., & RICHARDS, A.J. 1964. The effects of the severe weather of 1962/63 on birds in Britain. *British Birds, 57*, 373-434.

DOMINGUEZ, J., BARCENA, F., SOUZA, J.A., & VILLARINO, A. 1987. Breeding waders in Galicia, north-west Spain. *Wader Study Group Bulletin*, 50, 28-29.

DOODY, P. 1987. The impact of 'reclamation' on the natural environment of the Wash. *In: The Wash and its environment*, ed. by P. Doody and J. Barnett, 165-172. Peterborough, Nature Conservancy Council. (Research & survey in nature conservation No. 7)

DUGAN, P.J. 1981. *Seasonal movements of shorebirds in relation to spacing behaviour and prey availability*. Ph.D. Thesis, University of Durham.

DUGAN, P.J., EVANS, P.R., GOODYER, L.R., & DAVIDSON, N.C. 1981. Winter fat reserves in shorebirds: disturbance of regulated levels by severe weather conditions. *Ibis, 123*, 359-363.

DUNNET, G.M. 1986. Cormorant. *In: The atlas of wintering birds in Britain and Ireland*, compiled by P. Lack, 54-55. Calton, T. & A.D. Poyser.

EASTERBEE, N., STROUD, D.A., BIGNALL, E.M., & DICK, T.D. 1987. The arrival of Greenland Barnacle Geese at Loch Gruinart, Islay. *Scottish Birds, 14*, 175-179.

EBBINGE, B.S. 1985. Factors determining the population size of arctic-breeding geese wintering in western Europe. *Ardea, 73*, 123-128.

EBBINGE, B.S. 1987. In hoeverre bepalen lemmingen het broedresultaat van Rotganzen *Branta bernicla*? *Limosa, 60*, 147-149.

EBBINGE, B.S. 1989. A multifactorial explanation for variation in breeding performance of Brent Geese. *Ibis, 131*, 196-204.

EBBINGE, B.S., ST. JOSEPH, A., PROKOSCH, P., & SPAANS, B. 1982. The importance of spring staging areas for arctic-breeding geese, wintering in western Europe. *Aquila, 89*, 249-258.

ELLIOT, G. 1988. Montagu's Harrier conservation. *RSPB Conservation Review, 2*, 20-21.

ENS, B.J., PIERSMA, T., WOLFF, W.J., & ZWARTS, L., eds. 1989. Report of the Dutch-Mauritanian project Banc d'Arguin 1985-1986. *WIWO Report 25/RIN Report 89/6.* Ewijk, The Netherlands, WIWO.

EVANS, M.E. 1979a. Population composition, and return according to breeding status, of Bewick's Swans wintering at Slimbridge, 1963 to 1976. *Wildfowl, 30*, 118-128.

EVANS, P.R. 1979b. Adaptations shown by foraging shorebirds to cyclical variations in the activity and availability of their invertebrate prey. *In: Cyclic phenomena in marine plants and animals*, ed. by E.J. Naylor and R.G. Hartnoll, 357-366. New York, Pergamon Press.

EVANS, P.R., BREAREY, D.M., & GOODYER, L.R. 1980. Studies on Sanderling at Teesmouth, NE England. *Wader Study Group Bulletin, 30*, 18-20.

EVANS, P.R., DAVIDSON, P.R., PIERSMA, T., & PIENKOWSKI, M.W. In press. Effects of habitat loss at migration staging posts on shorebird populations. *Proceedings of the XX International Ornithological Congress.*

EVANS, P.R., & PIENKOWSKI, M.W. 1982. Behaviour of shelducks *Tadorna tadorna* in a winter flock: does regulation occur? *Journal of Animal Ecology, 51*, 242-262.

EVANS, P.R., & PIENKOWSKI, M.W. 1983. Implications for coastal engineering projects of studies, at the Tees estuary, on the effects of reclamation of intertidal land on shorebird populations. *Water, Science and Technology, 16*, 347-354.

EVANS, P.R., & PIENKOWSKI, M.W. 1984. Population dynamics of shorebirds. *In: Shorebirds: breeding behavior and populations*, ed. by J. Burger and B.L. Olla, 83-123. New York, Plenum Press.

EVANS, P.R., & TOWNSHEND, D.J. 1989. Site fidelity of waders during migration. *Proceedings of the XIX International Ornithological Congress.*

EVANS, P.R., UTTLEY, J.D., DAVIDSON, N.C., & WARD, P. 1987. Shorebirds (S.Os Charadrii and Scolopaci) as agents of transfer of heavy metals within and between estuarine ecosystems. *In: Pollutant transport and fate in ecosystems,* ed. by P.J. Coughtrey, M.H. Martin and M.H. Unsworth, 337-352. Oxford, Blackwell. (British Ecological Society Special Publication No. 6.)

EVERETT, M.J. 1987. The Elmley experiment. *RSPB Conservation Review, 1,* 31-33.

EVERETT, M.J. 1989. Reedbeds – a scarce resource. *RSPB Conservation Review, 3,* 14-19.

FERNS, P.N., GREEN, G.H., & ROUND, P.D. 1979. Significance of the Somerset and Gwent Levels in Britain as feeding areas for migrant whimbrels *Numenius phaeopus. Biological Conservation, 16,* 7-22.

FERNS, P.N. 1980a. The spring migration of Ringed Plovers through Britain in 1979. *Wader Study Group Bulletin, 29,* 10-13.

FERNS, P.N. 1980b. The spring migration of Sanderlings *Calidris alba* through Britain in 1979. *Wader Study Group Bulletin, 30,* 22-25.

FERNS, P.N. 1981a. The spring migration of Turnstones through Britain in 1979. *Wader Study Group Bulletin, 31,* 36-40.

FERNS, P.N. 1981b. The spring migration of Dunlins through Britain in 1979. *Wader Study Group Bulletin, 32,* 14-19.

FERNS, P.N. 1981c. Final comments on the spring migration of waders through Britain in 1979. *Wader Study Group Bulletin, 33,* 6-10.

FOX, A.D., & SALMON, D.G. 1988. Changes in non-breeding distribution and habitat of Pochard *Aythya ferina* in Britain. *Biological Conservation, 46,* 303-316.

FULLER, R.J. 1982. *Bird habitats in Britain.* Calton, T. & A.D. Poyser.

FULLER, R.J., & LANGSLOW, D.R. 1986. Ornithological evaluation for wildlife conservation. *In: Wildlife conservation evaluation,* ed. by M.B. Usher, 248-269. London, Chapman & Hall.

FULLER, R.J., REED, T.M., WEBB, A., WILLIAMS, T.D., & PIENKOWSKI, M.W. 1986. Populations of breeding waders *Charadrii* and their habitats on the crofting lands of the Outer Hebrides, Scotland. *Biological Conservation, 37,* 333-361.

FURNESS, R.W. 1973. Roost selection by waders. *Scottish Birds, 7,* 281-287.

FURNESS, R.W., GALBRAITH, H., GIBSON, I.P., & METCALFE, N.B. 1986. Recent changes in numbers of waders on the Clyde Estuary, and their significance for conservation. *Proceedings of the Royal Society of Edinburgh, 90B,* 171-184.

GALBRAITH, H., FURNESS, R.W., & FULLER, R.J. 1984. Habitats and distribution of waders breeding on Scottish agricultural land. *Scottish Birds, 13,* 98-107.

GAUTHIER, G., BEDARD, J., HUOT, J., & BEDARD, Y. 1984. Spring accumulation of fat by greater snow geese in two staging areas. *Condor, 86,* 192-199.

GLUE, D.E. 1986. Short-eared Owl. *In: The atlas of wintering birds in Britain and Ireland,* compiled by P. Lack, 278-279. Calton, T. & A.D. Poyser.

GOODYER, L.R., & EVANS, P.R. 1980. Movements of shorebirds into and through the Tees estuary, as revealed by ringing. *County of Cleveland Bird Report 1979,* 45-52.

GOSS-CUSTARD, J.D., KAY, D.G., & BLUNDELL, R.M. 1977. The density of migratory and overwintering redshanks *Tringa totanus* (L.) and curlew *Numenius arquata* (L.) in relation to the density of their prey in south-east England. *Estuarine, Coastal and Marine Science, 5,* 497-510.

GOSS-CUSTARD, J.D., & MOSER, M.E. 1988. Rates of change in the numbers of dunlin, *Calidris alpina,* wintering in British estuaries in relation to the spread of *Spartina anglica. Journal of Applied Ecology, 25,* 95-109.

GREEN, G.H., GREENWOOD, J.J.D., & LLOYD, C.S. 1977. The influence of snow conditions on the date of breeding of wading birds in north-east Greenland. *Journal of Zoology, London, 183,* 311-328.

GREEN, R.E. 1986. Skylark. *In: The atlas of wintering birds in Britain and Ireland,* compiled by P. Lack, 290-291. Calton, T. & A.D. Poyser.

GREEN, R.E. 1987. Breeding birds of the Wash saltmarshes. *In: The Wash and its Environment,* ed. by P. Doody and B. Barnett, 133-137. Peterborough, Nature Conservancy Council. (Research & survey in nature conservation No. 7.)

GREENHALGH, M.E., 1969. The populations of Redshank and Dunlin on saltmarshes in northwest England. *Bird Study, 16,* 63-64.

GREENHALGH, M.E., 1971. The breeding bird communities of Lancashire saltmarshes. *Bird Study, 18,* 199-212.

GREENHALGH, M.E. 1975. The breeding birds of the Ribble Estuary salt-marshes. *Nature in Lancashire, 5,* 11-19.

GRIBBLE, F.C. 1976. A census of Black-headed Gull colonies. *Bird Study, 23,* 135-145.

HANSON, H.C. 1962. The dynamics of condition factors in Canada Geese and their relation to seasonal stress. *Arctic Institute of North America Technical Papers, 12,* 1-68.

HEUBECK, M., ed. 1989. *Seabirds and sandeels: proceedings of a seminar held in Lerwick, Shetland, 15-16th October 1988.* Lerwick, Shetland Bird Club .

HOLZER, T.J., BEARDALL, C.H., & DRYDEN, R.C. 1989. Breeding waders and other waterfowl on Suffolk estuaries in 1988. *Wader Study Group Bulletin, 56,* 3-6.

HROMADKOVA, V. 1987. The distribution of breeding waders in Czechoslovakia in 1973-1977. *Wader Study Group Bulletin, 50,* 24-27.

HOWE, M.A., GEISSLER, P.H., & HARRINGTON, B.A. 1989. Population trends of North American shorebirds based on the International Shorebird Survey. *Biological Conservation, 49,* 185-199.

HUME, R.A. 1986a. Iceland Gull. *In: The atlas of wintering birds in Britain and Ireland,* compiled by P. Lack, 242-243. Calton, T. & A.D. Poyser.

HUME, R.A. 1986b. Glaucous Gull. *In: The atlas of wintering birds in Britain and Ireland,* compiled by P. Lack, 244-245. Calton, T. & A.D. Poyser.

HUTCHINSON, C.D. 1986. Little Gull. *In: The atlas of wintering birds in Britain and Ireland,* compiled by P. Lack, 230-231. Calton, T. & A.D. Poyser.

INSLEY, H., & YOUNG, L. 1981. Autumn passage of Ringed Plovers through Southampton Water. *Ringing & Migration, 3,* 157-164.

JONSSON, P.E. 1986. The migration and wintering of Baltic Dunlins *Calidris alpina schinzii. Var Fagelvarld Supplement, 11,* 71-78.

KERSTEN, M., PIERSMA, T., SMIT, C., & ZEGERS, P. 1983. Wader migration along the Atlantic coast of Morocco, March 1981. *RIN Report 83/20.* Texel, Research Institute for Nature Management.

KERSTEN, M., & SMIT, C.J. 1984. The Atlantic coast of Morocco. *In: Coastal waders and wildfowl in winter,* ed. by P.R. Evans, J.D. Goss-Custard and W.G. Hale, 276-292. Cambridge, Cambridge University Press.

KIRBY, J.S., CROSS, S., TAYLOR, J.E., & WOLFENDEN, I.H. 1988. The distribution and abundance of waders wintering on the Alt Estuary, Merseyside, England. *Wader Study Group Bulletin, 54,* 23-28.

LACK, P. 1986. *The atlas of wintering birds in Britain and Ireland.* Calton, T. & A.D. Poyser.

LAMBERT, R. 1986a. Snow Bunting. *In: The atlas of wintering birds in Britain and Ireland,* compiled by P. Lack, 410-411. Calton, T. & A.D. Poyser.

LAMBERT, R. 1986b. Shorelark. *In: The atlas of wintering birds in Britain and Ireland,* compiled by P. Lack, 292-293. Calton, T. & A.D. Poyser.

LAMBERT, R. 1986c. Lapland Bunting. *In: The atlas of wintering birds in Britain and Ireland,* compiled by P. Lack, 408-409. Calton, T. & A.D. Poyser.

LAMBERT, R. 1986d. Twite. *In: The atlas of wintering birds in Britain and Ireland,* compiled by P. Lack, 396-397. Calton, T. & A.D. Poyser.

LLOYD, C.S., TASKER, M.L., & PARTRIDGE, K.E. In press. *Status of seabirds in Britain and Ireland.* Calton, T. & A.D. Poyser.

MADSEN, J. 1984. Status of the Svalbard population of Light-bellied Brent Geese *Branta bernicla hrota* wintering in Denmark 1980-1983. *Polarinstitut Skrifter, 181,* 119-124.

MADSEN, J. 1985. Relations between change in spring habitat selection and daily energy energetics of Pink-footed Geese *Anser brachyrhynchus. Ornis Scandinavica, 16,* 222-228.

MADSEN, J. 1987. Status and management of goose populations in Europe, with special reference to populations resting and breeding in Denmark. *Danish Review of Game Biology, 12* (4), 1-76.

MADSEN, J., BREGNEBALLE, T., & MEHLUM,F. 1989. Study of the breeding ecology and behaviour of the Svalbard population of light-bellied brent goose *Branta bernicla hrota. Polar Research, 7,* 1-21.

MAINGUY, S.K., & THOMAS, V.G. 1985. Comparison of body reserve buildup and use in several groups of Canada Geese. *Canadian Journal of Zoology, 63,* 1765-1772.

MASMAN, D., DIETZ, M., & DAAN, S. 1986. Partitioning of energy for moult in the Kestrel *Falco tinnunculus. In: The annual cycle of the Kestrel* Falco tinnunculus, ed. by D. Masman, 141-184. Ph.D. Thesis, University of Groningen, The Netherlands.

MASMAN, D., & KLAASSEN, M. 1987. Energy expenditure during free flight in trained and free-living Eurasian Kestrels (*Falco tinnunculus*). *Auk, 104,* 603-616.

MAYR, E. 1970. *Populations, species and evolution.* Harvard, Harvard University Press.

MELTOFTE, H. 1985. Population and breeding schedules of waders, Charadrii, in high arctic Greenland. *Meddelelser om Gronland, Bioscience, 16,* 1-43.

MINTON, C.D.T. 1975. The waders of the Wash – ringing and biometric studies. Report of Scientific Study G, Wash Water Storage Feasibility Study.

MITCHELL, J.R., MOSER, M.E., & KIRBY, J.S. 1988. Declines in midwinter counts of waders roosting on the Dee estuary. *Bird Study, 35,* 191-198.

MITCHELL, O. 1983. The breeding status and distribution of Snipe, Redshank and Yellow Wagtail in Sussex. *Sussex Bird Report, 34* (1981), 65-71.

MONAGHAN, P., UTTLEY, J.D., BURNS, M.D., THAINE, C., & BLACKWOOD, J. 1989. The relationship between food supply, reproductive effort and breeding success in arctic terns *Sterna paradisaea. Journal of Animal Ecology, 58,* 261-274.

MORRISON, R.I.G. 1975. Migration and morphometrics of European Knot and Turnstone on Ellesmere Island, Canada. *Bird-Banding, 46,* 290-301.

MORRISON, R.I.G., & WILSON, J.R. 1972. Cambridge Iceland Expedition 1971 Report. Cambridge, University of Cambridge.

MORRISON, R.I.G., & ROSS, K.L. 1989. *Atlas of nearctic shorebirds on the coast of South America.* Ottawa, Canadian Wildlife Service.

MORRISON, R.I.G., & DAVIDSON, N.C. 1990. Migration, body condition and behaviour of shorebirds during spring migration at Alert, Ellesmere Island, N.W.T. *In: Canada's missing dimension. Science and history in the Canadian arctic islands*, ed. by C.R. Harington, 544-567. Ottawa, Canadian Museum of Nature.

MOSER, M.E. 1987. A revision of population estimates for waders (Charadrii) wintering on the coastline of Britain. *Biological Conservation, 39,* 153-164.

MOSER, M.E. 1988. Limits to the numbers of grey plovers *Pluvialis squatarola* wintering on British estuaries: an analysis of long-term population trends. *Journal of Applied Ecology, 25,* 473-485.

MOSER, M.E., BROAD, R.A., DENNIS, R.H., & MADDERS, M. 1986. The distribution and abundance of some coastal birds on the west and north-west coasts of Scotland in winter. *Scottish Birds, 14,* 61-67.

MOSER, M.E., & CARRIER, M. 1983. Patterns of population turnover in Ringed Plovers and Turnstones during their spring passage through the Solway Firth in 1983. *Wader Study Group Bulletin, 39,* 37-41.

MOSER, M.E., FERNS, P., & BAILLIE, S. 1985. BTO/WSG west coast spring passage project: a progress report. *Wader Study Group Bulletin, 43,* 9-13.

MOSER, M.E., & SUMMERS, R.W. 1987. Wader populations on the non-estuarine coasts of Britain and Northern Ireland: results of the 1984-85 Winter Shorebird Count. *Bird Study, 34,* 71-81.

MUDGE, G.P. 1983. The incidence and significance of ingested lead pellet poisoning in British wildfowl. *Biological Conservation, 27,* 333-372.

MUDGE, G.P. 1989. Night shooting of wildfowl in Great Britain: an assessment of its prevalence, intensity and disturbance impact. *Nature Conservancy Council, CSD Report,* No. 987.

MUDGE, G.P., & ALLEN, D.S. 1980. Wintering seaducks in the Moray and Dornoch Firths. *Wildfowl, 31,* 123-130.

MURFITT, R.C., & WEAVER, D.J. 1983. Survey of the breeding waders of wet meadows in Norfolk. *Norfolk Bird and Mammal Report, 26,* 196-201.

MURPHY, A.J., & BOAG, D.A. 1989. Body reserves and food use by incubating Canada Geese. *Auk, 106,* 439-446.

MYERS, J.P., SCHICK, C.T., & CASTRO, G. 1988. Structure in Sanderling (*Calidris alba*) populations: the magnitude of intra- and interyear dispersal during the non-breeding season. *Proceedings of the XIX International Ornithological Congress, Ottawa, 1986,* 604-615.

NAIRN, R.G.W., HERBERT, I.J., & HEERY, S. 1988. Breeding waders and other wet grassland birds of the River Shannon Callows, Ireland. *Irish Birds, 3,* 521-537.

NANKINOV, D. 1989. The status of waders in Bulgaria. *Wader Study Group Bulletin, 56,* 16-25.

NATURE CONSERVANCY COUNCIL. 1989. *Guidelines for the selection of biological SSSIs.* Peterborough.

NATURAL ENVIRONMENT RESEARCH COUNCIL. 1983. *Contaminants in top predators.* Swindon.

OAG MÜNSTER. 1987. The timing of autumn migration of some wader species in inland Europe: provisional results. *Wader Study Group Bulletin, 50, 7-16.*

O'BRIAIN, M., & HEALY, B. 1990. The pattern of winter distribution of light-bellied brent geese (*Branta bernicla hrota*) in Ireland. *Ardea,* in press.

OWEN, M. 1982. Population dynamics of Svalbard Barnacles 1970-1980. The rate, pattern and causes of mortality as determined by individual marking studies. *Aquila, 89,* 229-247.

OWEN, M. 1984. Dynamics and age structure of an increasing goose population, the Svalbard Barnacle Goose. *Norsk Polarinstitutt Skrifter, 181,* 37-47.

OWEN, M., & GULLESTAD, N. 1984. Migration routes of Svalbard Barnacle Geese *Branta leucopsis* with a preliminary report on the importance of the Bjornoya staging area. *Norsk Polarinstitut Skrifter, 181,* 67-77.

OWEN, M., ATKINSON-WILLES, G.L., & SALMON, D.G. 1986. *Wildfowl in Great Britain.* 2nd ed. Cambridge, Cambridge University Press.

OWEN, M., & BLACK, J.M. 1989. Factors affecting the survival of barnacle geese on migration from the breeding grounds. *Journal of Animal Ecology, 58,* 603-618.

PARISH, D., LANE, B., SAGAR, P., & TOMKOVICH, P. 1987. Wader migration systems in East Asia and Australasia. *Wader Study Group Bulletin, 49, Supplement. (IWRB Special Publication 7,* 4-14.)

PARISH, D. 1989. Population estimates of water birds using the east Asian/Australasian flyway. *In: Flyways and reserve networks for water birds,* ed. by H. Boyd and J.-Y. Pirot, 8-13. Slimbridge, IWRB. (IWRB Special Publication No. 9.)

PATTERSON, I.J. 1982. *The Shelduck.* Cambridge, Cambridge University Press.

PAYNE, R.B. 1972. Mechanisms and control of moult. *In: Avian biology, Volume 2,* ed. by D.S. Farner and J.R. King, 103-155. New York, Academic Press.

PIENKOWSKI, M.W., 1980. *Aspects of the ecology and behaviour of Ringed and Grey Plovers Charadrius hiaticula and Pluvialis squatarola.* Ph.D. Thesis, University of Durham.

PIENKOWSKI, M.W. 1983a. Surface activity of some intertidal invertebrates in relation to temperature and the foraging behaviour of their shorebird predators. *Marine Ecology Progress Series, 11,* 141-150.

PIENKOWSKI, M.W. 1983b. Identification of relative importance of sites by studies of movement and population turn-over. *In: Shorebirds and large waterbirds conservation,* ed. by P.R. Evans, H. Hafner and P. L'Hermite, 52-67. Brussels, Commission for the European Community.

PIENKOWSKI, M.W. 1984. Breeding biology and population dynamics of Ringed Plovers *Charadrius hiaticula* in Britain and Greenland: nest predation as a possible factor limiting distribution and timing of breeding. *Journal of Zoology, London, 202,* 83-114.

PIENKOWSKI, M.W. 1990. The role of long-term ornithological studies in target setting for conservation in Britain. *Ibis,* in press.

PIENKOWSKI, M.W., & DICK, W.J.A. 1975. The migration and wintering of Dunlin *Calidris alpina* in north-west Africa. *Ornis Scandinavica, 6,* 151-167.

PIENKOWSKI, M.W., & EVANS, P.R. 1982. Breeding behaviour, productivity and survival of colonial and non-colonial shelducks *Tadorna tadorna. Ornis Scandinavica, 13,* 101-116.

PIENKOWSKI, M.W., & EVANS, P.R. 1984. Migratory behavior of shorebirds in the western Palearctic. *In: Behavior of marine animals. Volume 6: Shorebirds,* ed. by J. Burger and B.L. Olla, 73-123. New York, Plenum Press.

PIENKOWSKI, M.W., & EVANS, P.R. 1985. The role of migratory behaviour in the population dynamics of birds. *In: Behavioural ecology: the ecological consequences of adaptive behaviour,* ed. by R. Sibly and R.H. Smith. Oxford, Blackwell. (*British Ecological Society Scientific Symposium, 24.*)

PIENKOWSKI, M.W., FERNS, P.N., DAVIDSON, N.C., & WORRALL, D.H. 1984. Balancing the budget: measuring the energy intake and requirements of shorebirds in the field. *In: Coastal waders and wildfowl in winter,* ed. P.R. Evans, J.D. Goss-Custard and W.G. Hale, 29-56. Cambridge, Cambridge University Press.

PIENKOWSKI, M.W., KNIGHT, P.J., STANYARD, D.J., & ARGYLE, F.B. 1976. The primary moult of waders on the Atlantic coast of Morocco. *Ibis, 118,* 347-365.

PIENKOWSKI, M.W., LLOYD, C.S., & MINTON, C.D.T. 1979. Seasonal and migrational weight changes in dunlins. *Bird Study, 26,* 134-148.

PIENKOWSKI, M.W., & PIENKOWSKI, A.E. 1983. WSG project on the movements of wader populations in western Europe, eighth progress report. *Wader Study Group Bulletin, 38,* 13-22.

PIENKOWSKI, M.W., & PIENKOWSKI, A.E. 1989. Limitation by nesting habitat of the density of breeding Ringed Plovers *Charadrius hiaticula*: a natural experiment. *Wildfowl, 40,* 115-126.

PIERSMA, T. 1986. Breeding waders in Europe. *Wader Study Group Bulletin, 48, Supplement,* 1-116.

PIERSMA, T. 1987. Hink, stap of sprong? Reisbeperkingen van arctische steltlopers door voedselzoeken, vetopbouw en vliegsnelheid. *Limosa, 60,* 185-194.

PIERSMA, T., BEINTEMA, A.J., DAVIDSON, N.C., OAG MUNSTER & PIENKOWSKI, M.W. 1987a. Wader migration systems in the east Atlantic. *Wader Study Group Bulletin, 49, Supplement, 7,* 35-56.

PIERSMA, T., BREDIN, D., & PROKOSCH, P. 1987b. Continuing mysteries of the spring migration of Siberian Knots: a progress note. *Wader Study Group Bulletin, 49,* 9-10.

PIERSMA, T., & JUKEMA, J. 1990. Budgeting the flight of a long-distance migrant: changes in the nutrient levels of Bar-tailed Godwits at successive spring staging sites. *Ardea, 78,* 315-337.

PIERSMA, T., & VAN BREDERODE, N.E. 1990. The estimation of fat reserves in coastal waders before their departure from north-west Africa in spring. *Ardea, 78,* 221-236.

PIROT, J.-Y., LAURSEN, K., MADSEN, J., & MONVAL, J.-Y. 1989. Population estimates of swans, ducks, and Eurasian Coot *Fulica atra* in the Western Palearctic and Sahelian Africa. *In: Flyways and reserve networks for water birds,* ed. by H. Boyd and J.-Y. Pirot, 14-23. (IWRB Special Publication No 9.)

PRATER, A.J. 1976a. The distribution of coastal waders in Europe and north Africa. *In: Proceedings of the 5th international conference on the conservation of wetlands and waterfowl, Heiligenhafen, 1974,* ed. by M. Smart, 255-271. Slimbridge, IWRB.

PRATER, A.J. 1976b. Breeding population of the Ringed Plover *Charadrius hiaticula* in Britain. *Bird Study, 23,* 155-161.

PRATER. A.J. 1981. *Estuary birds of Britain and Ireland.* Berkhamsted, T. & A.D. Poyser.

PRATER, A.J. 1989. Ringed Plover *Charadrius hiaticula* breeding population of the United Kingdom in 1984. *Bird Study, 36,* 154-159.

PRESTRUD, P., BLACK, J.M., & OWEN, M. 1989. The relationship between an increasing barnacle goose *Branta leucopsis* population and the number and size of colonies in Svalbard. *Wildfowl, 40,* 32-38.

PRINS, H.H.Th., & YDENBERG, R.C. 1985. Vegetation growth and a seasonal habitat shift of the barnacle goose (*Branta leucopsis*). *Oecologia (Berlin), 66,* 122-125.

PROKOSCH, P. 1984. Population, Jahresrhythmus und traditionelle Nahrungsplatzbindungen der Dunkelbauchigen Ringelgans (*Branta b. bernicla*, L. 1758) im Nordfriesischen Wattenmeer. *Oekologie der Voegel (Ecology of Birds)*, 6, 1-99.

PROKOSCH, P. 1988. Das Schleswig-Holsteinische Wattenmeer als Fruhjahrs-Aufenthaltsgebiet Arktischer Watvogel-Populationen am Beispiel von Kiebitzregenpfeifer (*Pluvialis squatarola*, L. 1758), Knutt (*Calidris canutus*, L. 1758) und Pfuhlschnepfe (*Limosa lapponica*, L. 1758). *Corax*, 12, 274-442.

PRYS-JONES, R.P., KIRBY, J.S., & EVANS, A. 1988. *The role of the Uists as a late spring staging post for some Nearctic-breeding waders*. BTO Research Report 38. Tring, British Trust for Ornithology.

RATCIFFE, D.A. 1986. Peregrine. *In: The atlas of wintering birds in Britain and Ireland*, compiled by P. Lack, 152-153. Calton, T. & A.D. Poyser.

REED, T. 1985. Estimates of British breeding wader populations. *Wader Study Group Bulletin*, 45, 11-12.

RIDGILL,S.C., & FOX, A.D. 1990. Cold weather movements of waterfowl in western Europe. Slimbridge, International Waterfowl and Wetlands Research Bureau. (*IWRB Special Publication* No. 13)

ROBERTS, P.J. 1988. Ornithological studies at Kingsnorth. Breeding birds. Report to Central Energy Generating Board (unpublished). (Kingsnorth 'B' Pre-application Studies.)

SALMON, D.G., PRYS-JONES, R., & KIRBY, J.S. 1987. *Wildfowl and wader counts 1986-87*. Slimbridge, Wildfowl Trust/Nature Conservancy Council/BTO/RSPB.

SALMON, D.G., PRYS-JONES, R., & KIRBY, J.S. 1989. *Wildfowl and wader counts 1988-89*. Slimbridge, Wildfowl Trust/Nature Conservancy Council/BTO/RSPB.

SALOMONSEN, F. 1968. The moult migration. *Wildfowl*, 19, 5-24.

SHARROCK, J.T.R. 1976. *The atlas of breeding birds of Britain and Ireland*. Berkhamsted, T. & D.A. Poyser.

SMIT, C., & PIERSMA, T. 1989. Numbers, midwinter distribution, and migration of wader populations using the East Atlantic Flyway. *In: Flyways and reserve networks for water birds*, ed. by H. Boyd and J.-Y. Pirot, 24-63. *IWRB Special Publication* No 9.

SMIT, C., & WOLFF, W.J. 1981. *Birds of the Wadden Sea*. Wadden Sea Working Group, Report 6. Rotterdam, A.A. Balkema.

SMITH, K.W. 1983. The status and distribution of waders breeding on wet lowland grasslands in England and Wales. *Bird Study*, 30, 177-192.

SMITH, K.W. 1988. BTO/WSG breeding wader monitoring scheme – the story so far. *Wader Study Group Bulletin*, 53, 3.

STANLEY, P.I., & MINTON, C.D.T. 1972. The unprecedented westwards migration of curlew sandpipers in autumn 1969. *British Birds*, 65, 365-380.

STEVENTON, D.J. 1977. Dunlin in Portsmouth, Langstone and Chichester Harbours. *Ringing and Migration*, 1, 141-147.

ST. JOSEPH, A.K.M. 1979. The seasonal distribution and movements of *Branta bernicla* in western Europe. *In: Proceedings of the first technical meeting on western palearctic migratory bird management*, ed. by M. Smart, 45-56. Slimbridge, International Waterfowl Research Bureau.

STRANN, K.-B. 1991. Numbers and distribution of Knot *Calidris c. islandica* during spring migration in north Norway, 1983-1989. *In: Recent advances in understanding knot migrations*, ed. by T. Piersma and N.C. Davidson. *Wader Study Group Bulletin, Supplement*.

STROUD, D.A. 1981. The distribution and abundance of Greenland White-fronted Geese in Eqalungmiut Nunaat. *In: Report of the 1979 Greenland White-fronted Goose Study expedition to Eqalungmiut Nunaat, west Greenland*, ed. by A.D. Fox and D.A. Stroud, 31-62. Aberystwyth, Greenland White-fronted Goose Study Group.

STROUD, D.A., CONDIE, M., HOLLOWAY, S.J., ROTHWELL, A.J., SHEPHERD, K.B., SIMONS, J.R., & TURNER, J. 1988. A survey of moorland birds on the Isle of Lewis in 1987. *Nature Conservancy Council, CSD Report*, No. 776.

STROUD, D.A., MUDGE, G.P., & PIENKOWSKI, M.W. 1990. *Protecting internationally important bird sites: a review of the EEC Special Protection Area network in Great Britain*. Peterborough, Nature Conservancy Council.

STROUD, D.A., REED, T.M., PIENKOWSKI, M.W., & LINDSAY, R.A. 1987. *Birds, bogs and forestry: the peatlands of Caithness and Sutherland*. Peterborough, Nature Conservancy Council.

SUMMERS, R.W. 1986. Breeding production of Dark-bellied Brent Geese *Branta bernicla bernicla* in relation to lemming cycles. *Bird Study*, 33, 105-108.

SUMMERS, R.W., UNDERHILL, L.G., PEARSON, D.J., & SCOTT, D.A. 1987. Wader migrations systems in southern and eastern Africa and western Asia. *Wader Study Group Bulletin*, 49, *Supplement*, 7, 15-34.

SUMMERS, R.W., & UNDERHILL, L.G. 1987. Factors relating to breeding production of Brent Geese *Branta b. bernicla* and waders *Charadrii* on the Taymyr Peninsula. *Bird Study*, 34, 161-171.

SWANN, R.L., & MUDGE, G.P. 1989. Moray Basin wader populations. *Scottish Birds*, 15, 97-105.

SWENNEN, C., & DUIVEN, P. 1983. Characteristics of oystercatchers killed by cold-stress in the Dutch Wadden Sea area. *Ardea*, 71, 155-159.

SYMONDS, F.L., & LANGSLOW, D. 1981. Wader movements in the Firth of Forth 1979-1981. *Nature Conservancy Council, CSD Report*, No. 375.

SYMONDS, F.L., LANGSLOW, D., & PIENKOWSKI, M.W. 1984. Movements of wintering shorebirds within the Firth of Forth: species differences in usage of an intertidal complex. *Biological Conservation, 28*, 187-215.

SYMONDS, F.L., & LANGSLOW, D. 1985. Shorebirds in the Moray Firth 1981-1985. *Nature Conservancy Council, CSD Report*, No. 603.

SYMONDS, F.L., & LANGSLOW, D. 1986. The distribution and local movements of shorebirds within the Moray Firth. *Royal Society of Edinburgh. Proceedings, 91B*, 143-167.

TASKER, M.L., & PIENKOWSKI, M.W. 1987. *Vulnerable concentrations of birds in the North Sea*. Peterborough, Nature Conservancy Council.

TASKER, M.L., WEBB, A., HALL, A.J., PIENKOWSKI, M.W., & LANGSLOW, D.L. 1987. *Seabirds in the North Sea*. Peterborough, Nature Conservancy Council.

TAYLOR, J. 1953. A possible moult migration of Pink-footed Geese. *Ibis, 95*, 638-642.

THOMAS, G.J. 1982. Breeding terns in Britain and Ireland, 1975-79. *Seabird, 6*, 59-69.

THOMAS, V.G. 1983. Spring migration: the prelude to goose reproduction and a review of its implications. *In: First western hemisphere waterfowl and waterbird symposium*, ed. by H. Boyd, 73-81. Ottawa, Canadian Wildlife Service/IWRB.

TINARELLI, R., & BACETTI, N. 1989. Breeding waders in Italy. *Wader Study Group Bulletin, 56*, 7-15.

TOWNSHEND, D.J. 1981. The importance of field feeding to the survival of wintering male and female Curlews *Numenius arquata* in the Tees estuary. *In: Feeding and survival strategies of estuarine organisms*, ed. by N.V. Jones and W.J. Wolff, 261-273. New York, Plenum Press.

TOWNSHEND, D.J. 1982. The Lazarus syndrome in Grey Plovers. *Wader Study Group Bulletin, 34*, 11-12.

TOWNSHEND, D.J. 1984. The effects of predators upon shorebird populations in the non-breeding season. *Wader Study Group Bulletin, 40*, 51-54.

TOWNSHEND, D.J. 1985. Decisions for a lifetime: establishment of spatial defence and movement patterns by juvenile grey plovers (*Pluvialis squatarola*). *Journal of Animal Ecology, 54*, 267-274.

TUBBS, C.R. In press. The population history of grey plovers *Pluvialis squatarola* in the Solent, southern England. *Wader Study Group Bulletin*.

TUITE, C.H., HANSON, P.R., & OWEN, M. 1984. Some ecological factors affecting winter wildfowl distribution on inland waters in England and Wales, and the influence of water-based recreation. *Journal of Applied Ecology, 21*, 41-62.

UNDERHILL, L.G., WALTNER, M., & SUMMERS, R.W. 1989. Three year cycles in breeding productivity of knots *Calidris canutus* wintering in southern Africa suggest Taymyr Peninsula provenance. *Bird Study, 36*, 83-87.

UTTLEY, J.D., THOMAS, C.J., DAVIDSON, N.C., STRANN, K.-B., & EVANS, P.R. 1987. The spring migration system of nearctic Knots *Calidris canutus islandica*: a re-appraisal. *Wader Study Group Bulletin, 49, Supplement*, 80-84.

VAN EERDEN, M. 1977. Vorstvlucht van watervogels door het oostelijk deel van de Nederlandse Waddenzee op 30 December 1976. *Watervogels, 2*, 11-14.

VAN IMPE, J. 1985. Estuarine pollution as a probable cause of increase in estuarine birds. *Marine Pollution Bulletin, 16, 271-276.*

WHITFIELD, D.P. 1985. Raptor predation on wintering waders in southeast Scotland. *Ibis, 127, 544-558.*

WILLIAMS, G., HENDERSON, A., GOLDSMITH, G., & SPREADBOROUGH, A. 1983. The effects on birds of land drainage improvements in the North Kent Marshes. *Wildfowl, 34*, 33-47.

WILSON, J.R. 1981. The migration of high arctic shorebirds through Iceland. *Bird Study, 28*, 21-32.

Contents

8.7.1 Introduction

Three groups of mammals are relevant to estuarine wildlife conservation: cetaceans, seals and otters. Although none is entirely dependent on estuaries, such places provide important feeding and breeding areas for otters and for seals, particularly common seals. The use of estuaries by cetaceans, chiefly dolphins, is less well understood, but some species are known to occur regularly in the outer parts of some British estuaries and so information on their known locations in review sites is included.

8.7.2 Cetaceans

Introduction

Twenty-four species of whales and dolphins have been recorded in British and Irish waters and most have been seen from the shore. Of these, 12 species are regularly seen close to our coasts. These include not only smaller species such as the harbour porpoise *Phocoena phocoena* but also larger whales including the 20-metre fin whale *Balaenoptera physalus* which has been seen mainly off western coasts. The small cetaceans characteristic of more inshore waters include the

harbour porpoise, the bottle-nosed dolphin *Tursiops truncatus* and Risso's dolphin *Grampus griseus*. Amongst the larger species, the minke whale *Balaenoptera acutorostrata* and the killer whale *Orcinus orca* are regularly seen from headlands and offshore islands.

A study of the status and distribution of British cetaceans is being carried out by the Cetacean Group, established in 1973 within the UK Mammal Society. A network of some 350 observers distributed throughout Britain and Ireland has contributed substantially to our knowledge of cetaceans in European seas. There is still much to learn, however, about the movements of cetaceans in British waters, and many of the early data have been drawn from records of strandings collected by the British Museum (Natural History).

Two species of cetacean are frequently found in enclosed coast Estuaries Review sites. These are the harbour porpoise *Phocoena phocoena* and the bottle-nosed dolphin *Tursiops truncatus*. Other species occur only infrequently and data for these species in review sites are very sparse.

Common or harbour porpoise

The harbour porpoise is the smallest British cetacean, measuring not more than two metres in length. It is a short, stout and robust-looking cetacean, with a black back, white belly and varying amounts of grey on the sides. It has a short blunt head; a snout or beak is absent. It is a slow swimmer and accordingly does not normally leap clear of the water as do dolphins (Purves 1977).

Porpoises are present in coastal waters throughout the year, favouring shallow calm waters, and the harbour porpoise has a very wide distribution in the North Atlantic. Adults with calves assemble in coastal waters on both sides of the North Atlantic from July to October, but breeding locations are unknown. The harbour porpoise is by far the most common cetacean species recorded from both strandings and sightings, although the frequency of its occurrence within review sites is not specifically documented. Between 1913 and 1978 there were 723 strandings, nearly four times as many as for the second most commonly stranded species, the bottle-nosed dolphin (Evans 1980). Porpoises are essentially coastal in occurrence, although individuals have been seen from time-to-time long distances up-river, notably in the estuarine systems feeding The Wash (R Mitchell pers. comm.).

Bottle-nosed dolphin

The bottle-nosed dolphin is a small cetacean which can grow to just less than four metres long. It has a robust slate grey or light brown body. The head possesses a distinct beak, the lower jaw of which protrudes beyond the tip of the snout. Streaks of lighter coloration stretch from the base of the beak to the blowhole located on the top of the head. The throat and belly are white or pale pink. There is a prominent dorsal fin which slopes backwards and has a concave hind margin (Purves 1977).

Bottle-nosed dolphins appear to be mainly coastal, often occurring in estuaries. Regular watching in recent years has revealed that certain estuaries and coastal areas either hold resident bottle-nosed dolphin populations or are visited regularly each year.

There are two main resident populations of bottle-nosed dolphins in British waters and one population can be found within or near to two review sites, the Moray and Cromarty Firths, whilst the other population is in Cardigan Bay in west Wales (outside review sites). Outside these areas most records of sightings are from south-west Britain and Ireland (Evans 1976). The Cardigan Bay population appears to be smaller than the population present in the Moray Firth. Research is currently under way to provide more information on both populations. Other places from which bottle-nosed dolphins are known include the Clyde Estuary and the hot water outflow from Dungeness Power Station on the Kent coast. Such areas are frequently used throughout the summer months.

In the Clyde, bottle-nosed dolphins have been observed in March feeding amongst herring shoals, and they have been seen feeding on salmon in the Cromarty and Moray Firths in the summer. Their diet is, however, rather poorly known. They are believed to feed mainly on inshore bottom-living fish including mullet, but will also take herring, mackerel and cod.

Bottle-nosed dolphins have been recorded most commonly in summer, earliest in the north of Britain and later further south. It is not clear whether apparent absence at other times of year is real or a consequence of varying intensity of observation.

Dolphins give birth mainly in spring/summer in lower latitudes, after mating 10-12 months before. After giving birth to their young, they move into higher latitudes to feed during the summer months. In Britain bottle-nosed dolphins can be occasionally be seen with calves. For example, there were two sightings of herds with young in Scotland in 1974, one of 40 adults and 10 small calves in April in the Cromarty Firth, the other on the Ballantrae Bank (outside review sites) in south-west Scotland in March, and groups in the Irish Sea have often been seen with attendant calves (E I S Rees pers. comm.).

Status and threats

The status of many species of cetaceans, especially the smaller species of dolphins and the larger species of whales, is of major concern. The harbour porpoise, although still the most frequently recorded species, is thought to have declined in recent years. Since 1980 noticeable declines have occurred in the southern North Sea, the English Channel and the Irish Sea (Evans 1980). This species was formerly very common near the French coast but is now one of the least common species there. The bottle-nosed dolphin seems to have become less common than formerly in the northern Irish Sea. It was seen frequently in parts of the North Sea until the late 1950s but had virtually disappeared from this area by the late 1960s (Gubbay 1988). Pollution, disturbance from ships and boats and over-exploitation of fish stocks have all been put forward as possible contributing factors, along with the incidental catching of cetaceans during fishing operations. High residues of chemicals, for example chlorinated hydrocarbon insecticides, have been found in the fat of porpoises from the North Sea (Holden & Marsden 1967), while drastic declines in planktonic stages of teleostean fish in the English Channel between 1933 and 1937 have been linked to an increase in stranding of porpoises (Russell 1973; Corbin 1948, 1949). Large incidental catches of cetaceans during fishing operations are thought to have been a major factor in, specifically, the decline of the harbour porpoise (Kayes 1985).

Conservation

As a result of the 1986 Quinquennial Review of the Wildlife & Countryside Act 1981, all cetaceans are afforded total protection. Prior to this only the harbour porpoise, common dolphin and bottle-nosed dolphin were so protected, although all species have been protected since 1934 from commercial whaling up to 200 miles from the English and Welsh coasts. Protection was extended because it was realised that the difficulties of differentiating threatened from unthreatened species as sea were so great that only protection of all would be effective. This also complied with international obligations under the Bern Convention (A Whitten pers. comm.).

Conclusions

Both harbour porpoises and bottle-nosed dolphins favour calm, shallow inshore waters, and clearly a number of the enclosed coast Estuaries Review sites provide such conditions. These areas also support populations of fish on which the species feed (see also Chapter 8.4). Data on the numbers of individuals which use these areas are limited, and the overall significance of review sites for both species is not understood, but individual locations such as the Moray Firth and Cardigan Bay are obviously of high conservation importance. The Moray Firth holds the largest known population of resident bottle-nosed dolphins in Europe.

8.7.3 Seals

Two species of seal, the grey seal *Halichoerus grypus* and the common seal *Phoca vitulina*, occur commonly and breed around the coasts of Britain.

Other species, including harp seal *Phoca groenlandica*, ringed seal *Phoca hispida* and hooded seal, have been recorded very occasionally in British waters, including some estuaries.

Grey seal

The world population of grey seals is distributed in three breeding groups, one in the Baltic Sea and the others in the western North Atlantic and eastern North Atlantic. 1985 surveys by the Sea Mammal Research Unit (SMRU) of the Natural Environment Research Council estimated the British population at about 92,000 grey seals (NERC 1987). This is about 50% of the world population. Grey seals favour exposed shores for their breeding sites, so breeding grey seals occur largely outside estuaries. Major breeding sites are in Shetland, the Orkneys, the Outer Hebrides, the Isle of May in the mouth of the Firth of Forth and the Farne Islands off the Northumberland coast. Grey seals also breed around some review sites in the far north of Scotland. Elsewhere there are a total of about 3,000 grey seals breeding in western Britain (on Anglesey, in Dyfed and in Cornwall) and grey seals also at Donna Nook on the Humber Estuary (Northridge 1990). Pups are born in autumn (December at Donna Nook) and remain on shore for several weeks. Grey seals do, however, regularly appear in estuaries throughout Britain, especially in the north and west, when they are away from their breeding sites. Individuals can move considerable distances along coasts and into estuaries for short periods; for example, Harwood (1988) describes a grey seal tracked by radio telemetry from the Farne Islands north up the east coast, into the inner Firth of Forth and north as far as the mouth of the Firth of Tay. Some estuaries are regularly used as haul-out sites: a non-breeding group using the Dee Estuary & North Wirral has increased from a few seals in the 1950s to over 300 individuals by the late 1980s. A recent review of seals in the Irish Sea (Northridge in press) notes that small numbers of grey seals are regularly recorded in the Mersey, Ribble, Morecambe Bay and Duddon Estuary. A similar pattern of appearance occurs in most other estuaries within the breeding range of grey seals.

Common seal

Common seals are less abundant than grey seals in Britain but their population is important in international terms. The estimated minimum population size of common seals in the early 1980s was 24,500 (NERC 1987), about 25% of the east Atlantic subspecies of common seal (Summers 1979). Common seals occur much more in sheltered inshore areas such as estuaries and sounds, where they use sand-banks and islands as haul-out sites. Estuaries therefore provide important areas for common seals in Britain. In contrast to grey seals, common seal pups can leave their sand-banks within a few hours of their birth in the summer. Two adjacent British estuaries, The Wash and North Norfolk Coast, are of very major

importance for common seals. Until recently these review sites supported about 6,600 common seals (27% of the British population and 7% of the east Atlantic subspecies), although numbers have now declined owing to viral disease (see below). A similar number breed on the sheltered shores, including review sites, of Orkney, so over half the British population breeds in just these two breeding areas.

Elsewhere much of the rest of the population occurs on the west coasts of mainland Scotland and the Inner and Outer Hebrides (5,800 seals), including the various sheltered review sites in these areas. There are 1,000 common seals breeding on the east coast of Scotland, mostly on the review sites of the Dornoch, Cromarty and Moray Firths and further south in the Firth of Tay and Eden Estuary (J Harwood pers. comm.). Common seals breed also at Donna Nook on the Humber Estuary (Northridge 1990). There are also small groups on some other east coast estuaries such as Teesmouth (D Jackson pers. comm.), where breeding is now being attempted again after the breeding population disappeared over a century ago, and also in north Wales (E I S Rees pers. comm.). Hence at least one-third, and probably considerably more, of the British population bred on estuaries before the spread of the virus (see below).

Outside the breeding season common seals, like grey seals, range widely around the coastlines of Britain and occur in most estuaries in northern and eastern Britain. They are however scarcer in the south and the west, occurring only occasionally in western England and Wales.

Recent population changes

Seal populations have been substantially reduced in Britain and in other major breeding areas such as the Wadden Sea since 1987 as a consequence of phocine distemper virus. This virus, similar to the canine distemper virus, was first noted in the Kattegat in April 1988. During the summer of 1988 it spread rapidly through the populations of the Wadden Sea and seals began dying in large numbers in Britain in August 1988. Common seals were much more seriously affected than grey seals, although there has also been concern about the effects that even a lesser impact of the virus may have on the small world population of grey seals, since most of the European population breed in Scotland.

All of the British populations of common and grey seals are thought to have been exposed to the virus, but different parts of the population have been affected to quite different extents. Extensive surveys of common seals in August 1989 found that numbers have decreased by 50-60% since before the epidemic in the Kattegat, the Wadden Sea, and on the east coast of England, including the major breeding area of The Wash, but that there has been only a 30% decline in the Irish Sea and little change in the Scottish common seal populations (Harwood

1990; P Thompson pers. comm.). Initial reports from 1989 suggest that the impact of the virus on common seals has been much less than in 1988, with only about 120 dead seals being reported up to August. Prior to the virus seal populations seem to have been fairly stable over many years, but the populations of common seals are now much reduced in Britain and elsewhere in Europe. The relatively slight impact of the virus in northern Britain means that the Scottish common and grey seals are now an even more important part of the European and British populations.

Conservation of seals

Adults and pups used to be killed in most places where they bred, mostly for commercial hunting and to prevent damage to fisheries, especially salmon fisheries. Although the 1914 and subsequent Grey Seals Protection Act imposed a closed season for hunting during the seal's breeding season, common seals had no such protection. Concern over the impact of extensive hunting of common seals on the The Wash, in Orkney and western Scotland led to the Conservation of Seals Act 1970, which imposed a close season for grey seals from 1 September to 31 December and for common seals from 1 June to 31 August. The Conservation of Seals (Scotland) Order 1973 afforded protection to common seals in Shetland all year. The Conservation of Seals Act permits licensed culling of seals for fisheries protection, population management and research. There has, however, been no hunting of common seals on The Wash since 1973 nor on Orkney or the west coast of Scotland since 1982. Similarly hunting of grey seal adults and pups in various parts of Scotland ceased in the early 1980s, and there has also been sporadic control of the adult grey seal population on the Farne Islands.

Seals can cause serious damage to fisheries and since the early 1980s licences have been issued mostly to fish farmers and salmon fishermen in Scotland to kill seals in the vicinity of their gear. In 1987 17 licences for common seals and 19 licences for grey seals were issued (Gubbay 1988) and in 1988 a total of 97 common seals were reported shot under licence. There is also concern over unlicensed killing in the vicinity of fishery operations, so the numbers killed may be well in excess of these figures. Since the viral epidemic the close season has been extended to give protection all year until 1990 to common seals throughout Britain and protection all year to grey seals in England and Wales.

The possible effects of pollutants on marine mammals in general and seals in particular were widely publicised as a possible contributor to the severity of the seal virus. It has been suggested that in particular polychlorinated biphenyls (PCBs) can affect mammalian immune systems, so rendering the animal more susceptible to disease, although no evidence is yet known to link pollution to the seal virus. PCBs are, however, known to be able to affect the reproduction of seals, and are of

particular current concern, although recent studies of seals on the east coast of England found levels of PCBs and other organochlorines mostly at the lower end of the range known for seals in the North Sea and Baltic Sea (Law et al. 1989). In general Irish Sea seal populations appear to have been less affected by pollution than those in the Baltic and the Wadden Sea (Northridge 1990 In press).

8.7.4 Otters

Introduction

The European otter *Lutra lutra* is a widespread largely fish- and shellfish-eating mammal that occurs in river systems, lakes and coasts throughout Europe and Asia. In Britain and Ireland it was formerly widespread and common throughout the country, but during the latter half of the twentieth century the distribution of otters has been substantially reduced in Britain and elsewhere in western Europe. In many parts of their European range otters remain scarce.

Many causes may have contributed to the decline in population and range of otters in Britain and Europe, but major factors were probably habitat loss associated with land drainage schemes that straightened and cleared rivers of the overhanging trees and other vegetation that provided cover for the otters, increasing pressure from waterborne and bankside recreation, and pollution (Lenton, Chanin & Jefferies 1980). Chanin & Jefferies (1978) have, however, identified persistent organochlorine pesticides as the key factor in the major decline in the otter population, as it was for the declines in populations of birds of prey. Other forms of pollution such as that from polychlorinated biphenyls (PCBs) and agricultural run-offs that kill invertebrates and fish may also now be involved (Andrews & Crawford 1986).

Concerns about the declining status of otters led to standardised surveys of the distribution of otters being made during 1977-79 over much of England (Lenton, Chanin & Jefferies 1980), Wales (Crawford et al. 1979) and Scotland (Green & Green 1980). These confirmed that otter distribution in England and Wales was very restricted, with only 6% and 20% respectively of surveyed sites showing signs of otters. The surveys found, however, that otters were widespread in Scotland. Because of the possibility of continuing declines in the British otter population, nationwide surveys were repeated during 1984-85 (Andrews & Crawford 1986; Green & Green 1987; Strachan et al. 1990). These have shown that there have been recent further declines in the populations of otters in two parts of Wales (Anglesey and mid-Glamorgan), but also that in some parts of England and Wales and in eastern Scotland there have been marked increases.

Otter surveys have concentrated on the freshwater parts of river systems, and otters are difficult to survey in tidal areas because signs such as spraints are rapidly washed away by the tide. Otters can,

Table 8.7.1 Numbers and percentages of review sites on which otters have been recorded recently

Country/region	On estuary	Upstream of estuary only	Absent
Scotland[a]	42 (82.4%)	7 (13.7%)	2 (3.9%)
W England/Wales	4 (10.0%)	16 (40.0%)	20 (50.0%)
S England	6 (17.6%)	8 (23.5%)	20 (58.9%)
E England	7 (21.9%)	7 (21.9%)	18 (56.2%)
Total	59 (38.1%)	36 (23.2%)	60 (38.7%)

[a] Includes Solway Firth
Percentages are of the total number of sites in that country/region

however, move considerable distances during a single night so although they are nocturnal and hence seldom seen in many parts of their range, and although signs of otters are difficult to find on estuaries, it is likely that otters regularly visit the tidal parts of many of the rivers on which they occur. They probably avoid, however, the heavily industrialised and polluted estuarine parts of river systems such as some of those in north-east England.

Distribution on British estuaries

Much of the information presented below on the distribution of otters on British estuaries has been gathered from otter surveyors past and present. Where appropriate this has been supplemented with information from the published surveys.

Otters have been recently recorded on 59 (38.1%) review sites (Table 8.7.1). In addition they are known to be present upstream of the tidal limit of a further 36 (23.2%) sites: in all otters are thus likely to occur on 61.3% of review sites. As would be expected from the general distribution of otters in Britain, otters are most frequently recorded on estuaries in Scotland, where 49 (96.1%) of sites have otters present or nearby (Figure 8.7.1; Table 8.7.1). There are only three estuaries in Wales on which otters are currently known to occur, although a further 10 review sites have recent records from above their tidal limits. Likewise there is only a scattered distribution in England, where most sites on which otters have recently been recorded are in Devon and Cornwall, and in eastern England between the Humber and north Suffolk. In all only 14 (17.7%) English review sites are currently known to support otters, and on only a further 21 sites are otters known to be present upstream. Otters are largely absent from the estuaries of south-east England, southern England east of Devon, south Wales, north Wales and north-west England (Fig 8.7.1).

In general there is a pattern of otters spreading back onto rivers in England and Wales so that both their range and their numbers are increasing. On some rivers such as the Severn otters are expanding their ranges downstream so that their use of estuaries is undoubtedly increasing. Otter

populations remain high or are currently expanding throughout most of Scotland – there has been a recent range expansion in southern Ayrshire, and the expansion in Fife noted by Green & Green (1987) is continuing. In addition reintroductions of otters such as those in East Anglia are helping to boost local populations and the extent of estuarine use.

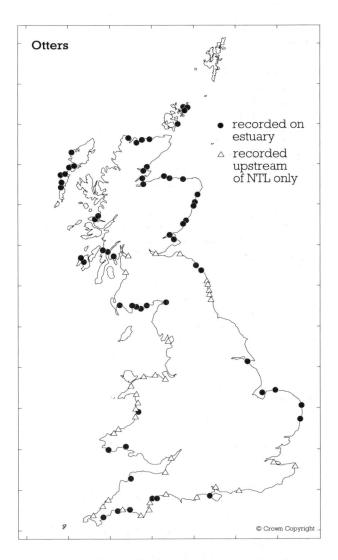

Figure 8.7.1 The distribution of otters on review sites

The ways in which otters use British estuaries seems to differ regionally. Over much of England, Wales and eastern Scotland otters are largely nocturnal, but in northern and western Scotland they are much more active by day. In south-west and west Scotland otters are widespread over much of the coastline, and use open coasts as well as estuaries, although in Dumfries and Galloway the sheltered estuaries and firths are preferred. Similarly otters are widespread and common on the sheltered coasts, including the review sites, of the mainland and islands of western Scotland. Otters are also widespread on Orkney and although the three review sites on Sanday have not been surveyed they, like the rest of the coastline of the Orkneys, are believed to be used by otters. On the north coast of Scotland otters mainly use the sheltered estuaries and bays and avoid the exposed open coasts between. In eastern Scotland otters are present chiefly in the estuaries and firths, and the river systems that feed into them. There is a similar distribution pattern over much of England and Wales, but in some places such as parts of the North Norfolk Coast the coastal marshes and reedbeds currently appear to be more important to otters than the adjacent rivers (H. Smith, pers. comm.).

Estuaries in Britain evidently support an important part of the British otter population throughout the year. In winter coasts and estuaries become additionally important to otters as refuges from severe weather. During these times when lakes and rivers freeze over making feeding difficult otters may move considerable distances to the tidal shores to find ice-free areas (Laidler 1982).

Threats to British otters

Although the otter population in Britain seems generally to be recovering after its severe decline induced by pesticide pollution, and some other pressures on the population such as otter hunting have eased, there are a number of concerns for otter conservation on estuaries and elsewhere . These include the risks of drowning in lobster pots and eel fyke nets in coastal parts of their range (although it is possible to fit fyke nets with guards to stop otters drowning), the impacts of increasing numbers of fish farms in otherwise little disturbed parts of their range, and the increasing recreational pressures on rivers and estuaries leading to increasing disturbance and the loss of safe shelters and breeding holts (Chanin & Jefferies 1978).

To counterbalance this, in some parts of Britain, notably the North Norfolk Coast, a re-introduction programme has resulted in local increases in the otter population.

The otter populations of Britain are of international importance in a west European context since northern and western Scotland supports one of the strongest remaining populations of the otter in north-western Europe outside Ireland (NCC 1989). Otters are fully protected through Schedule 5 of the Wildlife & Countryside Act 1981.

8.7.5 References

ANDREWS, E. & CRAWFORD, A.K. 1986. Otter survey of Wales 1984-85. London, The Vincent Wildlife Trust.

CHANIN, P.S. & JEFFERIES, D.J. 1978. The decline of the otter Lutra lutra in Britain: an analysis of hunting records and discussion of causes. Linnean Society. Biological Journal, 10, 305-328.

CORBIN, P.G. 1948. On the seasonal abundance of young fish. IX. Marine Biological Association of the United Kingdom. Journal, 27, 718-722.

CORBIN, P.G. 1949. On the seasonal abundance of young fish. X. Marine Biological Association of the United Kingdom. Journal, 28, 707-712.

CRAWFORD, A., EVANS, D., JONES, A. & McNULTY, J. 1979. Otter survey of Wales 1977-78. Lincoln, Society for the Promotion of Nature Conservation.

EVANS, P.G.H. 1976. An analysis of sightings of Cetacea in British waters. Mammal Review, 6, 5-14.

EVANS, P.G.H. 1980. Cetaceans in British waters. Mammal Review, 10, 1-52.

GREEN, J. & GREEN, R. 1980. Otter survey of Scotland 1977-79. London, The Vincent Wildlife Trust.

GREEN, J. & GREEN, R. 1987. Otter survey of Scotland 1984-85. London, The Vincent Wildlife Trust.

GUBBAY, S. 1988. A Coastal Directory for Marine Nature Conservation. Ross-on-Wye, Marine Conservation Society.

HARWOOD, J. 1988. Seals and whales plumb the depths. NERC News No. 5, 22-23.

HARWOOD, J. 1990. What have we learned from the 1988 seal epidemic? Biologist, 37(1), 7-8.

HOLDEN, A.V., & MARSDEN, K. 1967. Organochlorine residues in seals and porpoises. Nature, 216, 1274-1276.

KAYES, R.J. 1985. The decline of porpoises and dolphins in the southern North Sea. A current status report. Oxford, Political Ecology Research Group.

LAIDLER, L. 1982. Otters in Britain. Newton Abbot, David & Charles.

LAW, R.J., ALLCHIN, C.R. & HARWOOD, J. 1989. Concentrations of organochlorine compounds in the blubber of seals from eastern and Northeastern England, 1988. Marine Pollution Bulletin, 20(3), 110-115.

LENTON, E.J., CHANIN, P.R.F. & JEFFERIES, D.J. 1980. Otter survey of England 1977-79. Nature Conservancy Council, London.

NATURE CONSERVANCY COUNCIL, 1989. Guidelines for selection of biological SSSIs. Peterborough, Nature Conservancy Council.

NERC. 1987. Seal stocks in Great Britain: surveys

conducted in 1985. *NERC News* No. 1, 11-13.

NORTHRIDGE, S. 1990. Seals. *In: The Marine Forum for Environmental Issues, 1990 North Sea Report,* 85-88. London, The Marine Forum for Environmental Issues.

NORTHRIDGE, S. In prep. Mammals in the Irish Sea. Irish Sea Study Group Report. Liverpool, Irish Sea Study Group.

PURVES, P.E. 1977. Order Cetacea. Whales, dolphins and porpoises. *In: The Handbook of British mammals*, ed. by G.B. Corbet and H.N. Southern, 266-309. Oxford, Blackwell Scientific Publications

RUSSELL, F.S. 1973. A summary of the observations on the occurrence of planktonic stages of fish off Plymouth 1924-1972. *Marine Biological Association of the United Kingdom. Journal, 53,* 347-355.

STRACHAN, R., BIRKS, J.D.S., CHANIN, P.R.F. & JEFFERIES, D.J. in press. Otter survey of England 1984-86. Nature Conservancy Council, .

SUMMERS, C.F. 1979. The scientific background to seal stock management in Great Britain. *NERC Publications Series C*, No. 21, June 1979. Swindon, Natural Environment Research Council.

9 The conservation status of British estuaries

Contents

Summary

In recognition of the diverse and abundant wildlife importance of Britain's estuaries many parts of the estuarine resource have been designated or otherwise identified under a variety of domestic and international measures, both statutory and non-statutory. Some are designed specifically for nature conservation; others are primarily for landscape and amenity purposes. It is common for several different designations to be applied to parts of a single estuary, and to overlap.

Much of the current approach to nature conservation in Britain is site-based, but wildlife that is largely estuarine needs a wider land-use approach for its future safeguard. Land-use on estuaries is controlled by a great variety of domestic and, more recently, European legislation. This legal framework is particularly complicated, since it includes the local control of land-based activities, especially through the Town & Country Planning Acts, and the control of activities in the marine environment by 18 government departments and agencies. A great variety of consent mechanisms therefore operate on estuaries. Furthermore much of the intertidal and subtidal shore of estuaries is managed by the Crown Estate Commissioners, who control a variety of activities within these areas.

The protection of wildlife within British estuaries currently depends on a mixture of statutory designations, voluntary management agreements and consultation before development.

British conservation measures derive chiefly from the Wildlife & Countryside Act 1981 and its amendments. In addition the UK Government is party to a number of international agreements which oblige Britain to identify internationally important areas for birds and their habitats, especially the wetland habitats and the migrant waterfowl for which British estuaries are so important.

International conventions and directives

International conservation measures are essential for safeguarding wide-ranging species, for two key reasons. First, the long-term viability of such species depends on the maintenance of their geographic range and genetic diversity. Second, migratory species depend, individually and as groups, on networks of often widely scattered sites. All parts of the network need to be safeguarded, and British estuaries are critically important for many species.

The conservation of these species depends on countries in all parts of their range acting to safeguard habitats used during different parts of the annual cycle.

Estuaries are a recurrent theme of international conservation measures, both as wetlands and as habitat for very large populations of migratory animals, chiefly birds. The continuing worldwide losses of wetlands makes it vital to conserve those internationally important wetlands that remain. So far international wetland waterfowl conservation measures have been applied mostly for migratory bird populations, but their main aim is habitat safeguard since healthy habitats are as essential for birds as for other wildlife.

Some agreements are international conventions; others are European Community Directives, legally binding on member states. So far the most significant for estuarine conservation have been the 'Ramsar Convention' and the EEC 'Birds Directive'. Other international agreements and designations relevant to estuaries include the Council of Europe Convention on the Conservation of European Wildlife and Natural Habitats (the **'Berne Convention'**), the **'Bonn Convention'** on the Conservation of Migratory Species of Wild Animals, the **World Heritage Convention**, and **Biosphere Reserves**. A further EC directive on the protection of plant and animal species is in preparation.

The **Convention on Wetlands of International Importance especially as Waterfowl Habitat** (the 'Ramsar Convention') was adopted in 1971 and ratified by the UK Parliament in 1976. It aims to stem the progressive loss of wetlands, including all parts of estuaries down to six metres below low water.

Contracting Parties are required to designate wetlands of international importance, and to promote their conservation and 'wise use'. Criteria for identifying wetlands of international importance have been agreed by Contracting Parties. So far the most widely applied criteria relate to waterfowl populations and are especially relevant to estuaries. A wetland is regarded as internationally important if it regularly supports 20,000 waterfowl, or 1% of the individuals of a biogeographic population of one subspecies or species of waterfowl. By April 1989 there were 45 Contracting Parties worldwide and 468 Ramsar-listed wetlands (60% being in western Europe). In Britain the NCC is responsible for identifying suitable sites for designation by the UK Government.

Eighteen of the 39 designated British Ramsar sites cover parts of estuaries, and together they comprise almost 90% of the land designated. A further 43 estuarine Ramsar sites are currently amongst the 115 awaiting designation. Some Ramsar sites cover parts of more than one adjacent estuary, so that there are 66 estuaries in the Ramsar site network, 19 of them having designated Ramsar sites.

The European Council of Ministers adopted the **Directive on the Conservation of Wild Birds** (Directive 79/409/EEC) in 1979. It concerns the urgent need for European co-operation in bird conservation policies, and places emphasis on the need to conserve habitats as a means of protecting bird populations. In part this is achieved through the designation of Special Protection Areas (SPAs). 'Wider-countryside' measures are also stressed as complementary to site-based conservation.

The Directive requires Member States to take additional conservation measures for certain rare or vulnerable species, and regularly occurring migratory species. This is related especially to wetlands and migratory waterfowl. The Birds Directive therefore provides a statutory framework for international co-operation on safeguarding wetlands of international importance. It is explicit in the Directive that the network of SPAs must fulfil the overall objectives of the Directive, that population levels of many bird species should be increased, and that sites with particular importance as, for example, cold weather refuges, or where there is rapid turnover of individuals, can be included in the SPA network even where they do not fulfil quantitative criteria (e.g. 1% of the population). In order to safeguard migratory birds in their area of distribution, it is implicit that SPAs on estuaries need to cover subtidal areas, as well as the intertidal and terrestrial habitats.

The implementation of the Birds Directive in Britain is effected through the Wildlife & Countryside Act 1981, but this procedure has proved time-consuming and complex to apply. In particular the requirement that all sites must first have been notified as Sites of Special Scientific Interest has delayed the process, and has meant that SPAs usually cover only terrestrial and intertidal parts of an estuary, and then often only patchily.

In Britain there are 33 designated SPAs, out of a total of 761 designated by Member States by March 1989. British sites cover just over 127,000 ha (less than 1% of the land area), much less than some other states, for example Denmark (111 SPAs covering 22% of its territory) and Belgium (34 sites covering 12% of its area). Fourteen British SPAs are estuarine and comprise 84% of the designated SPA area in Britain. There are currently 47 estuarine proposed SPAs in Britain.

Overall, 68 estuaries (44%) are internationally important on quantitative criteria alone and are wholly or partly within the Ramsar and/or SPA site network.

Ramsar/SPA sites are mostly on large estuaries and so are not fully representative of the diversity of Britain's estuarine resource. Birds which concentrate on large estuaries are well represented, but those that are widely distributed around small estuaries also need effective site designations.

The Ramsar Convention and the EEC Birds Directive have greatly increased awareness of the international importance of Britain's estuaries. However, even where these designations apply, safeguards are not always maintained. Although the identification of internationally important sites has helped to safeguard some areas against damaging development proposals, habitat losses from internationally important sites still occur.

Consent for several recent major development proposals affecting internationally important estuaries, notably docks at Felixstowe on the Orwell Estuary and an 'amenity' barrage on the Taff/Ely Estuary (Severn Estuary), has been sought through Parliamentary Private Bills. Other major developments obtained consent through the local development planning process. Overall, internationally important British estuaries are still being damaged and destroyed rather than maintained and enhanced.

British wildlife conservation designations

A national policy framework for nature conservation in Britain was first set out in Government White Papers in 1947. In 1984 the NCC published *Nature conservation in Great Britain* which established a strategy in the context of a review of conservation progress. Nature conservation strategy in Britain currently has three main elements: managing key sites as National Nature Reserves (NNRs); notifying statutory Sites of Special Scientific Interest (SSSIs); and maintaining wildlife in the wider countryside. All are relevant to estuaries. In addition there is a variety of other designations, both statutory and voluntary, that apply to estuaries, often in overlapping patterns.

The detailed assessment and description of **Nature Conservation Review (NCR)** sites, which are biological sites of key importance and of NNR quality, was published by the NCC in 1977. By 1989 there were 943 NCR sites in Britain covering a total area of almost 1,057,900 ha. 150 (16%) are classified as coastal, over half of them estuarine.

The **Geological Conservation Review (GCR)**, begun by the NCC in 1977, is assessing and identifying key earth science conservation sites throughout Britain. There are some 3,000 GCR sites in Britain of which 7% are associated with estuaries. 144 GCR sites are cliff and foreshore exposures of rock and Quaternary deposits, on 60 estuaries. Only 58 estuarine GCR sites are geomorphological, on 48 estuaries. Sites include shingle features, sand-dunes, cliffs and shore platforms and saltmarshes, but tidal flats are not represented, nor are whole estuaries treated as single features.

Sites of Special Scientific Interest (SSSIs) are the major statutory site designations by which site-based wildlife conservation is delivered in Britain. SSSIs were first notified to local authorities under the National Parks and Access to the Countryside Act 1949. Subsequently the Wildlife and Countryside Act 1981 and its amendments strengthened the statutory process by which SSSIs are now notified to owners, occupiers, local planning authorities, the Secretaries of State, water authorities and drainage boards. Sites originally notified under the 1949 Act have had to be renotified under the 1981 Act, a process now largely complete.

There are currently 5,495 SSSIs covering almost 1,723,000 ha (about 7% of Britain). By early 1989 there were 334 SSSIs (6% of the total) associated with estuaries. Many estuarine SSSIs are large (averaging 1,166 ha, compared with the national average of 314 ha), so their total area of 389,300 ha is almost a quarter of notified SSSI land in Britain.

SSSIs are associated with 136 estuaries (88% of the total) throughout Britain. 70% of these SSSIs are at least partly intertidal, and the remainder are on associated terrestrial habitats such as sand-dunes, grazing marshes and maritime heaths. Some estuaries have only one large SSSI covering most of the core area; others have several SSSIs each covering part of the intertidal zone. Many estuarine SSSI boundaries have been drawn along the low water mark on intertidal flats, so dissecting the functional unit of an estuarine ecosystem. There are only 19 (mostly small) estuaries on which there are currently no SSSIs. SSSI designation makes consultation mandatory for developments likely to be damaging to the wildlife interest.

Even so, lasting damage to SSSIs continues to occur. In the three years from April 1986 to March 1989 146 SSSIs (about 3% of the total) were reported as permanently or lastingly damaged, and overall 564 (10%) were reported as suffering some damage. Estuarine SSSIs are even more threatened; during this period 56 estuarine SSSIs were damaged (17% of estuarine sites) and 27 of these (8% of the estuarine sites) suffered at least long-term damage. Planning and conservation legislation thus does not appear to be preventing continuing piecemeal habitat loss on estuaries.

National Nature Reserves (NNRs) are nationally important sites managed, by the NCC or on their behalf, specifically for nature conservation. 47 of the 234 declared NNRs are coastal and almost 90% of these are estuarine, on 35 estuaries.

Areas of Special Protection (AoSPs) (formerly designated as Bird Sanctuaries under the Protection of Birds Act 1954) are intended to safeguard particular bird species, but also protect all bird species for at least part of the year. Ten of the 38 Bird Sanctuaries/AoSPs in England and Wales are on estuaries. They provide strong statutory protection which can extend to open-water areas below the low water mark.

SSSIs and NNRs are terrestrial designations. The introduction of legislation for **Marine Nature Reserves (MNRs)** in the Wildlife & Countryside Act was intended to provide similar protection for marine areas. Designating an MNR is, however, more complex than designating a National Nature Reserve. The two MNRs so far designated are non-estuarine, but one of six proposed MNRs (Menai Strait) includes parts of five estuaries. Since MNRs can cover all parts of estuaries below the high water mark they can potentially help safeguard whole estuarine ecosystems.

In addition to the statutory MNRs two voluntary marine conservation designations have been applied to estuaries. Parts of four **Voluntary Marine Conservation Areas** cover five estuaries in southern England. One of 29 **Marine Consultation Areas (MCAs)** identified by the NCC in Scotland is an estuary (Traigh Cill-a-Rubha).

Local Nature Reserves (LNRs) increase public awareness of the value of estuarine wildlife. LNRs are declared by local planning authorities, can cover both intertidal and some subtidal areas, and can have bylaws controlling damaging activities, making them an effective way of managing estuarine habitats, especially close to urban centres. 33 LNRs (20% of the national total) are on 29 estuaries, mostly in southern England.

Several other conservation designations directed towards wildlife cover estuaries. Five **Environmentally Sensitive Areas (ESAs)** overlap parts of the upper reaches of 15 estuaries. 122 of the 1,800 **Wildlife Trust reserves** are associated with 52 estuaries, chiefly in eastern and southern England. The **Royal Society for the Protection of Birds** acquires and manages land supporting important bird populations. Thirty-four of its reserves are on 25 estuaries, and the RSPB is currently running a major campaign for more effective estuarine wildlife safeguards. Five **Wildfowl and Wetlands Trust Reserves** are on estuaries, three of them covering areas for major wintering and breeding waterfowl populations, and a variety of other organisations own or manage estuarine land for wildlife, often as privately run nature reserves, on 19 estuaries.

Landscape and amenity designations

Coasts and estuaries are important features of Britain's landscape. A variety of landscape designations afford protection to estuaries, including parts of four **National Parks** on 11 estuaries. In Scotland 15 estuaries lie within **National Scenic Areas**, with almost half the Scottish west coast estuaries covered by this Countryside Commission for Scotland designation. Twenty of the 38 **Areas of Outstanding Natural Beauty (AONBs)** designated in England and Wales by the Countryside Commission have coastal frontage, with 15 of them including parts of 38 estuaries, chiefly in southern England and East Anglia. Twenty-two **Country Parks** have been designated by local authorities on 20 estuaries. The only specifically coastal countryside designation, **Heritage Coast**, was first proposed by the Countryside Commission in 1970. Most of the 1,460 km of Heritage Coast coastline is, however, on rocky and sandy shores. None of the largest estuaries is substantially within a Heritage Coast, most of which end at or just within estuary mouths. The North Norfolk Coast is the only major estuary covered. The **National Trust** and **National Trust for Scotland** provide strong protection covering 825 km of coastline, and with 64 properties on 34 estuaries, mostly on the English south coast and the North Norfolk Coast.

Estuarine planning and management

Although some designations make strong requirements for wildlife safeguard, none yet entirely precludes land-use conflicts. Such conflicts are particularly difficult to resolve in estuaries, where much of the area not already claimed by man is under threat from further development and disturbance.

Recognition of the great wildlife importance of estuaries, and its acknowledgement in the local authority planning and control system, are key components of the future safeguarding of Britain's estuaries. Zoning policies with presumptions against damaging development on estuaries are essential to minimise the potential impacts of proposed developments. Environmental impact assessment, supported by the terms of the 1985 EC Directive on Environmental Assessment, can provide valuable guidance on the effects of estuarine development proposals, although the variety and complexity of estuarine ecosystems can make reliable impact prediction both difficult and costly.

Parliamentary Private Bills have been used instead of the local planning process to seek consent for some recent major damaging estuarine developments, where parts of the development affect statutory rights of access or navigation. The use of this procedure for developments on estuaries (and other habitats) of high wildlife importance causes concern, not least because such domestic legislation is exempt from the terms of the EC Directive on Environmental Assessment, although there are now proposals to change this.

The multiple pressures on coasts and estuaries have increasingly led to the demands for integrated coastal zone management plans and strategies. On some British estuaries the initiative has come from the NCC, on others from local authorities or voluntary conservation groups. Integrated coastal zone management can help safeguard the remaining estuaries and their wildlife by treating estuaries as functional units.

9.1 Introduction

Much of the safeguarding of wildlife in Britain has developed as a site-based approach in which the maintenance of the wildlife interest of an area depends on land-use decisions on specified sites, controlled through a great variety of domestic and, more recently, European legislation. The legal control over activities and developments is particularly complex in coastal areas such as estuaries. Estuarine ecosystems are subject to the authorities regulating land-based activity and development, notably through the Town & Country Planning Acts – legislation that affects both the associated terrestrial habitats surrounding estuaries and, usually, the intertidal foreshore. In

addition coasts and estuaries are subject to the legislation controlling the marine environment, for example that relating to fisheries and shell-fisheries. The complexity added by the marine component of the legislation is substantial: there are 18 government departments and agencies with responsibilities in the marine environment and at least 88 separate Parliamentary Acts with a direct bearing on the marine natural environment (NCC 1989a).

The legislation of this complex statutory framework affects wildlife conservation in several ways. Some laws, notably the Wildlife & Countryside Act 1981, are primarily designed to effect wildlife conservation. Others operate to permit or control a wide variety of activities and operations on land, sea and shore. The implications of such legislation often affect the interests of wildlife conservation. Some laws include provision to safeguard wildlife whilst others do not. In many cases the presence of a statutory site identified through primary wildlife legislation is the trigger for consultation over proposed operations or developments that may directly or indirectly affect the wildlife interest of a site. Other legislation, for example that for Sea Fisheries, controls other activities in a way not specifically designed as a conservation measure but which nevertheless is of benefit to wildlife.

Much of the safeguarding of wildlife on estuaries thus depends on statutory identification of important wildlife areas coupled with management agreements between the NCC and owners and occupiers, and is effected through consultation over potentially damaging changes to the environment.

Coastal and estuarine areas differ, however, from most terrestrial habitats in that most parts of the coastal and marine environment are not in private ownership. About half the foreshore around British coasts and in tidal rivers forms part of the Crown Estate and is managed by the Crown Estate Commissioners, although some parts of this foreshore are leased or managed by other organisations such as Local Authorities and the NCC. In addition to this, almost all the sea-bed below mean low water (or mean low water spring tides in Scotland) out to the limit of territorial water is under Crown control. Except where there are specific bylaws under, for example, sea fisheries legislation, all these Crown areas have public rights of access for fishing and navigation.

In addition to the domestic arrangements through which wildlife conservation is delivered, the UK Government is party to a number of international conventions, notably the 'Ramsar' Convention on the conservation of wetlands especially as waterfowl habitat. This places additional obligations on safeguarding sites of international importance. European Community legislation, notably the EEC Directive on the conservation of wild birds, places statutory obligations on member states to identify and safeguard internationally important wildlife areas. Both these and some other international wildlife measures are of particular importance for estuaries.

In response to this very complex pattern of legislation affecting estuaries, a wide variety of statutory and non-statutory designations and ownerships has evolved, affording varying levels of safeguard to estuarine wildlife and the landscape and environment in which it lives. This chapter describes each of these designations. It should be noted that in many cases a single estuary is the subject of many of these designations, which often overlap in the same geographical areas. A description of all relevant legislation and how it affects estuarine wildlife is, however, outside the scope of this review.

9.2 International conservation conventions and directives

9.2.1 Background

The maintenance of the geographic range and genetic diversity of populations of plants and animals is essential for maintaining the long-term viability of species (Soule 1987). International measures are thus essential for safeguarding species when they are widespread and their ranges cross national boundaries. Migratory species are governed by such boundaries even less. Since, during their lifetime, migratory species depend on an often widely scattered network of sites, their conservation depends on concerted action by countries in all parts of their range to safeguard habitats used during different times of the annual cycle (Stroud et al. 1990). Chapter 8.6 has described how many species of waterfowl depend on the network of British estuaries for their survival and on habitats and locations in many other countries during the various parts of their life-cycle.

Estuaries have become a particular focus of attention of international treaties, conventions and directives, since they both are wetlands and support very large populations of migratory animals, chiefly birds. The conservation of wetlands of all kinds is a major international concern since they fulfil vital life-support functions in many places but are intensely threatened as habitat (Maltby 1986). The continuing worldwide decline of wetlands through land drainage together with increasing developmental and recreational pressure on many of the remaining wetlands means that it is vital to conserve those wetlands already identified as being of international importance (Stroud et al. 1990). Overall, wetland losses of all kinds have become the target for major international action effected through both national wetland conservation strategies and international programmes. In addition, migratory species by their very nature are dependent for their survival on international co-operation to maintain the habitats on which they depend. These two international priorities come together on estuaries, which exemplify many of the habitats and species

that the international efforts at wetland habitat safeguard are designed to protect. So far this protection has largely been put into effect through provisions to safeguard migrant bird populations. It must be remembered, however, that the underlying thrust of these internationally-agreed measures is that of habitat safeguard, which benefits all the organisms using such places and not just the bird species which are the specific target. Recent initiatives have been aimed more directly at the conservation of habitats as well as the species of plants and animals that live there.

The need for international treaties to protect migratory species, particularly birds, is recognised very widely in the world (IUCN 1986). In Europe this recognition led to the agreeing of the 1902 Paris Treaty. In North America one of the earliest bilateral conservation treaties, the Convention for the Protection of Migratory Birds, was signed in 1916 by Britain (for Canada) and the United States of America. This convention formalised common concerns about, and responsibility for, migratory animal populations (Lyster 1985). More recently a voluntary network, dependent on local involvement including land and wildlife managers, has been established linking key waterfowl sites in North and South America. This network, the Western Hemisphere Shorebird Reserve Network (WHSRN), has expanded rapidly since its inception in 1983 and is also based on the recognition of the need to identify the links between the many places used by migratory animals and the need to conserve each through both international recognition and local involvement (Myers et al. 1987).

Bilateral treaties for migratory species have also been established elsewhere, for example the Japan-Australia Migratory Birds Convention (JAMBA) which was ratified in 1981. Co-operative research programmes are now underway under the auspices of this Convention, and, more recently (1986), a migratory birds agreement was signed by China and Australia (Lane & Sagar 1987).

International wildlife designations relevant to the conservation of estuarine wildlife in Britain and Europe fall into two main categories. One is the international conventions to which the UK Government is party and to whose terms it has agreed to be bound through ratification. The other category is the European Community Directives issued by the European Economic Community (EEC) and which are legally binding through European law on member states of the EEC. Two of these designations are particularly significant for estuarine wildlife conservation: the 'Ramsar' Convention on the conservation of wetlands especially as waterfowl habitat, and the EEC Directive on the conservation of wild birds, which requires the designation of Special Protection Areas (SPA). On estuaries these two measures are almost invariably applied in tandem as a mechanism for safeguarding internationally important bird populations and their wetland habitats. A further EC Directive on the protection of habitats and plant and animal species is currently under discussion by member states.

A recent NCC report (Stroud *et al.* 1990) has comprehensively reviewed the EEC Special Protection Area network in Great Britain. Much of the description below of the provisions and implementation of this Directive is taken from Stroud *et al.* (1990).

Other EC Directives currently in force are directed at broader environmental safeguards such as the quality of shellfish waters and the water quality of bathing beaches, rather than directly at wildlife safeguard. Nevertheless, measures aimed at maintaining and improving water quality and reducing marine and coastal pollution also benefit the quality of wildlife habitat on estuaries.

The various international measures and how they affect the conservation of British estuaries and their wildlife are described below.

9.2.2 Berne Convention

The 'Berne' **Council of Europe Convention on the conservation of European wildlife and natural habitats** covers the protection of mammals, birds, amphibians, reptiles, freshwater fish, invertebrates and plants. The requirements of the Berne Convention are mandatory on its contracting parties. This is not the case with some other conventions, which merely encourage certain actions. Britain is a party to this convention and ratified its provisions on 28 May 1982.

Article 4(1) of the Convention requires each party to take appropriate and necessary legislative and administrative measures to ensure the conservation of the habitats of the wild flora and fauna species, especially those specified in Appendices I (rare plants) and II (animals).

Article 4(3) is of particular relevance to estuarine wildlife since it requires parties to give special attention to the protection of areas of importance for migratory species that are appropriately situated in relation to migration routes as wintering, staging, feeding, breeding or moulting areas. Since British estuaries fulfil all these roles for internationally important waterfowl populations, the Berne Convention has great potential value as a means of safeguarding estuarine wildlife. Furthermore the protection directed by the Convention is not limited to signatories' own territories. Hence aid to African countries to maintain sites is envisaged as a means of conforming to Article 4(3) (Lyster 1985), and African states are being encouraged to join the Convention.

Unfortunately the requirements of the Berne Convention are rather general and states party to the Convention need guidance on the implementation of the provisions. To provide this advice a Standing Committee was formed. Progress has, however, been slow. Although a document was prepared as long ago as 1983 proposing the development of criteria for the identification of sites, the preparation of priority lists, the publication of a draft plan for the protection of sites on the priority list and conclusions as to which sites are to be protected, specific action through the Standing Committee had yet to be implemented in 1987 (Batten 1987). As a result, even though the convention recognised the importance of co-ordinated international measures to conserve wildlife, there are no estuarine (or other) sites yet identified in Britain for protection specifically under the terms of the Berne Convention. The EEC Wild Birds Directive (see below) does, however, serve to implement the Berne Convention for birds, and the additional SSSI protection afforded by the Wildlife & Countryside Act 1981 is also in line with the terms of the Convention.

9.2.3 Bonn Convention

Britain is a party to the **Convention on the conservation of migratory species of wild animals,** the 'Bonn Convention' which Britain signed in 1979 and ratified on 23 July 1985.

The Bonn Convention provides for strict protection of a number of endangered animals listed in its Appendix I. The Convention also provides the framework for a series of 'Agreements' between Range States for the conservation and management of species listed on its Appendix II. The Convention covers all species of migratory animals, including invertebrates, fishes, reptiles, mammals and birds. The Agreements can cover all aspects of the species' conservation, including habitat conservation, hunting, research, information exchange and status restoration.

For the measures to be effective, all states of a region need to join the Convention and then negotiate agreements, but as yet no Agreements have been negotiated. Working Groups are, however, currently preparing two Agreements, one on the white stork and the other on west palearctic Anatidae (ducks and geese) (Smart 1987). This latter has direct relevance for the conservation of many British estuaries since they support important migratory and wintering populations of ducks and geese (see Chapter 8.6).

The Convention makes provision for immediate action to be taken to safeguard endangered species listed in Appendix I, regardless of whether or not Agreements have been concluded.

As with the Berne Convention, however, the Bonn Convention has not yet led directly to any strengthening of safeguards for migratory animals on British estuaries, but the EEC Wild Birds Directive and the Wildlife & Countryside Act have provided protection measures consistent with the Bonn Convention.

9.2.4 World Heritage Convention

The **Convention concerning the protection of the world cultural and natural heritage**, the 'World Heritage Convention', was adopted by Unesco (the United Nations Educational, Scientific and Cultural Organisation) in 1972 with the aim of identifying and protecting sites that are outstanding for either natural or cultural reasons. Sites should be of such unique value that they form part of the heritage of mankind. The UK Government ratified the World Heritage Convention in 1984.

World Heritage Sites are nominated by the state within which they are situated and the nominations are then considered by a World Heritage Committee. Sites that are accepted are placed on the World Heritage List. World Heritage Sites must have strict legal protection and any management of the site must ensure that this continues; most sites are protected by the existing legislation of the country (Gubbay 1988).

Sites of world natural heritage status must either:

- be outstanding examples representing the major stages of the earth's evolutionary history; or

- be outstanding examples representing significant ongoing geological processes, biological evolution or man's interaction with his natural environment; or

- contain unique, rare or superlative natural phenomena, formations or features or areas of exceptional natural beauty; or

- be habitats where populations of rare or endangered species of plants and animals still survive (IUCN 1982).

Such sites must also fulfil 'conditions of integrity'. Thus, for example, a site listed for its rare or endangered plants and animals must be large enough to contain the habitat required to ensure the survival of the species (Gubbay 1988).

The United Kingdom currently has 14 World Heritage Sites, of which 11 are cultural sites. Only one of the three natural sites (St. Kilda; Giant's Causeway and Causeway Coast, Northern Ireland; and Henderson Island, Pitcairn Islands) is in Britain and none is estuarine. Amongst six further sites currently on the 'UK Tentative List' (sites for which nominations are in preparation) is 'The Wash and North Norfolk Coast' which covers two Estuaries Review sites. Elsewhere in Europe, the important estuarine wetland of the Wadden Sea is a World Heritage Site.

9.2.5 Biosphere Reserves

Biosphere Reserves were first promoted by Unesco in 1974 as areas of land forming a worldwide network of sites, linked by common international standards, protected for conservation purposes and the exchange of scientific information (Unesco 1974). Unesco basic criteria for biosphere reserves are that they must (i) be protected areas of representative terrestrial and coastal environments; (ii) have value in conservation terms; (iii) provide scientific knowledge, skills and human values to support sustainable development; and (iv) combine and harmonise the three concerns which characterise a Biosphere Reserve. These concerns are –

a) **Conservation concern:** the need to conserve genetic resources and ecosystems and maintain biological diversity.

b) **Logistic concern:** the need to set up a well identified international network of areas directly related to Man and Biosphere (MAB) field research and monitoring activities with training and information exchange.

c) **Development concern:** the need to associate clearly environmental protection and land resource development as a governing principle for research and education activities.

To enable these criteria to be met, IUCN (1979) proposed that an ideal Biosphere Reserve should contain –

a) a **Core Zone,** in which interference should be minimal, to serve as a baseline for the biological region and in which research, educational and training activities should be carefully controlled and must be non-manipulative.

b) a **Buffer Zone,** managed for research, education and training, where manipulative methods and techniques are permitted and traditional sustainable-use activities can be permitted in a controlled manner.

c) a **Restoration Zone,** managed to study and reclaim lands and natural resources, where heavy natural or human-caused alterations have passed ecological thresholds, where biological processes have been interrupted, or where species have become locally extinct.

d) a **Stable Cultural Zone,** managed to protect and study existing cultures and land-use practices that are in harmony with the environment.

This concept of the components needed to form an ideal Biosphere Reserve have been further discussed by von Droste & Gregg (1985).

There are currently 269 Biosphere Reserves in 70 countries (Goodier & Mayne 1988). Britain has 13 Biosphere Reserves, all of which were designated in 1976 and 1977, and all these British sites are also National Nature Reserves (see Section 9.3.5). This affords the necessary long-term legal protection to the sites as there is no additional legal protection for Biosphere Reserves.

The NCC acts as lead agency in Britain for Biosphere Reserve designation. There has been little progress in designation since the 1970s, a situation not helped by the UK Government's withdrawal from Unesco. Concern over the lack of progress led to the re-establishment of the UK MAB Committee which has since met to review the existing Biosphere Reserve network. Resource limitations continue, however, to make progress slow on any expansion of the reserve network. The current emphasis is on improving the knowledge and use of resources in existing reserves.

A substantial part of the British Biosphere Reserve network – four of the 13 reserves – is estuarine (Figure 9.1). It comprises the National Nature Reserves of Caerlaverock (Solway Firth), Dyfi Estuary, Braunton Burrows (Taw-Torridge Estuary) and Holkham and Scolt Head Island (North Norfolk Coast).

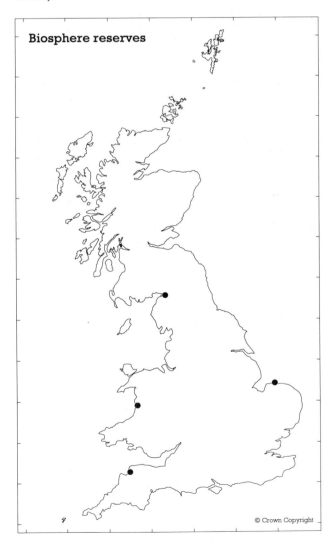

Biosphere reserves

© Crown Copyright

Figure 9.1 Estuaries Review sites with Biosphere Reserves

Goodier & Mayne (1988) have recently reviewed the characteristics of the British Biosphere Reserves and have concluded that most consist of the **Core Zone** only and are therefore by no means ideal Biosphere Reserves. Goodier & Mayne point out that there is thus considerable scope for further development of Biosphere Reserves. They also stress that the expansion of the Biosphere Reserve network would open up much wider conservation possibilities than are readily achievable through the narrower approaches such as are embodied in the concept of National Nature Reserves, since the former could facilitate more extensive management of semi-natural areas for a variety of uses but with the maintenance of ecological characteristics as an overriding aim. The zoning approach followed by the Biosphere Reserve programme may offer considerable benefits for its integration of complex patterns of sustainable land-use such as are widespread and necessary on British estuaries.

9.2.6 Ramsar Convention

The requirements of the Convention

The Convention on wetlands of international importance especially as waterfowl habitat was adopted at a meeting of countries concerned with wetland and waterfowl conservation held at Ramsar in Iran in 1971 (Carp 1972). This convention, usually known for convenience as the 'Ramsar Convention', was signed by the UK Government in 1973 and ratified by the UK Parliament in 1976.

The preamble to the Convention refers to the desire of the contracting parties "to stem the progressive encroachment on and loss of wetlands now and in the future".

The main provisions of the Ramsar Convention are described in several Articles, the key points of which are described below.

Article 1 defines wetlands as "areas of marsh, fen, peatlands or water, whether natural or artificial, permanent or temporary, with water that is static or flowing, fresh, brackish or salt, including areas of marine water the depth of which does not exceed six metres". Hence this broad definition includes both the intertidal and most subtidal parts of estuaries.

This Article also defines waterfowl as "birds ecologically dependent on wetlands". Under the terms of the Convention, waterfowl can therefore include a wide variety of birds including species of divers, grebes, terns, herons and egrets, storks and flamingos, as well as the waders, ducks, geese and swans that are the focus of attention on estuarine wetlands.

Article 2 requires each Contracting Party to designate suitable wetlands within its territory for inclusion in a list of wetlands of international importance. The boundaries of each wetland need to be described precisely and marked on a map, and may enclose riparian and coastal zones adjacent to the wetlands, islands and bodies of marine water deeper than 6 m at low tide lying within the wetlands, especially where these have importance as waterfowl habitat. On estuaries this means that Ramsar sites can include both the core Estuaries Review sites and also associated terrestrial habitats surrounding the core site.

Article 3 requires Contracting Parties to formulate and implement their plans so as to promote the conservation of wetlands included in the list and also, as far as possible, the 'wise use' of all wetlands in their territory. This Article also requires the Contracting Parties to inform the Bureau of the Convention, at the earliest possible time, if the ecological character of any wetland in the list has changed, is changing, or is likely to change as a result of technological developments, pollution or other human interference.

Article 4 requires Contracting Parties to promote the conservation of wetlands and waterfowl. It also requires that where a Contracting Party, in its own urgent national interest, deletes or restricts the boundaries of wetlands included in the list, it should compensate for any loss of wetland resources. This is to be undertaken in particular by the protection, in the same areas or elsewhere, of at least an equal area of the original habitat.

Article 5 requires contracting parties to consult with each other about implementation of the Convention. Such consultations should refer not only to trans-border wetlands but also to other matters, including north-south consultations on developments and projects affecting wetlands.

Article 6 requires Contracting Parties to convene conferences to consider matters relating to the Convention. Most recently conferences have been held at Regina (Canada) in 1987 (Ramsar Convention Bureau 1988) and Montreux (Switzerland) in 1990 (Ramsar Convention Bureau 1990). The UK Government is represented at all these conferences.

The 1987 conference clarified the definition of 'wise use' as specified in Article 3 and defined wise use as follows. "The wise use of wetlands is their sustainable utilisation for the benefit of humankind in a way compatible with the maintenance of the natural properties of the ecosystem".

Sustainable utilisation was further defined as "human use of a wetland so that it may yield the greatest continuous benefit to present generations while maintaining its potential to meet the needs and aspirations of future generations". Natural properties of the ecosystem were defined as its "physical, biological or chemical components, such as soil, water, plants, animals and nutrients, and the interactions between them".

Several of the conferences have considered guidance on the criteria for selecting sites of international importance. Although the basic themes have remained fairly constant throughout,

some modifications have been made, particularly to the criteria concerning general wetland types, as more information has become available on the assessment of sites on criteria other than their importance for birds (NCC 1988a). Most recently the criteria were revised and agreed at the Regina conference (Ramsar Convention Bureau 1988). These criteria, which have simplified and clarified some earlier criteria, are listed below. A wetland is identified as being of international importance if it meets at least one of the criteria.

1 **Criteria for assessing the value of representative or unique wetlands**

A wetland should be considered internationally important if it is a particularly good example of a specific type of wetland characteristic of its region (see also Guidelines below).

2 **General criteria for using plants or animals to identify wetlands of importance**

A wetland should be considered internationally important if:

a) it supports an appreciable assemblage of rare, vulnerable or endangered species or subspecies of plant or animal or an appreciable number of individuals of any one or more of these species; or

b) it is of special value for maintaining the genetic and ecological diversity of a region because of the quality and peculiarities of its flora and fauna; or

c) it is of special value as the habitat of plants or animals at a critical stage of their biological cycles; or

d) it is of special value for its endemic plant or animal species or communities.

3 **Specific criteria for using waterfowl to identify wetlands of importance**

A wetland should be considered internationally important if:

a) it regularly supports 20,000 waterfowl; or

b) it regularly supports substantial numbers of individuals from particular groups of waterfowl indicative of wetland values, productivity or diversity; or

c) where data on populations are available, it regularly supports 1% of the individuals of a population of one species or subspecies of waterfowl.

Guidelines

A wetland may be considered internationally important under Criterion 1 if:

a) it is an example of a type rare or unusual in the appropriate biogeographical region; or

b) it is a particularly good representative example of a wetland characteristic of the appropriate region; or

c) it is a particularly good representative of a common type where the site also qualifies for consideration under criteria 2a, 2b, or 2c; or

d) it is representative of a type by virtue of being part of a complex of high quality wetland habitats. A wetland of national value may be considered of international importance if it has a substantial hydrological, biological or ecological role in the functioning of an international river basin or coastal system; or

e) in developing countries, it is a wetland which, because of its outstanding hydrological, biological or ecological role, is of substantial socio-economic and cultural value within the framework of sustainable use and habitat conservation.

Further details of the implications of the criteria and guidelines, which have been subjected to further consideration at the recent Montreux conference, are given in Stroud *et al.* (1990). Criteria 1 and 2 listed above cover the whole range of wetland types and species and have been the subject of both national and international consideration. The NCC has as yet proposed few sites for designation under these criteria, while the deliberations have been continuing. (In Britain the NCC is responsible for proposing sites appropriate for designation to the UK Government (see below).)

Most sites identified for listing as wetlands of international importance in Britain have been identified under Criterion 3. Regina Criterion 3a, which indicates that a site is internationally important if it regularly supports 20,000 waterfowl, is a simplification of earlier criteria which used separate figures for different groups of waterfowl (waders and wildfowl). British estuarine Ramsar sites have generally been selected using this criterion and Criterion 3c, which refers to a site regularly supporting 1% of the individuals in a biogeographical population of one sub-species or species of waterfowl. The implications and complications of population assessments involving this 1% criterion have been described in Section 8.6.2 and also by Smit & Piersma (1989) and Stroud *et al.* (1990).

Ramsar sites in Britain and Europe

Since its adoption, the Ramsar Convention has proved extremely successful in focussing attention on the need for wetland conservation especially as habitat for waterfowl (Smart 1987) and 'Ramsar site' has become the flagship international designation aimed at safeguarding world wetlands for the future. Since 1987 the Convention has been administered through the Ramsar Convention

Bureau, based in Gland, Switzerland. Scientific support for the Convention is provided by the International Waterfowl and Wetlands Research Bureau (IWRB), based at Slimbridge (Gloucestershire) in Britain.

In Britain the NCC has the responsibility for identifying and advising the UK Government of sites worthy of designation as Ramsar sites. The procedure and its implications are the same as for the designation of Special Protection Areas under the EEC Birds Directive, and on estuaries these designations are usually applied simultaneously. The procedure is described further in Section 9.2.7 below.

By April 1990 there were a total of 468 Ramsar-listed wetlands distributed amongst the 45 contracting parties worldwide. Almost 60% (277 wetlands of international importance) of these have been listed by countries in western Europe. Although this is an impressive number, Smart (1990) points out that it is in reality small, considering that there are likely to be over 1,000 sites in western Europe, based on the bird-related criteria alone. Almost all countries in western Europe are now party to the Ramsar Convention but have so far designated widely differing numbers of sites (Figure 9.2). Britain, with 39 sites (plus a further one in Northern Ireland) designated by 1989, is amongst the countries that have designated the largest number of individual wetlands of international importance.

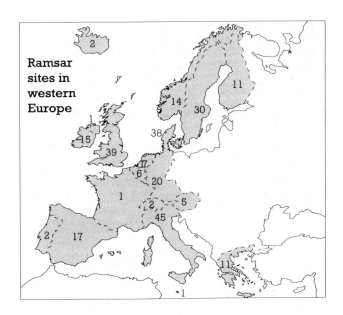

Figure 9.2 Countries in western Europe that have ratified the Ramsar Convention on the conservation of wetlands especially as waterfowl habitat, and the number of wetlands of international importance listed by each country (derived from Smart 1990). Ramsar Convention member countries are shown shaded. Note that it is the United Kingdom's Parliament that has ratified the Convention, but for consistency with the NCC's remit the numbers of Ramsar sites in Britain and Northern Ireland are shown separately.

This comparison of numbers of sites is, however, rather misleading for several reasons. Firstly, it takes no account of the relative size of the different countries, nor of the total area of designated sites. Secondly, Britain has a great many sites that qualify for inclusion as Ramsar sites: at total of 154 candidate Ramsar sites (including those already designated) have been identified, and at least 43 others have been proposed by various conservation bodies as likely to qualify (Stroud et al. 1990). It follows that the sites so far designated are only about 20-25% of the sites likely to qualify. Thirdly an increasing number of countries such as The Netherlands are placing greater emphasis on a more wide-ranging approach than simple site designation: the implementation of broad wetland conservation policies in the spirit of the wise-use part of the Convention.

Ramsar sites and Estuaries Review sites

Estuaries form an important part of the British Ramsar site network: by the end of 1989 15 (38%) of the 39 designated Ramsar sites were on core review sites, and a further three (Bure Marshes, Ouse Washes and Leighton Moss) were on associated terrestrial habitats adjacent to review sites. Hence almost half the current British Ramsar sites are associated with estuaries. These estuarine Ramsar sites are, however, larger on average than non-estuarine sites. They cover a total of 115,929 ha and so comprise almost 90% of the area in Britain protected by Ramsar designation. This is largely because of the inclusion of a few very large estuarine Ramsar sites, notably The Wash (over 63,000 ha) and the Dee Estuary (over 13,000 ha).

In addition there are a further 43 proposed Ramsar sites (37%) currently amongst the 115 listed by Stroud et al. (1990) that remain to be designated in Britain, and on the Severn Estuary the currently designated Ramsar site is a small part of the upper estuary, and a major extension to cover the whole estuary is proposed. Overall, therefore, 58 of the 154 British candidate Ramsar sites are on or closely associated with estuaries.

Most designated and proposed estuarine Ramsar sites, as described above, are also identified as Special Protection Areas under the EEC Birds Directive, since most have been selected largely because of their bird populations. A few Ramsar sites, for example Lindisfarne, were designated before the implementation of the Birds Directive and remain proposed SPAs. Two other Ramsar sites associated with estuaries, Cors Fochno and Dyfi (Dyfi Estuary) and Loch Fleet and The Mound (Loch Fleet), are not candidate SPAs, since they were selected on non-bird criteria.

The relationship between Ramsar sites and Estuaries Review sites is not straightforward, since Ramsar site boundaries are related to SSSIs whereas review sites cover areas wider than just the SSSIs within them. Furthermore some Ramsar sites are composed of a suite of SSSIs forming an ecological unit covering several adjacent estuaries.

This is particularly the case in Suffolk and Essex where the extensive continuous intertidal habitats are treated as separate but adjacent review sites. Two proposed Ramsar sites are formed from adjacent estuaries: the Orwell and Stour Estuaries form one Ramsar site, and the Colne and Blackwater Estuaries and Dengie Flats form another. Similarly Chichester and Langstone Harbours form one Ramsar site.

On some review sites there is, however, more than one Ramsar site. Such estuaries include the Firth of Forth where the Inner Forth and Outer Forth are currently proposed as separate Ramsar sites, and a third proposed Ramsar site, the Forth Islands, lies outside the review site boundary. On the Moray Firth also, inner and outer parts of the estuary are currently listed as separate proposed Ramsar sites. On some other review sites one Ramsar site covers the core site whilst others are on associated terrestrial habitats. An example is The Wash where the main estuary was designated in 1988. The adjacent Ouse Washes were designated as a Ramsar site in 1976, and the Nene Washes are a proposed site (Stroud et al. 1990).

The very great international importance of Britain's estuarine wetlands is clear from Figure 9.3. This shows that overall there are 66 review sites (42.6% of the total) that are within the British Ramsar site network, being partly or wholly proposed or designated as part or all of a Ramsar site. They are spread throughout Britain. 19 of these estuaries already have part or all of a designated Ramsar site and 47 are part of the proposed Ramsar site network. A further two review sites, Portsmouth Harbour and Milford Haven, are listed as possible Ramsar sites – sites whose qualifications are being further investigated – by Stroud et al. (1990). A third review core site, Breydon Water, also falls within this category of undergoing further investigation, but this is not apparent from Figure 9.3 since other parts of the grazing marsh systems adjacent to the tidal rivers of the Norfolk Broads are designated and proposed Ramsar sites.

It should be remembered that these estuarine Ramsar sites have almost all been selected on the basis of their bird populations (Criterion 3 above). Once Criteria 1 and 2 have become fully clarified and their provisions applied to Britain's estuaries it is likely that further estuaries may be identified as internationally important under the Ramsar Convention.

The use of the Ramsar Convention in safeguarding estuarine wetlands of international importance in Britain is closely linked with that of SPAs and is discussed in Section 9.2.7 below.

9.2.7 EEC Wild Birds Directive

The requirements of the Directive

The European Council of Ministers adopted the **Directive on the conservation of wild birds** (Directive 79/409) on 2 April 1979. This Directive

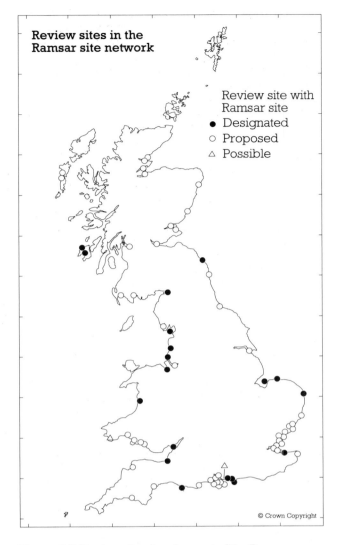

Review sites in the Ramsar site network

Review site with Ramsar site
- ● Designated
- ○ Proposed
- △ Possible

© Crown Copyright

Figure 9.3 Review sites forming part of the Ramsar network of wetlands of international importance. A review site is included if its core site or associated terrestrial habitats coincide with part or all of a candidate or designated Ramsar site.

(for convenience called the Birds Directive below) concerns the urgent need for European co-operation in bird conservation policies. This is because bird populations may move rapidly between different member states of the Community. Birds which range widely and which need to use habitats and areas in different member states will clearly benefit from a uniform positive approach to conservation.

Like all EC Directives the Birds Directive indicates what needs to be achieved but the way in which the objectives are attained is left to individual member states.

The conservation policies provide for a wide range of measures for bird protection, including standardisation of seasons in which gamebirds are protected and restrictions on certain methods of killing. Monitoring of bird populations is also stipulated by the Directive as a means of enabling the revision of conservation policies as and when needed.

The Birds Directive places emphasis on the need to conserve bird habitats as a means of maintaining populations. In part, such habitat protection is to be achieved by the establishment of a network of protected areas for birds throughout the Community. These are called Special Protection Areas (SPAs). The Birds Directive, as well as stating the need for SPAs, indicates that other means of protecting bird populations are necessary, especially where the populations are vulnerable and dispersed. These 'wider countryside' conservation measures are a necessary complement to site-based conservation.

The preamble to the Birds Directive states that "whereas the preservation, maintenance or restoration of a sufficient diversity and area of habitats is essential to the conservation of all species of birds; whereas certain species of birds should be the subject of special conservation measures concerning their habitats in order to ensure their survival and reproduction in their area of distribution; whereas such measures must also take account of migratory species and be co-ordinated with a view to setting up a coherent whole...".

Article 2 requires member states to "take requisite measures to maintain the population of the species referred to in Article 1 at a level that corresponds in particular to ecological, scientific and cultural requirements, while taking account of economic and recreational requirements, or to adapt the population of these species to that level." Species in **Article 1** all occur naturally in the wild state in the European territory of member states.

Article 3 of the Directive requires member states to preserve, maintain or re-establish a sufficient diversity and area of habitats for all species referred to in Article 1.

Article 4 requires member states to take additional special conservation measures, including the designation of SPAs, for two groups of birds. These are (under Article 4.1) certain listed rare or vulnerable species, which are listed in Annex 1 of the Directive (amended with some additions by Directives 81/854/EEC, 85/411/EEC and 86/122/EEC), and (under Article 4.2) regularly occurring migratory species.

For rare and vulnerable bird species, **Article 4.1** explains that "the species mentioned in Annex 1 shall be the subject of special conservation measures concerning their habitat in order to ensure their survival and reproduction in their area of distribution. In this connection account shall be taken of :

a) species in danger of extinction;

b) species vulnerable to specific changes in their habitat;

c) species considered rare because of small populations or restricted local distribution; and

d) other species requiring particular attention for reasons of the specific nature of their habitat.

Trends and variations in population levels shall be taken into account as a background for evaluations. Member states shall classify in particular the most suitable territories in number and size as special protection areas for the conservation of these species, taking into account their protection requirements in the geographical sea and land area where this Directive applies.''

The Birds Directive is reproduced in full in Stroud *et al.* (1990) and the NCC (1988b) lists 48 Annex I bird species which occur regularly in Britain. Estuaries and their environs are important as breeding or wintering areas for nine of these, Bewick's swan, whooper swan, Greenland white-fronted goose, barnacle goose, avocet, Sandwich tern, arctic tern, common tern and little tern.

Article 4.2 is of particular relevance to estuarine conservation. It directs that ''Member states shall take similar measures [to those in Article 4.1] for regularly occurring migratory species not listed in Annex I, bearing in mind their need for protection in the geographical sea and land areas where this Directive applies, as regards their breeding, moulting and wintering areas and staging posts along their migration routes. To this end, member states shall pay particular attention to the protection of wetlands and particularly to wetlands of international importance.''

This Article thus links the Birds Directive to the terms of the Ramsar Convention, and so provides a statutory framework within which the international co-operative measures of the Ramsar Convention, and in particular the safeguarding of sites designated as on the list of wetlands of international importance, can be implemented.

Article 4.4 also gives an important direction since it requires member states to take appropriate steps, in respect of SPAs, to ''avoid pollution or deterioration of habitats or any disturbances affecting the birds, in so far as these would be significant having regard to the objectives of this Article. Outside these protection areas, member states shall also strive to avoid pollution or deterioration of habitats''.

A Council Resolution of 2 April 1979 (reproduced in Stroud *et al.* 1990) made it clear that the Birds Directive, and its Special Protection Areas, should be used to further the conservation of biotopes wherever possible: ''In the designation of these areas [SPAs], account shall be taken of the need to protect biotopes and the flora and fauna without, however, delaying the action of primary importance for bird conservation, particularly in wetlands, to be taken under the programme of Action of the European Commission on the Environment.''

This resolution also called upon member states to notify the Commission within two years of the Directive (i.e. by 1981) of the list of SPAs to be notified, progress that had been made and progress that was intended.

There are several important features of the Birds Directive and how it should be implemented by member states. These have been highlighted by Temple Lang (1982), a legal adviser to the EEC Commission. A key point is the intention of the Directive that the network of candidate SPAs must fulfil the overall objectives of the Directive, in conserving bird habitats and populations, and not just the particular directions of Article 4. Furthermore there is a requirement to **increase** the population levels for many bird species rather than just maintain the *status quo*.

Another important point is that whilst Article 2 instructs member states to take account of economic and recreational needs, including hunting, these are subordinate to scientific needs. This is particularly relevant to the balance between the conservation of SPAs and national economic need in the determination of development proposals that affect SPAs, especially since, under Article 4.4, pollution, habitat deterioration and disturbance to birds should be avoided where they would significantly affect maintenance of the survival and reproduction of birds in their area of distribution.

Another important point relates to SPA site selection: that the failure of a site to meet quantitative criteria (such as a 1% population level) does not necessarily mean that the site should be excluded from the SPA network. Temple Lang (1982) cites the example of the importance of cold weather refuges (a key feature of many British estuarine areas – see Section 8.6.2) and the failure of quantitative criteria to give these appropriate prominence. Another example is the rapid turnover of individual migrant waders on estuaries which results in the use of an estuary by much larger numbers of individuals than are present at any one time (Section 8.6.2). Similarly Temple Lang (1982) points out that there is a need for alternative sites within the SPA network for mobile species such as terns.

The provisions of Article 4 for the conservation of habitats for birds in their areas of distribution are also significant as regards estuaries, as well as other marine areas, since they mean that the SPA network on estuaries should cover both terrestrial and intertidal habitats and also subtidal and marine areas for those species such as seabirds that depend for their survival on inshore and offshore feeding grounds. Hence all parts of review sites fall within the terms of the Birds Directive, and its provisions extend further geographically than the Ramsar Convention, which generally extends only as far as estuarine and coastal waters to a depth of 6 m subtidally.

The rationale and selection of a British network of SPA sites has been recently comprehensively developed by Stroud *et al.* (1990). They conclude that the network of candidate SPA sites currently identified (see below) must be regarded as an irreducible minimum, and will also need to be supplemented by land-use measures in the wider countryside. The importance of the general habitat protection clauses embodied in Article 3 of the Directive, especially for those species that have a dispersed distribution, is also stressed by Temple Lang (1982).

The designation of Special Protection Areas in Britain

The domestic legislation intended to permit the implementation of the Birds Directive is incorporated in the Wildlife & Countryside Act 1981. All sites identified as of international importance are, or will be, notified as Sites of Special Scientific Interest (SSSIs) (see Section 9.3.4). The international designation, whether it be as an SPA or a Ramsar site, places no further obligations on owners or occupiers of sites beyond those arising from SSSIs.

Both previous public statements and internal records give the impression that those involved in the drafting of the Directive and the Wildlife & Countryside Act believed that the two together would allow for a fairly rapid listing of appropriate SSSIs. This would have led to Britain fulfilling the requirements of the Directive not much later than the specified date of 1981 (Stroud et al. 1990).

In practice the process has proved to be time-consuming and complex. Firstly the requirements of renotification of SSSIs under the Wildlife & Countryside Act 1981 have proved more complex than anticipated, so that the requirement for sites to be SSSIs before they receive an international designation has delayed the first stage of the process. Many estuaries are large and have complex patterns of land-ownership and so have proved particularly time-consuming to notify as SSSIs.

Secondly, one of the many flaws in the drafting of the Act meant that dealing with international designations as part of the SSSI notification process was not legally possible. A second round of consultations with owners, occupiers and local authorities is therefore needed on the international designation, once the SSSI notification has been completed. During these consultations the NCC applies to the Government (the Department of the Environment (DoE) in England and Wales, the Scottish Development Department (SDD) in Scotland) for the designation of the site. DoE or SDD then consults with other government departments, this process running concurrently with NCC's local consultations, and considers comments from all interested parties before deciding whether to designate the site. This stage of government consultation has proved to take several years for some sites, particularly where there are unresolved questions on proposed developments affecting parts of sites. Once the Government decides to designate a site it agrees a date with the NCC. The NCC then informs owners, occupiers and local authorities, and the Government informs the European Commission (for SPAs) and/or IUCN (for Ramsar sites). Where, as for most estuaries, a site qualifies for designation as both a Ramsar site and an SPA, the consultations and designation are carried out for both simultaneously.

These procedures are summarised in Figure 9.4 and in NCC (1988b).

A further complication to the designation of all relevant internationally important areas arises from the limitations of the SSSI notification provisions of the Wildlife & Countryside Act. SSSIs can be designated normally only above the level of low tide. Hence although the Birds Directive applies to the whole territory of member states, it is not currently possible to designate SPAs covering inshore or offshore areas important for birds. This means that at present only the breeding colonies of seabirds can be designated (see Section 8.6.4), not their feeding areas. Nor can the inshore winter feeding grounds of many seabirds including divers, grebes and seaducks be afforded safeguard, even though the Government has an obligation through the Birds Directive to protect such areas. The outer parts of many estuaries include such feeding grounds. The only domestic legislative mechanism covering marine areas is that for Marine Nature Reserves, but these, however, are designed chiefly to conserve the sub-littoral marine environment and have proved to involve very great bureaucratic effort to achieve designation (Section 9.3.7). At the request of the Government a review of marine areas important for seabirds, under the terms of the Birds Directive, is being undertaken by the NCC's Ornithology Branch, based on information gathered by its Seabirds at Sea Team (Tasker et al. in prep.).

Special Protection Areas in Britain and Europe

By March 1989, 761 SPAs covering a total of 3,625,416 ha had been designated by the 12 member states of the European Community. Of these Britain had designated 33 sites as SPAs covering a total of 127,112 ha. Other EEC states have chosen to implement the Birds Directive in other ways in accordance with different domestic legislation or by incorporating the Birds Directive directly into domestic law. As a result they have designated markedly differing numbers of SPAs (Figure 9.5) and areas of land as SPAs. By far the most sites (382) have been designated by Germany although these are generally individually small sites. Denmark has designated 111 SPAs and these cover over 22% of its territory. It is actively evaluating other sites for SPA status. Although Belgium has designated only 34 sites these cover over 12% of its state area (Stroud et al. 1990). In contrast Britain's 33 SPAs cover less than 1% of its area.

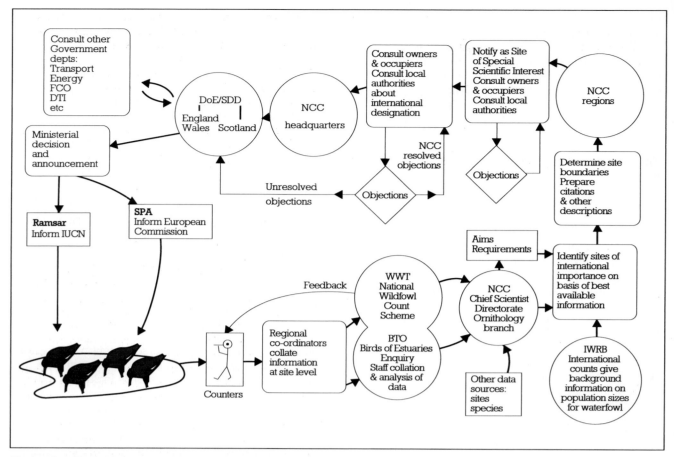

Figure 9.4 Summarised procedure for the designation of internationally important wetlands as SPA/Ramsar sites. The example shown is for a site selected for its bird populations.

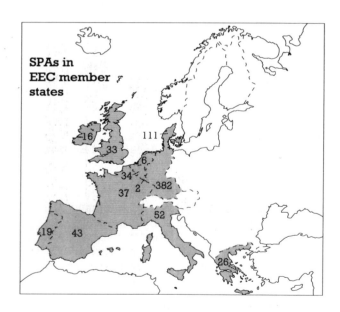

Figure 9.5 The number of Special Protection Areas (SPAs) designated under the EEC Birds Directive by March 1989 by different Member States

Special Protection Areas and Estuaries Review sites

As for Ramsar sites in Britain, estuarine SPAs are a major component of the network so far designated.

By March 1989, 14 designated SPAs (42% of the total) were on Estuaries Review core sites, with another SPA, Leighton Moss (Morecambe Bay) on associated terrestrial land. These 14 sites cover an area of 106,925 ha, 84% of the total area of SPAs in Britain. This very high estuarine proportion of British SPAs is, like that of British Ramsar sites, largely a consequence of the designation of The Wash and the Dee Estuary, which together cover over 66,000 ha.

In addition to these designated SPAs there are a further 47 SPAs among the 185 candidate sites proposed for designation. Overall the 62 SPA sites so far identified on or associated with British estuaries are thus 28% of the total covering all habitats and bird species. As might be expected for a designation that has been operative for a shorter time, a smaller proportion of estuarine candidate SPAs (22.6%) have so far been designated than have estuarine Ramsar sites (31%). With over three-quarters of SPAs yet to be designated there is clearly a great deal of work to still be done to comply fully with the terms of the Birds Directive in safeguarding British estuarine systems.

This is apparent also from Figure 9.6 which shows the review sites that fall partly or wholly within the SPA site network. As would be expected for sites selected chiefly for their wetland bird species and

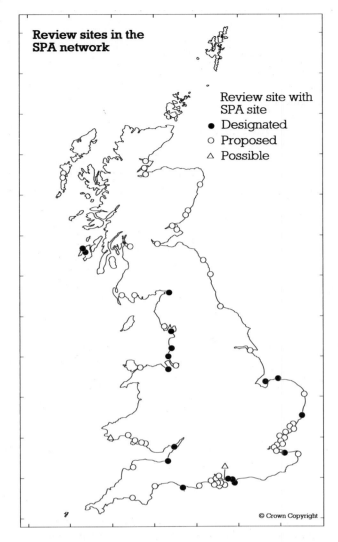

Review sites in the SPA network

Review site with SPA site
- ● Designated
- ○ Proposed
- △ Possible

© Crown Copyright

Figure 9.6 Estuaries Review sites within the Special Protection Area site network. Note that some adjacent review sites form part of a single SPA; other review sites cover more than one SPA (see text, and Stroud *et al.* 1990).

habitats, the distribution of estuarine SPAs closely follows that of estuarine Ramsar sites (Figure 9.3). There is a similarly complex relationship between the boundaries of review sites and those of SPAs, with multiple SPAs forming different parts of the core site and associated terrestrial habitats of some review sites (e.g. Firth of Forth, The Wash) and one SPA covering more than one review site (e.g. Orwell and Stour Estuaries, and Crouch and Blackwater Estuaries and Dengie Flats). On some review sites, e.g. The Wash, almost all significant parts of the core site are designated SPA, but on other estuaries, e.g. the Ore/Alde/Butley Estuary in Suffolk, the SPA currently covers only a small part of the core site.

Overall there are 17 review sites with part or all of their core area and environs already designated SPA and a further 49 review sites with areas proposed for designation as part of the SPA network (Figure 9.6). Hence overall, as for Ramsar sites, there are 66 review sites (42.6% of the total review sites) included at least partly within the

proposed SPA network, with the same additional three sites listed as under further investigation for possible inclusion as candidate sites.

Stroud *et al.* (1990) assessed generally high proportions (>90%) of the British wintering populations of typical estuarine waders, such as dunlin, knot and grey plover, to be within the proposed SPA network. This reflects the inclusion of all major British estuaries with the SPA network, but Figure 9.7 shows that, as might be expected from the way in which the designation criteria are implemented, small estuaries are very poorly represented in the network. Those small estuaries that are included are generally there as part of a wider SPA site, such as that around the Solent, or the Northumberland coast. This means, however, that the Ramsar/SPA site network is not fully representative of all parts of the British estuarine wetland resource. It also means that for species of bird that are widespread on small estuaries the network affords protection to a smaller proportion of their populations. This is exemplified by the redshank. The 25% of redshanks wintering in Britain are on small estuaries (Figure 8.6.47), and this part of the population amounts to some 17% of the international population, yet few of these small estuaries are within the SPA network. The result is that fewer redshanks (64%) than many other waders are within the network. It is clear that the 'wider countryside' approach embodied in the Birds Directive is needed for safeguarding the international importance of British estuaries, even when the Ramsar/SPA site network is in place.

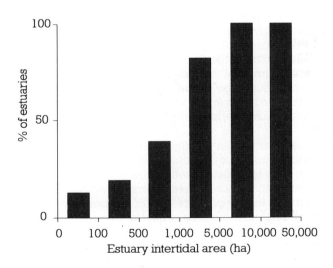

Figure 9.7 The percentage of review sites of different sizes that are within the SPA site network

The effectiveness of the Birds Directive and Ramsar Convention for estuarine wildlife safeguard

General implications

There are a number of obligations relevant to the conservation of estuarine wildlife that ensue from the Ramsar Convention and the Birds Directive, notably to designate and safeguard wetlands of international importance and SPAs; to formulate and implement planning so as to promote the conservation and wise use of wetlands; to take appropriate measures to increase waterfowl populations and to avoid disturbance to birds and other animals; and to take appropriate measures to avoid pollution and deterioration of habitats. Hence the general obligations on such internationally important sites are to maintain and improve their existing quality, and to prevent their deterioration through habitat loss or degradation by impacts such as pollution and to ensure that their existing future use is directed at 'wise-use' and sustainable development. Outside specifically designated sites there are also obligations to avoid pollution and deterioration of wild bird habitats (Article 4.4 of the Birds Directive).

Estuaries are the setting for many human activities, described in Chapter 10, that can affect the habitats and bird populations covered by these international obligations. Much of the current response in Britain to the needs of international wildlife conservation has been in the form of the designation of specific sites. Improvements to the environmental quality of estuaries have not generally been the result of the obligations imposed by these international conservation measures but more of other pressures for environmental quality. Such approaches include the reduction of pollutant levels in estuaries, being achieved through improved water quality standards directed by water authorities, and more recently by the National Rivers Authority (NRA). Estuarine and coastal water quality improvement is also driven by other EC Directives, on topics such as the environmental quality of bathing beaches, and by broader agreements such as the Ministerial Declaration of the Second North Sea Conference, which aimed at the reduction and ultimate elimination of pollution from the North Sea so as to safeguard the reproductive capacity of both the coastal and marine parts of the whole area.

The clear primary obligation of the Birds Directive is to maintain or enhance bird populations through the long-term protection, maintenance and restoration of a sufficient diversity and area of habitats for the conservation of all species of birds, with special measures of habitat protection for migratory species. The instruction to take account of economic and recreational needs, including hunting, (Article 2) is thus subordinate to the scientific needs (Temple Lang 1982). Neither the Birds Directive nor the Ramsar Convention, with its emphasis on sustainable wetland use, precludes the continuation of human activities, nor do they rule out further activity being started. The critical test, however, is that such new activity should not lead to the deterioration of existing habitats within or outside the protected site network. Indeed Article 3 of the Birds Directive directs that bird population maintenance shall be not only through the protection and maintenance of protected areas but also through the reinstatement of destroyed areas and the creation of new areas of habitat.

Since there is evidence that populations of at least one wader species have been restricted by intertidal habitat loss on British estuaries (Goss-Custard & Moser 1988), the requirements in the Directive to maintain and enhance the remaining areas of habitat are particularly apposite on British estuaries.

Government advice on development proposals affecting SPAs

In view of the requirements of the Birds Directive and Ramsar Convention described above, developments that would lead to the destruction of estuarine habitat are generally inappropriate under the terms of the Birds Directive, since habitat loss is inconsistent with the maintenance of suitable habitats for migratory and other species, unless such developments can be shown not to contravene the preamble and Articles of the Birds Directive.

Development proposals in Britain are generally dealt with by application to local planning authorities for consent under the Town & Country Planning legislation. Consent for some types of development proposal on estuaries is, however, increasingly being sought directly from the UK Parliament through the Private Bill procedure (see Chapter 9.6).

The most recent guidance to local planning authorities on the treatment of development proposals affecting sites of international wildlife importance is given in DoE Circular 27/87 (DoE 1987). Since under domestic requirements all SPAs will already have been notified as SSSIs, local planning authorities are required to consult the NCC before granting planning consent. Such consultations are also recommended by Circular 27/87 for developments outside site boundaries since, particularly in wetlands such as estuaries, indirect effects such as pollution and drainage can seriously affect the notified site. If the NCC believes that significant damage to the wildlife interest of the site will occur, it can request that the Secretary of State call-in the planning application for determination through a Public Inquiry.

Circular 27/87 points out that "the Government attaches great importance to the various international obligations it has assumed which now underlie the legislative framework for conservation". It also points out that "the UK is required to achieve the objectives set out in the [Birds] Directive and may be challenged in the European Court if it fails to do so".

The Circular indicates several points that need consideration in determining a planning application affecting an SPA:

a) whether any potential damage or disturbance to the birds or their habitats would be significant (in terms of the Directive) for the survival and reproduction of the species;

b) to what extent could the proposed development be undertaken or phased in ways which would ensure that there be the least possible damage and disturbance to the birds and their habitats;

c) where there is a threat of significant disturbance to birds, whether there are, or are likely to be, alternative suitable and available sites for the proposed development; and

d) the importance of the proposed development (either locally or nationally) in terms of the economic and recreational needs.

The Circular indicates that planning permission should be granted only where the planning authority is satisfied either that disturbance to Annex I or migratory birds, or damage to habitats, will not be significant in terms of the survival or reproduction of the species, or that any such disturbance or damage is outweighed by economic or recreational requirements.

In this and another reference using the words of Article 2 of the Birds Directive the Government advises planning authorities that in considering a planning application affecting an SPA they must carefully evaluate the balance between ecological, scientific and cultural requirements on the one hand and economic and recreational requirements on the other. Note that this would appear, however, to be at variance with interpretation of the balance of Article 2 of the Birds Directive by Temple Lang (1982). Temple Lang indicates that, in terms of the Birds Directive, economic and recreational needs are subordinate to scientific ones.

In general there is thus a presumption in the Directive against developments in SPAs unless they will demonstrably not affect the maintenance and enhancement of bird populations and their habitats. Stroud et al. (1990) conclude that the currently proposed SPA network is an irreducible minimum needed to implement parts of the Birds Directive, so this presumption must be very strong. It should be noted also that the requirements of the more recent EC Directive on Environmental Assessment for an environmental impact assessment (EIA) to be made before developments affecting sensitive wildlife sites are allowed mean that an EIA should be made where a development affects an SPA. On the 'polluter pays' principle embodied in the requirements of the Environmental Assessment Directive the onus of demonstrating the absence of damaging impacts on the SPA lies with the development's proposer.

The Circular indicates that proposed, but not yet designated, SPAs should be subject to the same considerations for planning applications as designated SPAs. This, however, poses some difficulty in determining within which area such considerations should be applied, since for some proposed SPAs the site boundaries have yet to be determined precisely. Such a situation can arise where more than one SSSI may be included in the Ramsar/SPA site, or where the SSSI has yet to be notified under the Wildlife & Countryside Act 1981.

There are also particular complications over dealing with the requirements of the Birds Directive in relation to planning applications on estuaries, whether affecting a designated or a proposed SPA. This difficulty stems at least in part from the limitations imposed by the restriction of SPAs to existing SSSIs and thus usually to only part of an estuary. Since each estuary consists of a linked mosaic of habitats used by bird populations, and since migratory birds depend on the continued existence of the whole network of estuaries both in Britain and internationally (see Chapter 8.6), it may be appropriate that development applications be considered in the terms described above wherever they occur in the British estuarine resource. Otherwise the objectives in Article 4 of the Birds Directive to take special measures to safeguard migratory bird populations are unlikely to be achieved, and neither will the stipulation that the SPA network fulfil the requirements of the whole Directive rather than just those of Article 4, i.e. those for rare and vulnerable species and migratory species (Temple Lang 1982).

Successes and failures of international site safeguard on Estuaries Review sites

The provisions and implementation of the Ramsar Convention and the Birds Directive have led to a much increased awareness of the major international importance of Britain's wetlands and other habitats and their rare, vulnerable and migrant bird populations. The combination of the two measures has been particularly effective in identifying the conservation importance of Britain's estuaries, since these places both are wetlands and support both rare and vulnerable bird species and migratory bird species. The designation of Ramsar sites and SPAs has contributed substantially to governmental and public understanding of the major national and international significance of these parts of Britain's wildlife resource. The high proportion of estuarine Ramsar sites and SPAs in the British networks is an illustration of the value of such places.

The implementation of these international measures in Britain has so far focussed on their site-related requirements, notably in the designation of Ramsar sites and SPAs. Much less attention has yet been paid to the wider, land-use based conservation measures needed to fulfil the requirements of both the Ramsar convention, through its wise-use articles, and the Birds Directive in dealing with the maintenance of populations of widespread species within their area of distribution. Wider-countryside measures as well as site designations may thus be needed to both safeguard the wildlife concerned and comply with the international obligations. Wider-countryside conservation appears to be needed even for some estuarine bird species, despite their localised and clearly defined distribution: for example species such as the redshank depend in part on the many small estuaries (which are mostly outside the current international site network) as well as the few large ones (see Chapter 8.6).

Stroud *et al.* (1990) summarise the adequacy of the currently proposed network of SPAs in Britain for Annex 1 and certain migratory species. They conclude, *inter alia*, that the currently proposed SPA network is adequate for the wintering population of only one species of wader typical of estuaries – the knot – and possibly for three others – avocet, black-tailed godwit and bar-tailed godwit. For 14 wader species typical of estuaries Stroud *et al.* (1990) indicate the need for additional wider-countryside measures to safeguard the wintering populations.

Even within the designated and proposed Ramsar/SPA site network there are limitations for estuarine conservation due to the requirement for all internationally designated sites to be SSSIs. The failure of this mechanism currently to permit SPA safeguard of marine bird populations such as those using the subtidal parts of estuaries as well as further out to sea has been described above, and by Stroud *et al.* (1990) and Tasker *et al.* (In prep.). The fragmentary nature of SSSIs, which has arisen often for historical legislative reasons unrelated to the current knowledge of the distribution and ecological influences on and requirements of internationally important bird populations, also means that it is not currently possible to designate all parts of the interlinked estuarine ecosystem utilised by a section of the population of any species.

What of the efficacy of these international measures as safeguards for the animals and habitats within the Ramsar/SPA site network? Certain legal actions are available to the EC Commission where the Commission considers that a Member State has failed to fulfil its obligation under the Treaty of Rome to apply the Directive. Through these infraction procedures the Commission can bring the matter to the attention to the European Court of Justice. A member state can also bring another member state before the Court of Justice for an alleged infringement. Such steps can ultimately result in the Court of Justice requiring the member state to take the necessary actions to comply with the terms of its judgement. This stage has, however, never yet been reached for matters under the Birds Directive (Batten 1987).

The provisions of the Birds Directive mean that adequate protection must be afforded to SPAs. Failure to give such sites protection against damaging developments can lead to the EC taking steps to prosecute a member state for breach of the Directive. Such intervention by the EC over a threat to an internationally important site can have positive effects for nature conservation (Batten 1987). In Britain one such instance of intervention by the EC involved wildfowl, although not on an estuary. In 1985, Duich Moss, on Islay, was proposed as a Ramsar/SPA site for its botanical and peatland importance and its internationally important wintering population of Greenland white-fronted geese. Planning consent was granted for peat extraction from the site inimical with the maintenance of its conservation importance, which

led to the intervention of the EC, with a threat of prosecution proceedings for breach of the Directive. The proposals were subsequently withdrawn, and less sensitive sites elsewhere were identified for the required peat extraction (Greenland White-fronted Goose Study Group 1986; Batten 1987).

The identified international importance of estuaries covered by the SPA network has at times been instrumental in safeguarding areas against damaging development proposals, by being the reason for the rejection of planning applications, for example the recent rejection of rubbish tipping proposals at Kinneil Kerse on the Firth of Forth. Many proposals and planning applications continue, however, to be made for developments that would lead to damage or loss of habitat on internationally important estuaries. When the Estuaries Review conducted its survey in early 1989, 36 (53%) of the 68 estuaries within the Ramsar/SPA network had proposals that would caused intertidal and subtidal loss of habitat (Figure 9.8). Since this figure is higher than the proportion of estuaries outside the international network that were subject to such proposals, it appears that the international importance of an estuary does little to deter the proposal of damaging developments (see also Chapter 10.5.5). Note, however, that there is a greater likelihood of development proposals being made for larger estuaries, and it is these larger estuaries that feature most strongly in the international site network (Figure 9.7). Nevertheless many potentially damaging proposals continue to be made relating to Ramsar/SPA estuaries. Whilst some of these proposals would result in only small incursions into the estuaries, such piecemeal loss of estuarine habitat is of general conservation concern and has resulted in the rejection of planning applications in places such as Langstone Harbour and Chichester Harbour. Other proposals may be outside the current Ramsar/SPA site boundaries, but, as described above, such proposals anywhere within an interlinked estuarine ecosystem can affect the international network.

Many development proposals may, however, have considerable and far-reaching impacts on the existing wildlife importance of estuaries and Ramsar/SPA sites and so would seem to breach the intent of the Birds Directive. These include proposals for marina developments on many internationally important estuaries especially in the south and west of England and Wales; tidal and 'amenity' barrage schemes on review sites such as the Severn Estuary, the Mersey Estuary, Morecambe Bay, the Duddon Estuary and the Humber Estuary; proposals for steel works adjacent to The Wash; road scheme proposals on the Dee Estuary in North Wales; and airport proposals on the Mersey Estuary. All these are of course in addition to existing activities such as rubbish tipping and spoil disposal that continue to cause permitted loss and damage to internationally important estuaries. These activities are described further in Chapter 10.

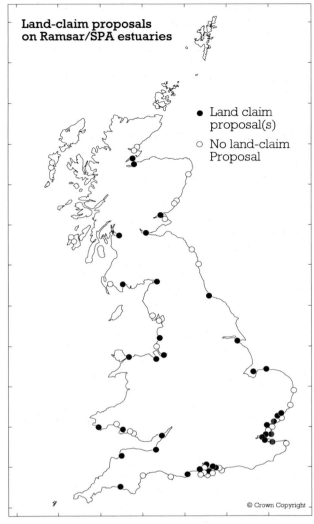

Figure 9.8 Review sites within the Ramsar/SPA site network affected by land-claim development proposals in early 1989

Not all these proposals whose development would lead to habitat loss or damage within estuarine Ramsar/SPA sites are, however, withdrawn or rejected. The most notorious recent example has been the allowing in 1988 of a major expansion of Felixstowe Docks in the Orwell Estuary. The Orwell Estuary forms part of the proposed Stour and Orwell Estuary Ramsar/SPA site. The development proposals, which were authorised by Parliamentary Private Bill (see also Chapter 9.6), will taken together directly destroy about 7% of the intertidal mudflats and 9% of the saltmarshes of the Orwell Estuary in three planned phases. As Davidson & Evans (1985) described, however, the overall magnitude of the impact of this loss was much greater than the area percentages alone indicate. This was because the area concerned, Fagbury Flats, formed a critical part of the Orwell and Stour Estuary ecosystem for birds using a much larger area of these and other estuaries, notably as high tidal level feeding areas, roost sites and as a cold weather refugium (see also Section 8.6.2).

Parliament passed the Felixstowe Dock and Railway Bill despite accepting that the development works it enabled would significantly damage the national nature conservation importance of the area, and the UK Government's international obligations to protect it. This decision was reached as a result of Parliament and its Committees accepting arguments that container port facilities could not be developed anywhere else in south-east England. The works were thus enabled on the basis that the urgent national need for dock facilities at this site outweighed the national and international conservation obligations, i.e. a view based chiefly on interpretation of Article 2 of the Birds Directive.

Another Parliamentary Private Bill, this time seriously affecting the proposed Ramsar/SPA site of the Severn Estuary, is also reaching its final stages. This proposes the construction of a barrage across the mouth of the Taff/Ely Estuary so as to create a permanently high water level in the impounded area as a recreational and leisure facility associated with waterside redevelopment. In doing so, the barrage would destroy the intertidal conservation importance of the estuary, which forms a key interlinked component of the unique Severn Estuary. At the time of writing consent for the passage of the Bill has been withheld pending clarification of the possibility of a potentially damaging raised water table in the surrounding urban area. Hence the national and international estuarine wildlife importance of the area would appear, as with the Felixstowe Dock Bill, to be overridden by developmental and recreational needs.

A third recent instance of serious permitted damage to an internationally important estuarine site is that of the construction of a pipeline facility across some of the most ecologically sensitive parts of the sand-dunes and intertidal flats of Morrich More on the Dornoch Firth. In this case consent was granted by the Secretary of State for Scotland about three years ago, following a Public Inquiry. Shell (UK) is now letting a contract to develop the facility.

All these examples are of sites also notified as SSSIs, and loss and damage to estuarine SSSIs is described further in Section 9.3.4. The overall trend is thus that even within these limited areas of key international importance within the Ramsar/SPA site network there continue to be proposals for developments that would cause direct or indirect damage to estuarine habitats, and some of these damaging developments continue to be authorised. This is despite the requirements of, for example, Article 3 of the Birds Directive to 'preserve, maintain or re-establish sufficient diversity and area of habitats for all species of birds through the protection of areas, the ecological management of habitats both inside and outside these protected areas, the re-establishment of destroyed habitats, and habitat creation.

Overall it would seem so far that the internationally important estuarine wildlife resource in Britain is being diminished through land-claim developments, rather than that the intent of the Birds Directive to enhance and increase the resource is being fulfilled. Even within the restricted Ramsar/SPA site network estuarine habitat losses are continuing, yet Stroud *et al.* (1990) conclude that even the maintenance of the existing site network does not provide adequate protection for most of the breeding and wintering bird species for which British estuaries are so nationally and internationally important.

9.3 British wildlife conservation designations

9.3.1 Introduction

The framework for a national policy for nature conservation in Britain was first formally set out in 1947 in two Government White Papers: *Conservation of nature in England and Wales* (Cmd. 7122) and *National Parks and the conservation of nature in Scotland* (Cmd. 7235). These set out the view that nature conservation in Britain would be most effectively implemented by the safeguarding of key areas representing the major examples of natural and semi-natural habitats with their characteristic plant and animal communities.

In 1984 the NCC published *Nature conservation in Great Britain* (NCC 1984) which set down a strategy for nature conservation in the context of a review of the progress of conservation and conserving key wildlife sites over the preceding few decades. This confirmed that safeguarding sites of special importance to nature conservation was the most powerful and cost-effective tool for nature conservation. At the same time increasing knowledge of the ecology, behaviour and needs of British wildlife cannot always be achieved by site-specific action. The maintenance of the current ranges and distributions of native plants and animals often depends on conservation measures, usually in terms of sympathetic land-uses, in the wider countryside outside key wildlife sites.

Hence there are currently three main elements of the nature conservation strategy in Britain:

a) the maintenance of wildlife in the wider countryside;

b) the notification of sites as Sites of Special Scientific Interest (SSSIs); and

c) the management of key sites as National Nature Reserves (NNRs).

This part describes the various designations, both statutory and non-statutory, applied to wildlife sites on estuaries in Britain. These domestic designations also provide the framework within which the international conservation measures described above are implemented.

Central to the delivery of wildlife conservation in Britain is the notification by the NCC of Sites of Special Scientific Interest (SSSIs). This, and the other statutory designations delivered through the main item of wildlife conservation legislation (the Wildlife & Countryside Act 1981) and described below – National Nature Reserves, Areas of Special Protection, Marine Nature Reserves – provide the mechanism for statutory safeguard of wildlife sites in Britain. In addition, statutory Local Nature Reserves can be declared by local authorities under the National Parks and Access to the Countryside Act 1949.

A number of non-statutory wildlife conservation organisations throughout Britain, notably county wildlife trusts, the Royal Society for the Protection of Birds and the Wildfowl and Wetlands Trust, own or manage further nature reserves and wildlife refuges.

The implementation and distribution of all these designations around Estuaries Review sites in Britain are covered in this part, which first describes two descriptive designations, Nature Conservation Review sites and Geological Conservation Review sites, applied by the NCC to sites as the initial identification of the key parts of the wildlife resource appropriate for subsequent statutory designation.

It is important to recognise two general points about the descriptions in this part. Firstly there can be multiple designations covering one location within an estuary. For instance an estuarine site may be notified as an SSSI by the NCC, with part or all of the SSSI designated as a National Nature Reserve, part of which is leased and operated as a Local Nature Reserve by a county wildlife trust. Secondly the detailed geographical relationships of the various designated areas within each estuary are outside the scope of this overview. Here we restrict analysis to reporting the presence of each feature on each estuary and, where possible, its presence in relation to core sites and associated terrestrial habitats. Most of the information presented here was collated during the first half of 1989, although in some cases more recent information has been incorporated where relevant.

9.3.2 Nature Conservation Review (NCR) sites

The NCC produced *A nature conservation review* (Ratcliffe 1977) in 1977. This major review set out why the key areas, identified as Nature Conservation Review (NCR) sites, are important for nature conservation and how the assessment of their quality is made. The safeguarding of these NCR sites listed by Ratcliffe (1977) is regarded as essential to the success of nature conservation in Britain.

A nature conservation review described the important characteristics of each wildlife habitat in turn and reviewed the sites then known to be of nature conservation importance. These became the priority sites for receiving management for nature conservation. The intention at that time was that these NCR sites would subsequently be designated on biological grounds as National Nature Reserves under the terms of the National Parks & Access to the Countryside Act 1949.

Subsequently the emphasis on ownership and declaration of all key wildlife sites has strengthened, particularly with the new provisions of the Wildlife & Countryside Act 1981. The NCC's current view is that all NCR land should be subject in perpetuity to nature conservation management of the highest quality. However, the ownership and management of a large part of the NCR series by others is now seen as both a necessary and an effective approach, provided that adequate management standards are maintained. Currently NCR sites help to identify suitable biological sites as candidates for National Nature Reserve status. Geological and geomorphological site selection has been undertaken through a similar approach, the Geological Conservation Review (GCR). This is described in Section 9.3.3 below.

In selecting key sites of national biological importance in *A nature conservation review*, Ratcliffe (1977) applied two basic principles for site selection. For most habitats the exemplary site principle was used. This selected the best examples of sites to give adequate representation of the countrywide range of variation in natural and semi-natural ecosystem types with their associated assemblages of plants and animals. In terms of estuaries, this approach selected sites with particular types of coastal habitats (see Chapter 8.3). For estuaries, however, the second approach also applies, in which all examples qualify for key site status when they are above an identified critical standard of nature conservation importance. Ratcliffe (1977) related this particularly to migrant and wintering waterfowl populations and colonial breeding bird assemblages. Such an approach is also embodied in the application on estuaries of the international conservation measures described above.

Estuaries fall within the 'coastlands' habitat type described by *A nature conservation review*. Ratcliffe (1977) points out that, unlike most other habitats, coastland NCR sites include all those supporting nationally and internationally important bird populations, as well as those holding the best representative examples of vegetative habitats. This is an important distinction when considering the appropriate overall estuarine conservation approach, since it emphasises the essential need for conservation of a widespread estuarine network rather than just representative sites.

Ratcliffe identified some 900 NCR sites in the original review. Subsequent revisions and deletions have maintained a similar total: by 1989 there were 943 NCR sites in Britain covering a total area of 1,057,875 ha (NCC in prep.). Of these, 150 (15.9%) are classified as coastal habitats.

Over half the coastal NCR sites are estuarine: there are 79 such NCR sites on review sites. Several review sites have more than one coastal NCR site within them, and some other NCR sites encompass more than one review site: 71 review sites (46% of the total) are entirely within the NCR site network, i.e. regarded as of national nature conservation importance for their coastal habitats and wildlife (Figure 9.9). The distribution of NCR coastal habitat features around British estuaries has been described in more detail in Chapter 8.3.

In addition to these coastal estuarine sites there are a further 20 NCR sites on associated terrestrial habitats adjoining 13 review sites. These associated terrestrial sites include woodland, peatland, lowland and open-water NCR sites, and include sites adjacent to six further review sites that are not within the coastal habitats NCR series (Figure 9.9), so that overall almost half the British estuaries and their associated terrestrial habitats (77 review sites) are within the NCR network.

9.3.3 Geological Conservation Review (GCR) sites

For its size Great Britain has an exceptionally diverse geological heritage. This comprises an unrivalled sequence of rocks and rich and varied fossils, mineral deposits and landforms, spanning much of the earth's long history including most since the appearance of life (Campbell & Bowen 1989). The geological importance of Britain is greatly increased by its very long coastline for such a small land area. On it there is an exceptional number of rock sections and coastal landforms accessible for research. Many of these sites have become recognised as of international importance after study and investigation by generations of geologists.

The NCC began its Geological Conservation Review (GCR) in late 1977. Its aim has been to assess, document and ultimately publish descriptions of all the British sites of national and international earth science importance. Hence the GCR provides the earth science equivalent of the Nature Conservation Review. The volumes of the GCR describe and assess key sites in the context of an aspect of the geology, palaeontology, mineralogy or geomorphology of Britain. The first GCR volume was published by the NCC in 1989 (Campbell & Bowen 1989). Once publication is completed the GCR will provide a comprehensive overview of the geology and geomorphology of Britain and a clear statement of the conservation value of the key earth science sites. To accompany this the NCC has recently published a strategy for earth science conservation in Great Britain (NCC 1990).

For practical reasons GCR site assessment and selection were organised within a framework of blocks, each of which represents a period of geological time, a particular subject or a geographical area. For each block a national

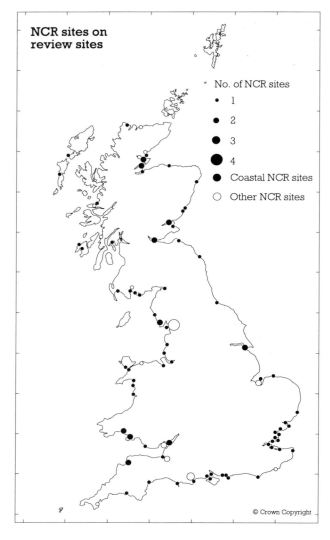

Figure 9.9 Review sites within the coastal NCR site series. Other NCR sites on associated terrestrial habitats adjacent to review sites are also shown. Note that some NCR sites overlap with more than one review site

9.1). The majority (144) of these sites are cliff and foreshore exposures of rock and Quaternary deposits. Between them these GCR sites display virtually the whole geological succession of Britain from pre-Cambrian times to the present. (The geological timescale is summarised in Figure 9.10.)

Era	System (Period)	Series (Epoch)	Age My B.P.
CENOZOIC	QUATERNARY	Holocene	
		Pleistocene	
			1.8
	TERTIARY	Pliocene	5.0
		Miocene	
		Oligocene	22.5
		Eocene	37.5
		Palaeocene	53.5
			65
MESOZOIC	CRETACEOUS		
			140
	JURASSIC		
			195
	TRIASSIC		225
PALAEOZOIC	PERMIAN		280
	CARBONIFEROUS		345
	DEVONIAN		395
	SILURIAN		435
	ORDOVICIAN		500
	CAMBRIAN		570
PRECAMBRIAN			

Figure 9.10 A summary of the geological timescale. Ages are shown in millions of years before present (My B.P.).

network has been identified of sites that incorporate the key features of the geology or geomorphology of that block. All GCR-block sites are regarded at least nationally important and are thus potential SSSIs.

Overall some 3,000 localities of individual GCR-block sites have been identified. Many of these sites overlap geographically. For example a particular stretch of coast can be nationally important in several respects for the rocks it demonstrates, the fossils they contain and the landforms that are present, each identified as a GCR-block site. So the final total of geological SSSIs resulting from notification of all these GCR sites will be rather less than the 3,000 GCR sites. The distribution of those that have been so far notified as SSSIs is described in Section 9.3.4 below.

Overall there are 202 GCR-block sites (*c.* 7% of the total) that are associated with review sites (Table

Only 58 estuarine GCR sites are geomorphological, but these are generally active geomorphological sites of considerable interest, since estuaries

Table 9.1 Numbers of different GCR-block sites located within Estuaries Review sites

GCR block		Number of sites
A Cliff exposures		
1	Pliocene	2
2	Paleogene (Eocene-Oligocene)	4
3	Cenomanian - Maastrichtian (Cretaceous)	4
4	Aptian-Albian (Cretaceous)	1
5	Wealden (Jurassic)	1
6	Kimmeridgian (Jurassic)	1
7	Oxfordian (Jurassic)	2
8	Callovian (Jurassic)	1
9	Bathonian (Jurassic)	1
10	Toarcian (Jurassic)	1
11	Hettangian - Pliensbachian	2
12	Rhaetian (Triassic)	4
13	Permo-Triassic	4
14	Westphalian	3
15	Dinantian	14
16	Devonian marine	2
17	Devonian non-marine	4
18	Devonian	3
19	Ludlow (Silurian)	1
20	Wenlock (Silurian)	1
21	Arenig Llanvirn (Ordovician)	3
22	Tremadoc Cambrian	1
23	Dalradian	3
24	Moine	2
25	Lewisian	2
26	Variscan structures	2
27	Caledonian structures	1
28	Igneous, Permo-Carboniferous	5
29	ORS Igneous	2
30	Mineralogy	3
31	Palaeobotany	17
32	Vertebrate palaeontology	17
33	Palaeoentomology	4
34	Arthropoda	1
35	Quaternary	25
Total cliff exposures		144
B Geomorphological sites		
36	Coastal geomorphology of Scotland	15
37	Coastal geomorphology of England	21
38	Coastal geomorphology of Wales	5
39	Saltmarshes	11
40	Miscellaneous geomorphology	6
Total geomorphological sites		58

provide particularly good illustrations of sedimentary processes. These are both post-glacial and modern-day processes and sites include shingle features, sand-dunes, cliffs and shore platforms and saltmarshes.

This section describes the nature and distribution of the various types of GCR site that occur on estuaries, first the cliff exposures and then the geomorphological sites.

Cliff exposures

Cliffs and associated foreshore exposures play a major role in geological studies in Britain: because of the length and height of exposure in most cliffs they are unrivalled for the study of large-scale features and variations in their geology that cannot otherwise be seen. Cliff exposures also provide continuous sequences of sedimentary rocks, unparalleled elsewhere, and it was from these that much of the geological history of Britain was first deduced. An estimated 30% of all the scientifically important British coastal cliff sites occur within estuaries. These include many classic locations for British geology.

Cliffs can be classified usefully as *durable* and *non-durable*, an important distinction for practical conservation purposes. Durable cliffs comprise granite, basalt, gneiss, slate, sandstone, limestone and a wide variety of other similar hard and strong rock-types. These are the product of long-term marine or fluvial erosion and, despite suffering occasional rock-falls, generally remain stable and well-exposed for long periods.

Estuaries with durable cliffs occur predominantly in south-west England, Wales, north-west England and around most of the Scottish coast. The estuarine localities selected by the GCR as being of national and international importance cover all fields of British stratigraphy, structural, igneous and metamorphic geology, mineralogy and palaeontology. In addition British estuaries also contain several hundred geological sites of local or regional scientific and educational importance, although such sites are as yet poorly documented. These local and regional geological sites include some prime teaching and fossil collecting sites.

Non-durable cliffs consist of clay, sand, gravel, weak mudstones, shales and other relatively weak materials. Such cliffs are often of more recent origin and rely on continuous erosion to maintain their exposure. They generally suffer repeated landslips and are the source of much of the sediment that is transported and redeposited along shores. The instability of non-durable cliffs has led to attempts at artificial stabilisation (see also Chapter 10). For conservation purposes, however, a degree of erosion needs to continue unless the exposure is to be lost.

Review sites with non-durable cliffs occur predominantly on the eastern and southern coasts of England, although there are also important examples in Wales, Scotland and in western England notable on the Severn Estuary. The localities selected by the GCR cover mostly British stratigraphy and particularly the Mesozoic, Tertiary and Quaternary deposits, i.e. the more recent parts of geological history (Figure 9.10). As with durable cliffs, there are also several hundred non-durable cliff sites of local or regional geological importance on review sites.

Examples of durable and non-durable cliff exposures of particular scientific importance occur, for example, on the Firth of Forth and the Newtown Estuary. The Kinghorn Coast section on the northern shore of the Firth of Forth exposes a richly fossiliferous succession of Carboniferous sandstones, coals and limestones interbedded with volcanic lavas. The fossils include fish scales, spines, teeth and bones, insects, and the best known plant assemblage of this period in the world. The succession and fossils form the basis for our

knowledge of the geological conditions and life of the Carboniferous period in the Midland Valley of Scotland. Hence the Kinghorn Coast is an important feature of the national network of sites which provides the geological record of this major period in Britain's geological history. The Newtown Estuary, on the northern shore of the Isle of Wight, has at Bouldnor a representative example of a non-durable cliff exposure. Here is exposed a long succession of clays, sands and weak sandstones of Tertiary age. These contain well preserved fossil mammals, birds, reptiles and plants which together constitute by far the best palaeontological assemblage from this period. These sediments and fossils have provided the main evidence for geological conditions throughout Britain during this period. The exposures continue to be of major importance for understanding the evolution of many plant and animal species.

The 144 cliff-exposure GCR-block sites are distributed around 60 review sites throughout Britain (Figure 9.11). The Severn Estuary, with 19 separate GCR-block sites, has more cliff-exposure sites than any other estuary in Britain and many

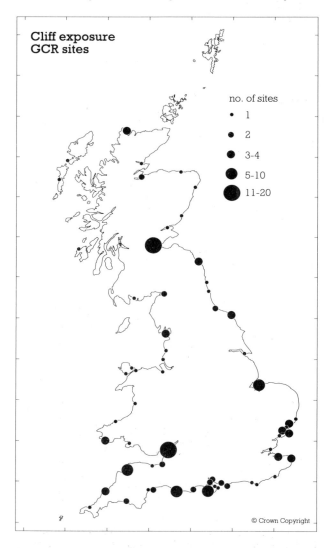

Figure 9.11 The distribution of cliff exposure Geological Conservation Review (GCR) sites on Estuaries Review sites

further sites of regional or local importance (NCC 1988c). Other estuaries with many cliff-exposure sites are the Firth of Forth (11 GCR sites), and the Newtown Estuary (10 sites) which for its size is particularly significant for its earth science interest.

Geomorphological sites

The soft coast geomorphology of Britain comprises three main landform types so far identified as of earth science interest: shingle structures, sand-dunes and saltmarshes. The GCR identifies a network of nationally and internationally important sites demonstrating the key features of each type. Many (46%) of these geomorphological GCR sites are associated with review sites, either as individual features (e.g. shingle bars) or as complex landform associations (e.g. sand-dunes developed on shingle bars). In the latter case it is important to note that the key interest of such sites from a geomorphological viewpoint lies in the total assemblage of features and the relationships between them (e.g. between sediment source and

resulting landforms). The distribution of geomorphological GCR sites on British estuaries is shown in Figure 9.12. Overall the 48 coastal geomorphological GCR sites are distributed around 48 (31%) of review sites throughout Britain (Figure 9.12). These sites include several, e.g. Blue Anchor – Lilstock (Blue Anchor Bay) selected for the geomorphology of their rocky shores. Most (37) estuarine geomorphological GCR sites demonstrate depositional processes, with a further seven being both erosional and depositional. Only four, all cliff and wave-cut platform sites, are purely erosional in character.

Tidal mudflats and sandflats, although a key geomorphological feature of estuaries (see Chapter 8.1), have not been systematically selected for the GCR, nor have estuarine systems in their entirety.

The key features of each major coastal geomorphological GCR type are described below.

Shingle landforms

Shingle is an important constituent of British coasts which occurs along almost 900 km of coastline. In southern Britain much of the shingle is formed from flint eroded from chalk sea-cliffs. Flints are then either deposited directly onto shingle foreshores or reworked from offshore banks. In contrast the Scottish shingle accumulations have more typically been transported to the coast by rivers draining from melting Pleistocene ice-sheets and nearby upland areas. A third source of shingle is material derived from glacial deposits on the nearshore seabed.

Shingle structures associated with estuaries are generally fringing beaches. These are a common landform comprising a strip of shingle running along the top of a beach, and occur frequently along the English Channel coast. Shingle spits form where there is an abrupt change in the direction of the coast, for example at Hurst Castle Spit (Lymington River) in The Solent. Hence they are most common on coasts which have an irregular outline. Shingle spits can have one or more recurved hooks and a recurved distal end that results from wave deflection by refraction round the end of the spit. Spits can form across estuary mouths as a bar or barrier with sometimes sand accreting over the shingle, for example Dawlish Warren on the Exe Estuary. Such places are classified as *bar-built estuaries* in this review (see Chapter 5).

There are some general patterns in the geographical distribution of shingle structures. Sediment is in short supply along the north Devon coast so shingle is scarce. A notable exception is at Westward Ho! where a large cobble ridge GCR site has been formed from material transported from the south. Towards the northern end of the ridge the sediment becomes finer and a spit has formed at the mouth of the Taw-Torridge Estuary. Here the dynamics of the estuary have played a

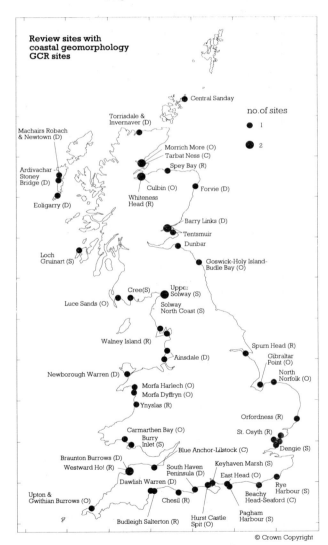

Figure 9.12 The distribution of coastal geomorphological GCR sites on Estuaries Review sites. GCR sites are named and their main geomorphological features are identified: D sand-dune, R shingle ridges, S saltmarsh, C cliff or wave-cut platform, and O complex (two or more features).

role in sorting and reworking the sediments. In contrast the shingle landforms of the Welsh coast have formed in areas with an abundant supply of sediment derived from glacial deposits. Shingle spits form constituent parts of many coastal depositional landforms. Many Welsh estuaries are bar-built (see Figure 5.6) and shingle bars and spits are notable features, identified as GCR sites, at Ynyslas (Dyfi Estuary), Morfa Dyffryn (Artro Estuary) and Morfa Harlech (Traeth Bach).

Shingle is only a minor component of coastal geomorphology from North Wales to Lancashire since sands and silts are relatively more abundant. At Walney Island, however, glacial sediments provide the material for the formation of shingle bars that are reworked and deposited in a macrotidal environment. Further north, in Scotland the shingle bars and spits at Whiteness Head (Moray Firth) and Spey Bay are notable for their massive size and the significant contribution of longshore drift to their formation.

In East Anglia two major shingle structures occur, within the North Norfolk Coast GCR site and at Orfordness. Orfordness is an important shingle spit, developed in association with the dynamics of the Ore/Alde/Butley Estuary (see also Figure 8.1.28). Further south along the English Channel coast shingle landforms have generally formed through reworking of material within estuaries. Chesil Beach (The Fleet) stands apart as an essentially fossil landform derived from a massive accumulation of shingle moved into place during the Holocene transgression under storm conditions. The shingle features at Rye Harbour, Pagham (Pagham Harbour) and East Head (Chichester Harbour) reflect the interaction between estuary mouth dynamics and shingle supply.

Overall then estuaries are important locations for the development of the shingle landforms where the tidal and current dynamics allow the transport and deposition of relatively large quantities of sedimentary materials. The vegetational importance of estuarine shingles is described in Section 8.1.7.

Sand-dunes

Sand-dunes form a distinctive component of the coastal geomorphology in Britain. They are commonest on coasts where a ready supply of sediment has been provided by the glacial and periglacial deposits of the last ice age. Sand-dunes are typically associated with estuaries where there are extensive tidal flats (see Figure 8.1.5) and so where abundant sand-sized sediment has been available for reworking by the wind.

Sand-dunes are associated with 55 review sites (Figure 8.1.23) and 23 of these have GCR sites identified for their dune systems (Figure 9.12). Major dune systems of GCR status occur within the estuaries of the Irish Sea coast, for example at Braunton Burrows (Taw-Torridge Estuary), Carmarthen Bay, Ynyslas (Dyfi Estuary), Morfa

Dyffryn (Artro Estuary), Morfa Harlech (Traeth Bach), Newborough Warren (Cefni Estuary), Ainsdale (Ribble Estuary) and Luce Sands (Luce Bay). On the North Sea coast important sand-dune systems are present at Forvie (Ythan Estuary), Barry Links and Tentsmuir (Tay Estuary), Holy Island (Lindisfarne and Budle Bay), and north Norfolk (North Norfolk Coast). Several beach complexes associated with review sites in the northern and western Scottish islands include sand-dunes and machair (dune grasslands), notably at Bagh nam Faoilean, Scarista, Torrisdale Bay and Cata Sand. On the south coast of England, however, sand-dune systems tend to be secondary features of the GCR sites that fall within estuaries.

The vegetation importance of sand-dunes has been described in Section 8.1.6.

Saltmarshes

Although saltmarshes are a common and characteristic feature of British estuaries (Section 8.1.5) those identified as of GCR quality form only a relatively small proportion (c. 10%) of the coastal geomorphology GCR site network. Saltmarshes have developed in places where shelter is provided by bars, spits and within estuaries. Saltmarshes also occur along predominantly rocky coasts in fjords and fjards where tidal energy is dissipated. In general saltmarshes of northern and western Britain are predominantly composed of fine sands and silts while their eastern counterparts are predominantly muddy (Adam 1978).

All of the 16 saltmarsh sites included in the GCR are located within estuaries (Figure 9.12). They are distributed from the Lymington Estuary (Hurst Castle) northwards to the Dornoch Firth (Morrich More) and include the extensive saltmarshes of the Solway Firth and North Norfolk Coast. The saltmarshes of Dengie Flats are notable for demonstrating important relationships between saltmarsh sedimentation and tidal flat dynamics.

Rock coast landforms

Five British estuaries include GCR sites that represent aspects of the geomorphology of rock coasts. Sites at Tarbat Ness (Dornoch Firth), Dunbar (Tyninghame Bay) and Blue Anchor – Lilstock (Blue Anchor Bay) have been selected for their shore platforms. GCR sites at Beachy Head – Seaforth (Cuckmere Estuary) and at Upton and Gwithian Towans (Hayle Estuary) are included for their cliff landforms.

9.3.4 Sites of Special Scientific Interest (SSSIs)

The National Parks & Access to the Countryside Act 1949 required the NCC to notify local planning authorities of Sites of Special Scientific Interest (SSSIs). This mechanism was essentially a means of ensuring consultation over planning applications.

Subsequently Section 28 of the Wildlife & Countryside Act 1981 extended the obligations and procedures relating to SSSIs. The 1981 Act requires the NCC to notify any area of land which in its opinion is "of special interest by reason of any of its flora, fauna or geological or physiographic features". These are now the Sites of Special Scientific Interest (SSSIs). The 1981 Act, and its 1985 amendments, require the notification of SSSIs to owners and occupiers, local planning authorities and the Secretary of State and the National Rivers Authority, the appropriate water and sewerage plcs, and internal drainage boards (under the provisions of the Water Act 1989). The functioning of the 1981 Act is further described by Adams (1984) and NCC (1988d).

Sites notified under the National Parks and Access to the Countryside Act 1949 remain SSSIs but the provisions of the 1981 Act relating to owners and occupiers do not apply until the land has been notified formally to them and to the Secretary of State. This process is generally called 'renotification' and has been largely completed. In addition to this renotification, surveys since 1981 have revealed further areas which are also of special interest but which were not previously notified as SSSIs. These areas, which in some cases involve the extension to the boundaries of existing SSSIs, are now being notified by the NCC. Conversely, some SSSIs or parts of SSSIs lose their special wildlife interest. The SSSI designation is then withdrawn by the NCC in a process of 'denotification'.

The 1981 Act also requires the NCC to advise owners and occupiers of any operations likely to damage the flora, fauna, geological or physiographical features that make the site of special interest. These activities are now known as Potentially Damaging Operations (PDOs). This list provides a mechanism for consultation between owners or occupiers and the NCC on the management of the SSSI, since an owner or occupier is required to advise the NCC of an intention to carry out an operation on the list. Where damage would be unavoidable the NCC can offer a settlement which will protect the wildlife interest. If resolution is not possible during a four-month consultation period, the NCC may request the Secretary of State to make a Nature Conservation Order under Section 29 of the Wildlife & Countryside Act 1981. This can lead to extension of the consultation period to 12 months (and in some circumstances up to 15 months) and prohibits third parties, as well as owners and occupiers, from undertaking PDOs. In the last resort the NCC may apply to the appropriate Secretary of State for a Compulsory Purchase Order.

There are two exemptions to the legal requirement for consultation on PDOs. One is if the operation is an emergency, in which case the NCC has to be notified as soon as is practicable. The other is where the operation is authorised by planning permission granted under the Town & Country Planning Act 1971 or the Town & Country Planning (Scotland) Act 1972. Owners and occupiers are not liable for the unauthorised actions of third parties such as trespassers or vandals.

Under Section 16 of the 1949 Act and Section 29 of the Wildlife & Countryside Act 1981 the NCC can enter into management agreements with owners and occupiers to enhance the conservation interest of the SSSI. It may also make grants (under Section 38 of the 1981 Act) or offer to lease or purchase the land (under Section 1 of the Nature Conservancy Council Act 1973). Such actions are usually taken for declaration of a National Nature Reserve (see Section 9.3.5).

The additional procedures and paperwork required for SSSI notification and renotification under the 1981 Act have proved extensive and complex. Large sites and those where ownership is complex have proved particularly time-consuming, and since many estuarine sites are of this type some remain to be notified or renotified as SSSIs under the 1981 Act.

Selection of SSSIs

Nature conservation in Great Britain (NCC 1984) stated that "the primary objective of nature conservation is to ensure that the national heritage of wild flora and fauna and geological and physiographic features remains as large and diverse as possible, so that society may use and appreciate its value to the fullest extent."

Site safeguard, the protection and management of the most important areas for wild flora and fauna and their habitat, is regarded as the cornerstone of conservation practice. Within this, SSSI notification is regarded as the principle statutory means of achieving this goal (NCC 1989b).

In the 1949 Act SSSIs were distinguished from nature reserves as "not being land for the time being managed as a nature reserve". Hence the original SSSI notification did not apply to National Nature Reserves (NNRs). The 1981 Act removed this distinction and made it a requirement to notify nature reserves of appropriate quality as SSSIs. The SSSI designation now applies to all National Nature Reserves and those identified as NCR sites and so qualifying for NNR status.

The biological SSSI series is intended to form a national network of areas representing in total the parts of Britain in which the natural features, especially those of greatest value to wildlife conservation, are most highly concentrated or of highest quality. Each SSSI represents a significant fragment of the much-depleted resource of wild nature remaining in Britain. NCC (1989b) points out that nature conservation in the wider countryside outside SSSIs is no less essential, since the ecological interdependence of SSSIs and the wider countryside is crucial, but wildlife conservation outside SSSIs has to be pursued through non-statutory approaches.

Guidelines for the selection of biological SSSIs are described in detail in NCC (1989b). The criteria for site evaluation continue to be those defined in *A nature conservation review* (Ratcliffe 1977). These are the primary criteria of:

size,

diversity,

naturalness,

rarity,

fragility,

typicalness,

and the secondary criteria of:

recorded history,

position in an ecological/geographical unit,

potential value, and

intrinsic appeal.

The application of these criteria is complex and they are used in different combinations or with different emphasis for different wildlife features. In relation to the wildlife features particularly relevant to estuaries, it is important that the two principles underlying NCR site selection be observed. One is the 'exemplary site' principle, used for selecting chiefly the best examples of sites representing a type within the countrywide variation in ecosystem types with their associated plant and animal assemblages. The second principle is that of 'minimum standards', applied chiefly to species populations, notably migrant and wintering waterfowl and colonial breeding bird populations. Site selection for the best examples of habitats and species groups is based on a subdivision of Britain into Areas of Search (AOS).

Sites and species that are individually of international importance are also, by definition, of special interest in their total national occurrence. In all such cases, all sites above a critical standard are selected. In addition to the key estuarine features and species already described in Chapter 9.2, NCC (1989b) lists several other categories of feature relevant to maritime and estuarine areas, including plant communities and species confined to the extreme western seaboard of Europe, large concentrations of breeding seabirds, endemic and island races, and globally rare animal species such as grey seal and gannet.

The selection of SSSIs for their bird populations is particularly important for estuaries. Here criteria analogous with those used in selecting internationally important sites (see Chapter 9.2) are used. For breeding populations, localities are eligible for selection where they contain 1% or more of the total British breeding population, or 10,000 breeding pairs. For non-breeding birds localities which regularly contain 1% or more of the total British non-breeding population of a species are eligible. In addition localities which contain 1%

or more of a British wintering population under irregular but definable conditions are also eligible. This is particularly relevant to estuaries used as severe weather refugia (see also Section 8.6.2).

SSSIs in Britain

About 8% of Great Britain is currently designated as biological and geological SSSIs. In addition there remain some new SSSI notifications to be completed, some sites in as yet unsurveyed areas may be discovered, and there may be further designations for under-represented groups of flora and fauna.

Overall in Britain by June 1990 3,331 of the SSSIs originally notified under the 1949 Act had been renotified, representing a renotification of 96% of these 1949 Act sites. In addition 2,018 (63%) of the 3,275 new SSSIs identified for notification under the 1981 Act have been notified. Allowing for denotifications, amalgamations and boundary changes, there are currently 5,495 SSSIs in Britain, and these cover a total of 1,722,887 ha. In some cases the sites remaining to be renotified have tended to be the large sites under complex ownership, for example some estuaries. This results in the average size (307 ha) of 1981 Act SSSIs (combining both renotifications and new sites) being smaller than the average size (543 ha) of 1949 Act SSSIs awaiting renotification. This arises partly because new SSSIs are generally much smaller than 1949 Act sites, averaging only 88 ha, but even so the renotified 1949 Act sites are still smaller, at an average 440 ha, than those awaiting renotification.

Most (69.5%) of these SSSIs have been notified for their biological interest. A further 10.6% have both biological and geological (i.e. mixed) interest and the remaining 19.4% have solely geological interest.

SSSIs and British estuaries

The numbers and sizes of SSSIs associated with review sites are summarised in Table 9.2. Since estuaries are of such great national and international wildlife importance (Chapters 8 and 9.2) it is not surprising that estuaries form a substantial part of the whole British SSSI resource. Overall by early 1989 there were 334 SSSIs associated with estuaries, amounting to 6.1% of notified SSSIs, and about 50% of coastal SSSIs are associated with estuaries. However, many estuarine SSSIs are large (the average size being 1,166 ha compared with the national average of 314 ha), and the total of 389,297 ha for these sites is 22.7% of the total area of SSSIs; in other words estuarine habitats make up almost one-quarter of the land safeguarded by SSSI notification in Britain.

These 334 notified SSSIs are distributed on the core sites, associated terrestrial and associated intertidal habitats of 136 review sites throughout Britain (Figure 9.13), so that at least part of 88% of review sites are covered by SSSI notification. Of these 334

Table 9.2 The numbers and areas of Sites of Special Scientific Interest (SSSIs) associated with Estuaries Review sites in late 1990. Both sites notified or renotified under the 1981 Wildlife & Countryside Act, and those 1949 Acts sites awaiting renotification, are included in the totals.

	No. of review sites	No. of SSSIs	Area (ha)
Core sites[a]			
Biological SSSIs	89	152	183,248
Mixed SSSIs	46	64	187,606
Geological SSSIs	13	16	2,079
Total	125	232	372,933
Associated terrestrial only			
Biological SSSIs	34	61	10,453
Mixed SSSIs	20	25	4,525
Geological SSSIs	10	11	749
Total	57	97	15,727
Associated intertidal only			
Biological SSSIs	2	2	437
Mixed SSSIs	1	1	97
Geological SSSIs	2	2	103
Total	5	5	637
Grand total	138	334	389,297

[a] Core site SSSIs include all those whose areas are partly or wholly below Extreme High Water Spring tides

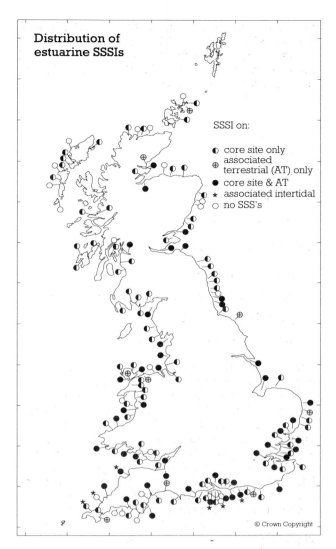

Distribution of estuarine SSSIs

SSSI on:
- ◐ core site only
- ⊕ associated terrestrial (AT) only
- ● core site & AT
- ∗ associated intertidal
- ○ no SSS's

© Crown Copyright

Figure 9.13 The distribution of SSSIs associated with Estuaries Review sites

SSSIs, 232 (69.5%) are located partly or wholly within core estuaries, i.e. below extreme high water on spring tides (see Chapter 4), 97 (29%) are wholly on associated terrestrial maritime habitats such as sand-dunes, grazing marshes and maritime heaths, and the remaining five are partly or wholly on areas of associated intertidal land linked to review sites. Note that the shore boundary of some terrestrial SSSIs is drawn on the mean high water mark as shown on Ordnance Survey maps. Hence some of the core review site SSSIs are largely on associated terrestrial habitat whilst others are entirely or almost entirely on the core estuary below high water mark.

Core site SSSIs are notified on 125 estuaries (81% of review sites), and there are SSSIs wholly on associated terrestrial land on 57 estuaries (37%) and on the associated intertidal areas of five estuaries (Table 9.2).

In addition to these notified SSSIs there are other parts of estuaries, as for other parts of the wildlife resource, that are currently under consideration for notification as SSSI. Such proposed sites range from those that are under investigation or need further survey and assessment to those actively undergoing the notification and consultation procedures between the NCC and owners and occupiers. The latter types of site will have identified boundaries, but, as with many proposed Ramsar/SPA sites, the boundaries and areas of others will still be under consideration. By the time of publication, some of these will have completed the notification procedure, as will some further renotifications of 1949 Act sites that involve substantial extensions to the existing site, as for example at Lindisfarne. At the time of the Estuaries Review survey in 1989 we were aware of 49 possible or proposed future SSSIs on 35 estuaries throughout Britain, several of these involving extensions to existing sites. At least one of these involves a review site which currently has no notified SSSIs associated with it, and on at least two other review sites there are potential SSSIs where the existing network does not cover intertidal habitat. Elsewhere further parts of core sites and associated terrestrial habitats are under

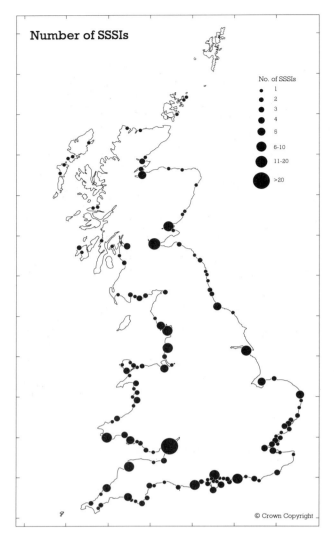

Figure 9.14 The number of notified SSSIs on each Estuaries Review site. Some of these SSSIs also include associated terrestrial habitats.

consideration for SSSI notification where other parts of the estuary are already notified.

Numbers of notified SSSIs differ greatly between estuaries (Figure 9.14). The intertidal of most estuaries is covered by one, or at most two, SSSIs: 75 estuaries (60%) of the 125 with core site SSSIs have only one, and a further 25 (16%) estuaries have two core site SSSIs. In part this is related to estuary size – most small estuaries are covered wholly or partly by one or two SSSIs – but this is not always the case, and some large estuaries, for example the Mersey Estuary (Figure 9.15), The Wash, the Solway Firth and estuaries in Essex and Kent, have only one or two core site SSSIs.

In contrast, the approach to SSSI notification on other large sites has been to notify numerous separate sections of shore as distinct SSSIs. Hence the Firth of Forth has 12 SSSIs covering parts of the core estuary plus another SSSI on the associated terrestrial area (Figure 9.16), the Humber has seven core site SSSIs and two associated terrestrial sites, and the Severn Estuary has nine core SSSIs and 12 on associated terrestrial habitats. In some

instances, for example the Severn Estuary, these large numbers of SSSIs result partly from the notification of generally small geological SSSIs.

The 19 review sites on which there are no SSSIs are mostly small. Only two such sites (Traigh Vallay and Bagh Nam Faoilean in the Outer Hebrides) have more than 500 ha of intertidal habitats, and most have intertidal areas of less than 100 ha. Almost all are in northern and western Britain, from South Devon to north-east Scotland, with one small site on the Northumberland coast.

Over half (50.8%) the estuarine area is on just seven review sites each with more than 10,000 ha of SSSI notified: Severn Estuary, Dee Estuary & North Wirral, Ribble Estuary, Morecambe Bay, Solway Firth, Moray Firth and The Wash (Figure 9.17), the largest being The Wash (64,384 ha) and Morecambe Bay (33,487 ha). In addition, SSSIs in the 'Greater Thames Estuary' form a further 5.9% of the estuarine SSSI resource.

It is not yet possible to calculate the precise area of estuaries below the high water mark that are within SSSI boundaries, since the relationship of overlaps is very complex. SSSI coverage of at least some habitats is, however, known to be extensive. For example Burd (1989) found that overall 82.2% of saltmarsh in Britain was covered by SSSI status, and that particularly in England the percentage is rather higher (Figure 9.18). Some of this area is notified as SSSI specifically for its saltmarsh of high conservation value. Other parts are included for other reasons, for example their geomorphological features or as feeding and roosting areas for nationally important bird populations.

SSSIs and estuarine site safeguard

SSSIs are essentially a terrestrial-based designation, with their safeguards related to local authority planning controls. Their efficacy is therefore limited generally to those areas of land that fall under local authority jurisdiction. With some exceptions these are areas above the mean low water mark in England and Wales, and low water mark of spring tides in Scotland. This poses complications for the notification of SSSIs in a way that effectively covers the interlinked mosaic of terrestrial, intertidal and subtidal habitats on estuaries. Many SSSI boundaries are drawn along the low water mark, thus cutting across the functional unit of the estuarine ecosystem. So it is difficult for SSSIs adequately to cover the whole range of wildlife interests on estuaries. Other statutory site designations, notably Marine Nature Reserves (see Section 9.3.7), have been designed to cover the marine and subtidal areas around the shores of Britain, but have yet to be applied to estuaries.

Within the area of an SSSI the provisions of the Wildlife & Countryside Act 1981 and its 1985 amendments aim to ensure that actions damaging to the wildlife interest of the area are not carried out by owners or occupiers, or consented to by local

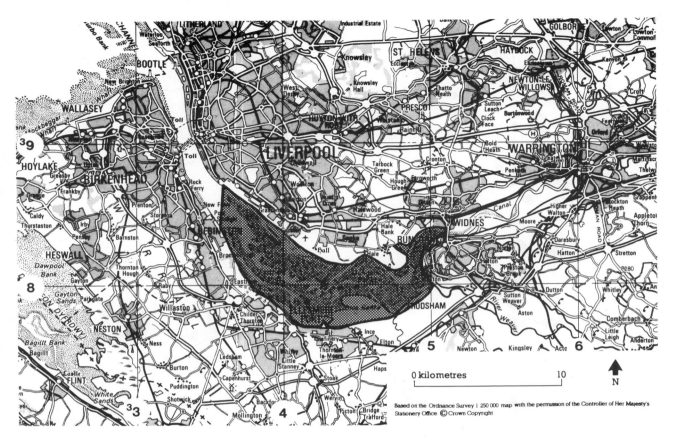

Figure 9.15 The Mersey Estuary SSSI.

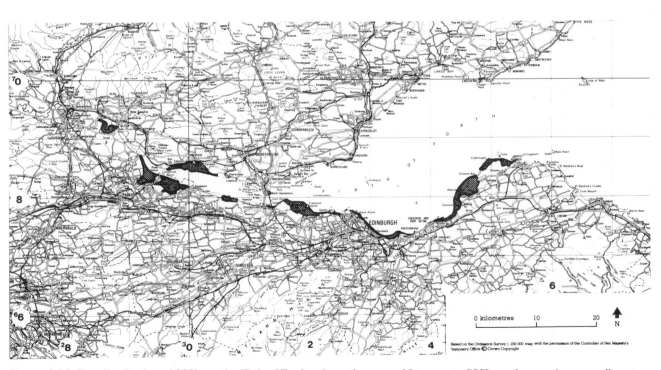

Figure 9.16 The distribution of SSSIs on the Firth of Forth, where there are 12 separate SSSIs each covering a small part of the intertidal area of the estuary

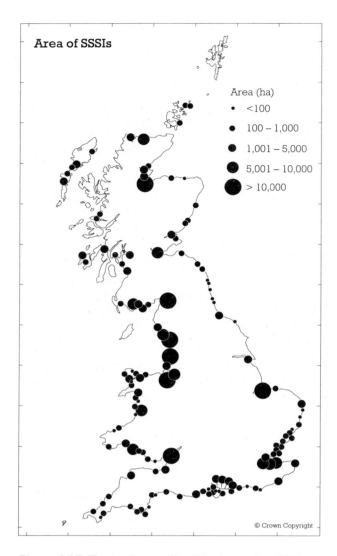

Figure 9.17 The total area of land designated as SSSI on and associated with Estuaries Review sites

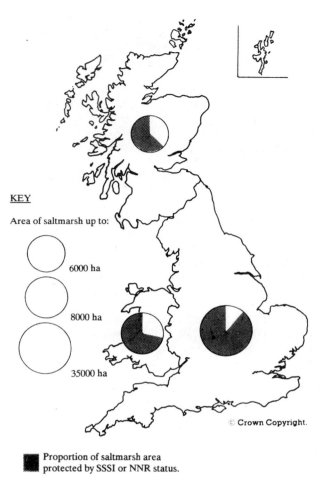

Figure 9.18 The proportions of the area of saltmarsh in England, Scotland and Wales that is covered by SSSI status, from Burd (1989)

authorities through the development control and minerals planning legislation, without appropriate consultation and agreement with the NCC. The notification of an SSSI does not therefore provide a complete safeguard against damage, although conditions written by local authorities into local and structure plans are increasingly indicating a presumption against damaging developments in such sensitive wildlife areas.

Local authorities are required by the Town & Country Planning General Development Order 1988 (in England and Wales) and the Town & Country Planning General Development Order 1981 (in Scotland) to consult the NCC before granting permission for the development of land in an SSSI. If the local planning authority is minded to grant permission for development against the advice of the NCC, they may inform the NCC so that if appropriate a request may be made to the relevant Secretary of State to call-in the application for determination by Public Inquiry.

These provisions apply to development proposals

directly affecting SSSIs, but local authorities are also encouraged (DoE 1987) to consult the NCC on policies and developments outside SSSI boundaries where they may cause indirect damage to the SSSI. Circular 27/87 specifically identifies estuaries, amongst other wetlands, as being particularly vulnerable to such indirect damage. Such guidance means that consultation on estuarine developments should take place on proposals affecting any part of an estuary including its associated terrestrial habitats, where any part of the estuary is afforded protection by SSSI status.

Although these provisions result in the appropriate involvement of the NCC in development planning and control decisions, they do not prevent damage to or loss of SSSIs. These may arise when economic arguments are considered, after a Public Inquiry, to override the national wildlife importance of the site. Alternatively the Secretary of State may refuse the NCC's request to call-in a planning application, as has happened recently for major development proposals on Rainham Marshes in the Thames Estuary. A major source of damage to

SSSIs is activity authorised through planning permission (NCC 1989c).

Damage to SSSIs can arise for a number of other reasons. Damage by third-parties is not covered by the provisions of the Wildlife & Countryside Act 1981. Such damage can be a serious problem on estuaries, for example damage to sand-dune systems by off-road vehicles. Damage and disturbance to estuarine SSSIs can also be by those exercising public rights of access, for example for private fishing and navigation. In Scotland there are also general rights of public access for foreshore wildfowling.

Another major cause of damage is work undertaken by public bodies (NCC 1989c). A great many organisations have wide freedom of action on estuaries, where responsibilities for the marine environment, particularly that below the low water mark, are spread between many government departments and agencies. These responsibilities include consent for fisheries and shell-fisheries from the Ministry of Agriculture, Fisheries and Food and for sediment extraction and other activities by the Crown Estate Commissioners. Other extensive powers, for example to undertake dredging and land-claim without reference to the controls of SSSI designation, are vested, often by private parliamentary legislation, in port and harbour authorities.

Parliamentary Private Bills are a third major source of damage to SSSIs, and the impact on estuaries of the availability of this process has been especially marked. It is described further in Chapter 9.6. A development authorised by a Private Bill provides a consent that circumvents local planning legislation, and the procedure has been the subject of considerable recent discussion. Recent development proposals on SSSIs (and internationally important sites) on estuaries include the extension of Felixstowe Docks in the Orwell Estuary and the Cardiff Bay Barrage Bill. The latter is currently approaching its final parliamentary stages and, if enacted, would entirely destroy the estuarine wildlife interest of the Taff/Ely SSSI and would also result in the destruction of the proposed Wentloog SSSI.

Overall there continues to be widespread lasting damage to SSSIs throughout Britain. In 1988/89 alone the conservation interest of almost 100 ha of SSSIs was destroyed and a further 1,100 ha suffered serious long-term damage (NCC 1989c). In addition, short-term damage to SSSIs was widespread. In the three years from April 1986 to March 1989, 146 SSSIs – c. 2.7% of all SSSIs – suffered permanent or long-term damage and overall 564 SSSIs (10.3%) suffered some damage (NCC 1987, 1988e, 1989c).

Estuarine SSSIs appear to be even more subject to actions causing loss and damage than are SSSIs in general. Between 1986 and 1989, 56 estuarine SSSIs were damaged – 16.8% of the total 334 estuarine SSSIs. Parts of 27 of these estuarine SSSIs (8.1% of the total area) were permanently destroyed or suffered long-term damage. This pattern of damage means that almost half (48%) of the damage to estuarine SSSIs was long-term damage or permanent destruction. This is almost twice the overall national proportion (26%) of cases of serious damage. Estuarine SSSIs are therefore under even more pressure of loss and damage than other parts of the SSSI series, and more at risk of serious damage.

Nevertheless the wildlife importance of estuaries as identified by SSSI status does in some cases lead to the rejection of development applications that would damage the wildlife interest of the site. For example two recent Public Inquiries, into proposals to extend rubbish tipping on tidal flats at Kinneil Kerse in the Firth of Forth and to route a by-pass road onto saltmarsh and tidal flats at Flint on the Welsh Dee Estuary, found in favour of maintaining the wildlife importance of the estuaries and regarded the further piecemeal loss of estuarine habitat as unacceptable. Similarly on the Solent no Public Inquiry since the 1960s has found in favour of a development proposal where the conservation of the shoreline or intertidal habitats has been at stake (Tubbs 1989).

In spite of such decisions to maintain the safeguarding of these estuarine areas of SSSI status, habitat loss in estuarine SSSIs continues and is part of a progressive and widespread piecemeal loss of estuarine habitat – further described in Chapter 10. Even for those parts of estuaries that can be and are afforded SSSI status, the designation is not always effective at safeguarding estuarine wildlife.

9.3.5 National Nature Reserves (NNRs)

The management of National Nature Reserves is a key part of Britain's current nature conservation strategy. The basis for the establishment of NNRs was set out in Cmd. 7122 and Cmd. 7235 in 1947. The NCC had the ability to establish NNRs under its charter of 1949, and legal provisions for the declaration by the NCC of key wildlife areas as NNRs were first made by the National Parks & Access to the Countryside Act 1949. Since then the provisions of the 1981 Wildlife & Countryside Act have led to a shift in emphasis from acquisition of all key sites by the NCC to its encouragement of sympathetic management by others of many sites, through the provisions made for SSSIs. A key point about NNRs is that they are managed by or on behalf of the NCC, specifically for wildlife conservation purposes. This is in contrast to SSSIs, where the primary land-use is not wildlife conservation but where the land is maintained, through management agreements, in a way sympathetic with the wildlife interest. New NNRs are designated under Section 35 of the Wildlife & Countryside Act.

'Nature reserves' are defined by Section 15 of the 1949 Act. Within this definition, NNRs are today seen as serving a variety of purposes, notably the conservation and preservation of sites, the maintenance of sites for research and study, the provision of advice on and the demonstration of conservation management, the furtherance of education, and providing facilities for amenity use and access for the quiet enjoyment of nature. Different NNRs provide for a variety of the range of functions, although the emphasis placed on each has fluctuated during the 40 years since the inception of the NNR idea. A review of the future strategy for NNRs is currently being prepared (NCC in prep.).

NNRs and British estuaries

By March 1989 the NCC had declared 234 NNRs throughout Britain, covering a total of 165,833 ha (NCC 1989c). These are managed by the NCC under a variety of terms: some are owned by the NCC, other are leased and others are managed under a nature reserve agreement. In addition 0.5% of the NNR area is held and managed by an approved body, and has been declared as NNR under Section 35 of the Wildlife & Countryside Act.

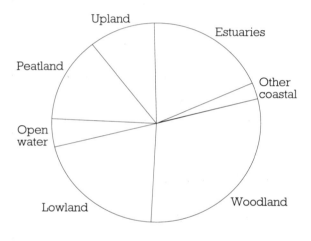

Figure 9.19 The proportion of National Nature Reserves in different NCR habitat types. Almost one-fifth of NNRs are estuarine

47 of the declared NNRs are on coastal habitats, and 42 of these are on review sites. So 18% of all NNRs, and almost 90% of coastal NNRs, are estuarine. These form a major part of the NNR network (Figure 9.19). NNRs are scattered around Britain's estuarine resource on 35 review sites (22.6% of the total) – see Figure 9.20.

In addition to these declared NNRs there are several further NNRs planned for estuaries. Notably it is intended to declare much of the remaining intertidal parts of the Tees Estuary as an NNR to safeguard the remaining parts of this much land-claimed estuary. The precise areas to be included depend on the outcome of proposed

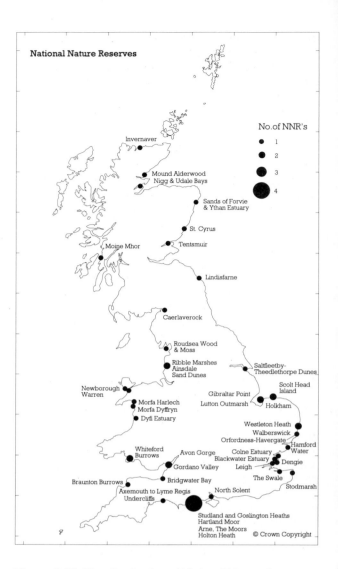

Figure 9.20 The distribution of National Nature Reserves on Estuaries Review sites

revisions to the Cleveland Structure Plan. Extensions to Dengie NNR in Essex are also proposed.

Since NNRs are managed specifically for nature conservation purposes and are owned or leased by the NCC, or are managed on their behalf, they provide a powerful safeguard for areas of critical estuarine wildlife importance.

9.3.6 Areas of Special Protection (AoSPs)

Areas of Special Protection (AoSP) are designated by Statutory Instrument of the Secretary of State under Section 3 of the Wildlife & Countryside Act 1981. AoSPs were formerly designated as Bird Sanctuaries by Sanctuary Orders made under Section 3 of the Protection of Birds Act 1954. Such sites are still called Bird Sanctuaries if designated before the Wildlife & Countryside Act. AoSPs can be designated only with the agreement of the owner or occupier of the area.

The object of designating an area is often to safeguard particular bird species, for example breeding colonies of little terns *Sterna albifrons*. The designation affords extra protection, however, to all species of birds within all or part of the area for all or part of the year. In addition access can be controlled for all or part of the year. There are special penalties for persons found guilty of taking or killing birds within the area.

Before the Wildlife & Countryside Act, wildfowling was prohibited in Bird Sanctuaries. The provisions under the Wildlife & Countryside Act mean that wildfowling can now be permitted on sites designated as AoSP where the object is, for example, to protect breeding species.

There are currently 38 designated Bird Sanctuaries/AoSPs in Great Britain. Ten of these areas are on estuaries, of which eight are in England and two in Wales (Figure 9.21). All designated sites give protection to all birds, and all the estuarine Bird Sanctuaries and AoSPs also give protection to eggs. The Bird Sanctuary on the Humber Estuary functions as a wildfowl refuge.

Although only a few AoSPs have been designated they provide strong statutory protection for wildlife. They also have the advantage that the designation can be used to confer protection on open-water areas, as for example in the areas adjacent to the seabird colonies at Berry Head (Devon). Here the designation prevents disturbance to breeding seabirds from tourist boats. This ability to cover both terrestrial and open-water areas may have particular advantages for safeguarding estuarine bird populations and hence estuarine ecosystems.

9.3.7 Marine Nature Reserves (MNRs)

SSSIs and NNRs are largely terrestrial site-safeguard designations, mostly designated in areas covered by local authority responsibility. Before the Wildlife & Countryside Act the nature conservation interest of any surrounding marine areas could not, therefore, be afforded protected status. In preparing the Wildlife & Countryside Act one possibility was to provide legislation for marine SSSIs. In the event an alternative approach for marine nature conservation was adopted, that of designating statutory marine nature reserves (MNRs).

Section 36 of the Wildlife & Countryside Act provides for the establishment of MNRs out to the limits of UK territorial waters and including both the sea and the sea-bed. The legislation provides for MNRs to be managed by the NCC for the purpose of –

a) conserving marine flora or fauna or geological or physiographical features of special interest in the area; or

b) providing, under suitable conditions and control, special opportunities for the study of, and research into, matters relating to marine flora and fauna and the physical conditions in which they live, or for the study of geological

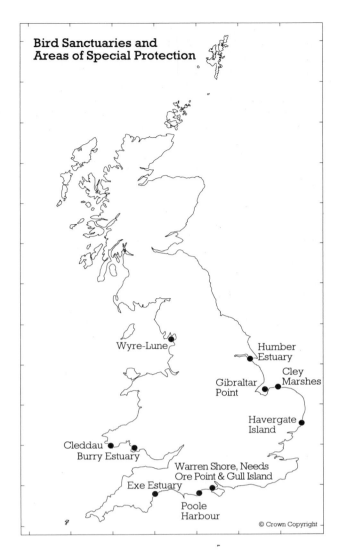

Figure 9.21 Bird Sanctuaries and Areas of Special Protection on Estuaries Review sites

and physiographical features of special interest in the area.

Section 37 of the Wildlife & Countryside Act makes provision for the NCC and other bodies to make bylaws covering MNRs. In practice, however, the ability of the NCC to make bylaws for MNRs has proved very limited since they cannot issue bylaws which interfere with the functions of local authorities, other bodies with statutory responsibilities or with anyone's rights, including those of fishing and navigation (Gubbay 1988; Warren 1989).

The process of designating an MNR is considerably more complex than that for a National Nature Reserve, since the NCC must make an application to the Secretary of State for an MNR designation. In general such a designation is acceptable only when it is based on the voluntary co-operation of all interested parties. So the procedures for establishing MNRs involve the NCC carrying out extensive consultations with the wide range of organisations who have interest in, jurisdiction over, or undertake activities within, the proposed MNR. Achieving agreement through such consultations has proved extremely complex, and even once achieved may not lead to the issuing of all bylaws needed to prevent damage within the MNR (Warren 1989).

Only two Marine Nature Reserves have so far been designated – Lundy Island in the outer Bristol Channel, designated in 1986, and Skomer Island in west Wales, designated in 1990. Neither is within an estuary. In addition there are six proposed MNRs in various stages of preparation for submission to the relevant Secretaries of State. One of these, Menai Strait in North Wales, has extensive estuarine areas, and includes parts of five review sites (Foryd Bay, Traeth Melynog, Cefni Estuary, Traeth Coch and Traeth Lavan) (Figure 9.22). The consultation document of this proposed MNR was issued in 1988. The site includes extensive intertidal soft shorelines, with extensive recreational, fishery and bait-digging usage. Restrictive bylaws would be kept to a minimum, with concentration on the educational potential of the MNR.

Marine Nature Reserves, because they can cover all areas from the high-water mark to the limit of territorial waters and can cover both the sea and the sea-bed, have considerable potential in the safeguarding of estuarine ecosystems as entities. This linking of intertidal and subtidal parts of review sites goes further, in principle, than is currently possible in practice with SSSI and NNR status. However, the legislative and consultative complexity of establishing MNRs has meant that this designation is of only limited value as yet in furthering the safeguarding of estuarine ecosystems in comparison to nearshore marine ecosystems.

Voluntary Marine Conservation Areas

In addition to statutory Marine Nature Reserves, several parts of the British coast have been established as Voluntary Marine Conservation Areas or Voluntary Marine Reserves. In such sites a consultative or management group of representatives of users of the area provides a forum for discussing issues and concerns (Gubbay 1986, 1988). This provides the opportunity for developing effective management strategies involving many of the user-groups of the area.

Several Voluntary Marine Conservation Areas have been established around Britain. The first of these, Lundy Island, is now a statutory MNR and several others are proposed MNRs. Five Voluntary Marine Conservation Areas include estuaries, usually the outer parts. The Cumbraes area includes parts of Hunterston Sands, the Seven Sisters area includes the mouth of the Cuckmere Estuary, the Wembury area includes the Yealm Estuary and an outer part of Plymouth Sound, and the Roseland area covers part of the eastern shore of the Fal Estuary. The Helford River Voluntary Marine Conservation Area covers all the Helford Estuary review site. The review sites covered by Voluntary Marine Conservation Areas are shown in Figure 9.22.

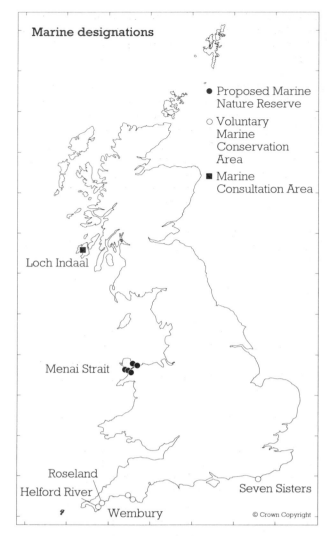

Figure 9.22 Review sites with proposed Marine Nature Reserves, Marine Consultation Areas and Voluntary Marine Conservation Areas

9.3.8 Marine Consultation Areas

In 1986 the NCC published a list of 14 coastal marine areas in Scotland that had been identified as being particularly important in respect of the quality and sensitivity of their marine environment and where there was sufficient scientific information available fully to substantiate their nature conservation importance (NCC 1990b). These Marine Consultation Areas (MCAs) have as yet no statutory status. However, in the absence of legislation allowing for the safeguarding of subtidal habitats, communities and species other than for Marine Nature Reserves (see above), MCAs are particularly valuable for identifying areas of marine conservation significance.

Identification of the location of MCAs provides a mechanism for other bodies with an interest, powers, or responsibilities in the marine environment to consult the NCC over activities in these important wildlife areas. In particular, in Scotland the Crown Estate Commissioners have an agreement with the NCC that they will not issue licences or leases in MCAs without prior consultation with the NCC. MCAs are therefore valuable in discussions over fish farming proposals, which are licensed by the Crown Estate Commissioners.

Since the initial identification of 14 MCAs, further scientific information and surveys have become available and a further 15 MCAs have been identified. All 29 MCAs are in Scotland and are listed in NCC (1990). For each MCA a citation, analogous to an SSSI citation, and map is produced. The citation summarises the intertidal and subtidal wildlife interest of the site, and key features including those of marine mammals and birds.

Most MCAs are rocky shores and sea-lochs in north-west Scotland. Only one, Loch Indaal, is on a review site (Figure 9.22). This is the Traigh Cill-a-Rubha review site on Islay, a sediment filled sea-loch of considerable marine and ornithological significance.

The MCA concept is currently being considered for extension into England and Wales. In the absence of statutory marine designations MCAs offer one way of promoting the needs of marine wildlife conservation.

9.3.9 Local Nature Reserves (LNRs)

Local Nature Reserves (LNRs) are designated by local authorities under Section 21 of the National Parks & Access to the Countryside Act 1949. District Councils have responsibility for LNR designation in England and Wales, whereas in Scotland designation is generally by Regional, Island or District Authorities. In all cases the LNR designation is made in consultation with the NCC, which provides advice on the suitability of the site. LNRs are established for the same purposes as NNRs, but in the local rather than the national interest of the site and its wildlife. Many LNRs are close to centres of population and provide visitor facilities and nature trails. Some are also of considerable wildlife importance and many are also SSSIs. Most LNRs are owned by local authorities, but some are managed on their behalf by other bodies such as local wildlife trusts.

Local nature reserves have a valuable role to play in conserving estuarine ecosystems throughout Britain. They are a particularly useful for a number of reasons. The 1949 Act gives local authorities powers to issue bylaws, subject to confirmation by the relevant Secretary of State, to protect the LNR. Hence control of potentially damaging activities such as bait-digging and wildfowling is possible through the LNR legislation. This is particularly significant in Scotland where LNR bylaws can provide for some of the few intertidal waterfowl refuge areas, since there is a general public right of access for shooting below the high water mark. Such control of shooting has been imposed through LNR bylaws on some Scottish estuaries of considerable wildlife importance, notably Montrose Basin and the Eden Estuary.

Secondly the establishment of an LNR can be effective at controlling further development damaging to wildlife in the area, since planning applications usually are considered by the same local authority as has established the LNR.

Many of the LNRs associated with estuaries include intertidal flats and saltmarshes as a major component of their area, and some have boundaries extending below the low water mark, although usually for practical reasons of drawing boundaries rather than specifically for marine wildlife conservation. Gubbay (1988) cites, however, one LNR – Saltern Cove, Devon – that specifically includes subtidal areas for their marine nature conservation significance.

By March 1989 local authorities had declared 166 LNRs – 146 in England, 14 in Wales and 6 in Scotland (NCC 1989d). 33 of these (20% of the total) are estuarine and fall within 29 review sites (Figure 9.23). The greatest concentration of declared estuarine Local Nature Reserves is in the Solent region of southern England, where there are 12 LNRs between Pagham Harbour in the east and

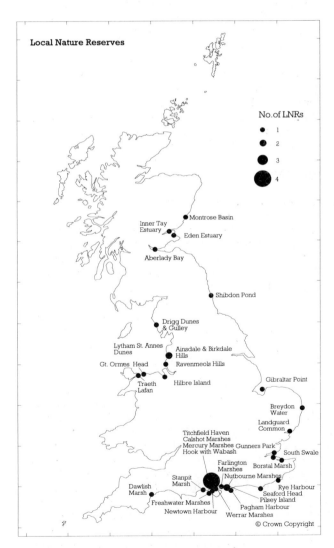

Figure 9.23 Declared Local Nature Reserves on review sites. LNRs are named.

Christchurch Harbour in the west. In 1989 there were also proposals for at least another 23 LNRs on 16 estuaries, including on nine estuaries which as yet have no designated LNR. So estuarine sites form a major part of the LNR network throughout Britain, and LNRs form an important element of the conservation of estuarine wildlife.

9.3.10 Environmentally Sensitive Areas (ESA)

Environmentally Sensitive Areas (ESAs) are designated by the UK Government with advice from the NCC and the Countryside Commission. They are areas where traditional farming methods have helped to create attractive landscapes and valuable habitats for wildlife. The ESA scheme is a way in which the UK Government seeks to encourage sensitive farming practices. The ESA approach was established by Article 19 of EC Council Regulation 797/85, as amended, and the UK Agricultural Act 1986. The EC regulation enables member states to make payments to farmers in designated areas of high conservation value to encourage farming practices favourable to the environment. The mechanism for such payments was established in Britain through Section 16 of the Agricultural Act 1986.

ESAs are targeted areas of high conservation value and are intended to provide incentives to farmers and crofters to protect and enhance environmental features of their land and to prevent damage to landscapes and wildlife which might result from some types of agricultural intensification (Johnston & Smith 1990).

Eighteen ESAs have so far been designated (10 in England, five in Scotland, two in Wales and one in Northern Ireland). Few ESAs are truly coastal, and most of the overlap with review sites is in the upper tidal reaches of the estuaries. ESAs also cover areas of associated terrestrial habitats adjacent to review sites. In relation to estuaries ESAs are particularly important in ensuring the continuation of sympathetic farming practices on areas of coastal grazing marsh and hay meadows, since such habitats have suffered major damage and loss over the last 50 years (see Chapter 10). These areas have major wildlife importance particularly for their aquatic flora and fauna and their wintering and breeding bird populations (see Chapters 8.1, 8.2 and 8.6).

Five ESAs are located partly on the agricultural land associated with 15 estuaries (Figure 9.24). Of particular significance is the Norfolk Broads ESA which has substantially halted the agricultural intensification of much of the traditional grazing marshes surrounding the tidal rivers feeding Breydon Water and Oulton Broad, and the Machairs of The Uists, Benbecula and Barra, which covers the extensive machair grassland systems associated with the estuaries and shores of the Outer Hebrides. Other ESAs overlapping estuaries are the Suffolk River Valleys ESA which touches the upper parts of the Blyth, Ore/Alde/Butley, Deben

and Stour Estuaries; the South Downs ESA adjacent to the Cuckmere, Adur and Arun estuaries where the tidal parts of these estuaries cut into the downs; and the Lleyn ESA associated with Traeth Bach in north Wales.

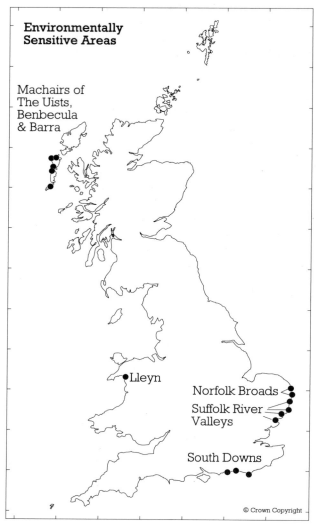

Figure 9.24 Environmentally Sensitive Areas associated with review sites

Non-statutory designations

In addition to the various statutory conservation designations designed to identify and safeguard the wildlife importance of estuaries, there are a large number of places where wildlife conservation is the primary land-use in areas managed by a wide range of non-statutory conservation bodies, groups and individuals. These, with the landscape and amenity designations described in Chapter 9.4, play a major part in the continued maintenance of natural estuaries and their wildlife. The various types of reserve are described below.

9.3.11 Wildlife trust reserves

Local wildlife trusts (many formerly called County Naturalists' Trusts) have been established to promote nature conservation at a local level. The first was the Norfolk Naturalists' Trust established in 1926, and there are now 48 trusts. In England and

Wales there is usually one trust covering a whole county or group of counties. Scotland is represented by a single trust, the Scottish Wildlife Trust. Each trust is an autonomous registered charity depending largely on subscriptions, grants and donations. Wildlife trusts are promoted and represented on national issues by a central body, the Royal Society for Nature Conservation (RSNC) – formerly the Society for the Promotion of Nature Conservation (SPNC).

Wildlife Trusts own, lease and manage, by agreement with owners, over 1,800 nature reserves covering more than 52,000 ha. The pattern of conservation designation on wildlife trust reserves is often complex. Many are of national and international wildlife importance and more than half are notified as SSSIs (Johnston & Smith 1990). Some are wholly or partly National Nature Reserves managed on behalf of the NCC. In addition a number of wildlife trusts manage Local Nature Reserves on behalf of local authorities, and operate others in conjunction with bodies such as the Royal Society for the Protection of Birds and the Ministry of Defence.

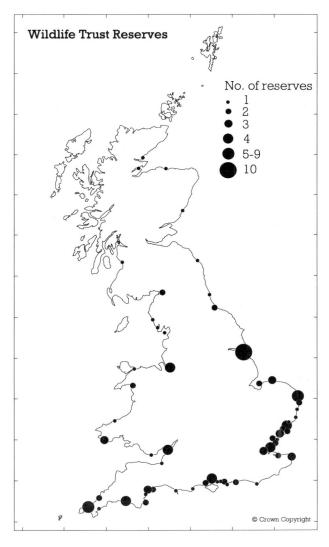

Figure 9.25 The number of wildlife trust reserves on review sites

122 wildlife trust reserves are associated with review sites and these are distributed around 57 estuaries (Figure 9.25). The Humber Estuary has a larger number (10) of wildlife trust reserves than any other single estuary, and there are major concentrations of reserves in Suffolk, Essex and Kent, around the Solent, and in south-west England. There are relatively few estuarine wildlife trust reserves in Wales, northern England and Scotland (Figure 9.25).

Unless such reserves are directly under wildlife trust ownership, they do not enjoy any protection additional to that afforded by SSSI, NNR or LNR status. Nevertheless the liaison between the wildlife trust and the local authorities on these and other sites ensures that comments can be made on development proposals that may affect their interests. In addition to their nature reserve holdings, wildlife trusts play an important part in dealing with wider countryside conservation matters and site safeguard. Firstly their survey work and local knowledge can help to identify appropriate new areas for consideration for notification as SSSIs. Secondly wildlife trusts maintain lists of sites of wildlife significance that fall outside the SSSI selection process. Such sites are known by various titles (Sites of Scientific Interest (SSI), Sites of Nature Conservation Interest (SNCI) etc.) and are similar in concept to the Regionally Important Geological/geomorphological Sites (RIGS) in earth science conservation. Liaison with local authorities means that wildlife trusts are generally consulted over development matters likely to affect these sites, and the local wildlife trust may take the lead in defending such sites against damaging developments.

9.3.12 Royal Society for the Protection of Birds (RSPB) reserves

The Royal Society for the Protection of Birds (RSPB) is the largest voluntary wildlife conservation body in Europe with in excess of 400,000 members. The major concern of the RSPB is the conservation of wild birds and their habitats. The RSPB was initially the Fur and Feather Group, formed in 1889 to protest about the widespread use of bird feather in the millinery trade. Its interests widened and in 1891 it became the Society for the Protection of Birds and was granted a Royal Charter in 1904.

A major thrust of RSPB policy is to acquire land so as to establish nature reserves. The majority of these reserves are wardened and allow access by visitors. Such sites provide major foci of information about wildlife and conservation in Britain. A few RSPB reserves are not open to the public, so as to avoid disturbance to sensitive bird populations. Wherever possible reserves are purchased, so that the level of safeguard for the wildlife and their habitats is high. Where reserves are leased, the RSPB aims to acquire long leases (longer than 21 years) with appropriate management rights.

In general the RSPB seeks to acquire land that is of

high wildlife value, for instance those areas which support major breeding or wintering populations of birds and those which support populations of rare breeding birds. So, many RSPB reserves are of high conservation value and are notified as SSSI or identified as Ramsar/SPA sites. Some may be within National Nature Reserves. In addition some reserves are maintained primarily as educational sites.

Overall the RSPB has substantial reserve holdings and currently manages over 120 reserves covering over 56,000 ha throughout Britain (RSPB 1989). Estuaries form a major focus of attention for reserves acquisition and the RSPB has 34 reserves on 25 review sites (Figure 9.26); so over one-quarter of reserves are associated with estuaries, and many include intertidal habitats. Some of these estuarine reserves are of major significance in the history of wildlife conservation – notably Havergate Island in the Ore/Alde/Butley Estuary in Suffolk where the avocet *Recurvirostra avosetta* returned to Britain to breed (see also Chapter 8.6).

The conservation of estuaries and their birds is currently a major priority in the work of the RSPB, and a major campaign for more effective safeguards for the future of estuaries – *Turning the tide* (Rothwell & Housden 1990) – was launched in late 1990.

9.3.13 Wildfowl and Wetlands Trust reserves

The Wildfowl and Wetlands Trust (formerly the Wildfowl Trust) was established by Sir Peter Scott in 1946, with a ringing station and wildfowl refuge at Slimbridge on the upper Severn Estuary in Gloucestershire. The work of the Wildfowl and Wetlands Trust (WWT) centres around conservation, education and research. At several of their wildfowl reserves extensive collections of captive wildfowl are maintained and captive breeding programmes have enabled the reintroduction to the wild of several endangered species of wildfowl. As part of their research programme, WWT have co-ordinated the National Wildfowl Counts (see Chapter 8.6).

As well as their wildfowl collections, used extensively for education, the Wildfowl and Wetlands Trust have established reserves in a number of key wintering areas for migrant wildfowl. The level of protection afforded to such sites is high since the land is either owned or held on long-term leases.

Five WWT reserves and refuges are associated with British estuaries (Figure 9.27). The saltmarshes and grazing marshes at Slimbridge, and the adjacent pools of the WWT reserve, are major wintering sites for the European white-fronted goose *Anser albifrons* and Bewick's swan *Cygnus columbianus*; the Caerlaverock reserve on the Solway Firth supports substantial parts of the world population of Svalbard barnacle geese *Branta leucopsis*; and the Welney reserve on the washlands of the Ouse Washes along the upper reaches of the tidal river Ouse (The Wash) supports some of the largest wintering populations of wigeon *Anas penelope* and Bewick's swans in Britain. Other WWT reserves at Washington (Wear Estuary) and Arundel (Arun Estuary) are mainly ornamental collections on largely marshland areas adjacent to upper tidal parts of estuaries.

9.3.14 Other non-statutory reserves and designations

Associated with 19 estuaries around Britain there are a variety of other places that have some form of protection or designation intended to provide a safeguard for wildlife (Figure 9.2.8). For example there are Bird Observatories at Gibraltar Point on The Wash, Holme-next-the-Sea on the North Norfolk Coast and Hilbre Island on the Dee Estuary. Observations on bird migration are made and birds are caught and ringed as part of migration studies.

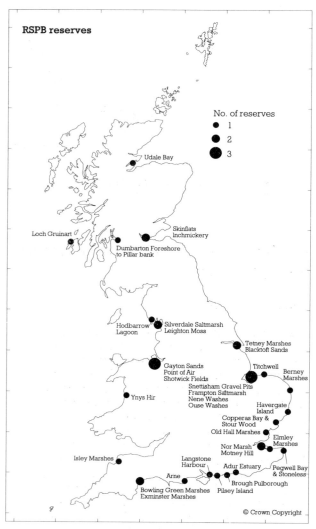

Figure 9.26 Royal Society for the Protection of Birds reserves on review sites. RSPB reserves are named.

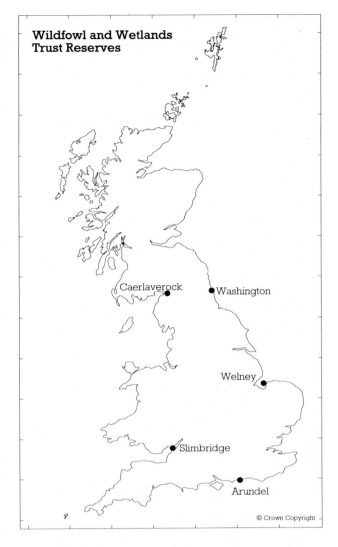

Figure 9.27 Wildfowl and Wetlands Trust reserves on review sites

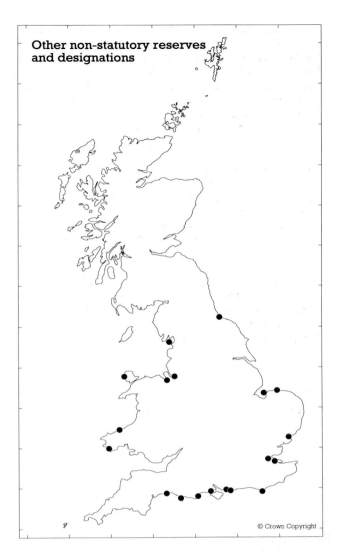

Figure 9.28 Review sites with other non-statutory conservation reserves and designations

The Woodland Trust, a non-statutory organisation which owns and manages woodlands throughout Britain, have two areas of woodland adjacent to estuaries: Copperas Wood on the Stour Estuary in Essex and Crag Wood on Morecambe Bay.

On a further 17 review sites there are reserves owned or managed by a considerable variety of groups and organisations, including wildfowlers' associations (Medway Estuary, South Thames Marshes, Langstone Harbour, Lymington Estuary), power generation companies (Milford Haven), harbour conservancies, local ornithologists' and wildlife associations (North Norfolk Coast, The Wash, Poole Harbour and Axe Estuary), industrial companies (Alaw Estuary, Tees Estuary), and private landowners and occupiers (The Fleet and Portland Harbour, Teifi Estuary).

9.4 British landscape and amenity designations

9.4.1 Introduction

In addition to the various statutory and non-statutory designations and controls designed to safeguard the wildlife interest of estuaries, described in Chapter 9.3 above, there are several designations affecting estuaries that provide for the identification and safeguarding of important and vulnerable landscape and amenity features of Britain's coastal countryside. In many cases such designations overlap geographically with wildlife designations, since in many cases the wildlife depends on the maintenance of wild and unspoilt landscapes. Although the primary objective of such designations is to protect the landscape, amenity and recreation value of a site, they are generally linked to the maintenance of wildlife interest. The various designations that cover review sites are described below.

9.4.2 National Parks

The National Parks & Access to the Countryside Act 1949 created the National Parks Commission for England and Wales, charged with establishing National Parks in England and Wales. This Commission has subsequently become the Countryside Commission which now has responsibility for the designation of Areas of Outstanding Natural Beauty and Heritage Coasts (see below). Since the scenic value provisions of the 1949 Act did not apply to Scotland there are no National Parks in Scotland.

Of the 10 National Parks in England and Wales that altogether cover 13,600 km², five have some coastal frontage and four of these overlap with parts of 11 review sites (Figure 9.29). These are the Esk Estuary (Yorkshire), whose upper tidal reaches touch the North York Moors National Park; the Esk Estuary (Cumbria), Duddon Estuary and Morecambe Bay in the Lake District National Park; Traeth Bach, and the Mawddach, Dysynni and Dyfi Estuaries in the Snowdonia National Park; and the Nyfer and Teifi Estuaries and Milford Haven in the Pembrokeshire Coast National Park. In addition there are two other areas in England, the Norfolk Broads and the New Forest, which have a similar status to a National Park. The Norfolk Broads, administered by the Broads Authority, covers the estuary of Breydon Water and its surrounding lands, and the New Forest abuts the Beaulieu River and Lymington Estuary review sites.

9.4.3 Areas of Outstanding Natural Beauty (AONBs)

As well as making provision for the establishment of National Parks, the National Parks & Access to the Countryside Act 1949 made provision for the designation of Areas of Outstanding Natural Beauty (AONBs). The need for such areas was first identified in 1945 (see Gubbay 1988), and the designation of AONBs (then by the National Parks Commission) was begun in 1955. The Countryside Commission is now the body which designates AONBs in England and Wales. AONBs can also be designated in Northern Ireland, where the designation is made by the Department of the Environment. As for National Parks, the legislation for AONBs does not extend to Scotland, where National Scenic Areas are designated instead (see below).

The main objectives for AONBs are set out by Countryside Commission (1989) as follows.

a) The primary purpose of AONB designation will be to conserve natural beauty.

b) Recreation will not be an objective of designation but AONBs should be used to meet the demands for recreation as far as this is consistent with the conservation of natural beauty and the needs of agriculture, forestry and other users.

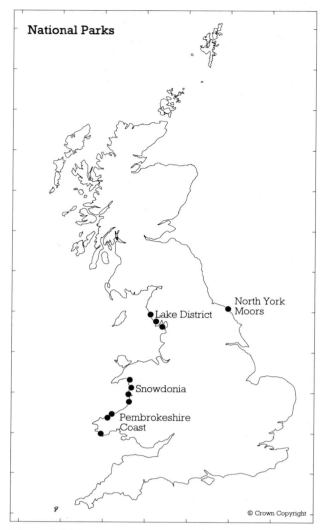

Figure 9.29 Review sites associated with National Parks in England and Wales

c) In pursuing the primary objective of designation, account should be taken of the need to safeguard agriculture, forestry and other rural industries, and of the economic and social needs of local communities.

These national objectives are set by the Countryside Commission, but responsibility for the local administration of an AONB lies with the local authority at county and/or district level. The designation of an AONB ensures that the advice of the Countryside Commission is sought by local authorities and government about planning applications and developments which could damage the natural beauty of the AONB. In general major industrial and urban developments are considered inappropriate within an AONB except when the development is in the national interest and cannot take place elsewhere. Large mineral workings are also subject to careful evaluation as are major road and motorway schemes (Countryside Commission 1983). There are also restrictions placed within AONBs and National Parks on permitted development rights under the General Development Order 1988. Local authorities are encouraged to produce a statement of intent for the planning and management for AONBs and to set up joint advisory committees with user and amenity groups. Many AONBs overlap with sites of wildlife conservation importance, and where they contain Sites of Special Scientific Interest, Local Nature Reserves or National Nature Reserves they have the additional protection afforded by those designations (see Chapter 9.3 above).

By 1989 there were 38 AONBs in England and Wales covering 19,287 km² (Countryside Commission 1989). The major landscape importance of the coast in Britain is emphasised by 20 of these AONBs having coastal frontage (Figure 9.30). Thirty-eight review sites are partly or wholly within 15 of the AONBs. AONBs often cover large areas of the countryside – generally much larger than SSSIs – and typically several estuaries fall within a Single AONB (Figure 9.30).

9.4.4 National Scenic Areas

In 1980 special development control measures were introduced by the Scottish Development Department (SDD Circular 20/1980) for 40 designated National Scenic Areas. National Scenic Areas are designated by the Countryside Commission for Scotland and are chosen as the best examples of Scotland's landscapes and part of the natural heritage of Scotland. This designation replaces two earlier categories of importance for scenic interest which served to fulfil some of the approaches embodied in the National Park and AONB designations in England and Wales. The first covered the five National Park Direction Areas and the second a variety of local authority-inspired regional landscape designations such as Areas of Great Landscape Value and Areas of Scenic Value.

The Countryside Commission for Scotland have recently concluded that the aims of the National Park designation – improving opportunities for the enjoyment of the countryside whilst conserving its recreational and scenic attributes – could be achieved by the National Scenic Area designation.

Most National Scenic Areas are in northern and western Scotland, and 15 of the 50 review sites in Scotland fall within National Scenic Areas (Figure 9.31). All but one NSA estuary (the Dornoch Firth) is on the west coast of Scotland between the Solway Firth and the north coast of Sutherland. Here 14 of the 29 estuaries (48%) are covered by this landscape designation.

9.4.5 Heritage Coasts

Heritage Coasts are the only British landscape designation that refers specifically to the coastal fringe. Heritage Coasts are selected as the finest stretches of undeveloped coast. The objective of the designation is to provide for their comprehensive conservation and management, and to facilitate and enhance their enjoyment by the promotion and encouragement of recreational activities consistent with the conservation of their

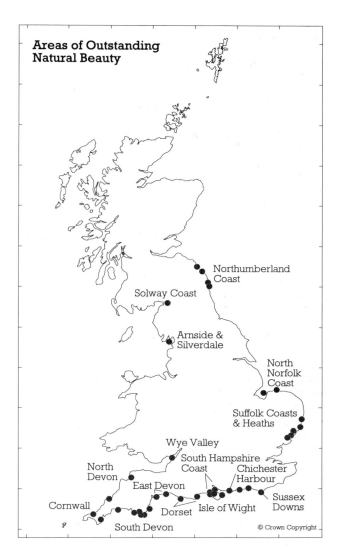

Figure 9.30 Review sites partly or wholly within Areas of Outstanding Natural Beauty (AONB). The relevant AONBs are named.

fine natural scenery and heritage features. These objectives contain elements of both protection and management, and also, implicitly, the 'Sandford principle' that where natural beauty and recreation are in irreconcilable conflict natural beauty must prevail (Countryside Commission 1990).

Heritage Coasts were first proposed in 1970 by the Countryside Commission as a statutory designation. Instead the Government ruled that Heritage Coasts should be treated as development plan definitions (DoE Circular 12/72; Welsh Office Circular 36/72). Although there is no statutory protection afforded directly to Heritage Coasts, many are also wholly or partly in AONBs and National Parks and so benefit from the protection afforded such sites. In addition almost one-third of Heritage Coast coastline is under the ownership of the National Trust (see below).

Policies for the control of developments within Heritage Coasts are generally incorporated in structure, local and district plans. Rigorous control of unsuitable developments, including the control of

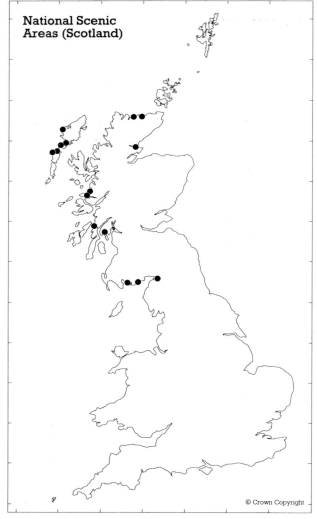

Figure 9.31 Review sites in Scotland covered by National Scenic Area designation.

recreational access, remains an important principle. Developments affecting intertidal areas and inshore waters along Heritage Coasts, such as oil exploration and production, marinas and fish farming, are regarded as also needing rigorous controls.

Most Heritage Coasts are managed by local authorities with guidance from the Countryside Commission through its Heritage Coast Forum established in 1988. Most Heritage Coasts now have management plans. Heritage Coast management needs to cover landscape conservation including agricultural practices and coastal protection; public enjoyment including tourism, sporting activities, information and interpretation; and nature conservation (Countryside Commission 1990). Most Heritage Coasts are now wardened and provided with interpretative facilities. Such wardening is regarded as a key part of Heritage Coast management.

Altogether, 44 Heritage Coasts have been identified, of which 43 have been defined. These are listed in the *Heritage Coast directory* (Heritage

Coast Forum 1989). The defined coasts cover 1,460 km of the coastline of England and Wales (Figure 9.32). The final area, North Devon and Exmoor Heritage Coast, remains to be defined. Of the 43, 16 have yet to have their inland boundaries defined. It is proposed that all such coasts should have their inland boundaries defined by local planning authorities acting in conjunction with the Countryside Commission. The Countryside Commission regards these 44 localities as adequate to fulfil the Heritage Coast functions.

Figure 9.32 Review sites partly or wholly within the Heritage Coast coastline, shown shaded.

Most Heritage Coasts have been defined on rocky and cliff coastlines and open sandy shores. Estuaries, especially where there are extensive soft shores, are generally outside the lateral boundaries of these coasts. Only 27 of the 104 review sites in England and Wales overlap with the Heritage Coast network and in most of these it is only the outer parts of the estuary, where rivers discharge into the sea, which overlap. Of the seven largest British estuaries, only the Humber Estuary features in the Heritage Coast network, and only then for a small area of Spurn Point at its tip (Figure 9.32). The only extensive estuarine feature covered by Heritage

Coast designation is the North Norfolk Coast. In some places only one side of an estuary is within a Heritage Coast, e.g. the Loughor Estuary; in others, as in Poole Harbour, the defined area covers coastline on either side of an estuary but little of the estuarine basin itself.

There would therefore seem to be potential for increasing the scale of inclusion in Heritage Coasts of estuarine coastlines as part of Britain's coastal heritage. In addition, it may be appropriate to draw on the valuable experience gained by local authorities managing Heritage Coasts and, in particular, the use of wardens, to develop public awareness of estuaries as coastal heritage, although great care will be needed in the development of management plans to ensure that the often very sensitive wildlife areas in estuaries are safeguarded from any increase in recreational or tourism pressure.

9.4.6 Country Parks

Country Parks, like Local Nature Reserves, are a local authority designation in this case made under Section 7 of the Countryside Act 1968. Unlike LNRs they are primarily designed for recreation and leisure and do not necessarily have nature conservation interest. Nevertheless many are in areas of semi-natural habitat and so form a valuable network of locations at which informal recreation and the natural environment co-exist. There are 22 Country Parks currently designated on 20 estuaries, of which all but three are in England (Figure 9.33). Most are on associated terrestrial land, but some such as at Tyninghame Bay and on the Colne Estuary also include intertidal habitats such as saltmarshes within their boundaries.

9.4.7 National Trust properties

The National Trust (NT) is an independent charity that is currently the largest private landowner in Britain. The National Trust was founded in 1895 to protect land and buildings for the nation. The society was responsible for establishing Britain's first nature reserve, at Wicken Fen in Cambridgeshire, in 1899. The National Trust covers England, Wales and Northern Ireland and now safeguards 228,713 ha of land, much of it in Trust ownership.

The National Trust for Scotland was established as a charity in 1931 with objectives similar to those of the National Trust, and now owns over 100 properties throughout Scotland. Land that is not owned by the Trust can be protected by a Conservation Agreement, a procedure authorised by Parliament in 1938. These are voluntary agreements with landowners who wish their property to come under a form of protection that is short of full Trust ownership. The objective of these agreements is to ensure safeguard in perpetuity and the agreement is binding on the title of the property (Johnston & Smith 1990).

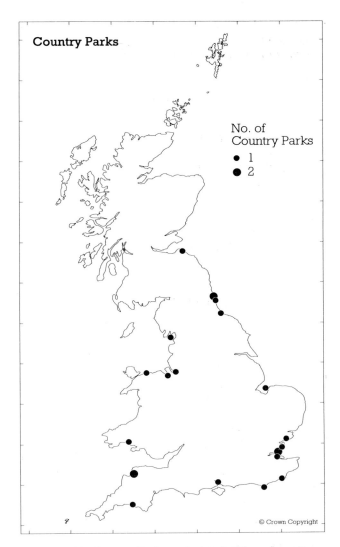

Figure 9.33 Country Parks associated with review sites

A 1907 Parliamentary Act gave the National Trust powers to declare its land and buildings inalienable. These properties cannot be sold or mortgaged although they can be leased, subject to approval by the Charity Commission. The Trust can also appeal to Parliament against any compulsory purchase order made on its inalienable land. Under National Trust ownership land is as fully protected against development as is currently possible. National Trust ownership is therefore an important part of the conservation safeguards for wildlife. Those NT sites that are of wildlife importance are generally managed for both public access and wildlife conservation, and many areas of National Trust land are covered by national and international conservation and landscape designations.

In 1965, owing to increasing concern over the loss of and damage to Britain's unspoilt coastlines, the National Trust launched its *Enterprise Neptune*. This was an appeal for funds to enable the Trust to purchase unspoilt coastal areas as they became available. *Enterprise Neptune* proved highly successful, and was relaunched in 1985. Overall the National Trust now protects 825 km of coastline.

This great emphasis on coastal land safeguard has meant that the National Trust now has extensive land-holdings on the British estuarine resource, although as with Heritage Coasts much of the focus has been on rocky and cliff shores and open sandy beaches. Overall there are 64 National Trust and National Trust for Scotland properties on 39 review sites (Figure 9.34). Most estuarine sites are on the south coast of England between Chichester Harbour and the Helford River, although the largest number of properties is on the North Norfolk Coast (Figure 9.34).

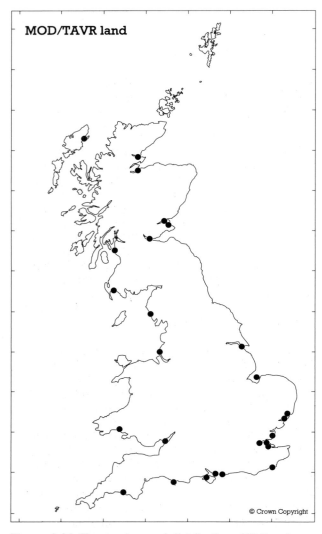

Figure 9.34 The number and distribution of National Trust and National Trust for Scotland properties associated with review sites

9.5 Other land holdings affecting estuarine protection

Land on some other parts of the estuarine resource is protected by virtue of its ownership, often by the restriction of public access. Of note are the areas of land held for a variety of purposes by the Ministry of Defence and the Territorial Army Volunteer Reserves (TAVR). Such places range from training camps and various military

installations and airfields on the flat lands surrounding estuaries through to rifle ranges and extensive bombing ranges on places such as the saltmarshes and tidal flats of The Wash and the Dornoch Firth.

The restrictions to public access imposed in the limitations to development in such places means that they can be amongst the most pristine areas of wildlife habitat. Many of these areas have considerable conservation significance and many are of national or international wildlife importance. Many have their own conservation groups overseeing the management of the areas, and some are managed by agreement with local wildlife trusts. Such areas of military land are associated with at least 26 review sites (Figure 9.35).

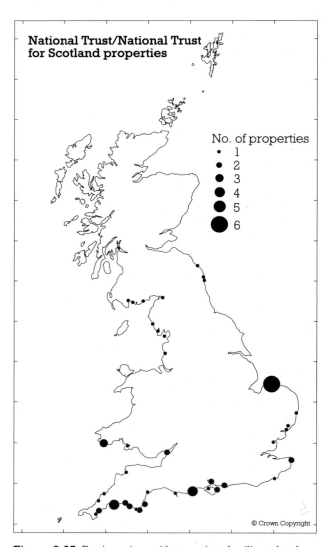

Figure 9.35 Review sites with associated military land-holdings

9.6 Estuarine development planning, development control and coastal zone management

All the designations and site identifications described above include mechanisms for the indication of high wildlife and landscape importance. Some, notably the international designations, place obligations on Britain to ensure that such sites remain safeguarded for the future. None, with the exception of National Trust ownership, is inalienable and so fully safeguards against damage or destruction, and not even such inalienable land is safe from indirect damage or disturbance arising from outside its boundaries. Estuaries have long been a focus of man's interests and activities, and land-use conflicts inevitably arise. Such conflicts are particularly difficult to resolve in places such as estuaries where there is a need and an obligation to safeguard a substantial part of the remaining area for its wildlife resource (see Chapter 8) and yet where there are a great many demands for further developmental and recreational land-uses for many purposes (Chapter 10).

Safeguarding wildlife sites on estuaries, as elsewhere, therefore depends on the recognition and consideration of their importance in the decision-making processes for individual developments. This in turn depends on sound overall policies to provide the framework and guidance for decision-making. Approaches to estuarine decision-making are described briefly below.

9.6.1 Local Authority control

Much of the responsibility for developing overall policies for future land-use and management is vested in local authorities by central government through the Town & Country Planning Acts. The system currently in force is a two-tier process established by the Town & Country Planning Act 1968. This requires the preparation of 'Structure Plans', usually at county level. These are primarily a statement of strategic policy and, after extensive public consultation, must be approved by the Secretary of State. 'Local Plans' provide detailed policies and land-use priorities for parts of the structure plan area or specific subjects of planning importance (e.g. landscape and wildlife conservation, transport or waste disposal). These local plans are prepared and approved by local authorities to conform with the general policies of the Structure Plan. More recently, metropolitan district councils have been required to prepare 'Unitary Development Plans' which deal with strategic planning on the smaller scale of a local authority district.

Most parts of Britain are now covered by structure plans, mostly prepared in the 1970s to cover the ensuing 20 years. Many have policies for wildlife conservation within them, although the strength of these policies, like those in local plans, varies

greatly. In general, however, there are intentions within structure and local plans that areas of high wildlife interest should not be the subject of damaging developments, unless in the urgent national interest. Many structure plans are currently under revision, and wildlife conservation policies for estuaries, as elsewhere, are being rewritten in the light of current awareness of the need for estuarine safeguard.

In general local planning authorities have a presumption against damaging developments that contravene structure or local plan policies or zoning. So the presence of strong policies is vital for ensuring continued estuarine wildlife safeguard.

Nevertheless, developments continue to be proposed for areas of high wildlife value on estuaries. Where it conflicts with the maintenance of high wildlife interest a development application can be the subject of call-in and examination by Public Inquiry by an Inspector appointed by the relevant Secretary of State. The final decision rests with the Secretary of State. In the absence of an overall national coastal policy the advice to local authorities embodied in Circular 27/87 is significant and indicates that consent for developments affecting wildlife areas, especially sites that are internationally important, should be given only in exceptional circumstances. Even so, and despite the multiplicity of conservation designations described in this chapter, damaging developments continue to take place on many estuaries. The cumulative effects are considerable throughout the estuarine resource, including both its national and international parts (see Chapter 10).

In addition to these county and local based plans, there have been some recent moves to develop strategic planning over larger areas, notably by SERPLAN, the South-east Regional Planning Forum formed from county councils in the south-east of England. SERPLAN has been examining approaches to strategic planning over this much larger area as a means of coping with the very great pressure for development in this part of the country. Guidance on this broad scale has the potential for ensuring that individual development proposals are considered in the wider framework of the planning needs of a substantial area.

The use of estuaries as boundaries complicates management and development planning on a 'whole-estuary' scale, since single estuaries form the boundaries between countries, counties, regions and local authority districts. Each of 15 review sites (10% of the total) are under the jurisdiction of two counties (or regions in Scotland) and six large review sites (Severn Estuary, Dee Estuary & North Wirral, Firth of Forth, The Wash and the Thames Estuary) are each covered by three counties/regions. Overall 60 review sites (39% of the total) are the responsibility of more than one local authority district. On large estuaries there can be considerable numbers of local authorities involved: for example the different parts of the Thames Estuary are covered by 20 local authorities, the Humber Estuary by 14, the Severn Estuary by 12, and The Wash and Firth of Forth by eight local authorities each. The fact that an estuary, although a single functional unit, can be covered by a multiplicity of planning authorities has important implications for the relationship between individual estuarine planning decisions and the overall impact of human activities on an estuary, and on the fate of the overall estuarine resource. Integrated conservation planning and management of estuaries will also become an issue of increased importance from 1991 for the NCC's three successor bodies (for England, Scotland and Wales) since four estuaries (the Severn Estuary, the Dee Estuary & North Wirral, the Solway Firth and the Tweed Estuary) form country boundaries.

The effective operation of the local authority development planning and control system is a key component of the future safeguarding of Britain's estuaries. Such powers are, however, limited because the area of local authority jurisdiction extends only to low water mark. These powers, whilst effective for terrestrial based developments, may therefore not extend to all parts of the functional estuarine ecosystem. Likewise, few conservation designations current in Britain extend to cover all relevant parts of an estuary, even where, as for the EEC Directive on the Conservation of Wild Birds, the requirement is for such overall coverage. The complications arising from the great number of consent authorities operating in the marine environment in relation to terrestrial development planning and control may therefore be crucial for future estuarine wildlife safeguards.

9.6.2 Parliamentary Private Bills

For developments which require the modification of statutory rights of access, for example for navigation or foreshore access for fishing, the procedure falls outside local authority planning powers. For such developments, consent is sought directly from Parliament in the form of a Private Bill. This effectively circumvents the local planning process and also makes local accountability and involvement difficult and costly, since an objector to such a development must petition Parliament. Such Private Bills on estuaries have proved particularly contentious over the last few years, since they have been used to obtain consent for a number of major development proposals, notably for docks and barrages, within nationally and internationally important estuaries. These developments, notably the Felixstowe Dock and Railway Bill (which allowed major dock expansion into the Orwell/Stour proposed Ramsar/SPA site) and the Lyndhurst Bypass Bill, have focused concerns about the Private Bill process. A joint parliamentary committee on Private Bill procedures has recently recommended substantial changes to the process, notably that such development proposals should first pass through the local authority planning process and only be laid before Parliament to deal with those matters requiring parliamentary consent. Private Bills are also currently excluded from the provisions of the EC Environmental Assessment Directive. The use of the Private Bill procedure, for example as currently for the Cardiff Bay Barrage which would destroy the Taff/Ely SSSI, remains a major concern for future estuarine site conservation safeguard.

9.6.3 EC Directive on environmental assessment

EC Directive 85/337 on the assessment of the effects of certain public and private projects on the environment came into effect in July 1988. It requires environmental impact assessments (EIA) to be made for a range of the potential impacts of developments on the environment. It currently lists a relatively small range of major undertakings for which an EIA is mandatory and, in Annex II, a wide range of developments for which the requirement for an EIA is at the discretion of the member state. In general such developments require EIAs where they are likely to have a damaging impact on the environment, and the presence of a wildlife site such as an SSSI is generally an indication of the need for an EIA. Under the terms of the Directive a developer is required to undertake the assessment and to provide an environmental statement covering a potentially wide variety of issues. This environmental statement accompanies the planning application, and so provides assistance to the consent authority in determining the application. Although the process in Britain is as yet in its early stages, and many environmental statements so far prepared have not fully investigated likely impacts, the process has great potential for ensuring that the impacts of a damaging development are fully understood early in the decision-making process. On estuaries, environmental assessment is particularly complicated since it requires the understanding and prediction of the subtle interactions of the many physical, chemical and biological processes in the estuarine ecosystem. Such assessments for major projects, for example the proposed Severn and Mersey tidal power barrages, are proving complex, and accurate predictions are difficult to make.

9.6.4 Coastal zone management

Coping in the future with the maintenance of wildlife interest in the linked estuarine resource around the coasts of Britain will undoubtedly require the co-operation and commitment of a great many estuary users and decision-makers, if the piecemeal loss and damage described in Chapter 10 is to be halted. There has been increasing interest in recent years in the integrated approach to coastal management as a way of strategically developing and controlling the management of coastal resources (see e.g. Houston & Jones 1990). Many parts of the British coastline are now the subject of projects developing coastal zone management priorities. In some places the initiative has come from voluntary conservation groups, such as the Dee and Mersey Estuaries Conservation Groups. Elsewhere, such as on the Sefton Coast in Lancashire, and SCOPAC in Sussex,

Hampshire and Dorset, the lead has been from local authorities and amenity groups; and in some places, such as The Wash, coastal management proposals have been initiated by the NCC.

There is much to be gained from ensuring that an integrated approach to coastal and estuarine management takes into account the very great wildlife importance and wide range of wildlife conservation designations on British estuaries in planning their future safeguard. Such approaches can be effective at the level of the single estuary (provided it is treated as a functional unit) as well as at the level of the entire estuarine resource of a region, if estuaries are incorporated into the regional management strategies for their importance as coastal wetlands.

9.7 References

ADAM, P. 1978. Geographical variation in British saltmarsh vegetation. *Journal of Ecology, 66,* 339-366.

ADAMS, W.M. 1984. *Implementing the Act. A study of habitat protection under Part II of the Wildlife and Countryside Act 1981.* Lincoln, British Association for Nature Conservationists/World Wildlife Fund.

BATTEN, L.A. 1987. The effectiveness of European agreements for wader conservation. *In: The conservation of international flyway populations of waders,* ed. by N.C.Davidson and M.W.Pienkowski. *Wader Study Group Bulletin, 49, Supplement,* 118-121. (IWRB Special Publication No.7.)

BURD, F. 1989. *The saltmarsh survey of Great Britain: an inventory of British saltmarshes.* Peterborough, Nature Conservancy Council. (Research & survey in nature conservation No. 17.)

CAMPBELL, S.C., & BOWEN, D.Q. 1989. *The Quaternary of Wales.* Peterborough, Nature Conservancy Council.

CARP, E. 1972. *Proceedings of the international conference on the conservation of wetlands and waterfowl. Ramsar, Iran, 30 January – 3 February 1971.* Slimbridge, International Waterfowl Research Bureau.

COUNTRYSIDE COMMISSION. 1983. *Areas of Outstanding Natural Beauty. A policy statement.* Cheltenham, Countryside Commission.

COUNTRYSIDE COMMISSION. 1989. *Directory of Areas of Outstanding Natural Beauty.* Cheltenham, Countryside Commission.

COUNTRYSIDE COMMISSION. 1990. *Heritage Coast policies and priorities: draft policy statement.* Cheltenham, Countryside Commission.

DAVIDSON, N.C., & EVANS, P.R. 1985. *The implications for nature conservation of the proposed Felixstowe Dock expansion.* Report to the Nature Conservancy Council (unpublished).

DEPARTMENT OF THE ENVIRONMENT/WELSH OFFICE. 1987. *Nature conservation.* DoE Circular 27/87 and Welsh Office Circular 52/87. London, HMSO.

GOODIER, R., & MAYNE, S. 1988. United Kingdom Biosphere Reserves: opportunities and limitations. *Ecos, 9,* 33-39.

GOSS-CUSTARD, J.D., & MOSER, M.E. 1988. Rates of change in the numbers of dunlin, *Calidris alpina,* wintering in British estuaries in relation to the spread of *Spartina anglica. Journal of Applied Ecology, 25,* 95-109.

GREENLAND WHITE-FRONTED GOOSE STUDY GROUP. 1986. Duich Moss: 'a minor administrative hitch'. *Ecos, 7* (2), 24-31.

GUBBAY, S. 1986. *Conservation of marine sites: a voluntary approach.* Ross-on-Wye, Marine Conservation Society.

GUBBAY, S. 1988. *A coastal directory for marine nature conservation.* Ross-on-Wye, Marine Conservation Society.

HERITAGE COAST FORUM. 1989. *Heritage Coast directory.* Manchester, Heritage Coast Forum.

HOUSTON, J., & JONES, C. 1990. *Planning and management of the coastal heritage.* Southport, Sefton Metropolitan Borough Council.

IUCN. 1979. *The Biosphere Reserve and its relationship with other protected areas.* Morges, International Union for the Conservation of Nature and Natural Resources.

IUCN. 1982. *The world's greatest natural areas. An indicative inventory of natural sites of World Heritage quality.* IUCN Commission on National Parks and Protective Areas for World Heritage Committee.

IUCN. 1986. *Migratory species in international instruments. An overview.* Gland, Switzerland, International Union for the Conservation of Nature and Natural Resources.

JOHNSTON, C., & SMITH, B. 1990. *Directory of the North Sea Coastal Margin.* Report to the UK Department of the Environment. Peterborough, Nature Conservancy Council.

LANE, B., & SAGAR, P. 1987. Conservation of wader habitats in Australasia. *In: The conservation of international flyway populations of waders,* ed. by N.C.Davidson & M.W.Pienkowski. *Wader Study Group Bulletin, 49, Supplement,* 135-138. (IWRB Special Publication No. 7.)

LYSTER, S. 1985. *International wildlife law. An analysis of international treaties concerned with the conservation of wildlife.* Cambridge, Grotius Publications.

MALTBY, E. 1986. *Waterlogged wealth. Why waste the world's wetlands.* London, Earthscan.

MYERS, J.P., MCLAIN, P.D., MORRISON, R.I.G., ANTAS, P.Z., CANEVARI, P., HARRINGTON, B.A., LOVEJOY, T.E., PULIDO, V., SALLABERRY, M., & SENNER, S.E. 1987. The western hemisphere shorebird reserve network. *In: The conservation of international flyway populations of waders,* ed. by N.C.Davidson & M.W.Pienkowski. *Wader Study Group Bulletin, 49, Supplement,* 122-124. (IWRB Special Publication No. 7.)

NATURE CONSERVANCY COUNCIL. 1984. *Nature conservation in Great Britain.* Peterborough, Nature Conservancy Council.

NATURE CONSERVANCY COUNCIL. 1987. *Thirteenth Report covering the period 1 April 1986 – 31 March 1987.* Peterborough, Nature Conservancy Council.

NATURE CONSERVANCY COUNCIL. 1988a. Development of criteria and guidelines for the identification of sites qualifying for Ramsar designation. *In: Convention on wetlands of international importance especially as waterfowl habitat. Proceedings of the third meeting of the conference of contracting parties. Regina, Saskatchewan, Canada, 27 May to 5 June 1987,* 318-336. Switzerland, Ramsar Convention Bureau.

NATURE CONSERVANCY COUNCIL. 1988b. *Internationally important wetlands and special protection area for birds.* Peterborough, Nature Conservancy Council.

NATURE CONSERVANCY COUNCIL. 1988c. The Severn Barrage and geological conservation. *Earth science conservation, 25,* 16-18.

NATURE CONSERVANCY COUNCIL. 1988d. *Sites of Special Scientific Interest.* Peterborough, Nature Conservancy Council.

NATURE CONSERVANCY COUNCIL. 1988e. *Fourteenth Report covering the period 1 April 1987 – 31 March 1988.* Peterborough, Nature Conservancy Council.

NATURE CONSERVANCY COUNCIL. 1989a. *Legislative responsibilities in the marine environment.* Peterborough, Nature Conservancy Council (Joint Marine Group).

NATURE CONSERVANCY COUNCIL. 1989b. *Guidelines for selection of biological SSSIs.* Peterborough, Nature Conservancy Council.

NATURE CONSERVANCY COUNCIL. 1989c. *Fifteenth Report covering the period 1 April 1988 – 31 March 1989.* Peterborough, Nature Conservancy Council.

NATURE CONSERVANCY COUNCIL. 1989d. *Local Nature Reserves.* Peterborough, Nature Conservancy Council. (Nature Conservancy Council Information Sheet No. 6.)

NATURE CONSERVANCY COUNCIL. 1990a. *Earth science conservation in Great Britain: a strategy.* Peterborough, Nature Conservancy Council.

NATURE CONSERVANCY COUNCIL. 1990b. *Marine Consultation Areas: Scotland.* Edinburgh, Nature Conservancy Council.

NATURE CONSERVANCY COUNCIL. In prep. *National Nature Reserve strategy.* Peterborough, Nature Conservancy Council.

RAMSAR CONVENTION BUREAU. 1988. *Convention on wetlands of international importance especially as waterfowl habitat. Proceedings of the third meeting of the conference of contracting parties, Regina, Saskatchewan, Canada; 27 May to 5 June 1987.* Switzerland, Ramsar Convention Bureau.

RAMSAR CONVENTION BUREAU. 1990. General program of the Montreux conference. *Ramsar,* No. 7, 8.

RATCLIFFE, D.A., ed. 1977. *A nature conservation review.* Cambridge, Cambridge University Press.

ROTHWELL, P., & HOUSDEN, S. 1990. *Turning the tide.* Sandy, Royal Society for the Protection of Birds.

ROYAL SOCIETY FOR THE PROTECTION OF BIRDS. 1989. *RSPB: where to go birdwatching. A guide to RSPB reserves.* London, BBC Books.

SMART, M. 1987. International conventions. *In: The conservation of international flyway populations of waders,* ed. by N.C.Davidson & M.W.Pienkowski. *Wader Study Group Bulletin, 49, Supplement,* 114-117.

SMART, M. 1990. Application of the Ramsar Convention in western Europe. *Ramsar,* No. 7, 2-3.

SMIT, C.J., & PIERSMA, T. 1989. Numbers, midwinter distribution and migration of wader populations using the East Atlantic Flyway. *In: Flyways and reserve networks,* ed. by H.Boyd and J.-Y.Pirot, 24-63. Slimbridge, IWRB. (IWRB Special Publication No. 9.)

SOULE, M.E. 1987. *Viable populations for conservation.* Cambridge, Cambridge University Press.

STROUD, D.A., MUDGE, G.P., & PIENKOWSKI, M.W. 1990. *Protecting internationally important bird sites. A review of the EEC Special Protection Area network in Great Britain.* Peterborough, Nature Conservancy Council.

TASKER, M.L., et al. In prep. Review of proposed marine Special Protection Areas. *Nature Conservancy Council, CSD Report.*

TEMPLE LANG, J.T. 1982. The European Community Directive on bird conservation. *Biological Conservation, 22,* 11-25.

TUBBS, C. 1989. The Solent: an estuarine system in flux. *BTO News,* 10-11.

UNITED NATIONS EDUCATIONAL, SCIENTIFIC
AND CULTURAL ORGANISATION. 1974.
*Programme on Man and the Biosphere (MAB).
Task Force on criteria and guidelines for the
choice and establishment of Biosphere Reserves.*
Paris, UNESCO. (MAB Report Series No. 22.)

VON DROSTE, B., & GREGG, W.P. 1985. Biosphere
Reserves: demonstrating the value of
conservation in sustaining society. *Parks, 10,* 2-5.

WARREN, L.M. 1989. *Statutory Marine Nature
Reserves in Britain. A progress report.*
Godalming, World Wide Fund for Nature.

Contents

Summary

Man has used estuaries for many centuries, at first mostly for supplies of food, for grazing animals, and as harbours. More recently the development of towns and cities on the shores of many estuaries, and the continuing expansion of industry and shipping, have led to extensive damage and destruction of habitat.

The widespread discharge of effluents produced by this urban and industrial society has caused heavy pollution of estuaries, and has contributed to the perception of estuaries as wastelands – areas of 'free land' suitable for waste disposal, tipping and land-claim for a variety of purposes. Most recently, leisure and recreational use has placed increasing infrastructure and disturbance pressure on the wildlife using the remaining parts of estuaries.

The Estuaries Review has collected information on the presence of over 250 different types of human activity (grouped into 100 major categories) taking place on estuaries in 1989. It has also identified estuaries on which these activities once occurred but have now ceased, and those for which there were proposals current at the time of the survey.

There are five key features of human use of estuaries:

● many different human activities occur on a single estuary at the same time;

● similar activities occur on many different estuaries simultaneously;

● there are many and widespread proposals for further developments on estuaries;

● current activities and new proposals are focussed on the remaining parts of a dwindling resource, large areas of which have already been claimed for human use; and

● many activities can and do have adverse impacts, both individually and cumulatively, on estuarine wildlife.

Overall activity patterns

Most estuaries have many different human activities: even on estuaries of less than 500 ha about one-quarter of all major activity categories occur. Although no one estuary had all possible activities recorded on it, some of the largest estuaries (Severn Estuary, Humber Estuary and Morecambe Bay) had over 90% of major activities current. Small estuaries had relatively more diverse activities for their size. Activities were particularly diverse in the Greater Thames Estuary, parts of Wales and north-west England, large Scottish firths, and the Humber Estuary, The Wash and the North Norfolk Coast.

Activity proposals were recorded on 108 estuaries, with a similar distribution pattern as for current activities. Proposals were relatively diverse on small estuaries, notably on the Hayle Estuary (where many were part of a single complex development proposal), parts of the Solent, the Greater Thames Estuary, and on the larger estuaries of the Humber and Firth of Forth.

The most widespread uses (on at least 60% of estuaries) were in these categories: linear sea defences and coast protection; dock, port and harbour facilities; bridges and tunnels; recreational activities including angling, dinghy sailing, boat moorings; exploitation of natural resources such as wildfowling and bait-digging; and scientific research and educational work. Docks and jetties are very widespread, on 147 estuaries, as are informal walking and bird-watching (at least 140 sites). Almost 40% of activities were, however, very localised, occurring on less than 20 estuaries each.

Patterns of activity type differ, ranging from typically 'urban' estuaries with over half the categories being urban, industrial and recreational, to 'rural' estuaries with mainly resource exploitation and recreation.

New proposals were diverse, although mostly less widespread than those activity categories are at present, except for tidal energy and 'amenity' barrages. The most widespread proposals (on 20 or more estuaries) were for 'amenity' barrages, dock, port and harbour facilities, capital dredging, road schemes, housing and car-parks, marinas, shellfish farming, and nature trails and information facilities.

The construction of linear sea defences has had a major impact on estuaries. 85% of estuaries have some artificial embankments restricting the tide. Sea defences are particularly extensive in eastern and south-eastern England. Land-claim was also widely promoted in the last century by the planting (on at least 39 estuaries) and subsequent spread of cord-grass.

Over one-third of the British population (18 million people) lives in towns and cities around estuaries. This places great recreational and urban development pressure on the remaining estuarine shores nearby. Seventeen estuaries have current housing and car-park developments, and 36 have proposals. Improved communications also lead to increased recreational pressure on more rural estuaries.

Many widespread human activities have the effect of degrading remaining parts of estuarine ecosystems through, for example, over-exploitation of their natural resources and excessive discharge and spillage of wastes and pollutants. Widespread water-based and land-based recreational use of estuaries is also of increasing concern both for habitat damage (e.g.. sand-dune erosion) and its ability to cause severe disturbance to wildlife, particularly nesting birds in summer and feeding and roosting waterfowl during the non-breeding seasons.

Such uses depend, however, on there being estuarine habitats left. The underlying key conservation issue, which also exacerbates the impacts of pollution, over-exploitation and recreation on the remaining parts of estuaries, is progressive habitat loss through land-claim.

Land-claim and habitat loss

Land-claim is part of a more general estuarine squeeze that is pushing the high water mark seawards (through land-claim, sea defences, barrages and rising sea levels) and low water mark landwards (through effects of dredging, barrages and rising sea level).

Land-claim has been widespread, cumulative and piecemeal. It has affected at least 85% of British estuaries, has removed over 25% of intertidal land from many estuaries, and over 80% in estuaries such as the Blyth (Suffolk), the Tees and the Tyne.

The largest area (47,000 ha) has been progressively claimed from The Wash since Roman times. On just 18 estuaries at least 89,000 ha have been claimed – 37% of their former area and overall an almost 25% loss from the British resource. In the last 200 years estuarine land has been claimed at 0.2-0.7% per year.

Widespread land-claim is continuing. 123 land-claims in progress in 1989 affected 45 estuaries. 72 of these cases were affecting the intertidal and subtidal parts of 32 estuaries.

Land-claim was for many purposes, but two-thirds was for rubbish and spoil disposal, transport (chiefly road) schemes, housing and car-parks, and marinas. Many individual claims were of less than 5 ha, but overall at least 1,100 ha are under active claim below high water mark, 61.5% of which is for rubbish and spoil tipping. Over 1,300 ha of associated terrestrial habitats were under claim, almost all for rubbish and spoil disposal.

Much agricultural land-claim in the past created coastal grazing marshes which have since developed substantial conservation interest. Much of this grazing marsh has now been secondarily claimed for intensive agriculture and for urban and industrial developments. Between 30 and 70% of the marshes that remained in the 1930s in different parts of south-east England have now been claimed. There are further major land-claim proposals for the remaining fragments such as Rainham Marshes on the Thames Estuary.

Many other estuarine development proposals would cause further land-claim: in 1989 there were 135 such proposals affecting 55 estuaries. Most are in the Greater Thames estuary, around the Solent, Milford Haven and the Severn Estuary. Housing schemes, marinas and barrage schemes together account for over half the proposals. There are fewer rubbish and spoil disposal proposals.

Overall future habitat losses will be considerable if all proposals are implemented. Barrage schemes alone may remove at least 8% of the remaining British intertidal resource. Continuing habitat loss will further reduce an already much diminished resource, and will force development and recreational land-uses into increasing conflict with wildlife on the remaining areas of estuarine habitat. Rising sea levels, especially in parts of southern Britain, will exacerbate the pressure because estuaries are not able to retreat landward beyond existing sea defences.

The recognised international wildlife importance of an estuary does not appear substantially to deflect land-claim: 26 estuaries in the Ramsar/SPA network have current habitat losses, 21 of these losing intertidal/subtidal areas.

Furthermore, land-claim proposals affect 36 Ramsar/SPA estuaries. In all, over 50% of internationally important estuaries face further habitat losses by direct land-claim. Proposals involve both small piecemeal incursions and major schemes such as barrages and airports.

Continuing land-claim has many impacts on estuarine wildlife, notably the disproportionate loss of saltmarshes and upper tidal flats, the overall reduction of estuarine biomass and production, and the reduction in the size of some internationally important bird populations, on at least individual estuaries.

10.1 Introduction

10.1.1 Background

Worldwide, the physical, chemical and biological characteristics of estuaries have made them of great value to human populations. Estuarine waters and sediments are rich in nutrients which are continually washed in-shore or down-river and provide abundant food for a wide variety of plants and animals. Man has harvested the products of these fertile conditions, including plants such as glass-wort *Salicornia*, traditionally collected as

'poor-man's asparagus', as well as grazing stock on saltmarshes. Estuaries have provided abundant supplies of shellfish and fish, including those migratory species such as salmon that pass through estuaries on their way to breed in the fresh waters upstream (see Chapter 8.4). The sheltered conditions which lead to the deposition of the fine sediments so characteristic of estuarine ecosystems have for many centuries also provided sheltered anchorage for fishing fleets plying the deeper waters out to sea. Such docks and anchorages have also long been vital for the import and export trades of these islands.

More recently the increasing industrialisation and urbanisation of the human population over the last 200 years have meant very great changes to many formerly rural estuaries and shores. Such places had till then been used by man chiefly for agriculture and fisheries. The industrial revolution and subsequent major technological advances have, however, had a profound impact on estuaries through changing patterns of human use. Estuaries have provided a plentiful supply of water for industry, and the development of many major industries alongside estuaries gave easy access for the import of raw materials and export of products. Initially many of these industries and the docks associated with them were many kilometres upstream. As shipping tonnages increased and ships became bigger many of the docks and ports have, however, moved to locations nearer the mouth of estuaries, and formerly shallow channels have been deepened by dredging. The overall effect has been the progressive loss of natural estuarine habitats.

Industry and the increasingly large urban populations associated with it have had another profound impact on estuaries – that of extensive waste discharge, often of untreated domestic and industrial effluents. The continual flow of river water down many estuaries, coupled with the daily tidal movements, have the effect of a repeated but partial flushing of the estuary, so that effluents are gradually diluted and eventually discharged into the sea. This widespread use of estuaries for waste discharge has, however, resulted in the serious long-term pollution of many areas. This has arisen in part because of the huge volumes of material discharged into estuaries and in part because it often takes some days for water reaching the top of a tidal river estuary to be discharged and further diluted in the open sea. During this time many pollutants in the water column become attached to turbid sediments and settle out into the mudflats and saltmarshes. There they are taken up by plants and are ingested by grazing and detritus-feeding animals, so that pollutants are concentrated and transported through the food chain.

High levels of pollutant can result in anoxic conditions – conditions in which many estuarine organisms cannot survive. Even low levels of some pollutants can make shellfish unfit for human consumption, so that the value to man of the natural resources of estuaries becomes diminished. The progressive industrialisation and degradation of estuaries has increasingly led to their being treated as wastelands with no value. Such places have been regarded as 'free land', readily available for claiming or modification for a wide variety of human uses. In many places the disposal of domestic refuse and spoil of many kinds has been particularly focussed on estuarine saltmarshes and mudflats. Such infill is seen as having the added advantage of subsequently providing cheap new dry land for industrial and urban developments.

This shift towards industrial and urban perceptions of estuaries has been accompanied by a shift in the way estuarine habitats have been claimed or modified. Early land-claims for agriculture, although sometimes very extensive, tended to claim saltmarsh areas and to leave the lower tidal levels of mudflats and sandflats untouched, although there were often subsequent changes to these tidal flat habitats through further accretion of saltmarsh, as for example on The Wash (Doody & Barnett 1987). Much of this piecemeal development of the upper tidal parts of estuaries is continuing for a variety of purposes (see Chapter 10.5). In addition, however, increasingly sophisticated technologies have led to the claiming of extensive areas for industrial uses. Many of these involve the claiming of all the intertidal area, down to low water mark, rather than just the upper parts.

In addition, in the 1960s major schemes to build barriers or barrages across the mouths of many estuaries were proposed, initially for water storage purposes. Subsequently such barriers, which with one development can dramatically alter the ecosystem of an entire large estuary, have become widely proposed for several purposes, notably tidal power generation and storm surge control and as part of recreational and urban renewal developments. In these last the stated aim is often to cover up the tidal flats and marshes so as to create a lake for water-based recreation. Hence the restoration of degraded estuaries is seem by some as requiring the eradication of the key estuarine features rather than the re-creation of more natural estuarine ecosystems.

Increasing prosperity during the 20th century, much of it involving industrial and port operations situated around and on estuaries, and the increasing time for leisure during the 20th century have placed further pressure on the remaining parts of Britain's estuarine resource. The extent of recreational and sporting use of estuaries, particularly the water-based activities such as sailing and board-sailing, has been increasing greatly, so raising the potential for conflict with the safeguarding of estuarine wildlife. Associated with this recreational use is considerable demand for shore-based facilities such as marinas and housing, which may in turn contribute to piecemeal development on further areas of estuarine habitat. In contrast to the 'wasteland' approach embodied in many of the human uses of estuaries, some of the most widespread activities on estuaries in Britain are the 'informal' recreational uses such as walking – thus many people continue to visit estuaries for their wildness, landscape and wildlife.

In general then, human use of estuaries has four key features –

1   There are many different types of human activity current on a single estuary at any one time.

2   Similar activities are current on many different estuaries simultaneously.

3   There are many proposals for further developments on estuaries, and these too are widespread.

4   The current activities and new proposals are focussed on the remaining parts of a diminishing resource.

Nevertheless, as described in Chapters 6, 8 and 9, the network of estuaries continues to be of major importance as a vital part of Britain's natural heritage. The challenge is to ensure that the national commitments and international obligations to safeguard, maintain and enhance this wildlife resource can be met alongside the long-term pattern of human estuarine usage. This chapter provides a synthesis of this pattern of human estuarine activities at present and for the future, as far as could be established, if current proposals are enacted.

10.1.2 Sources and analysis of information

As described in Chapter 3, the objective of this part of the review has been to provide a synthesis and overview of the range and variety of human activities that have and are occurring on British estuaries, and those for which there are known future plans. The 'overview' approach used below treats the British estuarine resource as a whole, on which is superimposed the pattern of distribution and the scale of each activity on its component parts. The analysis begins with a description of the overall patterning of activities around the estuarine resource, and ends (Chapter 10.5) with a description of the overall pattern of past, present and proposed land-claim on estuaries. This brings together information on those cases in each activity category known to cause direct loss of estuarine wildlife habitat on core review sites and their surroundings.

Although human activities data were collected for over 250 different categories of activity during the Estuaries Review surveys, these activities have been grouped into 117 types in 18 major broad categories for the synthesis in this chapter (Table 10.2.1). For analysis we have also condensed the 10 status categories for an activity into five: absent (includes known not to occur); old (recorded only as historical or recently ceased); current (including consented to and under development); proposed (including current proposed and consent applications); and defunct proposed. Since for some estuaries rather little information was available about some types of activity, the numbers and patterns of distribution are likely to be minima. Conversely, it is important to note that not all cases listed as current proposals will be pursued as far as a consent application or become operational; nevertheless, it is important to list all such publicly-announced proposals, since (a) it is impossible to tell which are likely to continue as firm proposals, and (b) in many past instances even a proposal that had been dropped has reappeared in either identical or similar form some time later.

Despite its size, this report cannot attempt to provide a comprehensive impact statement on each and every human activity on the wildlife and conservation significance of Britain's estuaries, since our assessment was designed to provide comparable information between, rather than within, estuaries. Furthermore detailed impact studies of wide application for particular activities are often lacking. The review does, however, bring together for the first time information on the distribution and scale of human activities over the whole resource and so provides directions for more detailed studies of key issues, some of which are already underway. Further analyses of the pattern and impact of the various key human activities are planned as future reports from the NCC's Estuaries Review.

The surveys analysed here provide a 'snap-shot' of activity patterns at the time of our surveys in early 1989. It is important to remember that we have not generally attempted to make a piecemeal update of activity status since then, as our objective was to provide a comparative overview of activity patterns at a particular time. We do, however, comment where major changes in the status of activities have occurred since then. Clearly it is in the nature of development proposals that many, particularly the small-scale proposals, will have moved through the consent process to development or current status, or have been rejected or dropped. Similarly some proposals that were reasonably believed defunct at the time of the survey have since been resurrected. This chapter should thus be read as a description of pattern and type in human activities and not as a definitive guide to individual locations and status at the date of publication. The analyses do, however, also provide the basis of assessing changes in patterns and pressures for the future.

10.2 Overall patterns of human activity

Activity records were collected for all 155 review sites, and in excess of 7,000 records (each record is one activity of one status on one review site) were compiled onto a computer database for analysis. On all estuaries we found evidence of human activities, and the nature of the activities varied between estuaries.

Figure 10.2.1 shows that there is generally a great

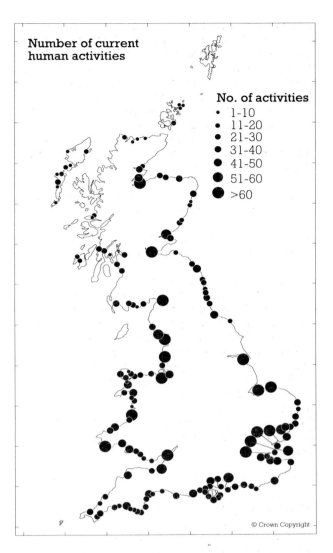

Figure 10.2.1 The number of current types of human activity on each review site, out of a possible 117 activity types

variety of different activities current or taking place on many review sites. This confirms the general perception that many of Britain's estuaries continue to be used extensively by man. It is usual for there to be over 30 different categories (of the total of 117) of activity on many estuaries, and on 25 estuaries there are over half the total types of activity going on simultaneously. The diversity of activities is greatest on a number of estuaries scattered around almost all parts of the resource. There are, however, some general patterns apparent from Figure 10.2.1, notably that the largest number of human activities occur on most of the 'Greater Thames' Estuaries Review sites in Essex and Kent, and on estuaries in Wales and north-west England, and the Humber Estuary, The Wash and the North Norfolk Coast. In general Figure 10.2.1 makes it clear that estuaries in most parts of Britain have extensive human influence and activities. Only in northern and western Scotland are there mostly small numbers of activities occurring on estuaries and even here there are exceptions, notably the Moray, Cromarty and Dornoch Firths as well as the Firths of Tay and Forth. The largest number of activities currently take place on the Severn Estuary (91 activities), Humber Estuary (90), Morecambe Bay (87), the Dee Estuary and North Wirral (77), The Wash (73) and the Firth of Forth (72).

There is a general relationship between the number of activities and estuary size, shown in Figure 10.2.2. On average, the smallest number of activities occurs on the smallest estuaries, and the diversity of activities increases with estuary size. Figure 10.2.2 shows, however, that this is not a linear relationship. Even on very small estuaries there is typically a pattern of about 15 types of activity. The number of activities rises steeply with increasing estuary size until on estuaries of 5,000-10,000 ha on average over 50% of activity categories are currently being undertaken. The rate of increase of types of activity then slows with further increases in estuary area. This means that most common or widespread activities almost invariably occur in some part of an estuary of 5,000 ha or larger, but that on larger estuaries it is still likely that some further, less frequent activities will occur somewhere within their bounds. Activities are also most diverse on estuaries surrounded by large urban populations.

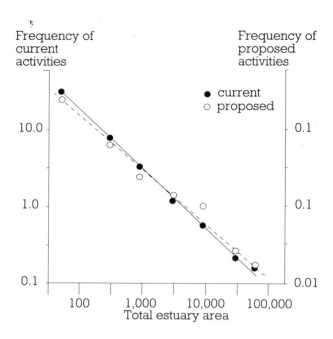

Figure 10.2.3 The frequency (no. ha⁻¹) of activity categories decreases with increasing estuary size

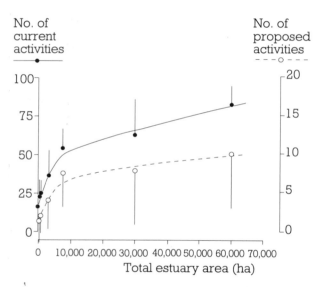

Figure 10.2.2 The number of current and proposed activity types on each review site in relation to total area of the site, shown as the average values (with 1 standard deviation) plotted in relation to the average area of estuaries in each size category.

An implication of the non-linear pattern of activity diversity with increasing estuary size is that, whilst on larger estuaries there are absolutely more types of activity taking place, on small estuaries there is a greater diversity of activity type per hectare of estuary. This is illustrated in Figure 10.2.3.

Such analyses of course do not provide information about the scale and overlap of individual activities on estuaries of different sizes, and in general common and widespread activities do occur throughout estuaries regardless of their size. Even

so, it is clear that the complexity of different and sometimes conflicting activities, and so pressures on the natural resources of estuaries, is generally almost as great on small sites as on large. Indeed the pressures on small estuaries can be even greater since they offer little flexibility in the form of, for example, segregated refuge areas for waterfowl facing human disturbance: whilst on a large estuary birds can move away from disturbance to other parts of the same system, on a small estuary the same level of activity would affect a much greater proportion of the available area. Small estuaries with diverse activity patterns may therefore pose some of the greatest challenges for implementing future estuarine conservation measures. Nevertheless, a single activity such as a barrage scheme can alone have a major impact on the entire ecosystem, so diversity of activity is, of course, not the only guide to patterns of estuarine pressure.

Out of the 155 review sites, the number on which each type of human activity was found to occur is shown in Table 10.2.1. The most widespread activity types on estuaries fall into a variety of categories including linear sea defences and other forms of coast protection, dock, port and harbour facilities, bridges and tunnels, recreational activities such as walking, bird-watching, angling and dinghy sailing, the non-marina moorings associated with sailing, exploitation of natural resources such as bait-digging and wildfowling, and scientific research and educational visits. All these activities were present or were taking place on at least 90 British estuaries (60%) in 1989. The most widespread of all proved to be ports, docks, jetties and wharf facilities on 147 review sites (95% of sites), and informal walking and bird-watching on 140 sites (90% of estuaries). Conversely many other types of activity are much more localised:

Table 10.2.1 The number of review sites out of the total of 155 sites on which each activity category was current and proposed during the Estuaries Review surveys in 1989. Note that a single estuary can have the activity both current and proposed, as for example an estuary with both existing marinas and proposals for new marinas.

Activity category	No. of estuaries with current activity	No. of estuaries with proposed activity
Coast protection and sea defences		
Linear defences	132	15
Training walls	5	0
Groynes	58	2
Brushwood fences	23	5
Spartina planting	2	0
Marram grass planting	20	0
Barrage schemes		
Weirs and barrages for river management	40	1
Storm surge barrages	3	3
Water storage barrages and bunds	2	3
Leisure barrages	7	20
Tidal power barrages	0	11
Tidal mills	6	0
Power generation		
Thermal power stations		
Generation facilities	22	10
Import/export jetties	8	1
Wind-power generation	2	3
Industrial, port and related development		
Dock, port and harbour facilities	147	29
Manufacturing industries	32	4
Chemical industries	33	3
Ship and boat building	65	1
Others	12	0
Extraction and processing of natural gas and oil		
Exploration	9	4
Production	5	0
Rig and platform construction	8	0
Pipeline installation	16	5
Import/export jetties and single-point moorings	19	2
Oil refineries	14	1
Mothballing of rigs and tankers	4	0
Military activities		
Military installations and facilities	31	0
Overflying by military aircraft	55	0
Others	14	0
Waste discharge		
Domestic waste disposal		
Sewage discharge and outfalls	122	12
Sewage treatment works	54	4
Rubbish tips	48	12
Industrial & agricultural waste discharge	40	0
Thermal discharges (power stations)	12	0
Dredge spoil	10	4
Accidental discharges	35	0
Aerial crop spraying	13	0
Waste incinerators	2	4
Sediment extraction		
Capital dredging	15	35

Table 10.2.1 (contd.)

Activity category	No. of estuaries with current activity	No. of estuaries with proposed activity
Maintenance dredging	72	4
Commercial estuarine aggregates extraction	11	0
Commercial terrestrial aggregates extraction	12	6
Non-commercial aggregates extraction	26	2
Hard-rock quarrying	1	0
Transport and communications		
Airports and helipads	34	2
Tunnels, bridges and aqueducts	106	17
Causeways and fords	46	4
Road schemes	15	23
Ferries	43	2
Cables	65	5
Urbanisation		
Housing and car parks	20	34
Tourism and recreation		
Infrastructure developments		
Marinas	51	41
Non-marina moorings	123	6
Dinghy and boat parks	59	2
Caravan parks and chalets	76	6
Leisure centres, complexes and piers	11	9
Aquatic-based recreation		
Power-boating and water-skiing	75	1
Jet-skiing	67	1
Sailing	127	4
Sailboarding and windsurfing	88	0
SCUBA and snorkling	23	1
Canoeing	77	0
Surfing	86	0
Rowing	13	0
Tourist boat trips/leisure barges	32	3
Angling	134	0
Other non-commercial fishing	40	0
Bathing and general beach recreation	106	0
Terrestrial and intertidal-based recreation		
Walking, including dog walking	116	3
Bird-watching	140	0
Sand-yachting	10	1
4WD and trial-biking	43	1
Car sand-racing	13	1
Horse-riding	69	1
Rock-climbing	5	0
Golf courses	48	9
Clay-pigeon shooting	21	1
Others	6	0
Airborne recreation		
Overflying by light aircraft	42	1
Radio-controlled model aircraft	10	0
Wildfowling and hunting		
Wildfowling	99	0
Other hunting-related activities	43	0
Bait-collecting		
Digging and pumping for lugworms and ragworms	96	0
Hydraulic dredging for worms	0	1
Others	5	0

Table 10.2.1 (contd.)

Activity category	No. of estuaries with current activity	No. of estuaries with proposed activity
Commercial fisheries		
Fish-netting and trawling	35	0
Fyke-netting for eels	29	0
Fish traps and other fixed devices and nets	35	0
Crustaceans	21	0
Molluscs		
Hand-gathering	44	0
Dredging	11	2
Hydraulic dredging	6	1
Cultivation of living resources		
Saltmarsh grazing	85	0
Sand-dune grazing	33	1
Agricultural land-claim	7	4
Fish-farming	9	0
Shellfish farming	59	22
Crustacea farming	0	0
Reeds for roofing	12	1
Glass-wort *Salicornia* picking	9	0
Others	27	3
Management killing of birds and mammals		
Killing of mammals	25	0
Killing of birds		
Adult fish-eating birds	23	0
Adult shellfish-eating birds	1	1
Gulls	16	3
Geese	43	3
Wildlife habitat management		
Cord-grass *Spartina* control	11	12
Education and scientific research		
Sampling, specimen collection and observation	103	0
Nature trails and interpretative facilities	85	27
Seismic studies and geological test drilling	17	0
Marine and terrestrial archaeology	34	1
Fossil collecting	6	0

47 different categories (almost 40% of the total) occurred on less than 20 estuaries each.

The pattern of human influence on individual estuaries varies greatly. On some review sites man has and is making extensive use of the estuary and its surroundings. Activities on such places are predominantly industrial, urban and recreational. On other 'rural' estuaries there has been much less urbanisation and here a greater proportion of uses exploit the living resources or are recreational pursuits. Examples of the relative frequency of activity types on urban and rural estuaries are shown in Figure 10.2.4.

The pattern of activity types for which there are new proposals is similar to the pattern for those already taking place. Categories for which there are proposals recorded are generally those which require some form of consent. A proposal in an activity category can be for a new activity for the estuary or for an extension of an existing activity. Many proposals are for types of development activity, for example marinas, docks or housing, and relate to the development of new sites. In some cases a single activity record may refer to a number of separate proposals in different parts of an estuary – for example where there are several marina developments proposed. Conversely a single development proposal can involve a record in several activity types, for instance where a major leisure development includes marina berths, housing and a golf course.

As for current activities there are many types of proposal for new activities or for new or expanded locations for activities. New proposals were recorded for 63 of the activity categories (53% of the total listed in Table 10.2.1). Proposals were generally less widespread that the existing

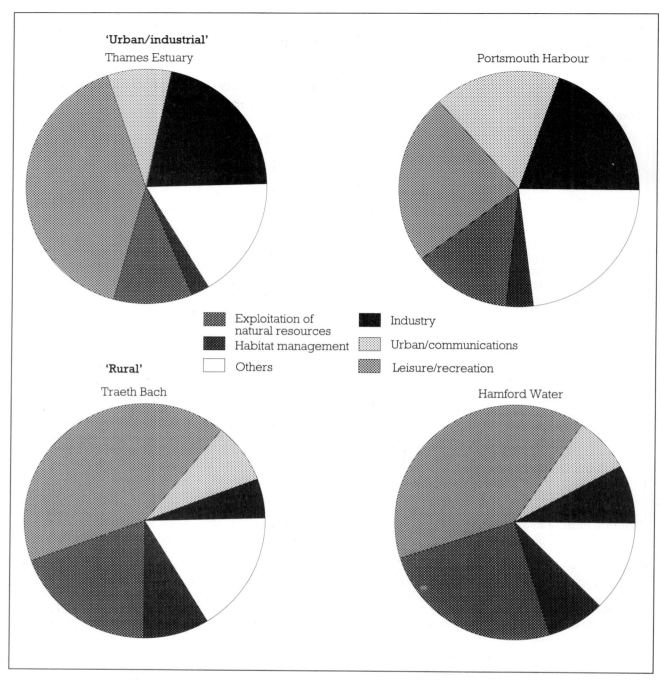

Figure 10.2.4 The relative frequency of human activities, grouped into different broad categories, for two examples each of 'urban' estuaries (Thames Estuary, Portsmouth Harbour) and 'rural' estuaries (Hamford Water, Traeth Bach)

distribution of the activity, although an exception is barrages for tidal energy and leisure development. For only eight activity categories were there proposals on 20 or more estuaries (13% of review sites). These were for leisure barrages, dock, port and harbour facilities, capital dredging, road schemes, housing and car parks, marinas, shellfish farming and nature trails and interpretative centres. With proposals on 41 estuaries (26% of review sites) marinas were the most widely proposed of all the categories of activity.

The distribution of proposed activity categories around review sites follows the pattern of existing activities, as is shown in Figure 10.2.5. Proposed activities were recorded for 108 of the 155 review

sites (70% of the total). Proposed activities were widespread around the estuarine resource, although as for current activities there is a relatively small range of activities proposed in most parts of northern and western Scotland. Proposals for activities are particularly abundant around the Greater Thames Estuary, the Solent and much of Wales and north-west England, and also on some individual estuaries such as the Humber Estuary, Tees Estuary, Firth of Forth, Morecambe Bay, the Severn Estuary and the Hayle Estuary.

As with current activities, there is a strong relationship between the diversity of proposed activities and estuary size (Figure 10.2.2), with a similar non-linear relationship apparent. Again the

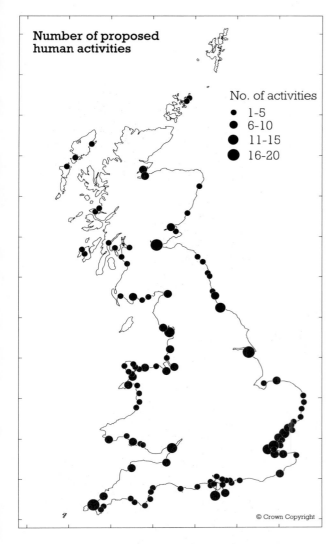

Number of proposed human activities

No. of activities
- • 1-5
- • 6-10
- ● 11-15
- ● 16-20

© Crown Copyright

Figure 10.2.5 The number of types of human activity on each review site for which there were new proposals, out of a possible 117 activity types

overall trend is for a greater diversity of proposed activities on larger estuaries. However, like the pattern for current activities, there are still relatively more activities proposed for their size on small estuaries than on large ones (Figure 10.2.3). Some individual estuaries stand out as having a particularly wide variety of activity proposals for their size. These include the small estuaries of the Hayle in Cornwall (where most categories are components of major leisure and recreational proposals then under consideration), the Medina on the Isle of Wight and the Tees Estuary, the larger Thames Estuary and the Colne Estuary and Southend-on-Sea in Essex. All of these are under 5,000 ha in total area. Amongst larger estuaries the Humber Estuary has a large range of activity proposals even allowing for its 30,000 ha area.

Such patterns of diversity have implications for future potential pressures on estuaries, since an understanding of the overall impact of future human use on an estuary may depend on an assessment of the pattern of all types of proposal and their interactions. Such issues are appropriate for consideration as much for small estuaries as for

large ones where the overall range of proposed activities is larger.

10.3 Sea defence and coast protection

10.3.1 Introduction

Sea defence (the maintenance of sea banks and walls to prevent flooding) and coast protection (the protection of cliff coastline from eroding) are important factors in the estuarine environment. In Britain as a whole, some 11.5% of the coastline is protected in some way by sea banks, walls, groynes and other artificial structures including promenades and coast protection features. In England this rises to 32%. The distribution of sea-walls and embankments, and other protection (notably groynes) around British coasts, is shown in Figure 10.3.1.

Most of Britain's major estuaries have developed in low-lying areas where the shores and hinterland slope only gently. By their very nature these areas are susceptible to flooding by sea water as a result of tidal incursion. The enclosure of saltmarsh with sea-walls greatly increases the threat of tidal incursion since the natural buffer zone is reduced during the process (see also Chapter 11). The main aim of most sea defence strategies is to maintain sea defence levels high enough to take account of a 50-100 year storm event.

In addition to flooding from the sea a major preoccupation in areas where sea level is rising (see below) is the effect of high tides which, when associated with heavy rainfall, can cause freshwater flooding upstream, as downstream drainage is impeded. Proposals to barrage several estuaries could have a similar effect and one of the major non-nature conservation issues in the Cardiff Bay Barrage debate is of the effect on groundwater levels.

10.3.2 Sea defence and estuaries

At the present time, as described in Chapter 8.1 for the enclosure of saltmarshes, substantial areas of tidal land in our major estuaries have been taken from the estuarine system (See also Chapter 10.5). The enclosure of saltmarsh and other areas has resulted in major losses of tidal land. Reductions of estuarine area by up to one third are not uncommon (Doody in prep.; see also Chapter 10.4). On the enclosed grazing marshes in Essex and Kent and around the Severn Estuary, the extent of land susceptible to flooding is immense. It is important to recognise that land 'won' from the sea is likely to be lower than the surviving saltmarsh to seaward of the sea bank. This is due partly to the shrinking of the enclosed land as it dries out and partly to the fact that the intertidal land continues to accrete sedimentary material outside the sea-wall. This obviously increases any threat from tidal flooding.

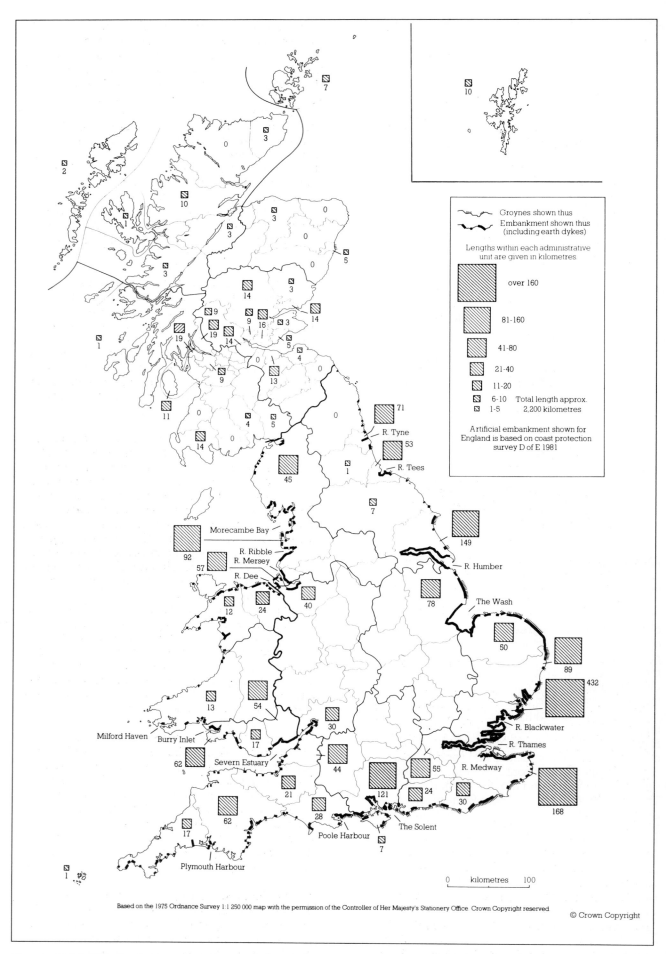

Figure 10.3.1 The distribution of artificial embankments and groynes around the coasts of Great Britain

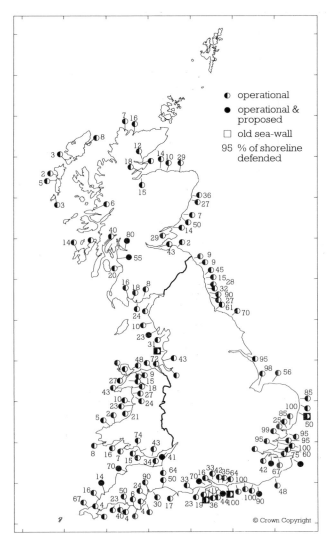

Figure 10.3.2 The distribution of linear defences (including sea-walls, embankments and revetments) on review sites. Operational, proposed and old (failed) defences are shown, with numbers indicating the percentage of the review site shoreline defended artificially.

The Estuaries Review has identified linear defences as the major sea defence category. Such defences include artificial sea-walls and embankments. There are only 19 review sites where some form of linear sea defence is not present. These are areas where the shorelines generally shelve steeply and so there is no need for artificial defences. 136 estuaries (88% of sites) are at least partly bounded by artificial defences, and often extensively so (Figure 10.3.2).

By their very nature linear defences require regular maintenance because wave attack and general deterioration of the structures cause decay. In a few areas the abandoning of sea-walls, particularly where associated with small 'reclaimed' islands, has allowed reversion of cultivated land to mudflats and saltmarsh. Examples include Alloa Inches in the Firth of Forth, the Blyth Estuary in Suffolk and a number of areas (such as Nor Marsh in the Medway) in south-east England.

The abandoning of sea-walls is as yet very much the exception and the majority of sites, notably in the south-east where sea level is generally rising relative to the land, have a very high proportion of their landward boundary made up of a sea-wall or earth bank which is actively maintained. From Humberside to the Thames Estuary 11 of 17 sites have more than 85% of their shore bounded by an artificial sea-wall. High figures are encountered also for the North Norfolk Coast and the Ore/Alde/Butley sites, with 56% and 50% respectively, even though these also have major natural sand-dune and shingle structures protecting the coast. (The Stour Estuary has a much more natural shoreline (only 11% embanked), but this site is bounded by relatively steeply shelving shores and there has been little past land-claim.)

Elsewhere a similar pattern emerges, notably where enclosure of tidal land for development has occurred. Thus the estuaries of the south coast around the Solent and in Liverpool Bay also have quite high proportions, with 72% of the Dee shoreline embanked. Large-scale linear defences are most commonly encountered at other sites where major port-related development has taken place, such as in the Clyde (80%) and Swansea Bay (74%).

The process of enclosure by linear sea defences has caused a direct loss of tidal land, particularly the upper parts of the intertidal zone, which has contributed greatly to the overall loss of intertidal habitats on British estuaries (Doody in prep.; see also Chapter 10.5). These enclosures have considerable implications for the future, particularly where sea level is rising relative to the land, since their maintenance is likely to become increasingly costly and difficult (see Chapter 11). Improvement to and repair of these sea defences also creates problems for conservation. In The Wash, for example, the traditional method of rehabilitating or raising the earth bank is to use excavated material from the seaward saltmarsh. This has the effect of removing the upper, often biologically the richest, sections from the natural zonation of the shore. Even after 30 years these seaward 'borrow-dykes' have patterns of vegetation very much less diverse than the surrounding unexcavated areas.

Even if, as in some other areas, material for maintaining or raising the sea-wall comes from the landward side of the wall and from some distance away, intertidal damage can occur. This arises because the general method of increasing their height is to extend the toe of the defence to seaward, further reducing the intertidal area. This process forms an appreciable proportion (6.6%) of the current incidence of land-claim on estuaries (Chapter 10.5).

The engineered ('hard') solution to the need for continued protection of land from flooding is still the most favoured option. Nevertheless, recognition is gaining ground that 'softer' solutions involving beach feeding, saltmarsh rehabilitation or even controlled retreat of the line of sea defences may

349

be more cost-effective options for the future in the face of possibly accelerated rates of sea-level rise. How these are followed through is considered in more detail in Chapter 11. However, the implications of global warming provide a challenge to the way in which we view sea defence strategies.

10.3.3 Coast protection and estuaries

Coast protection, which includes the erection of concrete sea-walls at the base of cliffs and the erection of groynes to slow down cliff erosion, has little direct effect on most parts of most review sites. However, by interfering with the natural processes of coastal erosion, long-shore drift and deposition, they may well upset the balance of shoreline change. This may in its turn put increased pressure on the coast elsewhere (including within estuaries) as sediment availability is reduced. Studies to quantify the sediment budget in these situations are extremely costly and few have been attempted. Such investigations as have been completed, for areas such as The Wash and its relationship with Humberside (Evans & Collins 1987), emphasise the interrelationship between coastal erosion and sea defence. The land eroded from one area becomes the sediment required for the building of beaches, sand-dunes, shingle bars or saltmarsh elsewhere. In time this may result in a gain of land.

The Estuaries Review has not collected data on this aspect of estuarine conservation, since the cliffs so eroded largely lie outside the boundaries of review sites. However, in developing policies for the conservation of estuaries, the integrated nature of the coastline is an important consideration. As for the various component parts of the estuarine resource, the interrelationships between estuaries and the coastal and wetland areas with which they are linked are vital to developing effective wetland resource management and management of the coastal zone.

10.3.4 'Natural' sea defences

The natural sea defence for many low-lying areas is the beach, sand-dune, shingle bar or saltmarsh. Each of these develops in response to natural sedimentary processes and wave action and forms a permeable, partly mobile, barrier to the sea. Because of their flexibility in responding to storm events they (especially sand-dunes and shingle structures) can provide very effective protection (see the response of the Lincolnshire coast in 1953 (Barnes & King 1953)). Over the years man has recognised this role and has attempted to reinforce some of these natural features, notably sand-dunes. The process of erecting brushwood or other fencing on sand-dunes to increase accretion has been carried out for centuries, particularly on the continent. When combined with the planting of marram grass (a major stabiliser of mobile dunes) considerable success can be achieved. To date there are 11 sites where brushwood fencing is being used to prevent dune erosion and a further 20 where marram has been planted. However, as described in Chapter 11, this may not always be the most appropriate solution to sand-dune erosion.

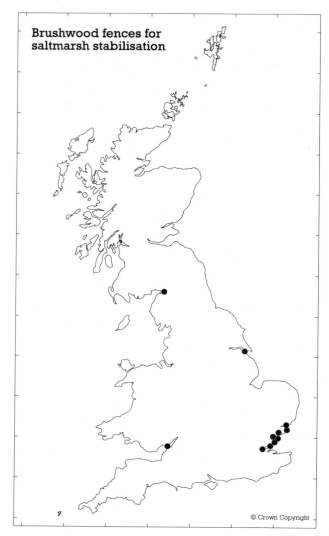

Figure 10.3.3 Review sites on which there are existing brushwood fence installations for saltmarsh protection

Brushwood fences are also increasingly being installed on saltmarshes and tidal flats, particularly in south-east England, in an attempt to halt saltmarsh erosion believed to be arising from sediment starvation and rising sea levels. Brushwood fences, erected in a variety of configurations, were reported as being installed at 21 locations on 11 review sites mostly on the Suffolk and Essex coasts (Figure 10.3.3). There were also proposals for a further three schemes on review sites.

In general the technique has been to erect polders formed from low lines of stakes interwoven with a variety of materials such as brushwood over the front part of eroding marshes. The objective is to reduce current velocities and so increase sediment deposition rates. In a number of instances cordgrass *Spartina anglica* has also been planted within the polders as a means of further enhancing sediment accretion (see also Section 10.3.7). A recent overview of the various Essex projects found that the method has so far apparently had only variable success, which may depend heavily on local conditions (Holder & Burd 1990).

10.3.5 Groynes

The erection of groynes is another method used to help stabilize beaches, dunes and shingle which takes as its cue the harnessing of natural processes. In this case the movement of material along the beach and coast (longshore drift) is one of the mechanisms which provide a continuous supply of sedimentary material at the base of cliffs or for accumulation above the level of the beach.

In an attempt to reinforce the value of the beach for sea defence, at many sites groynes have been placed at right angles to the shore to slow the movement of material and allow the beach to grow. The review has identified 57 such estuaries. Unfortunately, whilst these groynes may have the desired effect along some stretches of coast, they can lead to sediment starvation elsewhere.

One obvious manifestation of this is the ' terminal groyne problem'. Here the action of a sequence of groynes is to trap material on the beach and hence improve its coast protection function. If this succeeds, the beach beyond the final groyne is starved of material and starts to erode. The engineers' answer is to extend the groyne sequence, often pushing the erosion into someone else's territory. Considerations of this kind have important policy implications in relation to integrated coastal management schemes. In the above case the solution might be to remove rather than extend the groynes.

10.3.6 *Spartina* planting and the impacts of *Spartina*

The origins of *Spartina anglica* on the south coast and its subsequent colonisation through natural spread and introduction by man was briefly outlined in Chapter 8.1. The growth of *Spartina* on many estuaries, notably in England and Wales, has greatly altered their ecology and has led to an upsurge of interest in its colonisation, rate of spread, impact on nature conservation and methods of control (see Doody 1984).

The spread of *Spartina anglica* has been chronicled at a number of sites in several publications. A full review of its status was not carried out until 1967, however, by Hubbard and Stebbings. The NCC's *Saltmarsh survey of Great Britain* (Burd 1989) identified *Spartina* as one of the main communities which were mapped during the period of study (1986-1989). Table 10.3.1 gives a comparison of the information from these publications which gives some idea of the way in which the plant has developed and the implications for the conservation of British estuaries.

Planting of *Spartina* has been carried out extensively within at least 39 Estuaries Review sites (Figure 10.3.4). Whilst this has been mainly of the fertile *Spartina anglica*, in the earlier stages both this species and *Spartina townsendii*, the original sterile cross between *S. maritima* and *S. alterniflora*, may have also been introduced. However, it is the

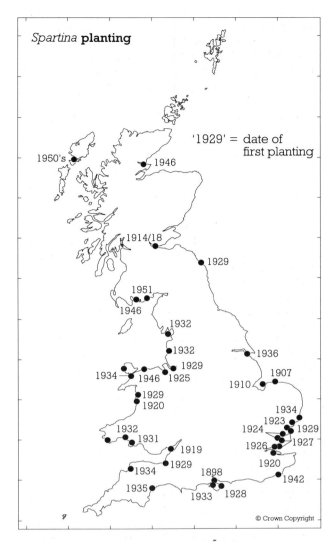

Figure 10.3.4 British estuaries on which cord-grass *Spartina anglica* is known to have been planted deliberately, derived largely from Hubbard & Stebbings (1967) and Doody (1984). Numerals give dates of first planting, where known.

fertile *Spartina anglica* which has made the most obvious impact on our estuaries.

The ability of this species rapidly to colonise open mudflats by a process of seedling establishment and subsequent vegetative growth to produce extensive monospecific swards is probably the single most important factor in assessing its value as a 'land-reclaiming agent'. Because of the ease with which *Spartina* trapped fine sediments and stabilised mudflats it was planted in the early days mainly as an aid to shoreline stabilisation and in some instances land-claim. As can be seen from the figures given in Chapter 8.1 the latter has amounted to a considerable area of land. Other factors which provided a positive view of the species were its high productivity (of possible value to the estuarine ecosystem), the creation by succession of grazing marsh, and its value for research (Doody 1990). It was recognised very early, however, that the rapid spread of this species might not always be such a 'good thing', and concern has often been expressed about its

Table 10.3.1 The spread of cord-grass *Spartina anglica* to estuaries in Great Britain, derived from information in A) Hubbard & Stebbings (1967) and B) NCC's saltmarsh survey of Great Britain (Burd 1989)

Estuary	Natural spread	Planting	Estimated area (ha) A	Estimated area (ha) B
Hayle Estuary	1958	–	<1	1
Taw/Torridge Estuary	–	1934	12	48
Bridgwater Bay	1918	1929	106	335
Severn Estuary	1930	1919	303	383
Tawe Estuary & Swansea Bay	–	–	<1	2
Loughor Estuary	–	1931	405	335
Carmarthen Bay	–	1932	20	103
Milford Haven	–	–	10	198
Dyfi Estuary	–	1920	(162-)243	287
Mawddach Estuary	–	1929	108	68
Traeth Bach	–	–	<1	65
Foryd Bay	–	1934	36	89
Cefni Estuary	–	–	2	1
Conwy Estuary	–	1946	<1	64
Dee Estuary	?1945	1925	405	321
Mersey Estuary	–	1929	40	11
Ribble Estuary	–	1932	405	330
Morecambe Bay	1942	1932	185	368
Solway Firth	1958	–	<1	0
Rough Firth/Auchencairn Bay	1947	1951	4	73
Water of Fleet	–	1946	<1	15
Cromarty Firth	–	1946	<1	2
Firth of Forth	–	1914/18	<1	1
Lindisfarne	–	1929	36	127
Humber Estuary	–	1936	162	120
The Wash	–	1910	1,914	138
North Norfolk Coast	–	1907	81	149
Blyth Estuary	–	–	<1	0
Ore-Alde-Butley Estuary	–	1934	49	18
Deben Estuary	–	–	2	62
Orwell Estuary	–	–	58	10
Stour Estuary	–	1923	149	119
Hamford Water	–	1927	1,129	33
Colne Estuary	–	1924	437	6
Blackwater Estuary	–	1924	469	35
Dengie Flat	–	1927	263	1
Crouch-Roach Estuary/Maplin Sands	–	1927	530	64
Southend-on-Sea	–	1926	298	18
Thames Estuary/South Thames Marshes	–	–	108	<1
Medway Estuary	–	1920	278	76
Swale Estuary	–	–	228	110
Pegwell Bay	1934	–	40	8
Rother Estuary	1922	1942	2	3
Cuckmere Estuary	–	–	2	14
Pagham Harbour	1919	–	100	14
Chichester Harbour	1896	–	715	815
Langstone Harbour	1900	–	193	65
Portsmouth Harbour	1900	–	263	172
Southhampton Water	1870	–	477	103
Beaulieu River	–	1898	182	188
Lymington Estuary	1893	–	498	360
Yar Estuary	1893	–	56	5
Newtown Estuary	1893	1933	63	24
Medina Estuary	1895	–	4	2
Wootton Creek & Ryde Sands	–	–	7	1
Bembridge Harbour	1923	1928	8	0
Christchurch Harbour	1913	–	15	1
Poole Harbour	1890	–	694	558
Exe Estuary	–	1935	6	24
Salcombe & Kingsbridge Estuary	1954	–	<1	0
Erme Estuary	–	–	2	10
Yealm Estuary	1955	–	<1	0

Notes 1 Dates of natural spread and planting are the earliest dates for that estuary. A dash (–) indicates no record of planting or natural spread in Hubbard & Stebbings (1967)
2 See Hubbard & Stebbings (1967) for details of dates and sources for column A

potential impact on wintering populations of wildfowl and waders.

There are four main reasons why *Spartina* spread might be considered detrimental to nature conservation interests in estuaries.

1   It invades intertidal flats which are rich in invertebrates and are the feeding grounds of large numbers of overwintering waders and wildfowl.

2   It replaces a more diverse pioneer plant community.

3   It produces dense, monospecific swards which change the course and pace of succession and are replaced, in ungrazed areas, by tall communities equally poor in species.

4   It promotes the reclamation of land for agriculture, thus destroying species-rich, high-level saltmarsh.

The pattern of development of *Spartina* may provide a clue to the future impact and need for control, so a brief resume of the sequence of colonisation and 'die-back' is given below for three main geographical areas, and is summarised in Table 10.3.1. It should be noted, however, that the precise extent of colonisation and especially of die-back is not as clear as Table 10.3.1 suggests, since survey methods differed and the 1967 surveys are now believed to have overestimated the extent of *Spartina* cover in at least some Essex estuaries.

South coast

Spartina anglica originated in the south and spread rapidly to all the major estuaries. By 1967 it covered approximately 12,000 ha in total, occurring as largely monospecific swards (Hubbard & Stebbings 1967). There are no accurate counts of bird populations in those areas at that time, since the Birds of Estuaries Enquiry (see Chapter 8.6) did not begin until 1969. It is difficult, therefore, to be categorical that this spread caused a reduction in feeding areas which was translated into fewer bird numbers. However, more recent evidence (notably that of Goss-Custard & Moser 1988) suggests that for dunlins at least a correlation can be found. Given the other human pressures on these estuaries from activities such as land-claim (see Chapter 10.5), it is clear that *Spartina* expansion has further exacerbated the effects of the cumulative losses of mudflats.

The occurrence of 'die-back', a process whereby *Spartina* plants lose vigour and die, was first observed around the 1930s. This has led to the erosion and slumping of the *Spartina* marsh throughout the south coast estuaries. There is some evidence that this reversal of the invasion of the flats is resulting in the increase in bird populations (Tubbs 1984) and Tubbs suggests that, given time, the adverse effects of *Spartina* may be reversed naturally. This conclusion remains,

however, as yet unproven and the reasons for 'die-back' are still the subject of considerable scientific uncertainty.

South-east England

Based on the findings of Hubbard & Stebbings (1967) it would appear that the pattern of invasion and 'die-back' has been similar here to that on the south coast, although later in origin. However, the figures given for the areas of *Spartina* in the Essex estuaries in particular may represent an over-estimate of the extent of invasion. The situation here was much less intensively studied than on the south coast, but despite this it is clear from individual site reports that concern was being expressed about the consequences of expansion on sites such as the North Norfolk Coast.

Today, whilst *Spartina* shows some signs of vigorous growth in the Stour, elsewhere the general picture is one of it forming a component part of the overall vegetation. As can be seen in Figure 8.1.18, overall there is much less *Spartina*, and the proportion of saltmarsh which is dominated by *Spartina* is also small, when compared with the position on the south coast of England.

North-west England and Wales

The situation is very different here. Rapid expansion of *Spartina* has been taking place on many sites during recent years. Morecambe Bay provides a particularly good example, described by Whiteside (1984). *Spartina* control has, not surprisingly, been a major preoccupation at many sites within this geographical area. Indeed it was mainly because of the upsurge in interest within this general geographical area that the Symposium reported in Doody (1984) was held.

10.3.7 *Spartina* control

With the increasing concern, described above, over the biological, wildlife conservation and recreational implications of the rapid spread of *Spartina* in many estuaries, various attempts have been, and are being, made to control its spread or reduce its area.

Figure 10.3.5 shows the distribution of the 11 estuaries where control is either active or of recent origin and the 12 estuaries where further attempts at control are proposed. These include proposals for eight estuaries where no previous control attempts have been made. Comparison with Figure 8.1.18 shows that these estuaries are generally those where *Spartina* is both extensive and still spreading. Way & Doody (In prep.) list 25 different places in which control has been or is still being attempted.

Methods of control have been many and various. The only effective ones are the use of herbicides (Dalapon) and weeding of seedlings (Way & Doody in prep.), and even these have proved effective only when operated at high intensity and over small

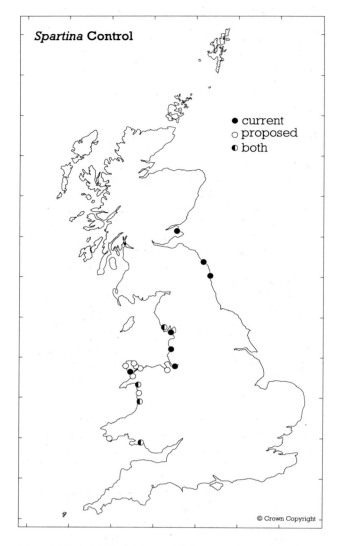

Figure 10.3.5 Estuaries on which attempts to control cord-grass *Spartina anglica* are current or proposed

areas in comparison with the overall areas of *Spartina* swards. The future control of this species depends on two factors.

1 Finding a suitable control agent (Dalapon can, in restricted circumstances, be used in estuarine waters; glyphosate is being used in trials at Lindisfarne).

2 Assessing the role of 'die-back'. Recent evidence from some sites in Wales, and even more recently at Lindisfarne, suggests that the pattern of development may be similar in these newer areas of colonisation to that of the spread and die-back now obvious on the south coast of England.

If there does prove to be some built-in obsolescence in *Spartina*, then it is important that this is fully researched before further large sums of money are spent on attempts to control this species.

10.4 Urbanisation

10.4.1 Human populations

As described above, man has had a long association with British estuaries for food, transport and industry. Many estuaries have large conurbations on their shores. In some cases towns and cities developed at river crossings and have been present since at least Roman times. Such places range in size from London to North and South Fambridge on the Crouch-Roach Estuary. In contrast other large urban areas, such as Middlesbrough on the Tees Estuary, have grown up in the last 150 years as ports and heavy industry have moved downstream into estuaries.

The present distribution and size of human populations associated with British estuaries is shown in Figure 10.4.1. This analysis shows the size of the population living in towns of 5,000 people or more, where the town abuts or comes within 1 km of the tidal shore of the estuary. Hence the analysis excludes small towns, villages, hamlets and farms, but provides a good overall picture of

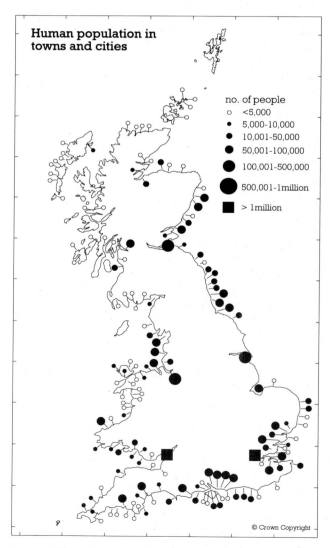

Figure 10.4.1 The size of the human populations associated with British estuaries

354

the distribution of the British population around the estuarine resource.

Overall some 18,186,000 people live in large towns and cities adjacent to estuaries, so at least one-third of Britain's population is associated with estuaries. However, as Figure 10.4.1 shows, this population is not evenly distributed. 73 review sites (47% of the total) have no town of 5,000 or more people associated with it. These 'rural' estuaries are scattered around the whole British coast, but are particularly found in western and northern Scotland, north Wales and parts of south-west England. Of course these population figures refer to the resident population; the major influxes of tourists in summer onto some of these estuaries particularly in southern and south-western England can greatly increase the human recreational pressure on them.

Of the 82 estuaries with large towns and cities beside them, most are in England. The most urban are the large estuaries of the Severn and the Thames. Almost eight million people live in and around London and the Thames Estuary – by far the largest conurbation in Britain. The Severn Estuary is the only other estuary with a population of over one million surrounding it. Three estuaries (Firth of Forth, Humber Estuary and Mersey Estuary) have associated populations of between 500,000 and 1,000,000 and a further 23 estuaries exceed a 100,000 population each. These are scattered throughout much of Britain, as far north as the Don and Dee Estuaries in north-east Scotland and the Clyde Estuary in west Scotland (Figure 10.4.1).

The presence of a large human population alongside an estuary can have a wide variety of consequences for the estuary and its wildlife. These include major industrial developments, which along with domestic effluent can have a substantial pollution impact on these urban estuaries. Recreational and leisure development pressure can be particularly high where there is a large local human population. Since people are becoming increasingly mobile this pressure can affect estuaries some distance from the main urban areas. Hence although there are relatively small populations directly alongside most Essex and Kent estuaries they are subject to major recreational use by people from London and its suburbs. Thirdly the needs of large urban populations for land for industry, housing, recreational and leisure uses and waste disposal contributes substantially to the overall pattern of piecemeal habitat loss on and around estuaries (see also Chapter 10.5). The impacts of housing land-claim are described further below. The discharge of large quantities of untreated or only partially treated domestic and industrial wastes into 'urban and industrial' estuaries has also resulted in many becoming grossly polluted, although efforts are now widespread to reduce pollutant levels and improve water quality, including the future setting of water quality standards including those appropriate to the maintenance of estuarine wildlife. Toxic pollutants

can, however, become trapped in sediments. These remain generally unavailable to estuarine plants and animals as long as the sediments remain undisturbed, but disturbance by other human activities such as dredging or bait-digging can subsequently result in the release of pollutants into a systems whose water quality has otherwise been improved.

10.4.2 Housing and car parks

The expansion of urban populations has resulted in considerable and continuing demand for building land for housing and associated services. House building is taking place on a variety of terrestrial areas around existing towns, some of which are marine-influenced habitats around estuaries (e.g. sand-dunes and coastal grasslands) and other former dock and port areas, notably in London's docklands. An increasing trend is for housing developments on estuaries to be associated with marina developments and both may form only part of a complex involving housing, marinas and boat berths, commercial and leisure facilities. Car parking is sometimes associated with these leisure complexes. Other car parks are developed to control or improve visitor access to recreational areas on estuaries.

The Estuaries Review found seven current housing developments associated with estuaries, three of which are part of marina developments. Two of these marina developments affect intertidal parts of estuaries and the remainder are on associated terrestrial areas, notably sand-dune systems, such as on the Ogmore Estuary. Several of the housing developments, such as on the Teifi Estuary and Portsmouth Harbour, are on land previously claimed from the intertidal parts of estuaries by a variety of landfills, either specifically for housing or speculatively.

Car parks were under construction or in active use on intertidal areas on nine estuaries as part of visitor leisure facilities or associated with housing developments. Four cases of car parks were on core estuaries – in one case the infilling of an old dock system, but the others were chiefly summer parking on sand-flats and saltmarshes. Altogether housing and car park developments were active on 17 estuaries, chiefly in Wales and western England (Figure 10.4.2).

Proposals for further housing and car park developments are more widespread: there are at least 36 proposals affecting 29 estuaries (19% of review sites) widely spread around the estuarine resource (Figure 10.4.3). At least 19 of these proposals involve housing, and of these 13 are for housing associated with marina developments. Fourteen of these housing developments would involve land-claim on intertidal parts of estuaries, and several others, for example on the Conwy Estuary and Langstone and Portsmouth Harbours are developments on earlier intertidal land-claims. In one proposal, in Langstone Harbour, the scheme reverses the marina development trend and

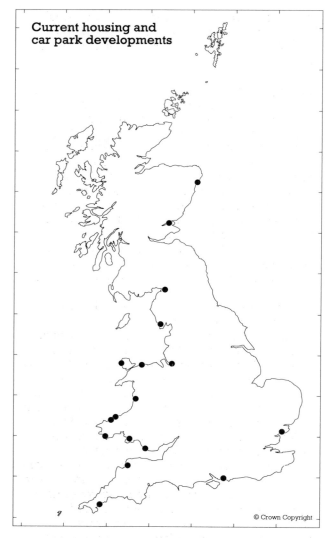

Figure 10.4.2 Current housing and car-park developments affecting intertidal and associated terrestrial habitats on review sites

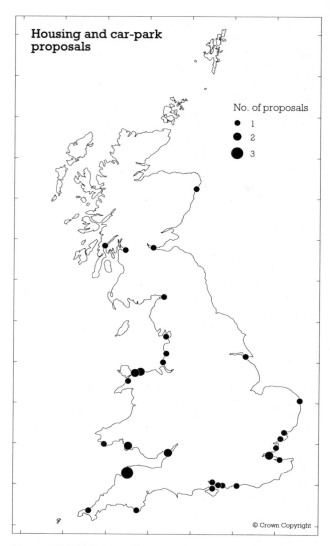

Figure 10.4.3 Proposed housing and car-park developments affecting intertidal and associated terrestrial habitats on review sites

proposes to infill much of an existing marina for house construction – a probable indication of the burgeoning demand for building land in parts of southern England in the last few years.

There are fewer car park proposals associated with leisure and housing developments and golf-courses, and most are small-scale. They affect at least eight estuaries, although the areas involved are small.

In addition to these extant proposals, at least eight further housing proposals have been dropped, or had planning applications rejected, on at least six estuaries during the last four years. Four of these defunct proposals would have also involved marina and other leisure developments.

Overall, housing and car park developments are a substantial contributor to piecemeal loss of habitat on estuaries. Current developments form 11.5% of land-claim cases, and housing and car park proposals are one of the most frequent contributors to the potentially major further losses of estuarine habitats, forming 18.5% of all known land-claim

proposals (Chapter 10.5). It is significant that 68% of housing proposals are part of marina developments, although it is often difficult to determine whether such proposals are primarily designed to provide further marina facilities, or housing. The linking of housing and marinas, and sometimes both developments as part of a complex of housing, retail, leisure and industrial facilities, seems to be an increasing trend on estuaries.

10.5 Land-claim and habitat loss

10.5.1 Introduction

The remaining estuarine wildlife habitats are amongst the most natural habitats in Britain (e.g. Ratcliffe 1977; Doody in prep.). Nevertheless man has been progressively, and in many places extensively, modifying estuarine habitats for a variety of purposes. This land-claim, often referred to as 'reclamation' or 'winning land from the sea', has generally been undertaken on the unspoken belief that estuarine intertidal (and occasionally subtidal) land is freely available and of no intrinsic value. Its conversion and modification has been viewed as being beneficial since it brings more land under man's direct control. The view of the intertidal land of estuaries as wasteland suitable only for covering up with land-fill, and subsequently use for a wide variety of activities, seems to have become increasingly prevalent with the increasing urbanisation of many estuaries. Formerly the major modifications to estuaries were for agricultural purposes; centuries ago most other forms of exploitation by man depended on the maintenance and health of intertidal flats and marshes from which, for example, fish, shellfish and wildfowl were gathered.

This Section summarises the patterns of overall estuarine habitat destruction set into the context of Britain's remaining estuarine resource, by bringing together the information on land-claim for each of the different human activities for which information has been collated by the Estuaries Review. It provides an overview of the variety of patterns of land-claim that have taken place on different estuaries. This is followed by a synthesis of the current distribution and causes of habitat loss, and the implications of the further proposals active in 1989, throughout the estuarine resource in Britain. Finally, the wider context of these habitat losses and the implications for wildlife conservation are considered.

This Section deals only with the direct loss of wildlife habitat and focuses on the intertidal and subtidal parts of estuaries, with additional information presented where relevant for the range of marine-influenced terrestrial habitats around the estuaries. Further description of coastal habitat losses, particularly of the range of associated coastal terrestrial habitats, is given in Doody (In prep.).

It is important to recognise that these direct losses of habitat, although very important, are only some of the types of pressure exerted by human activities on estuarine wildlife. The areas that remain after the land-claims described here are subject to a variety of pressures such as degradation through high levels of pollution and waste discharge, and damage to habitats and disturbance to wildlife by high levels of visitor and recreational pressure. Since, as described below, the area of estuarine habitat continues to diminish and recreational pressures tend to increase, the remaining areas of high wildlife conservation importance face constantly increasing pressures.

The episodes of land-claim described in this Section are chiefly 'terrestrial-based', i.e. they have originated from extension of human activities out from the existing shoreline. These encroachments have thus in general had a disproportionately large impact on the upper tidal flats and saltmarshes of estuaries. This has particular implications for the ways in which the remaining parts of estuaries can be used by wildlife (see e.g. Davidson & Evans 1986a). Only more recently have such 'land-based' encroachments begun to claim areas covering the whole range of intertidal shore levels down to low-water mark and below, as land-claim techniques have permitted the rapid covering of extensive areas of estuaries for docks and industrial developments and other similar purposes. These major land-claims can also have

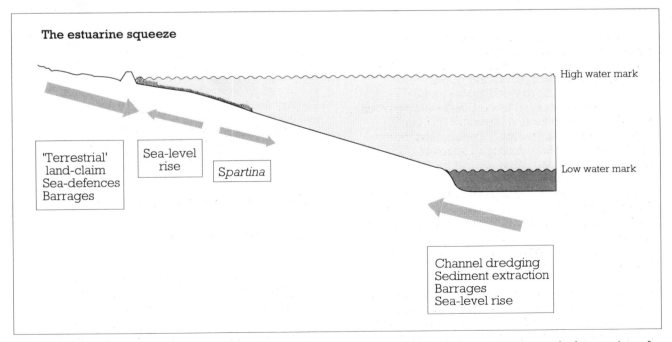

Figure 10.5.1 The 'estuarine squeeze' – the direction of pressure on intertidal habitats on estuaries tends, for a variety of reasons, to inundate or remove the lower intertidal levels and to depress or restrict the upper tidal levels. Some effects, such as the encroachment of cord-grass *Spartina*, tend to increase the proportion of saltmarsh at the expense of open tidal flats within this already restricted intertidal zone.

substantial and long-term indirect effects on the remaining habitats of an estuary, through their reduction of the tidal prism and hence modification of tidal currents, sediment transport and the location of tidal channels.

The land-claims described below are just one, albeit important, component of estuarine 'intertidal squeeze', illustrated in Figure 10.5.1. This squeeze works on both the existing high-water and low-water marks, and on the balance of habitats within the intertidal zone.

On the one hand there are factors affecting the low-water mark, notably dredging which deepens and widens the subtidal channels for shipping. This can directly remove parts of the subtidal and lower intertidal areas of estuaries, and can cause loss and damage by the indirect effects of increased scour and erosion on artificially steepened slopes and in some places from intertidal dumping of dredged spoil.

By definition, barrages and barriers, for whatever purpose, at the very least restrict tidal amplitude, effectively raising low water mark. In extreme cases, such as with leisure barrages, the tidal influence is entirely removed, so that low water is effectively raised to high-water level. This 'water-claim' has the same effect as land-claim, destroying all existing intertidal estuarine habitats within the barrage, and also tends to remove the brackish or sea-water influence on subtidal aquatic communities there.

In addition, the rise in sea level, especially if accelerated by global warming (see Chapter 11) will inundate existing lower tidal flats. The continued presence of intertidal areas in the face of rising sea levels depends, therefore, on rates of sediment deposition keeping pace with the rise in water level. This may not always occur.

There is also a squeeze at the high-water mark. Tidal and storm-surge barriers tend to depress the high-water mark, so that existing upper saltmarshes become dry and subsequently develop terrestrial vegetation. Sea-level rise would naturally move the high-water mark gradually further inland and altitudinally higher. But the construction and maintenance of sea-walls for sea defence (see Chapter 10.3) around parts of many of Britain's estuaries greatly restrict this. Their impact is complex depending on patterns of sediment redistribution. They can increase periods of tidal inundation at upper tidal levels or alter deposition patterns and steepen the shore.

The 'terrestrial land-claims' described below are an extension of the impact of sea defences since the effect of the land-claims is to shift the sea defence line further seaward so as to use the land behind it for another purpose. The spread of cord-grass *Spartina* acts in an analogous way to the other habitat loss impacts described here, since it raises marsh levels and moves the saltmarsh coverage further downshore, so claiming and reducing areas of intertidal mudflats and sandflats (see also

Chapters 8.1 and 10.3).

The overall impact of all these squeezes and land-claims is a general one of a narrowing and steepening of the shore profile, and in many cases particularly reducing areas of intertidal flats. There are some key points that emerge from the land-claim patterns described below. Firstly, on each British estuary land has been claimed at different times and for different purposes. Thus although overall the impacts have been broadly similar no two patterns are the same. Secondly in most estuaries the loss of areas and habitats has occurred, and continues to occur, in a piecemeal way in both time and space. The patterns are complex, with often a mixture of very small and very large land-claim episodes for a wide variety of purposes. Thirdly, land-claim on British estuaries has been reducing the overall size of the resource for many centuries and continues apparently unabated.

10.5.2 Historical patterns of estuarine land-claim

Land-claim on estuaries and coasts has been practised since at least Roman times. Much of the early land-claim was for the enclosure of saltmarshes with earth banks so as to restrict and control tidal inundation and provide better grazing conditions for stock. These agricultural land-claims have been very extensive and have been progressive over many centuries on many estuaries. They account for much of the overall area of estuarine habitat lost to man. In general it can be assumed that almost all of the low-lying land protected by sea-walls surrounding estuaries was originally enclosed for agricultural purposes, although the defences may in many cases subsequently have been extended or strengthened to protect housing and industry that later expanded onto the enclosed marshes. Figure 10.3.2 therefore suggests that parts of at least 136 of the 155 British estuaries (88% of the total) have lost intertidal habitat to agricultural land-claim in the past. In some estuaries such as The Wash and the Ribble Estuary the main reason for loss of estuarine habitats has continued to be for agricultural use, and these places have remained largely rural. Much of the agricultural land claimed from estuaries has been used ever since as pasture lands, often called coastal grazing marshes. Many of these areas have, however, subsequently been turned to arable crop production (see more detail below). Recent land-claims such as on The Wash and the Ribble Estuary have tended to be for immediate use as arable land.

On other estuaries most of the recent intertidal land-claims have been for a wider variety of industrial, urban and, very recently, recreational purposes. Such places as the Tees Estuary are now largely urban estuaries, and much of the land formerly claimed for agricultural purposes as well as recent intertidal land-claims has now been secondarily 'claimed' for urban and industrial uses (see below).

Some examples of the historical patterns of land-claim are given below.

Estuaries with predominantly agricultural land-claim

The Wash

The Wash and the vast area of marshland and swamp that formed the Fens upstream of the main embayment have been progressively embanked and drained since Roman times. Much of this area is now highly productive Grade 1 agricultural land on rich peat and alluvial soils. The overall land-claim has been very extensive (Figure 10.5.2). Land-claim has been progressive over the centuries since the construction of the Roman bank along much of the western and southern shores of

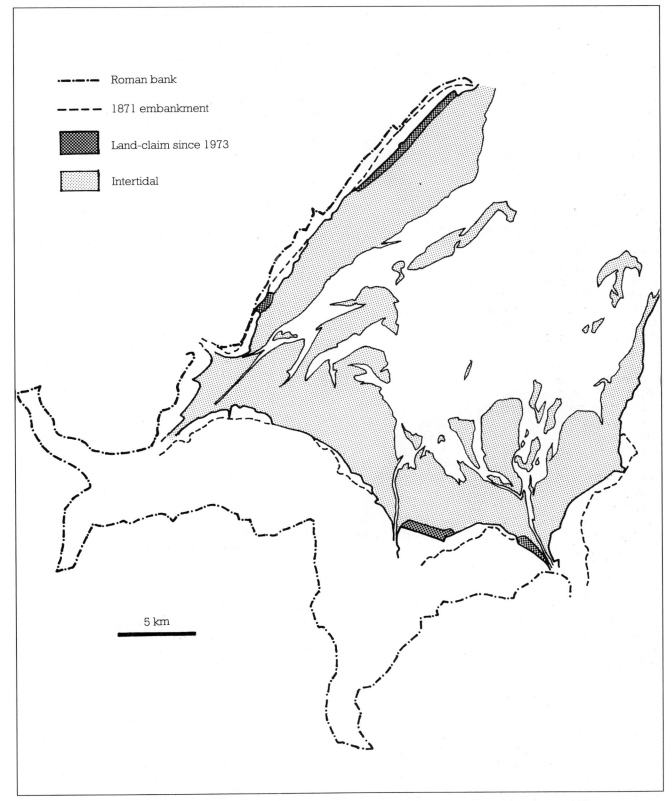

Figure 10.5.2 The overall extent of land-claim on The Wash since Roman times, after Doody & Barnett (1987)

the embayment, and each successive land-claim has involved the construction of an earth bank along the outer part of the saltmarsh. Subsequently new saltmarsh has accreted in front of this new sea-wall, permitting later saltmarsh land-claim episodes. As sea-level rises relative to the falling level of the land (see also Chapter 11) each successive sea-wall is higher and, because of sediment accretion, further to seaward than the last. Now some parts of the land behind the earliest sea-

walls are several metres below current sea level. Hence there are potentially serious implications here for the effects of future rises in sea level. This sequential land-claim pattern has continued well into the 20th century (Figures 10.5.2 and 10.5.3), with several further areas of land-claim during the early 1970s (Figure 10.5.2). Since then however there has been a moratorium on further agricultural land-claim as a development planning policy by Lincolnshire County Council. This, and the

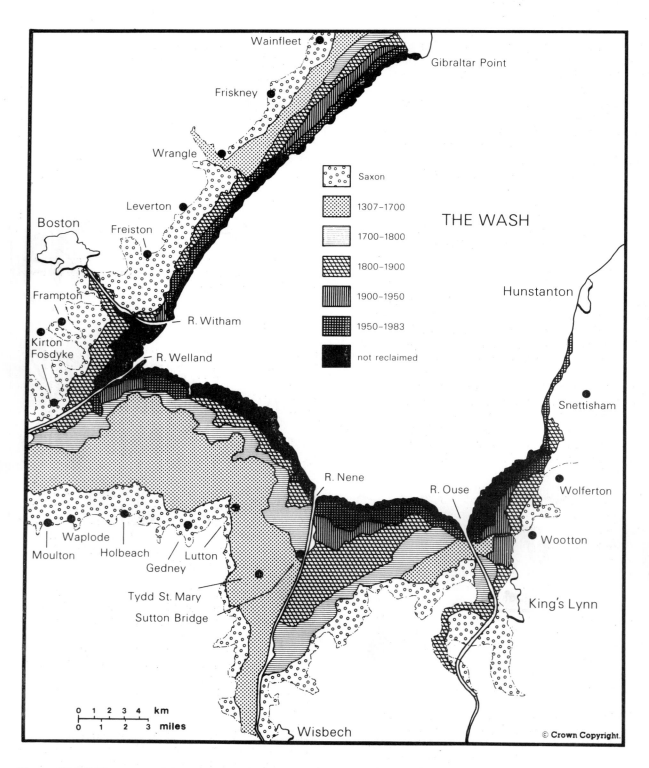

Figure 10.5.3 The sequential pattern of historical agricultural land-claim on The Wash, from Doody & Barnett (1987). Areas shown black are unreclaimed saltmarshes; intertidal mudflats and sandflats are not shown.

reduction in demand for agricultural land in the face of agricultural surpluses, means that there have been no further land-claims since 1979.

The low-water mark of The Wash has been static for at least the last 100 years (Doody in prep.), so the effect of successive land-claim episodes has been to squeeze the intertidal zone into a narrower width, so reducing its total area. This has resulted in a reduction in the total area of mudflats and sandflats of about 3% between 1971 and 1985 (Doody 1987; Hill & Randerson 1987). The subsequent development of saltmarsh outside each new sea-wall further reduces the area of intertidal flats remaining, although at over 25,000 ha they remain the second largest area of tidal flats in Britain (after Morecambe Bay) (Chapter 8.1).

The land-claims on The Wash are the largest recorded for any British estuary, and have amounted to about 47,000 ha since Saxon times (Prater 1981). Some 32,000 ha of this have been claimed since the 17th century, with about 3,000 ha going in the last 100 years (Dalby 1957; Doody in prep.).

The claiming of saltmarsh areas, but not the more difficult and costly claiming of tidal flats, is typical of the pattern of past historical land-claims.

Ribble Estuary

A similar pattern of progressive agricultural land-claim has occurred on the Ribble Estuary, where almost 2,000 ha of saltmarsh were claimed during the 19th century. Further areas were reclaimed in the early part of the 20th century (Figure 8.1.13), and here the cumulative effect of the direct loss through land-claim has been exacerbated by the planting and subsequent spread of *Spartina* which has extended the saltmarsh over the remaining tidal flats (Doody in prep.). Agricultural land-claim on the Ribble Estuary has continued until recently: the enclosure of about a further 600 ha was proposed in 1978. This would have had a highly damaging impact on saltmarshes of major conservation significance for their variety of plant communities and as feeding and breeding areas for waterfowl. It was avoided through substantial Government funding for purchase of the site which is now a National Nature Reserve. Nevertheless another reclamation of 320 ha was subsequently proposed adjacent to the previous area and as no funding was available for further acquisitions the area was claimed for agriculture in 1980 (Doody in prep.). Hence at least 18% of the intertidal of this estuary has been claimed since the beginning of the 19th century.

Dee Estuary and North Wirral

On the Dee Estuary and North Wirral there has been progressive land-claim chiefly for agriculture mostly since 1730 (Figures 10.5.4 and 10.5.5). The most extensive land-claims were during the 18th century, with progressive claiming resulting in the removal of all the intertidal habitat of the inner third of the estuary. There have also been smaller incursions from the western shore of the estuary, mostly during the 19th and 20th centuries (Figure 10.5.5). Overall since 1730 the estuary has declined from a total area of over 22,000 ha to only about 16,000 ha. This 6,000 ha loss is 27% of the former total area of the estuary. Figure 10.5.5 shows also that, as in other major estuaries, the land-claims have resulted in extensive growth of new saltmarsh out over the upper parts of the remaining tidal flats.

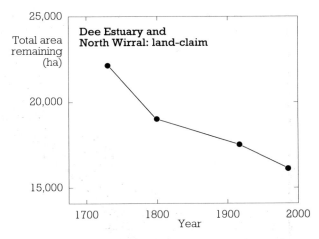

Figure 10.5.4 The total estuarine area remaining on the Dee Estuary and North Wirral after progressive, largely agricultural, land-claim since 1700

Other estuaries

Substantial land-claim of saltmarshes for agriculture has occurred on many other estuaries around Britain (Table 10.5.1). Doody (In prep.), quoting a variety of sources, lists 4,340 ha on the Greater Thames estuaries of Essex and north Kent, 1,300 ha of Morecambe Bay between the 13th and 19th centuries, over 4,600 ha (25% of the intertidal area) on the Humber Estuary between the 17th and mid-19th centuries, *c.* 8,000 ha (about one-third of the intertidal area) since Roman times on the Severn Estuary, 490 ha (8% of the intertidal area) on the Mersey Estuary during the 19th century and almost 150 ha (*c.* 3% of intertidal) on the Firth of Tay during the 1800s. Much of this information was drawn together originally as part of the work of the Royal Commission on Coastal Erosion (1911).

On the Suffolk coast, Beardall *et al.* (1988) have estimated that between 26.8% and 84.5% of the intertidal areas of Suffolk estuaries have been claimed, largely for agriculture, since the 12th century. These land-claims have been particularly extensive on the Blyth Estuary, the Deben Estuary and the Orwell Estuary, each of which appears to have lost over 60% of its intertidal area (Table 10.5.1).

Unlike many 'hard' land-claims for urban and industrial use, agricultural land-claim is not entirely irreversible. Failure to maintain earth banks and sea-walls leads to their erosion and the re-

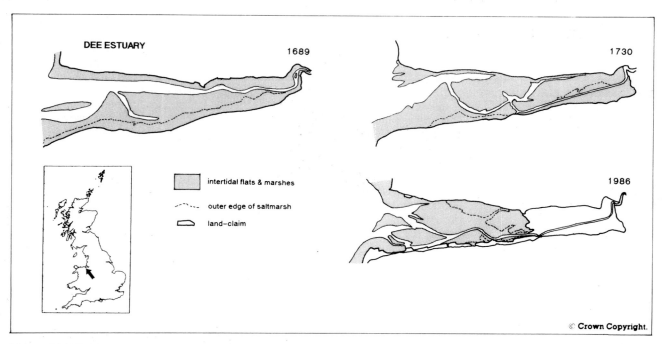

Figure 10.5.5 The shape of the Dee Estuary before and after successive land-claim episodes. Note the major changes in the location of saltmarsh areas

Table 10.5.1 Examples of areas of historical land-claim on some estuaries around Britain

	Area lost (ha)	Period	Source
The Wash	47,000	since Roman	Dalby (1957); Doody (1987)
Severn Estuary	c. 8,000	since Roman	Doody (In prep.)
Dee Estuary	6,000	since 1730	This study
Humber Estuary	4,600	1600-1850	Stickney (1908)
Greater Thames Estuary	4,340	mostly pre −1800	Macey (1974)
Tees Estuary	3,300	since 1720	This study
Ribble Estuary	2,320	since 1800	Doody (in prep.)
Firth of Forth (Inner)	2,280	since 1900	McLusky et al. (In press)
Morecambe Bay	1,320	1200-1900	Gray (1972)
Ore/Alde/Butley Estuary	3,640	since 1200	Beardall et al. (1988)
Deben Estuary	2,240	since 1200	Beardall et al. (1988)
Stour Estuary	1,600	since 1200	Beardall et al. (1988)
Blyth Estuary	1,280	since 1200	Beardall et al. (1988)
Orwell Estuary	980	since 1200	Beardall et al. (1988)
Southampton Water	690	since 1830	Coughlan (1979); Tubbs (1984)
Poole Harbour	530	since 1807	May (1969)
Portsmouth Harbour	490	since 1540	This study
Mersey Estuary	490	1800-1900	Doody (In prep.)
Tay Estuary	150	1800-1900	Doody (In Prep.)
Total	91,250		

inundation by the tide of former mudflats and saltmarshes. This has occurred in several places, particularly in southern England where sea-level rise relative to the land means that former intertidal areas are often well below the current high-water mark and so readily become reflooded. Pagham Harbour was bunded and claimed for agriculture during the 19th century but sea-wall breaches have now permitted the bay to revert to intertidal mudflats and saltmarshes, although these may not always exhibit the same type and variety of estuarine habitats and communities as before their initial claiming.

The Blyth Estuary in Suffolk provides another good example of such reversion to intertidal. By the middle of this century effectively all the intertidal flats and marshes of the estuary had been claimed for agriculture (chiefly grazing marsh), leaving only a narrow tidal channel. Since the 1940s, however, the progressive breakdown of unmaintained sea-walls has resulted in the incursion of tidal water

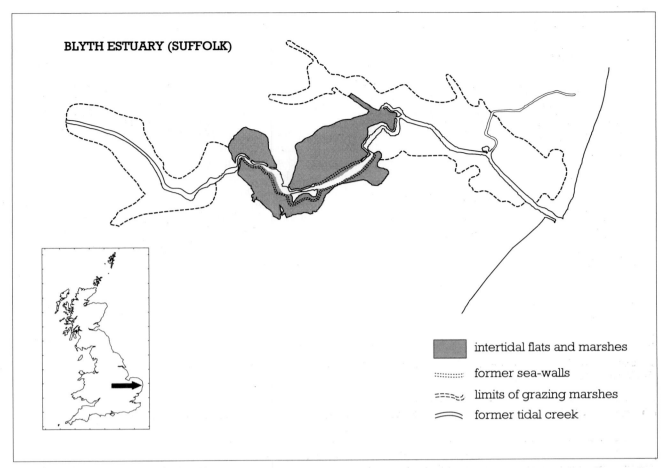

BLYTH ESTUARY (SUFFOLK)

- ▨ intertidal flats and marshes
- ·········· former sea-walls
- ==== limits of grazing marshes
- ⌒⌒ former tidal creek

Figure 10.5.6 Areas of intertidal land on the Blyth Estuary (Suffolk) that have reverted to mudflats after decay of sea-walls protecting grazing marsh

over 235 ha (about 16.5% of the original tidal area) of agricultural land, returning it to tidal mudflats (Figure 10.5.6). There has, however, been very little redevelopment of saltmarsh on these tidal flats, in contrast to the situation described at, for example, Pagham Harbour.

Current and proposed agricultural land-claim

Current agricultural surpluses and changing policies are now resulting in land being taken out of production through schemes such as 'set-aside' rather than more agricultural land being claimed. Nevertheless the practice has not entirely ceased. In 1989 we found seven estuaries with recently completed or ongoing agricultural land-claim, and four others with proposals for further land-claim for agriculture (Figure 10.5.7). Several of these are cases of continuing conversion to arable of grazing marshes formerly claimed from saltmarsh. Although these schemes are generally small-scale they contribute to the continuing piecemeal losses to estuarine habitats.

During the 1980s there have been a substantial number of other agricultural land-claim proposals for parts of several major estuaries, described further by Doody (In prep.).

Industrial, urban and leisure-related land-claim

Agricultural land-claim has almost invariably been undertaken on saltmarshes, where there is already a consolidated fine sediment substrate to provide the basis for the growth of grass or crops. Industrial and urban land-claim has no such requirement (Doody in prep.). All it needs is a firm base on which to construct housing, factories or other facilities. Where this is the purpose of claiming intertidal or subtidal land, the most common land-claim practice is to dump a variety of spoil materials onto the area or, especially for large areas, to pump dredged aggregates behind porous bunds constructed across the tidal flats and saltmarshes. Industrial and urban development often occurs subsequently on agricultural land claimed earlier from the estuary; in this case there is generally no need for substantial further infilling unless the area is now substantially below sea level.

Industrial land-claim is usually much less reversible than agricultural claims. This is partly because of the land-claim techniques involved and partly because, once claimed, such urban and industrial areas can develop high property and land values, so that there are strong financial reasons for their continued maintenance.

Major urban and industrial land-claim is of more recent origin than agricultural land-claim on

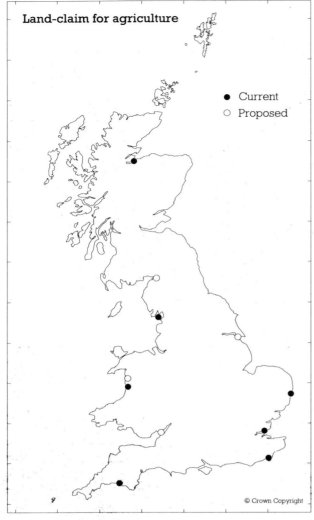

Figure 10.5.7 Estuaries with current and proposed agricultural land-claim

estuaries, and most has taken place over the last 200 years, since the Industrial Revolution. Port developments have a longer history, dating back to Roman times or the Middle Ages, but these were only very small incursions onto the shores of estuaries until the recent major developments in the techniques of land-claim and increases in the size of shipping.

Industrial and port-related land-claim has followed a similar pattern to that of agricultural enclosures in that it has been a largely piecemeal phenomenon, with many small incursions interspersed with some major episodes. As illustrated below the pattern and timing of the progressive industrial and urban land-claim differs between estuaries.

Taff/Ely (Severn) Estuary

A typical example of progressive alteration and claiming is the Taff/Ely Estuary in south Wales, which forms a side-arm of the Severn Estuary review site. The Taff/Ely Estuary has lost substantial intertidal areas to the progressive development of Cardiff Docks since the late 18th century (Figure 10.5.8). By 1985 a much smaller

tidal basin remained and the sediments outside the river mouth had altered substantially. The decline of trade passing through Cardiff Docks led to major proposals from the Cardiff Bay Development Corporation to revitalise the docks area of Cardiff with housing and new waterside industry and leisure facilities. To accompany these land-based developments a barrage across the narrow mouth of the bay has been proposed. This barrage is planned permanently to inundate the tidal mudflats and saltmarshes (which are an SSSI) so as to create a lake for recreational purposes. The barrage proposal has been the subject of a contentious Parliamentary Private Bill which was in its final stages in Parliament in late 1990. In addition to this major potential damage to the remaining part of the area there have been subsequent proposals for spoil tipping on parts of the saltmarshes irrespective of the future of the barrage proposal. This illustrates a typical situation in which progressive habitat loss from industrial and recreational development continues.

Part of the Taff/Ely Estuary does still remain, but some estuaries have effectively been claimed in their entirety. An example is the small Thaw Estuary in south Wales. In 1850 this was a typical small river discharge estuary, but now all that remains is the outer shore, with a power station constructed over much of the former tidal land (Figure 10.5.9).

Other examples of land-claim for industry are described below.

Orwell Estuary

In some estuaries recent land-claim has focussed on particular parts of the estuary. Although there has been substantial historical agricultural land-claim on the Orwell Estuary (Beardall *et al.* 1988), more recent land-claim pressures have been for a variety of purposes, including marinas and dock developments both on the upper parts of the estuary in Ipswich and close to its mouth at Felixstowe. Here the main area of former tidal flats in the lower estuary, Fagbury Flats, has now been almost entirely lost through the progressive expansion upstream of Felixstowe Docks, chiefly since the early 1800s (Figure 10.5.10).

The land-claim in this area has been most extensive since the 1950s, and by 1986 the area of saltmarshes, firm muddy sandflats and mussel beds had been reduced to only 40 ha. A further phase of dock development, authorised in 1988 by Private Bill, is now underway. The current works are the first in a planned three-phase development, with consent conditions from the Secretary of State to minimise the impact on the remaining parts of the internationally important estuary. Nevertheless during the land-claim works the remaining 20 ha of intertidal area were damaged by spoil dumping, run-off from pumped spoil used for the land-claim, and the cutting of drainage channels. This dock land-claim is typical in claiming all the intertidal down to the low-watermark, as well as the

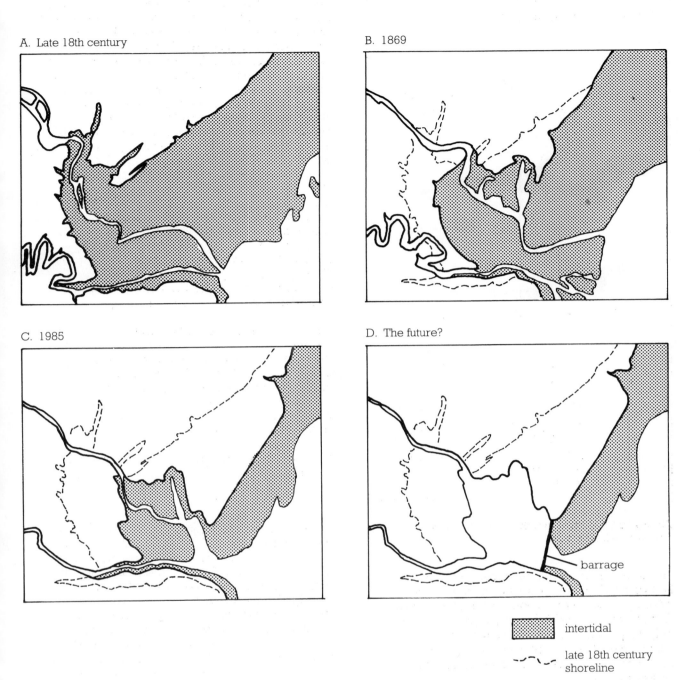

A. Late 18th century

B. 1869

C. 1985

D. The future?

barrage

░░░ intertidal

╌╌╌ late 18th century shoreline

Figure 10.5.8 The progressive alteration of the Taff/Ely Estuary (Severn Estuary) from dock and industrial development.

terrestrial hinterland, in contrast to agricultural land-claims which generally claim only the upper tidal zones on saltmarshes (see above). At Felixstowe this remaining area has outline consent for the two further expansion phases which will remove the last remnants of Fagbury Flats. Over the 1980s this phase of land-claim will have destroyed about 7% of the tidal flats and 10% of the saltmarsh in the Orwell Estuary (Davidson & Evans 1986b). In addition to the direct habitat loss and the indirect loss and damage from the land-claim methods the development also involves capital dredging into the mouth of the estuary, which may have further impacts on sediment transport and shore erosion.

The Fagbury Flats land-claim illustrates several typical features of industrial land-claims – the claiming of the whole intertidal zone, the progressive land-take and the chain of indirect effects on remaining parts of the estuary.

Portsmouth Harbour and the Solent

Portsmouth Harbour provides a particularly good example of a pattern of land-claim typical of many

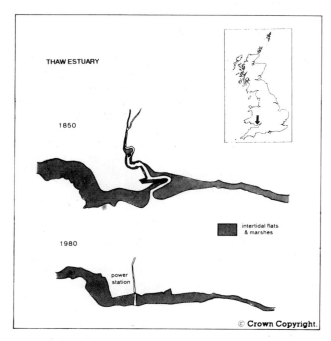

Figure 10.5.9 The Thaw Estuary in south Wales before and after land-claim

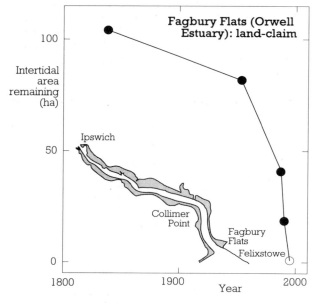

Figure 10.5.10 The progressive decline in the area of Fagbury Flats on the Orwell Estuary from land-claim associated with the expansion of Felixstowe Docks. The open symbol shows the area for which there is Parliamentary consent for further land-claim.

urban/industrial estuaries in Britain – that of piecemeal land-claim over several centuries (Figures 10.5.11 and 10.5.12). Many small land-claim episodes have occurred here since at least 1540. These early claims were often associated with the expansion of naval dockyards and subsequently other port facilities. Most recently a single very large area (240 ha) was claimed for motorway construction, rubbish tipping and just speculatively. The overall pattern is one of the loss of, particularly, the upper intertidal zones around much of the basin and the infilling of the smaller side-arms of the bay. In 1988 several further

intertidal areas remained threatened by land-claim (Figure 10.5.11).

The pattern of area loss is non-linear (Figure 10.5.12). There were only small losses of area here until the second half of the 19th century when there was a rapid period of land-claim over a 20 year period. Rates then slowed again until the 1960s when the single largest land-claim took place. Overall the 495 ha lost since 1540 was 24% of the

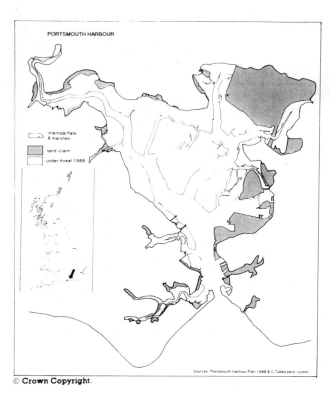

Figure 10.5.11 Areas of Portsmouth Harbour lost to land-claim since 1540, and areas under further threat of habitat loss, derived from Portsmouth City Council

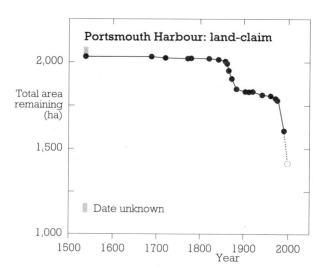

Figure 10.5.12 The timing of the decrease in total area of Portsmouth Harbour after progressive land-claims. The open circle shows the further decline if all areas currently subject to development proposals were to be claimed.

366

tidal basin, with 96% of this loss occurring since 1800. Since 1860, when the rapid land-claims began, 20% of the basin has gone – a rate of 0.16% per year.

Elsewhere in the estuaries of the Solent, industrial land-claim in Southampton Water has been taking place since at least the 1830s when 80 ha of saltmarsh and mudflats were claimed at Southampton, later to become the Old Docks. Further dock reclamation at Southampton took place between 1927 and 1933 (160 ha for the New Docks) and in the 1960s (c.100 ha for the container port). Further downstream, about 350 ha of intertidal in Dibden Bay was claimed by the disposal of dredged spoil, for the oil refinery and power station construction at Fawley (Tubbs 1984, in prep.). The overall losses to port and industrial development of at least 690 ha represents a loss of 33% of the intertidal area of Southampton Water since 1830, a rate of 0.2% per year.

Other review sites in the Solent have also lost intertidal habitats. For example rubbish tipping claimed 80 ha of Langstone Harbour (5% of the intertidal) in the 1960s and 1970s. The construction of half the 24 marinas in the Solent involved habitat loss by excavation of parts of the intertidal (Tubbs 1984 in prep.). Overall throughout the Solent system, Tubbs (1984) estimates that between 1930 and 1980 about 1,090 ha of intertidal land was claimed – some 11.5% of the total intertidal existing in the 1930s.

Tees Estuary

The history of the Tees Estuary provides one of the best known examples of the almost complete destruction of an intertidal estuary by port-related and industrial land-claim. The discovery of iron ore in the nearby Cleveland Hills and the abundant supplies of local coal from the Durham coalfield led to the development of an iron and steel industry in the upper parts of the estuary in the 18th century. With the exhaustion of local supplies of iron ore and the need to import raw materials, the steel works gradually moved further downstream with major new docks and urban areas developing at Middlesbrough in the early part of the 19th century.

Until then these industrial developments had left the main basin of the estuary largely untouched, since the developments had been in the narrower upper parts of the estuary, although there must have been some early land-claim in these places for agriculture as well as industry. In the 18th and early 19th centuries there had been some extensive agricultural land-claims of saltmarshes on both sides of the estuary (see below). Even so in 1850 the estuary remained a large expanse of intertidal mudflats and sandflats with small areas of fringing saltmarsh, with an intertidal area of about 2,740 ha. By the mid-1970s the total intertidal area of the estuary had been reduced by a succession of land-claims to 470 ha (Figure 10.5.13). This is an overall reduction of 83% at the high rate of 0.7% per year.

The pattern and sequence of piecemeal land-claim

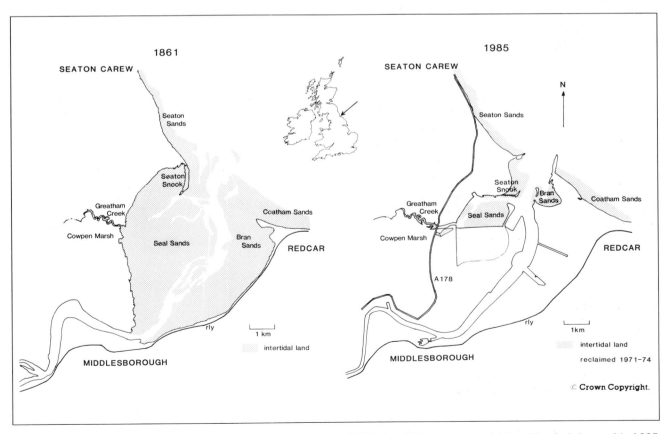

Figure 10.5.13 The intertidal areas of Teesmouth remaining in 1850 after 18th century agricultural land-claim, and in 1985 after major industrial and port-related land-claims (from Davidson & Evans 1986a)

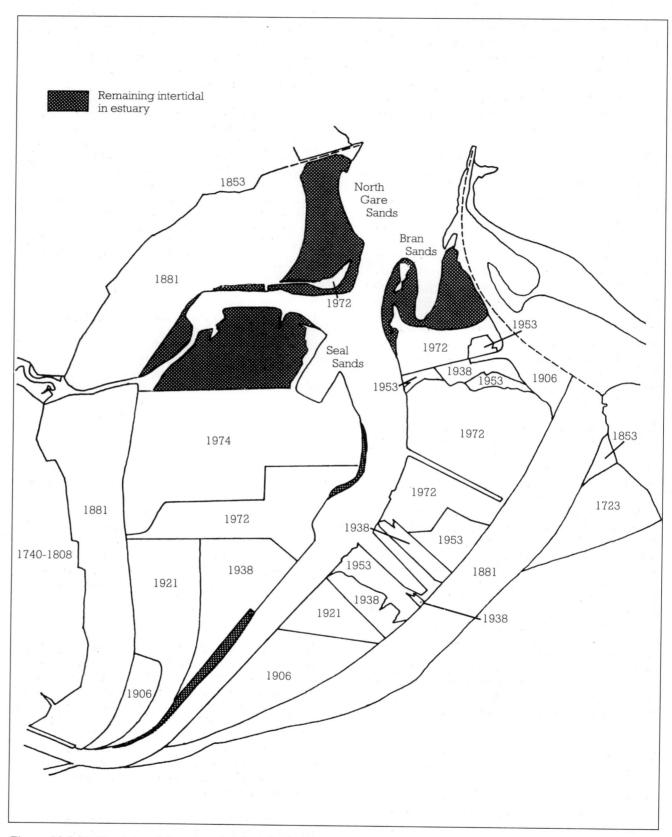

Figure 10.5.14 The dates of the progressive piecemeal land-claim episodes in the Tees Estuary. Dates within each block are those by when the land-claim is known to have been completed.

in the outer part of the Tees Estuary is shown in more detail in Figure 10.5.14. The first recorded land-claims were the agricultural enclosure of 84 ha of West Coatham Marsh in 1723. A subsequent major attempt in 1777 to enclose saltmarshes and tidal flats over much of this shore failed, apparently because the workmen were not paid shortly before the work was due to be completed. This resulted in the sea-wall not being capped with clay, so that it broke down in the next storm and quickly eroded away. This area remained tidal for another century.

On the northern shore of the estuary an earth bank was built enclosing at least 570 ha of saltmarshes at Cowpen, Saltholme and Billingham between 1740 and 1808, and a further 24 ha upstream at Haverton Hill were enclosed in 1800. At around the same time some further areas of the upper estuary must have been enclosed, since Port Clarence at the narrow neck of the estuary was originally an island but by 1850 was behind continuous sea-walls. A further sea-wall was built at Graythorpe and Seaton on the outer northern shore in 1853. It is noticeable that the 1850 Ordnance Survey map shows apparently very little saltmarsh development outside these early sea-walls in the century after their construction. This seems in marked contrast to the situation elsewhere such as The Wash where there has been rapid saltmarsh accretion outside new sea-walls (see above).

The single largest episode of land-claim was between 1850 and 1881, when a broad strip along the whole of both the northern and southern shores of the estuary was enclosed. This was apparently the first major incursion onto the tidal flats of the estuary, and took place during the period when the two outer breakwaters, at North Gare and South Gare, were being completed. It is not clear whether this land-claim was primarily intended for agriculture or was speculative land-claim to create industrial land. Whatever the purpose, much remained as grazing marsh for many years, and on the northern shore part of this 1881 land-claim is still grazing marsh. This area has been exploited for its underground salt deposits for use in the local chemical industries and so has been effectively rendered unusable for major industrial developments. At over 900 ha of intertidal land this was the single largest episode of land-claim, and land was claimed at the high average rate of over 33 ha per year – a rate not exceeded until the mid 1970s.

Late 19th and early 20th century land-claims involved mostly progressive excursions from the narrow inner part of the estuary, and the construction of docks and jetties on two parts of Bran Sands on the southern shore (Figure 10.5.14). These land-claims each involved relatively small areas and the rate of claim was slow (<15 ha per year) compared to the mid-19th century habitat losses. Much of the 20th century land-claim, up to and including the last major land-claim in 1972-74, was speculative, to create land for sale for industrial purposes. These works were undertaken first by the Tees Harbour Commissioners and later by their successors, the Tees and Hartlepool Port Authority. Bunded areas were not always fully infilled and these now provide part of a suite of peripheral wetlands of considerable significance to breeding, migrant and wintering waterfowl populations (Davidson & Evans 1986a). Even some fully claimed parts of these areas have never been used for any development, and remain 'wasteland'.

The last major land-claim took place on Seal Sands – the main north shore mudflats – in two phases between 1971 and 1974. At the same time there were major land-claims on the remaining part of Bran Sands, with the land being used for oil-related industry and steelworks expansion. The 1973/74 land-claim on Seal Sands, using porous bunds and infilling with dredged spoil, was both extensive and the most rapid, with over 400 ha being claimed at a rate of over 200 ha per year (Figure 10.5.15). This was a loss of over three-quarters of the intertidal flats remaining in the main part of the estuary.

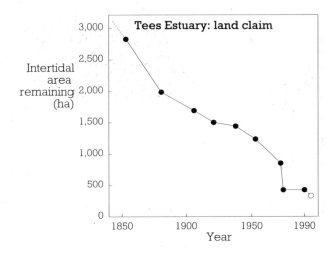

Figure 10.5.15 The areas lost to agricultural and port/industrial land-claim in the Tees Estuary in various time-periods since 1723. The average rates of loss during each period are also shown.

The loss of intertidal area at Teesmouth since 1850 is summarised in Figure 10.5.16. Overall at least 3,300 ha have been claimed since the early 18th century, representing an 86% loss of intertidal area. These areas of claimed land now support one of the largest industrial and port complexes in Britain, with major petrochemical refineries, stabilisation plants and export jetties, agrochemical plants, a variety of chemical works and chemical storage facilities, steelworks and offshore engineering, as well as general cargo port facilities.

There has been no further major land-claim at Teesmouth since 1974. In the early 1980s it seemed, however, that the remaining parts of Seal Sands would also be claimed for further port facilities, since they were designated for such use in the structure plan for the area. This designation was at the direction of the then Secretary of State who also instructed that, in recognition of the major

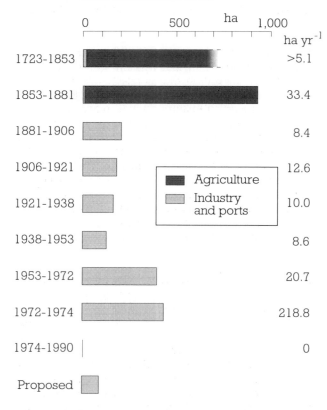

Tees Estuary: areas of intertidal land-claim since 1723

Period	ha yr⁻¹
1723-1853	>5.1
1853-1881	33.4
1881-1906	8.4
1906-1921	12.6
1921-1938	10.0
1938-1953	8.6
1953-1972	20.7
1972-1974	218.8
1974-1990	0
Proposed	

Legend: ■ Agriculture, ▦ Industry and ports

Figure 10.5.16 The decrease in the area of intertidal land since 1850

wildlife importance of the Seal Sands, alternative areas should be created to compensate for its loss (Davidson 1980). Although the Tees and Hartlepool Port Authority had parliamentary Private Bill consent to infill the remaining part of Seal Sands, this Bill was time-limited. In the event no land-claim works were undertaken before expiry of the consent, and both Seal Sands and Bran Sands remain intertidal.

More recently as part of the planned revitalisation of the Tees Estuary under the aegis of the Teesside Development Corporation, much of the area has been proposed as an international nature reserve. This recognition of the estuary as a significant feature of the Teesside environment is a major shift from the pro-development and land-claim attitude towards the estuary in the earlier parts of the century. Revisions to the county structure plan currently under consideration would re-zone the intertidal areas for wildlife conservation. Negotiations are now underway to safeguard these last vestiges of the intertidal estuary, with their nationally and internationally important wildlife, as a National Nature Reserve.

Other industrial and urban estuaries

Despite the very extensive land-claim Teesmouth

has retained some of intertidal flats and is used by nationally and internationally important bird populations. Some other estuaries have fared even less well. By 1873 John Hancock was bemoaning the changes to the Tyne Estuary: "A slake . . . was, until recently, found within the estuary of the Tyne. This is now, by the encroachments of man, in great measure destroyed as a resort of water fowl. . . . The beautiful sweeping reaches, and projecting headlands, that diversified both shores, are rapidly disappearing, and in their place the straight lines of the engineer are being substituted. Those gravelly and muddy shores, the delight of these birds, are all gone." In fact the last part of Jarrow Slake, to which Hancock was referring, was finally claimed in the late 1970s, and all that now remains of the intertidal of the Tyne Estuary is some small areas of sandflats close to the mouth and narrow fringing mudbanks along a canalised estuary further upstream.

Other estuaries, such as the Thaw Estuary described above, have changed almost entirely from their natural state as a result of land-claim. Extensive although less dramatic land-claim for industry and ports has been widespread in the last two centuries. For example Doody (In prep., citing May 1969) reports land-claims for docks, rubbish tipping, industry and railways in Poole Harbour amounting to 528 ha since 1807, a 20% reduction in intertidal area, and further losses for road schemes have occurred since. Similarly McLusky *et al.* (In press) found that almost 50% of the intertidal area of the Forth Estuary (i.e. the Firth of Forth upstream of the Queensferry bridges) has been claimed since the beginning of the 19th century. As with Teesmouth, major early claims were mostly for agriculture, but over 53% of the land-claim here has been for industry (much of it rubbish tipping and power station fuel ash disposal) and docks.

Other estuarine habitat losses

This section focuses on land-claim directly affecting the intertidal and subtidal areas of estuaries. In addition other pressures affect the surrounding terrestrial habitats, both through total loss of these habitats and damage to them. Doody (In prep.) describes the major pressures on sand-dunes, shingle and other coastal habitats both adjacent to estuaries and elsewhere on the coasts of Britain; for example, many dune systems have been extensively afforested, often in an attempt to stabilise mobile dunes, and on some areas such as the Culbin Forest and Findhorn adjacent to the Moray Firth afforestation covers in excess of 90% of the dune system. Other dune pressures cited by Doody (In prep.) include intensive agriculture, recreation (notably trampling and damage from off-road vehicles), golf-courses and a variety of other developments.

10.5.3 Overall patterns of wetland habitat loss in Britain and elsewhere

The full extent of the historical losses of estuarine habitats in Britain is not known. Minimum known areas of historical land-claim are, however, summarised for 19 British estuaries in Table 10.5.1. Although these estuaries numerically form only 14% of the British total they do include most of the largest estuaries so that they form almost half the present intertidal estuarine area in Britain. Many have been subject to extensive habitat losses, often amounting to at least one-quarter to one-third of their intertidal area. Known areas lost from these 19 estuaries alone amount to 91,250 ha of predominantly saltmarshes and tidal flats. Assuming that there has been no substantial compensatory expansion of intertidal areas elsewhere during this period, this means that at least 23% of British intertidal estuarine habitat has been lost since Roman times. Since there are many other estuaries on which extensive agricultural and urban land-claim has also occurred, overall losses are likely to be nearer one-third of estuarine intertidal area.

It is clear from the many examples described above, that progressive land-claim is typical of most British estuaries, and that such habitat loss has been occurring for many centuries. At first the loss was mainly of the estuarine fringe for agriculture and, over the last 200 years, for a wider variety of agricultural, urban and industrial needs. From the examples in Section 10.5.2 it seems typical for British estuaries to have lost between a quarter and a half of their intertidal habitats, often over the last 150-200 years. Rates and patterns of loss vary for different estuaries, but on average rates are generally between 0.2% and 0.7% of intertidal area per year. Such losses are continuing (see below).

Estuarine land-claim is not restricted to Britain. Progressive destruction of estuarine habitat, as of many other types of wetlands, is widespread worldwide. Coastal wetland losses elsewhere have been occurring at similar rates. For example Gosselink & Baumann (1980) report coastal wetland loss along the United States coast averaging 0.2% between 1922 and 1954 and 0.5% between 1954 and 1974. In this latter period there was a loss of about 374,000 ha at a rate of about 19,000 ha per year. A longer-term analysis of wetland loss on the north-east US coast found that rates of loss were slow before 1922, accelerated rapidly until 1954, and have slowed again more recently (Gosselink & Baumann 1980). The rate has slowed because most remaining wetlands are now in public ownership and so are protected. Many of the losses are attributable directly or indirectly to human activities. This study found also that rates of coastal wetland loss in the second half of the 20th century were highest in those areas with the largest human populations living nearby.

These coastal wetland losses reflect major wetland losses throughout the United States. Tiner (1984) estimates that over one-half of the coastal and estuarine wetland in the United States has been lost since early colonial days. This conforms to the general pattern of the destruction of wetlands in the US: Frayer et al. (1983) and Tiner (1984), quoted in

Howe (1987), estimate the overall cumulative loss of all types of wetlands in the US to be about 54% since pre-settlement days. In some states such as California and Iowa these losses are much higher, at over 90%.

Similar patterns of piecemeal land-claim on estuaries are occurring elsewhere in Europe, such as on the Seine Estuary in France (S Simon, pers. comm.). There have also been recent major modifications to the estuaries of the Delta region of The Netherlands, where estuarine areas have been barraged as part of major sea defence works. Sea-defence dikes have also been constructed over parts of the tidal flats and marshes of the Schleswig-Holstein and Danish parts of the Wadden Sea. In parts of the Mediterranean there are extensive coastal wetland drainage programmes affecting areas such as the internationally important Evros Delta in Greece and the Nile Delta wetlands in Egypt.

The British estuarine wetland losses coincide with extensive losses to other types of wetlands. For example surveys reported in Nature Conservancy Council (1982) found that 87% of the lowland raised bogs in southern Scotland and north-west England had been destroyed progressively between 1840 and 1978, a loss rate of about 0.6% per year. Most of these losses were initially through agricultural land-claim, with extensive afforestation in the 20th century. More recently much of the pressure has come from peat cutting for horticulture. The widespread losses of peat wetlands throughout Britain and Ireland are causing grave current concern and are the subject of a national peatlands campaign co-ordinated by voluntary conservation bodies.

Although there are no figures for the total losses of estuarine area in Britain, estimates have been made for some habitats. Doody (In prep.) estimates that approximately 57,000 ha of saltmarsh have been claimed for agriculture alone in Britain. This represents a 50% decline in saltmarsh habitat. The losses to coastal grazing marshes described below are just part of a widespread intensification of agricultural practice that has destroyed all but 3% of the area of semi-natural grassland in England and Wales during the last 50 years (Fuller 1987).

Coastal grazing marshes

Much of the agricultural land-claim of saltmarshes prior to the late 20th century created areas of semi-permanent wet lowland grasslands, with a variety of influence by fresh and brackish water. (Recent agricultural land-claims have been mostly for immediate use as arable land.) Many of these coastal grazing marshes have developed considerable wildlife conservation interest in their own right, notably their ditch flora and fauna (see Chapter 8.1). Coastal grazing marshes have themselves been under considerable pressure, particularly in south-east England and East Anglia. Losses of these grazing marshes through this

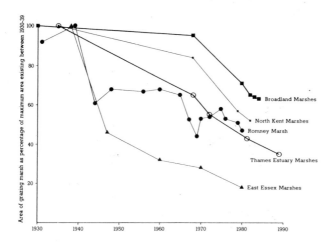

Figure 10.5.17 The decline in the extent of coastal grazing marshes in East Anglia and south-eastern England since 1930, from Thornton & Kite (1990)

grazing marsh present in the 1930s now remains, and proportional losses in some other areas such as in east Essex (around the Colne and Blackwater Estuaries and Dengie Flats) have been even greater, with an 82% decline in the last 50 years. Rates of loss have generally been 1-2% per year, even higher than most rates of intertidal loss.

As with land-claim on intertidal areas, grazing marshes have been claimed for a variety of purposes (Figure 10.5.18). Although much of the area has been destroyed by agricultural intensification – the ploughing and conversion of the grassland to arable land – the major loss of grazing marsh in the Thames Estuary, particularly in the inner part of the estuary, has been due to urbanisation, which overall accounts for 35% of the losses (Figure 10.5.18). This urbanisation covers a variety of purposes, including housing, industry, leisure facilities, rubbish tipping and spoil disposal. This last is a major cause of current habitat loss (see below).

The overall impact of this land-claim of grazing marshes has been immensely to fragment what was formerly, even as recently as 1935, a largely intact continuous spread of marshland alongside shores and estuaries. This loss of integrity of grazing marsh systems, which often depends critically on a coherent water level control system, further diminishes the effective losses of the resource beyond the area losses alone.

'secondary land-claim' have been very extensive and are reported in detail by Williams & Hall (1987) and Thornton & Kite (1990). These studies show very substantial declines in the remaining areas associated with estuaries in the Norfolk Broads, Essex, the Thames Estuary and north Kent (Figure 10.5.17). In the Thames Estuary only about 30% of

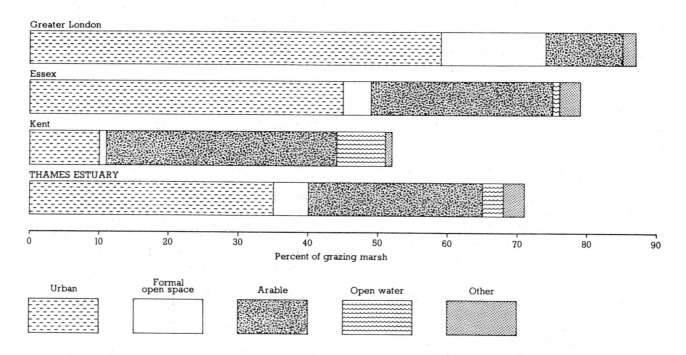

Figure 10.5.18 The proportion of grazing marsh claimed for other uses around the Thames Estuary between 1935 and 1989, from Thornton & Kite (1990)

372

This fragmentation and destruction of grazing marsh continues – for example, the last remaining large area of grazing marsh in the inner Thames Estuary, Rainham Marshes, is currently threatened by major infrastructure and leisure developments.

10.5.4 Current and future patterns of estuarine land-claim

The past pattern of progressive and piecemeal losses of estuarine habitats continues. The Estuaries Review surveys in 1989 identified widespread current human activities causing further losses of intertidal and surrounding terrestrial habitats. These are described below, and are likely to provide only minimum estimates of the extent and variety of land-claims.

Current estuarine land-claim

The 1989 surveys found 123 cases of current land-claim on British estuaries. These are land-claims that are either in progress now, or have been consented to. 72 cases (59% of the total) affected intertidal and subtidal parts of estuaries (and often also the surrounding terrestrial habitats), and 51 cases were entirely on associated terrestrial areas.

In 1989 land-claim causing loss of intertidal/subtidal habitats was ongoing on 32 of the 155 British estuaries (over 20% of the total). In addition a further 13 estuaries were being affected by terrestrial land-claim, so overall 45 estuaries (29%) are currently losing further areas of habitat (Figure 10.5.19).

Twenty-six of these estuaries (57% of those suffering land-claim) have more than one concurrent instance of land-claim. It appears that there are particular land-claim 'hot-spots', notably the Severn Estuary, the Greater Thames Estuary (particularly in Essex), the Solway Firth and the Moray Firth.

This habitat loss is currently occurring for a great variety of reasons and purposes. These are summarised in Figure 10.5.20. Overall the most frequent cause of current habitat loss is rubbish tipping (including domestic refuse, spoil disposal and power station ash disposal), which accounts for one-third of all cases. Transport schemes (chiefly road-building), housing, car parks and marinas together account for a further one-third of land-claims. Many other intended uses contribute to the remaining one-third of cases, but it is notable that as yet barrage schemes feature as only an infrequent reason for current claims.

Examination of the pattern of current land-claim reasons for England, Scotland and Wales separately (Figure 10.5.20) suggests some regional differences in the main causes of habitat loss. Scotland has relatively few current cases of land-claim for the number of estuaries, but almost half of these (i.e. more than the national average) are for rubbish tipping and spoil disposal. More proposals for marina developments cause land-claim in

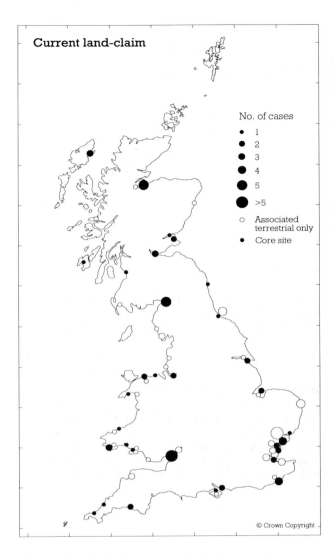

Figure 10.5.19 The number and distribution of current (1989) land-claim cases on British estuaries. Filled symbols are cases causing intertidal/subtidal habitat loss, and open circles are cases affecting surrounding terrestrial habitats only.

England than elsewhere, whereas in Wales major causes are housing and car parks, sea-defence and transport schemes as well as rubbish tipping.

Individual cases of current land-claim vary greatly in size. Area data are available for 56-59% of known cases. Many of these individual areas are small: 43 intertidal/subtidal and 31 terrestrial cases each involve a claim of less than 5 ha of land (Figure 10.5.21). Some others are, however, much bigger, with several exceeding 50 ha each. Many of these large areas of land-claim are long-term active rubbish tips and spoil disposal sites. The largest land-claims tend to be for spoil disposal sites on the associated terrestrial habitats, notably the remaining areas of coastal grazing marsh.

The prevalence of rubbish and spoil disposal as reasons for large land-claims results in these being by far the most significant current cause of habitat loss, by area (Table 10.5.2). Overall 61.5% of the intertidal area and 95.5% of the surrounding

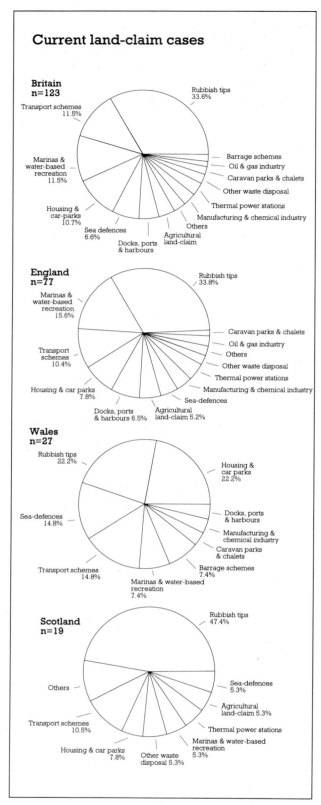

Current land-claim cases

Britain
n=123

- Rubbish tips 33.6%
- Transport schemes 11.5%
- Marinas & water-based recreation 11.5%
- Housing & car-parks 10.7%
- Sea defences 6.6%
- Docks, ports & harbours
- Agricultural land-claim
- Others
- Manufacturing & chemical industry
- Thermal power stations
- Other waste disposal
- Caravan parks & chalets
- Oil & gas industry
- Barrage schemes

England
n=77

- Rubbish tips 33.8%
- Marinas & water-based recreation 15.6%
- Transport schemes 10.4%
- Housing & car parks 7.8%
- Docks, ports & harbours 6.5%
- Agricultural land-claim 5.2%
- Sea-defences
- Manufacturing & chemical industry
- Thermal power stations
- Other waste disposal
- Others
- Oil & gas industry
- Caravan parks & chalets

Wales
n=27

- Rubbish tips 22.2%
- Housing & car parks 22.2%
- Sea-defences 14.8%
- Transport schemes 14.8%
- Docks, ports & harbours
- Manufacturing & chemical industry
- Caravan parks & chalets
- Barrage schemes 7.4%
- Marinas & water-based recreation 7.4%

Scotland
n=19

- Rubbish tips 47.4%
- Others
- Sea-defences 5.3%
- Agricultural land-claim 5.3%
- Thermal power stations
- Marinas & water-based recreation 5.3%
- Other waste disposal 5.3%
- Housing & car parks 7.8%
- Transport schemes 10.5%

Figure 10.5.20 The relative frequency of different activity types as causes of current estuarine land-claim, shown for the whole of Britain, and for England, Scotland and Wales separately

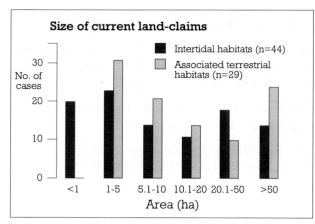

Size of current land-claims

- Intertidal habitats (n=44)
- Associated terrestrial habitats (n=29)

No. of cases

Area (ha): <1, 1-5, 5.1-10, 10.1-20, 20.1-50, >50

Figure 10.5.21 The frequency of current land-claims of different sizes on intertidal habitats and associated terrestrial habitats on British estuaries

Table 10.5.2 The percentages of estuarine habitat under current land-claim for different purposes, and the total areas being claimed

Activity	% current land-claim area	
	Intertidal	Adjacent terrestrial
Rubbish and spoil disposal	61.5	95.5
Docks and industry	15.2	2.2
Marinas, housing and car-parks	7.9	1.6
Others	15.4	0.7
Minimum area of land-claim (ha)	1,074	1,297
% of cases included	59	56

terrestrial area being claimed is for rubbish and spoil disposal. As a minimum estimate of areas currently under active land-claim or scheduled as part of long-term current land-claims, almost 1,100 ha of land below high-water mark (chiefly intertidal flats and saltmarshes) is under claim, as is almost 1,300 ha of the adjacent terrestrial land. The intertidal land-claim areas represent 0.35% of the total remaining intertidal resource on British estuaries. Since this area has been calculated from less than two-thirds of the known land-claim cases, the total area under current claim is likely to be closer to 0.5% of the resource. Some of these land-claims are taking place over periods of longer than one year, but nevertheless this amount of current overall loss implies that there has been little or no recent decrease in the annual rate of estuarine habitat loss compared with the long-term historical rates.

Proposed estuarine land-claim

Land-claim pressure on British estuaries continues unabated. In early 1989 the Estuaries Review survey found 135 proposed cases involving land-claim. These would, if all were carried through to development, affect 55 estuaries (35% of the British total). As for the current land-claims, proposals are scattered around almost the whole coastline of Britain, with the exception of north-west Scotland (Figure 10.5.22). There appear to be particular 'hot-spots' of future land-claim pressure in the Greater Thames Estuary, around the Solent, in the Severn Estuary, Milford Haven and the Humber Estuary.

As for current land-claims, developments leading to further estuarine habitat loss are proposed for a wide variety of purposes. The pattern differs, however, from current activities, in that proposals involve higher proportions of housing schemes, marinas and barrage schemes. These three activity categories account for over 50% of known land-claim proposals. There are indications that the 'wasteland' approach to estuaries may, however, be starting to lose favour since the proportion of proposals for waste disposal and rubbish tipping affecting estuaries is much less than

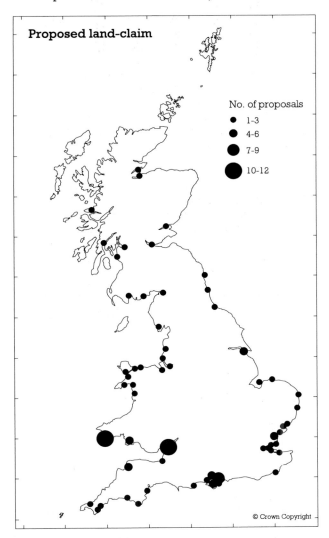

Figure 10.5.22 The numbers and distribution of different land-claim proposals on British estuaries

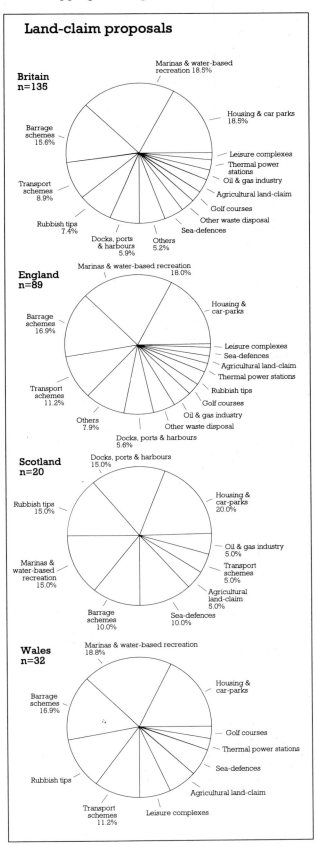

Figure 10.5.23 The relative frequency of different activity types as causes of proposed estuarine land-claim, shown for the whole of Britain, and for England, Scotland and Wales separately

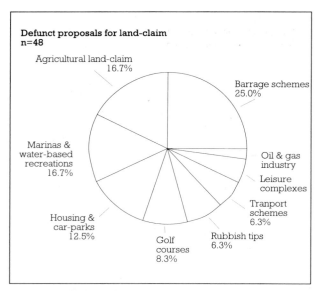

Figure 10.5.24 The relative frequency of different activity types as causes of defunct proposals for estuarine land-claim, shown for the whole of Britain

clear: that current development proposals on estuaries have the potential for causing a substantial further loss of estuarine habitat. Although the pressure for rubbish tipping, which causes some of the major losses of estuarine habitat at present, seems to be decreasing, other activities are on the increase. Notable amongst these are barrage schemes of various kinds.

Proposals for leisure barrages and tidal energy barrages currently affect 16 estuaries, with in some cases several proposals affecting parts of one estuary (Figure 10.5.25). Since leisure barrages are generally developed so as to provide a lake reaching to high-water level, they entirely inundate intertidal lands within them, so effectively claiming these areas – a 'water-claim' rather than strictly a 'land-claim' although the impact is the same for the intertidal flats and marshes. Tidal power barrages need to remain semi-permeable but almost inevitably reduce tidal amplitude within their impoundments, so substantially altering intertidal and subtidal areas upstream. The precise nature of

the current proportion of rubbish tipping.

As for current land-claims there are regional differences in the nature of proposals, and some similarities with the current regional patterns (Figure 10.5.23). Most proposals are in England, and there are relatively few proposals affecting Scottish estuaries. Rubbish and waste disposal still form a higher proportion of the proposed land-claims in Scotland than the national average, and land-claim for docks and ports is also a particularly prevalent type of proposal for Scotland. In Wales the pattern is broadly similar to the national picture, but again rubbish tipping is a more frequent proposal here than in the national pattern.

In addition to these proposals active at the time of our surveys, at least another 48 proposals for estuarine land-claim had been made during the previous five years but had become defunct for various reasons. The activities involved in these proposals are summarised in Figure 10.5.24, which shows considerable differences in the pattern of these dropped or rejected proposals from that of current land-claims and active proposals. One-quarter of the defunct proposals were for various kinds of barrage scheme, and almost another quarter were for agricultural land-claims. Golf-course proposals also contributed over 8% to the total. Neither golf-courses nor agricultural land-claim features amongst the most frequent current or proposed land-claims. Marinas, housing schemes and rubbish tips, which together formed 35.5% of defunct proposals, do however also feature strongly in the current and future pressures on estuarine habitats.

It is not possible to derive an assessment of the total area of estuarine habitat threatened by these active land-claim proposals, since for many the precise nature of the developments and their impacts remains uncertain. Nevertheless the implication is

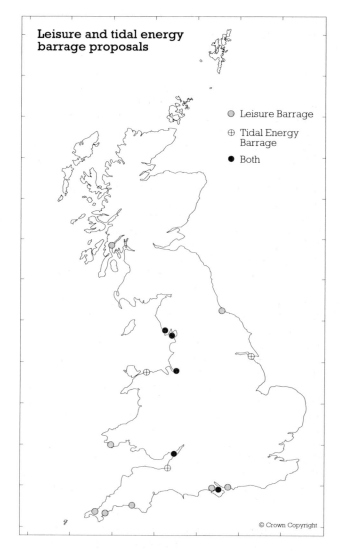

Figure 10.5.25 The distribution of proposed leisure and tidal energy barrages on British estuaries

376

these changes is complex and may depend greatly on the method of barrage operation. In some cases there may be a long-term restabilisation of a new intertidal regime, but the areas and habitats likely to be present are not yet known; equally, the short-term habitat loss and impact of the changes during construction and early operation phases of these semi-permeable barriers is not yet clear (e.g. Bolt & Mitchell in press).

Whatever their precise impacts on the area affected, the various proposed barrages would, if constructed, cause a very much greater overall habitat loss than any other single type of land-claim proposal. If only half the intertidal area was lost or damaged within barrages, this would amount to some 25,000 ha of intertidal flats and marshes from tidal power barrages alone – about 8% of the remaining intertidal area. If one adds to this the piecemeal habitat loss on other estuaries for the variety of purposes shown in Figure 10.5.23, the area under future threat of land-claim may approach 10% of the remaining intertidal resource on British estuaries.

10.5.5 Conservation implications of estuarine land-claim

The overall implications of the patterns of estuarine land-claim described above are that there has been a progressive long-term reduction in estuarine wildlife habitats and that this reduction is continuing. There is little evidence that rates of habitat loss and damage on estuaries are diminishing. Indeed the range and scale of current development proposals on estuaries would seem likely to increase the loss rate if these developments were consented. There is an inevitable finite limit to the long-term survival of this vital part of Britain's wildlife resource, determined by the continuing rates of loss. At current rates Britain's estuarine legacy would seem likely to disappear within about 200 years. Before that, however, the continuing piecemeal land-claims will continue to fragment the linked range of habitats that together form an estuarine ecosystem, further diminishing its wildlife value. In addition, the continuing loss of estuarine habitats places further land-use pressure on the remaining areas, through the focussing of further development proposals and the difficulty of reconciling the widespread and increasing recreational activities in restricted areas. Furthermore, the restriction of the development of estuarine habitats to landward imposed by sea-defence walls means that further losses of estuarine habitat from rising sea levels, especially in southern England, will become increasingly likely. Accretion rates will be less likely to keep pace with rising sea levels the faster the rate of rise becomes (see Chapter 11).

As described in Chapter 10 the major wildlife importance of Britain's estuaries is recognised; much of the network is designated as SSSIs, and 68 of the 155 estuaries are included in the Ramsar/SPA network of internationally important sites (Figures 9.3 and 9.6). Many of these internationally

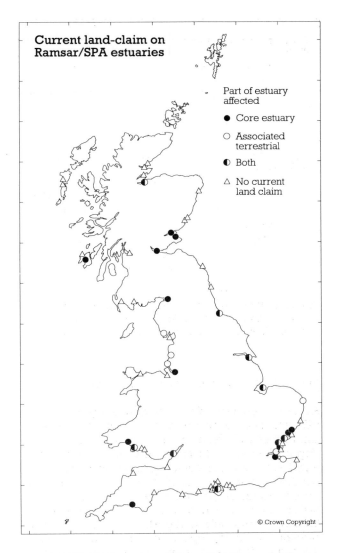

Current land-claim on Ramsar/SPA estuaries

- Part of estuary affected
- ● Core estuary
- ○ Associated terrestrial
- ◑ Both
- △ No current land claim

© Crown Copyright

Figure 10.5.26 Estuaries of international importance affected by current habitat loss through land-claim

important estuaries are, however, also those on which there is current and future land-claim pressure. Twenty-six of these internationally important estuaries (39% of the total) have current instances of land-claim and on 21 of these the land-claim involves the loss of intertidal habitats (Figure 10.5.26). The presence of an internationally important site does not seem substantially to deflect land-claim, although some of these instances are likely to have been the legacy of long-term consents issued before full identification of the wildlife significance of the area.

Even now, the recognition of the international importance of an estuary does not appear to deter proposals for further land-claim, since Figure 9.8 shows that there are current development proposals involving land-claim on 36 of the 68 internationally important estuaries (i.e., 53% of internationally important British estuaries face further habitat loss from human activities). Although some of these proposals are for estuarine areas outside currently defined Ramsar/SPA sites, for the variety of reasons described in Chapter 9.2 habitat loss outside the defined sites can be as significant as developments within sites, in terms of the impacts on the wildlife and the implementation of the international obligations. Ironically only 19 of the 87 British estuaries outside the international network are the subject of such proposals.

The maintenance of the diversity and variety of Britain's estuaries is vital for their continued health and to provide the conditions needed to support the great abundance of wildlife which depends upon them. One fundamental consequence of this progressive pattern of land-claim has been a reduction in the overall biomass and productivity of estuarine ecosystems. For example McLusky et al. (In press) have calculated that over half the invertebrate biomass and productivity and over half the biomass of fish populations have been lost from the inner parts of the Firth of Forth as a consequence of land-claim in the last 200 years. Such losses have substantial implications not only for wildlife conservation but also for the continued sustainable exploitation of living resources on estuaries.

Birds, as top predators, are good indicators of the overall health of estuarine ecosystems. There are, however, indications that habitat loss has already been instrumental in the decline of at least one species of wintering wader, the dunlin, for which British estuaries are of major international importance (Goss-Custard & Moser 1988). In this instance the decline appears to be the result of habitat loss due to the extensive spread of cord-grass Spartina over intertidal feeding grounds. As estuarine resources dwindle still further, such impacts will tend to become more rather than less widespread since bird populations cannot simply continue to fit into smaller areas at increasingly high densities: there is extensive evidence that there are upper limits to the 'carrying capacity' of each estuary because birds cease to be able to find adequate food when forced to feed at high densities (e.g. Moser 1988; Goss-Custard & Durell 1990).

Studies on the impacts of land-claim on bird populations have found that there is seldom a direct relationship between the size of the area lost and the extent of impact on the bird populations that depend on the estuary (Evans 1981; Evans et al. 1981; Evans & Pienkowski 1983; Davidson & Evans 1986a, 1986b; Lambeck et al. 1989; McLusky et al. in press). The populations of some species, particularly those that need to feed for long periods of the tidal cycle to achieve their required food intake and those that depend most on the claimed area, generally decline in greater proportion than would be expected from the size of the area lost alone. The full impact of such habitat loss may become apparent only during periods of severe weather when food requirements are highest. Since many British estuaries act as severe weather refugia for internationally important waterfowl populations (see Chapter 8.6) habitat loss on British estuaries that reduces the availability of food during severe weather is of particular concern.

Much of the piecemeal habitat loss has focussed on the upper tidal parts of estuaries, since many claims are land-based. In some of these cases such as on the Tees Estuary, post-claim redistribution of sediments has not been sufficient to re-create upper levels of tidal flats and saltmarshes (Evans et al. 1981; Davidson & Evans 1986a). This affects the ability of birds to find sufficient food both for daily survival in winter and also during migration periods. When migrating, birds need to accumulate reserves of fat and muscle protein to act as fuel for the flight and as reserves for their breeding attempt (Chapter 8.6). To achieve this they need abundant supplies of food, particularly in spring, and may need to feed unimpeded throughout periods of tidal exposure. Restriction of feeding opportunities by land-claim on upper parts of feeding grounds can jeopardise their ability to take sufficient reserves to the breeding grounds to breed successfully, and even jeopardise their own survival (e.g.. Davidson & Evans 1988; Evans et al. in prep.).

Upper tidal level land-claim also has a disproportionately large impact on saltmarshes, since saltmarshes are generally restricted to this zone. Even where saltmarsh does re-establish outside a land-claim the range and diversity of saltmarsh communities and plant species is generally reduced, so reducing its wildlife conservation importance (see Chapter 8.1). Furthermore, loss of upper tidal flats can interfere with macrobenthos populations throughout an estuary, since some important estuarine macrobenthic species such as Macoma depend on these areas for most of the settlement and survival of their spat before later redistribution throughout the estuary.

The impact of human activities on estuaries has been widespread and extensive and has already resulted in the loss of and damage to very substantial parts of Britain's estuarine resource. The pattern of land-claim and proliferating activities is continuing and there are indications that some forms of pressure are increasing. Superimposed on all this are the potential acceleration and exacerbation of the impacts of habitat loss and land-claim from rising sea levels, possibly accelerated by global warming (see Chapter 11 below).

The overall picture of continuing land-claims and habitat loss and damage that we have described for Britain's estuaries is difficult to reconcile with our international obligations embodied in measures such as the EEC Directive on the conservation of wild birds, to maintain and enhance the bird populations on estuaries, as elsewhere, by safeguarding the habitats on which they depend. The development of effective future safeguards for these vital wildlife areas must depend on resolving many of these land-use conflicts on estuaries. With further reductions in the estuarine resource such conflicts can only increase.

10.6 References

BARNES, F.A., & KING, A.M. 1953. The storm floods of 1 February 1953. The Lincolnshire coastline and the 1953 storm flood. *Geography, 38*, 141-160.

BEARDALL, C.H., DRYDEN, R.C., & HOLZER, T.J. 1988. *The Suffolk estuaries.* Saxmundham, Suffolk Wildlife Trust.

BOLT, S.R.L., & MITCHELL, R.M. In press. Estuarine barrages: ecological effects and nature conservation implications. *In: The changing coastline,* ed. by J. Pethick. Estuarine and Coastal Sciences Association, Symposium Series.

BURD, F. 1989. *The saltmarsh survey of Great Britain.* Peterborough, Nature Conservancy Council. (Research & survey in nature conservation, No. 17.)

COUGHLAN, J. 1979. Aspects of reclamation in Southampton Water. *In: Estuarine and coastal land reclamation and water storage,* ed. by B. Knights & A.J. Phillips, 99-124. Farnborough, Saxon House.

DALBY, R. 1957. Problems of land reclamation. 5. Saltmarsh in the Wash. *Agricultural Review, London, 2,* 31-37.

DAVIDSON, N.C. 1980. Seal Sands feasibility study. Report to Cleveland County Council and the Nature Conservancy Council (unpublished).

DAVIDSON, N.C., & EVANS, P.R. 1986a. The role and potential of man-made and man-modified wetlands in the enhancement of the survival of overwintering shorebirds. *Colonial Waterbirds, 9,* 176-188.

DAVIDSON, N.C., & EVANS, P.R. 1986b. Implications for nature conservation of the proposed Felixstowe Dock expansion. Report to the Nature Conservancy Council (unpublished).

DAVIDSON, N.C., & EVANS, P.R. 1988. Pre-breeding accumulation of fat and muscle protein by arctic-breeding shorebirds. *Proceedings of the XIX International Ornithological Congress,* 342-352.

DOODY, J.P., ed. 1984. *Spartina anglica* in Great Britain. Peterborough, Nature Conservancy Council. (Focus on nature conservation No. 5.)

DOODY, J.P. 1987. The impact of 'reclamation' on the natural environment of the Wash. *In: The Wash and its environment,* ed. by J.P.Doody & B.Barnett, 165-172. Peterborough, Nature Conservancy Council. (Research & survey in nature conservation No. 7.)

DOODY, J.P. 1990. Evidence to the House of Commons Committee on the Cardiff Bay Barrage Bill.

DOODY, J.P. In prep. *Coastal habitat loss: an historical review of man's impact on the coastline of Great Britain.*

DOODY, J.P., & BARNETT, B., eds. 1987. *The Wash and its environment.* Peterborough, Nature Conservancy Council. (Research & survey in nature conservation No. 7.)

EVANS, G., & COLLINS, M. 1987. Sediment supply and deposition in the Wash. *In: The Wash and its Environment,* ed. by J.P. Doody & B. Barnett, 48-63. Peterborough, Nature Conservancy Council. (Research & survey in nature conservation No. 7.)

EVANS, P.R. 1981. Reclamation of intertidal land: some effects on shelduck and wader populations in the Tees estuary. *Verhandlung Ornithologische Gesellschaft Bayern (1978/79) 23,* 147-168.

EVANS, P.R., DAVIDSON, N.C., PIERSMA, T., & PIENKOWSKI, M.W. In press. Implications of habitat loss at migration staging posts for shorebird populations. *Proceedings of the XX International Ornithological Congress.*

EVANS, P.R., HERDSON, D.M., KNIGHTS, P.J., & PEINKOWSKI, M.W. 1981. Short-term effects of reclamation of part of Seal Sands, Teesmouth, on wintering waders and shelduck. *Oecologia, 41,* 183-256.

EVANS, P.R., & PIENKOWSKI, M.W. 1983. Implications for coastal engineering projects of studies, at the Tees estuary, on the effects of reclamation of intertidal land on shorebird populations. *Water, Science and Technology, 16,* 347-354.

FRAYER, W.E., MONAHAN, T.J., BOWDEN, D.C., & GRAYBILL, F.A..1983. *Status and trends of wetlands and deep-water habitats in the coterminus United States, 1950s to 1970s.* Fort Collins, Department of Forest and Wood Services, Colorado State University.

FULLER, R.M. 1987. The changing extent and conservation interest of lowland grasslands in England and Wales: a review of grassland surveys 1930-84. *Biological Conservation, 40,* 281-300.

GOSS-CUSTARD, J.D., & MOSER, M.E. 1988. Rates of change in the numbers of dunlin, *Calidris alpina,* in relation to the spread of *Spartina anglica. Journal of Applied Ecology, 25,* 95-109.

GOSS-CUSTARD, J.D., & DURELL, S.E.A. le V. dit 1990. Bird behaviour and environmental planning: approaches in the study of wader populations. *Ibis, 132,* 273-289.

GOSSELINK, J.G. & BAUMANN, R.H. 1980. Wetland inventories: wetland loss along the United States coast. *Z. Geomorph. N.F. Suppl. Bd., 34,* 173-187.

GRAY, A.J. 1972. The ecology of Morecambe Bay. V. The saltmarshes of Morecambe Bay. *Journal of Applied Ecology, 9,* 207-220.

HANCOCK, J. 1873. A catalogue of the birds of Northumberland and Durham. *Natural History Transactions of Northumberland and Durham, Vol. VI.* London, Williams & Norgate.

HILL, M.I., & RANDERSON, P.F. 1987. Saltmarsh vegetation communities of the Wash and their recent development. *In: The Wash and its environment*, ed. by J.P. Doody & B. Barnett, 111-122. Peterborough, Nature Conservancy Council. (Research & survey in nature conservation No. 7.)

HOLDER, C.L. & BURD, F.H. 1990. Overview of saltmarsh restoration sites in Essex. An interim report. *Nature Conservancy Council, Contract Surveys*, No. 83.

HOWE, M.A. 1987. Wetlands and waterbird conservation. *American Birds, 41*, 204-209.

HUBBARD, J.C.E., & STEBBINGS, R.E. 1967. Distribution, dates of origin and acreage of *Spartina townshendii (s.l.)* marshes in Great Britain. *Botanical Society of the British Isles. Proceedings, 7*, 1-7.

LAMBECK, R.H.D., SANDEE, A.J.J., & DE WOLF, L. 1989. Long-term patterns in the wader usage of an intertidal flat in the Oosterschelde (SW Netherlands) and the impact of the closure of an adjacent estuary. *Journal of Applied Ecology, 26*, 419-431.

MACEY, M.A. 1974. Report 1d. Survey of semi-natural reclaimed marshes. *In: Aspects of the ecology of the coastal areas of the Outer Thames Estuary and the impact of the proposed Maplin Airport.* Report to the Department of the Environment. Natural Environment Research Council.

MAY, V.J. 1969. Reclamation and shoreline changes in Poole Harbour, Dorset. *Dorset Natural History and Archaelogical Society. Proceedings, 90*, 141-154.

MCLUSKY, D.S., BRYANT, D.M., & ELLIOT, M. In press. The impact of reclamation on benthic production and prey availability in the Forth Estuary, eastern Scotland. *In: The changing coastline*, ed. by J. Pethick. Estuarine and Coastal Sciences Association, Symposium Series.

MOSER, M.E. 1988. Limits to the numbers of grey plovers *Pluvialis squatarola* wintering on British estuaries: an analysis of long-term population trends. *Journal of Applied Ecology, 25*, 473-486.

PORTSMOUTH CITY COUNCIL. 1988. *Portsmouth Harbour Plan.* Portsmouth.

PRATER, A.J. 1981. *Estuary birds in Britain and Ireland.* Calton, T.& A.D.Poyser.

RATCLIFFE, D.E., ed.. 1977. *A nature conservation review.* Cambridge, Cambridge University Press.

STICKNEY, W.M. 1908. *Plan showing reclamation from the R. Humber to Holderness.* Appendix to evidence given to the Royal Commission on Coastal Erosion and Afforestation Second Report.

THORNTON, D., & KITE, D.J. 1990. *Changes in the extent of the Thames Estuary grazing marshes.* London, Nature Conservancy Council.

TINER, R.W.Jr. 1984. *Wetlands of the United States: current status and recent trends.* U.S. Fish and Wildlife Service, National Wetlands Inventory.

TUBBS, C.R. 1984. Conserving the Solent. *Ecos, 5*, 33-34.

WAY, L.S., & DOODY, J.P. In prep. *A review of* Spartina *control measures.* Peterborough, Nature Conservancy Council.

WHITESIDE, M. 1984. *Spartina* in Morecambe Bay. *In:* Spartina anglica *in Great Britain*, ed. by J.P.Doody, 30-33. Peterborough, Nature Conservancy Council. (Focus on nature conservation No. 5.)

WILLIAMS, G., & HALL, M. 1987. The loss of coastal grazing marshes in South and East England, with special reference to East Essex, England. *Biological Conservation, 39*, 243-253.

11 Global warming and sea-level change on British estuaries

Contents

11.1 Introduction

The climate of the world has undergone dramatic changes in the past. In recent years it has, however, been recognised that the concentration of 'greenhouse gases' in the earth's atmosphere has increased. Prominent amongst these gases is carbon dioxide which is a product of, amongst other activities, the burning of fossil fuels. The concentration of carbon dioxide in the atmosphere has been rising steadily over about the last 100 years. The report of the Intergovernmental Panel on Climate Change (IPCC)(Houghton *et al.* 1990) judges that over the same period there has been an increase in global temperatures of between 0.3-0.6°C. Neither of these changes are causally linked beyond doubt, and they still fall within the natural variability of the world's climate. At the same time there has also been an increase in global mean sea level of 10-20 cm. The IPCC report goes on to predict that, if there is no future cut in emissions of greenhouse gases then global mean temperature could rise during the next century by about 0.3°C per decade, a rise greater than that believed to have occurred over the last 10,000 years. The IPCC reports that from current models the best estimate of the resulting future change in global sea level is a rise of 18 cm by 2030, 44 cm by 2070 and 66 cm by 2100. This would represent an acceleration of 3-6 times the current rate.

As described in Chapter 10, rising sea levels can exert a compounding pressure on estuaries already being damaged or destroyed by other, more direct, human activities. In the light of the current evidence about global warming and rising sea levels it is appropriate to consider how both the current observed rise in sea level, and that predicted to occur over the next 100 years, might affect the British estuarine resource and its future conservation.

An accelerated rise in sea level may not be the only effect of global warming on estuarine ecosystems since changes in climate could alter the value of British estuaries to the plants and animals that currently depend on them. As yet, however, predictions of the detail of regional climate change are imprecise (Houghton *et al.* 1990), so the nature of any likely changes to ecosystems such as those of British estuaries are unclear.

11.2 Isostatic adjustment

An important complicating factor in measuring sea-level rise is the change in the height of the land due to crustal movements (isostatic change). Based on analysis of over 400 sea level index points, Shennan (1989) has assessed crustal movement in Great Britain since 8,800 b.p. Figure 11.1 shows these current estimated rates of crustal movement, which confirm an overall pattern of differential movement involving relative uplift in Highland Scotland and relative subsidence in southern England.

The effect this crustal movement has on the observed relative change in sea level is further complicated by the natural availability of sediment, which can raise the shoreline in some areas at a rate at least equal to that of sea-level rise. The imposition by man of other coastal changes through enclosure of tidal land, building of sea defences and coast protection measures serves only to confuse the understanding of the precise relative rates of change as measured by tide gauges, the most widely used method.

11.3 Recent patterns of change

This long-term historical picture gives an idea of the changes that have led to present-day conditions, but information about recent changes is also required so as to assess the implications of sea-level change on coastal systems. Analyses of recent sea-level change derived from tide-gauge data have been made by Woodworth (1987) and Carter (1989a) (see Figure 11.2). Carter (1989a) concludes that the British Isles "may be split into two provinces, one in the south-east where the tendency is for sea-level rise, and the other in the north and north-west where sea level is falling". Figure 11.2 illustrates a further feature of the pattern of sea-level change around Britain: the

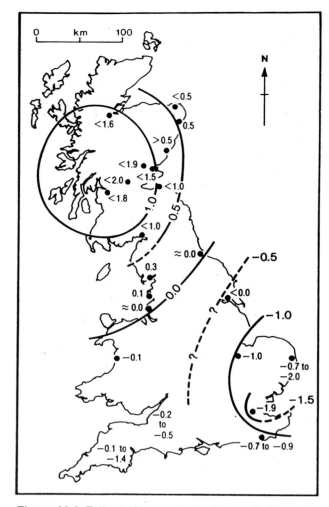

Figure 11.1 Estimated current rates (mm yr⁻¹) of crustal movement in Great Britain, from Shennan (1989). Isolines cannot be drawn for much of southern England and point estimates are shown for guidance.

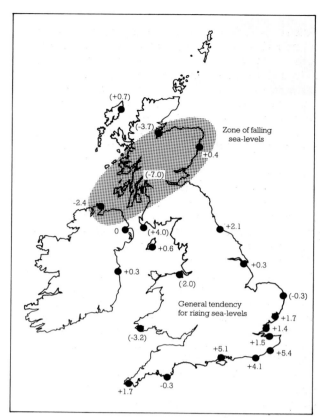

Figure 11.2 Recent sea-level changes (mm yr⁻¹) around the British Isles, from Carter (1989a). Note the considerable variation even between adjacent sites.

substantial differences between adjacent stations – compare for example the outer Thames basin (+1.4 to +1.5 mm yr⁻¹) with Dungeness (+5.4 mm yr⁻¹).

Some of the current problems attributable to sea-level change in different parts of Britain are described below since these illustrate the implications of sea-level change on coastal and estuarine systems and their conservation.

11.3.1 South and south-east England

For several reasons south and south-east England are of most concern when considering implications of sea-level rise. Land subsidence resulting from isostatic adjustments in this geographic area reinforces the current rate of sea-level rise and results in overall relative rates of rise higher than can be attributed to this eustatic change alone. It is generally believed that sea level is rising in Essex and north Kent at a rate of approximately 3 mm per annum relative to the land (Long & Mason 1983). Recent estimates by the National Rivers Authority (Anglia Region) for the East Anglian coast confirm this overall rise, although rates (1.75-2.75 mm yr⁻¹) are rather slower.

South and south-east England are also areas which have seen particularly massive enclosure of tidal land to create rich agricultural land. As described in Chapters 8 and 10, around The Wash and in Essex and Kent this has amounted to in excess of 33,000 hectares. Early maps of East Anglia show tidal swamp lands well inland, covering much of the District of Fenland in the county of Cambridgeshire. Despite the major drainage works carried out by Vermuyden and others in the early 1600s, the influence of the tide (although not of salt water) can still reach Earith, some 35 km inland of the sea and only 3 m above mean sea level, through the canalised River Ouse. The effect of these enclosures has been to reduce the extent of the intertidal and transitional zones. These would formerly have moved inland or seaward in response to changing patterns of tidal inundation, but are now restricted to a much narrower fringe around the coastline. Thus the natural flexible defence has been replaced with an unnatural inflexible concrete sea-wall or earth bank. Overall more than 75% of the soft estuarine coastline from the Humber to Dover has been protected in this way. On the south coast in the vicinity of the Solent, similar sea defences exist and some 50% of the coastline is protected by sea-walls (see Chapter 10).

In these areas there is, however, still a natural component to the sea defence capability of the coastline, despite the narrowing of the foreshore.

This is composed predominantly of sandflats and mudflats backed by saltmarshes which directly abut the toe of the sea defence. These provide a natural wave break, giving some protection to the toe of the sea defence. However, one of the consequences of sea-level rise already seems to be that the foreshore is becoming steeper and more prone to wave attack. This foreshore steepening undermines the ability of the fronting tidal flats and saltmarshes to dissipate wave energy.

There appear to be two underlying factors affecting these shoreline habitats: erosion pressure which affects both flats and saltmarshes, and decay of the saltmarsh itself. The implications of the loss of saltmarsh and its relationship with sea-level rise are the subject of current study by the Coastal Ecology Branch of the NCC's Chief Scientist Directorate. Using new surveys of saltmarsh vegetation in Essex and north Kent during 1988 and 1989, comparisons are being made with a survey carried out at the time of the proposals in 1973 for the development of Maplin Sands for a third London airport (Boorman & Ranwell 1977). The results are not yet complete, but a preliminary review confirms the generally held view that erosion is extensive and in some cases rapid.

Similar changes are occurring to the saltmarshes of Hampshire and the Isle of Wight. Here extensive saltmarsh expansion took place following the appearance of common cord-grass Spartina anglica at the end of the 19th century (see Section 8.1.5). This expansion continued until about 40 years ago, when a 'die-back' began. The loss of the extensive marshes seems to have followed the same pattern as in Essex and Kent, with a combination of decay within the marsh and erosion at the edge. Many theories have been postulated about the reasons for the demise of these cord-grass marshes, and a steepening of the foreshore and increasing tidal inundation and wave attack consequent on sea-level rise may be contributory (C Tubbs pers. comm.).

There is a markedly different pattern of change in The Wash. Here, with repeated agricultural land-claims (see Chapter 10), saltmarsh has continued to accrete (Hill 1988). The accretion has continued despite continuing enclosure of saltmarsh up to the 1970s. There is, however, no evidence of an extension seaward of low water mark so that the overall effect has been to reduce the area of the intertidal zone, as has occurred elsewhere. Three factors may be important in explaining the different response of the saltmarshes on The Wash. First, there is an abundant supply of sediment in the tidal waters; second, the embayment is large and sheltered and so encourages settlement of sediments; and thirdly there are extensive tidal flats (sand and mud) fronting the sea-walls and saltmarshes. All of these factors tend to encourage a rapid accretion of upper tidal flats, so permitting further saltmarsh development. This situation on The Wash highlights one of the difficulties of

interpreting impacts of sea-level rise: local conditions, notably of accretion, may mitigate effects of sea-level change.

By comparison, most the coastline of the rest of East Anglia has had little or no enclosure this century. The coastline is generally retreating not only as a result of saltmarsh erosion but also as some of the older sea-walls fall into disrepair. The loss of saltmarsh (which provides a buffer to wave attack) has helped to exacerbate the undermining of these old defences and this has led to attempts to rehabilitate saltings (Holder & Burd 1990).

The implications of these rising relative sea-levels for policies for the maintenance of sea defence structures require careful consideration. Improvements made to sea defences, notably those in East Anglia undertaken following the storm floods in 1953, are nearing the end of their life. This has provided an important opportunity to reappraise techniques and options for sea defence. In this context the National Rivers Authority's (NRA) Anglia Region review of policy, which includes alternative strategies such as beach nourishment, foreshore protection, saltmarsh rehabilitation and possible controlled retreat of the line of sea defences, is important. In the longer term these wide-ranging options may prove to have important implications for future sea defence strategies elsewhere, should the predictions of future increased sea-level rise, consequent upon global warming, be realised.

11.3.2 South-west England, Wales and north-west England

Whilst the south-west of Britain also lies in a zone of rising sea level, the problems of sea defence and loss of intertidal habitat are less acute than in south-east England. This is partly due to the nature of the land, which has a much lower proportion of low-lying alluvial landscapes fronted by sea defences (see Figure 10.3.2). Many of the smaller estuaries are drowned river valleys (see Chapter 5) and the opportunity for enclosure of tidal land and erosion of the shoreline is much less. Problems associated with saltmarsh loss do occur in the Severn Estuary, although whether this is due to changes in sea level or movement of tidal channels causing cyclical erosion is not clear.

More direct evidence of the effects of sea-level rise is, however, apparent notably on the Scilly Isles. Here fossil shingle beaches are being breached and overtopped; sand-dunes are retreating and intertidal areas are being submerged. This gradual inundation of the Scilly Isles is particularly obvious around Tresco, Samson and Bryher. It was formerly possible to walk dry-shod between these islands at low water, but now this is possible only in thigh-waders (P Sargeant pers. comm.).

Elsewhere throughout these western coasts of England and Wales accretion and extension of the foreshore is more generally the rule – so much so that, as has been described above, the extension of common cord-grass *Spartina anglica* marsh into many of the estuaries of west Wales and north-west England is considered to be much more of a threat to nature conservation interests than saltmarsh loss by inundation (Section 8.1.5). It appears at the present time that the combination of isostatic uplift (or stand-still) in this area and sediment availability make the coastline easily able to accommodate any rise in sea level. Whether this accommodation will continue is likely to depend on the extent of the increase in the rate of rise.

Even in this region of western Britain there are, however, considerable local variations in the impact of rising sea levels, as described for south-east England. On the Sefton Coast (Ribble and Alt Estuaries) in Lancashire, for example, a massive sand-dune erosion front is causing concern. The cause of the erosion is not yet clear, but any rise in sea level will certainly exacerbate the problem.

11.3.3 Scotland

The situation in Scotland generally appears to be the reverse of that in south-east England, with sea levels appearing to fall relative to the land (Figure 11.2). This is not the entire picture, however, since evidence from the Outer Hebrides suggests that retreat of the machair is taking place and that this could be attributed to the local effects of sea-level rise. It is possible that, in these outlying areas, the weight of the glacial ice-mass was much less than on the mainland, and that consequently the isostatic rebound is also less. Overall, the result is that the rate of sea-level rise has been greater than that of the rise of the land.

Local anomalies such as those described in the Outer Hebrides, the Sefton Coast and south-east England appear to be more frequent in Britain than elsewhere in the southern North Sea (P L Woodworth in litt.). Understanding their implications will be important for sensitive future planning for the effects of sea-level change.

11.4 Predictions of global warming and sea-level rise

So far this chapter has been largely concerned with a description of sea-level change as it currently appears to affect British coasts and estuaries, a coastline which is still adjusting to the last major glaciation. Mean sea-level rise worldwide is currently estimated to be 10 – 20 cm over the last 100 years according to the IPCC Report (Houghton *et al.* 1990), and is set to accelerate if the current predictions of sea-level rise induced by global warming are correct.

Precise estimates of future trends in sea-level rise, whether global, regional or local, are, however, very difficult and such attempts as have been made come to differing conclusions. The Ministry of Agriculture, Fisheries and Food has recently assumed a rate of 30 cm per century in the design

of sea defences "which is about double the observed rate over the past 100 years" (MAFF 1989). The National Rivers Authority (Anglia Region) currently assumes a 5 mm yr^{-1} rise in the design of sea-walls with a life of 30-70 years.

The recent IPCC predictions (Houghton *et al.* 1990) are for rises of about 20 cm by 2030 and 65 cm by 2100. On the basis of these figures considerable areas of lowland Britain become vulnerable to rising sea-levels, particularly when isostatic adjustments are also taken into account. Figure 11.3, based on Carter (1989b), represents a moderate case with sea-level rise within the predicted range and gives some indication of the areas of vulnerability.

11.5 Implications for estuarine and coastal wildlife

An assessment of the likely implications of these rates of rising sea levels for coastal habitats has been made by Doody (1990). The underlying implication is that if sea-level changes occur even at the lowest predicted rates, isostatic uplift will not compensate in the long term, even in Scotland. The implications for estuarine areas are fourfold:

1 As the sea level rises and the foreshore steepens there will be an accelerated loss of intertidal habitats of mudflats, sandflats and saltmarshes.

2 Where these habitats abut artificial sea defences the intertidal habitats will be squeezed into an ever narrower zone, with a consequent and perhaps catastrophic effect on coastal habitats and wintering bird populations.

3 In areas without sea defences the presence of other man-made structures, including housing on farmland, may suggest that prevention of erosion of sand-dunes and shingle and their subsequent movement landward is desirable. This will put further pressure on the remaining areas of natural habitat.

4 Wave attack at the base of cliffs (largely outside estuaries), and the consequent erosion, may elicit a similar response to (3) above. Certainly there is considerable local public pressure to prevent buildings falling into the sea on many parts of the south coast of England. However, the remedy may have significant adverse consequences for geological formations and biological features which rely on instability for their survival. In addition it is not always clear what the consequences may be for the sediment budget of an area. For example, some of the adjacent habitats may be sea defence features in their own right and rely for their continued existence on the sediments from the eroding cliffs. Furthermore many estuaries depend for large parts of their sediment supply on material transported from eroding shores

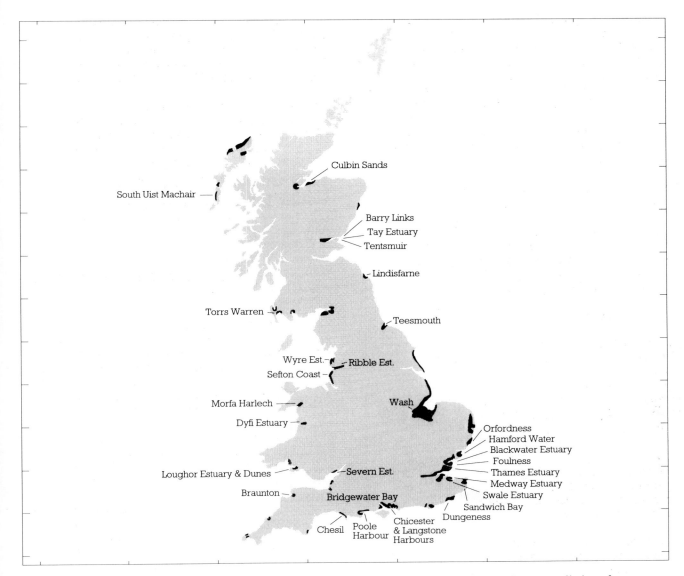

Figure 11.3 The main areas in Great Britain of vulnerability to further rises in sea level, based on a prediction of a moderate rise over 100 years (after Carter 1989b), and the main coastal features at risk in these areas. Effects of sea-level rise include flooding, land loss, salt-water intrusion and habitat loss of tidal flats, saltmarsh and sand-dunes.

outside their mouths. Starvation of such supplies by coast protection and sea defence works outside estuaries will thus exacerbate the direct effect of accelerated loss of intertidal habitats.

Many of the areas around the British coastline that will be most seriously affected by rising sea levels are the low-lying estuarine basins. Such changes resulting from sea-level rise would affect many estuarine wildlife sites of high importance (Figure 11.3). Overall, 51 review sites (33%) are within the areas identified by Carter (1989b) as the main areas of sea-level rise impact (Figure 11.4). These are scattered throughout Britain, but half are on the coasts of East Anglia and south-east and southern England, the area where impacts of rising relative sea level are greatest (see above).

The impacts of rising sea levels on estuarine wildlife are of course not restricted just to Britain; many of the main estuarine areas in, for example,

Ireland will also be affected (see Carter 1989b), as will other important wildlife areas in the southern North Sea.

If the predictions of global warming and consequent accelerated sea-level rise are correct, then a reappraisal of the way in which the coastline is managed and exploited becomes increasingly necessary. The potential impacts of rising sea levels on estuarine ecosystems are complex and point to a variety of policy options. These are considered in more detail in Boorman *et al.* (1989)

As described in Chapter 10.3, few gently sloping estuarine shores anywhere in Britain except in northern Scotland remain with their natural slopes unmodified by linear sea defences. Most parts of the lowland estuarine resource are thus prevented by sea-walls and industrial and dock frontages from responding naturally to continuing sea-level rise by a slow migration inland. In such places accelerated sea-level rise is likely to result in inundation of low

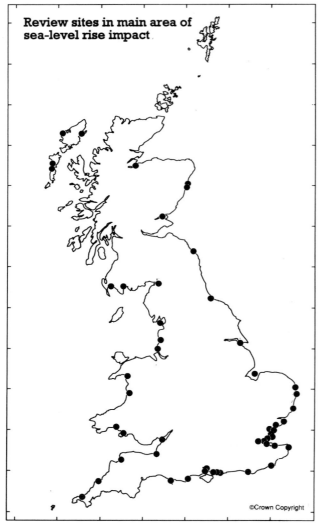

Review sites in main area of sea-level rise impact

©Crown Copyright

Figure 11.4 Estuaries Review sites in areas of sea-level rise impact in Britain, derived from Figure 11.3

tidal levels, steepened shore profiles and often increased erosion of higher tidal flats and saltmarshes. Rates of sedimentation on tidal flats may no longer be able to keep pace with such an increasingly rapid rise in tidal level. So the likely consequence is an overall loss of estuarine habitat area that will be additional to that from man's continuing land-claim incursions from the shore. Some coastal zone management options under consideration for parts of southern Britain (see Chapter 11.6 below) do, however, offer potential for maintenance of estuarine wildlife and their habitats through, for example, permitting inundation of buffer zones behind existing sea defences. The provision of such inundation zones does, however, have consequences of rising water-levels and increased brackish water penetration into other lowland habitats in the coastal zone, which may themselves be of current high wildlife value. They include the remaining areas of coastal grazing marshes, washlands, and the lowland fen systems such as those of the Norfolk Broads. These implications need careful balancing in developing management prescriptions for complex areas of wildlife interest.

Whatever the precise impacts on estuarine wildlife of sea-level rise and its coastal zone management, they will be additive to the pressures currently exerted on the wildlife by the many human activities described in Chapter 10. The indirect additional pressure of global warming on estuaries can only increase the urgency of the need to safeguard estuarine ecosystems against further unwarranted loss and damage.

11.6 Coastal zone management issues for the future

Although sea defence and coast protection issues now seem to be increasingly regarded as of importance and concern, the effectiveness of natural systems for sea defence is not always fully appreciated. Mudflats, sandy or shingle shorelines, saltmarshes, sand-dunes and shingle bars all develop in the highly unstable zone between the land and the sea. Each in their own way provides a flexible barrier which can adjust to changes in sea level and wave attack during storms. The terrestrial structures (sand-dunes and shingle) are themselves resilient, and have developed in response to the unstable environmental conditions.

The reintroduction of a more natural sea defence, by the creation of a higher and wider beach profile, rehabilitation of saltmarsh or creation of washlands behind existing sea-walls, are methods which at the very least will enhance the number of options for protecting the coastline. At best they may provide a more cost-effective alternative to the 'hard' solution of raising or replacing sea-walls. This 'softer' option will also provide opportunities for more positive nature conservation, through the retention and creation of estuarine habitats.

Furthermore there is much still to be understood about how the behaviour of coastal systems can be related to the creation of future sea defences. 'Stable instability', in which dunes and shingle bars in particular are given room to move so that they absorb the energy of the sea and protect the hinterland, is an important concept for future discussions on sea defence options.

The demands of rising sea level on such a crowded coastline as that round many parts of Britain enhances the need to view the coast as a vital resource and much more than a 'wasteland' fit only for unsustainable exploitation, development and recreation and without any intrinsic value.

The greatest difficulty in developing imaginative responses to the needs of estuarine conservation and management in the face of rising sea-levels may lie chiefly in the short term. The greatest impetus to consider new sea defence or coast protection strategies often follows a catastrophic event involving storm surges, breaches of sea-walls and flooding. The gradual rise in sea level will tend to exaggerate the effects of catastrophic events and increase their frequency. The immediate response is to deal with the local problems of defence of property and protection of life. The nature of these short-term responses may not, however, prove to be in the long-term interests of either coastal defence or estuarine wildlife.

11.7 References

BOORMAN, L.A., & RANWELL, D.S. 1977. *The ecology of Maplin Sands and the coastal zones of Suffolk, Essex and north Kent.* Cambridge, Institute of Terrestrial Ecology.

BOORMAN, L.A., GOSS-CUSTARD, J.D., & MCGRORTY, S. 1989. *Climate change, rising sea level and the British coast.* Institute of Terrestrial Ecology research publication no. 1. London, HMSO.

CARTER, R.W.G. 1989a. *Coastal environments.* An introduction to the physical, ecological and cultural systems of coastlines. London, Academic Press.

CARTER, R.W.G. 1989b. Rising sea level. *Geology Today, 5,* 63-67.

DOODY, P. 1990. Sea-level rise (coastal conservation). *North Sea Report 1990.* London, The Marine Forum.

HILL, M.I. 1988. *Saltmarsh vegetation of the Wash.* An assessment of change from 1971-1985. Peterborough, Nature Conservancy Council. (Research & survey in nature conservation No. 13).

HOLDER, C.L., & BURD, F.H. 1990. Overview of saltmarsh restoration sites in Essex. An interim report. *Nature Conservancy Council, Contract Surveys,* No. 83.

HOUGHTON, J.T., JENKINS, G.J., & EPHRAUMS, J.J. 1990. *Climatic change.* The Intergovernmental Panel on Climate Change. Scientific Assessment. Cambridge, Cambridge University Press.

LONG, S.P., & MASON, C.F. 1983. *Saltmarsh ecology.* Glasgow, Blackie.

MINISTRY OF AGRICULTURE, FISHERIES AND FOOD. 1989. *Caring for the future. Flood and coastal defence.* London, MAFF.

SHENNAN, I. 1989. Holocene crustal movements and sea-level changes in Great Britain. *Journal of Quaternary Science, 4,* 77-89.

WOODWORTH, P.L. 1987. Trends in UK mean sea level. *Marine Geodesy, 11,* 57-87.

12 Conclusions

This report is intended to provide a source of information on, and assessment of, the nature of Britain's estuarine resource, how successfully it and its wildlife are conserved, and the ways in which man uses this great variety of estuaries. Our objective has been to provide the basis for the development of future nature conservation strategies for estuaries in Britain, rather than to define such strategy here. These concluding remarks reiterate the key findings of this report, and also identify some of the most important issues that need to be addressed in developing future estuarine safeguards. The issues are identified from the analyses presented earlier in this report, and have been described in the preceding chapters.

12.1 Key findings of *Nature conservation and estuaries in Great Britain*

The key findings of the review reported here are that:

1 Britain has one of the largest and most diverse estuarine resource in Europe.

2 British estuaries are of great national and international importance for wildlife conservation.

3 Each estuary needs to be considered as an entire ecosystem consisting of a mosaic of subtidal, intertidal and surrounding terrestrial habitats.

4 Both small and large estuaries are vital components of the resource.

5 Effective conservation of estuaries for their wildlife requires both the maintenance of the range and diversity of the estuarine network, throughout Britain and internationally, and continued safeguard of individual estuaries.

6 The various domestic and international conservation safeguards are difficult to apply to estuaries because they occur at the interface between land and sea.

7 It appears, from the continuing widespread destruction of British estuarine ecosystems, including internationally important areas, that the existing conservation safeguards are not effective at maintaining the dwindling wildlife resource.

8 Britain's estuaries and their wildlife will depend for their survival on conservationists, decision-makers and estuary users co-operating over the conservation and management of this important part of Britain's natural heritage.

In this report, despite its size, we have not been able to describe the detailed distribution and impact of each of the many different human activities that take place on parts of the British estuarine resource, or on an estuary by estuary basis, or make a detailed analysis of the correlates between estuarine activities and the characteristics of the estuaries and their wildlife. Further Estuaries Review reports analysing these features are planned.

It is clear, however, that there are few assessments of the impact of different human activities on estuaries as a whole. In addition the complexity and variability of estuarine ecosystems means that most such studies are relevant only to the estuary, or part of estuary, on which they have been carried out. Furthermore there are very few impact assessments or similar studies that take an overall look at an activity or human pressure throughout the estuarine resource. Yet this review has confirmed that the piecemeal and concurrent loss of many parts of estuaries is a key problem for their future safeguard. For such an intricately linked wildlife resource as estuaries, assessing the cumulative impact of all proposals for a type of development on all estuaries is vital to the understanding of the impact and context of each development.

This review has also identified several other topics in which there is a need for integrated information, including the overall extent of habitat loss within estuaries during the last few centuries, the ways in which statutory site designations function in relation to development proposals and consents affecting parts of estuaries, and further understanding of the distribution of certain types of estuarine wildlife and way in which they depend on the estuarine resource. The information collected by the Estuaries Review provides a starting point for such analyses, as well as highlighting some of the key issues that must be addressed if estuarine ecosystems are to be afforded adequate safeguard in the future.

12.2 The future for estuarine conservation

Despite the present extensive and diverse site safeguard designations on estuaries, and increasing awareness of the importance of estuaries in the environment, widespread loss and damage continues. The future existence and health of Britain's estuaries and their wildlife now depends on imaginative resource management and on the improved implementation of conservation measures in partnership with decision-makers and estuarine users. The NCC and its successor bodies have a vital role in such partnerships.

12.2.1 The special needs of estuaries

Estuarine conservation is difficult to deliver effectively within the present statutory framework. Estuaries are diverse, often large, areas and straddle the boundary between land and sea. In addition, they are affected by a range of upstream, onshore and marine activities as well as those directly within their core areas.

Many estuaries cross country and county boundaries, and different parts fall within the jurisdiction of different authorities. Hence no one body can act independently to ensure their safeguard. The separation in 1991 of the NCC into three separate agencies (for England, Scotland, and Wales) does not alter the need for co-ordinated action to safeguard such a nationally and internationally-linked resource. The future health of estuaries depends on the co-operation of local authorities, developers and estuary users as well as conservationists.

Many issues and developments which can seriously damage the estuarine environment, such as power generation, port and harbour construction and recreational development, are subject to Government or Parliamentary control, consent or guidance. Government itself will have a key role in supporting the appropriate and sustainable use of estuaries without prejudicing their wildlife.

A 'sustainable development' approach is particularly relevant to estuaries since it presupposes that risks of damage to the environment will be anticipated and avoided. It depends on the maintenance of ecological processes and biodiversity in their own right, the establishment of 'minimum standards' for environmental assets, and environmental accounting of the state of those assets. Since so much of the estuarine resource has already been lost or damaged, and the remainder functions as a nationally and internationally important network, the 'minimum standard' for estuaries is very high, especially in the light of international obligations to maintain and enhance the resource of estuarine habitats and their wildlife.

12.2.2 Directions for the future

To improve the future safeguard of estuaries requires an understanding of the major national and international importance of estuaries in our natural environment, and the involvement and co-operation of many individuals and organisations.

Key issues for the future are:

● the need for a national policy to sustain the estuarine resource;

● the adoption of statutory site safeguard mechanisms on estuaries to ensure that effective conservation of estuarine ecosystems, including both terrestrial and marine features, is in line with international requirements;

● the need to work with individuals and organisations whose activities affect the health of estuaries and their wildlife, so as to ensure a greater awareness and acceptance of the value of estuarine and conservation needs; and

● the need to work with local interests at the level of individual estuaries to develop integrated management and development strategies, in line with the national and international estuarine network and its conservation needs.

We hope that this report has provided further insight into these issues, and will provide guidance for all who are interested in how estuaries and their wildlife can be conserved and managed as part of our coastal environment.

Without sympathetic and imaginative future treatment of these ecosystems, it seems inevitable that the piecemeal and cumulative damage and destruction of estuaries and their wildlife by a wide variety of activities and developments will continue. The estuarine resource is one of Britain's most valuable natural assets. We can no longer afford to treat it as wasteland.

Appendices

Appendix 1 Estuaries included in the Estuaries Review

This Appendix lists the code numbers, names, locations and and local authority areas of all Estuaries Review sites. Review sites are mapped in Figure 5.2 (Chapter 5).

Estuary		Centre grid	NCC region	County/ region(s)	District(s)
001	Hayle Estuary	SW5538	South-West England	Cornwall	Penwith
002	Gannel Estuary	SW8061	South-West England	Cornwall	Restormel
003	Camel Estuary	SW9375	South-West England	Cornwall	North Cornwall
004	Taw-Torridge Estuary	SS4631	South-West England	Devon	North Devon
					Torridge
005	Blue Anchor Bay	ST0244	South-West England	Somerset	West Somerset
006	Bridgwater Bay	ST2947	South-West England	Somerset	Sedgemoor
					West Somerset
007	Severn Estuary	ST4080	South-West England	Avon	Bristol
			West Midlands	Gloucestershire	Northavon
			South Wales	Somerset	Woodspring
				Gwent	Forest of Dean
				South Glamorgan	Gloucester
					Stroud
					Sedgemoor
					West Somerset
					Monmouth
					Newport
					Cardiff
					Vale of Glamorgan
008	Thaw Estuary	ST0366	South Wales	South Glamorgan	Vale of Glamorgan
009	Ogmore Estuary	SS8776	South Wales	Mid Glamorgan	Ogwr
010	Afan Estuary	SS7588	South Wales	West Glamorgan	Port Talbot
011	Neath Estuary	SS7292	South Wales	West Glamorgan	Neath
					Port Talbot
					Swansea
012	Tawe Estuary & Swansea Bay	SS6694	South Wales	West Glamorgan	Swansea
013	Loughor Estuary	SS4897	South Wales	Dyfed	Llanelli
				West Glamorgan	Lliw Valley
					Swansea
014	Carmarthen Bay	SN3408	Dyfed-Powys	Dyfed	Carmarthen
					Llanelli
015	Milford Haven	SM9403	Dyfed-Powys	Dyfed	Preseli
					South Pembrokeshire
016	Nyfer Estuary	SN0540	Dyfed-Powys	Dyfed	Preseli
017	Teifi Estuary	SN1648	Dyfed-Powys	Dyfed	Ceredigion
					Preseli
018	Aberystwyth	SN5980	Dyfed-Powys	Dyfed	Ceredigion
019	Dyfi Estuary	SN6495	North Wales	Dyfed	Ceredigion
			Dyfed-Powys	Gwynedd	Meironnydd
				Powys	Montgomeryshire
020	Dysynni Estuary	SH5802	North Wales	Gwynedd	Meironnydd
021	Mawddach Estuary	SH6416	North Wales	Gwynedd	Meironnydd
022	Artro Estuary	SH5725	North Wales	Gwynedd	Meironnydd
023	Traeth Bach	SH5736	North Wales	Gwynedd	Dwyfor
					Meironnydd
024	Pwllheli Harbour	SH3835	North Wales	Gwynedd	Dwyfor
025	Foryd Bay	SH4559	North Wales	Gwynedd	Arfon
					Ynys Mon
026	Traeth Melynog	SH4364	North Wales	Gwynedd	Arfon
					Ynys Mon
027	Cefni Estuary	SH4067	North Wales	Gwynedd	Ynys Mon
028	Alaw Estuary	SH3081	North Wales	Gwynedd	Ynys Mon

Estuary		Centre grid	NCC region	County/region(s)	District(s)
029	Trath Dulas	SH4888	North Wales	Gwynedd	Ynys Mon
030	Traeth Coch	SH5380	North Wales	Gwynedd	Ynys Mon
031	Traeth Lavan	SH6375	North Wales	Gwynedd	Aberconwy
					Arfon
					Ynys Mon
032	Conwy Estuary	SH7976	North Wales	Gwynedd	Aberconwy
033	Clwyd Estuary	SJ0080	North Wales	Clwyd	Colwyn
					Rhuddlan
034	Dee Estuary & North Wirral	SJ2674	West Midlands	Merseyside	Wirral
			North-West England	Cheshire	Ellesmere Port
			North Wales	Clwyd	Halton
					Vale Royal
					Warrington
					Alyn & Deeside
					Delyn
035	Mersey Estuary	SJ4180	North-West England	Merseyside	Liverpool
				Cheshire	Sefton
					Wirral
					Ellesmere Port
					Halton
					Vale Royal
					Warrington
036	Alt Estuary	SD2903	North-West England	Merseyside	Sefton
037	Ribble Estuary	SD3424	North-West England	Merseyside	Sefton
				Lancashire	Fylde
					Preston
					South Ribble
					West Lancashire
038	Morecambe Bay	SD3668	North-West England	Cumbria	Barrow-in-Furness
				Lancashire	South Lakeland
					Lancaster
					Wyre
039	Duddon Estuary	SD1977	North-West England	Cumbria	Barrow-in-Furness
					Copeland
040	Esk Estuary (Cumbria)	SD0896	North-West England	Cumbria	Copeland
041	Solway Firth	NY2762	North-West England	Cumbria	Allerdale
			South-West Scotland	Dumfries & Gal.	Carlisle
					Annandale & Eskdale
					Nithsdale
					Stewartry
042	Rough Firth & Auchencairn	NX8451	South-West Scotland	Dumfries & Gal.	Stewartry
043	Dee Estuary (Dumfries & Gal)	NX6747	South-West Scotland	Dumfries & Gal.	Stewartry
044	Water of Fleet	NX5753	South-West Scotland	Dumfries & Gal.	Stewartry
045	Cree Estuary	NX4655	South-West Scotland	Dumfries & Gal.	Wigtown
046	Luce Bay	NX1855	South-West Scotland	Dumfries & Gal.	Wigtown
047	Garnock Estuary	NS3039	South-West Scotland	Strathclyde	Cunninghame
					Kyle & Carrick
048	Hunterston sands	NS1953	South-West Scotland	Strathclyde	Cunninghame
049	Clyde Estuary	NS3675	South-West Scotland	Strathclyde	Bearsden & Milngavie
					Clydebank
					Dumbarton
					Glasgow
					Inverclyde
					Renfrew
050	Ruel Estuary	NS0079	South-West Scotland	Strathclyde	Argyll & Bute
051	Loch Gilp	NR8687	South-West Scotland	Strathclyde	Argyll & Bute
052	Tràigh Cill-a-Rubha	NR3362	South-West Scotland	Strathclyde	Argyll & Bute
053	Loch Gruinart	NR2971	South-West Scotland	Strathclyde	Argyll & Bute
054	Loch Crinan	NR7993	South-West Scotland	Strathclyde	Argyll & Bute

Estuary		Centre grid	NCC region	County/ region(s)	District(s)
055	Kentra Bay	NM6469	North-West Scotland	Highland	Lochaber
056	Loch Moidart	NM6873	North-West Scotland	Highland	Lochaber
057	Tràigh Mhór	NF7005	North-West Scotland	Western Isles	Barra
058	Bagh Nam Faoilean	NF7948	North-West Scotland	Western Isles	Benbecula
059	Oitir Mhór	NF8158	North-West Scotland	Western Isles	Benbecula
060	Tràigh Vallay	NF7875	North-West Scotland	Western Isles	North Uist
061	Oronsay	NF8575	North-West Scotland	Western Isles	North Uist
062	Scarista	NF9992	North-West Scotland	Western Isles	Harris
063	Tràigh Luskentyre	NG0798	North-West Scotland	Western Isles	Harris
064	Camus Uig	NB0433	North-West Scotland	Western Isles	Isle of Lewis
065	Laxdale Estuary	NB4434	North-West Scotland	Western Isles	Isle of Lewis
066	Kyle of Durness	NC3766	North-West Scotland	Highland	Sutherland
067	Kyle of Tongue	NC5858	North-West Scotland	Highland	Sutherland
068	Torrisdale Bay	NC6962	North-West Scotland	Highland	Sutherland
069	Melvich Bay	NC8964	North-West Scotland	Highland	Sutherland
070	Otters Wick	HY6843	North-East Scotland	Orkney	Sanday
071	Cata Sand	HY7041	North-East Scotland	Orkney	Sanday
072	Kettletoft Bay	HY6739	North-West Scotland	Orkney	Sanday
073	Deer Sound & Peter's Pool	HY5404	North-East Scotland	Orkney	Mainland
074	Loch Fleet	NH7996	North-West Scotland	Highland	Sutherland
075	Dornoch Firth	NH7087	North-West Scotland	Highland	Ross & Cromarty Sutherland
076	Cromarty Firth	NH6667	North-West Scotland	Highland	Ross & Cromarty
077	Moray Firth	NH7152	North-East Scotland North-West Scotland	Grampian Highland	Moray Inverness Nairn Ross & Cromarty
078	Lossie Estuary	NJ2470	North-East Scotland	Grampian	Moray
079	Spey Bay	NJ3465	North-East Scotland	Grampian	Moray
080	Banff Bay	NJ6964	North-East Scotland	Grampian	Banff & Buchan
081	Ythan Estuary	NK0026	North-East Scotland	Grampian	Gordon
082	Don Estuary	NJ9509	North-East Scotland	Grampian	Aberdeen
083	Dee Estuary (Grampian)	NJ9405	North-East Scotland	Grampian	Aberdeen
084	St Cyrus	NO7362	South-East Scotland North-East Scotland	Grampian Tayside	Kincardine & Deeside Angus
085	Montrose Basin	NO6957	South-East Scotland	Tayside	Angus
086	Firth of Tay	NO3527	South-East Scotland	Fife Tayside	North East Fife Angus Dundee Perth and Kinross
087	Eden Estuary	NO4819	South-East Scotland	Fife	North East Fife
088	Firth of Forth	NT0182	South-East Scotland	Central Fife Lothian	Clackmannan Falkirk Stirling Dunfermline Kirkcaldy East Lothian Edinburgh West Lothian
089	Tyninghame Bay	NT6480	South-East Scotland	Lothian	East Lothian
090	Tweed Estuary	NT9853	North-East England South-East Scotland	Northumberland Borders	Berwick-upon-Tweed Berwickshire
091	Lindisfarne & Budle Bay	NU1141	North-East England	Northumberland	Berwick-upon-Tweed
092	Alnmouth	NU2410	North-East England	Northumberland	Alnwick
093	Warkworth Harbour	NU2605	North-East England	Northumberland	Alnwick
094	Wansbeck Estuary	NZ3085	North-East England	Northumberland	Wansbeck
095	Blyth Estuary (Northumberland)	NZ3082	North-East England	Northumberland	Blyth Valley Wansbeck

Estuary		Centre grid	NCC region	County/ region(s)	District(s)
096	Tyne Estuary	NZ3466	North-East England	Tyne and Wear	Gateshead
					Newcastle upon Tyne
					North Tyneside
					South Tyneside
097	Wear Estuary	NZ3958	North-East England	Tyne and Wear	Sunderland
098	Tees Estuary	NZ5326	North-East England	Cleveland	Hartlepool
					Middlesbrough
					Stockton-on-Tees
099	Esk Estuary (Yorkshire)	NZ9010	North-East England	North Yorkshire	Scarborough
100	Humber Estuary	TA2118	East Midlands	Humberside	Beverley
			North-East England	Lincolnshire	Boothferry
				North Yorkshire	Cleethorpes
				Nottinghamshire	Glanford
					Great Grimsby
					Holderness
					Kingston upon Hull
					Scunthorpe
					East Lindsey
					West Lindsey
					Selby
					York
					Bassetlaw
					Newark & Sherwood
101	The Wash	TF5540	East Anglia	Cambridgeshire	East Cambridgeshire
			East Midlands	Lincolnshire	Fenland
				Norfolk	Peterborough
					South Cambridge
					Boston
					East Lindsey
					South Holland
					Kings Lynn & West Norfolk
102	North Norfolk Coast	TF8946	East Anglia	Norfolk	Kings Lynn & West Norfolk
					North Norfolk
103	Breydon Water	TG4907	East Anglia	Norfolk	Broadland
				Suffolk	Great Yarmouth
					South Norfolk
					Waveney
104	Oulton Broad	TM5192	East Anglia	Norfolk	South Norfolk
				Suffolk	Waveney
105	Blyth Estuary (Suffolk)	TM4776	East Anglia	Suffolk	Suffolk Coastal
					Waveney
106	Ore/Alde/Butley	TM4357	East Anglia	Suffolk	Suffolk Coastal
107	Deben Estuary	TM2945	East Anglia	Suffolk	Suffolk Coastal
108	Orwell Estuary	TM2338	East Anglia	Suffolk	Babergh
					Ipswich
					Suffolk Coastal
109	Stour Estuary	TM1833	East Anglia	Essex	Tendring
				Suffolk	Babergh
110	Hamford Water	TM2325	East Anglia	Essex	Tendring
111	Colne Estuary	TM0617	East Anglia	Essex	Colchester
					Maldon
					Tendring
112	Blackwater Estuary	TL9507	East Anglia	Essex	Colchester
					Maldon
113	Dengie Flat	TM0504	East Anglia	Essex	Maldon
114	Crouch-Roach Estuary	TQ9694	East Anglia	Essex	Basildon
					Chelmsford
					Maldon
					Rochford

Estuary		Centre grid	NCC region	County/region(s)	District(s)
115	Maplin Sands	TR0087	East Anglia	Essex	Rochford
116	Southend-on-Sea	TQ8984	East Anglia	Essex	Basildon
					Castle Point
					Rochford
					Southend-on-Sea
117	Thames Estuary	TQ6675	South-East England	London	City of London
			East Anglia	Essex	Greenwich
				Kent	Hammersmith & Kensington & Lambeth
					Lambeth
					Lewisham
					Southwark
					Tower Hamlets
					Wandsworth
					Westminster
					Barking & Dagenham
					Dagenham
					Bexley
					Havering
					Hounslow
					Newham
					Richmond-upon-Thames
					Thames
					Thurrock
					Dartford
					Gravesham
					Rochester upon Medway
118	South Thames Marshes	TQ8180	South-East England	Kent	Rochester upon Medway
119	Medway Estuary	TQ8471	South-East England	Kent	Gillingham
					Maidstone
					Rochester upon Medway
					Swale
					Tonbridge and Malling
120	Swale Estuary	TR0066	South-East England	Kent	Canterbury
					Swale
121	Pegwell Bay	TR3563	South-East England	Kent	Canterbury
					Dover
					Thanet
122	Rother Estuary	TQ9419	South-East England	East Sussex	Rother
123	Cuckmere Estuary	TV5198	South-East England	East Sussex	Lewes
					Wealden
124	Ouse Estuary	TQ4402	South-East England	East Sussex	Lewes
125	Adur Estuary	TQ2105	South-East England	East Sussex	Hove
				West Sussex	Adur
					Horsham
126	Arun Estuary	TQ0103	South-East England	West Sussex	Arun
127	Pagham Harbour	SZ8796	South-East England	West Sussex	Arun
					Chichester
128	Chichester Harbour	SU7600	South-East England	Hampshire	Havant
			South England	West Sussex	Chichester
129	Langstone Harbour	SU7002	South England	Hampshire	Havant
					Portsmouth
130	Portsmouth Harbour	SU6203	South England	Hampshire	Fareham
					Gosport
					Portsmouth

Estuary		Centre grid	NCC region	County/ region(s)	District(s)
131	Southampton Water	SU4506	South England	Hampshire	Eastleigh Fareham New Forest Portsmouth Southampton Test Valley
132	Beaulieu River	SU4100	South England	Hampshire	New Forest
133	Lymington Estuary	SZ3395	South England	Hampshire	New Forest
134	Bembridge Harbour	SZ6388	South England	Isle of Wight	Medina South Wight
135	Wootton Creek & Ryde Sands	SZ5592	South England	Isle of Wight	Medina
136	Medina Estuary	SZ5093	South England	Isle of Wight	Medina
137	Newtown Estuary	SZ4191	South England	Isle of Wight	South Wight
138	Yar Estuary	SZ3489	South England	Isle of Wight	South Wight
139	Christchurch Harbour	SZ1791	South-West England	Dorset	Bournemouth Christchurch
140	Poole Harbour	SZ0189	South-West England	Dorset	Poole Purbeck
141	The Fleet & Portland Harbour	SY6181	South-West England	Dorset	West Dorset Weymouth & Portland
142	Axe Estuary	SY2591	South-West England	Devon	East Devon
143	Otter Estuary	SY0782	South-West England	Devon	East Devon
144	Exe Estuary	SX9883	South-West England	Devon	East Devon Exeter Teignbridge
145	Teign Estuary	SX9172	South-West England	Devon	Teignbridge
146	Dart Estuary	SX8753	South-West England	Devon	South Hams
147	Salcombe & Kingsbridge Est.	SX7441	South-West England	Devon	South Hams
148	Avon Estuary	SX6745	South-West England	Devon	South Hams
149	Erme Estuary	SX6249	South-West England	Devon	South Hams
150	Yealm Estuary	SX5449	South-West England	Devon	South Hams
151	Plymouth Sound	SX4356	South-West England	Cornwall Devon	Caradon East Devon Plymouth
152	Looe Estuary	SX2554	South-West England	Cornwall	Caradon
153	Fowey Estuary	SX1255	South-West England	Cornwall	Caradon Restormel
154	Falmouth	SW8334	South-West England	Cornwall	Carrick Kerrier
155	Helford Estuary	SW7626	South-West England	Cornwall	Kerrier

Appendix 2 Area, shoreline and tidal channel measurements for Estuaries Review sites

Appendix 2a Core site areas and shorelines

Estuary		Total area ha	Intertidal area ha	Shoreline km	Tidal channel km
001	Hayle Estuary	115.0	89.0	11.9	2.4
002	Gannel Estuary	122.0	84.5	9.2	3.7
003	Camel Estuary	839.0	610.0	43.0	15.3
004	Taw-Torridge Estuary	1,592.5	1,147.5	79.0	20.8
005	Blue Anchor Bay	350.0	350.0	8.9	0.0
006	Bridgwater Bay	6,529.0	5,147.2	109.4	46.3
007	Severn Estuary	55,684.0	16,890.0	353.0	111.2
008	Thaw Estuary	160.0	160.0	4.7	0.0
009	Ogmore Estuary	25.0	15.0	3.2	1.6
010	Afan Estuary	37.5	17.5	4.9	2.5
011	Neath Estuary	1,128.5	1,078.5	26.9	10.6
012	Tawe Estuary & Swansea Bay	785.0	747.8	22.8	6.5
013	Loughor Estuary	9,524.0	6,552.5	84.7	30.2
014	Carmarthen Bay	8,295.0	5,359.5	115.7	30.7
015	Milford Haven	5,447.5	1,710.0	170.7	35.4
016	Nyfer Estuary	100.0	75.0	6.1	3.1
017	Teifi Estuary	301.5	180.9	21.0	10.0
018	Aberystwyth	17.5	5.0	7.1	2.4
019	Dyfi Estuary	1,954.0	1,524.6	52.2	19.6
020	Dysynni Estuary	116.5	69.0	9.9	4.4
021	Mawddach Estuary	999.0	816.0	33.2	13.8
022	Artro Estuary	120.0	114.0	7.4	1.7
023	Traeth Bach	2,050.0	1,749.5	54.0	15.7
024	Pwllheli Harbour	85.0	60.0	4.6	2.4
025	Foryd Bay	342.5	285.0	9.4	4.5
026	Traeth Melynog	365.0	314.0	10.9	5.4
027	Cefni Estuary	744.0	614.0	26.1	12.7
028	Alaw Estuary	1,085.0	721.0	38.2	10.4
029	Traeth Dulas	102.5	102.5	5.2	2.9
030	Traeth Coch	582.5	582.5	10.0	4.4
031	Traeth Lavan	304.0	293.2	16.1	2.9
032	Conwy Estuary	1,494.0	1,080.9	55.8	24.7
033	Clwyd Estuary	120.0	84.4	13.6	8.1
034	Dee Estuary & North Wirral	16,101.0	12,981.0	108.5	36.8
035	Mersey Estuary	8,914.0	5,607.5	102.9	15.6
036	Alt Estuary	1,412.5	1,412.5	14.0	5.2
037	Ribble Estuary	11,924.0	10,674.3	107.5	28.4
038	Morecambe Bay	44,872.5	33,749.3	256.1	40.3
039	Duddon Estuary	6,092.0	5,055.8	65.5	22.6
040	Esk Estuary (Cumbria)	456.0	371.0	31.2	11.4
041	Solway Firth	42,056.0	27,550.0	213.6	46.3
042	Rough Firth & Auchencairn	1,290.0	1,289.0	44.4	14.4
043	Dee Estuary (Dumfries & Galloway)	1,144.0	825.0	28.6	11.7
044	Water of Fleet	790.0	790.0	19.9	7.2

Estuary		Total area ha	Intertidal area ha	Shoreline km	Tidal channel km
045	Cree Estuary	4,727.5	3,340.0	24.3	63.2
046	Luce Bay	1,228.0	1,196.1	27.5	8.5
047	Garnock Estuary	204.0	161.0	14.7	5.6
048	Hunterston sands	291.0	291.4	16.4	0.0
049	Clyde Estuary	5,485.0	1,841.0	129.7	41.9
050	Ruel Estuary	426.0	184.0	15.4	6.7
051	Loch Gilp	245.0	142.5	6.8	3.4
052	Tràigh Cill-a-Rubha	639.0	288.0	8.6	3.0
053	Loch Gruinart	832.5	736.0	14.8	8.1
054	Loch Crinan	280.0	167.5	15.3	6.2
055	Kentra Bay	337.5	312.5	13.4	4.9
056	Loch Moidart	881.0	469.0	34.9	10.1
057	Tràigh Mhór	242.0	209.6	6.5	0.0
058	Bagh Nam Faoilean	2,144.0	1,264.0	37.5	10.9
059	Oitir Mhór	5,519.0	4,028.2	292.4	13.3
060	Tràigh Vallay	1,112.5	822.5	22.9	6.9
061	Oronsay	1,277.5	825.0	29.9	6.3
062	Scarista	290.0	290.0	7.5	0.0
063	Tràigh Luskentyre	344.0	344.0	11.5	4.1
064	Camus Uig	437.5	214.0	18.0	5.5
065	Laxdale Estuary	559.0	390.0	12.8	4.7
066	Kyle of Durness	1,327.5	561.0	28.9	12.7
067	Kyle of Tongue	1,818.0	442.0	37.2	14.2
068	Torrisdale Bay	199.6	138.9	9.8	2.9
069	Melvich Bay	78.0	32.9	6.9	3.0
070	Otters Wick	552.5	310.0	12.0	2.6
071	Cata Sand	217.5	204.0	7.9	1.3
072	Kettletoft Bay	190.5	121.9	6.7	1.9
073	Deer Sound and Peter's Pool	1,287.0	304.5	25.4	6.4
074	Loch Fleet	695.0	522.0	20.7	6.6
075	Dornoch Firth	11,663.0	4,397.0	284.5	42.8
076	Cromarty Firth	9,232.0	3,641.7	120.5	32.7
077	Moray Firth	11,149.5	4,782.5	169.6	32.3
078	Lossie Estuary	56.0	29.6	13.3	4.4
079	Spey Bay	49.0	29.3	4.9	0.9
080	Banff Bay	102.0	15.8	8.6	2.8
081	Ythan Estuary	282.0	200.5	28.2	10.9
082	Don Estuary	23.0	8.5	5.5	2.4
083	Dee Estuary (Grampian)	96.5	6.9	18.7	5.8
084	St Cyrus	35.0	25.7	6.7	2.1
085	Montrose Basin	841.5	739.4	21.9	8.0
086	Firth of Tay	12,128.0	5,583.3	165.0	53.7
087	Eden Estuary	1,041.0	937.4	27.7	11.1
088	Firth of Forth	8,401.0	4,798.3	272.5	54.8
089	Tyninghame Bay	507.0	400.3	25.8	5.9
090	Tweed Estuary	232.5	68.4	34.5	13.3
091	Lindisfarne & Budle Bay	3,274.0	2,840.6	32.8	8.5
092	Alnmouth	52.0	29.9	8.8	3.7
093	Warkworth Harbour	75.0	45.4	12.9	5.0

	Estuary	Total area ha	Intertidal area ha	Shoreline km	Tidal channel km
094	Wansbeck Estuary	15.0	11.5	1.7	5.0
095	Blyth Estuary (Northumberland)	168.0	8.7	21.5	6.6
096	Tyne Estuary	792.0	59.7	83.1	32.7
097	Wear Estuary	200.0	29.4	37.5	17.0
098	Tees Estuary	1,347.0	471.2	121.4	38.3
099	Esk Estuary (Yorkshire)	30.0	8.8	8.5	3.8
100	Humber Estuary	30,356.5	13,521.2	675.5	144.7
101	The Wash	66,654.0	29,769.8	359.0	90.2
102	North Norfolk Coast	6,292.0	5,874.1	70.2	6.0
103	Breydon Water	1,534.0	768.9	317.0	46.8
104	Oulton Broad	128.5	29.7	6.8	20.1
105	Blyth Estuary (Suffolk)	311.0	235.0	25.4	10.8
106	Ore-Alde-Butley	1,821.0	1,331.9	73.2	28.0
107	Deben Estuary	1,007.0	687.4	49.8	19.7
108	Orwell Estuary	1,785.5	576.3	50.7	20.1
109	Stour Estuary	2,531.0	1,637.0	48.1	19.6
110	Hamford Water	2,377.0	1,569.9	54.0	8.3
111	Colne Estuary	2,335.0	2,001.5	89.6	16.2
112	Blackwater Estuary	5,184.0	3,315.3	107.5	21.2
113	Dengie Flat	2,986.0	2,986.8	17.5	0.0
114	Crouch-Roach Estuary	2,754.0	1,536.2	158.5	29.6
115	Maplin Sands	11,519.0	9,442.9	18.2	0.0
116	Southend-on-Sea	2,737.0	2,528.0	71.7	8.8
117	Thames Estuary	4,745.0	1,126.3	232.0	82.5
118	South Thames Marshes	2,487.0	2,439.2	30.6	4.7
119	Medway Estuary	6,441.0	4,008.2	143.4	40.9
120	Swale Estuary	3,823.0	2,695.6	79.3	18.4
121	Pegwell Bay	863.0	708.6	79.9	35.1
122	Rother Estuary	376.0	344.1	23.0	6.6
123	Cuckmere Estuary	46.5	15.4	16.7	8.4
124	Ouse Estuary	124.0	6.0	20.3	49.2
125	Adur Estuary	153.0	45.7	46.5	20.6
126	Arun Estuary	171.0	3.0	80.3	37.1
127	Pagham Harbour	265.5	245.4	9.8	2.6
128	Chichester Harbour	2,946.0	2,341.8	80.6	8.1
129	Langstone Harbour	1,925.0	1,513.0	43.0	7.7
130	Portsmouth Harbour	1,593.0	963.9	55.2	10.8
131	Southampton Water	3,975.0	1,376.0	109.8	20.2
132	Beaulieu River	546.0	417.0	31.3	10.4
133	Lymington Estuary	1,366.5	589.4	18.1	4.2
134	Bembridge Harbour	145.0	117.3	5.6	2.3
135	Wootton Creek & Ryde Sands	32.0	23.4	4.7	1.8
136	Medina Estuary	219.0	100.6	19.6	7.4
137	Newtown Estuary	253.5	217.6	23.5	3.3
138	Yar Estuary	110.0	96.6	7.9	3.2
139	Christchurch Harbour	239.0	122.2	21.4	6.6
140	Poole Harbour	3,805.0	2,050.3	102.9	16.3
141	The Fleet & Portland Harbour	1,617.0	278.2	47.5	16.7
142	Axe Estuary	43.0	27.4	8.1	3.8

Estuary		Total area ha	Intertidal area ha	Shoreline km	Tidal channel km
143	Otter Estuary	36.0	18.9	6.1	1.1
144	Exe Estuary	1,874.0	1,200.9	47.8	16.7
145	Teign Estuary	370.0	219.3	20.4	9.1
146	Dart Estuary	863.0	312.7	60.5	19.8
147	Salcombe & Kingsbridge Estuary	674.0	446.4	48.6	8.3
148	Avon Estuary	213.5	146.2	19.8	7.8
149	Erme Estuary	145.0	71.5	17.1	6.0
150	Yealm Estuary	446.0	154.4	28.1	7.7
151	Plymouth Sound	3,962.0	1,809.2	208.6	34.1
152	Looe Estuary	56.0	42.5	12.6	4.1
153	Fowey Estuary	305.0	146.0	39.2	11.1
154	Falmouth	2,482.0	745.9	126.8	18.1
155	Helford Estuary	568.0	186.1	44.3	9.2
Total		524,842.6	303,443.4	9,090.8	2,451.3

Appendix 2b Associated intertidal areas and shorelines

Estuary		Associated intertidal area (ha)	Associated shoreline (km)
001	Hayle Estuary	227.0	7.6
004	Taw-Torridge Estuary	560.0	8.9
009	Ogmore Estuary	154.0	4.8
021	Mawddach Estuary	160.0	4.5
033	Clwyd Estuary	301.8	5.5
038	Morecambe Bay	589.3	10.4
040	Esk Estuary (Cumbria)	677.5	11.0
053	Loch Gruinart	140.0	3.9
077	Moray Firth	104.7	15.1
084	St Cyrus	110.1	4.1
086	Firth of Tay	136.6	5.3
090	Tweed Estuary	56.9	3.5
094	Wansbeck Estuary	25.7	1.5
098	Tees Estuary	453.7	19.1
120	Swale Estuary	244.4	12.3
137	Newtown Estuary	77.5	6.5
135	Wootton Creek & Ryde Sands	442.6	13.8
134	Bembridge Harbour	13.4	2.1
Total		4,475.2	139.8

Appendix 3 Geomorphological classification of Estuaries Review sites

The geomorphological and tidal range categories of the Estuaries Review classification are described in Chapter 5 and the location of each estuary is shown in Figure 5.2. Note that for simplicity in this listing only the major geomorphological type is given, but that some review sites also exhibit some features of other estuary types.

Estuary		Central grid	Geomorph. type	Tidal type
001	Hayle Estuary	SW5538	Bar Built Estuary	Macrotidal
002	Gannel Estuary	SW8061	Ria	Macrotidal
003	Camel Estuary	SW9375	Ria	Macrotidal
004	Taw-Torridge Estuary	SS4631	Bar Built Estuary	Macrotidal
005	Blue Anchor Bay	ST0244	Embayment	Exceptionally large
006	Bridgwater Bay	ST2947	Embayment	Exceptionally large
007	Severn Estuary	ST4080	Coastal Plain	Exceptionally large
008	Thaw Estuary	ST0366	Coastal Plain	Exceptionally large
009	Ogmore Estuary	SS8776	Coastal Plain	Macrotidal
010	Afan Estuary	SS7588	Bar Built Estuary	Macrotidal
011	Neath Estuary	SS7292	Ria	Macrotidal
012	Tawe Estuary & Swansea Bay	SS6694	Embayment	Macrotidal
013	Loughor Estuary	SS4897	Coastal Plain	Macrotidal
014	Carmarthen Bay	SN3408	Embayment	Macrotidal
015	Milford Haven	SM9403	Ria	Macrotidal
016	Nyfer Estuary	SN0540	Bar Built Estuary	Macrotidal
017	Teifi Estuary	SN1648	Bar Built Estuary	Macrotidal
018	Aberystwyth	SN5980	Bar Built Estuary	Macrotidal
019	Dyfi Estuary	SN6495	Bar Built Estuary	Macrotidal
020	Dysynni Estuary	SH5802	Bar Built Estuary	Macrotidal
021	Mawddach Estuary	SH6416	Bar Built Estuary	Macrotidal
022	Artro Estuary	SH5725	Bar Built Estuary	Macrotidal
023	Traeth Bach	SH5736	Bar Built Estuary	Macrotidal
024	Pwllheli Harbour	SH3835	Bar Built Estuary	Macrotidal
025	Foryd Bay	SH4559	Bar Built Estuary	Macrotidal
026	Traeth Melynog	SH4364	Bar Built Estuary	Macrotidal
027	Cefni Estuary	SH4067	Bar Built Estuary	Macrotidal
028	Alaw Estuary	SH3081	Fjard	Macrotidal
029	Traeth Dulas	SH4888	Bar Built Estuary	Macrotidal
030	Traeth Coch	SH5380	Linear Shore	Macrotidal
031	Traeth Lavan	SH6375	Embayment	Macrotidal
032	Conwy Estuary	SH7976	Coastal Plain	Macrotidal
033	Clwyd Estuary	SJ0080	Coastal Plain	Macrotidal
034	Dee Estuary & North Wirral	SJ2674	Coastal Plain	Macrotidal
035	Mersey Estuary	SJ4180	Coastal Plain	Macrotidal
036	Alt Estuary	SD2903	Coastal Plain	Macrotidal
037	Ribble Estuary	SD3424	Coastal Plain	Macrotidal
038	Morecambe Bay	SD3668	Embayment	Macrotidal
039	Duddon Estuary	SD1977	Coastal Plain	Macrotidal
040	Esk Estuary (Cumbria)	SD0896	Bar Built Estuary	Macrotidal
041	Solway Firth	NY2762	Complex	Macrotidal
042	Rough Firth & Auchencairn	NX8451	Fjard	Macrotidal
043	Dee Estuary (Dumfries)	NX6747	Fjard	Macrotidal

Estuary		Central grid	Geomorph. type	Tidal type
044	Water of Fleet	NX5753	Fjard	Macrotidal
045	Cree Estuary	NX4655	Fjard	Macrotidal
046	Luce Bay	NX1855	Linear Shore	Macrotidal
047	Garnock Estuary	NS3039	Bar Built Estuary	Mesotidal
048	Hunterston Sands	NS1953	Linear Shore	Mesotidal
049	Clyde Estuary	NS3675	Fjord	Mesotidal
050	Ruel Estuary	NS0079	Fjord	Mesotidal
051	Loch Gilp	NR8687	Fjord	Mesotidal
052	Tràigh Cill-a-Rubha	NR3362	Embayment	Microtidal
053	Loch Gruinart	NR2971	Fjard	Mesotidal
054	Loch Crinan	NR7993	Fjard	Mesotidall
055	Kentra Bay	NM6469	Fjard	Macrotidal
056	Loch Moidart	NM6873	Fjard	Macrotidal
057	Tràigh Mhór	NF7005	Embayment	Mesotidal
058	Bagh Nam Faoilean	NF7948	Fjard	Macrotidal
059	Oitir Mhór	NF8158	Fjard	Macrotidal
060	Tràigh Vallay	NF7875	Fjard	Macrotidal
061	Oronsay	NF8575	Fjard	Macrotidal
062	Scarista	NF9992	Embayment	Mesotidal
063	Tràigh Luskentyre	NG0798	Fjord	Mesotidal
064	Camus Uig	NB0433	Fjard	Mesotidal
065	Laxdale Estuary	NB4434	Fjard	Macrotidal
066	Kyle of Durness	NC3766	Fjord	Mesotidal
067	Kyle of Tongue	NC5858	Fjord	Macrotidal
068	Torrisdale Bay	NC6962	Fjard	Macrotidal
069	Melvich Bay	NC8964	Fjard	Macrotidal
070	Otters Wick	HY6843	Fjard	Mesotidal
071	Cata Sand	HY7041	Bar Built Estuary	Mesotidal
072	Kettletoft Bay	HY6739	Fjard	Mesotidal
073	Deer Sound & Peter's Pool	HY5404	Fjard	Mesotidal
074	Loch Fleet	NH7996	Bar Built Estuary	Mesotidal
075	Dornoch Firth	NH7087	Complex	Mesotidal
076	Cromarty Firth	NH6667	Complex	Mesotidal
077	Moray Firth	NH7152	Complex	Macrotidal
078	Lossie Estuary	NJ2470	Bar Built Estuary	Macrotidal
079	Spey Bay	NJ3465	Bar Built Estuary	Mesotidal
080	Banff Bay	NJ6964	Embayment	Mesotidal
081	Ythan Estuary	NK0026	Bar Built Estuary	Mesotidal
082	Don Estuary	NJ9509	Coastal Plain	Mesotidal
083	Dee Estuary (Grampian)	NJ9405	Coastal Plain	Mesotidal
084	St Cyrus	NO7362	Bar Built Estuary	Macrotidal
085	Montrose Basin	NO6957	Bar Built Estuary	Microtical
086	Firth of Tay	NO3527	Complex	Mesotidal
087	Eden Estuary	NO4819	Bar Built Estuary	Mesotidal
088	Firth of Forth	NT0182	Complex	Macrotidal
089	Tyninghame Bay	NT6480	Bar Built Estuary	Macrotidal
090	Tweed Estuary	NT9853	Complex	Macrotidal
091	Lindisfarne & Budle Bay	NU1141	Barrier Beach System	Macrotidal
092	Alnmouth	NU2410	Bar Built Estuary	Mesotidal
093	Warkworth Harbour	NU2605	Bar Built Estuary	Mesotidal

Estuary		Central grid	Geomorph. type	Tidal type
094	Wansbeck Estuary	NZ3085	Coastal Plain	Macrotidal
095	Blyth Estuary (Northumb)	NZ3082	Bar Built Estuary	Macrotidal
096	Tyne Estuary	NZ3466	Complex	Macrotidal
097	Wear Estuary	NZ3958	Complex	Macrotidal
098	Tees Estuary	NZ5326	Coastal Plain	Macrotidal
099	Esk Estuary (Yorkshire)	NZ9010	Complex	Macrotidal
100	Humber Estuary	TA2118	Coastal Plain	Macrotidal
101	The Wash	TF5540	Embayment	Macrotidal
102	North Norfolk Coast	TF8946	Barrier Beach System	Mesotidal
103	Breydon Water	TG4907	Bar Built Estuary	Microtidal
104	Oulton Broad	TM5192	Bar Built Estuary	Microtidal
105	Blyth Estuary (Suffolk)	TM4776	Bar Built Estuary	Mesotidal
106	Ore-Alde-Butley	TM4357	Bar Built Estuary	Mesotidal
107	Deben Estuary	TM2945	Coastal Plain	Mesotidal
108	Orwell Estuary	TM2338	Coastal Plain	Mesotidal
109	Stour Estuary	TM1833	Coastal Plain	Mesotidal
110	Hamford Water	TM2325	Embayment	Mesotidal
111	Colne Estuary	TM0617	Coastal Plain	Macrotidal
112	Blackwater Estuary	TL9507	Coastal Plain	Macrotidal
113	Dengie Flat	TM0504	Linear Shore	Macrotidal
114	Crouch-Roach Estuary	TQ9694	Coastal Plain	Macrotidal
115	Maplin Sands	TR0087	Linear Shore	Macrotidal
116	Southend-on-Sea	TQ8984	Linear Shore	Macrotidal
117	Thames Estuary	TQ6675	Coastal Plain	Macrotidal
118	South Thames Marshes	TQ8180	Linear Shore	Macrotidal
119	Medway Estuary	TQ8471	Coastal Plain	Macrotidal
120	Swale Estuary	TR0066	Coastal Plain	Macrotidal
121	Pegwell Bay	TR3563	Embayment	Macrotidal
122	Rother Estuary	TQ9419	Bar Built Estuary	Macrotidal
123	Cuckmere Estuary	TV5198	Coastal Plain	Macrotidal
124	Ouse Estuary	TQ4402	Coastal Plain	Macrotidal
125	Adur Estuary	TQ2105	Coastal Plain	Macrotidal
126	Arun Estuary	TQ0103	Coastal Plain	Macrotidal
127	Pagham Harbour	SZ8796	Bar Built Estuary	Macrotidal
128	Chichester Harbour	SU7600	Bar Built Estuary	Macrotidal
129	Langstone Harbour	SU7002	Bar Built Estuary	Macrotidal
130	Portsmouth Harbour	SU6203	Bar Built Estuary	Macrotidal
131	Southampton Water	SU4506	Coastal Plain	Mesotidal
132	Beaulieu River	SU4100	Bar Built Estuary	Mesotidal
133	Lymington Estuary	SZ3395	Coastal Plain	Mesotidal
134	Bembridge Harbour	SZ6388	Coastal Plain	Mesotidal
135	Wootton Creek & Ryde Sands	SZ5592	Coastal Plain	Mesotidal
136	Medina Estuary	SZ5093	Coastal Plain	Macrotidal
137	Newtown Estuary	SZ4191	Bar Built Estuary	Mesotidal
138	Yar Estuary	SZ3489	Coastal Plain	Mesotidal
139	Christchurch Harbour	SZ1791	Bar Built Estuary	Microtidal
140	Poole Harbour	SZ0189	Bar Built Estuary	Microtidal
141	The Fleet & Portland Harb.	SY6181	Bar Built Estuary	Microtidal
142	Axe Estuary	SY2591	Bar Built Estuary	Mesotidal
143	Otter Estuary	SY0782	Bar Built Estuary	Macrotidal

Estuary		Central grid	Geomorph. type	Tidal type
144	Exe Estuary	SX9883	Bar Built Estuary	Macrotidal
145	Teign Estuary	SX9172	Ria	Macrotidal
146	Dart Estuary	SX8753	Ria	Macrotidal
147	Salcombe & Kingsbridge Est	SX7441	Ria	Macrotidal
148	Avon Estuary	SX6745	Ria	Macrotidal
149	Erme Estuary	SX6249	Ria	Macrotidal
150	Yealm Estuary	SX5449	Ria	Macrotidal
151	Plymouth Sound	SX4356	Ria	Macrotidal
152	Looe Estuary	SX2554	Ria	Macrotidal
153	Fowey Estuary	SX1255	Ria	Macrotidal
154	Falmouth	SW8334	Ria	Macrotidal
155	Helford Estuary	SW7626	Ria	Macrotidal

Appendix 4 Categories of human activities

This Appendix lists the main categories and subdivisions of human activities for which information was collected between January and June 1989 for the Estuaries Review. Note that for some of the listed categories more detailed information was collected in subdivided categories. For example information on the killing of birds was collected individually for five species of geese and five species of gulls.

For the analysis of human activities in Chapter 10 the activity categories have in some instances been combined and re-ordered.

A. Coast protection and sea defences
Linear defences
Training walls
Groynes
Brushwood fences
Spartina planting
Marram grass planting

B. Industrial, port and related development
Dock, port and harbour facilities
Manufacturing industries
Chemical industries (excluding oil and gas)
Ship and boat building
    Shipbuilding & repair yards
    Boatbuilding & repair yards
Mothballing of ships and boats
Tidal mills
Commercial explosives testing

C. Barrage schemes
Water storage barrages & bunds
Storm surge barrages
Tidal power barrages
Leisure barrages
Weirs and barrages for river management

D. Waste discharge
Domestic waste discharge
    Sludge dumping
    Sewage discharge & outfalls
    Sewage treatment works
    Rubbish tips
Industrial and agricultural waste discharge
    Biodegradable waste
    Inorganic and persistent waste
    Thermal discharges (power stations)
    Dredge spoil
    Agricultural wastes
    Air-borne pollution
    Radioactive discharges
Accidental discharges
    Spillages
    Collisions
Aerial crop spraying
Waste incinerators

E. Sediment extraction
Capital dredging
Maintenance dredging
Commercial estuarine aggregates extraction
    Intertidal extraction
    Subtidal extraction
Commercial terrestrial aggregates extraction
Non-commercial aggregates extraction
    Estuarine extraction
    Terrestrial extraction
Hard-rock quarrying
    Estuarine extraction
    Terrestrial extraction

F. Transport
Airports and helipads
Road and rail tunnels
Road and rail bridges
Aqueducts
Causeways
Fords
Road schemes
Ferries

G. Communications
Overhead cables
Submarine cables

H. Urbanisation
Housing and car parks
Population sizes

I. Tourism and recreation
Infrastructure developments
    Marinas
    Non-marina moorings
    Dinghy and boat parks
    Pleasure piers
    Tidal paddling pools
    Caravan parks & chalets
    Leisure and conference centres
    Artificial island leisure complexes
Aquatic-based recreation
    Power-boating

Water-skiing
Paragliding
Sailing
Sailboarding and windsurfing
SCUBA and snorkeling
Canoeing
Surfing
Rowing
Tourist boat trips
Canal leisure barges
Bathing and general beach recreation
Terrestrial-based recreation
Walking, including dog-walking
Bird-watching
Sand-yachting
Off-road vehicles
Trial-biking
Hovercraft
Car sand-racing
Horse-riding
Rock-climbing
Golf courses
Wargames
Clay-pigeon shooting
Model railways
Hides for bird photography
Airborne recreation
Overflying by light aircraft
Radio-controlled model aircraft
Hang-gliding

J. Cultivation of living resources

Agriculture
Saltmarsh grazing
Sand-dune grazing
Agricultural land-claim
Fish farming
Salmon
Rainbow trout
Halibut
Turbot
Shellfish farming
Bottom and tray cultivation
Ostraea edulis
Crassostrea gigas
Tapes semidecussata
Tapes decussata
Mercenaria mercenaria
Mytilus edulis
Suspended cultivation
Mytilus edulis
Pecten
Chlamys

Crustacea farming
Nephrops
Lobster
Edible crab
Algal cultivation
Reeds for roofing
Salicornia picking
Sea lavender picking
Turf cutting
Collection of Hydrozoa

K. Management and killing of birds and mammals

Killing of mammals
Seals
Otters
Mink
Rats
Coypu
Fox
Grey squirrel
Rabbits
Roe deer
Killing of birds
Adult fish-eating birds
Heron
Cormorant
Sawbills
Adult shellfish-eating birds
Oystercatcher
Eider
Gulls
Killing of adults
Destruction of nests and eggs
Egg-pricking
Collection of gull eggs for human consumption
Adult grazing birds
Killing of adult geese
Goose egg-pricking
Control of corvids

L. Commercial fisheries

Finned fish
Seine-netting
Bag-netting
Long-line fishing
Trawling
Fyke-netting for eels
Fish traps and other fixed devices and nets
Salmon poaching
Crustacea
Lobster & crab potting
SCUBA diving

Tangle-netting
Trawling
Shrimping
Digging
Molluscs
Hand-gathering
Dredging
Hydraulic dredging

M. Non-commercial fishing
Spear fishing
Netting
Angling
Other small-scale collection e.g. mussels
Flounder trampling contest

N. Bait-collecting
Digging and pumping for lugworms & ragworms
Hydraulic dredging for worms
Boulder-turning for crabs
Razor shells
Mussels
Limpets
Sand-eels
Crab tiles

O. Military activities
Torpedo practice
Bombing, missile and artillery practice
Military exercise
Overflying by military aircraft
Other military installations

P. Education and scientific research
Sampling, specimen collection and observation
Nature trails and interpretative facilities
Seismic studies & geological test drilling
Marine & terrestrial archaeology
Fossil collecting

Q. Wildfowling and hunting
Wildfowling
Release of wildfowl
Feeding of wildfowl
Illegal shooting
Foxhunting

R. Extraction and processing of natural gas and oil
Exploration
Production
Rig and platform construction
Pipeline construction and installation
Import/export jetties
Single-point moorings

Oil refineries
Mothballing of rigs and tankers

S. Wildlife habitat management
Spartina control
Habitat creation
Mudflats
Sandflats
Saltmarsh
Grazing marsh
Ungrazed marsh
Brackish lagoons
Sand-dunes
Freshwater lagoons
Artificial islands
Shingle banks
Artificial marine reefs
Reed-beds
Habitat restoration
Mudflats
Sandflats
Saltmarsh
Grazing marsh
Ungrazed marsh
Brackish lagoons
Sand-dunes
Freshwater lagoons
Artificial islands
Shingle banks
Artificial marine reefs
Reed-beds
Habitat management
Mudflats
Sandflats
Saltmarsh
Grazing marsh
Ungrazed marsh
Brackish lagoons
Sand-dunes
Freshwater lagoons
Artificial islands
Shingle banks
Artificial marine reefs
Reed-beds
Beach feeding
Habitat translocation
Saltmarsh
Other habitats

T. Power generation
Nuclear power stations
Coal-fired power stations
Oil-fired power stations

Gas-turbine power stations
Import/export jetties (power generation)
Wind-power generation

U. Others

Coastguard rescue exercises
Lifeboat stations
Wildlife sanctuaries and releases
   Seal sanctuary
   Swanneries
   Wildfowl parks

Appendix 5 Distribution of nationally rare and scarce coastal vascular plant species on Estuaries Review sites

The distribution of nationally rare and scarce vascular plants on coasts and estuaries is described in Section 8.1.13.

A Nationally rare species

	Species	No. of 10 km squares in GB	British distribution	Review site(s)[b]
Lower saltmarshes, tidal flats and Creeks				
Carex recta	estuarine sedge	3	N	76, 77
Corrigiola litoralis	strapwort	1	SW	–
Eleocharis parvula	dwarf spike-rush	6	sc[a]	140, 149
Limosella australis	Welsh mudwort	2	W	20, 23
Scirpus holoschoenus	round-headed club-rush	3	SW	6, 20
Scirpus triquetrus	triangular club-rush	1	SW	152
Spartina alterniflora	smooth cord-grass	1	S	131
Mid and upper saltmarsh				
Atriplex longipes	long-stalked orache	7	sc	6, 14, 102
Halimione pendunculata	stalked sea-purslane	1	SE	+[c]
Limonium bellidifolium	matted sea-lavender	5	E	102
Shingle				
Geranium purpureum ssp. *forsteri*	little robin	2	S	127, 131
Geranium purpureum ssp. *purpureum*	little robin	6	SW	129
Polygonum maritimum	sea knotgrass	1	SW	–
Waste places, open areas and sandy shores				
Chenopodium vulvaria	stinking goosefoot	15	S	108
Petrorhagia nanteuilii	childing pink	1	S	127
Spergularia bocconii	Greek sea-spurrey	2	SW	155
Rocks				
Allium ampeloprasum	wild leek	2	SW	7
Allium babingtonii	Babington's leek	13	SW	1, 3, 154
Limonium paradoxum	sea-lavender	1	W	–
Rumex ruprestris	shore dock	3	SW	4, 9, 27
Tuberaria guttata ssp. *breweri*	spotted rock-rose	4	W	–
Dunes and dune-slacks				
Epipactis dunensis	dune helleborine	9	N	26, 37, 39, 91
Gentianella uliginosa	dune gentian	5	W	13, 14
Gnaphalium luteoalbum	Jersey cudweed	1	E	102
Orobanche caryophyllacea	bedstraw broomrape	2	SE	121
Teucrium scordium	water germander	3	sc	4

A Nationally rare species (contd.)

	Species	No. of 10 km squares in GB	British distribution	Review site(s)[b]
Sea cliffs				
Asparagus officinalis ssp. *prostratus*	wild asparagus	5	SW	–
Bupleurum baldense	small hare's-ear	2	S	–
Centaurium scilloides	perennial centaury	2	SW	16
Limonium recurvum	sea-lavender	1	S	–
Limonium transwallianum	sea-lavender	2	W	–
Matthiola incana	hoary stock	4	S	–
Matthiola sinuata	sea stock	2	W	4, 11
Orobanche maritima	carrot broomrape	9	S	151
Rhynchosinapis wrightii	Lundy cabbage	1	W	–
Coastal grassland				
Aster linosyris	goldilocks	7	W	7, 32, 38
Centaurium tenuiflorum	slender centaury	S	–	–
Gastridium ventricosum	nit-grass	9	S	–
Lactuca saligna	least lettuce	4	SE	116
Ononis reclinata	small restharrow	4	W	–
Ophioglossum lusitanicum	least adder's-tongue	1	SW	–
Orobanche purpurea	yarrow broomrape	7	S	–
Poa infirma	early meadow-grass	6	SW	3, 155
Romulea columnae	sand crocus	1	SW	144
Trifolium bocconei	twin-headed clover	2	SW	–
Trifolium incarnatum ssp. *molinerii*	long-headed clover	2	SW	–
Trifolium strictum	upright clover	3	W	–
Viola kitaibeliana	dwarf pansy	1	SW	–

a   sc = scattered distribution
b   See Appendix 1 for review site names and locations
c   + = present on review site
-   Present on coasts only outside review sites.

B Nationally scarce species

	Species	No. of 10 km squares in GB	British distribution
Lower saltmarshes, tidal flats and creeks			
Carex divisa	divided sedge	79	Sc.*
Chenopodium botryodes	saltmarsh goosefoot	17	SE
Parapholis incurva	curved hard-grass	36	SE
Puccinellia fasciculata	Borrer's saltmarsh-grass	53	SE
Ranunculus baudotii	brackish water-crowfoot	83	Sc.
Ruppia cirrhosa	spiral tasselweed	32	E
Spartina maritima	small cord-grass	25	SE
Zostera angustifolia	narrow-leaved eelgrass	29	Sc.
Zostera marina	eelgrass	74	Sc.
Zostera noltii	dwarf eelgrass	43	Sc.

	Species	No. of 10 km squares in GB	British distribution
Mud and upper saltmarsh			
Alopecurus bulbosus	bulbous foxtail	26	S
Althea officinalis	marsh-mallow	73	S
Bupleurum tenuissimum	slender hare's-ear	58	S
Frankenia laevis	sea-heath	25	SE
Inula crithmoides	golden-samphire	62	S
Limonium humile	lax-flowered sea-lavender	49	Sc.
Polypogon monspeliensis	annual beard-grass	18	SE
Salicornia perennis	perennial glasswort	37	SE
Salicornia pusilla	glasswort	32	SE
Shingle			
Crambe maritima	sea-kale	88	Sc.
Lathyrus japonicus	sea pea	16	E
Mertensia maritima	oysterplant	48	N
Suaeda fruticosa	shrubby sea-blite	30	S
Waste places, open areas, and sandy shores			
Carex maritima	curved sedge	26	N
Cochlearia scotica	Scottish scurvygrass	76	N
Erodium moschatum	musk stork's-bill	37	W
Fumaria capreolata	white ramping-fumitory	62	Sc.
Juncus acutus	sharp rush	25	S
Lavatera arborea	tree-mallow	70	W
Medicago polymorpha	toothed medick	43	S
Poa bulbosa	bulbous meadow-grass	23	S
Polygonum raii	Ray's knotgrass	66	Sc.
Puccinellia rupestris	stiff saltmarsh-grass	51	SE
Raphanus maritimus	sea radish	89	Sc.
Rhychosinapis monensis	Isle of Man cabbage	18	W
Trifolium glomeratum	clustered clover	37	SE
Trifolium ornithopodioides	bird's-foot clover	85	S
Vulpia ambigua	bearded fescue	40	SE
Rocks			
Adiantum capillus-veneris	maidenhair fern	21	SW
Asplenium billotii	lanceolate spleenwort	76	W
Carex punctata	dotted sedge	23	W
Limonium binervosum	rock sea-lavender	70	S
Dunes and dune-slacks			
Centaurium littorale	perennial centaury	42	N
Corynephorus canescens	grey hair-grass	16	E
Equisetum variegatum	variegated horsetail	89	Sc.
Erodium maritimum	sea stork's-bill	77	W
Euphorbia paralias	sea spurge	92	W
Euphorbia portlandica	Portland spurge	74	W
Festuca juncifolia	rush-leaved fescue	27	E
Hippophae rhamnoides	sea-buckthorn	36	Sc.
Juncus balticus	Baltic bush	47	N
Oenothera stricta	fragrant evening-primrose	32	S
Vulpia membranacea	dune fescue	44	W

B Nationally scarce species (contd.)

	Species	No. of 10 km squares in GB	British distribution
Sea cliffs			
Brassica oleracea	wild cabbage	33	S
Vicia bithynica	Bithynian vetch	25	S
Vicia lutea	yellow-vetch	19	Sc.
Coastal grassland			
Centaurium capitatum	tufted centaury	19	S
Hordeum marinum	sea barley	59	SE
Lotus hispidus	hairy bird's-foot trefoil	35	SW
Ophioglossum azoricum	small adder's-tongue	19	Sc.
Orobanche maritima	carrot broomrape	22	S
Parentucellia viscosa	yellow bartsia	66	SW
Primula scotica	Scottish primrose	28	N
Scilla autumnalis	autumn squill	28	SW
Trifolium squamosum	sea clover	41	S

* Sc. = scattered distribution

Appendix 6 The MNCR marine ecosystem classification

This appendix contains examples of working documents from the NCC's Marine Nature Conservation Review (MNCR) describing the habitat and community classification developed by the MNCR.

The MNCR site and habitat classification provides the catalogue of definitive terms for describing marine sites and habitats. It is the basis for the MNCR site and habitat recording sheets and has been used for two field seasons. The classification is reasonably compact and use has shown it to be robust.

The MNCR team are now developing a complementary approach for identifying the marine community types which are associated with major site and habitat groupings. For this, a definition of the classification on the basis of its characteristic species is required for the title, together with a more detailed description of the main species present and the structure of the community. This is likely to be a much more open-ended exercise than the classification of habitats and is being undertaken on a 'file-per-community' system.

To keep the number of types reasonably small, the community classification will be separated into littoral and sublittoral and then subdivided mainly by site or 'habitat' types, according to the substrata, wave exposure and by modifying factors which are considered to be of key importance in determining community type. These will usually be whole-site modifiers such as salinity and tidal stream exposure but will also include localised features determined by such factors as scour, shading, nitrification and the presence of crevices, rockpools, caves and underboulders.

Details of the MNCR habitat classification terms are given in Section A of this Appendix. Section B gives an example of how the classification can be used to described habitats and communities, in this instance in the Irish Sea.

The details of the MNCR marine classification, and its background and context will be considered in more detail in an MNCR theme report on Rationale and Methods currently in preparation for publication by the NCC.

Section A

The MNCR classification of marine habitats.

1

Physiographic features

Open coast

Straights/sounds/narrows

Shallow rapids

Enclosed coast (marine inlets, harbours)

Saline lagoons

2

Salinity

High

Normal

Variable

Low

3

Wave exposure

Extremely exposed

Very exposed

Exposed

Moderately exposed

Sheltered

Very sheltered

Extremely sheltered

4

Surface tidal steam strength

Very strong

Strong

Moderately strong

Weak

Very weak

5

Geology

Hard

    Igneous

    Chert/flint

    Slate

    Sand/mud stone

Medium

    Limestone

    Concrete

Friable

    Slate/shale

Soft

    Sand/mud stone

    Chalk

Very soft

    Clay

Habitat Classification

6

Biological/physical zones and subzones

Hard substrata

Supralittoral

Littoral

    Upper littoral fringe

    Lower littoral fringe

    Upper eulittoral

    Mid eulittoral

    Lower eulittoral

Sublittoral fringe

Sublittoral

    Upper infralittoral

    Lower infralittoral

    Upper circalittoral

    Lower circalittoral

Bathyal

Sediments

Littoral

Sublittoral

Water column

Surface

Midwater

Seabed

7

Substratum

Bedrock

Boulders – very large (>1m)

Boulders – large (500mm – 1m)

Boulders – small (256 – 500mm)

Cobbles – large (128 – 256mm)

Cobbles – small (64 – 128mm)

Slates (64 – 256mm)

Pebbles (4 – 64mm)

Rock gravel

Shell gravel

Maerl gravel (dead)

Coarse sand

Medium sand

Fine sand

Mud

Shells (empty)

Artificial

    Metal

    Concrete

    Wood

    Plastic

Tree/branch

Algae

Live maerl

Peat

Modifiers/indicators (features which modify the major habitat types or indicate particular conditions. This list can be added to)

Freshwater runoff

Wave surge

Tidal streams accelerated

Tidal streams decelerated

Grazing

Boulders/cobbles/pebbles/mobile

Rock surface even – rugged

Rock surface smooth – pitted

Rock non scoured – scoured

Rock clean – silted

Coarse sediment on rock

Boulders/cobbles/pebbles smooth – angular

Sediment surface even – uneven

Sediment firm – soft

Sediment stable – mobile

Sediment poor – well sorted

Sediment poor – well drained

Black layer absent – very shallow

Wave/dunes (>10cm)

Ripples (<10cm)

Mounds/casts

Burrows/holes

    Sediment

    Rock

Drainage channels

Vertical layering

Subsurface clay/mud

Surface silt on sediment

Habitat features/types (features on/in which particular communities develop within major habitat categories. This list can be added to)

Overhanging

Vertical (80° – 100°)

Very steep sloping (40° – 80°)

Upward facing (0° – 40°)

Fissures (>10mm)

Crevices (<10mm)

Large (>1m deep) rockpool

Large shallow rockpool

Small shallow rockpool

Gully

Cave

Tunnel

Rockhill/pothole

Sandy/sand-covered rock

Under boulder/cobble on rock

Under boulder/cobble on sediment

Boulder hole

Strandline

Wreck

Kelp holdfast

Kelp stipe

Kelp frond

Fucus serratus

Serpulid bed/clump

Modiolus bed/clump

Zostera leaves

Jetty pile

Section B

MNCR habitat classification for nearshore sublittoral areas. (Prepared for the Irish Sea and being used as a basis for a Great Britain classification.)

Key habitat features

	Substratum	Wave exposure	Tidal streams	Species/groups characterising different communities
1	Bedrock; boulders	Exposed	–	Infralittoral: *Laminaria hyperborea*; foliose red algae
2	"	"	–	Circalittoral: Fauna inc. erect sponges (*Polymastia* spp., *Axinella* spp., *Stelligera* spp., *Raspailia* spp.), hydroids, *Actinothoe*, *Corynactis*, *Caryophyllia*, erect bryozoans (*Crisia*, *Bugula*)
3	"	Sheltered	–	Infralittoral: *Laminaria saccharina*; foliose/filamentous red and brown algae; brown crusts
4	"	"	–	Circalittoral: Fauna inc. encrusting sponges (eg. Plocomionida), hydroids (*Halecium halecinum*, *Kirchenpaueria*, *Nemertesia* spp., *Obelia* spp.), *Pomatoceros*, encrusting bryozoans, *Thyone* spp., large solitary ascidians (*Ascidia* spp., *Ascidiella* spp.)
5	"	–	Very strong	*Balanus crenatus*, *Tubularia indivisa*, *Sertularia argentia*, *Halichondria panicea*, *Mytilus edulis*
6	"	–	Strong	*Alcyonium digitatum*, *Sertularia argentea*, *Actinothoe sphyrodeta*, *Sagartia elegans*, *Pachymatisma johnstonia*
7	Bedrock; boulders – sand scoured	–	Moderately strong	*Sabellaria* reefs
8	Bedrock – by/with sand	–	–	Infralittoral: *Halidrys siliquosa*; *Polyides/Furcellaria*; *L. saccharina* & *Desmarestia* spp.
9	"	–	–	Circalittoral: *Ciocalypta*, *Polymastia* spp., *Urticina felina* & *Flustra*
10	Bedrock – surge gulley	Surge	–	*Clathrina*, *Tubularia indivisa*, *Metridium*, *Sagartia elegans*, *Halichondria panicea*, polyclinids, *Dendrodoa*, *Pachymatisma*, *Mytilus*
11	"Bedrock – caves, overhangs	–	–	*Parazoanthus* spp., sponges (*Stryphnus*, *Stelleta*, *Dercitus*, *Thymosia*), *Parerythropodium*
12	Boulder, cobble & coarse sediment	–	Moderately strong	Hydroid/bryozoan turf (*Flustra*, *Securiflustra*, *Alcyonidium diaphanum*, *Eucratia*, *Vesicularia*, *Abietinaria abietina*, *Hydrallmania*)
13	Cobble, pebble & coarse sediment	–	Moderately strong	*Ophiothrix/Ophiocomina* beds
14	Cobble, pebble & gravel	–	Moderately strong	Ephemeral filamentous/foliose red algae (*Schmitzia*, *Scinaia*, *Naccaria*, *Dudresnaya*, *Actractophora*)
15	Gravel/shell gravel	–	–	Maerl beds
16	"	–	–	*Neopentadactyla*, *Glycymeris*; *Spatangus* (= infaunal community 1 and 6)
17	Gravel – muddy, with cobble & boulder	–	–	*Chaetopterus/Lanice/Pecten* (= infaunal community 5)
18	Sand – coarse, gravelly	–	–	*Ensis arcuatus/Mya truncata* (= infaunal community 8)
19	Sand – clean, mobile	–	–	Barren; *Ammodytes/Pagurus bernhardus* (= infaunal community 2 and 3)
20	Sand	–	–	*Zostera marina* bed
21	Sand	–	–	*Laminaria saccharina/Chorda*; filamentous algae (*Audouinella/Trailliella*)
22	" – fine	–	–	*Echinocardium cordatum*, *Amphiura brachiata* & *Labidoplax digitata* (= infaunal community 7)
23	" – muddy	–	–	*Virgularia/Amphiura* spp. with *Corymorpha*, *Thecocarpus*, *Molgula occulta*, *Arctica*, *Cerianthus*, *Ophiura* spp., *Turritella*, *Aporrhais*, *Astropecten* (= infaunal community 10)
24	Mud with shell	–	–	Modiolus beds
25	"	–	–	*Ascidiella aspersa/Sabella pavonina*
26	Mud	–	–	*Virgularia/Amphiura* spp. with *Philine aperta*
27	"	–	–	Megafaunal burrowers (*Nephrops*, *Goneplax*) (= infaunal community 12 and 13)

Appendix 7 The Estuaries Review aquatic estuarine habitat and community database

A7.1 The aquatic estuarine habitat and community database

The database developed for the Estuaries Review was designed to enable analysis to be made of the large quantity of marine habitat information available in surveys conducted by the NCC and outside bodies. Only a summary description is given here of the aquatic estuarine habitat and community database; for further information contact the Marine Science Branch of the NCC. The database was developed using Advanced Revelation database software. The database was developed in such a way that it shares common terminology with the NCC's Marine Nature Conservation Review (MNCR) database so that, at a later date, integration of the two will be possible. Just under 700 individual habitats were entered onto the database using standard MNCR terminology (see Appendix 6) although additional phrases were introduced to cope with the variability of data quality (see below).

Each habitat was classified according to salinity, wave exposure, tidal stream strength, biological/physical zone, major and minor substratum, dominant and secondary species, extent of record, and provisional conservation status. Each habitat description was linked to the original report from which it was extracted. The Estuaries Review terminology used was not hierachical in its layout but, through the relational indexing of Advanced Revelation software, it was possible to base searches on any one parameter or on combinations of parameters. Species information for individual habitats and communities was entered onto the database using the Marine Conservation Society Species Directory codings, and the taxonomy used was that chosen for the directory. Prior to data entry onto the computer of many of the older survey reports it was necessary to update species names due to taxonomic changes. In addition each review site was described in terms of its marine features and this information was stored as text on the database. Previously published sediment community names equivalent to Estuaries Review communities are listed in Table A7.1 The terminology used in the Estuaries Review aquatic estuarine database is given below (A7.2).

References cited in this Appendix are included in the reference listing for the aquatic estuarine communities chapter of the main report (Chapter 8.3).

Table A7.1 Sediment communities of the Estuaries Review which correspond to communities in the literature, adapted from Mitchell (1987).

Estuaries Review community	Equivalent community in literature	Association described by Jones (1950)
1 Gravel/shell gravel community	(a) *Spatangus purpureus-Venus fasciata* (Ford 1923) (b) *Spatangus-fasciata* (Bishop & Holme 1980) (c) ?*Spisula* (Bishop & Holme 1980) (d) ?'poor' *Spisula elliptica* (Einarrson 1941)	Boreal offshore gravel
2 Exposed sand community	(a) Crustacean-polychaete (Bishop & Holme 1980) (b) As described by Eleftheriou & McIntyre (1976) (c) Biocenoses of fast drying beaches (Augier 1982)	–
3 Clean sand community	(a) *Tellina* (Bishop & Holme 1980) (b) *Tellina tenuis* (Sparck 1937) (c) Biocenoses of fine surface sands (Augier 1982)	Boreal shallow sand
4 Current-swept sand community	(a) *Lanice* (Bishop & Holme 1980)	–
5 Muddy gravel community	(a) *Pullastra* (Bishop & Holme 1980) (b) Muddy gravel (Holme 1966)	–
6 Sand/muddy sand community	(a) *Echinocardium cordatum-Ensis siliqua* (Bishop & Holme 1980) (b) *Echinocardium cordatum-Venus gallina* (Ford 1923)	Boreal offshore sand
7 Muddy 'offshore' sand community	(a) *Echinocardium cordatum-Amphiura filiformis* (Petersen 1914)	Boreal offshore muddy sand community
8 Normal/variable salinity muddy sand community	(a) *Arenicola* (Bishop & Holme 1980) (b) *Macoma* (Petersen 1914)	Boreal shallow mud (in part)
9 Variable/reduced salinity mud community	(a) *Scrobicularia* (Bishop and Holme 1980) (b) *Macoma* (Petersen 1914)	Boreal shallow mud (in part) (in part)

A7.2 Terms used in the Estuaries Review aquatic estuarine database

Salinity

Normal
Variable
Reduced
Not recorded/not known*

Wave Exposure

Extremely exposed
Very exposed
Exposed
Moderately exposed
Sheltered
Very sheltered
Extremely sheltered
Not recorded/not known*

Tidal steam strength

Very strong
Strong
Moderately strong
Weak
Very weak
Significant*
Not recorded/not known*

Biological/physical zone

Supralittoral
Littoral fringe – upper
Littoral fringe – lower
Eulittoral
Eulittoral – upper
Eulittoral – mid
Eulittoral – lower
Sublittoral fringe
Infralittoral – upper
Infralittoral – lower
Circalittoral – upper
Circalittoral – lower
Bathyal
Littoral
Sublittoral
0-5m
5-10m
10-20m
20-30m
30-50m
>50m
Upper shore
Mid shore
Lower shore
Upper mid shore
Lower mid shore
Water column
Not known/not recorded*

Substratum (major & minor)

Artificial substratum
Bedrock
Boulder – large
Boulders
Boulder – small
Boulder – very large
Cobbles – large
Cobbles
Cobbles – small
Clay
Gravel – dead maerl
Maerl (live)
Mud
Pebbles
Rockpool
Sand
Sand – coarse
Sediment*
Sand – fine
Shell gravel
Hard*
Slates
Sand – medium
Gravel
Gravel – rock
Not known/not recorded*

Extent of record

Whole area surveyed
Biological subzone
Height band
Depth band
Restricted feature
Extensive*
Not recorded/not known*

Conservation status

International
National
Regional
Local
Not known/not recorded*

* Terms not compatible with the MNCR marine database, but introduced to allow usage of marine habitat information from a wide variety of sources.

A7.3 Names of aquatic estuarine communities

The aquatic estuarine community names used in the Estuaries Review are listed below. General descriptions of all the major communities are given in Chapter 8.3. These are mostly based on the MNCR draft classification of marine habitats and communities prepared mainly by D Connor, R Covey and K Hiscock. The major division is of communities which occur on soft substrata (Section A) and those which occur on hard substrata (Section B and Section C). Five communities which occur on hard substrata are not considered to be major estuarine community types and are not covered in Chapter 8.3. The names of these communities are listed in Section C below. Standardised descriptions of all the community types listed below are in preparation as a separate Estuaries Review report.

Section A

Major communities on soft substrata

Gravel/shell gravel community

Maerl community

Exposed sand community

Clean sand community

Beds of the common mussel *Mytilus edulis*

Beds of the horse mussel *Modiolus modiolus*

Beds of the European oyster *Ostrea edulis*

Algal community on sediment surface

Current-swept sand community

Sand/muddy sand community

Muddy gravel community

Muddy 'offshore' sand community

Normal/variable salinity muddy sand community

Eelgrass *Zostera* spp. beds

Variable/reduced salinity mud community

Reduced salinity mud community

Section B

Major communities on hard substrata

Exposed rocky shore community

Moderately exposed rocky shore community

Sheltered rocky shore community

Variable salinity rocky shore community

Variable (mainly reduced) salinity rocky shore community

Reduced salinity rocky shore community

Sabellaria reef community

Current-exposed sheltered rocky shore community

Exposed rock community

Sheltered rock community

Hydrozoan/bryozoan turf community

Beds of the slipper limpet *Crepidula fornicata*

Artificial substrata community

Variable salinity rock community

Variable salinity clay community

Variable (mainly reduced) salinity rock community

Reduced salinity rock community

Section C

Minor communities on hard substrata

Sand associated rock community

Rock scoured by sand

Current-swept mobile hard substratum

Rockpool communities

Underboulder communities

Appendix 8 Marine site conservation assessment criteria

This Appendix gives notes on the 14 comparative site assessment criteria (from Mitchell 1987) and definitions of the four qualifiers which are currently used to express the perceived conservation interest of marine habitats, communities and species.

Ecological/scientific criteria

Naturalness An area which is unmodified by human influence is desirable. Management techniques aimed at increasing diversity or maintaining a community at a sub-climax stage may thus be at variance with this criterion. Naturalness is found widely in the marine environment and this criterion will, for many types of biocenosis, be less important than other ones, although a necessary first qualifying attribute for a site in the selection process. (Biocenosis is equivalent to the word community or association.)

Representativeness It is not only necessary to choose areas which are in some way unusual or unique, but it is also desirable to represent the typical and ordinary sites which contain habitats, communities and species which occur commonly or are widespread. These areas may be particularly important for experimental purposes or may be desirable as controls in monitoring programmes.

Rarity While rarity on a national scale might be the grounds for the establishment of 'species reserves' it is probably better to regard rare species as a bonus on sites selected for other reasons. It is necessary to understand what factors are operating to make a species rare before its rarity is given weight in an evaluation excercise or its management needs are defined.

Diversity Variety in terms of species and communities is highly desirable and depends to a large extent on the physical diversity of an area and the number of different communities it supports.

Fragility This criterion reflects the sensitivity of habitats, communities and species to environmental change and has particular application to areas of low water exchange (e.g. saline lagoons and enclosed sea lochs) and low energy systems (e.g. low turbidity estuaries and sheltered inlets) which might be easily degraded by pollution, physical destruction or natural events.

Size Below a certain minimum size the communities or species conserved may be adversely affected by adjacent activities - the 'edge effect'. There is therefore a certain minimum size necessary to ensure the integrity of the site - the 'viable unit' concept.

Practical/pragmatic criteria

Situation Where practicable, it is desirable to include within a single geographic area as many as possible of the important and characteristic ecosystems, communities and species. This criterion is related to those of 'size' and 'diversity'.

Recorded history The extent to which a site has already been used for scientific study and research is a factor of some importance, and will elevate the value of such a site above another similar site which has little recorded history.

Research and education potential While most criteria are primarily directed at selecting sites for nature conservation purposes, the provision of protected areas to provide research and educational opportunities is often a linked purpose.

Restoration potential This criterion is concerned with the potential for rehabilitation of the sites or the creation de novo of an example of a particular ecosystem. Because 'naturalness' is found relatively widely in the marine environment, this may be a less important consideration.

Intrinsic appeal Certain ecosystems or organisms attract more interest than others because of the bias in human interest. Ease of collection and identification contributes to the bias. Despite the qualifications of this criterion, the 'expert eye' approach is considered a most important and valuable contribution to the identification of sites of potential conservation importance.

Vulnerability This criterion recognises the susceptibility of a habitat to a potential threat and may apply particularly to biocenoses that are intrinsically sensitive to damage (see 'fragility' above). Where there is a choice of examples of a particular biocenosis the one that is most remote from sources of damage is considered the most valuable.

Urgency The greater the likelihood of damage from an identified threat the more urgent is the need for protection, assuming a similar site cannot be found in a less vulnerable position.

Feasibility The availability of a site for acquisition for conservation management is an important consideration. The practical aspects of management are also important in assessing if a site will make an effective unit.

Qualifiers used to express perceived conservation importance

International Communities which are outstandingly good examples of their type in the north-east Atlantic. Communities recorded at only a few locations in the north-east Atlantic. Species which are recorded at only a few locations in the north-east Atlantic. Species recorded in higher abundance in the area under consideration than anywhere else in the north-east Atlantic or where the area is one of only a very few locations where large quantities are recorded.

National Communities which are outstandingly good examples of their type in Britain. Communities recorded in only a very few similar physiographic situations in Britain. Both of these definitions refer to communities which are or are likely to be widely occurring in other similar physiographic situations in the north-east Atlantic. Species which are recorded at only a few locations in Britain but are more widespread in other parts of the north-east Atlantic. Species recorded in higher abundance at locations under consideration than in any others elsewhere in Britain or where the site is one of only a very few locations where large quantities are recorded in Britain.

Regional Communities which are present in similar physiographic situations elsewhere in Britain but which are outstandingly good examples of their type in the location under consideration or are as good examples as similar communities present elsewhere in Britain. Communities recorded at only a few locations in the same biogeographic region. Species which are unrecorded or recorded at only a few locations in similar physiographic situations in Britain but which are widespread in other similar sites in other parts of Britain. Species recorded in higher abundance in the area under consideration than in any other part of Britain or where the site is one of only a very few locations where large quantities are recorded in Britain.

Local Communities which are widespread throughout Britain with as good or better examples at several other locations. The selection of only species which are of higher than local importance precludes the use of this category in the species lists.

Definitions of terms used to describe location

North-east Atlantic: North Cape to the Straits of Gibraltar

Region: These are the 15 biogeographical/physiographical regions defined for the Marine Nature Conservation Review

Area: This will most likely be a few kilometres of coastline but can be as large as a whole marine inlet or stretch of physiographically similar coast